PSYCHOLOGY

PSYCHOLOGY
The Study of Human Behaviour

SECOND EDITION

BRAJ KUMAR MISHRA

Formerly Professor and Head
Department of Psychology
Doranda College, Ranchi University
Ranchi

PHI Learning Private Limited

Delhi-110092

2026

In fond memory of ***Shri Asoke K. Ghosh*** *(October 1942 – February 2024), Founder Chairman and Managing Director of PHI Learning, whose vision endlessly inspires.*

The Legacy Continues....

Published by Pushpita Ghosh, PHI Learning Private Limited, Rimjhim House, 111, Patparganj Industrial Estate, Delhi-110092 and Mudrak, C-55, Sector 65, Noida, U.P.-201301.

₹895.00

PSYCHOLOGY: The Study of Human Behaviour, Second Edition
Braj Kumar Mishra

ISBN-978-81-203-5247-6 (Print Book)
ISBN-978-93-90669-71-4 (e-Book)

Reminiscence: O my glorious foreparents, without you where am I ?

Message

Onto the new generation
Ignorant but marvel in potentials
March onto marvel the commons and conquor
the odds to create a society—splendid in deed

Dedicated to my wife—MAMTA

Who lives in my heart
And she dwells in mine
That is all

—Braj Kumar Mishra

Contents

Preface *xxiii*
Preface to the First Edition *xxv*

PART I CURIOSITY OF MAN TO STUDY HIMSELF

1. Introduction 3–26

1.1 What is Psychology? *3*
1.2 Nature and Definition *4*
1.2.1 Diversity of Field *4*
1.2.2 Wider Range of Study *4*
1.3 Best Definition *6*
1.4 Some Fallacies about Psychology or Psychologists *7*
1.5 Subject Matter and Scope *8*
1.6 Is Psychology a Science? *9*
1.7 Nature of Psychology as a Science *9*
1.8 Is Psychology a Natural Science? *10*
1.9 Goals or Objectives of Psychology *11*
1.9.1 Describing the Behaviour *11*
1.9.2 Understanding the Behaviour *11*
1.9.3 Predicting the Behaviour *12*
1.9.4 Control *13*
1.10 Sub-fields or Branches of Psychology *13*
1.10.1 Theoretical Branches *14*
1.10.2 Applied Branches *16*
1.11 Psychology and Life *18*
1.12 Relationship of Psychology with other Disciplines *19*
1.12.1 Psychology and Anthropology *20*
1.12.2 Psychology and Sociology *20*

1.12.3 Psychology and Physiology *21*
1.12.4 Economics, Political Science and History *21*
1.12.5 Relationship of Psychology to other Natural Sciences *22*
1.12.6 Conclusive Remarks on the Relationship of Psychology with other Sciences *22*
1.13 Psychology Today *22*
1.14 New Frontiers of Psychology *23*
1.14.1 Neuro-Psychology *23*
1.14.2 Positive Psychology *24*
1.14.3 Military Psychology *24*
1.14.4 Assessment Psychology *24*
1.14.5 Computer Science *25*
Summary *25*

2. Historical Perspectives of Modern Psychology 27–43

2.1 Founding Ideas of Ancient Times *27*
2.2 Ancient Greeks' Views *27*
2.3 Philosophical Roots *28*
2.4 Biological Roots *29*
2.5 Beginning of Experimental Psychology *30*
2.6 Schools of Psychology *31*
2.6.1 Structuralism *31*
2.6.2 Functionalism *32*
2.6.3 Associationism *33*
2.6.4 Behaviourism *33*
2.6.5 Gestaltism *34*
2.6.6 Psychoanalysis *35*
2.6.7 Neo-Freudians *36*
2.6.8 Humanistic Psychology *37*
2.7 Modern Perspectives in Psychology—Current Views *39*
2.7.1 Modern Psychology *39*
2.8 Psychology Tomorrow *40*
2.9 Milestones in the History of Psychology *41*
2.9.1 Pre-19th Century Psychology *41*
2.9.2 19th Century Psychology *41*
2.9.3 20th Century Psychology *41*
2.9.4 21st Century Psychology *43*
Summary *43*

3. Methodology of Psychology 44–65

3.1 Introduction *44*
3.2 Meaning of Method *44*
3.3 Characteristics of a Scientific Method *45*
3.3.1 Objectivity *45*
3.3.2 Systematization *45*
3.3.3 Validity *46*
3.3.4 Reliability *46*
3.3.5 Standardization *46*
3.3.6 Controlled Conditions of Study *46*

3.4 Nature of Psychological Data 47
 3.4.1 Demographic Information 47
 3.4.2 Physical Information 47
 3.4.3 Physiological Data 47
 3.4.4 Psychological Data 48
3.5 Description of Major Methods of Psychology 48
 3.5.1 Observation—Introspection (Self-observation) and Objective Observation 48
 3.5.2 Experimental Method 53
 3.5.3 Interview Method 57
 3.5.4 Case Study Method 58
 3.5.5 Questionnaire Method 60
 3.5.6 Cross-sectional Method 62
 3.5.7 Longitudinal Method 62
 3.5.8 Sequential Method 63
 3.5.9 Survey Method 63
3.6 Conclusive Remarks Regarding Different Methods of Psychology 64
Summary 65

PART II BIOLOGY OF BEHAVIOUR

4. Biological Bases of Behaviour 69–109

4.1 Introduction 69
4.2 Evolutionary Perspectives 70
 4.2.1 Environmental Influences on Evolutionary Trend 71
4.3 Genes and Behaviour 72
 4.3.1 Threads of Life 72
 4.3.2 Chromosomes 72
4.4 Nature and nurture Controversy 73
 4.4.1 Socio-biology 74
4.5 Inherited Structures 75
4.6 Nervous System 75
4.7 Neurons as Building Blocks 76
 4.7.1 Structure and Functions of Nerve Cells (Neurons) 76
4.8 Monitoring of Neural Activities 78
 4.8.1 Law Governing Propagation of Action Potential (Nerve Impulse) 79
 4.8.2 Refractory Period 79
 4.8.3 Transmission of Nerve Impulse 80
 4.8.4 Synaptic Functions 80
 4.8.5 Synaptic Facilitation 80
4.9 Division of Nervous System 82
 4.9.1 Peripheral Nervous System (PNS) 82
 4.9.2 Central Nervous System (CNS) 84
 4.9.3 Specialization of Cerebral Hemisphere 92
 4.9.4 Divided Brain 95
 4.9.5 Methods Employed in Studying Brain Functions 96
 4.9.6 Theories of Brain Functions 99

4.10 The Endocrine System 104
4.10.1 The Characteristic Features of Endocrine Glands 104
Summary 108

5. Socio-Cultural Bases of Behaviour 110–125

5.1 Introduction 110
5.2 Socialization and Culture 110
5.2.1 Enculturation 112
5.2.2 Agencies of Socialization 112
5.2.3 Mechanisms of Socialization 117
5.3 Acculturation 119
5.4 Relationship between Behaviour and Socio-Cultural Environment 120
5.5 Social Structure 121
5.5.1 Status and Role 122
5.5.2 Multiple Status 122
5.5.3 Role Conflict 122
5.6 Social Class 123
5.7 Social Class and Behaviour 123
Summary 124

PART III KNOWING THE WORLD AROUND US

6. Sensory Process and Psychophysics 129–150

6.1 Introduction 129
6.2 Receptors and Effectors 129
6.2.1 Receptors 129
6.2.2 Effectors 131
6.3 Sensory Processes 132
6.4 Sensation: Nature and Definition 133
6.4.1 Properties or Attributes of Sensation 134
6.5 Sensory Channel: Processing 135
6.5.1 Sensory Stimuli 135
6.5.2 Transduction 136
6.5.3 Conduction 136
6.5.4 Afferent Code and Experience 137
6.6 Psychophysical Relations and Methods of Study 137
6.6.1 Detection Problems 138
6.6.2 Stimulus Scaling 139
6.7 Some Important Concepts of Psychophysics 141
6.8 Weber's Law 143
6.9 Gustav Fechner's Law (1860) 144
6.10 Stevens' Power Law 144
6.11 Modern Psychophysics 146
6.11.1 Helson's Adaptation Level Theory 147
6.11.2 Evaluation 149
Summary 149

7. Visual and Other Sensory Processes 151–179

7.1 Introduction *151*
7.2 Visual Sensation *151*
7.2.1 The Human Eye *153*
7.2.2 Detecting Blind Spot *155*
7.2.3 How Does the Visual Sensation Occur? *156*
7.3 Duplicity Theory of Vision *157*
7.4 Colour Vision *158*
7.4.1 Psychophysical Relationships *158*
7.4.2 Some Important Facts Relating to Colour Sensation *161*
7.4.3 Contrast Effect *164*
7.5 Theories of Colour Vision *165*
7.5.1 The Young-Helmholtz Theory *165*
7.5.2 The Hering's Theory *166*
7.5.3 The Ladd-Franklin Theory *167*
7.5.4 Edridge-Green Theory *167*
7.6 Current Trends in Understanding Colours *168*
7.7 The Auditory Sensation *168*
7.7.1 Stimulus for Hearing *168*
7.7.2 Characteristic Features of Sound Waves *169*
7.7.3 Auditory Sense Organ *170*
7.7.4 Anatomy of Human Ear *171*
7.7.5 How Does Auditory Sensation Take Place? *172*
7.8 Theories of Hearing (Audition) *172*
7.8.1 The Place or Resonance Theory *173*
7.8.2 The Frequency Theory *174*
7.8.3 The Volley Theory *174*
7.9 Current Trends *175*
7.10 Other Senses *175*
7.10.1 Smell *176*
7.10.2 Taste *176*
7.10.3 Skin Sensation *177*
Summary *179*

8. Perceptual Processes 180–227

8.1 Introduction *180*
8.2 Nature and Definition of Perception *180*
8.3 Characteristics of Perception *182*
8.3.1 Perception is a Complex Mental Process *182*
8.3.2 Perception is Immediate in Nature *182*
8.3.3 Perception is an Active Mental Process *183*
8.3.4 Perception is Selective in Nature *183*
8.3.5 Perception Involves Complex Receptor and Neural Processes *183*
8.3.6 Perception is Organization of Stimuli *183*
8.3.7 Perceptual Experience has the Attribute of Constancy *183*
8.3.8 Perceptual Experiences are also Flexible *184*

8.4 Processes Involved in Perception *184*
- 8.4.1 Receptor Process *184*
- 8.4.2 Symbolic Process *185*
- 8.4.3 Affective Processes *185*
- 8.4.4 Unifying Process *185*

8.5 Difference between Perception and Sensation *186*

8.6 Difference between Perception and Attention *187*

8.7 Role of Past Experience in Perception *188*
- 8.7.1 Experimental Evidence *189*

8.8 Organizational Processing in Perception *190*

8.9 Theories of Perception or Points of Views Towards Perceptual Phenomenon *191*
- 8.9.1 The Structuralist's View *191*
- 8.9.2 Gestaltist's Approach *192*
- 8.9.3 The Behaviouristic Approach *193*

8.10 Comparison between Gestaltist and Behaviouristic Approaches to Perception *195*
- 8.10.1 Points of Similarities *195*
- 8.10.2 Points of Differences *195*

8.11 Perceptual Organization (Grouping) *196*
- 8.11.1 The Peripheral Laws or Principles of Organization *197*
- 8.11.2 Central Laws or Principles *199*

8.12 Figure and Ground Perception *201*

8.13 Contour *203*

8.14 Perceptual Constancy (Stability) *204*
- 8.14.1 Size Constancy *204*
- 8.14.2 Shape Constancy *205*
- 8.14.3 Colour and Brightness Constancy *205*
- 8.14.4 Location Constancy *206*

8.15 Factors of Perception *206*
- 8.15.1 Redundancy of Sensory Cues *206*
- 8.15.2 Context *207*
- 8.15.3 Transposition *207*
- 8.15.4 Factors of Organization *207*
- 8.15.5 Effect of Learning *208*
- 8.15.6 Frame of Reference *208*

8.16 The Perceiver's (Personal) Factors *208*
- 8.16.1 Needs *209*
- 8.16.2 Value *210*
- 8.16.3 Symbolic Meaning *210*
- 8.16.4 Cognitive Style *211*
- 8.16.5 Expectations or Perceptual Sets *212*
- 8.16.6 Other Personal Factors *212*

8.17 Social Factors *212*
- 8.17.1 Social Norms *212*
- 8.17.2 Social Suggestion *212*
- 8.17.3 Cultural Influences *213*

8.18 Perceptual Defence *213*

8.19 Perceptual Vigilance *214*

8.20 Visual Space Perception *214*
8.20.1 Monocular Cues *215*
8.20.2 Binocular Cues *217*
8.21 Stereoscopic Vision *218*
8.22 Perception of Motion *218*
8.23 Space Perception of Sound *220*
8.23.1 Perceiving the Direction of Sound *221*
8.23.2 Perceiving the Distance of Sound *221*
8.24 Perception of Time *221*
8.24.1 Factors Affecting Perception of Time *221*
8.24.2 Methods Employed for Studying Time Perception *223*
8.25 Illusions *223*
8.26 Hallucinations *225*
8.27 Extra Sensory Perception (ESP) *226*
Summary *227*

9. Attentional Process **228–243**

9.1 Introduction *228*
9.2 Nature and Definition *228*
9.3 Some Aspects of Attention *230*
9.3.1 Attention as a Postural Adjustment *230*
9.3.2 Attention as a Clearness in Consciousness *230*
9.3.3 Attention as a Set Towards Action *230*
9.4 Span of Attention *231*
9.5 Fluctuation of Attention *232*
9.6 Division of Attention or Divided Attention *232*
9.7 Distraction of Attention *233*
9.8 Kinds of Attention *233*
9.8.1 Voluntary Attention *233*
9.8.2 Involuntary Attention *233*
9.8.3 Habitual Attention *233*
9.9 Selective Attention *234*
9.9.1 Factors of Selective Attention *235*
9.9.2 Theories of Selective Attention *236*
9.10 Sustained Attention *236*
9.10.1 Factors Influencing Sustained Attention *238*
9.11 Direction of Attention or Determinants of Attention or Conditions (Factors) of Attention *238*
9.11.1 External Factors *239*
9.11.2 Internal or Organismic or Subjective Determinants *240*
9.12 Attention Deficit Hyper-Activity Disorder (ADHD) *241*
9.12.1 Treatment *242*
Summary *242*

PART IV MODIFICATION OF BEHAVIOUR

10. Learning **247–280**

10.1 Introduction *247*
10.2 Nature and Definition of Learning *247*
10.3 Learning and Performance *249*
10.4 Learning and Maturation *250*
10.5 Kinds of Learning *250*
10.5.1 Verbal Learning *251*
10.5.2 Motor Learning *251*
10.5.3 Stimulus Learning *252*
10.5.4 Response Learning *252*
10.6 Learning Curve *253*
10.6.1 Plotting a Learning Curve *253*
10.6.2 Characteristics of Learning Curve *254*
10.7 Role of Motivation in Learning *254*
10.7.1 It is a Condition for Eliciting Learning Act or Behaviour *254*
10.7.2 Motivation is Necessary for Reinforcing the Response being Learnt *255*
10.7.3 Motivation Controls the Variability of Behaviour *255*
10.7.4 Some Examples of Role of Motivation on Human Beings *256*
10.7.5 Knowledge of Result *256*
10.8 How Do We Learn? *258*
10.9 Classical Conditioning *258*
10.9.1 Some Salient Features of Classical Conditioning Procedure *260*
10.9.2 Determinants (Factors) of Classical Conditioning *261*
10.9.3 Theories about Classical Conditioning *264*
10.9.4 Some Important Phenomenon of Classical Conditioning *265*
10.9.5 Discrimination *266*
10.9.6 Reinforcement *268*
10.9.7 Higher Order Conditioning *268*
10.9.8 Experimental Neurosis *269*
10.9.9 Counter Conditioning *269*
10.9.10 Pseudo-conditioning *269*
10.9.11 Significance of Classical Conditioning *270*
10.9.12 Shaping of Behaviour *275*
10.9.13 Some Important Phenomena of Instrumental (Operant) Conditioning *275*
10.9.14 Significance of Instrumental (Operant) Conditioning *278*
10.10 Current Thoughts Regarding Learning Activities *279*
Summary *280*

11. Some Other Principles (Theories) and Aspects of Learning **281–318**

11.1 Introduction *281*
11.2 Some Major Principles of Learning *282*
11.2.1 Thorndike's Connectionism *282*
11.3 Insight Theory *286*
11.3.1 Another Experiment *287*

11.4 C.L. Hull's Reinforcement Theory *288*
11.4.1 Some Definitions of Key Concepts in Hull's System *289*
11.4.2 Evaluation of Hull's System *292*
11.5 Tolman's Cognitive Theory *293*
11.5.1 Some Experimental Evidences (or Support) *295*
11.6 Comparison between Hull and Tolman's Theories of learning *297*
11.7 Guthrie's Contiguity Theory *298*
11.8 Observational Learning *300*
11.8.1 Imitation *301*
11.8.2 Vicarious Learning *301*
11.8.3 Live versus Symbolic Modelling *301*
11.9 Latent Learning *303*
11.10 Skill Learning *304*
11.10.1 Phases of Skill Acquisition *304*
11.11 Intentional and Incidental Learning *305*
11.11.1 Intentional Learning *305*
11.11.2 Incidental Learning *305*
11.12 Verbal Learning *306*
11.12.1 Materials Used to Study Verbal Learning *306*
11.12.2 Methods for Measuring Verbal Learning *307*
11.12.3 Methods of Verbal Learning *309*
11.13 Factors In Human Learning *311*
11.13.1 Methods of Learning *311*
11.13.2 Nature of Learning Materials *313*
11.14 Transfer of Learning *313*
11.14.1 Kinds of Transfer in Learning *314*
11.14.2 Bases of Transfer *316*
Summary *317*

PART V MEMORY PROCESS

12. Remembering and Forgetting **321–363**

12.1 Introduction *321*
12.2 What is Memory? *322*
12.3 Information Processing Model of Memory *323*
12.3.1 Input *323*
12.3.2 Attending and Organizing *324*
12.3.3 Storing and Holding *324*
12.3.4 Retrieving *324*
12.3.5 Deciding *325*
12.3.6 Output *325*
12.4 Atkinson–Shiffrin Model of Memory *325*
12.4.1 Sensory Memory *325*
12.4.2 Short-term Memory (STM) *327*
12.4.3 Long-term Memory (LTM) *328*

12.5 Types of Long-term Memory *332*
- 12.5.1 Episodic Memory *332*
- 12.5.2 Semantic Memory *333*
- 12.5.3 Procedural Memory *334*

12.6 Retention *334*
- 12.6.1 Measurement of Retention *334*
- 12.6.2 Some Implicit Measures of Memory *336*

12.7 The Process of Retrieval in Memory *337*
- 12.7.1 Tip of the Tongue Phenomenon *338*

12.8 Organization in Memory *338*
- 12.8.1 Concepts and Categories *338*
- 12.8.2 Schema *339*

12.9 Two Pioneering Research Studies done on Memory *341*
- 12.9.1 Herman Ebbinghaus' Study (1985) *341*
- 12.9.2 Fredrick Bartlett (1932) *342*

12.10 Construction and Reconstruction in Memory *342*
- 12.10.1 Memory is Not a Passive Rather an Active Process *344*
- 12.10.2 The Construction Occurs at the Time of Encoding the Experience before it is Stored in LTM *344*
- 12.10.3 Human Memory is an Active System *344*
- 12.10.4 Sensory Inputs are Perceptually Analysed and Interpreted before These Enter in LTM *344*

12.11 Some Important Phenomena of Memory *345*
- 12.11.1 Eyewitness Memory *345*
- 12.11.2 Implicit Memory *345*
- 12.11.3 False or Illusory Memory Syndrome *346*
- 12.11.4 Autobiographical Memories *346*
- 12.11.5 Flash Bulb Memories *346*
- 12.11.6 Inducing False Memories *347*

12.12 Forgetting *347*
- 12.12.1 Decay or Disuse Theory *347*
- 12.12.2 Interference Theory *349*
- 12.12.3 Bartlett's View Regarding Remembering and Forgetting *352*
- 12.12.4 Motivated Forgetting *352*
- 12.12.5 Reminiscence *353*

12.13 Causes of Forgetting *354*
- 12.13.1 Factors Relating to Poor Learning *354*
- 12.13.2 Factors Relating to Retention or Encoding Errors *355*
- 12.13.3 Retrieval Related Forgetting *356*

12.14 Do Memory Traces Fade out Completely? *357*

12.15 Memory Span *358*

12.16 Amnesia *359*
- 12.16.1 Transient Amnesia *359*
- 12.16.2 Organic Amnesia *359*

12.17 Improving Memory *360*
- 12.17.1 Mnemonics Using Images *360*
- 12.17.2 Mnemonics Using Organization *361*
- 12.17.3 Use of Multiple Methods and Strategies *362*

Summary *362*

PART VI SYMBOLIC PROCESSES

13. Thinking **367–418**

13.1 Introduction *367*
13.2 Nature of Thinking *367*
13.3 Defining Thinking *368*
13.4 Kinds of Thinking *369*
13.4.1 Autistic Thinking *369*
13.4.2 Realistic Thinking *370*
13.5 Tools of Thinking *371*
13.5.1 Role of Images in Thinking *372*
13.5.2 Kinds of Images *372*
13.5.3 Are Images Essential for Thinking? *374*
13.5.4 Cognitive Map and Thinking *376*
13.5.5 Role of Language *377*
13.6 Role of Set and Direction *380*
13.7 Trial and Error in Thinking *383*
13.8 Insight in Thinking *383*
13.9 Problem Solving *384*
13.9.1 Steps in Problem Solving *384*
13.9.2 Strategies of Problem Solving or Thinking *386*
13.9.3 Factors Affecting Problem Solving or Obstacles or Barriers of Problem Solving *387*
13.10 Problem Solving Behaviour as an Information Processing Model *390*
13.10.1 Input *393*
13.11 Theories of Thinking *393*
13.11.1 Central Theory *393*
13.11.2 Peripheral-Central Theory *394*
13.11.3 Comparison between Central and Peripheral Theories *396*
13.11.4 Some Experimental Evidences in Support of the Two Theories *397*
13.11.5 Piaget's Cognitive Theory *398*
13.12 Concepts *400*
13.12.1 Concepts and Thinking *402*
13.12.2 Characteristics of Concepts *403*
13.12.3 Kinds or Types of Concepts *404*
13.12.4 Differences between Artificial and Natural Concepts *406*
13.12.5 Formation or Determinant or Attainment of Concepts *407*
13.12.6 Factors of Concept Formation *408*
13.12.7 Other Factors *409*
13.13 Creative Thinking *410*
13.13.1 Some Characteristics of Creative Thinkers (People) *411*
13.13.2 Stages of Creative Thinking *411*
13.13.3 Nature of Creative Thinking *414*
13.13.4 Barriers to Creative Thinking *415*
13.13.5 Improving Creativity *417*
Summary *417*

PART VII CONATIVE ASPECTS OF BEHAVIOUR

14. Motivation **421–460**

14.1 Introduction *421*
14.2 Nature and Definition *421*
14.3 Motivational Cycle *423*
14.3.1 A Motivating State within the Individual *423*
14.3.2 Arousal and Directedness of Behaviour (Instrumental Behaviour) *424*
14.3.3 Attainment of the Goal *424*
14.3.4 Some Terminologies Related to Motives *425*
14.3.5 Influences of Motives on Behaviour *426*
14.4 Homeostasis *426*
14.5 Two Fundamental Theories of Motivation *427*
14.5.1 Instinct Theory *427*
14.5.2 Drive Theory *428*
14.6 Nature of Experimental Studies on Motivation *428*
14.7 Kinds of Motives *429*
14.7.1 Physiological Motives *430*
14.7.2 Unlearned/General Motives *435*
14.7.3 Social/Personal/Acquired Motives (Psychosociogenic Motives) *437*
14.8 Intrinsic and Extrinsic Framework of Motivation *444*
14.9 Measurement of Motives *444*
14.9.1 Activity Cage Method *445*
14.9.2 Obstruction Method *446*
14.9.3 Drive Competition Method *446*
14.9.4 Learning Method *446*
14.10 Measurement of Human Socio-psychogenic (Acquired) Motives *447*
14.10.1 Projective Tests *447*
14.10.2 Situational Tests *448*
14.10.3 Inventories or Self Report Techniques *448*
14.10.4 Experimental Studies *449*
14.11 Frustration of Motives *449*
14.11.1 Frustration *449*
14.12 Conflict *450*
14.12.1 Approach–Approach Conflict *450*
14.12.2 Approach–Avoidance Conflict *450*
14.12.3 Avoidance–Avoidance Conflict *451*
14.12.4 Double or Multiple Approach Avoidance Conflict *451*
14.13 Reactions to Frustrations *451*
14.14 Functions of Motivation or Role of Motivation on Performance *452*
14.14.1 The Energising Role *452*
14.14.2 The Directing Role *452*
14.14.3 The Emphasizing Role *453*
14.15 Some Basic Approaches or Theories of Motivation *453*
14.15.1 Need Hierarchy Theory *453*
14.15.2 Opponent–Process Theory *455*
14.15.3 Optimal Level Theory *456*

14.15.4 Valence–Vector Theory 457
14.15.5 Psychoanalytic Approach 458
14.16 Current Status of Motivational Psychology 459
Summary 460

PART VIII AFFECTIVE PROCESSES

15. Emotion **463–488**

15.1 Introduction 463
15.2 Nature, Meaning and Definition 463
15.3 Difference between Emotion and Feeling 465
15.4 Motives and Emotions 465
15.5 Some Basic Emotions 466
15.5.1 Anger 467
15.5.2 Fear 468
15.5.3 Love and Affection 469
15.6 Physiological Correlates of Emotion 470
15.6.1 Internal Changes in Emotion 470
15.6.2 Overt Expression or External Changes in Emotion 473
15.7 Judging a Situation 474
15.8 Theories of Emotion 474
15.8.1 The Common Sense View 475
15.8.2 James–Lange Theory 475
15.8.3 Cannon–Bard Theory 477
15.8.4 Activation Theory 479
15.8.5 Cognitive Theory of Emotion 480
15.8.6 Cognitive Appraisal Theory of Emotion 481
15.8.7 Theory of Relationships among Emotions 482
15.9 Role of Nervous System in Emotion 483
15.9.1 Role of Peripheral Nervous System (PNS) 483
15.9.2 Role of Central Nervous System (CNS) 484
15.9.3 Autonomic Nervous System (ANS) 485
15.9.4 Glandular Involvements in Emotions 485
15.10 Physiological Measures of Emotion 486
15.10.1 Polygraph and Lie Detector 486
15.11 Emotion and Competence 486
15.12 Emotion and Culture 487
Summary 487

PART IX INDIVIDUAL DIFFERENCES

16. Intelligence **491–528**

16.1 Introduction 491
16.2 Nature and Definition of Intelligence 492
16.2.1 Defining Intelligence 493

16.3 Theories of Intelligence *494*
 16.3.1 Some Classical Approaches or Theories of Intelligence *495*
 16.3.2 Contemporary Approaches to Intelligence *501*
 16.3.3 Some Process-oriented Approaches to Intelligence *502*
16.4 Assessing Intelligence *506*
 16.4.1 Individual Verbal Tests *508*
 16.4.2 Wechsler Adult Intelligence Scale (WAIS) *509*
 16.4.3 Group Intelligence Tests *511*
16.5 Culture Fair Tests *513*
 16.5.1 Evaluating Cattell's IPAT Test *513*
16.6 Some Intelligence Tests Constructed in India *514*
16.7 IQ Constancy *515*
 16.7.1 Factors Affecting Changes in IQ *515*
16.8 Uses of Intelligence Tests *516*
 16.8.1 Use of Intelligence Testing in Educational Institutions *516*
 16.8.2 Use of Intelligence Tests for Clinicians *516*
 16.8.3 Use of Intelligence Tests for Parents *517*
 16.8.4 Use of Intelligence Tests for Child Guidance Centres *517*
16.9 Genetic and Environmental Determinants of Intelligence—Controversy *517*
 16.9.1 Genetic (Heredity) and Environmental Influences on Intelligence *517*
16.10 Some Important Environmental Determinants of Intelligence *518*
 16.10.1 Gender Differences *519*
 16.10.2 Health *519*
 16.10.3 Family Structure and Size *520*
 16.10.4 Effects of Training *520*
 16.10.5 Cultural Factors *520*
16.11 Individual Differences in Intelligence *521*
 16.11.1 Giftedness (Genius) *522*
 16.11.2 Intellectually Retarded or Deficient *523*
16.12 Causes of Mental Retardation *524*
 16.12.1 Education and Treatment for Mentally Retarded *525*
16.13 Special Abilities: Aptitudes *525*
 16.13.1 Nature *525*
 16.13.2 Measurement of Aptitude *526*
16.14 Intelligence in Indian Context *526*
Summary *528*

17. Personality **529–586**

17.1 Introduction *529*
17.2 Meaning of Personality *530*
17.3 Approaches to the Study of Personality *531*
 17.3.1 Types and Traits: Development of Taxonomy (Trait and Type Classification) *531*
17.4 Dynamic Process-oriented view of Personality *539*
 17.4.1 Intra-psychic Theory *540*
 17.4.2 Post-Freudian Developments *544*
17.5 Behaviourist Approaches to Personality *555*
 17.5.1 Dollard and Miller: Early Social Learning Theory *555*
 17.5.2 Pavlov's Conditioning Principle *556*

17.5.3 Skinner's Radical Behaviourism 557
17.5.4 Bandura and Walters: Later Social Learning Theory 557
17.6 The Humanistic Theories of Personality 558
17.6.1 Rogers' Self Theory 558
17.6.2 Maslow's Theory of Self-actualization 559
17.6.3 A General Comment on Humanistic Aproaches to Personality 560
17.7 Kurt Lewin's Field Theory of Personality 560
17.8 New Advances: Five-Factor Model of Personality 562
17.9 Determinants of Personality 563
17.9.1 The Nature-Nurture Controversy 563
17.9.2 The Person-Situation Controversy 566
17.9.3 Factors of Personality 567
17.9.4 Social Factors of Personality 568
17.9.5 Cultural Factors 570
17.10 Assessment/Measurement of Personality 571
17.10.1 Holistic Approach 571
17.10.2 Trait Approach 571
17.10.3 Projective Approach 572
17.10.4 Some Important Measures or Tests of Personality 572
17.11 Some Indian Personality Inventories 583
17.12 Relationship of Personality Types and Cardiac Diseases (CHD) 584
Summary 585

Glossary **587–594**

Author Index **595–601**

Subject Index **603–617**

Preface

All students taking university courses in psychology and even lay readers interested in this subject will find this new, revised edition of the book—*Psychology: The Study of Human Behaviour*, not only of informative value but the book will also prove helpful in bringing the knowledge up-to-date in this field of science that is fast advancing.

In this new edition, an additional chapter—*Socio-cultural Bases of Behaviour* has been added in Part II as Chapter 5. Thus, the revised edition covers one of the important bases of behaviour which is no less important to biological bases (Part I, Chapter 4). No doubt, biological bases provide us with a reaction range, i.e., behavioural characteristics that one can possibly achieve. However, the social–cultural aspects provide the opportunities to achieve the genetically endowed reaction range. Hence, while dealing with behaviours of human this aspect can hardly be ignored.

Throughout the text, I have adopted a rigorous approach to this subject in keeping with the sophistication of today's students and higher academic standards of colleges and universities. Besides, due care has also been taken to incorporate the models set by UGC and various service commissions requirements.

The author gratefully acknowledges the assistance of Dilip Kumar Mishra and Vishesh Mrinal for their valuable suggestions and examples cited elsewhere in the text.

Hope, the students and teachers will find this new edition valuable and appreciate the descriptions of different chapters that meets with their requirements.

Suggestions, if any are most welcomed.

BRAJ KUMAR MISHRA

Preface to the First Edition

Psychology as a scientific discipline is a relatively much younger science that attempts to seek knowledge about 'what', 'why' and 'how' of behaviour events. However, it shares the features with somewhat unpolished ancient thoughts reflected in the ancient stories relating to the numerous questions for the knowledge of what, why and how of behaviour, including life and death.

Psychology shares with the common man's curiosities to know and understand the behaviour pattern. As a systematic body of knowledge, it encompasses research-based study of human behaviour. The knowledge facilitated by psychology provides invaluable perspectives for understanding ourselves as well as the other fellow human beings.

As psychology discovers more about human behaviour, our work becomes more and more difficult. It is so because there is a vast amount of literature available on the subject which had to be evaluated and incorporated precisely before conveying sensibly what is important and what is not. However, attempts have been made to lay emphasis on controllable and systematic studies to maintain various behavioural aspects—sensing, perceiving, modifying of behaviours, memorizing the past events, affective processes, abilities of humans and overall aspects of personality. Incorporation of the advances and discoveries in the field of different psychological processes, including the processes based on the Indian concepts, have made the text quite useful for the students as well as practitioners.

Students' interest should always be of paramount interest for the teaching community. Therefore, utmost care has been taken to include the updated sections of the syllabus as per the UGC guidelines according to which the syllabus of different universities have been recast. In order to make the abstract concepts understandable and graspable, the various facts of psychology have been presented in a lucid manner. The systematic and step-by-step interpretations of various psychological processes make the text highly productive to even a student of average ability. I hope the students who are taking this subject for their introductory courses in psychology or pursuing higher courses, will also find this text equally useful.

Besides, attempts have also been made to cater to the requirements of those readers who opt psychology as one of their optional papers for union and state level competitive examinations such as UPSC, various state public service commissions, NET, SLET, etc. To better serve the above objectives, efforts have also been made to make the text empirical with liberal use of experiments and examples.

I express my sincere thanks to all my family members for their encouragement and co-operation during the preparation of the manuscript. Thanks are also due to the authors and publishers of different texts which served as the reference materials in preparing the manuscript.

Finally, I am thankful to the editorial and production team of PHI Learning for careful processing of the manuscript.

BRAJ KUMAR MISHRA

PART I

Curiosity of Man to Study Himself

CHAPTER 1

Introduction

Psychology is a quest to know about self and others—a crowning characteristic of humans.

1.1 WHAT IS PSYCHOLOGY?

Curiosity to know and understand much about the self and that of the others is one of the most super-ordinated goals of mankind. In this sense, each one of us is curious enough to know and comprehend our ownselves as well as about others. It includes various aspects of environment around us—the objects, persons, natural events, and ever-changing environment in which we live. Psychology as a discipline, is also concerned with these curiosities. It has evolved as a systematic discipline out of the curiosities of mankind which is in existence ever since the evolution of man on earth. Primitive people used to depend largely upon superstitious beliefs to explain the 'what', 'why' and 'how' of behavioural events of human beings. Most of such explanations were offered in terms of good or bad evils of the cosmos. But with the advancement of knowledge, such superstitious beliefs gradually started fading away and scientific notions began to replace them. Consequently, in the current times, psychology as a scientific discipline of human behaviour is considered as a 'science of adjustive behaviour' of man. Its prime concern is to unearth the mystery **"what a piece of work is man, how noble in reason!, how infinite in faculty...."***

Man in fact, is superlatively excellent of animal's kingdom and is the leading organism in behaviour. This realization is the basis for the establishment of psychology as an independent science and to study the aspects of human behaviour in a systematic manner. 'Psychology' is one of the derivatives of this realization.

Psychology as an independent systematic science is concerned mainly to understand 'what',

* Shakespeare—*Hamlet*, Act II, Scene-II.

'why' and 'how' of behaviour which is done for the sake of adjustment with the various forces both back and forth in the ever-changing environment. Thus, psychology studies about the adjustive behaviour of man.

The present chapter deals with the nature of psychology, gradual refinements in its definitions and thus it clarifies what exactly psychology is?

1.2 NATURE AND DEFINITION

What is Psychology? It is a perennial question. To define any discipline or body of knowledge is important in the sense that it helps in understanding the exact nature of science or discipline under question. But to define psychology precisely is difficult on two counts: firstly, the field of psychology is diverse and secondly, there has been a multidirectional and rapid growth of psychology resulting in wider range of study about behavioural events.

1.2.1 Diversity of Field

Psychological studies include diverse kinds of simple and complex activities of human beings including animals. It includes the functions of brain, how one senses his external and internal environment, how one reciprocates the feelings, emotions and experiences of each other. Human behaviours are not only complex but also characterized by variousness. It varies in nature, strength, direction, continuity and other dimensions. All such diverse forms of behaviours come under the purview of psychological studies.

1.2.2 Wider Range of Study

Psychology is a pervasive science. Under its domain are covered a very wider range of behavioural phenomena such as behavioural events in the family, peer groups, neighbourhood, schools, various places of work, interactions with friends, various kinds of groups, playfields, recreational spots, marketplaces, trade and commerce, organizational set-ups etc. In all these diverse areas, man interacts with others and in doing so various kinds of mental and psychological activities take place in which psychologists ponder over and analyse.

Thus, psychology is a very vast field of studying behavioural aspects of mankind and this makes it difficult to define psychology precisely and in concrete terms. However, attempts have been made to define psychology in concrete forms and bring refinements in its definition from time to time.

The first such attempt was made to define psychology on the basis of terminological derivings. Psychology derives its origin from Greek terms—'**psyche**' and '**logos**'—the former (psyche) meaning 'soul' or 'mind' while the latter meaning 'to know about'. Thus psychology means 'the science or branch of knowledge that deals with soul'. Accordingly, the armchair speculative thinkers defined psychology as a '**discipline which studies about the soul**'.

But, later psychologists could not remain satisfied with this definition. To them, **soul** is ungraspable for man as it can neither be visualized nor can be described in concrete terms. Soul is an abstract term which is beyond scientific observation. Therefore, 'psychology as a science of soul' was not acceptable to them. They opined that in order to understand the nature of the organism, the mental activities of the organism should be the main concern of psychology and therefore, psychology can be better defined in terms of a science that studies the mind. Hence, '**study of mind**' was proposed as the definition of psychology.

Gradually, even this definition was rejected on the ground that like soul, mind is also unknown and unknowable. What is mind? It is a difficult question to answer in satisfactory terms. Mind at best can be viewed as a faculty that '**knows and knows that it knows**'. But this vision about mind is as abstract as soul. Hence, not accessible to scientific exploration.

Around the turn of later half of 19th century, enquiries about psychological aspects of mankind became the focal point of interest for many researchers and experimentalists. This focal point of interest is expressed in the systematic study of psychological aspects of mental experiences in a laboratory situation—marking the beginning of 'experimental psychology'. **Wilhelm Wundt** established a laboratory at Leipzig University in Germany and introduced the term 'conscious experience' to define psychology. The term **conscious experience** refers to the awareness of the mental activities of the organism. This awareness includes the stored mental impressions or representations of the past, the events or objects (or whatever is happening) at the moment (*i.e.*, in the present) and also of what the individual is likely to be aware of in the future.

Though, the term experience too is subjective because it has a personal reference, however, the term experience was subjected to investigation through experimental introspection method **Wundt** and many of his disciples such as Titchner followed the suit and thus, this definition of psychology is considered as the first refined definition in the literature of psychology. In this context, the contribution of Wundt is of paramount significance. He established the first laboratory for systematic study of conscious experience in the year **1879—a red lettered day in the history of psychology** because it was the beginning of systematic study of psychology as an independent branch of knowledge.

However, many ambitious psychologists considered **Wundtian thought** as despicable on the ground of scientific criterion of 'objectivity'. They aspired to develop psychology as a new science much like other natural and live sciences such as biology, physiology, neurology, physics, chemistry etc. They discard the term experience as a subject matter of psychology because, experience is something personal and private. Scientific exploration is impersonal or objective, *i.e.* science studies only those aspects which are accessible to direct observation and measurement. Such psychologists insisted on the term **behaviour** as the most suitable domain of psychological enquiry and accordingly, this group of psychologists were termed as **behaviourists** and **Watson** was the leader of this group. According to the behaviourists, the term **behaviour** refers to the activities overt (explicit) or covert (implicit) of the organism which could be observed or measured in objective terms. The explicit or overt behaviours include movement of limbs, fingers, eyes and other parts of the body. These activities are observable by others through naked eyes, *i.e.* **unaided observation**. The implicit or covert activities include functions of the lungs, the heart, the stomach or the circulatory, the digestive, the excretive systems of body which can be observed and measured by some instruments or sophisticated apparatus (**aided observation**). All these activities (explicit or implicit) are initiated by certain environmental (external or internal) forces or energies impinging on the human body. The impinging forces are called the **stimuli** (plural of stimulus) while the resultant explicit or implicit activities are termed as, **responses** (behaviours). Hence, the behaviourists are of the view that all our activities are responses to some sort of stimulus situation impinging on us and, therefore, behaviour is nothing but S-R affair (stimulus and response affair). Thus, they defined psychology '**as the science of behaviour**' and also emphasized to include the study of the behaviour of animals as a subject of psychological enquiry. They thought that human behaviour is a developed form what has evolved from animals and, therefore, there exists a good and high correlation between the patterns of human and animal's behaviour. Therefore, human behaviours can be better understood by understanding animal's behaviours. Accordingly, the behaviourists performed most of the experiments not only on human beings but also on animals and also put forward many principles and theories relating to learning, thinking, motivational aspects, and emotional feelings associated with human behaviours.

However, the definition of psychology offered by behaviourists limits its scope. Psychology cannot remain confined only to the study of explicit or implicit bodily activities. Behaviour, in fact, is not only initiated or triggered but are also regulated and controlled by mental activities. For example, when we perceive something alluring, we tend to approach them and when we perceive something as non-attractive or non-alluring, we tend to ignore them by avoiding or withdrawing behaviours. Hence our approaching or avoiding behaviour is determined by the way we perceive a thing which is a mental event. In other words, our bodily activities are directed to the stimulating situation by our perceptions while responding to any stimulus, we first attempt to evaluate and make a comparison among the several alternative courses of action, foresee the consequences of each action and then take a decision to respond to the situation in a particular manner. All these are the mental processes in which our perceptual experiences, past stored memories, thinking and other cognitive processes are involved. Similarly, bodily activities also initiate mental activities such as feelings of joy and sorrow, emotions of anger and love. These are termed as internal responses. Behaviourists also agree to label these mental activities as implicit behaviours. They also talk of thinking as sub-vocal talking. Thus, it is evident that the bodily activities and mental activities (experiences) both are not only interrelated but also interdependent. Hence, the two (behaviour and experiences) are inseparable. The organism or individual in fact, is an unified whole and psychology studies the individual as a whole. Therefore, experience and behaviour—both are included as subject matter of psychology. Accordingly, psychology is defined as—'A systematic science of experience and behaviour both' or more clearely—**'Psychology is a systematic science of the study of behaviour interpreted in terms of experience'**.

1.3 BEST DEFINITION

What follows from above is that Psychology studies the individuals in relation to the environment in which he lives and grows. The environment consists of various objects, persons and situations. The environment is full of complexities with which one has to deal with all through his life. Man has to deal with the past, present and also the happenings in the future. Thus, the interactions of a man with his environment stretches back to the past and extends forth in the future. Such interactions involve dealing with the various environmental forces—objects, persons, events around us. Dealing with the environment in such a long span of time—from birth till death, makes the environment more and more complex that poses challenges for the organism (man) to deal with them effectively. In so doing, human beings (or any organism) deliberate, select, decide and execute the pattern of behaviour that appear appropriate and adequate for effective dealings (adjustment) with the back and forth forces of the environment (environmental demand).

Environment, besides being vast and complex, is also dynamic. It is intangible, inpalpable and unstable. Human behaviours are constantly directed to adapt effectively with all these characteristic features of the environment (complex, vast, ungraspable, inpalpable, unstable features). In view of these features and adjustive purposes of behavioural responses, the science of psychology may be suitably defined in the following terms:

'Psychology is an objective science of mental experiences and behaviours in relation to over-all adjustment to the environment'.

The above definition seems most accurate and updated definition of Psychology with which most of the psychologists agree.

1.4 SOME FALLACIES ABOUT PSYCHOLOGY OR PSYCHOLOGISTS

It is usually observed that psychology is often misrepresented. In fact, many fallacies and wrong impressions about psychology or say psychologists have become popular in the society. Such popular wrong notions or fallacies are frequently and constantly conveyed through electronic media, films, stories of T.V. serials, newspapers and similar other agencies. For example, some of such popular fallacies are:

(a) The most common and popular notion about psychology is that psychologists are **mind readers**. This is a wrong notion. Psychologists, no doubt, try to understand what processes are going on in our mind (mental operation) in a particular situation by systematically observing what man does in a situation under reference. But it is not reading rather systematic analysis of mental operations based on objective or empirical observation.

(b) Another common fallacy is that psychologists are often considered as 'fortune-tellers'. Undoubtedly, 'prediction' of behaviour event is one of the chief goals of psychological studies, but it is not fortune-telling or reading of hand sketch lines. A psychologist systematically observes certain behavioural events occurring in various contexts and makes an attempt to discover the causal relationships of the event (cause and effect relationships) on the basis of which, he is able to predict about a particular behavioural event that may occur in future.

(c) Some misidentify psychology with **psychiatry**. This is still another false notion. Psychiatry is a branch of medicine devoted to the treatment of mental disorders. A psychiatrist is a professional doctor who has undergone a conventional medical training before specializing in the area of psychiatry. They, however, are not trained in the use of psychotherapeutic techniques and counselling. A group of psychologists called clinical psychologists gain expertise in clinically diagnosing and counselling of those who have psychopathic problems of adjusment and are thus emotionally disturbed persons. This a professionally applied branch of psychology in which those who have obtained at least postgraduation level of degree in psychology, are given special professional education and training in the field of clinical and counselling aspects of psychology.

Psychology, in fact, is a science or discipline in which, the behavioural events are systematically observed, the observed facts are arranged, analysed and certain conclusions about behaviour events are drawn which are described and explained, certain predictions are made and the ways of controlling the deviant behaviours are suggested. Thus, psychology is a discipline of knowing and understanding of human behaviours—both mental and physical.

1.5 SUBJECT MATTER AND SCOPE

From the above description, it is evident that psychology studies the behaviour of the man in particular and that of the organism in general. The term behaviour is used to refer to the activities of an individual—both the external (or overt) and the internal (or covert). The overt behaviours are bodily activities that can be subjected to direct observation through naked eyes, *i.e.* **unaided observation**, *viz.* talking, laughing, gesticulating, walking, communicating in verbal terms, etc. Covert behaviours, on the other hand, include the activities of internal organs that can be observed and measured only through delicate or sophisticated instruments. For example, blood circulation, respiratory behaviours, digestive functions etc. These can be observed or measured only through some delicate and sophisticated instruments and hence, are called **aided observation**.

Both of the above kinds of behaviours (activities) are initiated by different kinds of stimulating forces (physical energies) which act upon the body organs. These stimulating forces are called 'stimuli' (singular term stimulus) and the resultant overt or covert body activities are called **responses**. Thus, in course of pursuing the behavioural phenomenon, psychologists attempt to explain all such activities in terms of **stimulus** and **response** (S-R) **associations** or connections.

Psychology, however, is not confined to the study of bodily activities only. Psychologists also study the mental activities. These activities are implicit and include how do we think? How do we remember various past events or experiences? What and how do we forget? the processes involved in problem solving, understanding the situations of the environment, *i.e.* development of cognitive processes, attending, sensing of objects of the world, perceiving etc.

In addition to the above, the subject matter of psychology also include the development of concepts, acquisition of various kinds of verbal and motor skills, performance of task, *i.e.*, learning activities.

Man is also an emotional being. As an emotional being, he feels the moments of pleasure and pain, aggression and depression, becomes angry and afraid. Often he comes in the state of excitement or becomes calm, feels emotions of love and hatred etc. These are the affective aspects of human beings which are important to the study of behaviour because these affective states colour our behaviour. Emotional aspects serves spice to living by making our behaviour salty, spicy, sweet and often sour. Hence, emotions have additive value for describing and explaining the behaviours of human beings. Therefore, psychology also studies the emotional aspects of behaviours.

Besides, individuals differ in their abilities and personality features. These are the aspects that describe individual differences not only in abilities but also the differential patterns of behaviour, cognitive processes, modifications of behaviours etc. To understand and know about behaviours, psychologists also focus upon such individual differences and explain human behaviours by keeping the **individual** as the focal point of study. This refers to the study of abilities such as intelligence, aptitude, personal motivations, aspirations, conflicts, differential patterns of personality etc.

Psychological studies are also focused upon the application of psychological processes. Owing to this focus, the inconsistencies in behaviour, maladjustive patterns, and various forms of abnormalities, application of psychological principles in the fields of education, product manufacturing organizations, study of psychological aspects of social behaviours, interactions with the environment etc. are also the subject matter of psychology. Application of psychology in various areas/fields of human functioning have been described in some more detail in a separate section later in this chapter.

In short, psychology studies the behaviour and experiences of man in different areas ranging through the entire lifespan of man from birth till death. Thus, the subject matter and scope of Psychology is wide enough and is getting wider everyday on account of massive studies and researches being done on different psychological aspects of human beings.

1.6 IS PSYCHOLOGY A SCIENCE?

Is psychology a science? This question always haunts in mind and psychologists since centuries ago have been trying hard to establish psychology as a body of knowing what, why and how of behaviours on scientific footing. But, before we examine whether Psychology is a science, let as first examine what is a science?

Science refers to a systematic and bias-free study of the subject of study. This depends on scientific methods of study. Scientifically studied facts are objective, unbiased, reliable, valid, verifiable and standard. Science collects facts by employing scientific tools of data collection, arrangement of collected facts in a systematic order and then analyse them to arrive at a dependable conclusion which are described and explained in terms of governing principles. Such findings ultimately guide in formulating theories. Thus, science does four major functions. These are:

(a) Use of scientific methods to collect information (fact or data) relating to the subject matter in objective and impartial manner.
(b) Analysing the collected data systematically (*i.e.* in order).
(c) Formulation of general principles and theories based on the findings obtained through analysis of data.
(d) Applying the principles to solve human problems and thus, making human life happy.

In psychological studies, all the above-mentioned four chief functions are done. Psychologists use objective methods of observation and experimental methods to collect data relevant to the subject matter of psychology, observe the principle of impartiality in collecting data, arrange the collected facts in scientifically systematic manner, analyse the data by employing reliable and valid techniques of analysis and formulate general principles based on findings of the study which are subsequently described and explained. Thus, psychology too is a science much like other sciences.

Psychological studies have some more characteristics of a science. Like all other sciences, psychology is also a progressive discipline of knowledge. Psychologists are engaged in endless search of truth which are verifiable or subject to revision. Besides, psychological studies have also the attribute of applicability. Owing to these characteristics, psychology which started as small seedling during the last quarter decades of 19th century has today grown and developed into a giant tree with many prosperous branches bearing verifiable fruits.

1.7 NATURE OF PSYCHOLOGY AS A SCIENCE

Psychology in fact, is a **bio-social** science. It studies about the organism's behaviour. An organism is a living being, biologically structured and made of several interdependent biological organs and structures. These structures are interdependent in the sense that every building blocks (biological structures) of the organism work together to enable the organism to meet the demands made on it.

As is evident from the definition of psychology, its main concern is to study the adjustive behaviour through which an organism (or man) meets these demands—no matter, the demand is biologically originated or are social or environmental in origin.

Further, in order to meet the bio-social demands put on the organism, the organism responds in certain ways which are appropriate to the demanding situation. Responding involves the effectors (muscular or glandular). These effectors come into motion to enable the organism or individual to make appropriate response to the demands. The effectors (motor organs) are activated by motor nerve energies (impulses) which are generated by the motor area in the cerebral cortex. Generation of motor impulses involve interconnections by interneurons or connectors located in the cerebral cortex which on receiving afferent or sensory information interprets the sensing stimuli. Hence, responding or occurrence of behaviour event is a matter of physiological functioning of the biological structures or organs of which the organism or individual is made of. In this sense, psychology is a live science or say a 'biological science'.

But in true sense, behaviour is not only a matter of physiological functioning of the biological structures. Behaviours bear the stamp of socio-cultural contexts in which an individual is born, brought up and lives throughout the span of life. Most of our demands are socio-cultural in origin and our responses (behaviours) too are socio-culturally conditioned. Hence, while pursuing the study of behaviours, socio-cultural contexts can't be ignored. Besides, the organism, particularly, the human being in order to adjust effectively with his external and internal environ-mental demands, come in to interaction with others. Owing to such interactions, our behaviours are constantly modified, moulded and shaped in accordance with the socio-cultural norms, traditions, values, beliefs etc. Therefore, a psychologist while pursuing the study of adjustive behaviours also study the socio-cultural influences on behaviour.

Thus, psychology studies both aspects of behaviour—biological and socio-cultural aspects. In this sense, psychology is a **bio-social science**.

1.8 IS PSYCHOLOGY A NATURAL SCIENCE?

The nature of psychology as a science is also akin to natural sciences. The entire kingdom of organism including human beings is an integral part of this natural universe. Therefore, psychology can hardly be abstracted from natural science. In fact, it is believed that physical science or to say, the natural science is the basis of all sciences. It is also believed that ultimately, all sciences subsumes in physical science. So is the case with psychology. The science of psychology grew as a result of advances made in several natural sciences dealing with physical and chemical aspects of the universe. As a result, psychologists also began to take keen interests in applying the physio-chemical principles and laws to describe and explain the psychic phenomenon. This interest has resulted in the emergence of a new and vast area of research—establishing the relationship that exists between physical energies and their consequential psychological effects. This branch of psychology is known as **psycho-physics**.

In order to study the psycho-physical relations, application of mathematical principles is imperative. This made psychologists to be interested in the area of measurement of psychological processes by applying statistical measures—a branch of mathematics and fostered the emergence of still a new branch of psychology known as **psychometrics**.

From what has been discussed above, it is obvious that psychology besides being a bio-social science, is also intimately and intricately connected with other natural sciences. This is one reason that in many of the universities in India as well as abroad, study of psychology is offered in the faculty of science, both at the undergraduate and postgraduate levels. Students of these universities earn the degrees of B.Sc. or M.Sc. More recently, two other sciences have emerged, namely the **neuro science** and **computer science**. These two sciences also share much with psychology. For example, due to developments taking place in the area of neuroscience, the recent most brain imaging techniques such as MRI, EEG etc. are being widely used by neuropsychologists to study the brain functions in real time perspectives, *i.e.* when the brain functioning is actually occurring. Similarly, in IT sector, both human-computer interaction and artificial intelligence cannot possibly grow without psychological knowledge in cognitive processes.

Thus, psychology as a science or discipline today has two parallel streams. One which makes use of the methods in physical and biological sciences and the other which makes use of the methods of social and cultural sciences in studying various psychological and social phenomenon.

1.9 GOALS OR OBJECTIVES OF PSYCHOLOGY

Every science sets its definite goals and to achieve these goals is the main concern of scientific studies. Psychology, like other sciences is also a child of curiosity that aims at the following:

1.9.1 Describing the Behaviour

The primary major goal of any scientific discipline is to present accurate description of some aspects of the universe. Psychologists have chosen the behavioural aspect of the universe as the major concern to describe in objective terms.

To describe behaviour events in objective terms is extremely difficult. It is difficult because

(a) The nature of behaviour is very complex and intricate. Therefore, to unravel and describe complex knots of behavioural phenomenon becomes very difficult.

(b) Behaviour is not only complex rather also dynamic. Hence, description of a piece of behaviour on one occassion is likely to be falsified on another occassion. Behaviour, in fact, is such kind of variable that is susceptible to vary with every variations in time, place, sequence or other physical, social contexts.

Despite above difficulties, psychologists use objective observation method to collect large many facts to describe behavioural events. Describing behaviour on the basis of large many observations in an impartial manner, *i.e.* not allowing the observation being influenced by observer's personal views, prejudices, theoretical bindings, attitudes or impressions, etc. approximates the observation to the extent of highest possible accuracy. Thus, higher and dependable level of accuracy in the description of behaviour is achieved by employing proper control. Such objective observations are called 'controlled observation'.

1.9.2 Understanding the Behaviour

Second major goal of psychology is to understand the described behaviours by explaining the facts in a meaningful way. This involves explanation of the complexities or intricacies using classificatory categories of behavioural events on the basis of certain similarities in some aspects of behaviour. Usually two types of classificatory systems are most common. These are **qualitative** and **quantitative** classifications.

(a) **Qualitative classification:** In this system of classification, people (or any living being) are sorted and classified into groups and an appropriate label is assigned to the category. This sorting and group classification is done on the basis of certain common properties that they possess. For example, people may be sorted out on the basis of age level, socio-economic status (SES), gender, marital status, rationality or irrationality, level of education etc. Although, people who are put into a particular category may differ from each other in a number of ways, however, they possess some common similarity in attributes that is taken as the basis for classificatory category or categories as explained above.

(b) **Quantitative classification:** Quantitative classification is done on the basis of differences in degree of some measurable properties or characteristics. For example, people may be classified in terms of high or low in intelligence, achievement, level of aspiration, motivations, frequencies of approaching a target, personality dimensions etc. Quantitative classificatory system enables the psychologists to compare and determine the relationship between two variables, relative position of an individual on measured attribute in the population of the group etc. Psychologists use statistical techniques to determine all these.

With a view to achieve scientific understanding, psychologists make larger number of observations to substantiate the facts under study. This makes it possible to make meaningful generalizations about consistent relationship between various facts. This involves organization of facts to derive useful generalizations and understanding the behavioural facts.

Further, psychologists also organize the facts and principles in a logical frame which is orderly and consistent. This helps in relating the observed facts of behaviour to general principles and thus derive theories to explain the facts of behaviour and suggest some hypotheses to test in future studies.

Developing scientific understanding come under the domain of **pure science** which is distinct from **applied science**. Applied science concerns with practical application of scientific knowledge. However, in modern times, such a classification of science is not absolute rather relative. It is so because every scientific exploration is subjected to application in solving large number of problems relating to the exploratory facts.

1.9.3 Predicting the Behaviour

Like all other sciences, prediction is also one of the major goals of psychological studies. **Prediction** involves knowledge about the possible happenings in future. This is a natural curiosity of man. Throughout the history of mankind, people have been found curious enough to know the future and prepare oneself in advance for the predicted events. Owing to this natural curiosity of humans, the oracles and soothsayers in ancient times hold significantly honourable positions. However, in recent times, people rely more on scientific bases of such predictions. Scientific predictions are done on empirical basis of cause and effect relationship. On similar lines, psychologists discover the cause (that initiates a particular mode of response) and the effect (the particular mode of response that occurs under specific conditions) relationship of behaviour events and thus make predictions about the occurrence of a particular behavioural phenomenon in future. That is, what has led to what today is predicted what will lead to what in future. Such predictions are based on empirical facts of observed behavioural events which is distinct from the predictions of the soothsayers or oracles. It has a scientific base and verifiable in nature.

1.9.4 Control

Curiosity of men does not remain confined only to describe, understand and predict. Man also desires to influence and change what happens. This desire further creates another important goal to control the events to make or mould it in a desirable direction so that deviation in behaviour, if any, is brought under control and normalcy could be maintained. To achieve this goal, psychologists develop the ability to plan and direct behaviour. For example, psychologists work to guide individuals in selecting appropriate vocations as per predictable range of success, extend counselling services to reform disabilities of any kind, plan rehabilitative programme to help disabled individuals to improve their difficulties, reducing anxiety or stress, modify behavioural difficulties in adjusting with the environment, improving the adjustive patterns, treating psychological disorders and making life happy. These relate to teaching of art of living (AOL).

Thus, the goals of psychology are to describe, to understand, to predict and control behaviour events.

1.10 SUB-FIELDS OR BRANCHES OF PSYCHOLOGY

As has been described earlier, the scope of psychology is very vast. It covers all the aspects of human behaviour—physical or mental in relation to environment in which we live. Our environment is so vast and dynamic that all aspects of human behaviour in relation to environment cannot be embedded into a single discipline—'Psychology' by itself. In view of this, the interests of psychologists have grown ranging from simple reflexive activities to most complex behaviours that we display in course of dealing or interacting with the vast environment. As such, most psychologists hold the view that **'there is no psychology; there are only psychologies'**. This implies that psychology has pervaded almost to the entire life-spheres of human beings. This has resulted into growth and development of psychology into a **giant tree** of behavioural studies within a very short span of its emergence as a systematic discipline.

In the present section, attempt is made to acquaint the readers with main outline of the subject matter of some important fruit-bearing branches of this gaint tree—**psychology**.

Different subfields (or branches) of psychology can be put under two major categories—**theoretical** and **applied**. The 'theoretical branches' are concerned with general principles and theoretical models of behavioural phenomenon that explains the 'behaviour' that occurs in various environmental contexts. Such branches are labelled as **pure science**. On the other hand, **applied branches** have the major concern with the solution of practical psychological problems of different life situations in various environmental contexts. In other words, the acquired body of knowledge of psychology are applied to solve the problems of related areas of human activities.

Some of the important branches under the two heads are shown in **Table 1.1**.

TABLE 1.1 Major subfields (branches) of psychology

Theoretical branches	*Applied branches*
(i) General Psychology	(i) Educational Psychology
(ii) Abnormal Psychology	(ii) Clinical Psychology
(iii) Social Psychology	(iii) Industrial Psychology
(iv) Developmental Psychology	(iv) Medical Psychology
(v) Physiological Psychology	(v) Criminal Psychology
(vi) Experimental Psychology	(vi) Legal Psychology
(vii) Comparative Psychology	(vii) Engineering Psychology

1.10.1 Theoretical Branches

A brief description of each of the above branches are presented below:

General psychology: General Psychology deals with description and explanation of behaviour in general. It explains the behavioural events in terms of general principles and laws that govern various physical and mental activities of a normal person such as learning, perceiving, growth and development of personality, individual differences in abilities, memory, thought processes, motivations etc. that cause behaviours.

In sum, General Psychology is concerned mainly with collecting facts of behaviour in general terms, formulation of theories and principles, testing and verifying these theories and describing the behavioural phenomenon in the light of theoretical formulations, predicting and providing guidelines to control behaviours. These theoretical formulations and principles provide useful information to the psychologists working in other theoretical and applied fields.

Thus, General Psychology is a body of general knowledge about various behavioural phenomena which serve useful purpose to all other branches of psychology.

Abnormal psychology: Abnormal Psychology is concerned with description and study of abnormal forms of behaviour. Such behaviour forms are indicative of pathological state of mind and presents deviated pictures of normal behaviours. These deviated forms of behaviours are also called imbalanced or impaired behaviour patterns because they lead to maladjustment.

Abnormal behaviours take several forms such as—phobic reactions, hysterical states, obsessive and compulsive behaviours, disorders of mood, functional psychotic reactions, criminal behaviours, juvenile delinquencies, character disorders, psychosomatic disorders, alcoholism, drug addictions, psychological amnesia etc. Abnormal Psychology attempts to describe and explain the dynamics and theories concerning all such abnormal forms of behaviour or behavioural disorders.

Social psychology: This branch is also called 'Socio-cultural' Psychology. Man is a social being. Therefore, no individual can live or exist alone. Man lives with others throughout his lifespan (from birth till death). Every piece of individual behaviour bears the stamps or impressions of his socio-cultural context. This implies that in order to know and understand individual's behaviour, an account of his socio-cultural reference is imperative.

Socio-cultural Psychology studies the interactional patterns of individuals in reference to the socio-cultural settings at the following three different levels:

- Dyad interactional situations (interaction between two individuals).
- Interaction between one individual to a group of other individuals (individual-group situation).
- Interactions taking place between group of individuals (group to group situations).

All the above levels of interactions occur in mutual dimensions that a social psychologist pursues to study. In course of studying the patterns of interaction at the above levels, psychologists also take stock of cultural effects, *i.e.* the effects of values, traditions, standards and material aspects of a culture, *i.e.* arts, architecture, literature etc. These cultural aspects are internally linked with the nature and kind of individual's social interactions as these shape our attitudes, motives perceptions, belief systems, membership to a socio-cultural group, prejudices and many more psychological processes of an individual living in a particular socio-cultural milieu. Thus, the scope of Socio-cultural Psychology is vast enough and perhaps for this reason, it is generally remarked—**all psychology is Social Psychology**.

Developmental psychology: Developmental psychology concerns with the physiological as well as mental growth and development of children. Hence, it is also loosely named as **Child Psychology**. However, it is proper to call it as Developmental Psychology instead of Child Psychology because Developmental Psychology studies the growth and development of a man throughout his lifespan ranging from pre-natal state till old age, *i.e.* till death.

From psychological point of view, childhood is formative period of personality and various behavioural patterns. Growth and development of personality are based on the kind of foundation during early phases of development. This involves the study of the physical, social and psychological contexts.

Developmental Psychology studies the physical, social and psychological changes that occur at different ages and stages over a lifespan from conception to old age. The primary concern is to know and understand **how we become what we are**. In recent years, the focus of interest of increasing number of developmental psychologists in addition to childhood developments also include strong interest in adult development and aging. They focus on biological, sociocultural and environmental factors that influence psychological characteristics such as intelligence, cognition, emotion, temperament, morality and social relationship. Developmental psychologists collaborate with anthropologists, educationists, neurologists, social workers, counsellors and almost every branch of knowledge where there is concern for growth and development of a human being.

Physiological psychology: The basis of behaviour—mental or physical—is the physiological study. Psychology also incorporates the study of physiological bases of behaviours. This branch of psychology is also called **Biological Psychology**. It focuses on the relationship between behaviour and the physical system, including brain and the rest of the nervous system, the immune system and genetics. Physiological or biological psychologists often collaborate with neuro-scientists, zoologists and anthropologists. **Neuro Psychology** has recently emerged as a field of research where the psychologists and neuroscientists work together as a team. This branch of psychology includes research studies on the role of neurotransmitters or chemical substances which are responsible for neural communication in different areas of brain. Such communications are associated with various mental and congnitive functions. Neuro psychologists do their research on both kinds of people—those with normal brain functions as well as those with damaged brain. They use the advanced technologies like EEG, MRI, Scanning, PET etc. These techniques are recently developed to study brain function in real time perspective *i.e.* when it is actually going on.

Experimental psychology: Quite a good number of psychologists seem solely interested in experimental studies of psychological processes. They focus on knowing the fundamental causes of behaviour events. The major problems of experimental research include the areas of sensory processes, perceptual and attentional processes, modification of behaviours (learning), underlying motivational factors of behavioural events, affective processes (emotions and feelings) etc.

Following experimental procedures, psychologists collect objective facts about the various kinds of variables that cause a behaviour. Through experimentation, psychologists attempt to establish the various ways in which the observed facts are related or associated with the variable under study and accordingly, the psychologists formulate the laws and principles, test their soundness, The primary major objective of experimental psychologists lies in determining invariable relationships that exists between two or more than two variables. This objective of experimentation aims at discovering definite **cause and effect** relationships. Thus, an experimental psychologist tries to know and understands what and how an individual experiences his environment and discovers the variables that determine interpretation, what and how behaviour is modified and retained, retrieved, what factors facilitate remembering and what causes forgetting, what and how one get motivated to respond in a particular manner and not in any other way, what goes on inside while one thinks over a problem and how solutions are achieved, how does nervous system function to produce a behaviour etc.

Obviously, Experimental Psychology is a fundamental subfield of Psychology through which causal relationships of behavioural events are determined.

Comparative psychology: Experimental psychologists are particularly fond of controlled experimentation. To achieve adequate level of control, they prefer to use animals as subjects of experiment. Secondly, in order to better understand human behaviours, psychologists feel it necessary to trace back to evolutionary process of human beings who are supposed to have evolved in present form from simpler to complex animals. Hence, comparing the behaviours of human beings with other animals make significant contributions in understanding the behaviours of humans. This is what comparative psychology deals with.

The tradition of studying animal's behaviour has grown very fast and thus, a new subfield of psychology has emerged which is called Comparative Psychology or Animal Psychology.

Cognitive psychology: This is still another subfield of psychology which is concerned with the study of mental processes involved in acquisition, storage, manipulation and transformation of information received from the world around us. It also pursues the investigations as to how these processes are used and how do we communicate to others. All these mental processes are the congnitive processes involved in behaviour. The major cognitive processes are attention, perception, memory, reasoning, problem solving, decision-making and language. Though, all these topics are also covered in General Psychology, Cognitive Psychology has emerged as an offshoot of General Psychology which investigates the cognitive process extensively and has developed several models to explain cognitive processes based on **information processing models**. Cognitive psychologists conduct experiments in laboratory settings. Some of them also follow ecological approach, *i.e.* an approach that focuses on the environ-mental factors to study congnitive processes in natural setting. Congnitive psychologists often collaborate with neuroscientists and computer scientists.

1.10.2 Applied Branches

Educational psychology: Educational Psychology is concerned with solution of various psychological problems of educational institutions. It studies how people of all ages learn. The primary concern of educational psychologists is to help in developing instructional methods and materials used to train people in both educational and work settings. They are also concerned with research on issues of relevance for education, counselling and learning problems.

Educational Psychology is also concerned with the development of harmonious relationships between teacher and taught (pupil), improving teaching methods and learning processes, guiding, controlling and predicting behaviours of learners.

The professionals working in educational institutions have made many commendable works such as development of audio-visual aids in teaching, communication aid techniques etc. These developments are considered as landmark development in educational system. Similarly, educational psychologists have made significant contributions in educational settings by developing standardized tools of measurements to assess educational progress of pupils which are used to measure learning, memory, thinking, intelligence, aptitude, interests etc. The psychologists also work for bringing improvements in these processes on the basis of assessment through measurement and give useful advice.

A related field of educational psychology is known as **School Psychology** with focus on designing programmes that promote intellectual, social and emotional development of children, including those with special needs. They try to apply knowledge of psychology in a school setting.

Clinical psychology: Clinical Psychology is closely tied with Abnormal Psychology. Clinical Psychology deals with causes, treatment and prevention of different types of psychological disorders such as anxiety, depression, eating disorders and chronic substance abuse. A related area is **counselling**. The main concern of this related field is to improve everyday functioning by helping people solve problems in daily living and cope more effectively with challenging life situations. The work of clinical psychologists does not differ from that of counselling psychologists. However, counselling psychologists deal with people who have relatively less serious problems. In many instances counselling psychologists work with students, advising them about personal problems and career planning.

Clinical psychologists are professionally trained in the area of clinical problems relating to maladaptive forms of behaviour. They help people by diagnosing the form of abnormality and extending professional help to correct them by applying psychological principles inherent in psychotherapies, arranging for post-healthcare and launching of rehabilitative programmes. In discharging these responsibilities, clinical psychologists often collaborate with other professionals of clinical settings such as psychiatrists, social workers and other skilled staff.

The subject matter of this branch of psychology covers the subject matter of Abnormal Psychology (discussed earlier) with the difference that the clinical psychologists apply the general principles and theories of Abnormal Psychology in clinical settings.

Industrial/Organizational psychology: Industries and various organizational set-ups are concerned with human's important work sectors relating to economic aspects of behaviour. These set-ups are the major areas of man's total environment where psychological principles and theories are applied to handle various human problems of psychological nature. This branch of psychology deals with workplace behaviour focusing on both the workers and organizations that employ them. Industrial and organizational psychologists are concerned with training the employees, improving work conditions and developing criteria for selecting fit employees for the fit job. For example, suppose an organizational psychologist recommends to adopt a new management structure that may increase communication between managers and staff.

The background of industrial and organizational psychologists often includes training in Cognitive and Social Psychology such as improving interactional social relationships, betterment of worker's social life, launching social welfare programme etc. The critical issues with which industrial psychologists deal with include job analysis, enhancing work motivation, preventing accidents, solving the problems of turnover, labour wastage and appropriate management of human resources, enhancing work efficiency, reducing work fatigue, improving physical and psychological work conditions, solving industrial conflicts and increasing the morale.

Industrial/Organizational psychologists apply the psychological principles in industrial and organizational set-ups as an skilled professional who acquires these skills through special training and experience as industrial or organizational psychologist.

Medical or health psychology: Medical Psychology focuses on the role of psychological factors (*e.g.*, stress, anxiety) in the development, prevention and treatment of illness. Areas of interest for medical psychologists are stress and coping, the relationship between psychological factors and health, patient-doctor relationship, and ways of promoting health enhancing factors.

Criminal psychology: Criminal Psychology deals with criminals and delinquent behaviours. They analyse such behaviours on psychological principles and help the other professionals in identifying the criminals, their intentions, causes of criminal behaviours. Besides, criminal psychologists also try to help the criminals to bring reform and provide rehabilitative aids to lead their life like other normal human beings.

Application of psychology in some other fields: In addition to above-mentioned fields of psychology, there are many other fields as well where the principles of psychology are applied. It includes Legal Psychology, Engineering Psychology, Environmental Psychology, Sports Psychology etc. In fact, psychology has pervaded in all the spheres of human life such as administration, politics, trade and commerce, defence, police investigations, international relations, dealing with terrorists and extremists etc. Thus, the knowledge acquired by psychologists is so vast that it can be applied to any sphere of human life.

Obviously, the scope of applying knowledge and principles of psychology is very vast and hence, the statement that **there is no psychology, there is only psychologies** seems to hold true.

1.11 PSYCHOLOGY AND LIFE

From the point of view of a psychologist, psychology is the science of human and animal's behaviour including the application of this science in solving various human problems. What follows from this is that psychology has concern with real and practical problems of human life. Thus, psychology is not merely a subject that satisfies some of the curiosities about human nature, but it is a discipline that can offer solutions to a variety of human problems. These problems may range from purely personal (*e.g.* a daughter having to face an alcohalic father or a mother dealing with a problem child) to those that are rooted within the family (*e.g.* lack of familial relations and communication among family members) or in a larger group or community settings (*e.g.* terriorist groups, socially isolated communities) or it may have national or international dimensions.

Modern human life is encountered with various problems such as, problems related to education, health environment, intergroup relations, marital relations, daily life hassles etc. Solution of most of these problems involve political, economic and social reforms. However, interventions at individual levels are also needed to bring changes in human life and provide relief by easing the tension caused due to various problems that human beings are facing today.

Many of the human life problems are psychologically originated and these result from our ill-thinking, negative attitudes towards people and self and undesirable behavioural patterns. Analysis of these problems along psychological frames helps not only in having a deeper understanding of problems but also in finding their effective solutions.

Due to vital role of media, the potential of psychology in solving life problems is being greatly realized. Through several programmes on T.V. screens, we often see counsellors and psychotherapists suggesting solutions to a variety of problems related to children, adolescents, adults and aging people. We often also find these professionals analysing some vital social problems relating to the influence of social change and development, population, poverty, national integrity, intergroup or community violence and degradation of environment. Many psychologists now play an active role in designing and executing intervention programme with a view to provide better Quality of Life (QOL) to human beings. Realizing the vital and active role that a psychologist can play, quite a good number of psychologists are seen working in diverse areas such as schools, hospitals, industries, organizational set-ups, prisons, military establishments etc. An appreciable number of psychologists are also seen doing private practice as consultants and counsellors to help people in solving problems of concerned areas.

In addition to extending help in solving social problems and rendering social service, knowledge of psychology has also a relevance on personal level in handling daily life problems of the self. The principles and methods of psychology that we learn in psychology may be used in analysing and understanding oneself in relation to others.

No doubt, we do think about ourselves. But, often, some of us think very high of ourselves and feedback that contradicts our opinion about ourselves are rejected because our mind adopts defensive behaviour. Similarly often we develop a habit of running down ourselves. Both of these conditions are detrimental to our personal growth. We need to have a positive and balanced understanding of ourselves. If we are well-acquainted with psychological principles, we may use these principles in a positive manner that may help in healthy growth of mind. We may also develop good habits of study and improve our learning and memory and for solving personal and interpersonal problems by using appropriate decision-making strategies.

Knowledge of psychology may further help us in alleviating various kinds of stress that we often experience in our daily life situations and also make attempts to develop emotional intelligence.

Thus, the knowledge of psychology is of much use in our everyday life and is rewarding from personal as well as social points of views.

1.12 RELATIONSHIP OF PSYCHOLOGY WITH OTHER DISCIPLINES

While discussing the nature of psychology, we have seen that the discipline of psychology is concerned with the study of adjustive behaviour. Behaviour is determined by multiple complex factors—biological, social, anthropological and so on. This means that the study of behaviour is not the exclusive domain of psychology. There are other disciplines too, which study the human and animal behaviours. These disciplines include 'Anthropology', 'Sociology', 'Physiology', 'Economics', 'Political Science', 'History' etc. All these disciplines taken together are temed as **family of behavioural science** of which Psychology is a major member.

All behavioural sciences bear some resemblance with each other. More particularly, in respect of the use of empirical data and vigrous methods of study, all behavioural sciences display some points of similarity. However, different sciences possess some distinct identity in respect of priority of emphasis they lay upon.

In the following section, the major similarities between psychology and other sciences with points of differences are being briefly described.

1.12.1 Psychology and Anthropology

Anthropology is the study of human behaviour with emphasis on groups, most often larger groups. A branch of anthropology is concerned with the physical characteristics of people of different cultural and ethnic groups around the world. This includes the study of different races, societies, cultures—their physical characteristics as well as intellectual and emotional traits. Another branch of anthropology is 'socio-cultural'. This branch mainly concerns with the study of cultural and social structural aspects of various societies or groups, typical personality features of people of these societies or groups and how their socio-cultural traditions, values, customs influence specific personality features of the concerned societies or cultural groups. Besides, anthropology also examines primitive cultures, their habitats, rituals, customs etc. It also deals with evolution of culture from primitive to present, impacts of enculturation, acculturation and the process of cultural change.

All such studies by anthropologists have provided useful information or data in understanding the psychological processes of human beings that influence the behaviour. In this sense, anthropology is an important source of understanding the nature and cultural influences on individual's behavioural patterns. Thus, the two disciplines bear much similarity on the content of study.

However, the two sciences differ from each other on the emphasis laid by them. Psychology concerns with the individual as an unit of psychological studies whereas anthropologists concern themselves with the cultural group as a whole, of which individuals are the part.

But to understand individual, taking stock of cultures and vice versa is necessary because both the sciences have certain common problems and the specialists of these disciplines share each others' views by supplementing their areas of knowledge like a couple.

1.12.2 Psychology and Sociology

Psychology and sociology are intimately related to each other with the only difference in the emphasis laid on unit of study. For psychology, the unit of focus is individual while sociology focuses on the group of individuals. Thus, the two sciences differ from each other in terms of 'unit' of analysis—for psychologists the individual—building block of social group is subjected to be studied while for the sociologists, these building blocks do not matter much, rather they emphasize to study the social group as a whole. In this sense, psychologists follow the **'down top approach'**, *i.e.* from individual to group, whereas sociologists follow the **'top down approach'**, *i.e.* they study the group comprising the individuals and their collective interactional relations. Thus, for the sociological studies, individuals matter only in collective terms while in psychological studies what matters is the individual.

But it is important to note here that the study of behaviour of an individual in isolation from social and cultural context would not be possible because individual's behaviour is determined and shaped by social frame of reference. Hence, an individual's behaviour bears the stamp (impressions) of the society. The socio-cultural contexts and individual's behavioural events are so intricately weaved together that can hardly be separated. Therefore, psychologists do take into stock the socio-cultural contexts to know and understand individual behaviours.

Therefore, the two sciences are complimentary to each other. For example, psychologists study individual's motivations, attentional processes, perceptions, thoughts and many more psychological processes. On the other hand, a sociologist studies the nature and kind of social structure-groups and how the society functions, how social norms, traditions, customs etc. influence group functioning, the impacts of social change on the society etc. However, individual's psychological processes are constantly influenced by social forces. Thus, to understand how the psychological processes are changed or function, the study of social forces is indispensable. In this sense, the interests of the two sciences overlap with the principal distinction in approach.

Thus, the two disciplines are more collaborative than distinct.

1.12.3 Psychology and Physiology

Physiology (more appropriately called biology) is a life science which studies the functions of different biological organs such as the stomach, heart, glands, sensory organs, brain and various systems such as the digestive system, circulatory system, respiratory system, excretory system neural co-ordinating system etc. It mainly concerns how things go, repair, reproduce their kinds and how the life processes are carried on and regulated.

Psychologists also in course of pursuing adjustive behaviours concern with the physiological or biological bases of behaviour. Hence, knowledge of physiological process contributes much in gaining knowledge about human behaviour. More particularly the study of sensory processes, perceptual events, functions of organs of response and adjustor-effector coordinating systems (neural connections of the brain) along with biological injuries, impact of genetic processes on growth and development of an individual etc. are significant to understand the behavioural events of human beings. Thus, psychology is not only associated with physiology but also with biology, genetics, embryology etc.

1.12.4 Economics, Political Science and History

As sister social science disciplines, these three have drawn considerably from psychology and have enriched it as well. Psychology has contributed a great deal to the study of micro level economic behaviour, particularly in understanding consumer behaviour, savings behaviour and in decision-making behaviour. American economists are found utilizing data on consumer sentiments to produce products and foster economic growth. Three scientists who have worked on such problems have been awarded the nobel prize in economics, namely H. Simon, K. Kahneman and T. Schelling.

Like economics, political science also draws considerably from psychology. Particularly in understanding issues related to exercise of power, governance and authority, nature of political conflicts and their resolutions and voting behaviour etc.

History again is a behavioural science which attempts to reconstruct and understand the historical events. Such events are largely related to human behaviour that makes history. Psychologists too analyse the behavioural aspects related to such events. Hence, the two sciences are in close association with each other. To an extent, both make use of records of past events and hence, are historical.

1.12.5 Relationship of Psychology to other Natural Sciences

Natural sciences such as physics, chemistry, mathematics, zoology etc. are of course, not behavioural sciences. Yet, the researchers of these disciplines sometimes pursue the study of human behaviour. Some of our useful knowledge about sensory processes and perceptual events have come from physics who ventured to measure human reactions to different kinds of physical stimuli. This has led to the development of a new branch of psychology—**Psychophysics**.

Mathematics has also a significant bearing in developing psychology as a scientific study of behavioural phenomenon. Statistics is one of the applied branches of mathematics which psychologists use for analysing descriptive data in a precised, concrete and systematic way. Use of mathematics or statistical principles has undoubtedly brought psychology very near to natural sciences and a new branch of psychology—**'Psychometrics'** has emerged.

1.12.6 Conclusive Remarks on the Relationship of Psychology with other Sciences

What follows from the above discussion of relationship of psychology with other disciplines, it is obvious that to sketch any absolute demarketing line between different sciences is increasingly difficult. The distinctions between different related sciences are not watertight. They differ only in emphasis. Rather, the specialists of different disciplines work side-by-side, often collaborating with each other on the study of behavioural phenomenon. In fact, psychology can be located at some point of convergence where it interacts with other disciplines—physiology or biology, computer science, neuroscience and other natural sciences. Psychologists gather facts about human behaviour from all these sciences to analyse them from psychological perspectives. Similarly, other sciences too take in the psychological facts of human behaviour to study and analyse them from their respective perspectives.

As we have seen, different social sciences too borrow much from psychology and vice versa. However, different social science disciplines study the behavioural phenomenon from their respective perspectives and approaches.

Thus, psychology and all other sciences subsume with each other and has resulted in multidisciplinary approach of analysing behavioural events. Accordingly psychology, today is known as **eclectic science** as it takes stock of interdisciplinary approach of viewing individual's behaviour.

1.13 PSYCHOLOGY TODAY

The nature of contemporary psychology is pervasive. The developments in contemporary psychology showing advances in theory and application are wide-ranging. The range of psychology today has widened its concerns and psychologists are vigorously working to reconstruct psychological theories and principles on the basis of advances being made in other disciplines. Psychologists of the day have begun to realize the cultural contexts of psychology and thus try to study psychological processes in cultural frame of contexts and discard the Euro-American based principles of psychology.

Today, we are moving towards the age of information. Such transitions call for inter-dependence and sharing. In view of such demands, psychologists today are repositioning themselves by striking a balance between local realities and global concerns. These developments are exciting and psychologists now are also aggressively moving towards adopting eclectic principles to study the psychological processes of mankind. This has resulted in the development of computer related information processing models of behaviour and mental activities. As a result, most of the cognitive processes are being described in terms of information processing processes.

1.14 NEW FRONTIERS OF PSYCHOLOGY

Psychology is growing very fast in many directions. Since psychology is applicable in various areas of human life situations and in order to improve quality of life (QOL), the theoretical and methodological concerns of psychology too has become vast enough. Researchers are taking greater interests in studying biological, socio-cultural, cognitive, community, and health related issues of human life. In each and every field, new ideas are emerging and large number of findings are being obtained. This is posing a challenge to the psychologists to encompass the entire facts of voluminous research findings into a limited body of knowledge about psychology. To meet these challenges, many new subfields of psychology have emerged. Some of the recently emerged subfields are described below.

1.14.1 Neuro-Psychology

In this emerging field, researchers concern themselves in understanding the functioning of intact-brain (without damaging or injuring) as it relates to mental functions. Advances are being made in many directions. One of the most recent areas is the study of **neural communication**. Researchers are uncovering the working of neurotransmitters—a kind of chemical which is responsible for neural communication. At present, about 40 such neurotransmitting substances have been made known. These transmitting substances can be put under three categories as under:

(a) **Monomines:** Such as dopamine, norepinephrine, serotonine etc. These substances play vital role in emotion, movement, learning and memory.

(b) **Acetylcholine:** This substance is important for memory.

(c) **Gama-aminobutyric acid (GABA):** It is the major inhibitory transmitter. It is important for emotion, anxiety and arousal.

(d) **Endophins:** It regulates pain and pleasure.

These neurotransmitters are found in different parts of the brain, particularly in limbic system, thalamus, brain stem and frontal cortex. Knowledge of these neurotransmitters is unravelling the mystery of mental functions and has proved very much useful in fighting with various diseases. Thus, it is of great significance in enhancing the well-being of human beings.

1.14.2 Positive Psychology

In the face of ever-increasing trends of competition and fast life throughout the globe, the human lifestyle has tremendously changed than before. This has resulted in two types of mutually antagonistic changes in our lifestyle. On the one hand, we are moving fast towards consuming all available products of comfort and luxury and competing in all spheres of human life. On the other hand, the limitations of resources are putting hurdles in our desire to consume and compete. Modern life is characterized by **survival of the fittest as well as fastest**. This characteristic feature of modern life has brought forth many difficulties and we are passing through great stress and strain. In view of this, there has been greater interest among psychologists in topics like hope, optimism, happiness, and flow (spontaneity). Taken together all these constructs deal with positive side of human existence and as such, has paved the way for the emergence of still a new branch of Psychology—we call **Positive Psychology**. Positive Psychology is concerned with evolving strategies to manage negative emotions, enhancing positive emotions, developing and strengthening of self-concept and identity, strategies to cope with life challenges posed by stressful life events and developing hope, optimism, abilities to compete and overall psychological well-being.

1.14.3 Military Psychology

Military is the greatest power of a country and occupies super-ordinated postion as national security agency. Hence, application of psychology in defence agency is of paramount significance. In defence sectors, psychology is applied to perform the following main purposes:

(a) for selecting defence personnel of different levels.

(b) for designing appropriate training programmes such as strategies for defence, attack, escape strategies, learning these strategies, coping with stress in battlefields and defending the personnel from mental shock. Such designs prepared by psychologists are much useful.

(c) preparing or designing programme to learn leadership qualities called officer-like qualities (OLQ).

(d) arranging mass level campaign programmes to maintain defence personnel's morale within and outside the forces.

(e) conducting research studies to solve some problems such as tension, stress problems associated with mountaineering exercises etc.

Obviously, military psychology is concerned with the psychological problems at human level among defence sector personnel and construction of psychological tests to measure different kinds of abilities which are expected in military.

1.14.4 Assessment Psychology

This is one of the most important areas of psychological applications. Measurement of aptitude, intelligence, personality, attitudes, values and many other psychological attributes are useful in research. Providing guidance to people, selecting and training them for different jobs in different organizations are some of the important areas for which assessment of human competencies are required. In recent past, psychologists have been focussing their attention to these requirements and have developed quite a large number of psychological tests for assessing these competencies. This trend has led to the emergence of a new field of psychological testing and assessment called 'Assessment Pshychology'.

1.14.5 Computer Science

From the very beginning, the computer scientists have been working on stimulating the human mind. This can be evident by knowing how a computer is structured and function, how memories are organized and stored through simultaneous and successive processing. Computer scientists are eagerly trying to make computer intelligent as well as devising the software by dint of which computer can also sense and feel like human beings. Developments in both these disciplines (computer and psychology) have brought about significant advancements in the area of **cognitive science**.

There are many new frontiers of psychology that includes 'Aerospace Psychology', 'Correctional Psychology', 'Forensic Psychology', 'Geriatic (Aged) Psychology', 'Environmental Psychology' etc. where the application of psychological principles are relevant. In addition, today psychologists are also seen seriously involved in exploring the role of mental processes about which we are usually unaware—a field known as unconscious mental systems.

Thus, it is crystal clear that psychology is such a discipline that has pervaded in almost all spheres of human activities and quite a good number of new areas of research are being included within the peripheries of psychological studies and application and opening of new frontiers day-by-day.

SUMMARY

- Psychology is a systematic study of behaviours of the organism, more particularly the man and describe them. Hence, it is a behavioural science.
- Psychology has variously been described from time to time and underwent gradual refinements. Currently, psychology is defined in terms of an objective science of adjustive behaviour that includes both overt and covert—physical as well as mental activities—experience.
- There are some wrong notions prevalent in society about psychology and or psychologists. Media play an important role in popularizing such fallacies. However, psychology as a discipline has a scientific base of objective and systematic studies of behavioural facts and predictions are based on such objective observations.
- The field or scope of psychology is very vast. It studies all activities of human beings in diverse areas.
- The major goals of psychology are to describe, explain, predict and control behaviours.
- Psychology is a science much like other natural sciences. However, the psychology as a science is bio-social in nature because it studies behavioural phenomenon in association with socio-cultural contexts.
- Psychology, in fact, is a giant tree with many branches that concern difficult areas of human activities. All these branches are known as independent subfields of psychology as these concern specific areas of study and application.

- The different branches of psychology can be broadly divided into two types—Theoretical and Applied. The Theoretical branches include 'General Psychology', Abnormal Psychology', Social Psychology', 'Cognitive Psychology', 'Developmental Psychology', 'Physiological-Psychology', 'Comparative Psychology' and 'Experimental Psychology'. The applied branches include the 'Clinical Psychology', 'Educational Psychology', 'Industrial/Organizational Psychology', 'Medical Psychology', 'Criminal Psychology' etc.
- Psychology is in fact a life science. Hence, it is intimately related to human life situations. In all walks of life, psychological principles seem to apply to solve human problems on social as well as personal levels.
- Psychology is an integral part of behavioural science family. Hence, it has close associations with other behavioural sciences such as anthropology, sociology, economics, political science, history etc. Besides, it is also related to biology, and other natural sciences including computer science.
- In modern times, psychology is considered as an eclectic science and emphasis is laid on multidisciplinary approach of studying behavioural phenomenon.
- There has been a very fast and rapid growth in the application of psychology in different areas of human activities. This trend has led to convergence of vast number of new frontiers of study such as Neuro Psychology, Sports Psychology, Military Psychology and so on.

CHAPTER 2

Historical Perspectives of Modern Psychology

2.1 FOUNDING IDEAS OF ANCIENT TIMES

As we have seen earlier, psychology has a long past with a short history. A long past because the roots of psychology lie in our curiosities to know about ourselves and our fellowmen. This curiosity has always remained a crowning characteristic of mankind ever since its evolution in the present form. But, psychology has a short history because it has emerged as an organized body of scientific enquiry recently—hardly over a century ago.

If we look at the historical records of evolution, it would be observed that many divergent systems and views existed right from the ancient times. However, the most early people were not able to understand and predict natural events objectively. They mostly used to explain such events in terms of supernatural powers and or good/evil spirits. Such views of ancient people are known as **demonology**. Ancient people gradually developed the idea of **soul** and considered that soul is an entity that rests inside mortal body. The soul itself is immortal that exists even after death. The basis of this explanation was the experience that soul could leave one's body and visit other places as we visualize during dreams. Such prevalent ideas led to the development of various mythologies which gradually became powerful and complex enough to explain various curiosities of human beings during ancient times.

2.2 ANCIENT GREEKS' VIEWS

Against these mythologies and analogies, ancient Greeks made some significant and valuable contributions in diverse areas such as 'art', 'literature' and 'Philosophy'. Their beliefs no doubt brought some notable changes in ideas about the universe that people hold. People now began to realize the efficiency of reasoning in calculating and understanding the natural events. Their beliefs presented the world as a very orderly place to live in. Such beliefs were the basic thoughts of western thinkers and it is believed that the modern psychology also began in western philosophical thoughts. The western philosophical perspectives that developed in Greece had two divergent approaches—the **empiricist view** led by **Aristotle** and the latter view that derived from Aristotle's view is known as **rationalism** led by **Plato**. Aristotle promoted the idea of **elementalism** meaning thereby that anything **complex** may be understood through reducing it to its elements. In psychology, this idea of elementalism took the form of **analysing mind by reducing it to sensation and associations.**

The latter view of **Plato** emphasized the **rationalism** as opposed to **empiricism**. This view lays emphasis on **reasoning**. For him, knowledge is derived from **reason** which is as valid as the knowledge itself. Accordingly, the sensory inputs were considered as imperfect source of knowledge and therefore by analysing the mind into sensations would not be as valid as knowing the mind through reasoning.

2.3 PHILOSOPHICAL ROOTS

Against the aforementioned background of ancient Greeks, there was a significant transition of human thought from **middle age** to modern times. This transition period is known as **Renaissance of Science**. During this period, the trade was on the increase, explorations were being made and ancient writings were being rediscovered. Such discoveries and rediscoveries particularly in cosmic sciences (astronomy) and physical sciences provided some realistic picture about the universe and human thoughts began to analyse and think of various events in somewhat realistic terms. **Francis Bacon's** thought of logic is a good evidence of such transitions to new approach. He bitterly criticized the method of **deducing** knowledge from ancient sources which were applied by the medieval scholars as it was unfruitful or unprofitable. Instead, he proposed **inductive method** and insisted upon observation of natural events to formulate laws that can explain the events. His insistence on inducing knowledge through observation influenced psychology to study various aspects of behaviour applying inductive method based on empirical facts gathered through observation of behavioural events such as habits, education, friendship, praise, reproof etc. Perhaps for this reason, Bacon is often regarded as the **originator** of Social Psychology (Durant, 1949). His method however lacked precision and systematization which could be possible only in a well-equipped laboratory of modern psychology. Further, he also believed that certain truths are beyond the scope of human investigation as they relate to **divine realm.** Hence, not accessible by reasoning. For this reason, he could not get entry into **theology**.

Rene Descarte (1596–1650) is another important figure who influenced the development of modern psychology. He emerged in France and is famous for his assertion—**cogito ergo sum**—meaning **I think therefore I exist**. He proposed that mind and body are separate but interact with each other. He also argued that animals lacked soul and therefore are essentially machines. To Descarte, ideas are put in mind by God and visualized by mental faculties through intuition.

Obviously, Descarte emphasizes that ideas are innate or inherited (because put by God) which are reasoned by mind. Though, Descarte was a mathematician, his views were not scientific in the modern sense. Yet, his emphasis on induction and reasoning influenced psychology in moving towards empirical concepts of psychological facts. Therefore, his contributions are considered significant in founding of modern psychology as an empirical science.

Later, philosophers like **St. Augustine** and **St. Thomas** also made significant contributions in founding of psychology as a systematic body of knowledge. They advocated the concept of **dualism**, *i.e.,* mind and body are two distinct aspects of human being. These two are not interrelated in any way. Hence, there exists a complete division between mind and body. This kind of concept is evidenced from expressions about certain aspects of behavioural events such as: 'while spirit or soul is willing but flesh is weak', 'He may act dumb, but he has got a mind like a steel trap' (Witting and Williams-III, 1929). These expressions obviously provide evidences to the fact that mind and body are two separate and distinct aspects. But some other philosophers like Leibnitz, Descarte and Spinoza attempted to relate mind and body in different ways. Descarte offered the concept of **interactionism** as solution to the problem. He viewed mind and body as separate aspects but proposed that the two interact with each other. **Leibnitz** formulated the theory of **psychological parallelism** that presumes that mind and body both functions as parallel system. **Spinoza**, on the other hand, proposed that mind and body are inseparable aspects. This view is known as **psychological double aspectism**. Thus, the philosophers held **monismic** view about mind and body. This view suggests that though mind and body are two different aspects but these two can be related to one another in certain ways and accordingly, the concepts of interconnectionism, parallelism or double aspectism etc. were proposed.

Around the same period, some British philosophers such as **John Locke**, **George Berkeley** and **David Hume** came forward to protest the above views of the philosophers and launched a movement known as **empiricism**. This movement in fact had a very profound impact on founding of psychology as a prosperous science.

Subsequently, a movement known as **associationism** was derived from empiricism. This new movement was led by **David Hartley**, **James** and **John Stuart Mill**, **Alexander Bain** and **Herbert Spencer**. They were primarily concerned with formulating the principles or laws that govern ideas getting hooked together or get associated together. This movement had again a very deep impact upon the principles of structuralism and modern principles of learning. The principle of **associationism** in fact served as the founding stone for formulating learning theories of **I.V. Pavlov's Conditioning** and **Edward Thorndike's Connectionism.**

Thus, we see that the ancient philosophical thoughts have directly influenced the founding of psychology as a modern systematic science.

2.4 BIOLOGICAL ROOTS

The physiological foundations of modern medicine were laid during 1800–1870 with the works of **Johannes Muller** and **Claude Bernard** in experimental physiology. Their works had greatly influenced psychology in laying the foundation of physiological psychology. **Muller** had proposed the doctrine of **specific nerve energies** which states that 'each sensory nerve yields a specific kind of sensation irrespective of how it might be stimulated'. Thus, Muller holds that we become aware of our world indirectly through stimuli which in turn generate nerve impulses in our sense organs, travels through nerve fibres and terminates in the brain centres. Further, **Marshall Hall**, **Pierre Flourens** and **Paul Broca** studied Brain functions.

Charls Darwin, a British scientist, worked in the fields of biology and genetics. His works brought revolutionary changes in the area of genetics. His book—**Origin of Species** published in 1859 was very much influential. He proposed the theory of **evolution.** According to this theory, human beings are one species on a continuum. Hence, like other species, human beings are also regulated by similar nature of selective pressure as other organisms. This theory further proposes that since human beings share the behavioural characteristics of other organisms on the evolutionary continuum, much can be known about human behaviours by studying the behaviours of other organisms. This paved the way for psychologists to conduct experiments using rats, cats and monkeys and further led to the emergence of a new field of psychology—**Comparative Psychology**.

2.5 BEGINNING OF EXPERIMENTAL PSYCHOLOGY

During the first half of 19th century, scientific studies in various fields such as physiology, physics and Darwin's theory of evolution had greatly influenced the emergence of scientific psychology. Beginning of experimentation on psychological process can be rooted in the discoveries about brain, nervous system and anatomical studies relating to localization of psychological functioning (phrenology), sense physiology etc. These studies stimulated many psychologists to study the physiological or biological bases of human thoughts, feelings and behaviours. In order to study the biological basis of psychological processes, the experimental methods of natural sciences were applied. In this context, the works of **Sir Charles Bell** (1774–1842), **Muller's** (1801–1858) doctrine of specific nerve energies and **Herman Helmholtz's** study to measure the speed of nerve impulse are some of the outstanding contributions in the emergence of modern experimental psychology.

Further, advances made in the field of physiology gave rise to a new field of experimental psychology which is known as **psycho-physics**. Psycho-physics is mainly concerned with detecting the relationship between physical stimuli and their mental experiences. The works of **W.H. Weber** (1795–1878) and **G.T. Fechner** (1801–1857) are the notable contributors who have evolved psycho-physical methods to solve **detection** problems of psycho-physical relations and proposed laws that govern detection of absolute and differential (AL and DL or j.n.d.) limens.

Again the concept of phrenology originally practised by **Franz Gall** (1758–1828) which subsequently was modified and expanded by **Spurzheim** (1776–1832), had also greatly influenced psychology in developing an understanding about various mental faculties and their locations in brain. Their works helped psychologists as well as the physiologists or neuroscientists in localizing the sensory, motor and associative areas in the brain.

Sir Francis Galton (1832–1911), cousin of Darwin, was still another genius British scientist who gave a sudden stroke to the intellectual's world by publishing a book—**Hereditary Genius** and came with a conclusion that outstanding abilities or powerful mental functions are inherited. He was also highly impressed by the concept of variation and became staunch supporter of constant variations from generation to generation and the concept of **individual differences**. His emphasis on individual differences generated a lot of researches which led to the founding of a new branch of psychology called—**psychometrics**—a great contribution to psychological studies. These contributions attracted many psychologists to develop psychological tests for assessing various mental abilities by following scientific criteria.

Thus, we see that right from ancient times, various mythologies and analogies, philosophical thoughts, empiricists movements, developments in the field of neuro physiology, phrenology, psycho-physics and evolutionary doctrines—all were instrumental in founding of modern experimental psychology.

2.6 SCHOOLS OF PSYCHOLOGY

As is evident from the foregoing discussion that different fields of natural and biological sciences had deeply influenced psychology to emerge as a science of human behaviour in the sense that they could forge ahead to use scientific methods of study. This led to the development of a good number of schools of thoughts or 'isms'. These schools differed in their views of man, objectives of psychology and approaches to study. Often these schools clashed with each other resulting in many lively clashes. Yet, these schools of thoughts have significantly enriched our understanding of man and his behaviour. Thus, these schools too have made significant contributions in making psychology a potential science of behavioural studies. The controversies have led to constructive refinements in explaining behavioural events. Therefore, it seems important to briefly discuss the main thrusts of these schools that have brought forth to understand and explain human behaviour.

2.6.1 Structuralism

Structuralism was one of the earliest schools of psychology. Customarily, it is traced back to the year 1879 when **Wilhelm Wundt** at the university of Leipzig in Germany established the first psychological laboratory and made psychology as independent systematic science to study psychological processes. For this reason the year 1879 is considered a **red lettered day in the history of psychology**. Wundt was dissatisfied with the philosophical approach to the study of mind. He emphasized that psychology should acquire the status of an independent system of studying mental processes using objective techniques and this thought prompted him to establish a laboratory to study mental experiences by analysing them into elements that constitute the experience. His laboratory attracted students from all parts of the world.

Wundt and his colleague **Edward Titchner** were interested in analysing human consciousness and identifying its basic elements. They emphasized on mental structures. Structuralists defined psychology as a science that studies about the **conscious experience** and used **introspection** as the method of study.

Wundt was, in fact, a philosopher turned psychologist. As a philosopher he was highly influenced by **John Locke's** views and accordingly believed in gaining knowledge about mental activities through studying the experience aspect of mind. He was also influenced by **Stuart Mill's** concept of mental chemistry. He also possessed adequate knowledge of physiology due to his close associations with **Helmholtz** with whom he worked in his laboratory. Having been influenced by all these he proceeded towards advancing psychology as a systematic independent science by using experimental introspection to analyse experiences in the laboratory which he had founded. Experimental introspection means introspecting one's own experiences and feelings in a systematic manner and analysing such self-observed experiences in objective terms as far as practicable. Structuralists have made distinctions between immediate and mediate experiences. For example—experiencing the toothache is the immediate experience and when an individual based on this immediate experience proceeds to locate the particular teeth with cavity, is mediate experience. Structuralists lay emphasis on the study of immediate experience and called it the conscious experience and stated that psychology studies this conscious experiences which is the immediate experience.

Having been influenced by Mill's mental chemistry, structuralists also viewed that conscious experiences can be analyzed into elements and designated the **sensation** as objective element and associated feelings are the subjective elements of experience.

Wundt also introduced **tridimensional theory** of feeling to explain the feeling element of experience. Structuralists also dealt with the phenomenon of **apperception** as cognition which is a mental activity. As for the **mind-body** problem, structuralists favour **parallelism** and discard the notion of **interactionism**.

Structuralists conducted experimental studies on various psychological aspects that included (i) sensation and perception; (ii) reaction time experiments; (iii) association experiments (iv) attention; and (v) feeling aspects. Experimental waves on all these aspects could reveal many new things of psychological significance.

As for conscious experiences, structuralists hold the view that human consciousness consists of three basic elements, namely sensations, images and affective states (feeling aspects). Therefore, conscious experiences could be understood as combination of all these three elements.

However, structuralists' views have met with certain severe criticism. The critics hold the view that structuralism as a system is **mentalist** because it relies excessively on inner processes of mind which are neither observable nor verifiable. Hence, far from scientific system of exploration.

2.6.2 Functionalism

A group of psychologists of Chicago University founded a school around 1930 which is known as **Functionalism**. This school of thought came into existence as a protest against structuralism and is considered as a flexible school of American psychologists.

Some forces worked as antecedent factor in the development of this thought of psychology. Important among them were the evolutionary principles of **Darwin**, **Spencer** and **Galton**. Besides, James principles also was an important antecedent force to the origin of functionalism. In fact, James is considered as the forerunner of functionalism.

Functionalism was founded by **John Dewey** of Chicago University and his student **James, Angel** and **Harvey Carr** of the same university followed him and developed Functionalism as a system of psychology.

The main assumption of functionalists was that human mind was continuously adapting to environmental demands. Following this basic assumption (which is based on evolutionary principle), John Dewey emphasized that an organism's practical goal is to adapt to its environment to function effectively. Therefore, psychology deals with the functional processes of mind and not with elements or contents of consciousness as structuralists hold. Hence, psychology studies the mental activities or adaptive behaviours. In this sense psychology has concern with adjustive behaviour to the environment. So far method of adjustment is concerned, individuals evolve effective ways to improve his adjustment through the process of learning.

William James, another functionalist thinker, was particularly interested in consciousness, memory and emotions. He published a book in 1890—**Principles of Psychology**—which is considered as one of the classic books on psychology. Functionalists like structuralists do consider consciousness as the core of psychology which according to James is an ongoing stream. Functionalists also relied upon introspection method but they also added observation and experimentation (with some caution) as desirable methods of collecting data to enable interpret psychological processes in objective terms. Thus, the functionalists did not adhere to any single method rather emphasized the usefulness of both kinds of data—subjective as well as objective.

Another focus of functionalist research programme was related to the area of learning. They hold that learning is a process of association or connection which is governed by certain laws or principles such as law of similarity, law of contiguity, law of frequency and law of finality. Besides, they also studied the attention and motive as the primary agents of selective behaviour that operates as a mechanism of adaptive behaviour.

Today, this school of thought has merged into the main stream of psychology and hence, no longer exists as a distinct school of thought. But there is no denying the fact that its impact in developing modern psychology has been wide enough. Its impact can be most prominently seen in the areas of learning memory, mental testing, Educational Psychology, Animal Psychology and Abnormal Psychology. In the context of the wide ranging impacts of functionalism in different areas of Modern Psychology, it can be assumed that in fact the assimilation of functionalist thought into the main stream can be termed as 'rebirth' of the school in a newer form.

2.6.3 Associationism

Associationism in fact was a principle and not a distinct school of thought. The principle of associationism had its existence even prior and subsequent to Wundt's experimental psychology.

Associationism as a principle has two forms—older and modern. **David Hartley** is considered the pioneer associationistic thinker. Later on the names of James Hill, John Stuart Mill, Alexander Bain, and Herbert Spencer also got associated with associationistic movement who developed and elaborated this thought of principle. These associationistic thoughts are considered older associationism.

The 'Champions of modern associationism' include the names of Ebbinghaus, Pavlov, Bectrev and Thorndike. They laid emphasis on association of either stimulus with stimulus (S-S association) or stimulus and response (S-R association) as the fundamental principle of learning. The discovery of nonsense syllables by Ebbinghaus, classical conditioning phenomenon by Pavlov and Thorndike's connectionism along with his works on intelligence are considered as most significant contributions in developing modern psychology.

2.6.4 Behaviourism

This school emerged as a result against structuralism. **J.B. Watson** (1878–1958) is considered as the main champion of this school of thought. Behaviourists emphatically stated that the mentalistic concepts such as consciousness, images or mind has no place in a scientific and objective science. The method of introspection was also declared as faulty because introspective data are subjective and also because the observer and the subject of study are the same. Behaviourists view psychology as the science of **behaviour** that can be objectively observed and described. This observation can be done in terms of stimuli and responses. Thus, the behaviourists propagated the use of objective observation of behavioural events systematically much like other natural scientists who observe the facts relevant to their disciplines.

Behaviourism is characterised by three basic characteristics:

(a) Behaviourists lay emphasis on conditioned reflexes as building blocks of behaviour and conditioning is a method that can be employed to analyse behaviour. Complex behaviours are built up by elementary blocks. In this sense, behaviourism bears similarity with structuralism. However, the behaviourists differ from structuralists in the sense that behaviourists consider these elementary blocks as conditioned reflexes and not the sensations as structuralists think of.

(b) Behaviourists emphasize behaviour as learned rather than unlearned. Thus, behaviourists reject the idea of instinct or any inborn tendencies. This becomes obvious from what Watson had once claimed that through proper training and providing conducive environment, any infant can be turned into what he likes such as a begger, a lawyer or any kind of person he desires. In this context, Watson is also considered as an **environmentalist thinker**—who has also suggested some **environmental ethics** for bringing improvements in the society through launching of **rehabilitative** and **reeducative programme**.

(c) Behaviourists are also characterized by their emphasis on animal behaviour. They do not see any tangible difference in behaviour between human beings and animals. Hence, we can gain useful knowledge about the psychological aspects of human behaviours through studying animal's behaviours. Such studies continue to be done even today and its significant contributions have been providing solutions to a large number of psychological problems of human beings.

With the characteristic features of behaviourism as discussed above, the most salient contributions of behaviourism can be enumerated as follows:

(a) Behaviourists strongly refuted subjectivism and subjective data collected through introspection. They rather emphasized objective observation that can be accessible to observation by any observer and verify the same as and when one desires. Therefore, 'behaviour' was thought as the subject matter of study which is open to all for objective observation in a systematic way. Psychology is defined as the study of behaviour even today.

(b) Behaviourists also inspired many other psychologists to undertake experimental works on psychological aspects of behaviour. This trend led to the emergence of a newer school of behaviourism during the period 1940s–1950s. These newer schools attempted to develop some general theories of behaviour based on experimental works on animals such as Skinner, Hull, Tolman, Guthrie etc. However, these theories often arose serious debates relating to the correctness of predictions about behaviours based on their theoretical frames.

Behaviourism, in fact, is a S-R approach which emphatically reject conscious experience. However, the importance of conscious experience cannot be outrightly rejected because it plays a mediating role between stimulus event and resultant observable behaviour event, *i.e.* response. Owing to this, behaviouristic approach has also been subjected to serious criticism.

2.6.5 Gestaltism

While behaviourism was gaining ground in America, another school of thought was appearing in Germany under the leadership of **Max Wertheimer** (1880–1943). This is known as **Gestaltism**. Some more psychologists also got associated with this school. Important among them were **K. Koffka**, **W. Kohler** and **K. Lewin**.

'Gestal' is a German term that refers to **form**, **organization** or **configuration**. The main thrust of Gestalists was that psychology studies the pattern of behaviour and experience. This pattern is 'organized whole' and not the sum total of their elements. Thus, Gestaltists opposed 'atomism' rigorously and stated emphatically that our mental experiences and behaviours are not compounds of simple elements rather they have patterns of organization. Such organized patterns produce an experience of the **whole** with certain characteristics distinct from the characteristics of separate parts or elements. Therefore, the experience of whole cannot be analyzed into elements. This concept is opposed to the concepts of structuralism and behaviourism both because both of these approaches look for the elements.

The 'whole' consists of some unique attributes. Such unique characteristics are destroyed as soon as the whole is broken down into elements. Therefore, analysing the experience (whole) into elements is not a correct approach as such this approach would give no useful results.

Gestaltists have also refined the constancy hypothesis of experience which states that there exists a point to point correspondence between physical stimuli in the environment and consequent arousal of experience. Instead, Gestaltists hold the view that the relationship between what we perceive and what remains in the physical environment does not correspond point to point, *i.e.* there is no complete constancy between the two events (mental experience and physical environment).

In describing the wholeness of perceptual phenomenon, Gestalists have put forward certain laws of organization that govern perceptual experiences into a whole organized pattern. These laws or principles are the laws of similarity, proximity, continuity, closure, symmetry, figure and ground etc.

Gestaltists have also made attempts to explain learning, thinking, memory and other cognitive processes in terms of **Gestalten**, *i.e.* configuration of the situation. In this context, the insight theory of learning is considered a very significant contribution of Gestaltists.

2.6.6 Psychoanalysis

Although, psychoanalysis is not a major school of psychology as it is not based on any kind of academic research (experimental or non-experimental) on general psychological processes such as learning, perception, memory, thinking etc. rather, it originated from non-academic field—medical practice. However, its impact was revolutionary. In fact, psychoanalysis as system brought international recognition and fame to **Sigmund Freud** who founded this system during the early years of 20th century.

Freud was a neurophysician who hailed from Vienna. During his medical practice, he frequently used to get vexed in handling the problems of patients who complained of physiological disorders without any recognized physiological aetiology (cause). Freud concerned himself very deeply with all such vexing and confounding patients and began to collect empirical data by deeply interviewing the patients, developed hypotheses and tested them in course of interviewing and treating the patients.

Out of his experience, Freud developed a system for diagnosing and treating mental disorders and also attempted to explain personality in line with his system which is known as **Psychoanalysis**. Thus, psychoanalysis as a system is used in three senses—(a) It is an elaborate system of diagnosing and classifying mental disorders. (b) It refers to the treatment method with emphasis on **Free association**. In this technique, the patient is inspired to freely associate or think and narrate whatever comes to his mind. Psychoanalysts use all such information revealed during free association to analyse the underneath hidden causes of patient's difficulty. (c) It is also a theory of personality. The theory elaborates and stresses the role of unconscious repressed motives. According to **Dollard**, psychoanalysis as a theory of personality is much more interesting than as a method of treatment because it describes many aspects of personality that develop in a periodical sequence from birth till maturity. Besides, it also contains many unverified assertions which in due course tempted many psychologists towards proposing several theories and quite a good number of personality theories following the psychoanalytic tradition could be proposed subsequently.

The entire system of psychoanalysis is based on the concept of **unconscious** which remained untouched by previous thinkers or schools of psychology. The concept of unconscious served as stimulus for further systematic research in various behaviour disorders such as criminal behaviours, juvenile delinquencies, anti-social behaviours, psychopathies, psychosomatic disorders, social pathologies, conflicts of motivations, anxiety states, phobic reactions and so on.

However, soon this system had to face split. **Alfred Adler** and **Carl Jung**, close associates of Freud, disagreed with him on certain assertions like the concept of unconscious and libidinal energies. Their disagreement led to the foundation of two distinct approaches—**Analytical Psychology** of Carl Jung and **Individual Psychology** of Adler.

Besides, the formation of two separate systems of thought, psychoanalytic movement is also marked by changes in views of Freud himself and some others. This led to the development of a new system of psychoanalysis, popularly known as **Neo-Freudian thoughts**.

Despite changes in views and split by close associates, Freud's views has significantly influenced psychology and is marked by a turning point in the history of psychology. Psychoanalysis indeed had widened the scope of psychology in application that covered almost all aspects of behaviour disorders and maladjustment. Perhaps for this reason, Freud is sometimes called as the **father of modern psychology.**

2.6.7 Neo-Freudians

Psychoanalytic thought has grown in many directions. But Freud's rigidity in emphasizing the role of biological forces, more particularly the libidinal energies in determining behaviour is considered as orthodox. Inspired by this, a group of psychologists attempted to modify Freud's thought and bring flexibility by emphasizing socio-cultural forces also as important determinant of behaviour. This group of psychologists are known as **Neo-Freudians**. Among the important contributors, the name of K. Horney, Eric Fromm, H.S. Sullivan and E. Erickson are worth mentioning.

Karen Horney's approach is known as **Social Foundations of Personality**. She argued that the difference between gender (males and females) are the results of social factors more than biological factors, because there exists no innate cause of inferiority among females. According to her, each sex has attributes which are admired by the others. Therefore, neither should be viewed as superior or inferior.

Horney also argues that psychological disorders are not solely caused by fixation of psychic energies but are the outcomes of disturbed interpersonal relationships during childhood. When parents' behaviour towards a child is that of indifference, disparaging and erratic, the child develops feelings of insecurity which Horney terms as **basic anxiety**. She also holds that deep resentment towards parents or basic hostility occurs due to basic anxiety.

Eric Fromm another constituent of Neo-Freudians thought was both—a psychologist and a sociologist. As a social analyst, he was much influenced by social theory of Karl Marx. Fromm published a very famous book—**Escape from Freedom**—in the year 1941. In this book he has described man as a social animal. Therefore, people can be better understood in terms of their relationship with others. Fromm had argued that psychological qualities of the people such as growth and realising potentials are outcomes of a **desire for freedom** and **striving for justice and truth**. Obviously, Fromm's approach is socially oriented and is thus contrary to Freudian's approach which is a biologically-oriented approach of viewing man. For this reason, Fromm's approach is known as **Human Concern Approach**.

H.S. Sullivan also laid greater emphasis on social and cultural factors of personality but, unlike Horney and Fromm he was much influenced by non-psychological sources. So, he deviated from Freud. In his principles, he dropped most of the concepts of Freud such as 'id', 'ego' 'super ego', 'sex theory' etc. But at the same time, he also accepted some of the concepts of Freud such as 'needs', 'tension,' 'anxiety', 'unconscious', 'motivations', 'defence mechanisms' and 'dream interpretations'. Sullivan formulated a distinct theory which is known as **interpersonal theory**. According to him, personality is an enduring pattern of recurrent interpersonal situations that characterizes human life. Interpersonal interaction is the characteristic feature of human life which begins right from birth. This interaction shapes our behaviour, and personality develops in the context of our interactions with others. 'Sullivan' has also mentioned three major aspects of personality—**dynamics of personality, euduring aspects of personality** and **developmental stages of personality**. Thus, Sullivan's theory is full and systematic description of personality and is very widely accepted as valuable contribution in understanding personality.

Erik Erickson also developed a theory of personality development with a focus on social adaptation. **Erickson** while retaining the basic frame of Freud's system broadened it by adding some more sensible interpretations which are based on observation of human behaviours. He considered 'ego' as more important than either 'id' or 'super ego'. He views 'ego' as having the potentials to unify experiences with a blend of creativity in solving problems. Further, ego is not only an inner force but also a socio-cultural force as it is also determined by socio-cultural factors. The influence of socio-cultural factors on ego is reflected in **ego qualities** that emerges in different stages of development.

Erickson has also given emphasis on psycho-social aspects of personality development and described 8 different stages. These stages include the 5 stages of Freud's psycho-sexual development (oral, anal, phallic, latent and genital). In addition, he has included three more stages, namely, early childhood, middle adulthood and old age. Erickson's 8-stage model is also marked by distinct developmental characteristics and each stage has a crisis (turning point). These turning points in personality development are brought about by interaction between increased physical maturity and demand placed by others around the child such as parents, teachers, society etc. The 'crisis' is usually resolved by the **ego qualities** of the concerned period.

Thus, 'Erickson' basically belongs to psychoanalytic tradition, but has brought some refinements and added new thoughts incorporating the socio-cultural contexts.

2.6.8 Humanistic Psychology

Humanistic movement is considered as third force in the history of psychology. The another two forces are behaviourism and psychoanalysis.

'Humanistic movement' shows a definite shift of focus from prominent roles of inner dynamic forces to the qualities of creativity, competence and problem solving abilities of human beings. Thus, the major focus are within the individual himself, realization of basic human potentials within the human beings and providing human to develop and strengthen their **own self** and 'identity' is the central theme of this movement.

'Humanism' grew as a movement around 1960s under the leadership of **Abraham Maslow**—a spiritual father of the movement in America. 'Maslow' argues that human beings are basically good and creative and, therefore, a favourable environment is likely to favour the realization of one's own potentialities and abilities. They are worthy of respect and **self-actualisation.**

Carl Rogers is another stalwart of humanistic approach who formulated **Self-theory** and developed client-centred technique of therapy.

In essence, humanistic approach is opposed to the pessimistic conflict and despair of psycho-analysis as well as the mechanical man concept of behaviourism and lay emphasis on creative growth and healthy potentials of human beings.

Though different humanistic psychologists have adopted different lines of thought, there are some common lines of approach that bind them together. These common approaches are as follows:

(a) Man is an integrated, unique and organized 'Whole'. So, we need to know and understand man as a whole rather than to analyse any single piece of behaviour in isolation.

(b) To enable to understand a man as a whole, we need to collect information about a person's whole life history.

(c) Self-realization or actualisation is the basic and ultimate goal of one's life and occupies the topmost hierarchy of different needs arranged in order of dominance such as the primary physiological needs, safety needs, love and belongingness, esteem needs and finally the self-actualisation need.

(d) The nature of man is basically good and possesses creative potentialities. However, the evil or destructiveness in man's nature is the outcome of unfavourable environment.

(e) Humanistic psychologists do not consider animal's study to be of any value in understanding man's nature. They argue that animal's study ignores the basic human attributes such as ideas, values, art, humour etc. Therefore, they lay emphasis on studying human beings rather than drawing any conclusion on the basis of animal's study.

(f) Humanistic psychologists, more particularly 'Maslow', assume creativeness as an inborn potentiality found in every human being. Hence, it is a common feature of all humans which are self-expressed in different forms.

(g) Humanistic psychology lays emphasis on the study of mental health of every person. They have severely criticized 'Freud' for having concentrated upon the study of abnormal individuals only. Such one sided study would make psychology crippled. Therefore, we need to study the mental health of all—normal and abnormal as well as matured and immatured.

Obviously, humanistic psychologists emphasize on healthy functioning of human beings, his mode of living and goals of life as a whole.

From perusal of different schools of psychology, it is evident that modern psychology has grown through various schools of thought, modifying and widening the scope of each others' thoughts. Consequently, modern psychology today tend towards specialization.

2.7 MODERN PERSPECTIVES IN PSYCHOLOGY—CURRENT VIEWS

Like a child, sciences do take time to mature gradually. So is the case with psychology. As we have seen, couriosity to know and understand man has been in existence ever since man began to think in abstract terms. However, systematic thinking over what, why and how of behaviour could start from the year 1879 when Wundt established a systematic laboratory of psychology at Leipzig University in Germany. This year is marked by emphasis on empirical data which are to be used to understand the basic nature of human behaviour interpreted in terms of experience. It was followed by emphasis on objective observation and use of experimental method to establish cause and effect relationship of behavioural events. This trend led to a large number of experimental research on various aspects of psychological processes that helped psychology in establishing itself as a sytematic giant body of psychological knowledge based on scientific methods of data collection and interpreting those data with scientific vigour. This resulted in development of various thoughts or schools. This period is characterized by differing views about various psychological processes. However, the different views had a very positive effect in enriching the discipline with divergent concepts and approaches refining and reconstructing or even adding some new ideas. Moreover, the periods of these schools are also considered valuable in the sense that this helped psychology to grow and mature very rapidly.

As the psychology matured, it had made a turn towards 'eclecticism', *i.e.* it began to select the best from all thoughts. Hence, one may discern that the present status of psychology is assimilation and integration of ideas and concepts of various schools and has taken in the knowledge gained through other sciences. This trend has led to the emergence of multidisciplinary approach of viewing psychological processes of behavioural events of human beings and other organisms. Nowadays, psychologists are also seen fast moving towards specialization. Consequently our knowledge about various aspects of psychological process and related behavioural phenomenon are growing voluminously. As a result, large many branches have emerged that cover very wide range of areas of human activities and many more are in the offing.

2.7.1 Modern Psychology

Modern psychology is also seem to have been influenced by information theory borrowed from engineering and computer science fields. 'Cognitive science' is a good example that has over-lapped the disciplines like computer science, linguistic philosophy and neuroscience. Similarly, computer science has also borrowed much from psychology in developing certain programming in such a way that computers can also perform intellectual works (artificial intelligence—AI) as human mind does and also stores vast amount of memory, think like human mind and process various activities like composing music, medical diagnosis, solve complex problems etc.

In view of growing professionalization of knowledge due to changes taking place at global level, modern psychology is characterized by three faces—Teaching, Application and Research.

1. **The teaching of psychology:** Psychologists engaged in teaching profession are concerned mainly with the following:

    (a) To supply existing body of knowledge to students so that they can gain a good knowledge of psychological principles and laws that govern inter-personal adjustive behaviours.

(b) To help the students in making him a good citizen of his community and nation to enable them to do the best for the modernization of the society to which they belong.

(c) To develop open-minded attitude to enquire into different aspects of human behaviour and experience—to help them to develop new insights and application of scientific methods in solving human problems.

(d) To keep the students apprised with basic vocabulary, methodologies, established facts and principles of psychology.

2. **The application of psychology:** Approximately 50% or more members of American Psychological Association (APA) are engaged in numerous fields of applied psychology. These are non-academic psychologists. They are concerned mainly with helping troubled people and solving their problems of adjustment. Others work for schools, business industries, military and similar other agencies including solving problems of environment and creating an atmosphere of environment-friendly behaviours. However, these applied psychologists frequently engage themselves in teaching and/or research as per the needs of the organizations they are associated with. Such psychologists are designated as 'clinical psychologists', 'school psychologists', 'industrial psychologists', 'organizational psychologists', 'research and design (R&D) psychologists', 'adminis-trative psychologists' etc. Some psychologists also do private practices.

3. **Research psychologists:** About 30% of psychologists today are found engaged in research. They devote themselves to increase our knowledge of the principles of psychology on the one hand and application of human psychological problems on the other. In so doing, a research psychologist make use of a variety of procedures such as description, understanding, qualitative and quantitative classifications, predicting behaviours, controlling the situations and behaviours and so on.

2.8 PSYCHOLOGY TOMORROW

Though, it is difficult to say precisely about the fate of psychology in future. However, the present day trends are reflective of the future. Psychology is rapidly moving towards an inter-disciplinary discipline. Almost all disciplines of natural and social science streams, humanities, trade and commerce have started adopting and researching the principles of psychology and psychology too is borrowing much useful informations from these sciences/disciplines to explain the facts of behaviour. Further, in course of time to come, it is expected that psychology is likely to be subsumed and made integral parts of philosophy, physiology, biology, neuroscience, human engineering, trade and commerce, defence and administrative organizations, various service sectors, art and literature, politics, governance, history, music, religion, economics etc. This expectation is based on the realization of its significance in understanding human behaviour in all such spheres of environment. However, we will have to wait and see how and in what direction the things move on into future.

2.9 MILESTONES IN THE HISTORY OF PSYCHOLOGY

2.9.1 Pre-19th Century Psychology

The history of modern psychology during this period has greatly been influenced by the developments taking place in different fields of scientific explorations and discoveries. Some of the important events in the field of psychology are:

- Early psychology was a part of philosophy.
- Philosophers considered psychology as the study of soul.
- Philosophers used armed chair speculation method to know and understand human nature and behaviours through soul.

2.9.2 19th Century Psychology

The studies done in various areas of natural and life sciences such as physics, chemistry, mathematics, biology, phrenology and Darwinian principles of evolution had greatly influenced the emergence of modern scientific attitudes to view psychological phenomenon. Some of the salient events are as follows:

Year	Major events
1875	First psychology course was offered by William James.
1878	First American Ph.D. was awarded.
1879	Wilhelm Wundt established first psychological laboratory at Leipzig University in Germany from where systematic study of psychological processes began and thus psychology as an independent discipline came into existence.
1883	First psychological laboratory was established in America at John Hopkins University.
1885	Ebbinghaus's famous book **'On Memory'** was published.
1886	First American text on psychology was published by John Dewey.
1889	Edward Titchner advances the structuralism school of thought based on introspection of conscious experiences.
1890	William James published a classical book—**Principles of Psychology**.
1892	Foundation of American Psychological Association—APA.

2.9.3 20th Century Psychology

The early part of this century is characterized by the emergence of various schools of thought in psychology. Another salient feature of this century has been that quite a good number of scientists were attracted towards study of psychological processes. Some of the major such events are listed below:

1900	Sigmund Freud established psychoanalytic school by publishing a book entitled Interpretations of Dreams.

1906	First psychological laboratory was established at Calcutta University in the department of philosophy.
1912	Max Wertheimer and others advanced Gestalt viewpoint.
1913	John Watson proposed Behaviourism.
1916	First separate department of psychology at Calcutta University came into existence.
1922	Psychology was included in Indian Science Congress.
1924	Indian Psychological Association (IPA) was established.
1925	Publication of Indian Journal of Psychology started.
1928	N.N. Sengupta and Radha Kamal Mukherjee published a book on Social Psychology (Allen and Unwin: London).
1940	Mental Health Hospital in Lumbini Park at Calcutta was founded.
1945	Institute of Psychological Research and Services (IPRS) was established in Patna University.
1947	Hindu Psychology was published by Akhilananda (Allen and Unwin: London).
1948	Psychological Research wing of defence service in India come into existence.
1953	Gardner Murphy published a book—*In the Minds of Man* based on partition violence in India.
1955	National Institute of Mental Health and Neuro Sciences (NIMHANS) was established in Bangalore.
1957	Herbert Simon was awarded with prestigious Nobel Prize for his research in decision process.
1960	The study of Jean Piaqet was introduced to English speaking world.
1962	Establishment of a hospital for mental disorders in Ranchi, Jharkhand.
1963	S.D. Singh publishes his works on monkeys in the Journal of Scientific American.
1969	Durganand Singh publishes—*Indian Villages in Transition.*
1972	First Research Survey published in India.
1878	Sudhir Kakar publishes 'Inner World'—A psychoanalytic study of childhood and society in India (Oxford University Press, New Delhi).
1981	David Hubel and Torsten Wiesel got Nobel Prize for studies on neurons in visual cortex.
1983	Ashish Nandi publishes Intimate Enemy: Loss and Recovery of Self Under Colonialism (Oxford University Press, New Delhi)
1984	Anand C. Paranjpe publishes Theoretical Psychology, The Meeting of East and West (Plenum Press, N.Y.)
1989	National Academy of Psychology (NAOP) was established.

2.9.4 21st Century Psychology

By the advent of 21st century—the new millennium, psychology gradually turned towards eclectic approach and thus is liberal in pursuing studies of psychological processes by taking help of advances made in other disciplines. Moreover, psychologists are working as team member of different scientific areas of research and application relating natural life sciences and social sciences.

Three of the outstanding events of this century are:

1. Janak Pandey publishes Psychology in India: Revisited (2000, 2001, 2004), (Vols. I, II and III)—Sage Publication, New Delhi.
2. Significant advances have been made in the field of 'neuro psychology'.
3. Some new branches of psychology are emerging in both directions—as a branch of basic knowledge and as a branch of application.

SUMMARY

- Origin of psychology is relatively new but has a long past.
- Early people used to understand natural events as caused by supernatural powers—both the evil and good spirits which is known as 'demonology'.
- Ancient Greek philosophers learned a great deal about people and attempted to speculate and explain behavioural events in some orderly way.
- Orderly speculative ideas of philosophy gradually encompassed larger areas of concern and led to the development of a good number of specialists of different departments of knowledge such as natural philosophy, natural sciences, phrenology, biological sciences, physiology, physics etc.
- Emergence of psychology is also rooted to the field of biological science and the influence of Darwin's theory of evolution is greatly recognized.
- Psychology as a systematic independent discipline came into being in the 1879 when Wundt established the first systematic laboratory of psychology and did several research studies on psychological processes involved in mental experiences. He employed introspection as the method of study and defined psychology as the study of soul.
- Soon systematic observation and empirical studies became the centre of emphasis. This was followed by experimental method.
- In the meanwhile, various schools of thought emerged to explain psychological processes in the contextual frames of different schools. Important such schools are 'Structuralism', 'Functionalism', 'Behaviourism', 'Gestalt', 'Psychoanalysis', 'Neo-Freudian School' and 'Humanism'.
- All the above-mentioned schools differed widely from one another in their approach to explain the psychological events. But they significantly influenced psychology in widening its scope and moving towards modern thoughts and develop this discipline as a full blooming discipline of knowledge and application.
- Though, now no such school is in existence, their impact is still felt.
- Psychology of modern times has taken a turn towards eclecticism by selecting the best from other disciplines and working in collaboration with scientists of other areas.
- As for the future prospect, the current indications are reflective of still wider application and prosperous growth of psychology in times to come.

CHAPTER 3

Methodology of Psychology

3.1 INTRODUCTION

Psychology has been defined as the study of behaviour of human beings and other animals. This area is highly difficult to study. It is difficult because the 'behaviour' of an organism is a dynamic variable. It is not static rather everchanging phenomena in different times and space. Hence, difficult to predict and control. Further, behaviour of a man also varies from man to man in the same situation and socio-cultural contexts. Therefore, to study behaviour in an objective and unbiased manner is difficult. Yet, psychologists have evolved certain scientific and standard methods to study behaviour much in the manner a natural scientist studies the various aspects of natural universe.

The scientific status of psychology comes from the use of scientific methods, *i.e.* 'how' and 'what' does it study? The question of what relates to the subject matter or the phenomenon that a discipline pursues to study. Answer to this question has extensively been described in Chapter 1. The present chapter is concerned with the question—'how' does it study the behaviour and experiences (subject matter) of man.

Psychology uses various scientific procedures and methods to study the facts of behaviour. But, before we discuss various methods, let us first consider the meaning and characteristics of a scientific method.

3.2 MEANING OF METHOD

Methods refer to the procedures followed in collecting the facts pertaining to the subject matter with which a particular descipline deals with, *i.e.* 'what' it studies. Methods also refer to how the collected facts are arranged, analysed and interpreted to arrive at a dependable conclusion about the subject matter being studied. Every discipline has well-defined methods to study. Likewise, psychology too uses certain methods.

Before we discuss the various methods or procedures used in psychological enquiries, let us first discuss the major characteristics of a scientific method because it has earlier been stated that psychology uses scientific methods much like the other sciences.

3.3 CHARACTERISTICS OF A SCIENTIFIC METHOD

Scientific methods are distinguished from other methods on the basis of certain salient characteristics. These characteristics are as follows:

3.3.1 Objectivity

Objectivity is the foremost characteristic feature of a scientific exploration or enquiry. It refers to 'bias free' (*i.e.* impartial) study. This implies that the explorations are uninfluenced by any prenotion, prejudices, beliefs, attitudes, and personal biases of the explorer (one who pursues the study). The observations of an event (which are subjected to study) are done exactly in the same form in which it occurs. In other words, the concerned events are studied or observed on 'as is where is' basis. In natural sciences (physics, chemistry etc.), it is easy to achieve objectivity because the subject matter of study is concrete and stable to a great extent. But, in behavioural sciences, such as psychology, the unit of analysis is the behavioural events of the organism or man which is dynamic and unstable. Hence, not so easy to control. However, psychologists with proper control over possible influences of other variables to the maximum extent, are able to make objective study of the psychological processes. They plan and adopt such processess that minimize the chance error of any bias to a negligible limit and thus, makes objective observation of the behaviour events.

3.3.2 Systematization

Systematization is another striking feature of a scientific study. Systemization refers to preplanned orderly manner of collecting information and arranging them and use preplanned procedures of analysis. No doubt, observation and experiments are considered essential to science, but these are of little use if disorderly or unsystematic. The observation must 'make a sense' that can be achieved only if the observation is done in predetermined order and follows the 'economy of effort'. Psychologists use observation and experimentation in a systematic order, prepare a planned sketch of study using a limited number of variables and principles. Systematic studies follow an orderly circular path from observation to principle and again back to the observation. All natural sciences adhere to this circular path and psychologists too proceed their observations along this path. Psychologists make observations whatever is possible (without any rhyme or reason), carefully analyse them and formulate tentative or provisional principles which they consider fairly well and summarize their observations. This part of the circular path is called **'induction'**. Then psychologists proceed further to track another part of the circle called **'deduction'**. After that, the psychologists reason and determine possible predictions and go ahead with a new observation based on some plan to test the tenability of the summarized principle that may either prove to be correct or incorrect (wholly or partially). If found incorrect, the results are analyzed again and this new deduction is again put to test. Even if the deduction is found correct, further analysis at primary level is warranted or it may suggest some other analysis. It is a fundamental fact that **in science, no deduction is final**. Hence, the scientists are found continually engaged in formulating, modifying and extending principles and in so doing, they follow the circular path, *i.e.* systematic order of observation to induce and deduce conclusions.

3.3.3 Validity

Validity is a fundamental characteristic of any scientific measurement. Validity refers to the extent to which a measurement or procedure of observation accomplishes the intended purpose. For example, suppose a test of mathematical aptitude has been constructed and it is found that those with high scores on this measurement, are successful in solving mathematical problems while those with low scores are unsuccessful. Thus, the scale or instrument constructed to measure mathematical problem is taken as a valid instrument because of inherent good dis-crimination power in mathematical aptitude and thus, it meets the intended purpose. Psychologists use several kinds of tools of measurement to study various characteristics such as intellectual abilities, aptitudes, interests, personality, motivational levels etc. for which they select valid measures.

3.3.4 Reliability

Reliability is also an essential characteristic of a scientific method. It refers to the consistency of a test or observation. If a test or observation yields similar results on different occasions under similar situations, then it is considered reliable. For example, suppose you administer a test of intelligence on an individual and find him genius and repeat the test on him after an interval of two or three months and the individual's score is indicative of the same category of intelligence then, the test will be considered as reliable one. Thus, reliability refers to stability or consistency of finding on different occasions.

3.3.5 Standardization

Standardization is also an important feature of scientific study. This refers to standard conditions of study on the basis of which a 'norm' for the population may be developed. To achieve this goal, psychologists conduct their studies on larger number of people who represent the defined population. Then they determine the standard score on the basis of average and a 'norm' is developed to predict the relative position of an individual on the dimension of measure in the population of which he is a part.

3.3.6 Controlled Conditions of Study

In addition to the above properties, precision, definiteness, and accuracy are also the esential features of a scientific study. These salient features depend upon controlled conditions of study. A scientist pursues his studies under rigorous control of extraneous relevant variables that may impact the findings and cause error or doubt. For this, psychologists identify the relevant extraneous variables and devise the appropriate ways to control their possible impacts.

Psychologists employ various methods of study as per their need. In behavioural studies, no single method is appropriate or adequate in all phenomena of behaviour or situations. Therefore, psychologists employ various methods and most often more than one method to accomplish maximum accuracy. The chief methods employed by psychologists include observation, experimentation, interview, case study etc. Besides, psychologists also use various kinds of psychological tests. All these methods possess properties or attributes of a scientific study as described above. Hence, psychology uses scientific methods of study.

3.4 NATURE OF PSYCHOLOGICAL DATA

As compared to other natural or live sciences, psychological data are somewhat different. Psychologists collect a variety of information from different sources employing different methods and tools of data collection. All such information are called 'data' (singular datum).

These relate to individual's covert or overt behaviours, personal experiences and mental processes. These data serve as 'input' to the psychologists that approximates the reality to some extent and provide opportunities to the psychologists to verify or falsify our common ideas about behavioural events, and develop scientific notions about the behaviour.

Data are not independent of the physical or social contexts, *i.e.* the persons involved and the time when behaviour occurs. We behave differently when alone than in group or at home and in office.

The nature and quality of data are also influenced by the method we employ for collecting information, such as introspective data, experimental data, objectively observed facts, information gathered through interview, case studies, questionnaire etc. Besides, we also collect certain information about the participating subjects such as age, sex, socio-economic status (SES), educational status, marital status etc.

One of the significant features of data are that they do not speak itself about the reality. A researcher interprets them and attaches meaning to the data by placing them in the proper context.

In psychological studies, different types of data are collected. Some of these types are as follows:

3.4.1 Demographic Information

It includes personal information such as name, age, gender, ordinal position, size of the family, socio-economic status (SES), marital status, residence, caste, community etc.

3.4.2 Physical Information

It includes information relating to ecological conditions (hilly/desert/forest), mode of economy, housing conditions, size of rooms, facilities available at home, in the neighbour, in the school, mode of transportation etc.

3.4.3 Physiological Data

In some studies data about health conditions, height and weight, heart conditions, level of fatigue, galvenic skin responses, electrical activity of the brain, blood oxygen levels, reaction time, duration of sleep, blood pressure, pattern of dream, amount of salivation, digestive functioning, running and jumping rates (in case of animals) etc. are collected to analyse behavioural events.

3.4.4 Psychological Data

Psychological information relates to intellectual level, personality, interest, aptitude, values, creativity, emotions, motivations, psychological disorders, illusions, delusions, hallucinations, perceptual judgement, thought process, consciousness, subjective experiences etc. These throw much light on the mental processes involved in behaviour.

The above information may be either in the qualitative categorical forms or quantitative forms. The qualitative data are analysed separately by applying qualitative methods such as categorization, (high/low; male female, upper SES or low SES categories etc). These are used for cross-category comparisons. The quantitative data are analyzed by applying statistical techniques—descriptive, variabilities or inferential statistics.

3.5 DESCRIPTION OF MAJOR METHODS OF PSYCHOLOGY

Some of the most widely used methods of psychology are listed below:

(i) Observation—Introspection (self-observation) and objective observation
(ii) Experimental method
(iii) Interview
(iv) Case study method
(v) Questionnaire
(vi) Cross-sectional method
(vii) Longitudinal method
(viii) Sequential method and
(ix) Survey method.

Let us briefly describe the above methods one by one.

3.5.1 Observation—Introspection (Self-observation) and Objective Observation

Observation is a basic method of scientific study employed by all sciences. For this reason, it is generally remarked—‘a science begins and also ends with observation’.

‘Observation’ means ‘to look’ or ‘to view’. One may view or observe an event either directly or through sophisticated equipments/instruments. Direct observation is referred to **unaided observation** while observing by using instruments is called **aided observation**. In psychology, we use both kinds of observation—‘aided’ and ‘unaided’. Aided observations are employed to observe implicit activities under a particular state or situation. For example, in a state of emotional feeling observing the level of blood pressure by using sphygmomanometer (B.P. instrument), heart beat by using stethoscope, changes occurring in cardiovascular mechanism through electro cardiogram (ECG), respiratory changes through phneumograph etc. All such observations are aided observations. Direct or unaided observation is used to observe explicit or overt behaviours such as walking, laughing, smiling, jumping, sneezing etc. All such behaviours can be observed by anybody with naked eyes.

Observation, whether aided or unaided, is important to describe any fact or event. So, in order to describe facts of behaviour, psychologists also use observation. Through observation, he becomes aware of the individual or the organism, he discovers the interrelationships of various activities and the conditions under which particular activity occurs. Such observations enable him to explain the behaviour of the individual or the organism.

However, as we know, psychology studies behaviour as well as mental experiences. Hence, psychologists try to observe both kinds of events—experiences and overt or covert bodily activities. Thus, in psychological studies, observation takes two distinct forms—(a) Introspective observation (self-observation) and (b) objective observation. Let us examine these two forms of observations separately.

Introspection (self-observation): The term introspection is made of two terms—'inter + inspection'; meaning **to look within the self** or **viewing within the self**. Obviously, this refers to self-observation. When an individual describes his subjective experiences, affective states—feelings and emotions, the flow of ideas, what mental operations go on when he encounters a problem, what solutions come to his mind, how he takes a decision or reasons to solve a problem etc. are called introspection or self-observation. The subjects by observing his own personal feelings, ideas, thoughts, etc. are able to describe or report about conscious activities of his mind in verbal terms either in writing or orally. Such introspective reports yield useful information to the psychologists for analysing the mental process (implicit mental activities). Certain aspects of psychological problems such as secrets about the sexual relationships between husband and wife and similar other aspects of one's private life affairs can be studied only by introspection.

Introspection is a very common and simple procedure. Anybody may turn his thoughts inward and inspect or reflect upon his experiences. This is what we call introspection or self-observation. Introspection indeed is a classical method of psychology. 'Wilhelm Wundt' and 'Titchner' introduced this method for the first time in their system—structuralism. But, Wundt's procedure of introspection was somewhat different. Wundt thought of analysing the sensory experiences into elements just as the chemists analyse the chemical compounds into elements. Wundt also used apparatus to measure and manipulate stimuli (in laboratory condition) to arouse experiences and the subjects were asked to inspect their own experiences and report systematically. This procedure of self-observation is termed as **experimental introspection**. 'Wundt' also used especially trained introspectionists who were able to describe an object in terms of its impact on one's senses, *i.e.* in terms of certain attributes of sensory experiences (e.g. quality, intensity, duration, vividness etc.). For example, suppose a subject is shown a piece of chalk which he describes as follows: **I am seeing a cylindrical thin white object which I felt as hard and lacked flavour or smell**.

Merits and limitations/demerits: Since psychology studies the experience and behaviour both, no doubt, introspection is an useful method to study conscious experience aspect as well as its relationship with certain forms or patterns of behaviour. Some of the important points of its advantages are as follows:

(a) To study the implicit mental experiences, introspection is the only appropriate option, because, what goes on inside our mind is inaccessible by any other direct method or observation.
(b) Introspection is a useful technique for other objective methods of study as it can supplement the facts which cannot be accessible by other direct methods and thus, makes the study more useful. Besides, the facts gathered through introspection can be used as a 'check' to the facts gathered by other techniques or procedures. Hence,

introspective observation is advantageous in the sense that it makes the study perfect and dependable. This is the reason that even today, psychologists consider introspection as indispensable technique for psychological studies.

(c) Introspection also bears historical significance. Psychology as an experimental science was formally founded by 'Wundt' when he established first psychological laboratory at Leipzig University in Germany (1879) and where he trained 'Kant' and 'Titchner' as **introspectionist** and a formal school—**structuralism**—emerged. Thus, psychology as an independent scientific discipline came into existence with **introspection** as a method.

(d) Introspection is an unique method that distinguishes psychology as a science from other natural sciences. For example, judgements regarding relative differences between two weights are done by both the psychologists as well as by physicists. But, a psychologist comes to a conclusion (accuracy and possible extent of error) about the judgement basing upon introspective statement of a subject's mental experience whereas a physicist uses a measuring balance to weigh the two weights and then judge which one is heavier or lighter. Thus, introspection is an unique method that distinguishes the science of psychology from the other natural sciences.

Limitations/demerits: However, the method suffers from certain demerits. Some of the salient demerits are as follows:

(a) Introspection is a subjective method. Hence, the described facts about mental experiences concern only to the experiencing individual. Therefore, any generalization on this basis is likely to be erroneous. Hence, not practicable for generalization.

(b) Introspection does not fulfil the scientific criteria of a method. In similar situations, the experiences of two individuals and even of the same individual on two different occasions are likely to vary. Thus, no concrete and definite conclusions can be drawn.

(c) While introspecting, the same individual has to get himself involved in two kinds of mental activities—to experience the stimuli and to observe what goes on in his mind. Experiencing and observing are two distinct activities which cannot run parallel to each other. What we call introspection is in fact **retrospection** (post facto observation), *i.e.* observing the facts of experience after experiencing event is over. Such observations are likely to be erroneous because of the limited duration and capacity of our immediate memory (working memory that goes on in short term memory). Under the situation, most of the experienced facts are likely to be forgotten as they may drop off from immediate memory very soon.

(d) Introspection also suffers from limitations of applicability. This method cannot be used with animals, young children, the feeble-minded, and those who are suffering from mental pathologies. Similarly, the geriatric individuals, colour blinds, tone-deaf or taste blinds also cannot introspect their mental experiences properly.

(e) Our most of the experiences are either wholly or partially repressed into unconscious which are inaccessible to self-observation or introspection.

(f) Self-observed facts are unverifiable and cannot be checked by other observers. Hence, not dependable. Self-observation reports are likely to be misreported or not honestly reported. Hence, not much reliable and analysis may go wrong.

Considering the above-mentioned demerits or limitations of introspection method, psychologists also use some other methods that can be relied upon as well as yield useful information about the problem of psychological study.

Objective observation: Objective observation is a basic method of any science. Since psychology is also a systematic science, objective observation is a basic method of this science too.

Observation is a deliberate inspection for collecting facts (data). Psychologists employ this method to gather information about 'what' a person does in a particular situational context, 'how' he does and 'what makes' him to act in a particular way out of many other alternative courses of action. For example, in a state of anger, one can objectively observe the changes in facial expression, vocal changes, postural changes etc. and on the basis of these observed changes, the observer can conclude that the person is angry. Similarly, other external activities can also be subjected to observation by others. These are called **unaided observation**. Objective observation also includes internal activities such as pounding of heart, increase in blood pressure, changes in sugar level, psycho-galvanic responses etc. To observe such internal changes, psychologists use some delicate devices such as ECG, sphygmomanometer, stethoscope, pneumograph etc. These are in fact **aided observation**.

Psychology also studies about mental activities, we call experience. These are not subjected to objective observation. However, while making aided or unaided observation, psychologists also obtain verbal responses relating to experiential aspects. This is called introspection. Psychologists inspire the subjects (participants of study) to think inwardly, visualize his personal experiences through inner eyes and make a report. Such introspective reports are collaborated with the data gathered through objective observation and are analyzed objectively.

Observation as a method of study in psychology takes two distinct forms as per the setting of observation. These are **naturalistic observation** and **controlled observation**.

Naturalistic observation: When observations are done in a natural or real life setting, it is called naturalistic observation. In this case, the observer makes no effort to control or manipulate the situation for making an observation. This type of observation is conducted in hospitals, homes, schools, day care centre etc. For example, suppose Principal of a school is interested to know how children studying in a particular class spend their time in school. Two things are possible. As a researcher, the Principal has a fairly good idea of different activities in the class. He may prepare a list of all these activities and go to the class to find out their occurrences. Now suppose, the Principal is a new one. He has no prehand idea about the activities of the children in the class. In this case, he silently enters the classroom from backdoor and occupies a vacant seat in the remote rear row. He observes different activities of the children and makes a record for analysis.

Controlled observation: Controlled observations are done in laboratory situation. On many occasions, we need to control certain factors that may influence the behaviour as they are not the focus of study. Such observations are called experimental observations. This will be discussed later in some detail.

Observations sometimes also take the form of 'participant' or 'non-participant' observation.

Non-participant vs. participant observation: Observation can be done in two ways. A researcher may decide to observe the person or event from a distance or he may decide to become an active associate of the group to be observed. The former is called non-participant observation while the latter is participant observation. For example, a researcher may want to observe the patterns of interaction between teachers and students in a particular class. For this the researcher may instal a video camera to record the classroom activities that he can see later and analyse. Alternatively, the researcher may decide to take active participation in the activities of children.

In participant observation, it may take sometime to establish rapport with the group being observed and when the group begins to accept the researcher as a member of group, observation starts. However, the degree of involvement of the observer with the group being observed would vary according to the focus of study.

Merits and limitations of objective observation method (in general): Observation is a basic method of data collection in objective manner. It has certain merits or advantages as well as certain limitations or shortcomings. The salient merits and limitations/demerits are as follows:

(a) **It is an objective and impersonal method:** Objective observation, as it is called conducts observation of behavioural phenomenon objectively. The observer neither makes any alteration or manipulation in the occurrence of the event nor does he allow his personal views, beliefs or principles to guide or influence what he is observing. Hence, it is an impersonal method of collecting data on the behavioural phenomenon under study. Thus, observation is done in exactly the same manner in which the events occur.

(b) **Possibility of quantitative study:** In objective observation, the observed data or facts are usually in quantitative form *viz.* the temporal sequence and interval in which the behaviour occurs, the frequency or number of times of occurrences, etc. Hence, such quantitative forms of data are subjected to quantitative analysis and thus, it allows the study to be done in quantitative forms.

(c) **Wider scope of application:** Objective observation has a wider scope of application. One may observe the behaviours of all others—normal or abnormal, children or aged persons, literates or illiterates. Hence, unlike introspection, objective observation has wider scope of use.

(d) **It is possible to study more than one individual at a time:** One can observe the behaviour of one individual or a group of individuals. This saves time and effort whenever group observation, *i.e.* observing the same phenomenon under similar situation of more than one individual. Thus simultaneous observation is economical in time and effort both.

(e) **Deep study is possible:** In naturalistic observation, deep and intensive study can be done. For this, the observer plans participative form of observation in which he actively involves in the activities of the group or community selected for observation. While observing, he uses the recording devices such as video camera, diary notes of the events etc. Active participation facilitates close watch and inspection and thus very valuable information particularly relating to personal and confidential nature are easily obtained.

Limitations/demerits: Though, objective observation is an important and useful method of study, it suffers from certain great limitations or demerits as under:

(a) The findings based on observation are likely to suffer from **halo-effect**, *i.e.* a tendency of the observer to judge consistently the behaviour of an individual in a particular direction—favourable or unfavourable, based on the personal knowledge or belief about the person. In other words, the observer cannot absolutely isolate the behaviour being observed from his personal knowledge about the person (who is under observation) as a whole. For example, an observer may be highly impressed with the subject who is genius. This prior knowledge about the inellectual geniousness may influence his judgement about other aspects of his behaviour also in a favourable direction. Similarly, prior information or knowledge may influence to judge the person in unfavourable direction also. Thus, the observation is not objective or impartial (bias-free) in absolute sense.

(b) Study of implicit behaviour, particularly the mental activities such as, perceptual experiences, ongoing thinking processes, processes involved in decision-making and judgements, reasoning etc. are not accessible to objective observation. These processes can at best be inferred on the basis of certain overt behavioural pattern. But, such inferences are likely to be erroneous because behavioural patterns cannot be taken as **true reflection** of mental processes.

(c) Since in naturalistic observation or in participant observation, no control over the possible impacts of certain extraneous relevant variables is exercised, it is difficult to establish perfect **cause and effect relationship** of the behavioural event.

(d) From practical point of view, certain aspects of behavioural event such as sexual behaviours or similar other delicate behaviours are not possible to observe despite the fact that these aspects may have significant relevance for the behaviour under study.

(e) Often individuals tend to hesitate in expressing the crude realities of his behavioural patterns because such patterns are considered not good in taste. So, he may express the disguised form of the realities which is unreal. Obviously, this makes the observation erroneous.

Though objective observation is likely to suffer from certain limitations, an experienced observer takes due care and precautions to keep himself free from personal biases and also controls other sources of error. In that case, objective observation may yield bias-free and dependable or reliable information in a concrete and precised way.

3.5.2 Experimental Method

Experimental method is also a form of observation—we call controlled observation. Experiment is considered as most scientific method of study because through experimental observation the gathered facts are highly reliable or dependable, valid and standard.

The major and sole objective of experimental study is to establish an invariable relationship between two or more than two variables. To achieve this objective, the experimenter does the following three main functions: (i) he changes or varies something (*i.e.* manupulative function), (ii) keeps other conditions constant or under control and (iii) looks for the resultant changes or variations upon the behaviour selected for observation. Thus, the method is very simple. But, it is highly technical and follows a preplanned systematic order of observation. Preplanning involves: (i) careful definition and explanation of problem of study in a simple, precised and concrete terms, (ii) formulation of hypothesis, (iii) classification of variables, (iv) techniques or strategies of controlling extraneous relevant variables and (v) detailing the systematic procedures of observation. Hence, an experiment is defined as **systematic or pre-planned observation under controlled conditions.**

Variables: As has been stated above, experiment involves variables. **A variable is that which varies**. Ideally, variables are those attributes of objects, events, situations or things and beings that can be varied and measured. For example, sudden noise is a factual event of the physical environment. Such events are not static rather they can vary or can be varied in terms of quality or quantity (intensity). The noise can vary in intensity of loudness, temporal sequence or interval, continuity etc. Breathing is also a variable in the sense that it may vary in terms of rapidity, slowness or deepness or shallowness. In the similar way, all events, facts, or things, attributes or properties are variables because these can vary.

Types of variables: In the context of cause and effect relationship, variables are classified into two types. These are (a) **independent variables** and (b) **dependent variables**.

(a) **Independent variables:** Independent variables are those whose effects are studied in an experiment.

(b) **Dependent variables:** Dependent variables in an experiment is a factor about which the experimenter makes a prediction regarding the possible changes due to manipulation of the independent variable in a certain way.

Obviously, independent variables are the causes while the dependent variables are the effects of causative factor (independent variable). Thus, the experimenter attempts to observe the resultant effects or impacts due to manipulation of independent variable (cause) on the behaviour event, *i.e.* the dependent variable.

To understand the above, let us examine an example. Suppose, a medical scientist plans an experiment to study the effect of vitamin 'X' on maze learning activity of rats. Here vitamin X is an **independent variable** because the experimenter in his experiment will vary this element by manipulating it in certain ways (*e.g.* injecting vitamin X to some rats while not giving this vitamin to others or giving more to some others). The resultant effects or changes on learning ability of rats will be the **dependent variable** in this experiment.

On the basis of how the experimenter manipulates an independent variable in experimental studies, the independent variables take two forms: Type E variable and type S variable.

Type E variable refers to direct attempt to bring variations in quality or intensity or duration, presence or absence etc. Here, the experimenter directly manipulates the variable (independent) and observes their effects on dependent variables.

Type S variable refers to certain subject related factors such as age, sex, status etc. These variables cannot be directly manipulated or varied. To examine the impacts of such variables, the experimenter follows the principle of **selection**. For example, to study the effect of ordinal position on intelligence or achievement. In this case, the experimenter would select subjects of different ordinal positions—1st born, middle born and youngest born and then measure their intelligence and compare the intelligence scores of each group of subjects selected for the study.

Extraneous relevant variables: In course of planning an experiment, the experimenter also identifies some more independent variable that may influence the dependent variables. These variables are relevant in the sense that these also may exert their impacts. Such relevant variables are also called as extraneous, because these are not the focus for the study. These relevant variables are beyond the purview of experimental study. The experimenter, during the period of his experiment, attempts to control their possible impacts by employing certain strategies such as counter balancing, determining the priorities of experimental and controlled conditions of experiment, maintaining constancy of their impacts etc. The strategy that the experimenter employs to control are adopted keeping in view to ensure maximum possible accuracy and clarity of findings.

Thus, the purpose of an experiment is to establish an invariable relationship between two or more than two variables. This relationship explains the **cause and effect relations** of behavioural events. This purpose is achieved by manipulating the independent variable in a preplanned manner and observing the resultant effects in a systematic manner under controlled conditions.

Designing an experiment: Operationally, defining the variables in an experiment is followed by designing the experiment. Designing refers to the 'blueprint' of an experiment. It involves detailing of the entire experimental procedures such as determination of different levels of independent variables, procedures of manipulation, detailing the materials and tools to be used in the experiment, control of extraneous variables, sequence of conditions of experiments. Their nature, instructions to be given to the subjects, nature of data to be collected and the procedures to analyse the collected data. Thus, design of an experiment is a precised and clear description of the entire experimental procedures in concrete terms. In fact, success of an experimental study depends on how well an experiment is designed.

In psychological studies, various forms of designs are used depending upon the purpose, objective and nature of the problem. It requires expertised deliberation in selecting a particular experimental design for the study.

In psychological studies, various kinds of experimental designs are used. These are **factorial design, counterbalancing design, before and after design, within and between group design** etc. To describe these designs in detail is beyond the scope of this book. Students may look for books on research methodology or experimental research.

Merits and limitations: Experimental method is most highly developed, formalized and accurate of all other methods. The salient features of this method are as follows:

Most objective and impartial: One of the major features of psychological study is objective collection of facts about behavioural events. In experiment, the experimenter records what the subject does and not what he feels or thinks. Thus, the method is objective and bias-free.

Control: Control is another important characteristic. Since, experiments are perfomed under controlled conditions, the obtained facts are most reliable, dependable and accurate. It is so because the extraneous variables are kept under control. Therefore, the observed facts are influenced only by the manipulation of the experimental independent variable and not by any other variables.

Replication: Replication refers to verification of the previous finding by conducting study again and again on different occasions. Replication ensures the dependability of the earlier finding or it may suggest revision of the study. This is one of the significant attributes of a scientific study which experimental methods possess. We can repeat an experiment again and again to become sure of the observation.

Quantitative analysis: Through experiment, data are made available in quantity form. Hence, statistical analysis is possible that makes the analysis precised and solid.

Applicability: Experimental method has wider applicability in the sense that it can be applied on categories of living beings of all ages.

Standardization: Experiments are performed under standard conditions and on the basis of larger number of experimental observations, **norms** are developed to predict the behaviour in relation to the population of the individual's behaviour selected for experimentation.

Limitations: No doubt, experimental method is a highly developed method of scientific research, it also suffers from certain limitations which are:

(a) **Experiment cannot be always used.** In the area of psychology, experimenter works with living beings who are not docile. Therefore, they are not always willing to participate as subjects for the experiment at the sweet will of the experimenter. This limits the scope of its application. Besides, certain aspects of human behaviour are practically not accessible for experimentation. For example, it is almost very difficult to experimentally examine what makes marriages happy?

(b) Experiments are conducted in artificially created situations that may resemble natural settings but cannot be taken as true natural setting. Therefore, the expression of behaviour under experimental situation is also likely to be artificial. Such expressive behaviours may have some resemblence with the natural behaviour but cannot be taken as natural expressions in true sense.

(c) Since, experiment is highly technical, it requires well-trained experimenter who possesses the knowledge of technical implications involved in experimentation. Normally such well-trained experimental psychologists are few in number.

(d) Most of the experiments require sophisticated and delicate instruments and well-developed laboratory conditions with all requisite facilities. This requires huge financial involvements which is a great constraint.

(e) Most of the variables are beyond control of the experimenter. Hence, accuracy of observation in absolute sense is not practicable.

Despite the above limitations of experimental method, it is the only method that meets all the criteria of a scientific enquiry and is, thus, most reliable and dependable. The limitations of this method are not too great that cannot be solved. The only need for the psychologist is to gain adequate efficiency and expertise in experimentation. Moreover, the aspects of behaviour that are inaccessible to experiment need to be complemented by using other methods in collaboration with experimentation. This is the reason that psychologists use introspection as supplementary method of experiment.

In addition to the above-mentioned methods of experiments, psychologists also use some other forms of experimentation which are different from laboratory experiments. These are **Field experiment** and **Quasi experiment**.

Field experiments and quasi experiments

(a) **Field experiment:** In situations in which any behaviour event is not possible to be studied in laboratory settings and the psychologists want to study such a phenomenon with a view to achieve high generalizability, the psychologists go to the field or natural setting where the particular phenomenon actually exists. This is what we call **field experiment**. For example, a researcher may be willing to determine which of the two methods of teaching—lecture method and demonstration method—is more effective in learning? For this problem, the researcher would prefer to conduct an experiment in school. He will select two groups of students matched in several attributes such as age level, class level, gender, intellectual abilities and so on. Both the groups will be taught the same topic by the same teacher with difference that one group would be taught by lecture method while the other group would be taught by demonstration method. After teaching both the groups, they would be tested on the basis of their performances and their performances would be compared.

In such experiments, control over the relevant variable is relatively less than what we find in laboratory experiments.

(b) **Quasi-experiment:** There are several such variables that cannot be manipulated in laboratory settings. Besides, there are some ethical problems also that unables an experimenter to conduct experimental studies. For example, if someone wants to study the effect of an earthquake on victims, such a situation cannot be created in a laboratory. In such situations, the researcher opts for 'quasi' experiments (quasi is a latin word that means 'as if'). In such types of experiments, the independent variable is selected rather than manipulated by the experimenter. For example, in the experimental group we can select people who are victims of earthquake and in the control group those people who have experienced the earthquake but has not lost anything, *i.e.* not directly victimized. Thus, in quasi experiments, the independent variables are not manipulated rather selected from natural setting.

3.5.3 Interview Method

In psychological studies, **interview** is an important tool of data collection. This technique is mostly used by clinical psychologists in the study and treatment of personality/behaviour disorders. Interview is also widely used by social psychologists to study attitudes, beliefs, public opinion etc. In addition, interview is also a chief method for selecting new workers in different industrial and organizational settings, government jobs and similar other semi-government organizations.

Interview is a **face-to-face conversation or verbal exchange** between at least two individuals who are known as the interviewee (respondents) and interviewer. Thus, interview is a **social process of mutual interaction** between the interviewer and the interviewee. The interviewer puts certain questions to the interviewee to which he responds. In this sense, interview involves a process of verbal exchange of ideas, emotions, feelings etc. In this way data are collected and are subsequently subjected to analysis for assessing one's personality, patterns of responses, needs, beliefs, attitudes, emotions and other affective states, and self-concept etc.

Interview is classified in several ways according to the purpose of interview. However, broadly, it is classified into two types—**structured interview** and **unstructured interview**.

Structured interview: Structured interview refers to predetermined interview situation. Such a situation is fully structured, *i.e.* the set of questions to put, order of questions, response patterns, method of scoring, initiation and termination of interview session etc. Every aspect of interview is pre-planned and is conducted systematically in a standard condition. Therefore, it is also called standard interview. Often, this type of interview is also termed as formal or patterned interview because it follows a systematic, predetermined patterned process of gathering data in an uniform way.

Structured interview is often preferred because of three basic reasons:

(a) The situation of interview is highly structured.
(b) Since the interview situation is highly structured and formalized, relatively less trained interviewer can also conduct the interview smoothly.
(c) It is less time consuming and meaningful. Meaning can be drawn with precised system of analysis. Hence, economical in conduction as well as analysis.

However, structured interview suffers from two major limitations. These are as follows:

(a) Structured interviews are expensive.
(b) It is relatively less valid than some other methods such as bio-data analysis, standardized psychological tests etc.

Because of the above limitations, structured interview is preferred only when unstructured or informal interview is considered impracticable.

Unstructured interview: It is just opposite of structured interview. In this type of interview, there is neither any predetermined or preplanned set of questions, nor any fixed response category or pattern. It is a kind of free deliberation between the interviewee and the interviewer. The role of initiation, continuation, termination and even pattern of responding—everything rests on the respondent (interviewee). Hence, the entire interview situation is unstructured and informal. This type of interview is most commonly used in clinical settings. It is not a fixed method rather a flexible instrument of data collection. In this type of interview, the interviewer is able to dig deeper, *i.e.* he can have deeper understanding about the respondent's behaviour.

However, this type of interview also has certain limitations such as:

(a) There is greater scope for personal influences.
(b) It requires greater skill on the part of the interviewer. He should be tactful, intelligent, possess a social sense and should have deeper knowledge of the subject.
(c) Data obtained through unstructured interview are by and large more descriptive. Hence, it is a cumbersome task to convert the qualitative data into quantitative form or interpret them meaningfully.

Despite the above-mentioned limitations, both types of interviews are very useful and popular tools of data collection. However, structured interview is more preferred by psychologists interested in collecting data on socio-cultural perspectives while unstructured interview is more popular among clinical psychologists. Both kinds of interviews require a good deal of skill on the part of the interviewer.

3.5.4 Case Study Method

'Case study' is also an important method employed in psychological studies. It is mostly used in clinical situations. For this reason, often **'case study'** is also known as **'clinical method'**.

Case study involves study of a particular case, *i.e.* the individual (one at a time). In this method, emphasis is given on 'in-depth' study of the particular case. The psychologists focus on the cases which can provide critical information or new learning on less understood phenomena. The case can be an individual with certain distinguishing characteristics (*e.g.* patient with psychological disorders), a small group of individuals showing some commonness (*e.g.* creative writers), institutions (*e.g.* poorly or successful functioning) and specific events (*e.g.* devastation by tsunami, war, or bomb blasting events by terriorists, vehicular pollutions etc). The cases selected for study are usually unique and, therefore, can provide rich information.

Case study method, in clinical cases, involves preparation of the life history of the case by collecting information from various sources. The basic sources are as follows:

Day book: This method is often used in child study. Child's development is carefully watched and recorded day-by-day. It may contain some questions like—when the baby first began to stand, sit, walk and talk etc. Such records help the psychologist in judging the normality of the developmental processes of the individual child.

Clinical examination: It is an elaboration and extension of day book records. This involves exploration of past life history and present life situation of the case on the basis of information received from the case itself, his close associates like parents, teachers, peers, friends or others who relate to the case. Such informations help the psychologist to discover **the cause of** and **solution to** some emotional or adjustment related problems. It also involves three types of professionals—the physicians, the social workers and the psychometricians. Physician examines the case for signs of physical illness, social worker searches out the home or family atmosphere and the psychometrician administers certain psychological tests to measure psychological attributes such as aptitude, intelligence, various dimensions of personality etc.

Autobiography and/or biography: Such records contain full records of the past life of history of the case in detail. Such records help the clinicians to understand the antecedents that may be associated with the development of the present patterns of behaviours.

Thus, case study method in fact, is an important tool of obtaining information about a particular case. It is a combination of features of clinical observation, experiment and systematic observation.

Following are the merits and demerits/limitations of case study method.

Merits

(a) Case study method makes intensive and in-depth study of the particular case because it examines the full life history of the case.
(b) This method traces back to the stage to which the present form of behaviour relates.
(c) This method is particularly useful in handling the behaviour disorders in various areas of interaction, such as in schools, at home or in work situations.
(d) It is also useful in validating the facts gathered by other methods.

Demerits/Limitations

(a) The conclusions based on case study are relatively less reliable and dependable as the information passed on by the close associates of the case often do not reveal all the relevant facts honestly and try to maintain confidentiality.
(b) The close associates or those who relate to the case also present the facts as per their own subjective interpretations. Hence, most of such facts are not objective rather biased.
(c) Historical records of life events largely depend on memory which are likely to be transformed or restructured or possibly one may fail to retrieve some relevant events accurately.
(d) Variations in biographical records may be found. Such variations may confound the researcher to come to a conclusion.
(e) Often it becomes cumbersome to arrange case history records systematically. It so happens because the past life event histories are not presented in orderly manner.

Hence, though the case history method is useful for clinical purposes as well as for other areas of research, the researcher should be cautious enough in interpreting the records keeping in mind the above outlined limitations.

3.5.5 Questionnaire Method

'Questionnaire' is also an important tool of data collections which is very widely used in researches involving behavioural studies. It is in fact, most common, simple, versatile and low cost self-report method.

Questionnaire consists of a predetermined set of questions and the respondents are required to answer them as instructed to respond. This device is used to collect factual information from the respondent himself. The questionnaire can be administered both in the individual and in group situations.

The set of questions in questionnaire is prepared with due precaution and following the norms such as simplicity of language, clarity of meaning, using short sentences, avoiding the use of double meaning words in the sentence etc.

Types of questionnaire

Questionnaires are classified in different types on the following bases:

(a) On the basis of type of response required.
(b) On the basis of administration of questionnaire and
(c) On the basis of purpose of study.

On the basis of type of response required: Based on the type or modes of response, questionnaires are classified in two types:

(a) Closed-end questionnaire and
(b) Open-end questionnaire

(a) **Closed-end questionnaire:** In closed-end type of questionnaire, the questions and their probable answers in fixed categories are given and the respondents are required to exercise a selection of the category that best fits or suits him. The fixed categories of answer may be like yes/no, true/false/doubtful categories. Some questionnaires also contain multichoice options (multi option response—MOR) arranged in a scale such as 3 point, 5 point or 7 point, 9 point, 11 point etc. In some cases, the subjects are asked to rank a number of things in preferential order. For example, look at the following sample:

1. Do you feel shy in group? Yes/No
2. Do you enjoy when you are with your friends? Yes/No

(b) **Open-end questionnaire:** In this type of questionnaire, the respondent is free to write whatever answers he/she considers appropriate. It contains no fixed alternative categories of answer or response. For example, look at the following sample:

- What are the causes of youth unrest?
- Why someone feels afraid when he meets a stranger?

Here, the respondent is free to mention several factors that he thinks are appropriate.

On the basis of administration of questionnaire: On this basis, a questionnaire may be either a 'mailed' questionnaire or a 'face-to-face' questionnaire. The former form of questionnaire is used on the designated outstation respondents by mailing through post on their addresses. While mailing the questionnaire, return addressed stamped envelop is enclosed for returning the filled-in questionnaire. However, one of the demerits in the use of mailed questionnaire is that most of the respondents do not take due care to fill up and return the questionnaire to the researcher.

The latter form of questionnaire is administered in a face-to-face situation either individually or in group situation. The respondents are requested to complete the questionnaire as instructed and return the same to the researcher as soon as they complete responding to the questionnaire.

On the basis of purpose of study: The form and content of questionnaire varies according to purpose, such as, sample questionnaire, diagnostic questionnaire, crime detection questionnaire, lie detection etc. All these questionnaires may be of any form—open end or close end—and may be administered either through mail or in face-to-face situation. The question items are framed as per the purpose which the investigator intends to study.

Following are the merits and demerits/limitations of questionnaire method.

Merits: Questionnaire method is a very useful tool of data collection because:

(a) Questions (items) are easily scored or coded. This facilitates quantification and interpretation.
(b) Questionnaire method is easy in administration. It does not require much skilled persons for administration.
(c) This method also proves easy for the respondents who are required to exercise minimum effort in selecting appropriate response out of the fixed categories of response.
(d) Questionnaire method is economical in time consumption as it can be administered on group and also that it takes less time in completion when closed-end questionnaire is used.
(e) Since questions in this method are indirect, simple and in shorter sentences, respondents find it quite easy to express their feelings, emotions, ideas, thoughts, opinions etc. without any fear or hesitation in revealing their inner subjective feelings and ideas.

Demerits/Limitations: However, questionnaire method has certain limitations too. These are:

(a) This method is applicable in the case of literates only. Children or very old persons cannot be studied through this method.
(b) Administration of this method is also difficult in the case of those who are not conversant with the script or language of questionnaire.
(c) While preparing the questionnaire, due care in selecting simple words, correctness of sentence, clarity in expression etc. are required; otherwise reliable and valid information cannot be obtained. Questionnaire construction requires skill and good deal of experience.
(d) Reliability and validity of questionnaire must be determined before final administration. This involves labour and separate research.
(e) At times, questionnaire also proves wastage of time and money as most of the respondents either do not return or return the incomplete questionnaire.

The above limitations, in fact, are in construction of questionnaire and their use. These do not reflect any demerit of the method itself. If questionnaire is properly constructed and used, it can yield most useful information.

3.5.6 Cross-sectional Method

This is a strategy in which children or individuals of different age levels (chronological or biological age) or socio-economic status are compared at one point of time. For example, if someone wants to study the developmental changes in memory, the subjects may be divided in three or five groups representing 10 years old, 15 years old, 20 years old, 25 years old and 30 years old. All these groups may be given a task to memorise and their performances can be compared. This may leads to understand the trends of development in memory. Similarly, other cognitive processes may be cross-sectionally compared.

The success of this method depends upon representative selection of sample. For this, usually random selection procedure is adopted. In random sampling technique, each member of the larger group of the same chronological age level has equal chance of being selected in the designated section (sample). Following are the merits and demerits/limitations of cross-sectional method.

Merits

(a) This method is less time consuming as the same study is not required to be repeated over time interval.
(b) This method is also economical in expenditure and effort because, the entire study is completed in one stroke.
(c) The limitations of longitudinal method are removed such as shortage of number of subjects for several reasons, keeping patience for relatively longer duration etc.

Demerits/Limitations

(a) It is difficult to achieve equivalency in different groups.
(b) It is difficult to know the changes in behavioural patterns of individuals comprising a group because, the study is not repeated over time intervals.
(c) In this study, individual study is not possible.

3.5.7 Longitudinal Method

This is also a popular method in psychological studies. In this method, same individual or group of individuals are repeatedly studied over time intervals. The span of time interval and the number of times to repeat the study is based on the rational decision of the researcher depending upon the nature and objectives of the study.

This method is mostly used to study the developmental aspects of children such as language development, sensory and motor development, cognitive development, social development, emotional development etc. At the same time, this method is also used to make a comparative study of the developmental process of an aspect. **Kagan and Moss** have used this method to study the development of personality traits among children which is popularly known as 'birth to maturity'. On the basis of this study, they have stated that the development of personality traits begins among children from their childhood itself.

Following are the merits and demerits/limitations of longitudinal method.

Merits

(a) This method is useful to study the systematic and orderly changes that occur in behaviour during different stages of development of children.

(b) The problem of equivalency as in cross-sectional method is automatically solved in this method and the study is repeated every time after predetermined interval on the same individual or group.

(c) This method is facilitative in establishing **cause and effect** relationship.

Demerits/Limitations

(a) This method requires a lot of time and cost.

(b) The researcher is required to maintain his patience for a longer duration of time.

(c) Since the study is carried over for a longer duration (period) owing to certain intervening factors, gradually, the number of participating subjects go on decreasing. These factors are related to certain unavoidable situations such as death, change of place, ill-health etc. These factors cause decrement in their availability on subsequent occasions over time intervals.

(d) On different time intervals, changes in environment do occur. This poses difficulty in isolating uncontrolled changes in environment. This affects reliability and objectivity of the findings.

3.5.8 Sequential Method

This method includes both the cross-sectional and longitudinal methods. The researcher begins his study with cross-sectional studies and after some time interval (*e.g.* after a month or a year) the same individual or group of individuals are studied and a new group of subject at each level is also included. This approach of study has the advantages of both the cross-sectional and longitudinal methods.

However, this method is neither cost effective nor economical in time and effort.

3.5.9 Survey Method

Among several methods of psychological research, survey method is also very widely used method of study. This method is frequently used to study the prevalent patterns of behaviour in a particular group in a given period of time. For example, suppose a pharmaceutical company conducts a survey plan of a group of medical practitioners to find out the causes for unsatisfactory sale or sale decline of a particular brand of medicine. Similarly, surveying the domestic women to find out the causes of sale decline of a particular brand of detergent powder is also an example of survey research.

In survey research method, some other tools of data gathering are also used. These include interview, questionnaire, scale to measure attitudes etc. What we mean to say that survey is a very widespread and extensive method of study employed to collect or gather some specific kinds of information. Survey is used for seeking information on various socio-political issues such as provision of reservation for women in jobs.

In the current times, we often find the electronic media like various T.V. channels, conducting survey research during elections, voting patterns and several predictions and generalizations are made.

Survey can also be used to test the hypotheses about relationship among variables. Researcher may try to find out the effect of some event on people's behaviour. For example, surveys have been conducted after earthquakes at Bhuj in Gujarat to find out the impact of earthquakes on people's life.

To conduct surveys, the researcher defines the population to be studied and selects representative sample from the defined population. There are several techniques of sampling, *viz.* random sampling, stratified random sampling, cluster sampling etc. In random sampling, every member of the population has equal opportunity to be included in the sample. In stratified sampling, two or more sub-samples are represented according to some predetermined proportion, generally in the same proportion as they exist in the population. In cluster sampling, groups are selected by using clusters or groupings from a larger population.

In survey, size of the sample is also determined because, the generalizations about the population depends on the size of the sample that has been drawn from the population.

In survey, while using questionnaires and interviews as tools of data collection, these are often used through mail or on telephone.

3.6 CONCLUSIVE REMARKS REGARDING DIFFERENT METHODS OF PSYCHOLOGY

What follows from the description of different mehtods, it is evident that from the ancient times to the current modern age, the methods of study has gradually travelled through subjective techniques to more objective and impartial procedures of collecting facts, arranging them in order and interpreting them to arrive at the conclusive finding. Systematic studies in the field of psychology started with **introspection**—a subjective method which was resisted by behaviourists with emphasis on empirical method—objective observation. Later on, with the advancement of scientific approaches, psychology developed towards perfection and today, **experimental method** is being used as the chief method. Psychologists realized that objective observation limits the psychologists to observe the events and things that naturally occur and observations are done in a natural condition. Experimental method, on the other hand, enables the psychologists to make those events happen which they need to observe and they observe the events under the conditions of their own choice and that too under controlled conditions. Hence, experimental findings are more solid, concrete and definite.

As we have seen, each of the method described so far has some merits as well as certain limitations. But, most of the limitations of different methods do not discredit the use of method. These discredits relate to defective use. Each method may be equally useful, if these are used in a proper and efficient way by a well-trained and competent researcher with due precautions. Moreover, there are certain aspects which can be more efficiently studied by introspection or self-observation. In certain cases, objective observation is more useful and convenient.

Similarly, for clinical purposes, in-depth studies, various forms of interviews and/or case study method are preferable. When a researcher wants to conduct research studies, about the trends or attitudes towards certain issues, impacts of certain events, survey method is much useful by employing various tools of data collection such as questionnaire. In studying the developmental aspects of infants and children, usually cross-sectional and/or longitudinal method is used. Hence, what we find is that for different purposes and areas of research, different methods are chosen keeping in view, which of these several methods would be more useful or practicable. Therefore, in psychological enquiries, psychologists do not remain confined to any one mehtod rather they keep their mind open to choose the method that may be more profitable for the subject or topic of research. Often, psychologists use more than one method to enquire the same area of research and thus, try to arrive at a dependable conclusion in a precisely accurate manner.

Hence, all the above-described methods are useful for psychological studies.

SUMMARY

- Psychology as a science, makes use of scientific methods.
- Scientific methods are characterized by objectivity, systematisation, validity, reliability, verifiability (replication) and standardization.
- In psychological studies, the nature of data are qualitative and quantitative that are collected from various sources such as demographic information, physical information, physiological facts and psychological information.
- The major methods of psychological enquiries include observation (introspective and objective), experimentation, interview, questionnaire, cross-sectional method, longitudinal method and survey method.
- Observation is a basic method used in all sciences. In psychology, observation takes several forms such as introspection (self-observation) and objective observation. This includes naturalistic observation, controlled observation, participant observation and non-participant observation.
- Experiment refers to observation under controlled conditions where the possible impacts of extraneous relevant variables are controlled by the experimenter through several strategies that predetermines the entire procedure of observation to establish cause and effect relationship between two or more than two variables.
- Interview means face-to-face social interaction between the interviewer and the interviewee. This procedure is mostly used in clinical settings.
- Questionnaire is a set of predetermined questions with fixed or open modes of responses.
- Case study is also an important method of study which aims at in-depth study of the particular case.
- Cross-sectional method and longitudinal method are successfully used to study the developmental aspects of children.
- Survey is a method employed to study larger groups in the population to know their opinions, attitudes, post-effects of certain natural calamities etc.
- Each method has certain merits, limitations and their applicability. Psychologists usually choose a particular method in view of the nature, purpose and feasibility of application.
- Psychologists often use more than one method to study the same problem with a view to accomplish maximum possible perfection and definiteness.

PART II

Biology of Behaviour

CHAPTER 4

Biological Bases of Behaviour

4.1 INTRODUCTION

The nature of psychology is 'bio-social'. It thrusts upon the behavioural events of human beings. Human beings, the *Homosapiens* are superordinately developed of all the organisms found on this earth. They are characterized by specialized brain tissues that make them distinct from the other species.

Man during the entire lifespan, consistently engages himself interacting with others of his environment. He sees or observes various objects around him, hears different kinds of sounds, touches the objects, smells and tastes. All these activities take place with the help of specialized sense organs and brain tissues. The sense organs receive these diverse kinds of objects known as 'stimuli' (physical energy of the objects) that stimulate various organs of reception. The physical energy is then immediately converted or transformed into neural energy, called **nerve impulse** through the process of **transduction** which is carried over or conducted through neural paths to the centre *i.e.* the 'Brain'. The centre evaluates the messages received in coded form and decides about the particular response to be made which we call **behaviour**. Thus, behaviour is a response to the stimulus event in the environment. Responding involves the motor organs (effectors) which are also called 'organs of response'. In the process of response to the stimulus event, the brain mediates with 'receptor-effector mechanisms'. The involvement of these mechanisms in producing behaviour event is what we call physiological or biological basis of behaviour.

Studies have shown that in humans, biological features of larger brain (in size) and specialized brain tissues have evolved through millions of years and have enabled them to engage in several complex behaviours. Owing to this, the human beings are distinguished from other species and occupy the uppermost ladder of world creatures.

The present chapter is concerned mainly with the biological bases of behaviour. However, attempt has been made to describe the evolutionary processes which are relevant to understand the development of behaviour. Thus, the present chapter also includes the evolutions of human behaviours, genetics and receptor-effector-connector mechanisms—the biological and neural bases of behaviour.

4.2 EVOLUTIONARY PERSPECTIVES

We may often think that man on this earth is perhaps the smallest being in comparison to angels. But, we perhaps forget that in the kingdom of millions of different organisms, human beings are the most developed organism who belong to *Homosapiens* category of species. It is also observed that different organisms of this world enormously vary in their physical (size, shape, colour etc.) and behavioural characteristics. Such variations are noted not only 'between the species' but also 'within the species'. Biologists believe that such a large number of species have come into existence today as a result of evolutionary process and 'the between' and 'within' variations in physical and psychological characteristics result from the interaction of their genetic endowments and environmental demands.

'Evolution' refers to gradual and orderly biological changes that result in a species from their pre-existing forms in response to the changing adaptational demands of the environment. The physiological and behavioural changes that occur due to evolutionary processes are so slow that they become visible after hundreds of generations (see **Figure 4.1**).

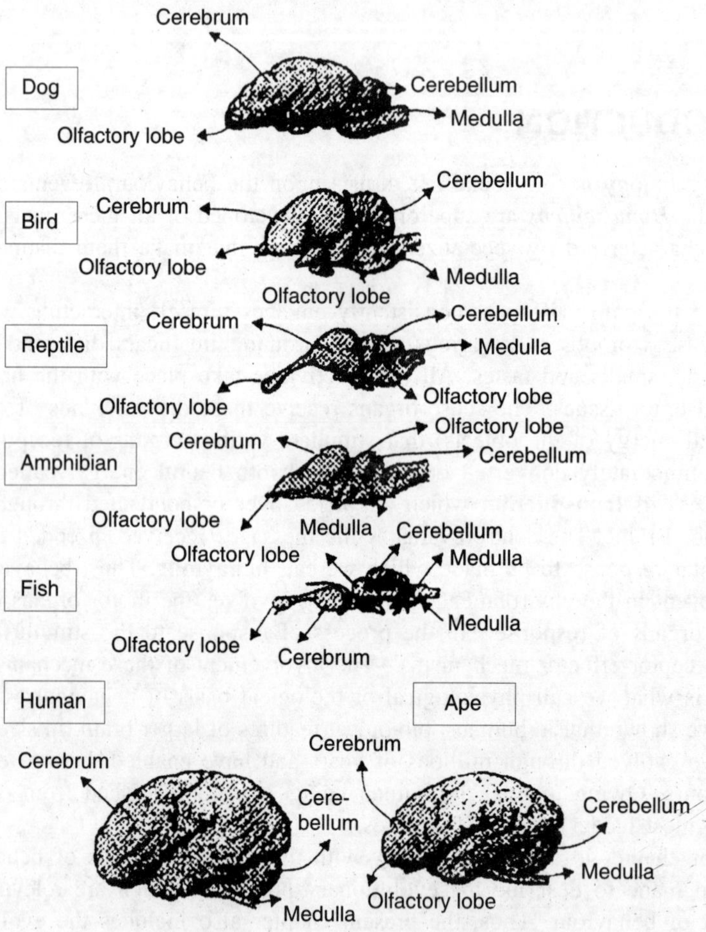

FIGURE 4.1 The evolution of the brain.

Evolution follows the process of **natural selection**. As we know, members of each species vary greatly in their physical structure and behaviour. The traits or attributes that are related to higher rate of survival and reproduction of those species are most likely ones to be passed on to the next generation. The process of natural selection leads to the evolution of new species that are more effectively adapted to their specific environment. It is similar to selective horse-breeding or breeding of other animals which is prevalent now-a-days. The breeders select the fittest and fastest male-female horses from their stock and promote them for selective breeding to get the fittest horses. **Fitness** refers to the ability of the organism to survive and contribute its genes to the next generation.

If we look at the evolutionary history of human species, three landmark features distinguish human beings from other species. These are (a) Bipedalism, (b) Encephalization and (c) Language development.

(a) **Bipedalism:** It refers to the abilities of human beings to walk upright. The human beings evolved in a manner that they developed the capacity to stand and walk uprightly on the strength of two legs (bipedal) only, *i.e.* by the movement of different joints of the two lower limbs. Thus, the upper two limbs (two hands) became free to perform other tasks such as holding, grasping and operating tools with the help of hands. This helped humans to develop and acquire some new skills using hands. Consequently, the human beings became better able to explore the environment.

(b) **Encephalization:** This refers to evolutionary changes in the size and structure of brain. Gradually, brain size increased which was followed by increased proportion of specialized brain tissues. The weight of human brain is 2.35 per cent of total body weight which is two to three times more than the monkeys or apes.

Owing to increase in specialized brain tissues human beings' became capable of complex thinking, reasoning, remembering and problem solving uniform space selling and thus, human brain became the centre of higher cognitive processes (see **Figure 4.1**).

(c) **Language development:** The third landmark evolutionary changes that occurred in humans was the advent of language. Language made human interactions much more effective than any other animal. Language is also the basis of **cultural evolution**. It is a vehicle of thought because it serves as most important tool and medium of effective communication.

Thus, through the process of biological process of evolution, human beings are at the top of the ladder of evolution. The biologists also hold the view that the process of evolution is continuing ever since it began millions of years ago (approximately 50,00,000 years ago) and we are still evolving and it will continue.

4.2.1 Environmental Influences on Evolutionary Trend

The human beings as we find today is a unique creature on this earth. Every human being differs with respect to physical and psychological characteristics. This uniqueness of individuals has resulted from not only biological evolutionary process but also due to interaction of the environment.

In early human societies, perhaps there existed a system of division of labour. This division was based on gender division, *viz.* hunting and gathering of food from distant places was assigned to men while women used to focus on household activities and child care. In course of gradual evolution of species, different demands and role expectations began to be placed on men and women both. Accordingly, their roles began to differ from what it was earlier. Women gradually became better efficient in fine motor tasks while men became better in laborious and hard muscular tasks. In the present day, due to wide ranging impacts of industrialised cultures, significant shift in expectation is seen. Present day industrialized society has began to demand for more specialised levels of different abilities and competencies in various fields of human activities. In this context, today, the gender-based differentiation in role playing has started to disappear. Today, women are being employed in military and police services while men are working as cooks in hotels and other food industries. Differences between men and women are fast ceasing and now-a-days the members of either of the sexes have gained the competency to perform most of the tasks.

These developments evidently show that biological and behavioural changes are caused by the changes in environmental demands over a period of time. Environmental changes in fact, create competition for resources among members of species. This competition is based on the principle of **survival of the fittest**. According to this principle, only those would survive or cope with change and reproduce who possess the characteristics which are instrumental in coping.

4.3 GENES AND BEHAVIOUR

According to **Conkun, E.G.** (1923) of America, **development of human beings ... is the climax of all wonders.** This remark is not an exaggeration, but truth. Man has developed from a tiny thread-like structure. This threadlike structure is subdivided into billions of cells resulting in the development of human being with infinite and extraordinary physical and psychological potentials. In poetic style this tiny threadlike structure is called **threads of life**.

4.3.1 Threads of Life

At the time of conception, two germ cells—one **sperm cell** from father's testes and another an 'egg cell' or 'ovum' from mother's ovary—unite together to form a **new individual** called **gametes**. The cell structured from gametes is called 'zygote'. The sperm and ovum cells also contain a very tiny structure, called **chromosomes** which are 23 in each (23 in sperm from father's testes and 23 from mother's ovum). Thus, together there are 46, or 23 pairs of chromosomes which unite together to form a new individual. These **chromosomes** are called the **threads of life**.

4.3.2 Chromosomes

The term **chromosomes** means coloured body. It is so called because when the chromosomes are treated with special dyes dark stains appear. Chromosomes are composed mainly of a substance called **DNA** (Deoxyribonucleic Acid). **'Francis Crick'**, **'James Watson'** and **'Maurice Wilkins'** have extensively studied the chemistry of DNA who have been awarded with Nobel Prize in the year 1962. By composition, DNA is an acid. It is nucleic acid because it is found chiefly on the nucleus of cell. **Genes** are composed chiefly of DNA molecules containing atoms which are long stringlike structures giving an appearance of a twisted string. In the centre of each atom is found a microscopic area which is known as **'genes'**. 'Genes' are known as bearers of heredity. These genes are also called **'master code'**, *i.e.* blueprint of the process of physiological and psychological characteristics. The science that studies the mechanism of heredity is called 'biology of genetics'.

Human zygote normally has 46 chromosomes. But, sometimes one additional pair of chromosome may also be found that provides abnormal structure, *viz.* two heads, larger size of brain, 6 fingers etc.

When the zygote is formed, the chromosomes from two parents **line up** and function in pair form. Then the zygote divides and redivides into many cells. The process of division takes place in such a way that the chromosomes do divide in similar way so that there are the same number in each cell. But, when gamete develops to maturity, there is another process of division, called **reduction division**. As a result, the mature egg or sperm contains only one chromosome from each pair. Thus, only half of each parents' chromosomes are transmitted to each child which is determined by the process of **chance selection**. This is one reason that different offsprings of the same parent differ in some hereditary characteristics. Thus, the familial similarities or differences in hereditary attributes are determined by transmission of genes as governed by the process of chance selection.

Each chromosome contains thousands of genes. However, the sperm cell differs from egg cell in one respect. The 23rd chromosome of the sperm cell (father's) can either be 'x' (the larger) type or 'y' (the smaller) type whereas the 23rd chromosome of egg cell (mother's) is always large, *i.e.* 'x' type. If the 'x' type sperm fertilizes the egg cell, the fertilized egg will have 'xx' 23rd chromosome pair and the child will be a female. On the contrary, if 'y' type chromosome of sperm fertilizes the egg, the 23rd chromosome will be male. Thus, the sex of the child depends entirely on the chromosome of the sperm cell of father.

Every chromosome stores thousands of genetic commands, each engraved in a gene which is the basic unit of hereditary transmission and the full set of genes inherited from both parents is called 'genotype' which determines the similarities and differences. The set of characteristics, the organism actually develops and by which an individual is recognized such as body built, colour of eye and behavioural traits (the observable features) is termed as 'phenotype'.

A given gene can exist in several different forms. Change of a gene from one form to another is called **mutation**. The type of mutation that occurs spontaneously in nature provides variation in 'genotypes' and permits the evolution of a new species. **Mutation** also permits recombination of new genes with the genes already present. This new combination is then put to test in the environment which can select out those genotypes that turn out to be appropriately fitted for the environment.

The science that focuses on identifying the genetic bases of behavioural traits such as intelligence, mental disorders etc. is called **behavioural genetics**.

4.4 NATURE AND NURTURE CONTROVERSY

Usually it is observed that despite similarity in inheritance, children differ from their parents in behavioural and psychological attributes. For example, a two-year-old child may be found throwing things while another child of the same age and the same parent may be calm and quite, *i.e.* may have no tendency to throw things. To explain this, the genetic scientists hold that the two children might be possessing unique combination of 'genes' unlike that of the parents. In such instances, the mother and the father pass on to their children a part of what they have receive from their own past generations.

However, so far the evolution of behavioural characteristics is concerned, there are severa controversial issues such as **nature versus nurture, passivity versus activity, continuous versu discontinuous** developments etc. Out of these, the heredity versus environment (nature versu nurture) is perhaps the most enduring.

The research studies done so far provide ample evidences in support of both of these view and as such, the issue is still unresolved. In the context of this unresolved controversy, moder scientists take compromising position. They hold the view that the nature-nurture debate in fact concern relative impact of both heredity and environment. Neither heredity nor the environmen alone determines the complete development of behavioural attributes. Heredity provides a frame work of behavioural tendencies. Hence, heredity is the base of behaviour in which genes pla significant role in transmitting the stored tendencies. But, in course of time, under the influenc of environment, traits of personality develop that provides adjustable patterns to behavioura tendencies. Thus, the developmental levels of behaviour patterns may be expressed in equatio form like this

$$H \times E \times T = \text{Developmental level*}$$

Hence, heredity and environment both have significant role to play in the development c behaviour. Heredity endows us with various behaviour patterns that determine the range or limit c level whereas the nature and quality (or kind) of environment influence the operation and attainmer of the determined range or limit of heredity. It is so because the environmental conditions go o constantly changing and in order to cope with such changes, one is required to bring modificatior in the inborn tendencies in accordance with the demands and expectations of the environmen Hence, it is evident that acquisition of such adaptive modifications depends upon the nature an quality of environment in which one is nurtured.

In view of the above relative significance of heredity and environment—both the moder psychologists and biologists have started taking interest in the field of 'socio-biology' which ha led to the emergence of a new discipline—called 'ethology'.

4.4.1 Socio-biology

Socio-biology is a systematic study of biological bases of social behaviours. The centr assumption of **socio-biology** is that the key purpose of human life is to pass along genes future generation. In this context, **'Charles Darwin'** has proposed the principle of natur selection. This principle states that in order to better adapt to the environment, the evolutiona forces are at work so that the survival of the species may be ensured to pass on the genes the next generation. Thus, **the study** of biological evolution of adaptive social behaviour **human beings and animals is the main concern of socio-biology**. Studies done by many soci bilogical scientists on animals lend much support to the evolutionary basis of social organization Further, the **biograms** of human beings evolutionary history also evidences the fact that hum beings possess built-in programmed behavioural predispositions (which are only broad tendenci to behave in certain ways and the details of behaviours are provided by learning and one own experiences). There are several examples of such tendencies such as tendencies towa

* H = Heredity, E = Environment and T = Time.

competition and aggression, especially among males are claimed to be innate. Similarly, territoriality, the need for a social organization with leaders, certain things that we do in child rearing, male-female roles, sacrifice or altruism etc. are all assumed to be innate behavioural potentialities which may have a basis in the evolution of our species.

Like nature-nurture controversy, the socio-biologists and psychologists too may be in controversy on the issue. However, the socio-biologists' assertion on deep-seated evolutionary basis of social behaviour needs to be extensively studied.

4.5 INHERITED STRUCTURES

Under the guidance of heredity, the organism living in a normal environment, undergoes a process of growth involving three major sets of structures: the nervous system, the endocrine glands and the muscles. In the sections to follow, we shall be describing the nervous system and endocrine glands as the biological basis of behaviour. As for the study about muscles, see the chapter—**Sensory Processes and Psychophysics**.

4.6 NERVOUS SYSTEM

Behaviour of an organism involves co-ordination of three types of organs. These are the receptors, the effectors and the adjustors. The receptors receive the stimuli while the effectors respond to the stimuli. The adjustor mediates between these two types of organs, *i.e.* functions to integrate or co-ordinate. This co-ordinating function is done with the help of a network of neural mechanisms called 'nervous system'. Therefore, in order to develop a better understanding of the behaviour events, it is desirable to know and understand nervous system (see **Figure 4.2**).

FIGURE 4.2 Nervous system.

Nervous system is a complex network of neural connections that connects the receptors and effectors by conveying the sensory and motor impulses from sensory organs to the centre and from centre to the motor organs *i.e.* organs of response. Since, the nervous system is a complex structure, we can better understand the functions of nervous system by understanding its structural units or building blocks.

4.7 NEURONS AS BUILDING BLOCKS

Nervous system is a group or bunch of several nerve cells. Hence, it is obvious that the smallest building block of nervous system is a nerve cell or neuron. It is practically not possible to estimate the exact number of nerve cells in the body because there are billions of nerve cells spread along throughout the body with the help of which the functions of various receptors and effectors are conducted, regulated and controlled.

4.7.1 Structure and Functions of Nerve Cells (Neurons)

A neuron is a nerve cell with a cell body and nerve fibres. It is the smallest building block of nervous system. It has all the characteristics of a living cell in general. In addition, neurons are also specialized to receive stimuli from environment and convert them into an electro-chemical energy form called nerve impulse. This is considered as a unique characteristic of a neuron which is termed as **biological transduction**. This nerve energy contains the encoded form of physical characteristics of a stimulus which is conveyed from receptors in the peripheries to the central processor (spinal cord and the brain) and from central nervous system (CNS) to the effectors in the peripheries.

Structure of neurons

Broadly, a neuron has following three major structural parts as shown in **Figure 4.3**:

(a) **Cell body or soma:** It is a membraneous structure which has no definite shape but almost spherical (like a tiny bag). It has very tiny pores. The pores enable the charged particulars (ions) to move through it. The inner side of this membraneous structure contains liquid substance called 'cytoplasm' with a floating microorganism structure 'nucleus' which keeps the cell active (see **Figure 4.3**). Cell body is also called **'cyton'**.

Functions: Cell body receives the nerve impulses and pass on 'axon' fibres for onward transmission to another neuron.

Fibres: All neurons have two types of fibrelike extensions of cyton; various members of dendrites and one axon.

(b) **Dendrites:** Dendrites are typically short, multiple and branched fibres found at the end of the cell body or cyton. It is formed by dendrons containing **nisale bodies**.

Function: Its main function is to receive the stimuli and carry the stimuli to the cell body (cyton or soma).

(c) **Axon:** Axon is relatively a long fibre coming out from **axon hillock** at the another end of the cell body. It is uniform in thickness. It is formed by neurofibril and is covered by **Axioplasm (myelin sheath)**. It is branched at the terminal end (terminal bottoms) called **'end brush'**.

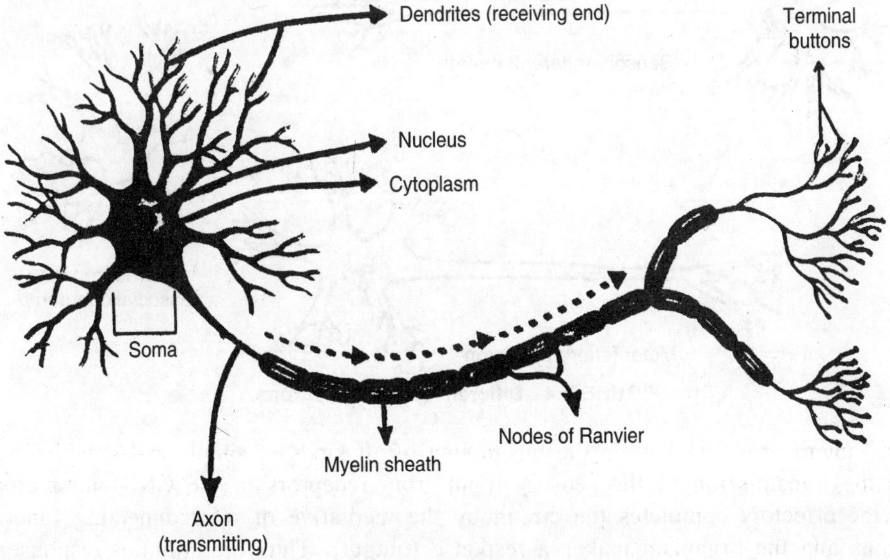

FIGURE 4.3 Different kinds of neurons.

Function: Main function of an axon is to transmit the stimuli or nerve impulse to another nearby neurons, glands and muscles. Neurons transmit the information only in one direction, *i.e.* from the dendrite through the cell body (soma) to the axon to the terminal buttons (see **Figure 4.3**).

Kinds of neurons

Following are the three types of neurons:

Sensory or afferent neurons: Sensory neurons receive the information from receptors (input) and transmit the same to the centre (brain or spinal cord) for interpretation and subsequent action command. These are located at the nerve root outside the spinal cord. The inter-neurons or connectors found in spinal cord are merely conductors.

Motor or efferent neurons: These neurons carry the message impulses (motor impulse) from central nervous system (CNS) to the effector (motor) organs, *i.e.* muscles and glands which are involved in action (organs of response). The cell bodies of those neurons are located in the spinal cord and the axon fibre is long enough to reach the neighbouring neuron or even the muscles or glands to which it relays the input.

Inter or connector neurons: These are located mainly in the CNS—spinal cord and brain. They receive the incoming impulses from the sense organs or body's internal environment, process the information and pass it for action to the motor neurons. These neurons make many contacts with each other before reaching a motor neuron (see **Figure 4.4**).

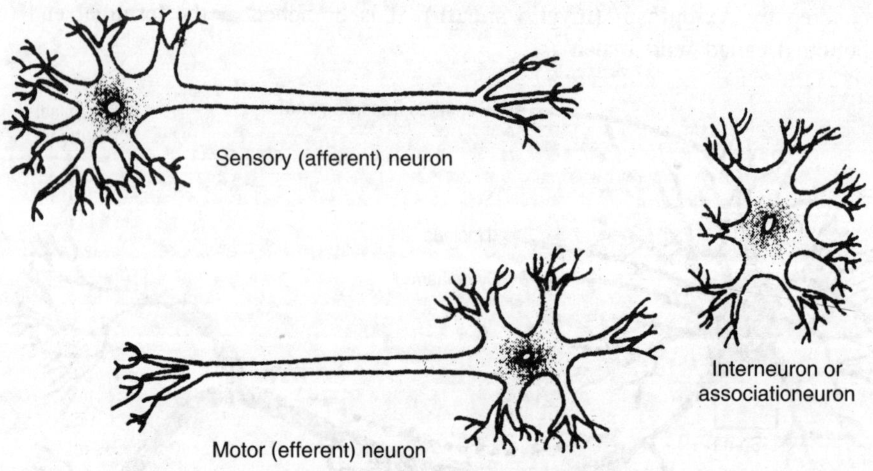

FIGURE 4.4 Different kinds of neurons.

Thus, interneurons mediate in the functioning of all kinds of simple and complex activities and thus the transmission of the sensory input from receptors to the CNS and motor input down to the effectors completes the circuit by the mediative or interconnecting functions of interneurons and the organism makes a response (output). Thus the stimulus-response circuit (S-R circuit) is completed.

Basic differences between peripheral nervous system neurons (afferent and efferent) and interneurons (association neurons).

(a) Afferent and efferent neurons have usually long conducting fibres while the fibres (dendrites and axons) of interneurons are short in structure.

(b) Afferent and efferent neurons constitute the parts of peripheral system whereas interneurons are mostly located in the central nervous system—brain and spinal cord.

4.8 MONITORING OF NEURAL ACTIVITIES

Neurons are, in fact, information carriers of the nervous system. The neurons are of three kinds—afferent, efferent and interneurons. Each carries different kinds of information (input). Afferent neurons conduct the afferent nerve impulse from receptors in the periphery to the central nervous system (CNS). Motor or efferent neurons carry the motor impulse from CNS onto the effectors (organ of response), *i.e.* muscles and glands. The interneurons are largely found in spinal cord and brain. It receives afferent impulses conducted through afferent neurons and passes it onto the motor neuron to conduct the impulses down to the organs of response. Thus, it connects the two neurons or bring association between them.

Thus, the function of the neuron is to generate neural energy (nerve impulse) and with the help of axon fibres it transmits neural impulses from one place to another in the nervous system. In this context, let us first consider how a neural impulse is generated? Nerve impulses are electrical events of a very short duration that travel from dendrites to the axon terminals. The nerve impulse is brief and sharp. It is called a 'spike'. It is rapid, reversible change in the electrical charges inside and outside a neuron. This electrical change is a matter of excitation of the neuron caused by electrical energy from stimulus. A nerve cell, comparable to a battery, has negative and positive poles which on being interconnected by an electric wire, produces electric current.

Likewise, the outer and inner sides of the cell's membrane are positively charged with sodium ion (Na^+) and negatively charged potassium ion (K^-) respectively when it is in resting stage (rest potential). On being excited by a stimulus energy, it makes the inside ion a little less negative. At a critical point (threshold), the membrane surrounding the neuron will change its characteristics. The channels (small pores) open briefly allowing charged particle of sodium ion (Na^+) floating into the cell which are positively charged. Thus, the inside of the neuron becomes more positive than the area outside the cell for a short duration (about a millisecond). This brief change to inside positive is called the 'action potential' or 'neural impulse'.

In other words, when a neuron is at rest, there is difference between the electrical charge inside and outside the neuron (the inside being more negative). When the neuron is stimulated, the difference suddenly reverses so that inside suddenly becomes slightly positive. This brief change to inside positivity is the 'neural impulse'.

After the nerve impulse has occurred, the neuron is restored to its original resting charge by an outward flow of potassium ion and is ready to fire again. The electrical nerve impulse travels along an axon exciting the next region and so on continuously down the axon. The function of neural conductivity is regulated by certain functions and laws. These are described below:

4.8.1 Law Governing Propagation of Action Potential (Nerve Impulse)

The propagation of nerve impuse or action potential is governed by a law which is called **all or none-law**. According to this law, the strength of propagation of nerve impulse or action potential does not depend upon the intensity or strength of stimulus which initiates it, instead, it depends upon characteristics of the fibre itself. The only necessity is that **threshold**, *i.e.* minimum strength of stimulus to propagate or fire be reached. After this a self-propagation series of events, which cannot be stopped, takes place in the membrane of the fibre.

This law makes it clear that a weak stimulus is unable to propagate a nerve impulse. The intensity of the stimulus which is just adequate to cause an impulse is called **threshold stimulus**. A stimulus below the threshold fails to propagate any action potential. Further, once the impulse is created, it travels along the entire length of the axon in both directions without loss of strength of nerve impulse. Hence, **all or none-law** states that if cell responds, it responds in full, provided the stimulus is just adequate (*i.e.* of threshold value). It does not vary in size according to the strength of stimulus.

4.8.2 Refractory Period

Refractory period refers to the repolarization of the membrane. Once, nerve fibre is fired, it cannot fire again for a brief interval even in response to strong stimuli. This is a period of complete irresponsiveness and called **absolute refractory period**. This period is approximately one thousandth of a second. It is followed by a **relative refractory period**. During this period, a very strong stimulus is needed to produce new impulse in the nerve fibre.

Thus, reexcitation of a nerve fibre is possible only after the membrane restores the original resting potential. This is called **repolarization** and the period elapsing between excitation and repolarization is called **refractory period** which has two phases—absolute and relative. This refractory period is a **natural defence** against nerve fatigue.

It is also important to note that during relative phase of refractory period, the propagation of neural impulse follows the governing principle of **all or none-law**.

4.8.3 Transmission of Nerve Impulse

In transmission of nerve impulses from the point of origin (receptors) to its destination point, the nerve impulses are required to take a longer course to travel through several fibres. Thus, several neurons are involved. But the two fibres of the two separate neurons do not join each other rather show a gap in-between. Each branch of an end-brush of axon terminates in a synaptic knob, a rounded expansion applied against the dendrites of another neuron. This is a junction point of the **pre-synaptic** and **post-synaptic** fibres which is called **synapse**. **Thus the junction of axon fibre of one neuron and dendrite fibre of another neuron is called synapse.**

The synapse serves as one-way vault, *i.e.* the nerve impulse crosses from one end-brush of the pre-synaptic axon to post-synaptic dendrite only. Thus, the direction of transmission is always forward, *i.e.* from dendrite of a neuron along axon tips to the dendrite of another neuron and not in reverse (opposite) direction. When a nerve impulse reaches a synaptic knob (the terminal point of pre-synaptic axon fibre), there is a potential change in the membrane of the next neuron (post-synaptic neuron) and the impulse is mediated by **neurotransmitting substance*** found in the vesicles at the synaptic cleft.

4.8.4 Synaptic Functions

The effect of neurotransmitter on the post-synaptic (receiving) cell is either to increase its tendency to fire nerve impulses—excitation' or to decrease this tendency—'inhibition'. The excitatory function is also termed as facilitating function.

4.8.5 Synaptic Facilitation

Synapse is a case of **contiguity** without **continuity**. As the nerve impulse passes across the synapse between two neurons, there is a difference in their rate of travel. Some impulses are weak to evoke potential change in another neuron. Therefore, such impulses never cross the synapse at all unless it reaches a certain size (threshold). These facts are indicative of discontinuity at the synapse. Here two types of facilitating summations take place, namely special summation and temporal summation.

Special summation: Nerve impulses from two pre-synaptic neurons emerging out from two different special points, reach a synapse and combine together. Their combined or summated effects help the weaker impulse to cross the synapse.

Temporal summation: Sometimes at some intervals, two nerve impulses through the same pre-synaptic neuron combine together within the life period of the weaker nerve impulse at

* The vesicles at the synaptic cleft usually contain certain substances like Adrenaline, Acetylcholine which begin to release and impulse is mediated.

the synapse. Combined or summated effects of these two impulses facilitate the weaker impulses to cross the synapse.

Hence, arrival of a nerve impulse at synaptic knob either from two different points or in two different temporal sequences facilitates in depolarization of post-synaptic neuron which is known as excitatory post-synaptic potential (EPSP). The best known transmitter involved in generating EPSP is Acetylcholine (ACH).

Synaptic inhibition: In addition to facilitating function at synapse, inhibitory function also takes place. This is called inhibitory post-synaptic potential (IPSP). A synapse is not only filled with vesicles of excitatory substances but also with inhibitory substances. Inhibitory substances hyperpolarize the post-synaptic neuron making it more negative, *i.e.* driving the neuron away from firing level and thus, inhibits post-synaptic potential.

Vesicles with excitatory substances are relatively round in shape while vesicles with inhibitory substances are egg-shaped.

Figure 4.5 shows the anatomy of structure of different kinds of neurons, synapse and functional continuity of nerve impulses at the synapse.

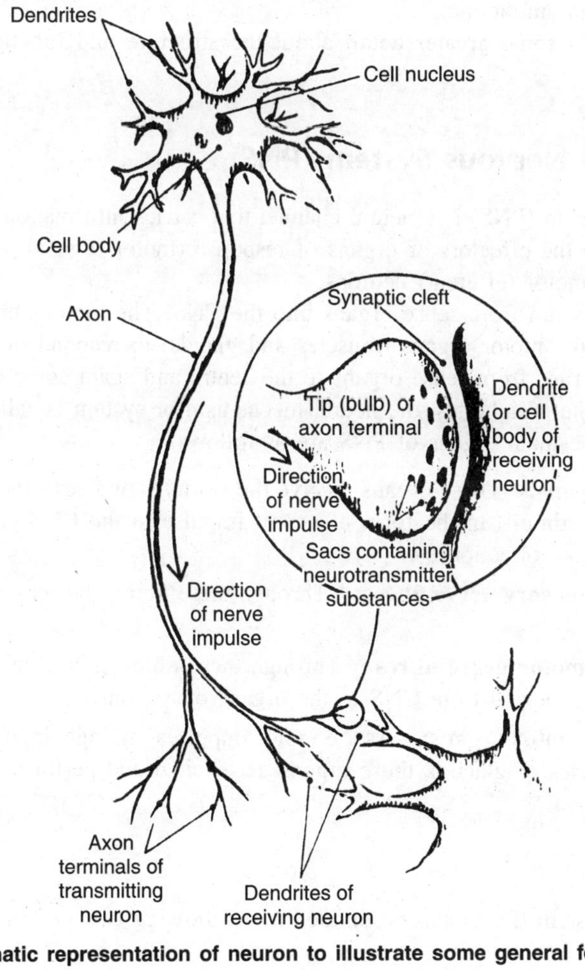

FIGURE 4.5 A schematic representation of neuron to illustrate some general features of nerve cells.

4.9 DIVISION OF NERVOUS SYSTEM

Nervous system consists of neural mechanisms that conduct and transmit nerve impulse (information) and carry messages throughout the body.

Nervous system can be divided in to three main types which are as follows:

1. Peripheral Nervous System (PNS) consisting of fibres of sensory and motor neurons and forming a channel that carries information to and from the Central Nervous System (CNS).
2. Central Nervous System (CNS) consisting of brain and spinal cord which recognizes and transforms some of the information received through PNS, collates it with other information, stores some of it and sends out signals through motor part of PNS.
3. Autonomic Nervous System (ANS) consists of many nerves leading from the brain and spinal cord out to the smooth muscles of the various organs of the body, to the heart, certain glands and to the blood vessels.

In fact, ANS is a division of PNS based on autonomy of functions. On this basis, PNS in divided into somatic and autonomic.

Let us describe in some greater detail about the structure and functions of these nervous systems one by one.

4.9.1 Peripheral Nervous System (PNS)

Peripheral Nervous System (PNS) is a neural channel that carries information from receptors to the CNS and from CNS to the effectors or organs of response (motor organs). It consists of fibres of sensory (afferent) and motor (efferent) neurons.

The sensory fibres run from sense organs into the CNS. The motor fibres run out from CNS and activate or excite the motor organs (muscles and glands) to respond or act. Since, the entire neural channel of PNS runs from sense organs to the centre and again come out from centre to the organs of response in the peripheries, the neural mechanism or system is called peripheral nervous system—PNS. Thus, the main organs of PNS are as follows.

(a) **Receptor organs:** These organs receive the stimulus and send the impressions (sensory codes of the stimuli) in the form of neural impulse to the CNS causing sensations, *viz.* vision, addition, olfaction etc.

(b) **Afferent or sensory nerve fibres:** Through these fibres, the sensory input is transmitted to the CNS.

(c) **Efferent or motor nerve fibres:** Through these fibres, motor nerve impulses (response messages) are carried from CNS to the organs of response.

(d) **Effectors or motor organs:** As the motor impulses impinge upon the effectors or motor organs (muscles or glands), these organs get excited and perform the act as response to the stimuli.

Division of PNS

Peripheral Nervous System (PNS) can be divided into following two main types:

(a) Sensory Peripheral Nervous System (SPNS) and
(b) Motor Peripheral Nervous System (MPSN).

(i) **Sensory peripheral nervous system (SPNS):** Sensory peripheral nervous system consists of afferent nerve fibres originating from receptors and passing through the central nervous system (CNS) and thus, makes a connection between sensory organs in the peripheries and CNS. These fibres carry afferent or sensory nerve impulses and enter CNS through the **dorsal** or **sensory root**.

(ii) **Motor peripheral nervous system (MPNS):** Motor peripheral nervous system consists of efferent nerve fibres coming out from CNS and passing through down to the motor organs or organs of response (effectors), *i.e.* the muscles and glands. Thus, it connects the brain with the effector organs and carries the efferent nerve impulses to stimulate or excite the organs of response. The efferent fibres leave the CNS through **ventral** or **motor root**.

Anatomy of PNS

PNS includes cranial and spinal nerves* that connect the CNS with the receptors and effectors of the body.

Cranial nerves

Twelve pairs of cranial nerves arise from brain. Of them four pairs are sensory in nature and concerned with the sensation of vision, olfactory, audition and balance.

Other four pairs are motor in nature and are concerned with eye movements, regulation of pupils size, visceral reflexes, shoulder movements and tongue movements.

Another four pairs are mixed nerves connecting both kinds of fibres—sensory and motor and concerned with taste, swallowing, secretion of saliva, facial expression, properioception, abduction of eye and visceral reflexes associated with pharynx, larynx, thoracic and abdominal viscera.

Spanial nerves: All spanial nerves are of mixed type. 31 pairs of them arise from the spinal cord. These are as follows:

Cervical nerves	8 pairs
Thoracic nerves	12 pairs
Lumbar nerves	5 pairs
Sacral nerves	5 pairs
Coccygeal nerves	1 pair
	31 pairs

All spinal nerves arise from two roots of spinal cord—dorsal or sensory root and ventrăl or motor root. Dorsal root is formed of only fibres, the cell bodies which are located in the dorsal root ganglion. Sensory impulses from receptors travel through 'dorsal root'. Ventral roots are formed by motor fibres, the cell bodies of which are located in the ventro-lateral horn of grey matter and their axons lead to the muscles in the peripheral tissues.

* A nerve is formed of several fibres enclosed in a connective tissue sheath.

4.9.2 Central Nervous System (CNS)

Central Nervous System (CNS) is the most significant part of nervous system because it is the centre of all kinds of neural activities. It performs integrative functions of all incoming information (input), thought processes, decision-making (central processing) and issues neural messages to the effector or motor organs to perform a particular act (output). Thus, it functions like a central processor unit (CPU) in a computer system that correlates and integrates the information, collates with other information, recognizes them and interprets the information, stores some of it and sends out signals through motor part of PNS. All these functions of CNS are parts of integrative activities. Thus, it is especially organized as an integrator of information.

CNS is made of two major parts—spinal cord and brain. Let us consider these two constituents separately.

Spinal cord: In the middle of the back, there is a spinal bone (tail bone). It extends from lowest part of the back (waist) to the neck. Inside it, there is a semi-solid substance or nervous tissue. This tissue also extends from bottom of the back to the lowest part of the skull. It thus, forms a thick string or cord and is therefore called spinal cord.

A cross-section of spinal cord shows that its centre (inside) contains gray matter and looks like a butterfly (H-shaped). It consists of cell bodies of association or interneurons and motor nerves. The gray matter appears penetrating into white matter which consists of the axon fibres of the sensory and motor neurons in the form of horns which conduct the impulses to and fro in the peripheries (**Figure 4.6**).

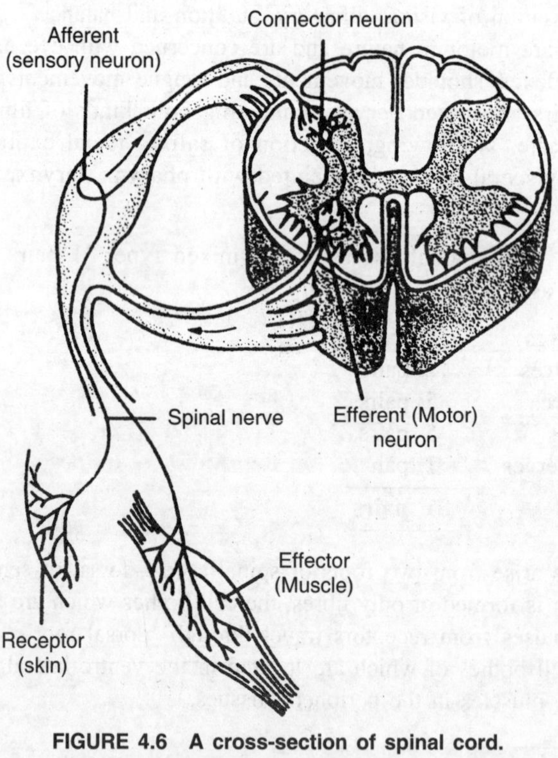

FIGURE 4.6 A cross-section of spinal cord.

Pathways or nerve tracts

Nerve tracts are bundle of nerve fibres that ascend or descend along white matter of the spinal cord. They originate and terminate at similar sites. There are two types of nerve tracts as mentioned below:

(a) **Ascending nerve tracts:** Ascending nerve tracts are those that conduct nerve impulses from spinal cord to the brain. Hence, the nerve impulses from periphery are brought by incoming spinal nerves to ascending tract and conveyed to the brain to produce sensation.

(b) **Descending nerve tracts:** Descending nerve tracts are those that conduct nerve impulses from brain to different levels of spinal cord. Such impulses evoke response via spinal nerves to muscles and glands.

The cord: The cord is cylindrical with two swellings—one in cervical region and one in lumbar region. It is approximately 18" string of nerve fibres. There are 31 pairs of spinal nerves arising at intervals from dorsal and ventral roots. The 'dorsal root' is sensory and contains sensory nerve fibres. 'Ventral root' is motor and has motor fibres.

The motor nerves emerge from ventral root of the cord which carries motor impulses into the muscles and glands in the peripheries. The dorsal root fibres bring in the information to spinal cord from periphery giving sensation of vision, audition, touch etc.

Functions: Spinal cord functions in two ways as mentioned below:

(a) It acts as a main centre of reflex action.
(b) It acts as a link between spinal nerves and brain.

Thus, it participates in conscious action. In other words, it is the conducting pathway of signals, both sensory and motor.

Reflex action: A reflex action is the spontaneous and involuntary action of the body. These are performed to cope with the emergent situations. Such actions are sudden and immediate without involving neuronal analysis and integration. These actions occur very fast, even before one can feel the stimulus through brain. Such actions are described as **autonomic response to stimuli**. Reflex actions are simplest and inborn actions which are controlled and regulated by the spinal cord of CNS.

Some examples of common human reflex actions are mentioned below:

(a) Knee jerk reflexes
(b) Ankle jerk reflexes
(c) Blinking reflexes
(d) Sneezing reflexes
(e) Salivation or watering of mouth on sight, smell or thought of food.
(f) Withdrawal reflexes, *viz.* withdrawal of hand or finger on touching a hot plate surface etc.

Reflex arch: The body responds to external or internal changes. The above-mentioned reflex actions are done in response to certain external and internal changes which call for immediate action. Therefore, the spinal cord as second-in-charge (2ic) of the centre (brain) passes the motor signals to the organ of response in the periphery and thus, evokes immediate action to cope with the emergency situation caused by sudden stimulus exciting the receptors in the periphery.

Reflex arch is a simple nervous pathway connecting a receptor and an effector. It consists of the following parts:

(a) **The receptors:** It is situated in the sensory organs which receive a stimulus and generate sensory nerve impulse.

(b) **Afferent or sensory neuron:** It connects the receptors to the spinal cord where it enters through 'dorsal root'. It conveys afferent or sensory nerve impulse to the spinal cord.

(c) **Association neuron or interneuron:** It is situated in the spinal cord which connects and passes impulses conveyed by afferent neurons to the motor or efferent neurons. Generally, there is only one association neuron in reflex arch. But, sometimes two such neurons may be present in a reflex arch. On this basis, two types of reflex archs have been differentiated.

(d) **Efferent or motor neuron:** It comes out from ventral root of spinal cord and extends to muscles or glands in the periphery. It transmits motor impulses to the organs of response which may be a muscle or a gland.

(e) **Effector organ:** It is the organ of response which responds to the exciting stimulus on receiving the motor impulse through motor neurons. These organs may be either a muscle or a gland.

Thus, it is clear that **reflex arch** is a path of flow for the signals from receptor to spinal cord and again down to the effector and a response to the stimuli is evoked which we call **reflex action** (see **Table 4.1**).

TABLE 4.1 The Path of Reflex Arch

Stimulus (*viz.* pinprick)	→	*Receptor organ* (*viz.* skin)	→	*Sensory or afferent nerve*	→	*Spinal cord*
Reflex action spontaneous	←	Effector organ	←	Motor nerves	←	↓
Removal of skin or part of body pricked	←	Muscles	←	Efferent nerves	←	Connector neuron

The path of reflex arch is shown in Figure 4.7.

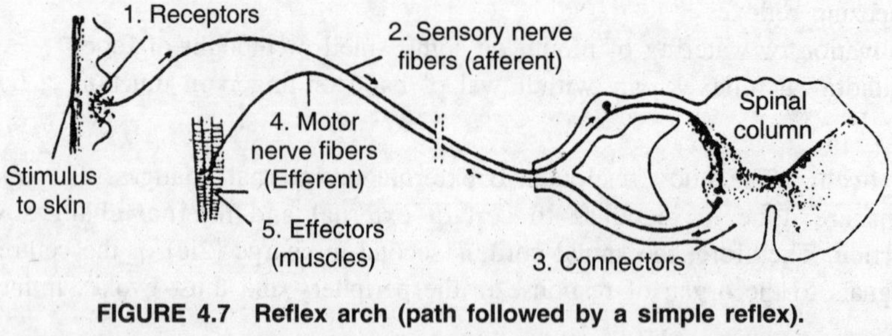

FIGURE 4.7 Reflex arch (path followed by a simple reflex).

Brain: Brain is the major part of CNS. It is the most complex as well as delicate structure that plays a central role in all our activities—simple or complex—such as walking, talking etc. as simple activities and learning, thinking, decision-making, use of language, etc. as complex activities.

The brain is said to be a great ravelled knot and contains billions of nerves which are spread all over the body. It controls and regulates the activities of all the parts of our body.

The brain is divided into two hemispheres (right and left). The upper layer is called the cortex that lies inside the cavity of skull. Sometimes, it is also referred to **neocortex** because, it is assumed that in the process of evolution, this is the latest developed part of the brain. In brain, the neurons appear grey and hence, is commonly called as grey matter. Tracing back to the process of evolution from earliest to recent most development, brain structure may be divided into three distinguishing levels—

(a) The brain stem and cerebellum
(b) The limbic system, and
(c) The cortex.

The brain stem and cerebellum: Brain stem, in fact, is an extension of spinal cord which is the **centre of life support**. For example, it is the centre of breathing, heartbeat, waking and sleeping. It contains the following structures (see **Figure 4.8**):

(a) Medulla oblongata
(b) Pons
(c) Cerebellum

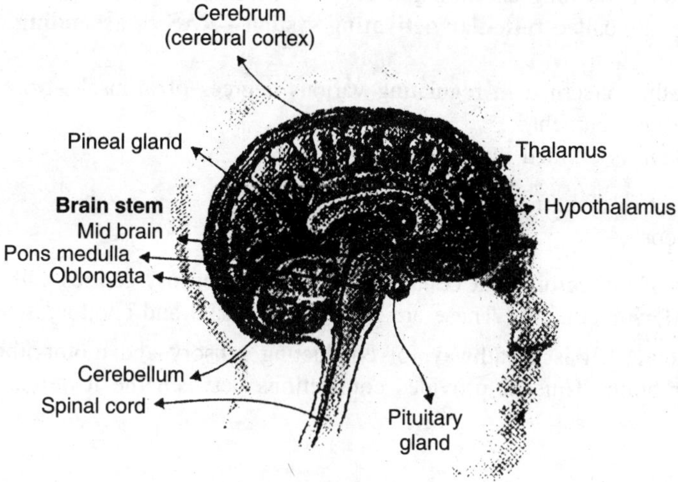

FIGURE 4.8 Brain stem.

- **Medulla oblongata:** Medulla oblongata is one of the constituents of brain stem—ventral portion of the hind-brain. It is approximately 2″ long and is the apex extension of spinal cord entering into the brain. The medulla contains vital centres for breathing and heart. It also includes centres that relay impulses upward to the middle and forebrain and thus, it connects the brain with spinal cord.

- **Pons:** It is the second constituent of ventral portion of hind brain. It is situated just above the medulla and functions as a bridge made up of nerve fibres that connect the two hemispheres of cerebellum and also cerebrum. It also connects other parts of the brain with cerebellum and cerebrum. Its main function is to provide pathways for sensory and motor impulses to and from hemispheres.
- **Cerebellum:** It is situated at the posterior part of the brain (dorsal portion) below occipital lobe of cerebrum. It is divided into two hemispheres. One hemisphere is connected to spinal cord with the help of several fibres and the other one is connected with the cerebrum through pons.

Cerebellum (Latin—little brain) is concerned with neuromuscular control of body movements, postures, muscle tone, coordination of muscular movements, reflex, control and makes necessary adjustments (modulates) of voluntary movements initiated by cerebral cortex. All its functions are unconscious.

Mid-brain

Mid-brain connects cerebellum with cerebrum. It contains a large number of nerve cells scattered in white matter. Some of these cells control muscle tone and modify motor activities. Some act as centres for auditory and visual reflexes. In the centre or core of brain stem running up from medullar to mid-brain is a complex region containing many small clumps (thick pieces of mass) of neurons and a number of long and short nerve fibres. It appears like a **network** (Latin word is reticulum). Thus, this region is named as **reticular formation**. Later on, it was discovered that this network through its long ascending fibres was involved in activation or arousal of cerebral cortex and hence, are called **reticular activating system—RAS** or **ascending reticular activating system—ARAS**.

It is critically concerned in regulating various degrees of arousal—from deep sleep to alert awareness of the environment.

The mid-brain is divided into two main parts:

(a) The roof or tectum and
(b) The floor

- **The roof or tectum:** It contains two pairs of sensory centres called **superior colliculi** and **inferior colliculi**. These are involved in visual and auditory sensation respectively.
- **The floor:** It is a pathway for conducting sensory and motor fibres to and from the higher brain. Thus, it provides connections between the lower and higher centres of brain.

Fore-brain

The higher centre of brain is called the **forebrain**. This is broadly divided into four major parts:

(i) Thalamus
(ii) Hypothalamus
(iii) Limbic system and
(iv) Cerebrum.

(i) **Thalamus:** It is located above the mid-brain but below cerebrum. It consists of the round bulged masses of grey matter. It serves as a relay centre for sensory and motor impulses coming from spinal cord and brain stem to various parts of cerebrum. Because of this, 'thalamus' is called **exact centre of the human brain**. Thus, the 'thalamus' alerts the different centres of brain by relaying the incoming messages (sensory signals) to the appropriate areas of the cortex for processing. In this sense, it functions as **Chetak**. Each hemisphere has a thalamus and the two function in harmony with each other.

(ii) **Hypothalamus:** It is directly below and a merging part of thalamus. It is formed of patches of grey matter of neurosecretory cells. It is divisible in two parts—posterior or lateral portion and anterior or central portion. The former helps in the functions of sympathetic system of ANS while the latter helps in parasympathetic system of ANS. Thus, the two centres together form the higher centre of ANS that controls hunger, thirst, sleep, fatigue, emotions, satisfaction, anger, pleasure and penance. Hypothalamus also links nervous system to endocrine glands and regulate its functioning by secreting neuro hormones. It also controls carbohydrate and fat metabolism, body temperature, blood pressure, and water balance.

(iii) **The limbic system:** The **limbic system** is found in all mammals. It is composed of a number of structures grouped together around the central part of brain area. This group of structures is called limbic system (from Latin meaning **'boarder'**). These lay along the innermost border of the cerebral hemisphere. It is the complex arrangement of pathways and centres. It also includes part of hypothalamus, septal area, the amygdala, the hippocampus and cingulate gyrus. The cingulate gyrus is a cortical part of the limbic system.

Limbic system is considered important in regulating and controlling emotional and motivational behaviours. The system is also associated with the regulatory functions of heart and stomach. Perhaps due to this, the region **limbic system** is called as **visceral brain**.

The significance of this region of brain in emotional and motivational behaviour has been well-established. For example, in animals, it has been found that the nerve impulses arising in the septal area inhibits the expression of anger while the nerve impulses originating from amygdala increases its intensity. It has further been observed that when the limbic system is injured or damaged, phenomena like irregular memory, hallucinations, epileptic syndromes etc. are seen. According to **MacClean** the limbic system is also associated with subjective feelings and experiences of emotions.

On the basis of studies conducted on some important roles of various areas of limbic systems, the following facts have been observed:

- The hippocampus is the largest of limbic structure. It has a significant role to play in memory, particularly in the storage of long-term information.
- The amygdala has important role to play in aggression. It is also involved in memory, emotion, and certain basic motives.
- The hypothalamus is the smallest structure in brain with a vital role to play in behaviour. It is concerned with regulation of physiological processes relating to emotional and motivational behaviours—eating, drinking, temperature regulation and sexual arousal. It is also concerned with regulation of endocrine system. Basically, hypothalamus involves in the maintenance of homeostasis in the body (see **Figure 4.9**).

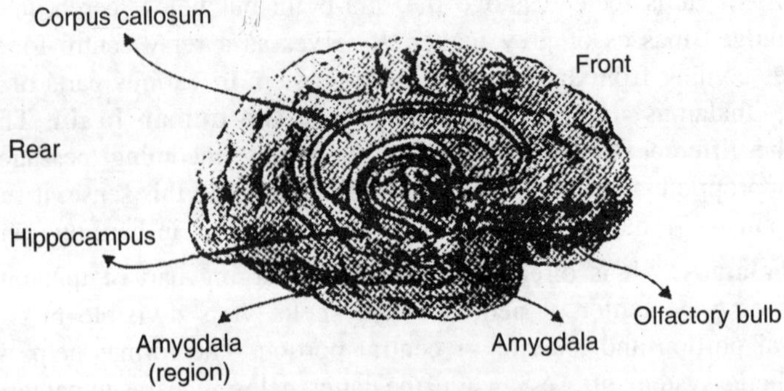

FIGURE 4.9 The lymbic system.

(iv) **Cerebrum:** Cerebrum is the largest and most prominent part of brain. It represents a highly complex structure of forebrain, *i.e.* uppermost layer of brain. It consists of an inner core of white matter and outer layer of grey. Inner white is composed of fibres running to and from the cells in outer layer or **cerebral cortex**. Cerebrum encloses almost all forebrain and mid-brain. It is covered by the cortex. The cortex looks like rumpled piece of cloth that has many ridges and valleys. Ridges are called **gyrus** while valleys are known as **sulcus** or **fissures**.

Cerebrum is divided in two halves—the **right** and **left hemispheres**. In general, the right hemisphere controls the left side of the body while the left hemisphere controls the right side of the body. Impulses are also received accordingly, *i.e.* the right hemisphere receives impulses from left side and left hemisphere receives impulses from the right side of the body. Each hemisphere is connected by a bundle of large many sensory and motor fibres called **'corpus callosum'**. The corpus callosum coordinates the two hemispheres and provide the form of a single unit, *i.e.* **unison**. In the event of damage to this bundle, there would be **'two minds in a single brain'**, *i.e.* **'divided brain or mind.'**

Cerebrum contains higher centres which regulate higher levels of cognitive and emotional functions. As has been stated earlier, the uppermost layer of cerebrum is called cortex. Without cortex, there can be no planning, no complex movements, *viz.* movements involved in dancing. Cortex is also important in perception, speech etc. The entire surface of cortex is covered by 4 mm thick mass of **neurons, glial, neural nets** and **bundle** of **axons.** These enable us to perform organized actions, create images, symbols, associations, memories, wishes and fantasies. Though, the two hemispheres appear identical, in most of us, one hemisphere is more dominant than the other. In human beings, usually the left hemisphere is more dominant which controls the right side of the body. It is also found that some functions are specific to one hemisphere, *viz.* speech is generally controlled by the left hemisphere. However, in some left-handed individuals, the centre of speech is in the right hemisphere (see **Figure 4.10**).

The upper layer of cortex looks grey because it contains concentrated neurons which give the appearance of grey and therefore called grey matter. The inner side of cortex looks white because it has myelinated fibres and hence appear white (called white matter).

The cortex has many large deep and small thin ridges and valleys (gyrus and fissures). Of them, two fissures (valleys or sulcus) are most prominent. These are called **'central or fissure of Rolando'** and **'lateral or fissure of sylvius'**. These two fissures divide each hemisphere vertically and horizontally, both. Thus, the brain is divided into 4 lobes with specialized functions. These are called cortical lobes. These cortical lobes are as follows:

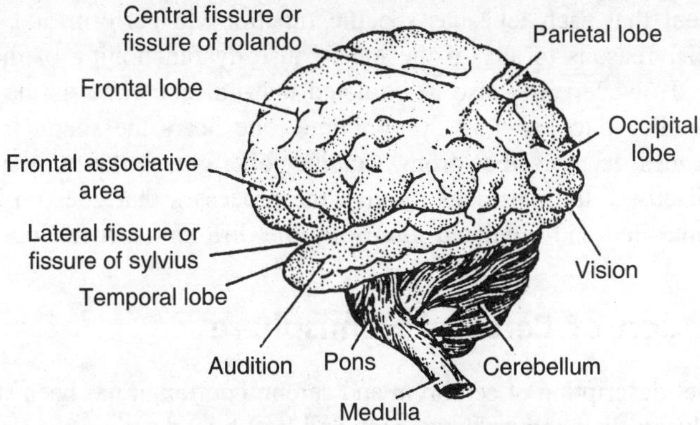

FIGURE 4.10 Cerebral cortex and different lobes.

(a) **Frontal lobe:** It is located in front, of central fissure or fissure of Rolando and above fissure of sylvius. Some of the important functions performed by this lobe are as follows:

- ◆ It initiates, sustains and controls various voluntary movements and actions such as eating, talking, walking etc.
- ◆ It is involved in motor control and higher level cognitive activities. It facilitates proper coordination of psycho-motor activities.
- ◆ It is also concerned with conscious processes such as thinking, planning, decision-making, pursuing goals etc.
- ◆ Damage to frontal lobe adversely affects human behaviour and personality including speech and intellectual impairment.
- ◆ It inhibits and controls autonomic and emotional responses.

(b) **Parietal lobe:** It is located in both the hemispheres behind the central fissure and involve in the following activities:

- ◆ Co-ordination between sensory input and motor output
- ◆ Speech
- ◆ Comprehending and co-ordinating the stimuli at tridimensional level
- ◆ Activities relating to touch sensations

(c) **Temporal lobe:** This lobe is located below the fissure of sylvius lying just inside the two temples. The main functions are as follows:

- ◆ Auditory sensation
- ◆ Processing of auditory information such as sound, words etc.
- ◆ Storage of verbal and visual memory

(d) **Occipital lobe:** It is located in the back of the brain and involved in the following functions:

- ◆ Receiving nerve impulses from visual receptors
- ◆ Interpretation of visual impulses
- ◆ Memory for visual stimuli and colour orientation

Thus, it is evident that each lobe has specific functions to perform and, therefore, damage due to accident or other reasons to any of the lobe, cause dysfunctioning of the functions related to the concerned lobe. However, it is also to be noted that no lobe controls the specific behaviour alone. For example, while watching a T.V. programme, one hears the sound from temporal lobe, visually locates the scenes on the screen from occipital lobe, grasps the programme with the help of parietal lobe and discusses the messages through the processes that goes on in the frontal lobe. Thus, behaviour is controlled and regulated jointly by the different cortical lobes.

4.9.3 Specialization of Cerebral Hemisphere

While presenting a brief description of cerebrum and cerebral cortex, it has been stated that cerebrum is divided into two halves called hemispheres (right and left) by a deep groove (longitudinal fissure). This fissure stretches from front to the back of cerebrum (forehead to the back of neck). It has also been stated that in general, the two halves or hemispheres control and regulate the bodily activities of the various parts of the body just in opposite directions, *i.e.* the left hemisphere is responsive to the right side of the body while the right hemisphere is responsive to the left side of the body and the impulses too are conveyed to the respective hemispheres in the like manner, *i.e.* in opposite direction, *i.e.* from right side to the left hemisphere and from left side to the right hemisphere. It has also been made clear that the two hemispheres function in unison with one another failing which, there would be a case of two minds in one brain. This 'unison' of functioning is attributed to the white bundle of fibres that arch between the two hemispheres and called **Corpus Callosum**.

But the research studies done in this area have also shown that the two hemispheres are specialized in certain specific functions. Their specified functions are described below:

Left hemisphere

Left hemisphere is supposed to be specialized in language functioning and as such is very often called as **'language brain'**. This fact would be obviously evidenced if we observe people with brain injury as in the case of **stroke**. Those with right side paralysis (*i.e.* with left hemisphere strokes) are likely to exhibit some language problem as compared to those who are suffering from left side paralysis (right hemisphere stroke). In recent years, neuroscientists have developed a very convenient 'test' to study the localization of speech hemisphere in normal individual. **Sodium amytal**—a sedative drug is injected into main artery serving one hemisphere. While the sedative drug is taking effect, the subject is instructed to talk. It is observed that gradually, the speech starts disintegrating and as soon as the drug reaches to one side of the hemisphere, the speech completely drops. From this, one can easily conclude the particular side of the cortex in which speech is localized. Results of such tests have indicated that speech is localized in the left hemisphere. It has also been established that left hemisphere is specialized for language functions in 95% of the right-handed persons and in about 65% in left-handed people (Milner 1974).

Analyzing the results in some greater details of the left hemisphere, it has been found that the upper temporal lobe and the lower frontal lobe are the main localized centres of language functions. The temporal lobe language centre is known as **Wernicke's lobe** (after 'Carl Wernicke' who studied language disorder due to brain injury in this area in the year 1870). The language centre in the frontal lobe area is known as **'Broca's area'** (after Paul Broca—a French physician, who in 1860, discovered the language functions of this area). Damage to either of the two areas results in language problem specific to the area of damage.

Aphasia is a very common disorder of language that occurs due to brain damage. This is reflected in loss of communication, understanding of language, talking or abilities to express through writing.

'Wernicke's area' is involved mainly in understanding of spoken and written language. Therefore, the ability to comprehend is seriously impaired due to injury or lesion in this area of the cortex. It also plays a role in the formation of sentences, figuring out what one wants to say or write, searching the appropriate words to express etc. It has been found that after injury, a person with fluent speech and pronunciation, experiences difficulty in finding out the appropriate words. Consequently, his communication is weak and vague, *i.e.* deficient in meaning.

Other language problems that are related to Wernicke's area are as mentioned below:

(a) Impaired ability to repeat spoken words
(b) Reading and writing problems
(c) Difficulty in naming common objects
(d) Intrusion of incorrect sounds or words into the flow of speech, *viz.* 'streeb' in place of street or daughter in place of mother.

Symptoms of 'Broca's area' are somewhat different from 'Wernicke's area'. This area is mainly concerned with spatial relationships and fluency of speech. In the event of damage to this area, it has been found that though the comprehension of spoken or written language generally remain intact (unimpaired), there may be some problem of minor nature. But the big difficulty may be found in the fluency of speech. Such people speak very slowly, with great difficulty, articulation is poor, tend to omit pronouns, adjectives, adverbs, articles, use of singular nouns, has trouble with tenses of verbs etc. In a nutshell, the speech is nonfluent and ungrammatical. For example, one may speak in the following manner:

"He go ... school ... yesterday ... 8 o'clock" in place of correct sentence—"He went to school yesterday at 8 o'clock".

In the light of the above observations of aphasic patients, **Geschwind** (1970, 1979) formulated a theory that describes the **anatomy of language**. This theory is known as **Wernicke's-Geschwind model**. The model explains how an individual listens words, how he speaks and what he speaks after understanding the written words. To understand this model, let us examine **Figure 4.11** that shows the anatomy of language.

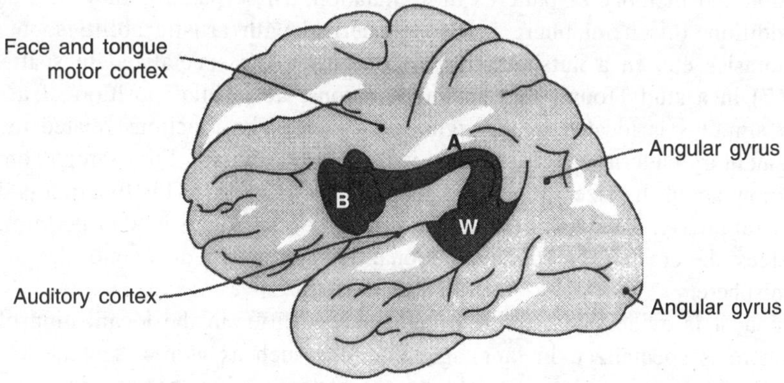

FIGURE 4.11 The language areas of the cerebral cortex. W—Wernicke's area; A—arcuate fasciculus; B—Broca's area.

The figure shows that the Wernicke's and Broca's areas are interconnected by a bundle of nerve fibres called the **arcuate fasciculus** (Latin word for arc-shaped bundle). These fibres run through white matter beneath the cortex. Besides the auditory cortex, the face and tongue motor cortex and the angular gyrus (cortical region) have also been shown in the figure. This cortical region is important in brain for the processes involved in reading. In the event of injury to angular gyrus, a person is able to communicate and understand speech but, has difficulty in reading.

The theory states that each of the anatomical areas plays a particular role in various aspects of language. Spontaneous speech originates in Wernicke's area. But, when one is required to speak and link the listened word into a meaningful sentence to speak, the activity patterns of Wernicke's area are sent to Broca's area through the 'arcuate fasciculus'. This area contains the programmes for complex patterns of muscle movements needed in speech. The Broca area programmes are then relayed to motor cortex region that controls the lips, tongue and vocal cords which produce the vocal speech sounds. Thus, when one has to reply to someone's communication or to repeat the listened words or sentences, the input from auditory cortex goes to Wernicke's area. Here, the reply is organized. The organized pattern then is sent to Broca's area through **arcuate fasciculus** from where it is relayed to motor cortex for expression. In reading a passage or listening the words too, **the Wernicke's area—arcuate fasciculus** and **Broca's area—motor cortex** pathways get involved. But in this case, the Wernicke's area receives the input from visual cortex via angular gyrus.

Though, this theory is not an agreed theory to all the scientists who study brain and language, yet this model is useful in helping to understand and organize our knowledge about the location of language function in the left hemisphere.

Right hemisphere

In somewhat different way, right hemisphere of cerebrum also seems to be the specialized centre of language. The remaining question about language is pattern, *i.e.* how is the language represented in the brain? How are the words searched and assembled in a sentence? What is Broca's regions programme? All these questions relate to electrical and chemical patterns of language functions. This is known as the **physiology of language**. But unfortunately, not much in this regard is known to us.

Studies done so far reveal that right hemisphere is specialized in certain functions of language such as recognition and memory of patterns of stimulation. These patterns may be visual, tactical or spatial. In addition, this hemisphere is also concerned with artistic abilities, music, dance, imaginations, fantasies etc. In a nutshell, this area seems to be specialized in spatial relations. **Gazzaniga** (1967) in a study found that spatial functions, *i.e.* spatial position of a stimulus in relation to other stimulus is located in the right hemisphere. The functions related to knowledge about visual and auditory patterns are also located in this region of brain. For example, on visualizing a stimulus, we know about the size, colour and shape of the stimulus. This function is done by the right hemisphere. Similarly, knowledge about the direction of a sound is also performed by right hemisphere. Besides, the creative functions, emotional expressions are also controlled and regulated by the right hemisphere.

In conclusion, it is evident that the two hemispheres differ in the localization of functions. The left hemisphere is specialized in language functions such as words, sentences, speech etc. while the right hemisphere is specialized in neural patterns of space, relations, recognitions, memory etc.

However, the specialization function is not water-tight. The two halves are interconnected and, therefore, often they takeover the functions of one another as and when either of one gets damaged.

4.9.4 Divided Brain

Evidences gathered from the studies of those people who have undergone surgical procedures of connecting the disconnection of the two hemispheres are perhaps the most dramatic way to demonstrate that the two hemispheres perform different functions. Several bands of nerve fibres called **'corpus callosum'** and anterior commissure interconnect the right and left hemispheres. These connect the areas of one hemisphere to the corresponding areas of the other. When the connections are intact, information is passed back and forth between the two hemisphares. However, when connections are cut to provide relief by controlling epileptic attacks, passage of information does not occur (Sperry). This paved the way to study what each isolated hemisphere can do? To demonstrate the distinctive functions of each hemisphare, let us examine an experimental paradigm, described below:

As we know, in a visual field input from the right visual field goes to the left hemisphere, while input from left visual field goes to the right hemisphere. To test that only the left or right receives input from the visual field, the patient must be tested by making him to concentrate his vision on the centre of visual display and while fixating his vision, he cannot move his eyes and head as shown in **Figure 4.12**.

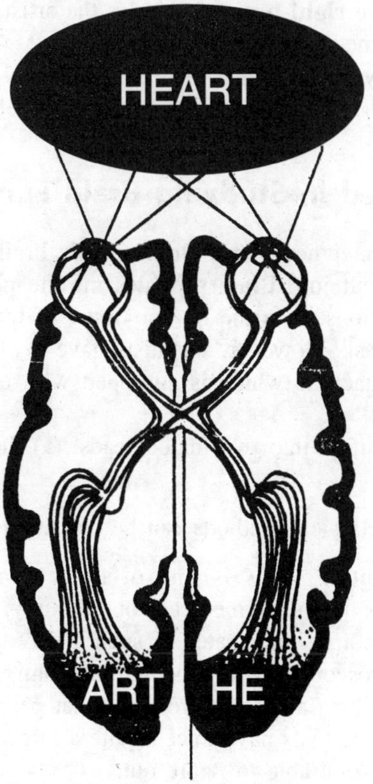

FIGURE 4.12 Experiment on divided brain.

In the test, the split brain patient looks at the centre of the visual display and a word, 'HEART' is displayed quickly. It was displayed so quickly that the subject had no time to move his eyes or head and thus, the scanning of the display was restricted. In this way, the image of letters HE reaches the left hemisphere while ART reaches the right hemisphere. The split brain patients in this case only report the information reaching left hemisphere and thus says HE. They give no verbal report to the input reaching the right hemisphere ART; thus, part of the word is verbally ignored. This indicates that the speech is organized in the left hemisphere because, this hemisphere can verbally make report about the input reaching in this hemisphere. In the split brain patients, the left hemisphere does not receive information from the right hemisphere and therefore it could not incorporate the information in verbal report reaching in right hemisphere. On the other hand, those with intact brain would say HEART because the information from right hemisphere reaches the left hemisphere or verbal report organization cortex and thus, the input is incorporated into verbal report. However, the right hemisphere can show that it has received information about the part of the word—ART, provided the subject is given a chance to express in a non-verbal way.

The difference between the two hemispheres that we have discussed till now leads us to some fascinating speculations on the type of thinking done by left and right hemispheres. The left brain is said to be analytical, logical and mathematical hemisphere which is concerned with scientific thought of cause and effect relationships. The right hemisphere, on the other hand, is concerned with images, pattern of sensory input and synthesis of information. As such, this part of the brain is more concerned with the thought processes involved in creation of paintings, or musical compositions. Some people are found **left brained** such as the scientists, accountants, physicians, and the like. Others are **right-brained** such as the artists, composers, architects, and so on. Rare people are both left-brained and right-brained.

However, in reality, we may only say that there seems to be some hemispheric specialization of function and not that there are two distinctly divided brains—left and right.

4.9.5 Methods Employed in Studying Brain Functions

'Charles Sherrington', an eminent neurophysiologist, calls brain as the 'great ravelled knot'. Hence, to study brain is a difficult job. Brain provides infinite neural patterns for each infinite human feelings, thoughts and actions. It is the master tissue of human body. Hence, to study its functions is a most challenging task. However, scientists have evolved certain methods to explore inner functions of this elegant machine which is equipped with electronic and chemical control systems.

These methods can be classified into two major heads: (a) the classical methods and (b) the modern methods.

Classical methods: The classical methods can be classified into the following parts:

(a) **The anatomical method:** This is one of the classical methods mostly used by anatomists and/or those pursuing medical course study. In this method, the tissues of posthumous bodies or corpse are treated in such a way that nerve tracks can be viewed with the help of a microscope. By this method, anatomists learn as to which parts of the sense organs send the fibres and to where, and what parts of brain sends motor fibres to the spinal cord. The anatomists have traced quite a large number of connections that the physiologists have not been able to figure out.

(b) **The method of extirpation or ablation:** Extirpation refers to cutting out or destroying. Behavioural scientists in their curiosity to know how the brain functions, take help of neurosurgeons and get removed the portions of brain tissues from the test animals through surgery or destructive electric current applied through electrodes and the resultant behavioural changes are observed. The method is used systematically. First, the behaviour of the test animal is carefully observed and measured. Next, the part of the brain is removed (ablation—a Latin word meaning removal) and changes in behaviour are observed and compared.

One of the difficulties in applying this method is that this method can be applied on animals only. In humans' case, this method can be used only when the person's part is either diseased or injured. But under such conditions, the diseased or destroyed parts are not sharply localized. This poses difficulty in studying brain functions.

(c) **Action potential method:** During the recent past decades researchers have devised some sensitive electrical recording devices. The neurons, while conducting the process, produce electrical currents and the underlying potentials can be recorded. These records are available in tiny changes in the electrical waves and some monitoring devices can detect differences in the amount of work going on in different sections of the brain, moment by moment. Such devices permit naturalistic observation. These devices can also be used for experimental observations. For example, subjects can be made to think and the changes in the map of the brain (portrait) can be observed as dependent variable while thinking.

(d) **Method of stimulation:** The area of brain associated with sensation can be mapped by stimulating patient's brain during surgical operation and introspective report of the sensory experiences can be obtained. Similarly, areas associated with muscular activities can be mapped by stimulating different areas of brain and then observe as to which muscular part of the body makes movement. In this way, the experimenter can correlate exact brain spots with particular activity.

In recent times, some refined techniques of stimulation have been developed with the help of electrodes fixed in the designated area of stimulation. In this technique, a stiff wire is positioned by a **rack-and-pinion device** which is clamped to the head. This helps to reach deep nuclei or pathways for stimulation.

(e) **Chemical method:** This is a very common method. Some measured amount of drugs or hormones are injected into test animals and resultant reactions are observed. In this case, the injected chemicals (drugs or hormones) are independent variables while the consequent physical or behavioural changes are dependent variables.

In some cases, various chemicals are applied within or on the surface of the brain through advanced surgical techniques. More recently, there has been some advancement in the technique. In this improved technique, tiny tubes (cannulae) are inserted with precision into specific nuclei, deep in the brain. This functions as a passageway for minute amount of chemical crystals. Observing which of these crystals activate particular nuclei, indicate the type of transmitter substance employed in the synapses there (Grossman, 1960).

Changes in the chemical composition of brain regions, even of single neurons, help in learning the chemical aspects of neurons.

(f) **Selective breeding:** This is another part of classical method. In this method, the experimenter raises a number of generations of plants or animals and systematically sorts out each generation member with inherited attributes or properties. This method is more useful in studying hereditary genesis of behaviour.

Thus, we find that several methods are employed to study about how brain functions.

Modern techniques

In modern times, owing to modern advances and development of new sophisticated techniques, it is possible to know and understand the functions of brain without causing any harm to it, or destroying any of its tissues. Such techniques are highly sensitive that can study the live brain in real time perspective, *i.e.* now as it is functioning. Such techniques are called brain imaging techniques (BIT). Currently, the researchers have evolved 6 such brain imaging techniques (BIT) which are most widely used to study live brain in real time perspectives. To acquaint the students with this technique, a brief description of these techniques is given below:

(a) **Computerized Tomography (C.T. scanning):** This is an advanced technology of 'x-ray'. In this technique, x-rays are passed through the brain at different angles which detects the fine and soft brain tissues that normal x-rays are unable to detect. Tomography facilitates viewing different cross-sections of brain from different angles.

(b) **Positron Emission Tomography (PET scanning):** It measures neural functioning. It traces the movement of radioactive substances in the active regions of the brain. This technique depends or relies on detected positron particles emitted by the radioactive dye or colour. The technique is considered good in tracking brain functioning.

(c) **Magnetic Resonance Imaging (MRI):** It uses radio waves and a strong magnetic field to produce signals that can be interpreted by computer. In this technique, the patient's head is positioned within a strong magnetic field. This causes the hydrogen atoms to spin in the same direction. The radio waves directed at the brain cause the hydrogen atom to emit signal. A computer amplifies and analyses these signals to construct picture of brain tissues. MRI details are considered much better than CT scan because this technique distinguishes between closely related brain structures in a better way. This technique is most popular to diagnose brain injuries and other neurological problems.

(d) **Single Photon Emission Computerized Tomography (SPECT):** This is another computer aided technique in which cerebral blood flow is tracked. In this technique, photon, a single particle of light, is used as opposed to energy wave.

(e) **Super Conducting Quantum Interference Device (SCQID):** It senses tiny changes in brain's magnetic field and shows the pattern of neural activity in three-dimensional output.

(f) **Electroencephalogram (EEG):** It is an electrical activity recording device of the brain. The researchers use electrodes to record the electrical activity of the brain as it responds to the environmental situations. Electrodes are positioned over the surface of the skull and transmit signals that are amplified and recorded. This technique has been very much useful in studying the processes involved in sleeping and dreaming. Clinicians also use EEG for the diagnosis of abnormalities associated with brain functioning and the activities involved in speech.

Obviously, several classical and modern techniques are used to study brain functions that give significant clues to determine what sensory or motor functions are associated with which part or region of brain and how brain processes the information received from external or internal environment.

4.9.6 Theories of Brain Functions

Since long past, the functioning of brain has been a controversial topic. Some researchers opine that each part of the cerebrum performs some definite specified functions while others hold that different parts of the brain are functionally more or less interchangeable. These two approaches are discussed separately herein below.

Localization theory of functions

Those who contend that each part of the cerebrum is specialized to perform a particular function, have localized different parts which are responsible to perform specific functions such as sensory functions, motor functions and association functions. Thus, for each specific function, there are specific portions or areas in the cortex which if impaired, the related function is also abolished or impaired.

In the light of above assumption, let us consider the sensory, motor and association areas of the cortex that perform sensory, motor and associative functions.

(a) **Sensory functions:** Most of the senses (smell is an exception) have specific areas in the cerebral cortex which are called as **primary sensory areas**. In general, the sensory impulses when generated by a receptor on being excited by the appropriate stimulus, travels through peripheral sensory nerves pathways in the CNS with varying numbers of synapses in them. A synaptic relaying function in the thalamus, enable the impulses to reach the appropriate primary sensory area in the cortex. For example, the visual input reaches in the occipital lobe, tactical impulses go to body sense or somatosensory region in parietal lobe, auditory input reaches the portion of temporal lobe, input representing taste arrives at temporal lobe cortex burried in the lateral fissure and cannot be seen on the brain surface. Thus, specific sensory informations (input) reach to the specific sensory cortical regions of the cortex, *i.e.* primary sensory areas.

The primary sensory areas process the input and send it to association cortex or other parts of the brain where further processing takes place.

Though, much of the details are still unknown, most of the neuroscientists consider that our experience of the environment or perception depends upon activity patterns occurring in the sensory system of which the primary sensory areas of the cortex are important parts. For example, when we perceive a familiar face, there is a pattern of activity in our visual system (inclusive of primary visual area of the cortex) that stands for, represents or codes for that particular face.

The entire sensory functions can be grouped into four categories and for each of these, the specific primary areas are shown in **Table 4.2**.

At this point, it is important to note that though stimulation of different sensory nerves produce different kinds of sensory experiences, however, the differences are not because of the fact that impulses are different. Specify in fact lie in the **kind of neuron** located in the part of the brain where specific nerve ends.

TABLE 4.2 Categorization of sensory functions

Sl. No.	*Sensory experiences*	*Related sensory organs*	*Specified areas in brain to perform related functions*
1.	Taste and smell	(i) Tongue (Taste)	(i) Temporal lobe cortex burried in the lateral fissure
		(ii) Nose (Smell)	(ii) Olfactory bulbs of the subcortical region
2.	Kinesthetic or somesthetic	Skin	Parietal lobe called somatosensory
3.	Visual	Eyes	Occipital lobe (visual area of the left hemisphere)
4.	Audition	Ears	A portion of temporal lobe

(b) **Motor functions:** The motor areas in the brain are relatively narrower than the sensory areas. The neurons of motor area are pyramidal in structure and therefore are called **pyramidal tract**. Three areas in the brain have been identified as performing motor functions. One such area is **primary area** concentrated immediately in front of the fissure of Rolando which extends both forward and backward. Long axons lead down from this area through spinal cord to the motoneurons supplying motor nerve impulses to the muscles and extremities. On stimulation of this area, some voluntary muscle groups have been found to respond. Conversely when areas in this region are destroyed, impairment of movements occur.

Another projection of body muscle has been located near the fissure of sylvius. It is called **secondary motor** area. But little is known about the functions of this area.

Third projection of body muscle has been found in the **supplementary motor area**. It is located in the longitudinal fissure near middle line of the brain. These areas are involved not only in muscular movements but also in muscle tensions (muscle tone) and postural controls.

Secondary and supplementary motor areas send small axons and form a chain of small axons. These axons extend to the nuclei in the interior of the cerebral hemisphere. From here, another small axon goes to the nuclei in the brain stem and action of such neurons lead to the spinal cord.

The short neuron system is suspected to play a major role in the control of movements. If uncontrolled, disorderly movements such as trembling, jerks etc. are caused as some parts of it are damaged and can be cured only by destroying others through surgery.

(c) **Association area:** Many large areas of the cortex are not connected with sensory-motor processes. These are association areas that perform integrative functions of the inputs coming from more than one sensory channel and are also supposed to perform higher order functions such as learning, thinking, remembering, decision-making, reasoning etc.

Though, our knowledge about association areas is still incomplete, recent researches have shown that they perform a number of functions. For example, the frontal association areas (the parts of the frontal lobes anterior to the motor area) play an important role in thinking processes involved in problem solving situation.

French and Harlow (1962) have found that in monkeys, the ability to solve a delayed response problem is destroyed due to lesions in the frontal lobe. **Milner** (1964) has found that even in human beings, if someone is suffering from damaged frontal lobe shows deficiency similar to monkeys, eventhough his intellectual performances are normal.

The posterior association areas are located along various primary sensory areas. They consist of such areas that serve a particular sense, *viz.* lower portion of temporal lobe is associated with visual perception. Several areas in and near temporal lobes are concerned with language while some of the areas in the temporal lobe are concerned with memory.

Association areas of the brain are by and large concerned with higher order functions called higher centres of the brain. These higher order functions include a wide variety of functions—learning, memory reasoning, thinking, emotionally charged activities, motivational behaviours etc.

Damage or injury in the various association areas of the left hemisphere have been found to cause loss of connected functions. This area is just above the fissure of sylvius. Part of this area near the mouth, has later come to be known as **'Broca's area'**.

Disease or injury to certain area causes failure to recognize familiar objects. Such patients though have normal sensation of the object, fail to organize elementary sensory elements into normal perception. Similar disorders of perceptions are found in other sensory fields called **agnosia,** *i.e.* **inability to know**. Similarly, disorders in association areas related to language are called **'aphasias'**. The 'agnosia' and 'aphasias' on the basis of nature of the functions are of the following three types:

Asterognosis: Loss of ability to recognize solid objects through sense of touch.

Alexia: Inability to recognize printed words *i.e.* **word blindness**.

Sensory aphasia: Inability to recognize spoken words. This disorder is associated with lesions in the association areas close to sensory areas of the cortex.

Similar impairments of the association areas near motor areas have been found to cause motor disturbances.

From the above-mentioned descriptions and supporting evidences, it is possible to localize specific areas of the brain that perform specific functions.

Mass action theory

Contrary to localization theory, some investigators hold that brain functions as a whole and therefore localization theory does not hold good enough. According to these theorists, different areas or parts of the brain area are more or less functionally interchangeable. The propounders of this view are **Franz, Lashley, Goltz, Monakow** etc. This assertion is based on experimental observations. It has been observed that impairment or injury in a particular area, though cause disturbance or almost complete loss of function. Gradually, owing to practice, the lost function recurs. It so happens because the adjoining areas of the injured part takes over to discharge the function of injured part. Such evidences go to prove that each area in the brain is equally capable to perform similar functions. Hence, the theory is also known as **equipotential theory**.

The rationale behind this theory is that the loss of activity is proportionate to the area of brain damaged. Hence, complete loss of a particular function is rare. The supporters of this theory also argue that the living structures in the adjoining areas of the damaged structures are **equipotential** and, therefore, they take over to discharge their functions.

In a nutshell, equipotential or mass action theory holds that brain functions as a whole and thus discards localization theory of brain functions.

Conclusions: Though the rationale put forward by **equipotential** theorists are tenable, however, modern studies show that various parts of the brain are responsible for different functions. Therefore, a compromising position appears to be more tenable.

Autonomic nervous system (ANS)

Autonomic nervous system (ANS) is concerned with regulation and governance of involuntary activities of visceral organs (see **Figure 4.13**). Hence, it is also known as **visceral nervous system** (VNS). The term **autonomic** here does not mean that system is self-regulating (autonomous) or automatic, rather it refers to the system that is concerned with such neural mechanism that regulates and controls those organic functions over which the organism has no conscious control, *i.e.* these organic activities are involuntary. Such organic functions include functions of heart, maintenance of blood pressure, digestive functions etc. These are the vital functions of visceral organs and essential for sustenance and growth of life.

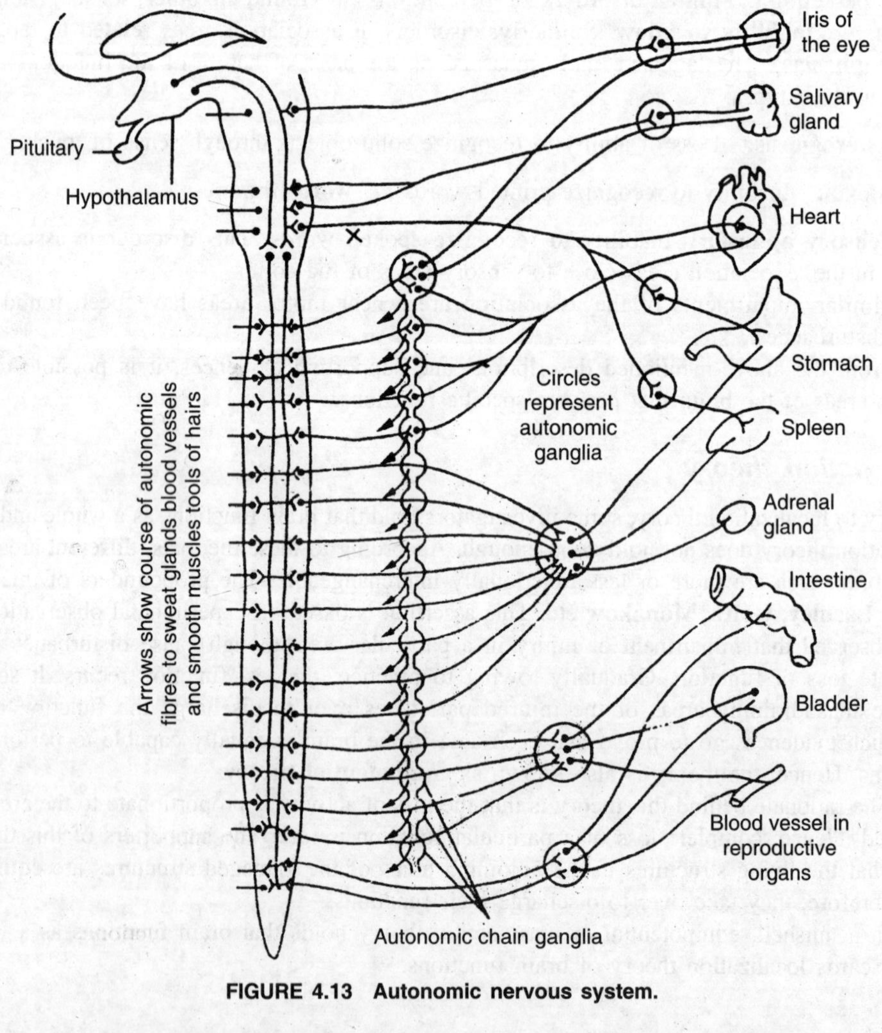

FIGURE 4.13 Autonomic nervous system.

The autonomic nervous system consists of many nerves leading from the brain and spinal cord out to smooth muscles of the various organs of the body. Autonomic nervous system (ANS) is made up of a set of reflex areas which are subjected to control of certain centres in the brain (see **Figure 4.13**). Some efferent (motor) fibres emerge from central nervous system (CNS) and pass onto a mass of cell bodies called **autonomic ganglia**. It consists of (i) autonomic ganglia and (ii) pre- and post-ganglionic fibres. Thus, the motor impulses to the autonomic effectors are supplied by two efferent neurons, namely the pre- and post-ganglionic fibres.

Hence, the autonomic nervous system (ANS) constitutes three major parts:
(i) Autonomic ganglia, (ii) pre- ganglionic fibres and (ii) post-ganglionic fibres.

Division of autonomic nervous system (ANS): The autonomic nervous system (ANS) is classified into two parts:

(a) The sympathetic system
(b) The para-sympathetic system

Each of these two systems passes their own pre- and post-ganglionic fibres and ganglia.

(a) **The sympathetic nervous system:** This system branches off from centre of the spinal nerve roots. These are small bundle of fibres and run to a chain of ganglia on either side of the spinal cord. The fibres run up or down in this chain and then form a synapse with effector neurons that run to smooth muscles and glands of the skin, via nerve branches which rejoin the spinal nerves. At certain points, nerves leave this chain and pass to distant ganglia. Here, their fibres synapse with others that run to the visceral organs. It is evident that the fibres of this system originate from spinal cord segments in the middle of the back, known as **thoraco-lumbar** and reach the structures from head to the toe and thus form a sympathetic chain. It is a distributing mechanism which has many fibres running up and down that give off numerous subordinates. Anatomists hold the view that the main function of this system is to make the visceral organs work in **sympathy** and hence, it is called sympathetic nervous system.

(b) **The para-sympathetic system:** The nerves of this system branches off from lower segments of the spinal cord and brain stem. These nerves give an appearance of ordinary spinal and cranial nerves. But these pass to visceral structures and not to skeletal muscles. Further, like sympathetic system, these are also interrupted by a synapse outside central nervous system (CNS), often in the walls of innervated organs. Since, this system branches off from CNS above and below the sympathetic system, it is called **para-sympathetic** or **cranial-sacro division** of ANS.

Most organs of chest and abdomen receive fibres from both of these systems. Wherever this happens, the two divisions function antagonistically to each other. Thus, when one becomes more active to excite the organs to increase its activities, the another inhibits or decreases the activity. Hence, ANS makes a very effective control over visceral organs and maintains the equilibrium. The two systems are comparable to the accelerator and the break of an automobile. However, which system accelerates or breaks depends upon what the concerned organ does.

Division of labour in ANS: The sympathetic system is chiefly concerned with protective responses in times of emergency. The para-sympathetic system is associated largely with the activities concerned with normal functioning.

In addition, the two systems are also concerned with visceral sensations, *viz.* palpitation of heart, colic pain, excretory needs etc. Hence, there is division of labour between the two divisions of ANS.

4.10 THE ENDOCRINE SYSTEM

In adjustive behaviours, in addition to the **nervous system**, another group of biological structure also play important role. This group of biological structure is called the **glandular system** which works in close association or co-operation with 'nervous system'.

The glandular system consists of various glands found in human body which secrete various chemical substances necessary for the growth and maintenance of body. These glands are of two types—**exocrine** and **endocrine**. The exocrines have ducts and as such called **duct-glands**. The duct or exocrine glands secrete chemical substances other than the hormones which are carried to different parts of the body through ducts or tubes, *viz.* tear glands, the salivary glands, the sweat glands, the bile glands etc.

The endocrine glands secrete hormones and are directly poured into blood stream. These glands do not have any duct. Hence, these are called ductless glands. The endocrine glands do not initiate any specific activity by themselves but influence the activity of various organs such as heart, liver, circulation of blood etc. The activities of these organs are either accelerated or slowed down depending upon the hyper or hypo secretions of hormones which are reflected in various physiological and psychological behaviour events. Therefore, from psychological point of view, endocrine glands are important.

At this point, it is important to note that the endocrine glands work in conjunction with hypothalamus and, therefore, this link is often called as Hypothalamus Pituitary Adrenal (HPA) Axis.

4.10.1 The Characteristic Features of Endocrine Glands

There are certain characteristic features of endocrine glands which are as follows:

- Endocrine glands are ductless. Hence, are called ductless glands.
- Endocrine glands secrete complex chemicals called hormones which are directly poured into blood stream.
- The circulatory system provides passageway for the hormones to be carried to various organs and systems of the body.
- Endocrine system is controlled by autonomic nervous system. As such, its activities are not under concious control.
- Endocrine system helps in maintaining bodily homeostasis.
- The hormones of endocrine glands take longer to exert their effects than those produced by ANS and may be highly specific in their action by influencing only the target organ. For example, secretion of pituitary gland stimulates only the sex organs. Some may have general effects, *e.g.* pancreas secretes insulin which facilitates glucose uptake by the body cells.
- Hormonal excesses or deficiencies often have dramatic effects on behaviour.

Following are the description of different endocrine glands. **Figure 4.14** shows some of the endocrine glands.

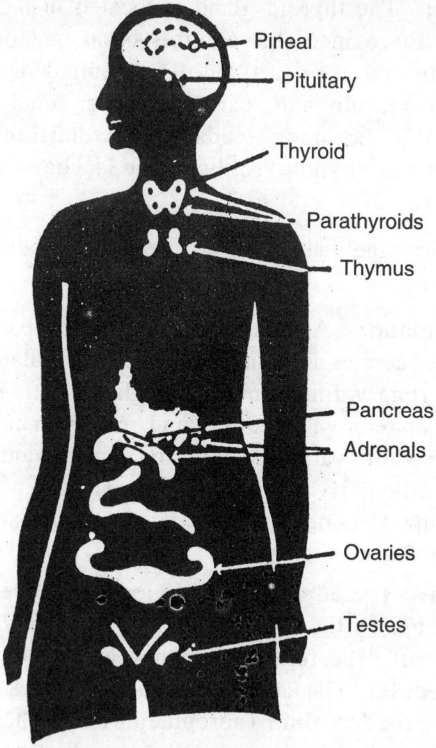

FIGURE 4.14 Endocrine glands.

(a) **The pineal gland:** The pineal gland is about the size of a 'pea' and located in the brain. The chief hormone secreted by it is called **melatonin** which regulates growth of body and reproductive functions. This hormone also influences our daily life activities. For example, in the morning hours, due to sunrise, there is an increase in the level of temperature resulting in general stimulation of pineal gland and relatively hyper secretion of **melatonin** hormone. This causes us to be active during the day hours. By evening, when the sun sets, the general level of our activities slow down because of relatively lower secretion of **melatonin** and as darkness spreads, we become relaxed or inactive and go to sleep.

(b) **The pituitary gland:** Pituitary gland is located below the brain stem within **cranium.** This gland is also known as **master gland** because it directs the activities of most of the glands in our body. It secretes nine kinds of hormones which regulate the other endocrine glands and body functions. The other glands which are influenced by pituitary gland are adrenal gland, thyroid gland, testes, ovaries etc. It has been found that dwarfs generally have underactive pituitary gland while the giants have overactive pituitary gland. Thus, hypo or hyper secretions of pituitary hormones are related to body growth. Similarly, excessive or deficient secretions also lead to under or oversexual activities because they produce sex cells as well as hormones. The hormones secreted by pituitary gland is regulated by hypothalamus which exercise control over major and vital processes of the body.

(c) **The thyroid gland:** The thyroid gland is located in the lower portion of the neck region. It produces thyroxine. This controls basal metabolic rate. Early deprivation of thyroxine leads to cretinism (a type of feeblemindedness). Undersecretion of this hormone results in neurological, cardiovascular, renal and respiratory disorders. Oversecretion of this hormone leads to a condition known as **myxoedema*** (a clinical syndrome of hypothyroidism). It is characterized by overweight and general sluggishness.

The hypersecretion of thyroxine make us more energetic, irritative and active, loss of weight, hypertension and overanxiety.

(d) **The parathyroid gland:** A small structure called parathyroid is situated below thyroid. This gland secretes parathormone which regulates calcium and phosphorus metabolism. The primary function of this gland is to maintain bony structure of the body. Damage or removal of this gland results in neural disorder called **tetany** (development of fear of water, muscle and spasm) and this state is related with muscular spasms particularly of hands, feet, and jaw bones. Damage to this gland also leads to weaking of bones due to loss of calcium and is often characterized by aches, pains and groans.

(e) **The adrenal gland:** The adrenal gland is located above each kidney, sits like three corner hats on the top of the kidneys. Each adrenal gland has two parts—an outer part and an inner part. The former is named as **adrenal cortex** while the latter is called **adrenal medulla**. The adrenal medulla secretes two hormones—adrenaline (epinephrine) and noradrenaline (norepinephrine). These hormones are produced during stress due to fear, anger, aggression, conflict etc. Insufficient secretions of these hormones cause fatigue, loss of appetite, anaemia, sleeplessness, darkening of skin etc. These syndromes are known as **Adison's disease**.

Adrenal cortex (outer part) secretes three kinds of hormones, namely **aldosterone**, **cortisol** and **sex hormone**. The hypo or hypersecretions of these hormones result in:

(a) Imbalanced metabolism of carbohydrate and salt
(b) Development of **'Cushing syndrome'** in adult males resulting in obesity, hirsutism (excessive growth of hair), diabetes and hypogonadism (inactivity) of gonads.
(c) In adult women, development of masculinization or virilism due to excessive androgens and in adult males excessive estrogens may cause feminization, particularly breast enlargement.
(d) In children, excessive sex hormones cause precocious puberty, *i.e.* early sexual maturity.

ACTH (Adreno-corticotrophic hormone) prompts the secretion of adrenal hormones from the anterior pituitary gland. All hormones of adrenal gland taken together as a group is called 'corticoids'. Normal levels of these hormones are utilized by the body for a number of purposes, *e.g.* regulation of blood pressure. However, excessive production of corticosteroids is detrimental to the body as is seen when an individual is constantly under stress.

---

* **Myxoedema:** A clinical syndrome of hypothyroidism in which the patient becomes slow in movement and mentally dull, bradycardia, low temperature, dry skin, and swelling of limbs and face, associated with low serum thyroxine and raised thyrotrophin levels.

(f) **Pancreas:** It is situated in the middle part of the body. In secretory function, it is both—exocrine and endocrine (duct gland and ductless gland). The exocrine cells of pancreas are responsible for the enzyme-rich pancreatic secretions. The endocrine part secretes insulin which regulates the blood sugar by increasing the deposition of glucose in liver and muscles as glycogen*. It also secretes glucagon† which acts antagonistically to insulin.

(g) **The gonads:** The gonads that produce sex hormones in females is called ovaries and the testes in males. Together, they are called gonads.

The important male hormones are **androgens** or **testosterone**. This hormone is concerned with sexual maturity in males reflected in growth of facial hair, change of voice at puberty etc. Androgen is also responsible for bone growth and changes related to sex drive.

Ovaries secrete two important hormones—**oestrogen** and **progesterone**. **Oestrogen** is responsible for female internal reproductive structure and emergence and growth of secondary sex characteristics such as breasts and pubic hairs. This hormone also plays an important role in regulat-ing menstrual cycle.

Progesterone prepares uterus for implantation of the fertilized egg and nourishes the embryo during early stage of prenatal development.

A summary of different endocrine glands, hormones and their effects are shown in **Table 4.3.**

TABLE 4.3 Summary of endocrine glands, hormones and their effects

Sl. no.	*Name of glands*	*Names of hormones secreted by the glands*	*Effects on behaviour*
1.	Pineal gland	Melatonin	Regulates growth and reproduction
2.	Pituitary or hypophysis	9 kinds of growth hormone	Controls the growth of bones and muscles Regulate protein, carbohydrate and fat for metabolism
3.	Thyroid	Thyroxin (TSH)	Regulates and maintains basal metabolism
4.	Parathyroid	Parathomone	Regulation of level of calcium and phosphate
5.	Adrenal gland	(a) Aldesterone	Controls water level in the body, regulates carbohydrate metabolism
	(a) Adrenal cortex	(b) Gluco corticoids	Regulates sex growth
		(c) Sex hormone	Regulates body functions
	(b) Adrenal medulla	(a) Adrenaline (b) Noradrenaline	These are produced under stress, fear, anger, conflict, cause fatigue, anaemia etc.
6.	Pancreas	(a) Insulin (b) Glucagon	Regulates sugar in blood and storage of glucose
7.	Gonads	Androgens	Promotion of male sex characteristics and growth
	(a) males	(a) Oestrogens	Regulation of menstrual cycle
	(b) females	(b) Progesterone	Maintenance of pregnancy

* Glycogen — The main carbohydrate storage compound in which glucose molecules are linked in branched chains.

† Glucagon — Hormone produced in alphacells of pancreas that causes break down of glycogen in to glucose.

It is obvious that like nervous system endocrine glands also play a significant role in determining and regulating behaviour at different stages of life. But, it is worth remembering that the endocrine glands do not function independently rather are controlled and regulated by various centres of the brain.

SUMMARY

- Psychology as a bio-social science is the study of adjustive behaviour. Behaviours are initiated, regulated and controlled by physiological system called organs of adjustment.
- Man in the present form has gradually evolved and so is the case with the development of complex behaviours which has followed the evolutionary process from simple to complex behaviours.
- There are three landmarks in the evolution of human beings. These are bipedalism, encephalization and language development.
- Genes are important sources of biological bases of behaviour that endow us with biological structures that receive stimuli from the environment, interpret them and signal the command to respond.
- The organs of response have their base in neural functioning. A neuron is a nerve cell with a cell body and fibres—dendrites and axons. Neurons are the basic building blocks of larger systems of neural mechanism.
- Neurons are classified as sensory, motor and association neurons. Sensory neurons carry information in the form of nerve impulses from receptors to CNS. Motor neurons carry response related messages of the centre down to the effector organs or organs of response. The association neurons interconnect the sensory and motor neurons and perform integrative functions.
- Nervous system has three main divisions—peripheral nervous system, central nervous system and autonomic nervous system.
- Peripheral nervous system has two divisions—sensory peripheral nervous system and motor peripheral nervous system.
- Central nervous system has two major parts—spinal cord and brain.
- Spinal cord is the 2(ic) of brain. It is concerned with controlling and regulating reflex actions following the path forming an arch and therefore called reflex arch.
- Spinal cord also connects peripheral organs (sensory and motor) with the centre, *i.e.* brain.
- Brain is a great revelled knot. It contains billions of nerves spread all over our body.
- Broadly, brain is divided into three major parts—brain stem, limbic system and cerebrum.
- All these major parts are further divided in several parts such as medulla oblongata, pons, cerebellum, midbrain—reticular activating system, roof or tectum, floor.
- Cerebrum consists of limbic system, thalamus, hypothalamus and cortex.
- Cerebrum is divided into two hemispheres—right and left. These hemispheres work in opposite directions to receive stimuli and control or regulate behaviours.
- Several methods of studying brain functions are employed. Some of these methods are classical while others are modern.

- The modern methods include CT scanning, PET scanning, MRI, SPECT, SCQUID and EEG.
- As regards brain functions, two approaches have been advanced. Some contend that specific parts of brain perform specific functions. Others hold that each part of brain is equally capable to perform any task.
- Recent studies have shown that left hemisphere is specialized to perform language functions. This is evidenced by studies done on split brain.
- Endocrine systems are also important bases of behaviour. These are ductless glands. Pineal, thyroid, parathyroid, adrenal glands, pancreas and gonads are the endocrine glands that influence our behaviour.

CHAPTER 5

Socio-Cultural Bases of Behaviour

5.1 INTRODUCTION

As has been explained earlier, human beings are 'bio-social' in nature. Hence, psychology studies the human behaviours not only as a biological unit, rather it studies the behavioural aspects in the context of 'socio-cultural' set-ups of human beings. In the preceding chapter, we discussed biological and hormonal bases of behaviours. But, these do not explain all our behaviours. The biological and hormonal bases play important role in regulating physiological aspects of behaviour, but they do not completely control human behaviour. Therefore, biological factors alone cannot help us much in understanding human behaviour. It is so because, the nature of human behaviour evolves through an interplay of biological and socio-cultural forces. This is the reason that many of the human behaviours often appear similar to others while on most occasions manifest differences. Such differences are because of the fact that **customs and conventions govern our actions**.

Socio-cultural factors shape our behaviours into a socio-cultural 'templets' and provide 'socio-cultural identity'. This helps not only in shaping our behaviours but also in developing ***social self*** by moulding, modifying and refining the patterns of behaviour that are conducive to the demands of social adjustment. In other words, such moulding or refinements in behaviours can be termed as **social conditioning** of behaviours in which various 'socio-cultural factors' play important role, and thus, the man forms his social identity and develops as a **socio-cultural being**.

The present chapter therefore, deals with socio-cultural factors that operates in the growth and development of humans as a **social being**.

5.2 SOCIALIZATION AND CULTURE

Socialization is a **process of social learning**. This process enable individuals acquire knowledge, skills and dispositions that make him fit into the 'social frame' of his society. The individuals acquire or adopt the prevalent traditions, customs, rituals, beliefs, attitudes, values, norms, standards, opinions and interactional patterns. Such learnings help the individual to participate as an active and effective member of the groups and society. The process of socialization is a continuous process throughout the life span of an individual. Hence, over the entire life span, an individual learns and develops ways of effective functioning. Socialization is also seen as a process of socio-cultural transmission from one generation to another. In absence of such transmissions, the society would face the danger of its own survival.

As stated above, the process of socialization enables us to acquire or adopt the social traditions, beliefs, opinions, etc. During infancy, we acquire all these through the process of child rearing. As **Ruth Benedict** states:

> **The life history of the individual is first and foremost an accommodation to the patterns and standards traditionally handed down in his community. From the moment of his birth, the custom into which he is born shapes his life experiences and behaviour. By the time he can talk, he is a little creature of his culture, and by the time he is grown and able to take part in its activities, its habits are its habits, its beliefs are its beliefs, its impossibilities are his impossibilities. Every child that is born into his group will share them with him, and no child born into one on the opposite side of the globe can ever achieve the thousandth part.***

The process of socialization makes it certain that the new member in the family—the young and growing infants or children—learn what his primary or secondary group has to say about, and fit in the world with other people by getting along with them. They learn the culture of his society (into which he is born). A neonate is incapable of doing any activity except inborn reflexive actions. He is **'a-social being'**, *i.e.* neither social nor unsocial. But in course of growing and developing, he emerges as an active and effective member of his group and society either automatically or by willful choice. Thus, gradually he/she learns to interact with others.

From the above, it is evident that all human beings are capable of a far greater repertoire of behaviours than they ever exhibit. We begin life in a particular social context, and there we learn to make certain responses and not others. For example, let us think of our linguistic behaviour. Although, we can speak any language of the world, we learn to speak only the language which people around us speak (*i.e.* **mother tongue**), *viz.*, a baby born in a Bengali family, learns Bengali, a baby born into a Marathi family, begins to speak Marathi, and so on. In the same way, we also learn many other things within the social context (*e.g.* when and how to express emotions and when to suppress them, how to greet somebody, how to respond to others, etc.).

From the above, it is also evident that the probability of our behaving in a particular way is greatly influenced by those who relate to us. Thus, any one in our society who possess power of relating, can socialize us. Such people are termed as **socialization agents**. This include parents, teachers and other elders who are supposed to be more knowledgeable in the ways of their society. In certain conditions, even our age peers may also affect socialization.

The process of socialization is not always glossy or smooth transition between the socializing agents and the individual. Often it involves conflicts. In such conditions, some of the patterns of behaviours are punished, some are blocked or hindered. Such punitive measures or blocking are imposed by those who either relate to us in some way or even by others. It is so done in an effective manner to restrain undesirable patterns of behaviours.

In the same way, some of our behaviours or responses need to be reinforced so that the same may acquire the strength to be repeated. Thus, **reward** and **punishment** is one of the mechanisms that serve as basic means to achieve the goals of socialization. This amply shows that all socialization involve efforts by others to direct behaviour in a desirable direction and control the undesirable ones.

* Benedict, R., 1959, *Patterns of Culture*, 2nd ed., Boston: Houghton Miffin, pp. 474–507.

The process of socialization is never unidirectional despite the fact that the process primarily consists of deliberate teachings to produce **acceptable behaviour**. In fact, socialization process is a two-way traffic. Individuals are not only influenced by the people around him, rather he also exert influence over them. Society of an individual is comprised of several social groups, and individuals are likely to choose the group which they wish to belong. Further, since people also migrate from one society to another, they are socialized not only once, rather are re-socialized whenever they move from one society to another. This is called **enculturation**.

5.2.1 Enculturation

Enculturation refers to all social learning that takes place without direct, deliberate teaching or preaching. We learn many ideas, concepts, values, beliefs, attitudes, traditions, customs, etc. simply because these are available in our socio-cultural contexts. For example, what is vegitable?, what is noise?, and similar other things. The meanings of all such concepts are learnt indeliberately simply because, these concepts are readily available as labelled and agreed upon by people at large in the society. Thus, the process of socialization is made possible by both—**socialization** and **enculturation** *i.e.* deliberately and indeliberately.

What follows from above, is that enculturation refers to all learning that occur in our life because of their availability in the socio-cultural context. The key element in enculturation is observation. Individuals observe others in their social environment and imitate their behaviour. Therefore, whenever an individual observes and follows, he learns or acquires the pattern. This evidences the process of **enculturation**. Generally, we learn many complex activities of the society, such as cooking, stitching, several etiquettes, manners, etc. Though, the effects of enculturation are obvious, hardly we are aware of its effects. It is so because, the deliberate and indeliberate processes of socialization are so intermingled together that we hardly can differentiate their effects.

For example, we learn many languages spontaneously while the same is refined by deliberate teaching by others. Similarly, we learn several languages only through teaching by others. (*e.g.* To cite for example, a Hindi knowing boy learns Bengali spontaneously by virtue of living among Bengali speaking groups. Similarly, many Indian students acquire the knowledge of French through learning a defined course by the teachers of French language. Even spontaneous learning of languages are refined by teaching of grammar or acquiring the meanings of words or sentences. Thus, it is obvious that 'enculturation' and 'socialization'—both are intermingled, and hence, difficult to differentiate their effects.

5.2.2 Agencies of Socialization

While discussing the process of socialization (Section 5.2.1), mention of agents of socialization has been made. What follows from the afore-mentioned discussions about the nature of socialization, it is a complex process indeed. Several people who relate to us in some way or other, possess the power to socialize. Such people are called **agents of socialization**. Parents and family members are the primary agents, and hence, occupy most significant position as an agency. Even, child care is also a legal responsibility of the parents. They are concerned with nurturing of the children in such a way that their natural inherited potentialities are maximized and negative potentials or tendencies are minimized or controlled. However, since each child is also a part of a larger society, several other agents, such as teachers, school, neighbours, peer groups, etc. also operate on his/her life, and thus, exert their influence to socialize them. In the present section, a brief description of some chief agencies are being presented below:

Parents or the family

During the early years of an individual, when his personality and behaviours are being moulded rapidly, the family (and particularly parents) have most direct and significant impact on development. Hence, family functions as most powerful agent in socializing the child. Family socializes the child through specific training procedures as well as by creating proper atmosphere. Children make responses to their parents differently in different situations. Parents encourage certain behaviours by reinforcing or rewarding (*e.g.* praising) or in other perceptible ways (*e.g.* giving chocolates or child's desired objects). Parents also discourage certain behaviours by non-approving the undesirable behaviours. In this sense, **family functions as craftsman who carry the socio-cultural norms, values, standards etc. to the child**. The family or the parents also arrange to put children in a variety of situations that provide them with a variety of positive experiences, learning opportunities and challenges. This enable the child to learn socially valued skills like manners and social poise (social dignity), social values about right and wrong, good and bad, approachable and avoidable, desirable and undesirable behaviours. Parents also discourage children in the direction of emotional intelligence and encourage to control outbursts of emotions, aggressive tendencies, tantrums and hatred of others (*Janis, et al.,* 1969).*

Family infact is built upon a network of interrelations in which inter cooperation and threads of emotionality are found. Basically, family functions as carriers of culture but, at the same time, the parents present a model before the child. They reinforce some of the behaviours while discourage others. By so doing, they help determine the personality traits, goals and values. For example, one child discovers that his mother will let him have his own way if he throws a temper tantrum. Another child in another family may find that temper tantrum does not work but pretending illness does. The technique a child develops in dealing with his parents, is naturally carried over into his contacts with others. Suppose, a grown-up man becomes **sullen** with his wife. This might have probably been learnt in his response while dealing with his mother during childhood.

The process of sex typing is a good example to see how a parent trains owing to this sort of training, children of two sexes develop the responses and interests that fits well to his or her gender. Generally, boys are reinforced for rough and aggressive play, inhibiting emotional displays, showing an interest in the working of mechanical things etc. On the other hand, girls are generally reinforced for being more submissive, sweet and emotionally expressive. They are also discouraged from developing interest in mechanical devices. Though, due to **acculturation**, we can find noticeable transition in the above trends today. Despite this, parents play a very dominating role in shaping the behaviours of boys and girls differently.

In the family, child also interacts with siblings. Therefore, interactional patterns among the siblings also influence behaviours of a developing child.

Acquisition of interactional behaviours in the family also depends on the strategies adopted by the parents. Different parents adopt different strategies that relates to

(a) level or degree of behaviour exhibited by parents,
(b) degree of control imposed by parents, and
(c) degree of affection shown by parents. All such things are known as **Parenting styles**.

---

* Janis, I.L., Mahi, G.F., Keegan J. and Holt. P.R., 'Personality, Dynamics, Developmental and Assessment', New York: Harcourt Brace and World, 1969.

These styles can be broadly categorized into four distinct categories. These are:

(a) Authoritarian—autocratic style,
(b) Indulgent—permissive style,
(c) Authoritarian—reciprocal style, and
(d) Indifferent or uninvolved style.

(a) Authoritarian—autocratic style: In this style of parenting, the parents are usually very strict and disciplinarian. They presume as the authority and master of all sorts of decisions that a child must follow. Child's freedom is almost totally restricted. The desires and goals of parents occupy supreme position. This kind of parenting style is not conducive for child's social development. Child's growth is hampered and intellectual output declines. He becomes dependent on parents, and is unable to take independent decisions.

(b) Indulgent—permissive style: In this style of parenting, parents are liberal and perseverant *i.e.*, take care of the child with great patience. Such parents do not thrust upon his own thoughts, opinions, attitudes directly. Such parenting permit independent decision-making. However, in some cases negativism is also likely to develop resulting in increased aggressiveness and incompetency in social dealings, adopting escaping attitude to take up any responsibility, etc.

(c) Authoritative—reciprocal style: This is a combination of above two styles in a balanced manner. Such parents determine a parameter (standard) of behavioural patterns for the children to follow. Along with this, children are also permitted for independence and to an extent freedom is permissible. The parents are open in discussing any problem with the child and assent to the outcomes of reciprocal discussions. The parents and child mutually accept and agree to their personal rights and duties. Such styles favour the development of cognitive abilities, decision taking and fosters the development of respect for one another. Thus, provides a base for mutual social interactions in a positive and healthy direction. Aggressive tendencies are also controlled to a great extent and the child is able to develop positive attitudes towards the self as well as others

(d) Indifferent—uninvolved style: Such parents do not recognize their parental role. They remain uninvolved in the activities of their children and maintain a sort of rigid uncooperative atitude. In such styles of parenting, child's development is badly hampered and consequently children become aggressive. They hardly care for anybody in the society. Often they indulge in criminal activities.

We have seen how different parenting styles influence the growth and development of child's behaviour as a social being.

However, before leaving this discussion of role of parents and their styles of parenting child's behaviour, we must take into account a key point: Children are not shapeless mass of hot metal waiting to be shaped by parents. The longitudinal studies of **Thomas** and **Chess** (1977, 1980) indicate that children may be born with **styles** of their own in the form of basic temperament patterns. Parental styles influence the way these patterns are expressed. Secondly, parental style is also partly a **response** to child's style. Parents and children—both influence one another which is an **ongoing cycle**. Obviously, we cannot view parent as the **cause** and the child as the **effect**. This would be serious mistake. We cannot think every troubled child as a product of poor parenting. There are various other factors too.

Peer groups

As the child grows and enters into middle childhood, his social network is extended beyond home. Children establish friendship with other children of the neighbourhood, playgrounds, school/classmates, etc. These friends are contemporary in age, and hence, **horizontal communication** is possible. In this respect, peer group acquires great significance in the process of socialization. It provides children an opportunity to be in the company of others, and at the same time, these children also involve themselves in organizing various activities (*e.g.* play), collectively. Qualities like sharing, trust, mutual understanding, role acceptance and fulfilment, develop in interaction with 'peers' Children also learn to assert their own point of view as well as accept and adapt to those of others. Peer group also greatly facilitate in the development of **self-identity**.

In peer group, children are often found involved in **cooperative play**. This is a direct child to child relationship and require some complementary role taking. For example, in 'pretend games' we can find such role taking patterns. Children use to explore mysteries as adult relationships (*e.g.* games of **Mommy** and **Daddy**) and other children's anatomy (*e.g.* games of **Doctor**). In peer groups, children also exhibit their faithfulness to one another when they choose playmates or friends or form teams of players. Children also begin to prefer playmates of the same gender—a preliminary step to the stable sense of **gender identity**.

Thus, peer group do play a significant role in socializing process.

School

School is also an important socializing agent. Since children spend almost half of waking time in schools that provide them a fairly organized set-up for interaction with teachers and peers. Schools are in fact second most powerful agency of socialization after parents. In schools, children learn not only cognitive skills (*e.g.* reading, writing, doing mathematics, etc.) but also many social skills, such as—ways of behaving with elders, age mates, establishing **vertical** and **horizontal** interactional patterns, fulfilling responsibilities, etc. schools also provide opportunities to internalize the norms and rules of society and several other qualities, such as 'self-initiative, 'self-control', 'responsibility', etc. In addition, schools also encourage 'creativity'. These opportunities make children more self-reliant. In the event of successful transactions in schools, the acquired knowledge through curriculum or interaction with others, are likely to be transferred to other fields of children's life.

Thus, for over all development and shaping of personality, school plays a very significant role.

Media

In recent years, 'media' such as television, cinema, internet, newspapers, radio, books, magazines, etc. has also acquired the property of socializing agent. While children learn many things from these sources, the adolescents and young adults do derive their models from them, more particularly from television and cinema. For example, violence on TV has become an important issue for discussion. It is so because, in studies, it has been observed that violence on TV enhances aggressive behaviours among children and adolescents. This agent need to be used in a better way to prevent children from developing undesirable behaviours and desirable ones are prompted. TV and cinema both present life like experiences, and hence, give a symbolic satisfaction to the viewer. Therefore, the lively contents of these media channels easily get instilled into the minds in an effective manner. Thus, different media channels do have the property of socializing process.

Day care homes

In the present times, in most of the families, both the members of parental figure are involved in earning livelihood for which they have to go out of homes. Consequently, there remains none to take care and look after the babies. Such parents usually put their babies to **day care homes** specially meant for small babies from 2 to 8 years. The day care homes function as play schools where children are looked after by staffs of the care homes. In cities and metros, such care homes are flourishing as a good profession. In such centres, children are not only fed, but also learn many arts of social life such as—reciprocal responses, co-living, sympathies, co-operation, competition, helping others, empathetic feelings, mutual interactional patterns, etc. Side-by-side, children also learn reading, writing, recognition of objects, concepts, living manners, discipline, ability to communicate, etc. Thus, **day care homes** also function as primary group in socializing and enculturating children.

In India, under the banner of 'Integrated, Child Development Services' (ICDS), **Anganbadi** runs as an institution to care for poor and deprived children as **creche homes.** Such **Anganbadis** are Government sponsored where only the children coming from below poverty line (BPL) families are taken care of.

Group

Till now we have been discussing different socializing agents covered under primary group. But, people do not remain restricted to primary groups only. As children move to later childhood, their social world expands and learn to form one-to-one relationships with friends and learn to organize themselves in groups. Groups have certain defining characteristics such as, goals shared by its members, rules of conduct (often implied or understood) and a hierarchical structure. The structure resemble the organizational chart. There are leaders at the apex and followers at the lower level. Every member possess some identifiable relationship to one another.

Groups are of different types, such as formal–informal groups, in and out groups, small and large groups, etc. Membership to these groups also have the property of socializing a person. Membership to a group fosters development of cognitive and social themes, leadership qualities, interrelationships. Co-operation, sympathy, role playing, intergroup role conflicts, etc. Hence, groups do play a significant role in the social growth and development of individuals. Hence, functions as socializing agent.

Religion

Religion is an integral part of any society. It refers to the activities that is **ownable**. It means what one must adopt or do and what not. Every religion has a set of certain norms, values, rules of conduct. All these are concerned with character formation. Hence, religious faiths are aimed at controlling and regulating behaviours.

Every religion has some fundamental principles that motivate or drive people of a society to form positive attitudes towards humanity. However, religions differ in their rituals and members of a society follow the rituals of the religion that are prevalent in a particular society. For example, Hinduism lay emphasis on **Karma** and **rebirth**. Being motivated by this, almost all Hindu individuals follow these beliefs and perform the related rituals. In 'Islam'—worship of statue is forbidden. Therefore, Islamic people worship God (Allah) as an abstract entity.

All religious rituals and ceremonies are in fact our daily social life activities. The festive occasions of religions determine direction to imitate and follow others of the religious group. The religious stories, musics, songs, mantrochar, etc. exert durable and stable impact on us, and our behaviours are guided, regulated and controlled by them. Thus, religious ceremonies, festive occasions, rituals, etc. acquire the property of socializing agent and these help in character formation as per particular socio-cultural demands of the society and in turn, our religious faiths also provide us energy to counter social life challenges.

Thus, we find several social agencies that operate as agents of socialization process and make us a **socio-cultural being**.

5.2.3 Mechanisms of Socialization

Since socialization is a process of social learning, certain mechanisms operate in the process. Some of the important mechanisms that operate in the process are as under:

(a) Reward and punishment
(b) Imitation and modeling
(c) Identification and internationalization
(d) Cooperation and competition
(e) Sympathy
(f) Child rearing practices
(g) Acculturation

Reward and punishment

Any kind of learning is influenced by **reward** and **punishment**. Those patterns of behaviour which are satisfying, give pleasing experiences, hence, are positive in valence, and make the acquisition of behaviour stable. On the contrary, the undesirable patterns of behaviours are dissatisfying or annoying. So, such patterns have negative valence and are therefore subjected to punishment. Therefore, individuals reject such response patterns and **unlearn** them. In short, the positively valued behaviours are reinforced owing to which such behavioural patterns are most likely to be repeated in future while, the undesirable patterns are not reinforced, and hence, not likely to be repeated in future. Consequently, the reinforced behaviours become stable while the non-reinforced behaviours are weakened and unlearnt. For this reason, parents not only denounce undesirable behaviours of children, but also impose punishment in some form or other. In schools also the teachers the principle of reward and punishment is followed to make the pupil learn the desirable behaviours and to unlearn the undesirable ones. Reward (reinforcement) is usually given in the form of medals, appreciations, merit certificates, etc. for good discipline, good attendance, obtaining good grades, etc. Punishment (non-reinforcement) is given in the form of inappreciation, disapproving, complaints to parents, heads of institutions, threats to struck off the names from school, etc. for any sort of unbecoming behaviours.

Gewirtz, J.L. and Ross, H. (1959) have also experimentally evidenced the effects of reward and punishment on social learning.

Imitation and modelling

In learning social behaviours, imitation do play important role. Following consciously or unconsciously the behaviours of others is what we call imitation. By imitating others, the individual wants to conform with others so that he may be recognized and obtain the position similar to other members of the group or society. By imitating others, we learn many social and cultural behaviours such as—conformity, cooperation, competition, sympathy, empathetic behaviours, discipline, compliance, religiosity, traditions, norms, values, etiquettes, communication skills, mannerism, obedience, etc.

Modelling resembles imitation. In modelling, one or more than one is assumed as model and by observing the behaviour patterns of the model, the individual imitates the behaviour pattern of the chosen model. For example, many of us treat a celebrity (film star, cricket player, political man, leaders of army, etc.) and try to imitate their styles of dress, hair, speaking, talking, walking, etc. of the model. Sometimes, the individual is unable to decide as to what and how to behave or act in a particular situation. Under such circumstances, the individual observes others and follows the same pattern, *i.e.* imitates. On the basis of imitation and modelling, **Bandura** and **Walter** (1963) proposed a theory of learning known as ***observational learning*** or ***imitative learning*** (see Chapter 11) .

Identification and internalization

In social situations, learning by imitation is very common. However, on certain occasions children often learn to behave the very same (not different) person due to satisfying interpersonal relationships or due to some special characterization. This is what we call identification—*i.e.* identifying oneself the same as other with whom he is identifying. It is the process of identification due to which one treats himself Indian or a part of a particular religion, caste or community.

Sometimes, we not only identify but also make the quality of some one's act or behaviour as our own internal quality. This process is called internalization. In this process, the individual himself becomes the part and parcel of the person he is introjecting, *i.e.* he incorporates his qualities as his own. There stands a very fine difference between 'identification' and 'introjection'. In identification, an individual attempts to become similar to his model while in introjection, the individual experiences the shades of characteristics of models, *i.e.* he internalizes the qualities in himself. For example, a son begins to speak as his father (model) is what we shall call identification. But, when one internalizes most of his qualities within his own self would be called introjection or internalization. In other words, in identification an individual imitates the model, whereas in internalization, the individual assimilates within the self the attributes or qualities of the model.

Obviously, the mechanisms of identification and internalization occupy significance in the process of socialization.

Cooperation and competition

Cooperation and competition also fosters the process of socialization. Cohabitation or co-living, respect for one another, inter exchange of ideas and objects are some of the salient features of social life and these features have roots in cooperative and competitive feelings that emerges in social life of human beings. In fact, co-operation is the base pillars of social relations. In longitudinal studies, it has been found that feelings of co-operation engraved during childhood is reflected in co-operative tendencies on attaining adulthood.

When two or more than two individuals give similar value to a certain goal to achieve, the feelings of competition arises. In course of competitive behaviours, the individual automatically learn many of the social behaviours. A person enriched with competitive feelings, have higher aspirations, he gets motivated on various social behaviours. For example, a political leader while fighting elections, focuses his attention on the sensitive issues of the electorate, concentrates on it and actively involves in solving the issue. In this way, he comes close to the mass and learns to communicate with them, moulds their attitudes in his own favour, and makes them unfavourable to his rival. Some research studies have shown that those who lack competitiveness are also poor in acquiring social behaviours.

The cooperative and competitive feelings are universal in nature because, these feelings are found almost in every individuals of all societies and cultures. However, in some, it is not much while in some it is very strong. The research studies on this issue have shown that such feelings are developed in course of mutual social interactions. Hence, co-operation and competition functions as a mechanism in social learning process.

Sympathy and empathy

Sympathy and **empathy** are two very important feelings of social life. Sympathy is a sort of fellow feeling, a compassion or the quality of being affected. Empathy, on the other hand, refers to imaginatively experiencing others experiences as his own. All our favourable or unfavourable attitudes root from these two social feelings and guide our social interactions accordingly. Both of these feelings are essential gradients of **pro-social behaviours** such as helping others and rendering services to them. Lack of such feelings are likely to make our behavioural interactions anti-social. Hence, undesirable.

We learn the attributes of sympathy and empathy through socialization process in which these affective feelings operate as mechanism. In many cases of anti-social behaviours, or socio-pathic behavioural patterns, lack of sympathetic and empathetic nurturing has been found as important causative factor.

Thus, these two serve as mechanism of socialization.

Rearing practices

As we have seen earlier, child rearing practices are very dominant mechanism involved in socializing a child. In different families of the same socio-cultural frame, rearing practices differ. The primary function of a family is to rear up every new member in the family in such a way as to make him a social being. Obviously then, the varied patterns of child rearing practices (*i.e.* variations from one child to another of the same family as well as variations from one family to another) will influence child's socializations variantly. For example, in certain families, in course of rearing itself, children are trained for independence while in others children are reared with exaggerated love and care. In the former case, children are able to take independent decisions to face the social life situations, while in the later case, children become dependent upon their parents and are not able to take independent decisions.

Much of the negative social behaviours, such as juvenile delinquency criminal behaviours, etc. emerge only due to freely rearing practices.

Therefore, it is evident that rearing practices operate as a mechanism in socialization process of a child.

5.3 ACCULTURATION

Acculturation refers to a process of intercultural borrowing marked by the continuous transmission of traits and elements between diverse peoples of different cultural groups resulting in new and blended patterns.

Usually, such contacts come into effect in reference to socio-political contexts. For example, historical and contemporary experiences, colonial experiences due to foreign rules, international trade, attack and cultural exchanges between the two cultures. All these bring about changes in cultural values, standards and norms of the original culture. For example, during Mughal empire, many Indians adopted Islamic religion, during British rules, our life styles were accultured that resulted in notable changes in our social structure, educational system and economy of the Indian culture. These changes can be clearly seen in dress, language, normal living manners and religiosity. The incidences of acculturation may happen any time or period of our life time, and therefore, we need to relearn to acquire modes of adjustment in a new way. Acculturation produce many new problems as well as provide new opportunities. This is why, we need to bring changes in our older patterns of behaviour. Migration is one such example. As a result of migration, people come in contact with people of another culture and in order to have a proper adjustment with other people of migrating cultures, the migrants have to bring changes in their language, dress, living manners climatic conditions, habits, religious rituals, etc. which put challenge to change. Similarly, colonial countries do experience changes.

People's reactions to acculturative changes are varied. Some readily accept the contents of other cultures while others oppose.

The consequences of acculturation are many fold, such as, expansion of population, discrimination based on cultural differences changes in attitudes, changes in policies and so on. The resultant phenomenal changes are seen in educational patterns, urbanization, political participation, communication, customs, rituals, etc.

In order to make proper adjustment with such changes due to acculturation, the following ways are helpful. These are:

(a) Assimilation: The individual departs from his original cultural identity and assimilates with the other culture.

(b) Separation: The individual wants to maintain his original cultural features and attempts to preserve them.

(c) Integration: The individual interacts with other cultures and integrates it with his own original culture.

(d) Marginalization: The individual is least interested in preserving his original culture.

Generally, acculturation is a stressful experience. Hence, the way an individual evaluates his experiences and use the available skills to cope with the resultant stress, both of these influence the degree of stress.

5.4 RELATIONSHIP BETWEEN BEHAVIOUR AND SOCIO-CULTURAL ENVIRONMENT

Human behaviour is also determined and regulated by the 'socio-cultural' environment. In fact, these two (**social** and **cultural**) are inseparable constituents of our environment. Socio-cultural aspects of our behaviour in which we live and grow, represent our environment in totality. Every culture varies in its values, norms, standards, customs, traditions, institutions and art. Cultures on one hand put restrictions on our behaviours to regulate it in the context of cultural norms and standards and on the other hand, it also motivates us to acquire, ones learn new skills and patterns of behaviour which are useful and incongruence with the socio-cultural growth.

Each culture has its unique templates in which culture grows and behaviours also grow/ develop in accordance with the cultural template.

Culture determine the experiences an individual has, the frustrations and adjustments he must leal with, and standards of conduct required of him. Each culture with its distinctive values, morals nd ways of living, laysdown its own rules for child rearing and relationship within a family. In a ense, it dictates the pattern of behaviour person should acquire, and thus, influences the individual ɔ grow and develop as a member of the socio-cultural group.

Socio-cultural environment selectively reinforces certain patterns of behaviour, determine ıe primacy of behaviours in accordance with significance, motivate to develop potentials, acquire kills, etc. in reference to the socio-cultural group to which the individual come from.

What has been discussed above, one should not construe, that biological bases of behaviours re of no significance. In fact, biological bases provide a basis of reaction range of behaviour, *i.e.* range of possible levels that an individual may ultimately reach. However, different patterns of ehaviours and mental experiences are shaped into a specific templet by our experiences in socio-ultural environment. Psychologists today are in agreement that biological bases and socio-cultural nvironment, both interact with one another in such a way that our emotions, perceptions, cognitive rocesses, reaction patterns, sensory experiences, ability to learn and memorize, etc. are all determined y the biological bases while the socio-cultural bases of human life make these environmental specific. his can be evidenced by a simple example of child rearing processes. There is a universal process f rearing a newly born child. However, the practices of rearing differs from family to family and ılture to culture. Such differences or variations cause specificity of behaviour.

Thus, it is clear that biological bases provide a basis for range of reaction *i.e.* a range of ɔssible levels that one may ultimately attain while the level of attaining the level depends on the ɹality of experiences one gains in his socio-cultural environment.

The influence of culture on our behavioural development has typically been described by **uth Benedict** (1959) in his book 'Patterns of Culture'. He describes:

> **The moment an infant is born in a cultural group, the traditions and customs of the group begin to shape his behaviours. As he heeds towards maturity, the cultural traditions and customs are embedded into his habits. The traditions, customs, attitudes, beliefs, etc. are cultural elements of his group become a part of his habit, and thus, he becomes a fully encultured person of his group.***

From what has been discussed in the foregoing paras, it is evident that our socio-cultural ıvironment influence our behaviour very strongly. The power of their influence is so much that ′en if an individual attains to adulthood, he cannot find himself free from controls of the society.

.5 SOCIAL STRUCTURE

ıe culture, in fact, is characterized by a distinctive pattern. Thus, each culture has its own social ′ucture that is involved in socialization of individuals. Each component of the social structure ntribute in some way or other to the socialization of a person.

Social structure involves assignment of ranks to people and expects the kind of work to done by every rank holders. For example, families are constituted in a certain way and each nstituent member of the family is expected of certain attitudes, beliefs, roles, etc. Social structure some societies are rigid, while in others, it is flexible. But, it is sure that no society is without me degree of structuring.

ꓤuth Benedict (1954), *Patterns of Culture*, 2nd ed., Boston: Hughton.

The basic structural components include status and role, multiple status, role conflict, socia classes, groups, leadership, etc.

5.5.1 Status and Role

Though, in shaping social structure, 'division of labour' is one of the important factor, but, th positions of different members in the family is also most significant contributors. It is the positio of a member in the family that determines how and what needs would be fulfilled by a particula member of the family or society. Thus, category-wise, each member is assigned a particular tas that is expected of him. This is what the social scientists call **status**. Each status is a position tha represents differences in the exchange of goods and services for the satisfaction of needs in th society. This status also depends on one's profession, and power to affect one's daily interaction with others.

Status often is changeable. It can be noted in family and other social groups also. Fc example, a person's status in the family may change to a parental figure (father or mother), an the same individual becomes grand parental figure in course of time. Thus, in different times, a individual's status changes, and accordingly his influence on others also changes. Similarly, in professional group, a teacher or any junior staff's status changes as principal, or senior staff, office and even employer, and accordingly, he plays his role and influence other's behaviours. 'Statu and roles' are indeed a key concept in understanding social structure. 'Status' refers to position i society while 'role' refers to the behaviour that goes with that position.

5.5.2 Multiple Status

The system by which statuses are arranged in a social structure permits a person to be categorize in many ways. For instance, as head of the family, teacher, priest of a temple, member of a clul etc. An individual therefore holds several statuses at the same time and on different occasions, h roles do vary accordingly. For example, his role as a house hold head, as a father as a grandfathe as a teacher, etc. varies as he is expected to play his role with a particular status.

5.5.3 Role Conflict

Often, a person is caught in a conflict or roles. It is a common phenomenon found in a society the social structure is complex as well as mobile. To cite for example, a foreman in a worksho who drives his men with an iron hand, may find his methods unsuccessful when he is promote as an executive. Similarly, a student leader who is accustomed to the role of president of a colleg union in a small town, may not find his role befitting when he enters a university in a metro cit A middle class professor used to the manners of cocktail party may find himself uncomfortable a gathering of poors.

Such changes put conflict of roles. He finds that the roles he is accustomed to a particul status is not appropriate in a new status. This makes him uncertain as to what role should play. If however, he is forced to decide the appropriate role, he may have little confidence in h choice. This situation may result in frustration, anxiety, hostility and failure to adjust. Many of t problems of the adolescents in the society are related to the difficulties to the changing behaviou or roles expected of him as he progresses from childhood to adulthood.

Role conflict is a universal phenomenon. Many people solve such conflicts and go ahead very conveniently by applying their experiences, intellect, etc. However, for some, role conflicts make serious problems. Through, the process of socialization, an individual better understands his multiple status and roles expected of him, and can better learn the skills to cope with the situations—posed before him.

5.6 SOCIAL CLASS

Social class is also an important component of social structure. In every society, people are arranged along a scale of prestige—based on their status, wealth, power, respect and honour. Though, there is no one-to-one relationship between status and wealth, because, people of the same status and prestige may differ on the measures of wealth, one may have relatively more wealth than the others. However, in the society, people are situated on scales of prestige, and accordingly, he is honoured by others in the society. Thus, in social structure, people are put into different categories on the basis of their prestige rank. Those who are placed at the apex of 'prestige scale' are put in to different category as compared to middle and lower rank holders. People in the past societies were generally categorized as **noble class**, **freeman class** and **slave class** and their social interactions were also determined accordingly, viz. people of a class were allowed to choose a profession that were found befitting to the class they belong to. Even interactional behaviours between two different categories were also determined in accordance with the class division (**Cattel**, 1942).

In the modern times, however, there is neither any rigid demarcation line between two classes nor people of a particular class is associated with a particular profession or occupation. Despite this, in every society **social class group** is found that determines social environment.

Division of people in a society influences individuals behaviours and experiences in a massive way, viz. whom to meet, get together, with whom one spends his leisure time, the kind of profession one chooses, the kind of things he wants to possess, how one perceives others, etc. all are influenced by the class one comes from.

Though, the measures to classify people in a society is not well-defined, usually ones profession, occupation, sources of income, education, kind of residential homes/houses, social prestige, moral status, etc. are some of the measures on which people are situated in different class categories.

5.7 SOCIAL CLASS AND BEHAVIOUR

Social class differ not only in status, and things that go along with status but, they also differ in attitudes and personalities of the members of a class. Political scientists, philosophers, sociologists do opine that social class differ in their political beliefs and social philosophies, *i.e.* either on the occupational scale or in the social class he thinks he belongs to the more likely he is to hold conservative political views.

Kinesy, et al. (1948) in a research study of pattern of sexual behaviours among the American male, revealed a significant relationship between sexual conduct and social class as measured by occupation. The semi-skilled labour group was seen to have relatively frequent pre-marital musturbation and relatively in frequent masturbation. The pattern was however, reversed among professional groups and lower-white-collar group. These groups showed an intermediate or transitional pattern of sexual behaviour. In this context, it is interesting to note that Kinesy found marked departure in the pattern of sexual conduct when an individual moves from one class to another. The study revealed that a person born in a skilled labour group when moves in to a professional class, shows a youthful sexual pattern incongruence with the class in which he eventually moves. Similarly, a person born in a skilled labour class when located in unskilled labour class, resemble the pattern of individuals born in to that class (**Krech, et al.** 1962/334).

Thus, knowledge of the social environment of the individual facilitates understanding of his sexual attitudes and behaviours.

As regards, differences in personality due to differences in class, it is not widely recognized. In fact, personality depends on the kind of home, neighbourhood, kind of work he does the kind of play, the kind of facilities they have, etc. that go along social class and help to determine personality pattern. Even more important in the training and education of a child that differs according to social class. Several studies of social class differences in child rearing practices provide information on this point (**Bronfenbrenner**, 1958), **McClelland**, 1958), (**Curry**, 1962), **Mishra, B.K.**, 1974) etc.

The findings of their studies provide definite information that on the measure of socio-economic status (SES) differences, shaping of personality patterns do differ. This also include child's aspirations, ambitions, increased level of need for achievement and reaction patterns.

From the above, it is clear that a number of significant differences in behavioural patterns occur in individuals coming from different classes. They differ in attitudes, beliefs, perceptions, child rearing practices, educational goals and even in certain motivations.

In addition to socialization (their agents and techniques), cultural bases, social structure and social class, there are several other components of society such as structure of social groups, characteristics, types or kinds leadership, etc. all influence behaviour. These components develop certain behaviour such as social facilitation, loafing, conformity, compliance, co-operation and competition, social inhibition, etc. But, in the view of the limitations of this book, these are not described here. Interested students may consult any standard textbook on Social Psychology or Sociology. For reference one such book by Krech, Cructchfield and Ballsey, 'Individual and society' is referred for convenience.

SUMMARY

- While introducing the chapter, it has been stated that behaviour is moulded to a large degree by social forces. It is for this reason that man is considered not only a biological unit rather he is 'bio-social'. It is so because, our behaviours are governed not only by biological structures and their functions but also by customs and conventions of socio-cultural milieu.
- In shaping and moulding of behaviour, the process of socialization play a vital role. It is because, the process of socialization crafts our behaviours in a socio-cultural templates.
- Certain agencies function as founding pillars in socializing a child. Among such pillars, the family (or parents) is one of the most important agent. The family socializes a child through specific training procedures as well as creating a proper atmosphere.
- While socializing a child by the parents or family rearing styles such as authoritarian-autocratic style, indulgent-permissive style, and authoritative reciprocal styles and in different or uninvolved style are of great significance. Each style has its different impacts in making a child's social life.
- Another important agents are media, peer groups, school, and religion.

- The process of socialization, involve certain mechanisms or techniques that operate. Important such mechanisms are (a) imitation and modelling (b) reward and punishment (c) identification and internalization (d) co-operation and competition (e) sympathy (f) child rearing practices and (g) cultural acculturation.
- Human behaviours are determined and regulated by the socio-cultural environment. Socio-cultural environment reinforces certain patterns of behaviours, determine their primacy, motivate to develop potentials, acquire skills, etc. in the context of society or culture of which he is a member.
- However, biological bases as discussed in Chapter 4, is equally important. In fact, the biological bases determine the range of possible level that one can attain while the socio-cultural environment shapes the behaviours in a particular socio-cultural templates.
- Social structure involves assignment of ranks of people within a social frame and put them into categories of class group. Such categorizations usually bases upon certain measures adopted in a society, such as profession, status, honour, etc.
- Differences in social behavioural patterns, beliefs, attitudes, etc. have been found in accordance with the class group from which one comes from.
- The basic structural components of social class include status and role, multiplicity of status, role conflict, social class, groups, leadership, etc.
- Society or the socio-cultural environment influences our behaviours in many ways such as, social facilitation, social inhibition, competition, co-operation, etc.

PART III

Knowing the World Around Us

CHAPTER 6

Sensory Process and Psychophysics

6.1 INTRODUCTION

The world in which human beings live and transact, consists of innumerable kinds of objects, individuals and varied situations. Psychology is a science of adjustive behaviour. Adjustment involves knowing the world in which one lives and transacts. To know the world that surrounds us, it is essential to receive the information about the surrounding objects of the world, integrate the information in a meaningful way and then to display the desired response. Thus, adjustive behaviour involves three-tier processes—receiving the information from the external and internal environment (input), integrating and interpreting the information (central processing) and finally, responding to the information (output). Hence, three kinds of organs operate in making adjustive behaviours. These are the **receptors** that receive information from the external and internal environment, the **effectors** that move to respond and the **adjustors** or **conductors** that interpret the information.

In Chapter 4, we have discussed the central processor, *i.e.* the central nervous system and other neural mechanisms that function as adjustor. The present chapter is devoted to the discussion of receptors and effectors and also to the discussion of the channel through which the input is conveyed to the central processor involved in knowing the world around us.

6.2 RECEPTORS AND EFFECTORS

6.2.1 Receptors

The receptors are the stimuli receiving organs of the body. These are called **sense organs**. Sense organs are in fact, **windows** through which information about the objects of the world is gathered.

These are the primary organs of contact with the physical environment because our cognition or awareness about the world depends upon sense organs. The stimuli of the external world stimulate or activate the receptor mechanism of the sense organs, produce nerve impulses of information about the present stimulating conditions, the impulses are carried over through afferent fibres to the corresponding sensory areas in the brain. We precisely become aware of the present stimulus. Thus, the windows or the receptors are the senses which function as primary channel of mental awareness (cognition) which is termed as **sensation**. The major sense organs are the eyes, ears, nose, tongue and skin. Each of these organs is capable of being stimulated by specific stimuli and produced specific sensations. Thus, we have visual sensation when the eye (visual sense organ) is stimulated, auditory sensation is the resultant stimulation of ear (auditory sense organ), olfactory sensations of different kinds of smells take place when olfactory organ (nose) is stimulated. We also sense cold, warmth, smoothness or hardness of a surface when we touch something and tactile sense organ (skin) is stimulated. Thus, receptors are the sense organs that are stimulated by the physical energy of the stimuli in the environment.

Types of receptors or sensory organs

Psychologists in fact, do not know exactly how many sensory organs one possesses. There are certainly more than traditionally known five sense organs, *i.e.* eyes, ears, nose, skin and tongue. Other senses are hidden within the body which are involved in knowing the position of one's body in space, its movements, internal changes and physiological tensions, when one is hungry, thirsty or tired. All these sensory organs can be broadly classified into the following three categories:

(a) **Exteroceptors:** Exteroceptors are related to (concerned with) receiving information on getting stimulated from stimuli present in the external world. There are five known exteroceptors—the eyes, the ears, the nose, the skin and the tongue. Appropriate external stimulus that stimulates the receptor cells within these organs as a result of which sensory nerve impulses are produced and conveyed to the appropriate sensory area in the brain and thus, the individual becomes aware of the external stimuli, *viz.* wave-lengths of light enter into eyes and the receptors within eyes get stimulated from where the sensory impulses of visual features of the object are transmitted to the visual area in the brain and then the visual sensation takes place. Similarly, various frequencies of sound waves are received by hair cells (receptors) inside the ears and resultant nerve impulses are conveyed to the auditory area in the brain and thus, we have auditory sensation. Similar is the case with other senses—olfactory, tactile and taste sensations.

(b) **Interoceptors:** Interoceptors are related to (concerned with) the visceral organs of the body such as lungs, intestines, heart etc. These get stimulation from changes taking place in our visceral or internal organs of the body and produce sensations of the changes taking place in our internal environment, *i.e.* within the body, *viz.* stomach pain, chest pain, headache, palpitation etc. Since these receptors are found inside the body organs and are stimulated by internal stimuli only, they are termed interoceptors.

(c) **Proprioceptors:** Proprioceptors are found in the peripheral regions of the body and are responsible for **kinesthetic sensations**, *i.e.* sensations of movements of joints, tendons and muscles. Sensing of tiredness, fatigue or muscular pains etc. are the examples of **kinesthetic sensations**. It should be clear here that the muscles in themselves are not the receptors, rather they are the effectors or organs of response. But the muscles also contain receptor structures which give sensations whenever muscles make any movement to respond.

From the above description of the receptors and their typology, it is evident that the exteroceptors, interoceptors and proprioceptors are associated with receiving and conveying of information from external, internal and peripheral regions respectively and thus, function co-operatively in our adjustive behaviour by making us aware of the environment we live in.

6.2.2 Effectors

Effectors are the organs of response. These respond to the stimuli through diverse ways of movements. These are also called motor organs. Effectors are of two types: (i) Muscles and (ii) Glands.

Muscles

Human body is a skeleton structure. That is, it is a framework of bones covered with muscles. Muscles protect the body and provide good appearance to the body. In addition, they also perform various kinds of motor activities through the process of contraction and relaxation. All our body functions, simple or complex, gross or fine are the outcomes of contraction and relaxation of muscles. Muscles are of three types as mentioned below:

Smooth muscles: Such muscles are automatic and perform involuntary functions of several body organs such as, the intestine, stomach, respiratory organs, blood vessels, iris etc. Accordingly, the smooth muscles are also termed as **involuntary muscles**. These muscles are not concerned with any bone. Therefore, these are inaccessible to external observation. Their contracting and relaxing functions are regulated by autonomous nervous system (ANS) and hence are automatic. Smooth muscles are the linings along the walls of vicarious organs right from alimentary canal to anus and appear as spindle. It contains fibrile substances which make the muscles contract and relax. Another important role of smooth muscles is that since these muscles are linings over the walls of delicate visceral organs, they provide support to them.

Cardiac muscles: Cardiac muscles are found in the heart and are responsible for cardiac functions. Cardiac muscles are similar to striped muscles in appearance but differ on two counts: (i) the striped linings are not parallel as are found in striped muscles and (ii) cardiac muscles have no coat over it as is found in striped muscles. Cardiac muscles are regulated and controlled by autonomic nervous system (ANS).

Striped muscles: Striped muscles are voluntary muscles because they perform voluntary functions. Such muscles are connected with the skeleton structure of body with the help of either ligaments or joint sockets wherever required. Accordingly, striped muscles are also termed as **skeletal muscles** and contain two types of stripes.

Striped muscles make the locomotive organs to move (provide motion to the locomotive organs) and thus, perform the motion actions such as walking, bending, turning, making back and forth motions of upper and lower limbs, laughing, spreading of eyebrows, speaking etc. These activities are performed with the help of cell structures found in these muscles. The connecting muscles of different bones are found in pairs. One of the pairs is called **flexor** while the another is called **relaxor**. When flexor contracts, the connected piece of bone bends in a particular direction and when the relaxor contracts, it bends in just the opposite direction. For this reason, striped muscles are called 'antagonistic' muscles. Thus, one of the chief characteristics of this muscle is that when one of the pairs, say, the flexor is activated the relaxor too is activated, Therefore, in a given time, the skeletal activity connected with these muscles often depends much on the balanced joint action of the pairs and when the balance of joint action is disturbed for any reason, the connected bone does not make motion.

Another characteristic of striped muscle is that all its actions are conscious. That is, the individual is well aware of its actions and he has conscious control over its actions. As such, striped muscles are known as voluntary muscles.

In striped muscles, two types of corpuscles are found. One of the corpuscles is red while the another one is white. Red shadow corpuscles contain energy elements more than the white corpuscles. As such, it is commonly observed that former can remain active for relatively longer period to the latter.

Glands

Glands too are motor organs of the individual which respond to the stimuli by secreting chemical substances. There are two types of glands—duct glands and ductless glands.

Duct glands: Duct glands are exocrine which secrete chemical substances (not hormones). These substances are carried to different parts of the body through tubes or ducts. For example, mammary glands, salivary glands, pancreas gastric glands, intestinal glands, sweat glands etc. are the duct glands. The secreted chemicals of these glands do not mix with blood. Some of these secretions act upon digestive functions while some come out of the body providing outlets for waste products inside the body, *viz.* gastric glands secrete gastric juice which act upon the swallowed food particles inside the stomach and thus, help in digestion. On the other hand, the sweat gland secretions or secretions from bladder excrete the waste products of the inner body organs.

Ductless glands: Ductless glands are endocrine that respond by secreting hormones and poured into blood directly without the help of any duct or tube. The secreted hormones mixed with blood are circulated to different organs and cells through blood circulatory system. There are several ductless glands. These have been described in Chapter 4—Biological Bases of Behaviour in a separate section—**endocrine system.**

6.3 SENSORY PROCESSES

We know that psychology is a science of adjustive behaviour of the organism in general and of the man in particular. Adjustive behaviour is a S-R bound (stimulus-response association), *i.e.* a response (behaviour) is elicited by a stimulus. This implies that in order to respond to any stimulus (object, situation, person or event), the individual must be aware of the present stimulus in the environment to which he makes a response. All such awareness or knowledge come through senses in the form of sensory experience.

The study of knowing the world through **sensory experiences** leads to two different but closely related approaches: (i) One such approach aims at discovering the aspects of environment to which the sense organs respond to by registering the information and conveying the registered information to the brain where integrative, interpretative and decision-making processes for making a response take place. (ii) Another approach on sensory processes is applied one. This approach aims to determine man's ability to discriminate and interpret sensory stimuli so that one's capability can be matched to the task requirement.

Both of these approaches to the analysis of sensory mechanisms are of great importance in psychology which is the main theme of discussion in this section.

To have a better understanding of the organism's behaviours, we need to know how sensory mechanisms are constructed and how they mediate the sensations of light, touch, taste and the like. This is the first stage of knowing the world around us which is being discussed hereafter.

6.4 SENSATION: NATURE AND DEFINITION

Sensation is a primary experience of knowing the world around us. To know, recognize and evaluate the objects of the world, we need to obtain information about them. These informations are gathered through information gathering system that include receiving of information through receptor mechanisms in the sense organs. These mechanisms convert the physical energy of the stimulus into neural energy which are conveyed through sensory peripheral nervous system to the sensory areas in the brain and then we have the first-hand knowledge about the stimulus (object) present in the environment. This entire channel of process streching from reception leading to transmission of impulses to the sensory area is what we call **sensory process** and sensing of the object is **sensation**.

Sensation is the simplest mental activity which provides mere awareness of the stimulus present in the environment. This results from combined cooperative activity of the sensory mechanism involving the reception, neural transmissions and central nervous system that decode the encoded messages in the form of neural energy and recognize the physical object. Sensation is also a primary process of knowing the object or sensing the object because, it is the first step in understanding the more complex higher order cognitive processes such as, perceiving the object, thinking, problem solving etc.

The process of sensation is very simple. Any object present in the environment impinges on the sense organs that respond to it by producing nerve impulses followed by communicating (transmitting) the same to the corresponding sensory areas in the brain via spinal cord. This whole process is called **sensing** and information received centrally by means of this process is known as **sense data**. Study of all these sensory activities comes under the perview of **sensation**.

The term sensation is used in three different senses—(a) it means a primary sense datum (plural data), (b) it refers to the process or activity of sensing and (c) it denotes a topic in psychology dealing with sense datum and process of sensing. Combining the above three uses of the term, sensation can be defined as follows:

Sensation is a simple, primary cognitive mental process in which the individual merely becomes aware of immediate present stimuli in the environment.

The process of sensation takes place when receptor cells of a sense organ are stimulated, nerve impulses are initiated and travel along the sensory pathways to the sensory area in the cortex.

From the above description about the nature of sensation, one can discern the following salient features of this process:

(a) It is a simple mental activity.
(b) It is a primary process of cognition because it is the first stage of awareness in understanding more complex higher order cognitive processes.
(c) Through sensation, we become merely aware of the environmental stimuli. That is, it does not provide meaningful or complete cognition of the present stimuli.
(d) Sensation is always of the immediate stimuli and follows sensory channels of awareness or cognition from receptor to the sensory areas of the central nervous system (CNS).

Hence, sensation is a primary process of registering the information about the world around us by means of sensory channels.

6.4.1 Properties or Attributes of Sensation

'Sensations' are characterized by certain characteristics. Some of these characteristics are specific in nature that have the reference to the particular sense modalities. But, sensory experiences have certain general attributes or properties which are common in all kinds of sensations or all sense modalities. These properties are—(i) quality, (ii) intensity, (iii) vividness and (iv) duration.

(i) **The quality:** Quality is one of the such attributes of sensation that differentiates object on the basis of stimulus quality, *viz.* a visual sensation may be of one colour or of another. The quality of a taste sensation may be sweet, bitter, sour, etc. Similar is the case with other sensations like auditory, olfactory, tactile etc.

(ii) **The intensity:** Intensity is another important attribute of sensations. Stimuli of the same class and quality produce different sensations. For example, a bright colour produces a sensation different from a dull colour. Similarly, we distinguish a loud sound from mild sound and mild sound from whisper. Such differences in sensations are possible because of inherent attribute of intensity. Differences in sensations due to difference in intensity of stimuli depend upon two factors—(a) intensity of the stimulus itself and (b) sensitivity of the receptor cells.

 (a) More intense is the stimulus, more number of receptor cells inside the specific sense organ are stimulated; just opposite is the case with relatively less intense stimuli. This causes differences in sensing different intensities of stimuli.
 (b) The receptor cells within a particular sense organ differ in their sensitivity, *viz.* the receptor cells located around cheeks and lips are much more sensitive than the receptor cells located in the back region. As such, the same amount of pressure on these two points are sensed differently.

(iii) **Vividness:** Vividness refers to the clarity of the stimulus. It is a corollary of the attribute of intensity. More intense is a stimulus more vivid and clear sensation is produced. This attribute of sensation makes our sensory experience standing out different from sensations produced by an ambiguous or relatively less vivid stimuli.

(iv) **Duration:** All sensations contain the attribute of duration. Sensations may be momentary or longer in duration which are easily distinguishable from each other, *viz.* at the point of time if an alarm watch which is allowed to ring for a minute and at another point of time it is allowed to ring for two minutes. The listener of the two rings from equal distance will experience distinct sensations. This difference in sensory experience is due to difference in duration (persistence) of the stimulus. Longer duration allows persistence of the stimulus for long causing continuity of stimulation of receptor cells and resultant communication of nerve impulses to the sensory area in the brain. Momentary duration is relatively less persistent. Thus, different sensory experiences are produced.

In addition to the above four attributes, often two more attributes are added. These are **extensity** (spreadoutness) and **local sign**. Sensations produced by a stimulus on a larger part or area of the sense organ is distinguishable from sensations produced by the same stimuli on a relatively smaller area or part. This difference is due to the attribute of **extensity**. Secondly, whenever a stimulus impinges on a sense organ, it leaves its impressions for some time over the impinged area or part of the organ. Owing to this, one is able to localize the affected part or area of the organ even when the stimulus or stimulating conditions are absent. Obviously, the localization of the affected area of the sense organ is due to the characteristic feature of **local sign** that the sensory experiences possess.

6.5 SENSORY CHANNEL: PROCESSING

The greatest mystery of sensory experience is that the organism or man does not experience physical energy itself directly. The organism or individual only senses the activity in nervous system. Thus, whatever idea or information or image we get about the world is only what we sense and perceive through our senses.

Sensory process involves a succession of events beginning with stimulation of receptors, encoding the message, transmission of the coded message in the form of nerve impulse and decoding of the message by the sensory cortex in the brain. Nerve impulses go to centres in the spinal cord and/or brain stem. They are then relayed to the appropriate cortex region. The meaningfulness of nerve impulses—the sensory information that they provide, depends upon the specific receptor from where they were initiated (point of origin) and the centre in the cortex, *i.e.* the destination. The nerve impulses reaching their destination are decoded and integrated with other information and the outcome is the awareness about the world outside and about our own body. This whole process of sensory activity (stimulation of the receptor organ), encoding, conveying, reaching the message to its destination is the process of **input** about which we are concerned at the moment.

6.5.1 Sensory Stimuli

A stimulus (inside or outside our body) initiates some kinds of activities. Sensory stimuli are those that activate our sense organs (often called as the gateway or windows of knowledge). Sensory stimuli are classified according to the gateways (receptors or sense organs) triggered by them. Human body is equipped with a variety of **sensors** each attuned to a specific stimulus. For example, the receptors in the ear are called **mechanoreceptors** because they are sensitive to the mechanical forces of sound waves. 'Mechanoreceptors' also serve the sense of touch among others. **Chemoreceptors** are sensitive to substances in solution such as sugar in water. Our **olfactory** (smell) receptors are also attuned to certain chemicals in gaseous form. **Thermoreceptors** (skin) are activated by heat and cold. They are also attuned or sensitive to some mechanical stimulation, giving information about tactile properties of objects. Then, there are **photoreceptors** in the eyes that respond to light energy. **Kinesthesis** depends upon stimulation provided by movement in muscles, tendons and joints. The stimuli are **pressure** and **pull** on these structures. **Static sensitivity** is attuned to stimulation associated with movements of the head and body as a whole. Such movements activate receptors in the **equilibratory** mechanism in our inner ear. The stimuli for **organic sensitivity** are gases, tissue changes and chemical activities associated with gastric and other internal processes.

6.5.2 Transduction

Receptor process begins with changes in the physical environment of the organisms that affect the receptor cells. The immediate effect is conversion of physical energy into neural energy which travels through afferent (sensory) neurons to the brain. This conversion of one energy form to another is called **transduction.** The receptor cells converting or translating the physical energy into nerve impulse (*i.e.* another energy form) are called the **transducers**, *viz.* a telephone is a transducer which changes sound input into an electrical output. Similarly, the rays of light when impinges on photoreceptors in the eyes, the rays are converted into optic nerve impulses which are carried through optic nerves to the visual area in the brain. Here, the photoreceptors in the eyes are the **transducers** and the process of transforming the rays into optic nerve impulses is called the process of **transduction**. Each receptor cell is specialized for conversion of specific type of physical energy.

The process of transduction takes place in sequential order as shown in **Figure 6.1**.

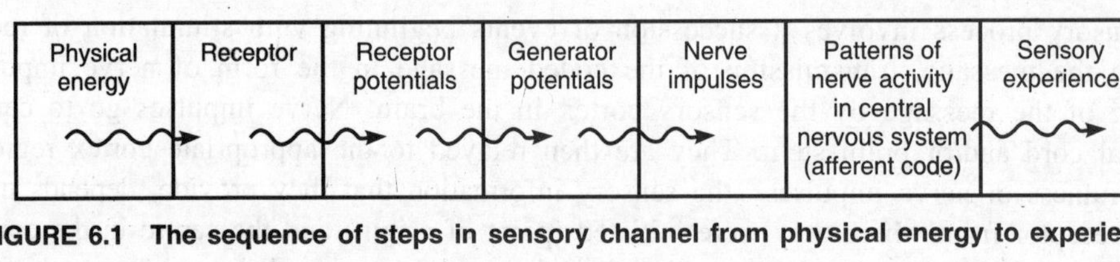

FIGURE 6.1 The sequence of steps in sensory channel from physical energy to experience.

The above sequences are explained as hereunder:

(a) First of all the physical energy (stimuli) impinges on a specialized receptor cell.
(b) The receptor cells when affected by a physical stimulus, respond by slowly changing electrical voltages, which are technically called 'receptor' and 'generator potentials'.
(c) The generator potential acts upon the nerve cells and fibres to produce nerve impulses which travel towards the brain. The process of transduction in fact, mobilizes several hundreds of nerve cells and fibres, each conducts the nerve impulses at a different rate of transmission and reaches the brain centres at slightly different times.
(d) The nerve impulses reaching the brain centres form a spatial pattern of sensory input serving as raw sense data.
(e) The raw sense data become the basis for **sensory experience** or **sensation**. This experience occurs in the brain and we become aware of the physical stimuli in the environment.

6.5.3 Conduction

Nerve cells or neurons are specialized for conducting information from receptors to their centres in the brain. Each neuron has a cell body and fibres leading to and from it. Information is conducted over these fibres in the form of nerve impulse or **spikes**. The spikes are triggered by generator potentials. Spikes are very brief electrical pulses lasting for about 0.5 to 1.5 milliseconds.* However, the rate of travel depends upon the size of the fibre. Research studies on the phenomenon indicate that larger the size of the fibres, the larger is the spike and faster it travels. This obviously means that the size of the spike depends upon the size of the fibre and not on the strength of the stimulus which triggers it. Spikes, in any particular fibre are always of the same size. This rule about spike action is known as **all or none-law**.

Neurons form junctions known as **synapse**. When a spike reaches the end of a fibre (the terminal button of axon), it secretes chemical substances from its sacs or vesicles which are poured into synapse. This chemical substance is called 'neurotransmitter'.

The neurotransmitter may either **excite** or **inhibit** the adjacent cell depending on the kind of chemicals. When neurotransmitter substance is able to build up a generator potential strong enough to trigger the adjacent neuron, the spike potential is likely to set off further. But, if the neurotransmitter substance is of inhibiting nature, the spike potential is unlikely to advance further. Thus, the nerve impulses are conducted to the sensory area in the cortex through several fibres and this process of transmission is called conduction.

6.5.4 Afferent Code and Experience

The nerve impulses reaching their destination (corresponding sensory areas in the cortex) take the form of organized patterns of spikes called **afferent code** or the **input code**. The afferent code generally corresponds to the stimulating conditions which are translated (decoded) by the brain as an actual experience. How afferent code is deciphered (decoded or translated) into an experience, that too so rich in quality and variety, is still a mystery and scientists are vigorously trying to find out an answer to this question.

6.6 PSYCHOPHYSICAL RELATIONS AND METHODS OF STUDY

Sensory experiences are of the physical energies that stimulate the sense organs or the receptor channels. Hence, the sensory experiences are the outcomes of receptor stimulation or excitation. Thus, at the initial end of the sensory channel, there is physical stimulation and experience of the stimulation at the other end. Therefore, it is obvious that there exists some sort of relationship between the physical stimulation and resultant sensory experience. The study of this relationship in quantitative form is known as **psychophysics**. Hence, **psychophysics is the study of quantitative relationship between physical energy (stimulus) and resultant sensory experience of the stimulus**.

In recent times, **psychophysics** has emerged as a major field of Experimental Psychology that deals with some basic problems related to the relationship that exists between psychological events (experience) and the physical events (stimulus) that impinges upon sense organs. The basic problems are—(a) Detection problems and (b) Stimulus scaling problems.

---

* A millisecond is one thousandth of a second.

6.6.1 Detection Problems

We know that each receptor requires some minimum amount of stimulus intensity for being stimulated or excited and thus, make detection possible. This minimum value or magnitude of stimulus is called **threshold** or **limen**. When the stimulus value is below this level, no detection occurs and when it is above this value, detection becomes possible. Thus, **threshold or limen is a distinct border or a boundary line between sensing and not sensing**. For example, some lights are too weak to be visible while some lights are strong enough to be visible. In between these two intensities, there would be a minimum value or magnitude of light that may serve as distinct border below which we may not sense the presence of light and above which, we more frequently sense the presence of light. This minimum required magnitude of light is the threshold for vision. Similar is the case with other sensations—auditory, tactile, olfactory or taste.

Psychophysicists usually talk of two kinds of thresholds—absolute threshold or limen (AL) and differential threshold or limen (DL), which is also called just noticeable difference (j.n.d.).

Absolute limen (AL)

This limen is also called Reizlimen (R.L.) which refers to the least amount of physical energy which can be experienced or detected. For example, if you add a granule of sugar to a glass of water, you may not experience any sweetness in that water. Addition of a second granule to water may also not make it taste sweet. But, if you go on adding sugar granules one after another, there will come a point when you may say that the water is now sweet. In this case, the minimum number of sugar granules required to make you experience that the water is sweet, will be the absolute limen (AL) of sweetness (see **Figure 6.2**).

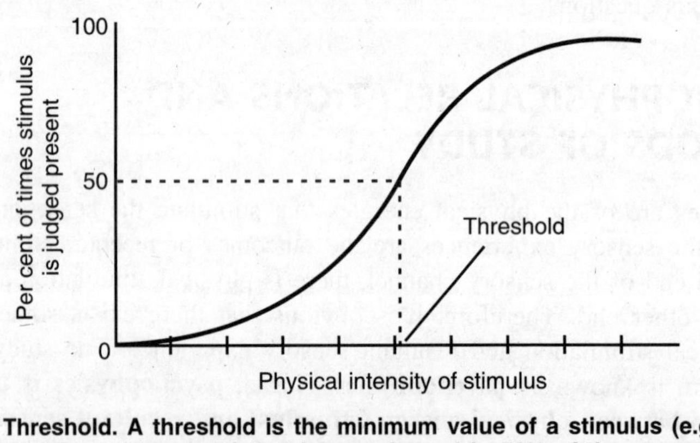

FIGURE 6.2 Threshold. A threshold is the minimum value of a stimulus (e.g. brightness of light, loudness of tone etc.) that is experienced in 50% of the exposure time.

It may be noted at this point that AL or RL of any physical stimuli is not a fixed point, instead it varies considerably across individuals and situations depending upon one's organic and motivational states. Hence, we need to assess it on the basis of number of trials. Thus, in technical terms, absolute limen (AL) refers to the smallest value of physical stimuli that produces a response in 50 per cent of exposures, i.e. one experiences the stimulus in 50 per cent of time and in remaining 50 per cent of time, he does not experience the stimulus. Thus, the number of sugar granules that may produce the experience of **sweetness** in water on 50 per cent of occasions will be called absolute limen (AL) of sweetness. If more number of sugar granules are added, the chances are greater that the sweetness will be experienced more often than plain. This is depicted in Figure 6.2.

Differential threshold or limen (DL) or just noticeable difference (j.n.d.)

Second threshold with which psychophysicists are concerned is **differential limen (DL)** or just noticeable difference (j.n.d). This is an experience of difference between a standard value of some kind of stimulus and a variable of the same kind of stimulus. As it is not possible to notice all stimuli, it is also not possible to notice all differences in the magnitude of a stimuli. In order to notice two stimuli as different in their magnitude, there has to be some minimum difference between value or magnitude of those stimuli. Thus, **the smallest difference in the value of two stimuli that is necessary to notice them different is called differential threshold or limen (DL).**

To understand, let us repeat the above example of sweetness in water. As you have seen, the plain water is experienced as sweet after the addition of certain quantity of sugar granules. Try to remember the magnitude of experienced sweetness of the water. The next question is how many sugar granules will be needed to experience the water sweeter than before (*i.e.* difference in sweetness). Go on adding sugar granules one after another tasting the water each time. After addition of a few granules, you may notice at a point that the water is now sweeter than before. The quantity of sugar granules added to the water to generate an experience of sweetness that is different from the previous one on 50 per cent of occasions will be called the DL or j.n.d. of sweetness. **Thus, difference threshold is the minimum amount of change in a physical stimulus that is capable of producing a sensation of difference on 50 per cent of the trials.**

What determines these thresholds (AL & DL), has extensively been studied and theories have suggested several factors such as the characteristic features of stimulus, organic conditions of sense organs, personal factors relating to affective and motivational states, the physical environmental conditions and certain contextual references. In addition to these AL and DL or j.n.d. also vary across individuals.

6.6.2 Stimulus Scaling

Stimulus scaling concerns with psychophysical methods employed to measure the relationship between the characteristics of physical energy and reported experience. There are various psychophysical methods. Some of the most commonly used methods are as follows:

(a) Method of average error or adjustment.
(b) Method of limit or minimal changes or successive exploration.
(c) Method of constant stimuli and constant stimulus difference.

The above-named methods are though classical methods, these are even today employed by psychologists.

Psychophysicists by using these methods have put forward certain principles or laws that govern our sensory experiences of the physical stimuli. One such law is that the relationship between physical event and psychological event (experience) is regular or lawful. Amount of change in experience is found to be related to the changes in the intensity of physical energy.

But, this relationship does not correspond point to point or one to one with the physical changes in intensity.

Psychophysical methods are also used to determine errors of judgement based on the experience of the physical stimuli, determining the amount of change to produce a psychological change in experience, determining the threshold and governing laws etc. Such experimental studies and researches are possible by scaling the physical stimuli on the one hand and scaling the aroused experiences (sensations) on the other.

Let us now discuss the different psychophysical methods one by one.

Method of average error or adjustment

As is evident from its name, this method is used to determine the average magnitude of error in one's perception or judgement of value of the object or stimuli. In using this method, the investigator repeatedly presents to the subject a stimulus of fixed or constant value called **standard stimulus** together with a **variable stimulus** whose value can be varied either by increasing or decreasing its value. The variable stimulus is also named as **comparison stimulus**. Subject is required to adjust the **comparison stimulus** either by increasing or decreasing its magnitude (in either one direction in a trial) until it appears equal to him. The difference in the value of standard stimulus and the value of comparison stimulus that appears to the subject as equal, gives an estimate of the magnitude of error in judgement by the subject. The 'mean' of the differences obtained from several observations provide the average or mean error in perception. Since the subject adjusts the value of comparison or variable stimulus to the value of equality of standard stimulus, it is also called 'method of adjustment'.

Sometimes, the constant or standard stimulus alone is presented and the subject is asked to reproduce. For example, a line of fixed length (magnitude) is presented and the subject is asked to reproduce a line of the same length on a sheet of paper. A number of such reproductions are taken and the mean difference of the reproduced lengths with the constant or fixed length of the line would give an estimate of average error in perception. Thus, the method is also called 'reproduction method'.

Methods of limit or minimal changes or successive exploration

This method is principally used to determine absolute limen (AL or RL) and differential limen (DL or j.n.d.). The procedure involves presentation of variable in ascending or descending order alternatively by increasing and decreasing its magnitude (value) with minimal units of change in the magnitude or (value) of the stimulus. The subjects are required to respond the point where he perceives the variable stimulus equal to the standard stimulus. Hence, in both the alternative orders of presentations of the variable stimulus, the transition points (change of response) of the subject are recorded which are subjected to treatment or analysis to determine the RL or DL values. Thus, in this method, the experimenter presents the variable stimulus alternatively in ascending and descending orders and the subjects are required only to respond to the value where he perceives a transition (change) in judgement of perceived value. This method is also called method of minimal changes because the experimenter presents the variable stimulus by bringing minimal changes in value or magnitude alternatively in ascending and descending orders. The procedure for determining RL or DL involves the presentation of the variable stimulus in a successive or serial order, *i.e.* by increasing or decreasing its magnitude gradually (successively or sequentially). Therefore, it is also named as successive or serial reproduction method.

Method of constant stimuli or method of frequency

In this method, the comparison (variable) and standard stimulus—both are presented before the subject either side by side or one after the another in random order for equal number of times repeatedly for a number of times. Each time the standard stimulus (fixed magnitude stimulus) either precedes or follows the comparison variable but this sequence (preceding or following) of presenting the two stimuli is altered in a random sequence for equal number of times. In other words, the variable stimulus value precedes or follows the standard stimulus value for equal number of times randomly. The subjects are required to respond whether the preceding stimulus value is smaller in magnitude (shorter or lighter) or equal or larger (heavier or longer) as compared to the comparison or variable (that follows) stimulus value. Hence, on all the occasions of comparison, the subject is required to give his response in only one way—whether the stimulus that precedes another stimulus is larger, equal or shorter.

When the method is used to determine RL, it is called method of constant stimulus and when used to determine DL, it is named as method of constant stimulus difference. The method is also named frequency method that relates to the manner in which data are treated by this method. The frequency of each kind of responses that the subject makes in respect of each value of the variable stimulus is counted and RL or DL is calculated on this basis.

Since, different constant values of variable stimulus are presented (though in chance order) throughout the entire set of observations that the experimenter decides to take in the experiment, it is called the method of constant stimulus.

The methods of limit and constant stimulus are similar in one respect as compared to the method of average error. In average error method, the subject himself manipulates the variable stimulus (*i.e.* he himself either increases or decreases its magnitude) or reproduces the standard stimulus. In other two methods (limits and constant stimulus methods) the experimenter manipulates the variable stimulus. The subject only judges and makes a verbal response to express his perceived judgement.

6.7 SOME IMPORTANT CONCEPTS OF PSYCHOPHYSICS

Psychophysics has two words—'Psyche' *i.e.* mental event and physics, *i.e.* physical events. Hence, psychophysics pursues the study and measurement of experimental aspects (mind or psyche) about the physical events or energies. In course of pursuing the experiential aspects about the physical energies that impinge on our sense organs, the psychophysicists use certain terminologies that we need to know and understand. These are as follows:

Sensitivity

Sensitivity refers to the limited and selective response capacities of sense organs. This is an indicative of the functional limitations of sense organs. We know that we have specialized sense organs that are attuned to specific physical energies of the stimulus. For example, eyes are sensitive to light energies, ears are sensitive to sound waves, nose is sensitive to certain kinds of gaseous forms of chemical substances, skin is sensitive to touch and tongue is sensitive to the gustatory chemicals. However, these sense organs have limited capacity to respond and are selective in nature to respond. For example, our eyes cannot visualise things which are very dim or very bright. Similarly, our ears also cannot hear sounds below 20 Hz or above 20,000 Hz. Thus, auditory receptors can respond to sound waves between 20 Hz and 20,000 Hz only. The same is true for other sense organs also. As human beings, we function within a limited range of stimulation. For being noticed by a sensory receptor, a stimulus has to be of an optimal intensity or magnitude.

Psychophysicists usually talk of two kinds of sensitivities—absolute and differential sensitivities.

(a) **Absolute sensitivity:** Absolute sensitivity refers to the least magnitude of a stimulus to which a sense organ is able to be excited or respond.

(b) **Differential sensitivity:** This refers to the capacity to respond to the qualitative or quantitative differences of stimulus.

Threshold or limen

Threshold or limen refers to the border line limits of the stimulus value that produces an experience of either presence or none presence of a stimulus. Thus, this border is indicative of sensing or not sensing of the stimulus. There are two kinds of limens—AL and DL—which have been described earlier in this chapter.

Point of subjective equality (PSE)

When we sense or perceive a stimulus we tend to make an estimation about the stimulus being sensed or perceived. Such estimations are subjected to two kinds of possible errors. Either we may overestimate or underestimate the stimulus value from reality. This means that while sensing, we tend to estimate equality or similarity that may be erroneous either in the direction of over-estimation or underestimation. Thus, the point of subjective equality (PSE) refers to the point or value at which we experience the stimulus to be equal or similar. For example, in **Muller-Lyer illusion**, while adjusting the feather-headed line equal to the constant length of arrow-headed line (say 50 mm), the subject on the average experiences the two lengths equal at 47 mm. Thus, this 47 mm is the point of subjective equality (PSE) of the subject and the direction of error in estimated experience is underestimation by 3 mm. This means that the subject experiences 47 mm length as equal to 50 mm length of the standard stimulus (see **Figure 6.3**)

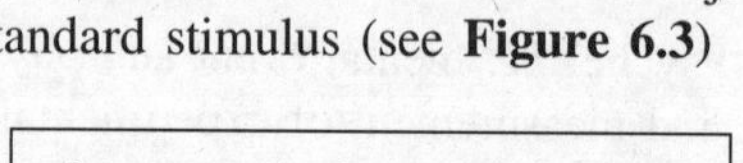

FIGURE 6.3 Muller-Lyer illusion.

Constant error

When an individual expresses his subjective estimation about the stimulus based on sensing or perceiving the stimulus, usually, he tends to make error either in direction of over (excess) or under (less). This, tendency of estimation error is found consistent in either of the directions in almost all or most number of the observations. This is what we call **constant error**, *i.e.* a consistent tendency either to overestimate or underestimate. This kind of error in estimation is determined by subtracting the mean value of point of subjective equality (PSE) from standard value (M_{PSE} – standard). In case M_{PSE} is more than the standard value—it would mean a constant error in the direction of over estimation and if the same is less than standard value, it would mean constant error in the direction of underestimation.

Variable error

Variable error is different from constant error. In constant error, the experiencing individual makes estimation error consistently in either of the two directions in all his observational trials. On the other hand, the variable error varies in different trials of observations in one trial the subject overestimates while in another trial he underestimates. Thus, there is no consistency of direction rather it varies from trial to trial. There are various sources of variable errors. Some of the important sources are as follows:

(a) Inconsistency of sensitivity
(b) Lack of full control over experimental situations
(c) Mental state of the subject during experimentation
(d) Some other subjective factors such as attitude, interest, mental inconsistency
(e) Defects of sense organs etc.

6.8 WEBER'S LAW

We have discussed earlier the differential limen (DL) or j.n.d. In this context, an important question is—whether the value of j.n.d. for a stimulus or sensory area is constant? In course of finding, it could be revealed that the unit of psychological dimension is not constant for different ranges of the corresponding physical scale. At first, this created an obstacle in an attempt to develop measures of psychological processes. **Earnest Weber** solved this difficulty by discovering that though the unit of psychological scale is not absolutely constant, it is relatively constant. **The DL for stimulus bear a constant ratio to the stimulus irrespective of the value of stimulus. In other words, though the DL increases with the increase in the size or magnitude of the stimulus, the increase is always proportional to the size of the stimulus.** Thus, if an addition of 1 gram makes noticeable difference in a weight of 20 grams, an addition of 5 grams will make noticeable difference to a weight of 100 grams. The DL increases in the same proportion as the stimulus. Hence, in the above example, 1/20 or .05 gram will be a constant ratio according to Weber for all values of weight. This is known as **Weber's ratio** or **Weber's fraction**. Weber's Law is expressed in equation form as:

$$K = \frac{\Delta R}{R}$$. Here, K = constant, ΔR = DL and R = stimulus value

Let us try to understand this law with the help of an example. Suppose, for 50 grams of weight the obtained j.n.d. is 2 grams. Then for 100 grams of weight, the j.n.d. will be 4 grams. In equation form—

$$\text{1st condition } \frac{2}{50} = .04 \text{ gm}$$

$$\text{2nd condition } \frac{4}{100} = .04 \text{ gm}$$

Hence, in both the above-mentioned conditions the proportion of j.n.d. is .04 gm which is Weber's fraction.

However, further researches have shown that Weber's Law hold good in respect of middle or moderate range of stimulus intensities only and also that this law differs with different sense modalities as shown in **Table 6.1**.

TABLE 6.1 Some Weber's constant ratios

Sense modalities	*Weber's constant ratios*
Vision (bright light)	1/60
Kinesthetic (lifted weights)	1/50
Audition (tone loudness)	1/10
Taste (for salt)	1/3

6.9 GUSTAV FECHNER'S LAW (1860)

'Gustav Fechner' has modified Weber's Law and used it for a direct measurement of the intensity of sensations. **Weber** found that a particular stimulus value would be just noticeably different from another value, if the other value is increased by a constant fraction of the first value. Thus, if Weber's ratio for a particular kind of sensation is 1/5, a stimulus of the value of 20 should be increased by 1/5 of its magnitude, *i.e.* by 24 to be just noticeably different from 20. Again, the other value that would be just noticeably different from 20 would be 1/5 of 24 added to 24 or 28.8. Still another magnitude of the stimulus that would be sensed as different should be 1/5 of 28.8 added to 28.8 or 34.56 and so on. What we see in this case is that j.n.d. values can also be determined by using constant multiple of 12/10; $20 \times \frac{12}{10} = 24$; $24 \times \frac{12}{10} = 28.8$, $28.8 \times \frac{12}{10} = 34.56$; $34.56 \times \frac{12}{10} = 41.47$ and so on.

'Fechner' thus noticed that by multiplying the stimulus magnitude each time by constant value, we should produce one unit change in sensation. Starting with 20 as the initial magnitude, the first change will occur at 24, the second at 28.8, 3rd at 34.56 and so on. What we notice is that while the stimulus value progresses by the process of multiplication, the sensation increases by the process of addition. Increase by the process of multiplication is called geometrical progression; that by the process of addition is called arithmetical progression. If the two variables so correspond with each other that when one increases geometrically, the other increases arithmetically. The relation between them is termed logarithmic. Hence, the sensation values may be thought as the logarithms of corresponding stimulus. Those familiar with the use of log tables know that log 1 = 0, log 10 = 1, log 100 = 2, log 1000 = 3, log 10,000 = 4 and so on. Fechner's discovery of logarithmic relationships between values of the stimulus and units of sensation led him to restate Weber's Law as: **Sensations are proportional to the logarithm of the exciting stimuli**. Thus Fechner expressed the law in equation form: $S = C \log R$. Here S = Sensation, C = Weber's constant, R = Stimulus magnitude.

Thus, Fechner provided an equation for direct measurement of sensation.

6.10 STEVENS' POWER LAW

Fechner's revision of Weber's Law has been used by many scientists and attempts to refine the revised forms have been made. In this endeavour, **Stevens'** (1961) revision and refinement is important and has proposed **Power Law** of sensation. In fact, in Weber's or Fechner's Law, judgements regarding sensations or sensory experiences are expressed in categories. For example, the lightest stimulus is kept in category 1 and extremely heavy stimulus is kept in category 6. Now the experiencing individual expresses his judgement by sorting out from the categories lying in between those two extremes—such as 2nd, 3rd, or 4th categories. While sorting one's own sensory experiences out of the categories, certain subjective factors may also get involved in influencing one's judgement. To remove this limitation Stevens has proposed the method of **magnitude estimation** in which there is no definite category of stimulus intensity and the subject can give his judgement in any manner. The only thing is that such judgement does not contain any zero value. For example, suppose the standard stimulus weight is 100 grams, which has a power value 10. After this any weight may be presented one by one. In this condition, suppose the subject experiences the 2nd weight twice heavier than the standard weight (with a value of 10) he may say it 20, if he experiences thrice heavier, he may say 30 and so on. Similarly, if the subject estimates a stimulus just half of the standard, he may say 5, 1/4th lesser than the standard, his estimation would be 2.5 or 1/5th lesser will be estimated as 2. Thus, there is no 0 (zero) estimation. In magnitude estimation method, the value assigned to the standard stimulus is called **modules** which is 10 in the above example.

According to Stevens, the relationship between intensity of stimulus and magnitude of sensory experience is not logarithmic rather, sensory experience is an outcome or result of extent of increase in stimulus intensity in terms of exponent or power. It can be expressed in equation form as mentioned below:

$$S = K R^N$$

Here S = magnitude of sensation
K = constant
R = intensity of stimulus
N = exponent

Thus, in terms of Stevens' Law, the increment in sensation along with the increase in stimulus intensity depends upon the size of the exponent. Hence, if the exponent is 1, then the increase in sensory experience will correspond to the increase in stimulus intensity.

Stevens has obtained exponents for different sense modalities which is approximately stable and definite (see **Table 6.2**).

TABLE 6.2 Stevens' exponents for different sense modalities

Loudness of sound	6
Lines of varying lengths	1
Salty taste	1.3
Weightlifting	1.45
Electric shock	3.50

We should remember here that with the change in exponent, the interrelationships between stimulus intensity (R) and the magnitude of sensation (S) also change. It has been shown in **Figure 6.4**.

Evaluation: Stevens' exponent or power law is comparatively more objective to Weber's or Fechner's Law. Therefore, we can better understand the relationship between stimulus intensity and magnitude of sensation.

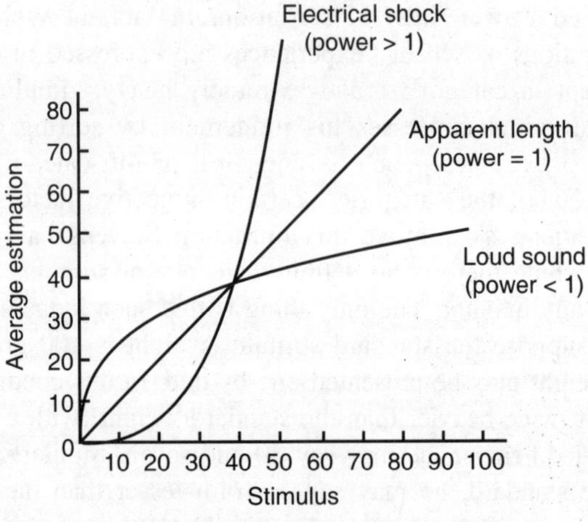

FIGURE 6.4 Power curves for electric shock, line length and loudness of sound.

6.11 MODERN PSYCHOPHYSICS

The classical psychophysical methods deals mainly with determination of thresholds or limens. But, this could be possible or appropriate in ideal conditions only and not in ordinary conditions. **Green and Sweat** (1966) have instead proposed a new theory—**Theory of Signal Detection**—TSD. According to this theory, psychophysical judgements are determined by both—observer's sensory ability as well as non-sensory biases. Therefore, on the basis of signal detection analysis, it is possible to abstract (or separate) the sensory and non-sensory factors affecting judgement of perceptions. In this context, the study of **Buckout** (1970) is important. In order to analyse signal detection, the following four kinds of alternatives are recorded. These are:

1. *Hit responses:* Signal (*i.e.* stimulus) is present and the subject is successful in identifying the signal, *i.e.* hits correctly.
2. *Miss responses:* The subject misses to identify the presence of signal (stimulus).
3. *False alarm response:* In a trial, the signal (stimulus) is absent but the subject identifies the same as present. Here, the hit is incorrect or false.
4. *Correct rejection:* In a trial, the signal (stimulus) is not present and the subject also identifies the signal as absent, *i.e.* the presence of stimulus is correctly rejected.

The above four kinds of responses can be presented in a tabular form like the one as shown in **Table 6.3**.

TABLE 6.3 Signal responses

		Yes	*No*
Stimulus or signal	Present	Correct hit	Wrong (incorrect hit)
	Absent	Wrong (incorrect hit)	Correct (correct rejection)

Table 6.3 shows four possible consequences of combining the two signal situations—present and absent with two response options—Yes or No. If one recognizes a real signal despite noise,

he scores **hit**, if fails to recognize, he scores **miss**. Responding **Yes** when signal is not present, qualifies on **incorrect hit** and accurate recognition that signal (stimulus) is not present, counts as correct rejection.

According to signal detection theory, the threshold identification by the subject is a form of **decision making**. The subject must decide whether he/she detects signal (the stimulus). This detection depends on motivation, sensitivity and nature of stimulus.

We can plot a graph on the basis of correct yes (hit) and false alarm responses. The curve so made is called **'receiver operating characteristic curve'**—ROC curve. A sample of this type of curve is shown in **Figure 6.5**.

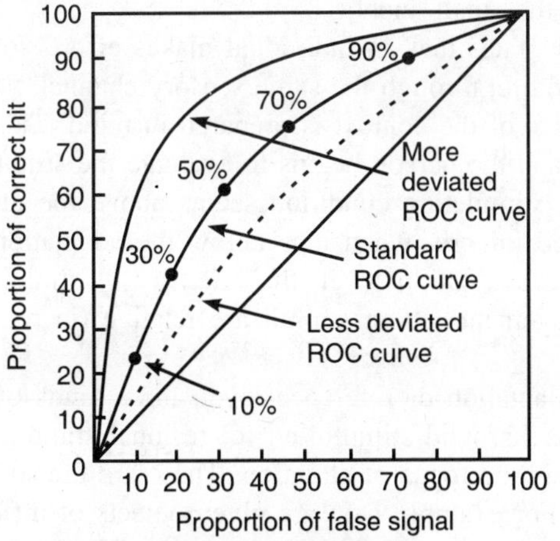

FIGURE 6.5 ROC cure.

6.11.1 Helson's Adaptation Level Theory

Research studies done in modern times on the contextual and relational determinants of perceptual experiences prompted **Helson** (1964) to propose **adaptation level theory** of perceptual experiences. This theory offers to explain that what we experience about an object or event and then react to it depends upon the context in which the object or event appears. An event or any stimulus is experienced against a background of other events or stimulus. For example, it is observed that in order to suppress the undesirable behaviour of children, **punishment** (an event) by loving parents is experienced quite differently than when it is given by callous or indifferent parents. Similarly, even reactions to such experiences also differ accordingly (Sears et al., 1957). With the help of this instance, the general idea is discernible about the effect of context. Helson's adaptation level theory is based on this general idea about the significance of contextual references in perceiving or sensing aspects of the world.

Helson has developed the concept of adaptation level to quantify and provide general theory concerning context effects. The central idea of the theory is that the context or background acts to set a **standard** against which events or objects are sensed and perceived. For example, although a mediocre student looks like a poor student in a class of good students, he may seem quite good in a class of dolts. To substantiate this fact, Helson (1964) conducted an experiment that shows the way, perception is affected by distributing stimuli or the context to which the subject is exposed.

Helson investigated the perception or judgement under several different contextual conditions. The subjects were required to perceive and judge the size of the squares. The subjects judged the squares on a scale, ranging from very-very small to very-very large. The context was manipulated by using 'anchors'—extreme stimuli which biases distribution of stimuli in one direction or another. The 7 sizes of squares to be judged ranged from 1.0 to 3.82 inches on a side, and the two extreme anchors were squares of 0.30 and 9.00 inches on a side. These anchors were used to distort the distribution of square sizes and to provide a particular background or context against which the stimuli were perceived and judged. With the large 9.00 inch square, the other stimuli might be expected to look small by contrast. With the small anchor, we might expect the stimuli to look relatively large. This is what happened. The stimuli with the large anchor were judged to be smaller than those with the small anchor.

In essence, the theory states that an individual makes efforts to adapt with the dynamic and variable environment. Therefore, through the same sensory channel, various stimuli impinge on the sense organ, a reference level of the context is prepared in mind. This mental level of reference is known as adaptation level and the person begins to evaluate the stimuli in context of the reference level. When the impinging stimulating condition seems above the mental adaptation or reference level, the stimulus is judged intense, when it is below the adaptation level, it is judged dim and when it seems equal to the adaptation level, the intensity of stimulus is judged as moderate or intermediate. Thus, our judgements about stimuli are relative (in relation to level of reference or context) and not absolute.

In determining the adaptation or reference level, three kinds of stimuli are involved. These are: (a) focal stimuli, (b) background stimuli and (c) residual stimuli.

The focal stimuli are in the focus of attention. These are the stimuli about which experiential judgements are warranted. For example, you are given objects of different weights to judge which weight is heavier, lighter or equal to the standard weight. Here the weight stimuli are the focal stimuli. **Helson** and **Nash** (1960) on the basis of an experiment using weights, found that when the series of weight stimuli are used as focal stimuli, the subjects adaptation level used to increase with the increment in the series of weights (focal stimuli).

Background stimuli are those which are in the background of focal stimuli and act as a reference to judge the focal stimuli. For example, in weightlifting experiments, the subject picks up a 100-gram weight and estimates its weight. Second time he picks up a 75-gram weight which is a focal stimuli to judge whether it is heavier, lighter or equal to the first weight. Here, the 1st weight stimulus (100-gm weight) serves as background stimulus in the context of which the subject is required to give his judgement about the focal stimulus (75-gm weight).

The residual stimuli in loose sense are the past experiences. These are the residual parts of previously experienced stimuli that serve as reference in making judgement about the current or present focal stimulus. Previously experienced parts also act as reference or context in determining the adaptation or reference level about the present stimulus which is in focus.

The above descriptions of the adaptation level theory depict the qualitative aspect of the theory. However, it has a quantitative aspect also. In quantitative terms the adaptation level is the weighted product of focal, background and residual stimuli which is represented in equation form as:

$$\text{Adaptation level} = FW^1\ BW^2\ RW^3$$

Here FW^1 = Weighted coefficient of focal stimuli

BW^2 = Weighted coefficient of background stimuli

RW^3 = Weighted coefficient of residual stimuli

The weighted coefficient values of all the three kinds of stimuli are different and thus, are indicative of their relative significance in determining the adaptation level. Therefore, greater the coefficient value of a kind of stimulus relatively greater is its significance in determining the adaptation level.

6.11.2 Evaluation

Though, from modern viewpoints of psychophysics, the adaptation level theory occupies a significant position. Its significance lies in the fact that the qualitative and quantitative aspects of this theory is much helpful in understanding the complexities of sensory processes in contextual frame of reference. However, the theory suffers from certain limitations such as

1. In this theory, only the context of external stimuli has been emphasized whereas our sensory or perceptual experiences are also determined by the subjective contexts. Subjective contexts in fact have been ignored that play a crucial role in determining the adaptation level.
2. To know the weighted coefficient values of different categories of stimuli (focal, background and residual) is a very complex task.

SUMMARY

- In adjustive behaviours, sensory process plays an important role in which the involvement of receptors and effectors are crucial.
- The receptors receive the input and communicate the same to the centre while effectors respond to the environmental stimuli.
- In sensory processes, the sensory channel plays an important role by processing the information.
- Receptors are the windows of human body or serve as the gateway for information about the physical world.
- Receptors are of three types—exteroceptors, interoceptors and proprioceptors.
- Exteroceptors include eyes, ears, nose, skin and tongue. Interoceptors are within the body that gather information from internal environmental changes such as changes in heart, respiratory organs, digestive organs etc. Proprioceptors are found in the joints, tendons and provide kinesthetic information.
- Effectors refer to motor organs or organs of response such as muscles and glands.
- Muscles are of three types—smooth muscles, cardiac muscles and striped muscles. Glands are classified in two major types—duct glands and ductless or endocrine glands.
- Sensory process is a mechanism that receives the stimuli, transduces the physical energy into neural energy, transmit the encoded afferent message to the CNS through afferent fibres by establishing synaptic connections, and the CNS decodes the message that is experienced as sensation.
- Sensation is a primary and simplemost process of awareness about the world. It provides mere awareness.
- Sensations have the attributes of quality, intensity, duration, vividness, extensity and local sign.

- Psychophysics has contributed much towards the study of relationship between psychological events and physical events.
- Psychophysics is mainly concerned with detection problem, *i.e.* determination of absolute and differential limen.
- Three major psychophysical methods are employed to study psychophysical relation-ship. These are method of average error, method of limit and method of constant stimulus.
- Sensitivity, threshold, point of subjective equality, constant error and variable error are some of the basic concepts of psychophysics.
- In psychophysics, Weber, Fechner and Stevens' have significantly contributed by formulating laws to explain and measure the psychophysical relations in sensing objects and giving judgements.
- In modern psychophysics, the theories of signal detection and Helson's adaptation level are much popular.

CHAPTER 7

Visual and Other Sensory Processes

7.1 INTRODUCTION

We have seen in the preceding chapter that man lives and interacts in the environment that consists of various individuals, objects and situations. Such interactions are important to transact and adjust with the diverse world around us. We need to know and understand the varieties of objects, persons, situations and events that surround us. In knowing the various forces of the physical world, we gather information about our surroundings through sensory channels. The receptors as the primary level of sensory channel receive the characteristic features of the physical energies, and through processings of the sensory mechanism, we become aware of the impinging stimulus. We have also seen that these receiving mechanisms are within the sense organs. There are various sense organs and each sense organ is attuned to a specific kind of physical energy. The receptors inside these sense organs are excited by the specific energies, convert these physical energies into neural energy through the process of transduction and thus, the encoded message or information is communicated through afferent fibres to the respective sensory areas in the cortex where the encoded information is decoded and makes us to 'sense' the stimuli present in the environment.

Since, each sense organ has specialized receptors to transform the specific physical energies into specific afferent codes, it is important to know and understand the mechanism and functioning of different sense organs. The present chapter is thus devoted to the description of different sense organs, facts and theories related to the various sensory experiences, more particularly, the visual and auditory sensations that constitute the major source of gathering information from the environment.

7.2 VISUAL SENSATION

In humans, there are eight different kinds of sensations. These are visual, auditory, tactile or cutaneous, olfactory or smell, gustation or taste and kinesthetic sensations. In addition, we also sense the temperature and pain that give sensations of warm, cold and pain.

Of the eight sensations, the visualization is highly developed, complex and important in humans. According to an estimate, vision is used by human beings in approximately 80 per cent of transactions with the external world. In order of significance, audition is just next to vision. There are some other senses also that contribute to enrich our information we collect from external world. However, we shall discuss in detail about visual and auditory sensations with a precised or summarized description of the important features of other senses.

The stimulus for vision

Stimulus for vision is a small portion of electromagnetic energy travelling through space, commonly known as sunlight. When sun's light is absent, lights produced by other sources (*e.g.* candle light, or electric light) form the stimulus for vision. Electromagnetic energy (sun's light) travels in waves with varying lengths (the distance from one crest of wave to the next). Wave-length varies from the shortest cosmic rays (10 trillionths of an inch) to long radiowaves that may measure many miles. The wavelengths to which human eyes become sensitive (visible spectrum) ranges from nearly 380 nanometres (nm) to about 780 nm*. Thus, it is clear that visible energy is a very small section of the total electromagnetic spectrum (entire range of wave-lengths).

'Sir Isaac Newton' (1666) found that sunlight passing through a prism, breaks down into a component wavelength (a band of varicoloured light) as is seen in rainbow. A prism' in fact, spreads all the wavelengths out in a band so that we can see and measure each wavelength in a mixed beam of light wavelengths in the visible spectrum. These relate to the experience of colour (see **Figure 7.1**).

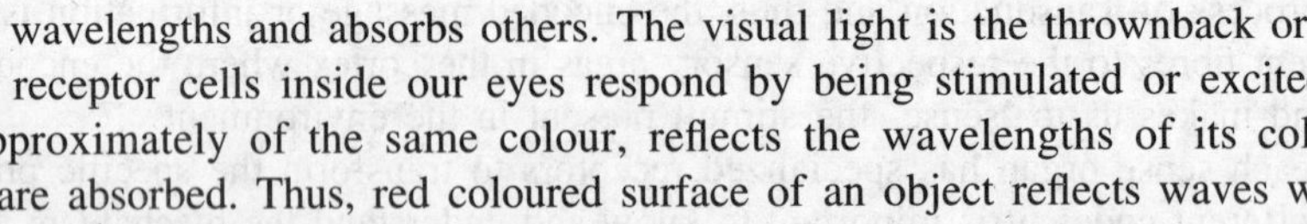

FIGURE 7.1 Light waves of different lengths and height.

Sunlight is a mixture of different wavelengths. But when it falls on any object, the object reflects some wavelengths and absorbs others. The visual light is the thrownback or reflected light to which the receptor cells inside our eyes respond by being stimulated or excited. The objects which are approximately of the same colour, reflects the wavelengths of its colour and other wavelengths are absorbed. Thus, red coloured surface of an object reflects waves whose length is nearabout 700 mμ† and abosrbs waves of other lights.

The visible light stimulus does not differ only in wavelength but also in strength or intensity which is expressed in height or amplitude. The source of light may be weak or strong. Besides, difference may also be found in the complexity of light. It may be pure (unmixed) or a mixture of different wavelengths.

* A nanometer (nm) is one billionth of a metre.

† A millimicron (mμ) is millionth of a metre or one thousandth of a millimetre.

The light reflected by an object falls upon the eyes and stimulates the receptor cells that produce visual sensation. Before, we discuss the other details of visual sensation, let us first examine the structure and function of eye mechanism.

7.2.1 The Human Eye

The human eye is like a photographic camera. In a camera, there is a plate to focus the image of an object. Likewise, human eye has a 'retina' to focus the image of the object being visualized. In a camera, the photographer moves lens to obtain desired focus on the plate and adjusts its refraction or bent. In the like manner, this adjustment of lens to bent or refract light on to retina is done by 'cornea' and 'lens' with the help of **cilliary muscles** connected with it. The contraction and relaxation of the muscles bring changes in the shape or form of the lens depending upon the distance of the object. For viewing the distant objects, the lens becomes thinner while for near objects, the shape of the lens becomes wider and thicker. This function of lens adjustment is called **accommodation**.

The eye, as shown in **Figure 7.2**, is situated just below eyebrows in head region in a hallow cavity called sockets. Eyes are ball-shaped and hence, called eyeballs. Its circumfrence is about 25 mm and weighs roughly 7 grams. A little portion of eyeball is externally visible as it is on the upper surface of the socket and the remaining portions are covered within the sockets. Eyeball has three layers or coats namely, (i) **the sclerotic coat**, (ii) **the choroid coat** and (iii) **the retina**.

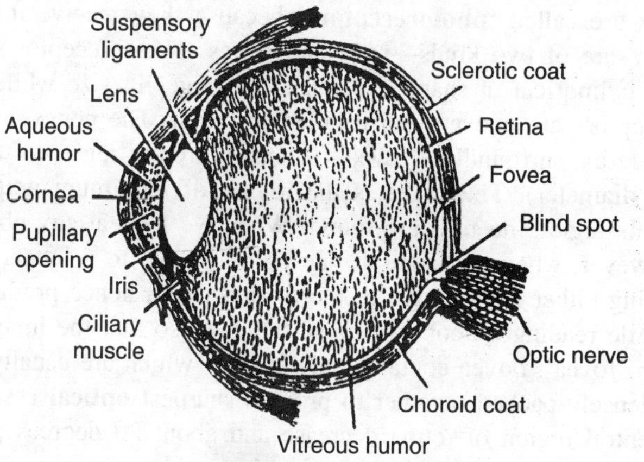

FIGURE 7.2 The human eye.

The sclerotic or sclera

Sclerotic coat is the outermost layer of the eyeball. It is tough and firm. It is made up of approximately 5 mm thick fibrous material that protects and preserves the shape of eyeball. Hence, it is a security guard of the eye. It is white in colour and forms the white part of the eye when the eye is open. It is opaque (non-transparent) but the front portion of this opaque coat bulges out and is called 'cornea' which is transparent. The sclera layer is attached to extra 'ocular muscles' which make the eyeball turn.

The choroid

It consists of large many tiny blood vessels which contain **brownish-black pigments**. The front portion is called **'iris'**. The blank portion in-between cornea and iris is filled with a liquid substance called **aqueous humour**. In the centre of iris is a very very small gap point called **'pupil'** of the eye and serves as entry door through which the light rays enter into the eye. The size of pupil may become wider or constricted depending upon the brightness of the light. This helps in allowing only the permeable amount of light to enter. This is also a kind of adjustment to the intensity of light which is governed by the autonomic nervous system (ANS) and the **cilliary muscles** are involved in its operation. Just behind the pupil is **'lens'**—a membranous transparent structure that hinges with the help of connecting 'suspensory ligaments' from both sides. It is a thread-like muscular structure. These ligaments maintain the balanced position of lens and change its shape into convex or concave forms depending upon the distance or nearness of the object being visualized. This process is called accommodation.

The space behind lens is filled with a liquid substance called **'vitreous humour'**. This substance preserves the round shape of the eyeball. When the vitreous humour comes out due to injury to eyeball, the sensitivity of the eye is lost and people become blind.

The retina

This is the thirdmost important layer of eyeball. The light rays pass through vitreous humour and approaches to visual path through different layers of retina (there are 10 layers in retina). The tenth layer of retina is the most sensitive layer as it contains the receptive cells of vision. These receptive cells are called **'photoreceptors'** because they receive the photic images of the object. Photoreceptors are of two kinds—**rods** and **cones**. These receptor structures differ in size and shape. Rods are cylindrical in shape and relatively larger in size while the cones are tapered and short. These receptors are unevenly distributed in retina. The cones are more plentiful in the central region of the retina surrounding 'fovea'—a small circular region of the size of a pea (about 2 degrees of arc in diameter). The fovea is the region of maximum **acquity**, *i.e.* **the point of clearest vision**. In this region, no rods are found. When we look at any object directly, the image falls on 'fovea'. However, when we fixate at one point, only 5 to 6 letters of a word can be read and other words falling either left or right to the fixated point, hence produce blurred vision. This is the reason that while reading a book, we move our eyes so that the image of subsequent words or letters may fall on 'fovea'. Fovea contains only 'cones' which are usually long and slender. The cones in fovea are densely packed together to provide sharpest **optical resolution**.

Rods in the central region of retina decrease and about 20 degrees away from fovea, more number of rods are found. Again in the peripheries, its number decreases.

From evolutionary point of view, the rods and cones are assumed as two separate visua systems. This is known as **duplicity theory of vision** (Vonkries, 1834). This theory states tha we have two distinct types of visual receptors and they differ in structure as well as function (see **Figure 7.3**). One is the **cone system** while other is the **rod system**. The cones are the retina elements active in bright light or daylight. Rods, on the other hand, are active in dimlight. I addition, the former receptor elements (cones) produce colour vision—**chromatic sensation** whil the latter (rods) produce colourless vision—**achromatic sensation**. Colour blindness is caused b the absence or damage of cone system of vision. This fact regarding chromatic and achromati sensations, in fact, represents the biological division of labour, based on the principle of evolutio and the **duplicity theory** do is based on this evolutionary concept of vision.

The structural differences of rods and cones are shown in **Figure 7.3**.

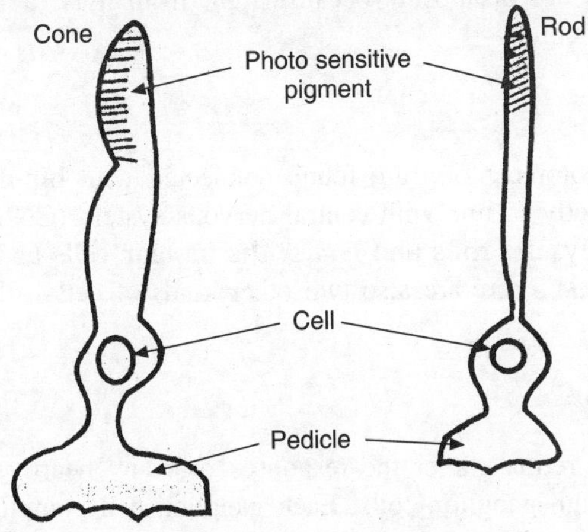

FIGURE 7.3 The structure of rods and cones.

The area or point in retina from where optic nerves exit is called **'blindspot'** as there is no photoreceptors (either cones or rods). Normally, we fail to notice blindness in this area because what we miss in one eye is registered by another eye and the information is filled by the brain that matches the background. **Table 7.1** shows the main differences between the rods and cones.

TABLE 7.1 Differences between rods and cones

Rods	*Cones*
1. Photoreceptors for scotopic (night) vision	1. Photoreceptors for photopic (daylight) vision
2. Sensitive to dim light	2. Sensitive to higher level of illumination
3. Responsible for colourless vision (*i.e.* white or grey sensations)	3. Responsible for chromatic (colour) vision
4. Useful to detect large and moving objects in periphery of vision	4. Structurally short and tapered
5. Structurally thin and cylindrical in shape	5. Cones provide acuity of visiont

7.2.2 Detecting Blind Spot

One may find his own blind spot by doing the following:

Cover the left eye and stare (gazing intently) at the × (see **Figure 7.4**) while moving the book closer. Move the book slowly, when it is very close (a few inches away from eye), the dot

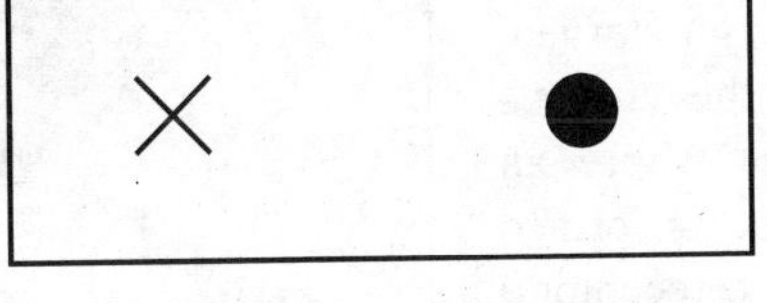

FIGURE 7.4 Detecting the blind spot.

will disappear. You may also need to move the book up and down a little. You need to stare hard at × for this work. The dot disappears because light from it is falling on the blind spot which contain neither rods nor cones.

The optic nerves

The rods and cones (photoreceptors) are found connected with **bipolar cells** and **ganglion cells**. These two cells are directly in line with central nervous system (CNS). Thus, the 'axon' fibres of three-layered cells namely, **the rods and cones**, **the bipolar cells** and **the ganglion cells** together make up the **optic nerves**. There are also two other kinds of cells—the **horizontal** and **amacrine cells** in the optic disc.

Pathways to brain

The bipolar cells in the retina gather the responses of many nearby receptors and send them to the cerebral cortex through ganglion cells. Each ganglion cell combines the impulses from many bipolar cells and transmit them to the brain through the visual pathway. The axon fibres of the ganglion cells bundled together, making up the optic nerves and carries the visual information from eye to brain.

The optic nerve leads to specialized area at the back of the brain called 'occipital lobe'. It decodes the encoded messages sent by the photoreceptors (nerve impulses) and conveyed through the optic nerves. In decoding the message, help of memory is taken through the mental process of retrieval and thus, we are able to recognize (perceive or sense) what is out there?

The bundled axons of the ganglion cells from both eyes (optic nerves of the two eyes) first travel to the base of the brain and from the 'optic chiasm' (×-shaped intersection). At the 'optic chiasm', stimuli from the left visual field are sent to the right occipital lobe and from the right visual field to the left occipital lobe for further processing (see **Figure 7.5**).

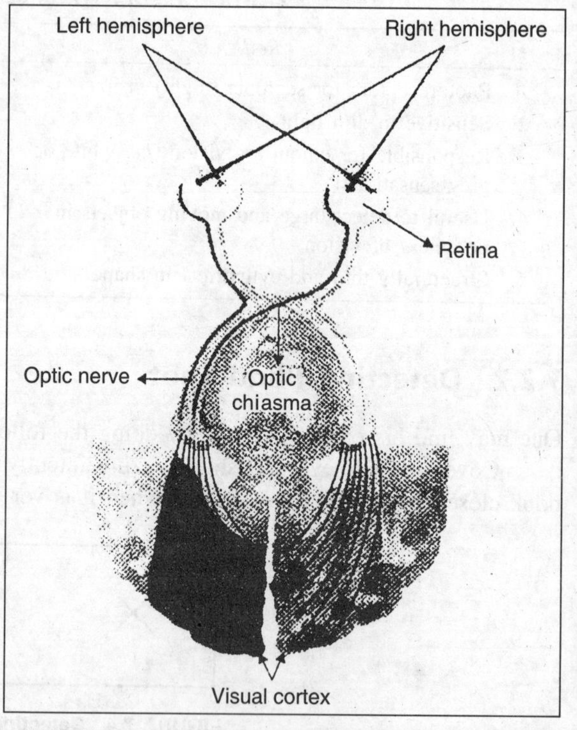

FIGURE 7.5 Pathways in the human visual system.

7.2.3 How Does the Visual Sensation Occur?

The visual stimulus (rays of light) that impinges on eye are partly cut off by the iris and by the sclera. Thus, only those rays that pupils admit are allowed to enter. These rays, in turn, pass through cornea, the aqueous humour, the lens, the vitreous humour and fall on the retina where an image of the light reflecting object is formed and the sensitive elements (photo-receptors) on the retina get excited. These receptors are specialized in encoding the photic stimulation and transforming or converting into neural energy which are conveyed through axon fibres of optic nerves via visual pathways to the visual cortex (occipital lobe) in the brain and thus, the visual sensation takes place. In the process of light rays passing through the transparent elements from cornea onto retina, some reflexive adjustments do occur by flexing and relaxing functions of ciliary muscles and suspensory ligaments that permit the only admittable amount and intensity of light rays to enter the visual mechanism.

7.3 DUPLICITY THEORY OF VISION

In course of discussing the anatomical structure of retina and the photoreceptors found on retina, a reference of 'duplicity theory of vision' has been made. This theory has been propounded by **Von-Kries** (1834) and **Schultz** (1876). They believe that all the phenomena of visual sensations can be explained in terms of the functional characteristics of two systems of vision—the **rod system** and the **cone system** (duplicity theory). The main assumptions of the theory are:

(a) Rods and cones are the two main sensitive elements of visual sensations.
(b) These two systems are not uniformly distributed on the retina, rather are evenly distributed.
(c) Rods are active in dim light and are responsible for achromatic sensations of varying brightness such as white, grey and black. The cones on the contrary are responsible for chromatic sensations (sensations of colour—red, green, yellow, etc.) and are active in bright daylight vision.

Most of the phenomenal aspects of visual sensations can be explained on the basis of this two-tier system of vision. For example, some of the facts are explained below:

Visual threshold: Visual threshold refers to the minimal amount of physical stimulus energy that can make the rod and cone systems (the two sensitive elements of retina) active. In case, the physical energy is below this minimal level or amount, the two systems do not respond. According to the duplicity theory, the visual threshold depends upon the portion of retina excited. In the middle portion of retina, the rod system is more in number and, therefore, we may sense even the dim-lighted object as larger portion of this system in the retina get excited and make a response. Whereas, we may have visual sensation of the object only when the illuminating condition is strong enough to excite the focal area (fovea) where more number of cones are found.

Spectrum: The spectral luminosity such as photopic vision and scotopic vision differs because of the difference in the luminous area of the spectrum. In photopic vision the entire visual spectrum is visible and the most luminous part is somewhat near to 555 mμ, *i.e.* greenish-yellowish. In twilight, the reddish end of the spectrum is relatively poor in brightness resulting in dark visibility whereas no decrement in brightness is found at the violet end of the spectrum. Hence, in twilight, the visual spectrum becomes narrower. These phenomena in photopic and scotopic visions are known as **Parkinje phenomenon** or **effect**. **Parkinje** was a physiologist who belonged to **Bohemia** and studied the length of visual spectrum under bright and dim luminous states. In everyday life situations also, we may find the instances of Parkinje effect, *viz.* during darkness of night, the greener leaves of the rose plant is visualized as brighter than the red coloured flowers of the plant.

Visual adaptation: The receptors constantly adapt to the varying (different) intensities of light. When an individual is exposed to illuminating environment from a dark, immediately for a while, he feels difficulty in visualizing anything. But after a few moments (approx. 30 to 60 seconds), the receptor cells become adapted to the illuminating conditions of the environment and he finds no difficulty in visualizing the things. This is **light adaptation**. Similarly when one moves to the dark from bright illuminous environment, nothing is visible for a while but after a few moments he is able to see things in dark environment. This is called **dark adaptation**. However, dark adaptation takes some longer duration as compared to light adaptation. Such phenomena are due to the attribute of adaptiveness of the photoreceptors.

Visual acquity: According to duplicity theory of vision, the visual acquity depends upon intensity of light, distance of stimuli, duration of vision, background and angle of retinal stimulation.

Colourblindness: According to Von-Kries, the phenomenon of colourblindness is the result of deficiency of cone receptors or their weaknesses. Complete colourblindness occurs when the cone system is damaged either due to injury or any kind of disease.

No doubt, the duplicity theory of vision hold good in explaining some important phenomena or facts of visual sensation as discussed above. However, many other facts remain unanswered.

7.4 COLOUR VISION

The visual sensory mechanism or system receives, transduces and conducts the encoded light energy (nerve impulses) reflected by the stimulus (objects) and not the object itself such as the silver plane in the sky, or a red flower or a blue pencil. Each of these stimuli reflects light energy that act upon the transducers (rods and cones). But, the viewers of the objects experience them in their characteristic colours. Colours are actually in the brain. **Dr. Earnest W. Kent**, a Professor of Physiological Psychology at the University of Illinois (1981) expressed the view that 'redness' and other perceptions of colours are in our brain. To quote him:

> 'A moment's reflection will demonstrate that, strictly speaking, there can be no such things as a red object. The object's redness is solely determined by whether or not it possesses those properties necessary to reflect light of a particular wavelength.... Can we say that 'redness' is a property of the light. 'No, because the only relevant property of the light is its wavelength, and wavelength is not colour. Colour is a property of your sensation' (Kent, 1981, p. 46).

It is evident that experience of colour is a mental event, but it is also related to physical characteristics of the stimuli. Hence, there exists a psychophysical relationship between the physical stimuli (light) and the experience of colour. Let us now examine this relationship in some greater detail.

7.4.1 Psychophysical Relationships

Visual experience indeed is not just the patches of light and shadows, rather sensory input of vision are processed to produce various experiences about the quality or properties inherent in an object such as size, shape, form, hue (colour), distance, brightness etc. This evidences the fact that there exists some relationship between the physical stimulus and various aspects of experiences that result from processings. Form, brightness and hue are the salient characteristic features of any visual experience. Further, the hue may be more or less mixed with white, *i.e.* more or less saturated. Thus, the characteristic features of visual experiences are form, brightness and hue which are briefly discussed below:

Form

As a basic rule, perception of any form depends upon differences in the amount of energy focused on the retina. Thus, some parts of the perceived scene are lighter than others with an outline that seperates the darker portion from the lighter ones. In other words, it is the pattern of energy that is projected on the retina and determine 'form' in vision. For example, when we look at the sun, a patch on the retina will be extremely bright and the light projected by the sky will be relatively less bright.

Hue

Hues refer to names of colours that we ordinarily experience such as red, green, yellow etc. Thus when we say a visualized object is red, it means a red hue, greenish-blue a greenish blue hue and so on. Hue depends primarily on wavelength of light. But, if several wavelengths mix together, the hue will depend upon the dominant wavelength in the mixture. If, however, all wavelengths of the visible spectrum are mixed together, the experience is 'white light'. The experience of hue (colour) and corresponding wavelengths are shown in **Table 7.2**.

TABLE 7.2 Colours with corresponding wavelengths

Wavelengths	*Experience of colour*
760 mμ	
	Red
580 mμ	
	Yellow
510 mμ	
	Green
480 mμ	
	Blue

Thus, hue is a sensory experience which is produced on stimulation by a particular wavelength of light. Such light is called homogenous light.

Although, hue primarily depends upon the wavelength of the radiant energy, intensity of stimulation is also a contributing factor. In addition, experience of hue is also dependant upon the background against which an object is viewed. This is known as **contrast effect**.

The relationship of hue to wavelength is shown in **Figure 7.6** in which the experienced hue and their corresponding wavelengths are depicted in an arranged order in the colour circle.

Brightness

Physical basis of brightness is primarily the energy of the light source. It corresponds to the amplitude (height) of the wave. But, brightness also depends upon the wavelength. For instance, yellow appears relatively slightly brighter than certain red and blue wavelengths even though all three are of equal amplitudes. Brightness in fact is the perceived intensity of light as is with loudness which represents the perceived intensity of sound.

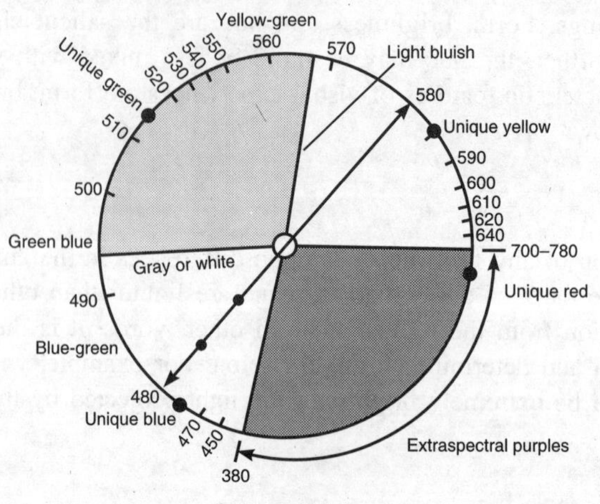

Colour circle

FIGURE 7.6 The arrangement of various hues and their corresponding wavelengths on a colour circle. Points opposite each other in the unshaded sections represent complementary hues while those in the lightly shaded sectors have no complements in the visible spectrum.

Saturation

Saturation refers to the apparent purity of colour or hue. Saturation is the degree to which a light colour is diluted or not diluted by whiteness. Many colours appear as mixed grey. A highly saturated colour appears to be pure hues without any grey, whereas, low saturated colour appears close to grey. Saturation depends upon the complexity of lightwaves. A wave composed of only one or minimum number of wavelengths will produce highly saturated colour. But, light waves composed of many components will result in low-saturated colour. Saturation also depends upon brightness. As a colour becomes brighter (merges with bright) or darker (merges with dark or black) begins to lose its apparent purity and looks less saturated. Thus, change in brightness is accompanied by a reduction in saturation. For example, let us examine pink and deep red. Both have almost similar hues but pink is relatively less saturated than deep red. Hence, lightness or deepness of a colour or hue depend on the degree of saturation. For instance, you take 1 gm of a colour and mix it in a glass of water. Next, you mix two glasses of water in the same amount of colour (1 gram) and inspect the two solutions. You will find that the former solution is deeper than the latter because the former is relatively highly saturated than the latter solution. However, the hue of the two solutions is the same. Saturation can also be explained with the help of a spindle as shown in **Figure 7.7**.

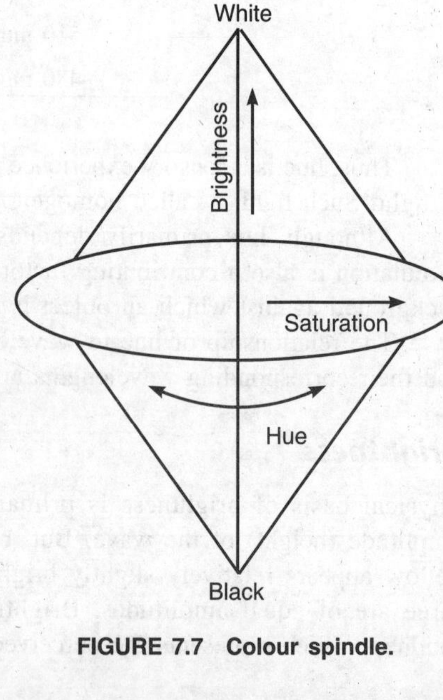

FIGURE 7.7 Colour spindle.

In Figure 7.7, saturation is the distance outward from the central axis. The pure colours (highly saturated colour) lying on the outer edge have the highest saturation.

Grey at the centre (zero saturation) and the muted muddy and pastel colours with intermediate saturation lie in-between.

7.4.2 Some Important Facts Relating to Colour Sensation

Colour mixture

Human beings with normal vision are wonderfully prepotent to distinguish large many colour shades—approximately 7 million different shades. Hence, as human beings, we are rich enough in our sensitivity to different kinds of colours and shades. The sensitivity of females in distinguishing large many colour shades is far more richer than males. The relevant question is that the primary colours are only four in number. Other colour shades are the products of mixture of these primary colours in different proportions. The colours produced by mixing the primary colours are called secondary colours. The shade of secondary colours depends upon the proportion in which two primary colours are mixed together. For instance, suppose in a mixture, the red is more in proportion than yellow, it will produce an orange hue with dominant shade of red. Similarly, if in a mixture, the proportion of blue is more than red, it will appear violet with dominant bluishness.

An important fact in this context is that some colours are complementary while others are non-complementary. When two complementary colours are mixed together in equal proportions, the two cancel out each other and produce the sensation of grey. But if the two non-comple-mentary colours are mixed together, the two instead of cancelling out each other, produce the experience of a new colour, *viz.* red-yellow, red-blue etc.

Mixing any two or more than two colours is what we call **colour mixing**. There are three ways of mixing colours:

(a) **Retinal mixture:** In this method, two or more colours on a revolving wheel are very rapidly moved together in such a way that the two wavelengths are fused and projected onto the retina that give an experience of a new third colour.

(b) **Additive mixture:** In this method, different wavelengths of primary colours are added together and projected onto a screen in such a way that produce an experience of outrightly a different colour as we see on T.V. screens.

(c) **Subtractive mixture:** In this method, the pigments and not the light waves are mixed together. This method is most frequently used by painters and artists in their paintings.

On the basis of above methods of colour mixing, the researchers have formulated some laws of colour mixing. These are as follows:

(a) When two complementary colours are mixed together in a particular proportion, the two cancel out each other and produce the sensation of grey with brightness equal to the average brightness of the two colours.

(b) When two non-complementary colours are mixed together, it produces an experience of a new colour with brightness equal to the average brightness of the two.

(c) When the pairs of complementary colours (*e.g.* red-green or blue-yellow) are mixed together, it produces the experience of grey with brightness which is equal to the average brightness of the pair.

It should be remembered here that when the two primary colours are mixed together, some parts of the wavelengths of each other are absorbed and thus the experience of another colour corresponds to the reflected wavelength, *i.e.* post-absorption length of the wave.

At this point, it is also worth knowing that in the colour mixture, the sensation of another colour is determined by the dominant colour of the mixture.

After-image effect

For every colour, there is a complementary colour (hue). Sensation of this complementary colour is second sensation of colour that follows the original colour sensation. This is called after-image. In other words, when we see a colour for some time, a visual image of the seen colour persists for a while onto the retina. As a result, when the originally visualized colour stimulus is removed, the person experiences the presence of the visualized colour that gradually appears as grey.

After-image is of two types—**positive after-image** and **negative after-image**.

Positive after-image: Positive after-image refers to experiencing the same colour after the original colour is removed. For example, if you fixate your eyes on a red-coloured object for some time and when the object is removed from your visual field you still experience the presence or visualize the same colour even after its removal, this phenomenon is called positive after-image. It so happens because of the persistence or continuation of the neural processings in the retina following stimulation of the original stimulation with characteristic colour for sometimes. However, this phenomenon is rare and very brief in duration.

Negative after-image: In this event, the after-image takes complementary colour. If you fixate your eyes on a piece of yellow paper (without allowing your eyes to waver), the border of the papers will soon take on a bluish tinge (complementary colour). Even the yellow itself would appear to fade (*i.e.* seem to lose saturation). For example, look at a white paper, you will see a patch of blue—which is complementary to yellow. Most of the researchers opine that this happens due to retinal fatigue.

A negative after-image, such as the above mixes with a currently sensed colour which may be predicted on the basis of law of colour mixture, *viz.* if a blue after-sensation is projected on orange surface, the orange and blue after-images are combined and produce the sensation of red-purple.

Colourblindness

Normal individuals are able to recognize different colours of the spectrum and differentiate the hues which appear different to them. But, there are some such persons who even sense the different colours differently but are unable to differentiate the apparent differences in their hues (colour). Such persons are referred to **colour-weak**. Again, there are some who are unable to see colours. Such persons are called **colour-blind**. This state is largely genetic and sex-linked characteristics which is mostly found in males (approximately 0.8 per cent) while in females, the percentage is low (0.3 per cent).

Thus, the basic difference between normal person and colour-blind is that hues which apppear different to the normal person look the same to the colour-blind. Normal persons are able to differentiate all kinds of colours based on three wavelengths—700 mμ (red), 546 mμ (green and yellow) and 435 mμ (blue). Though primary colours are four in number—red, green, yellow and blue, however, on the basis of only three wavelengths, a normal person is able to recognize all the four primary colours. The wavelength of yellow is able to produce sensation of two hues—yellow and green. Thus, this is known as **trichromatic theory of colour sensation**.

'John Dalton', an eminent British chemist, was the first to recognize this defect (colour-blindness). He was himself a colour-blind who described his own state of colour sensation in 1794 stating that the blood looked to him 'not unlike the colour called bottle green'. This description by Dalton was the beginning of a systematic study of colour blindness.

The colour-blind defect has been found to take several forms such as red-green blindness, blue-yellow blindness and total colourblindness.

Red-green blindness: The study of red-green blindness is important on two counts—first because of the frequency with which it occurs and second, because of the colours which are confusing. As the name suggests, such persons experience difficulty in recognizing or differentiating these two colours. In males, this kind of partial colourblindness are found to be approximately 4 per cent while in females the percentage is approximately .088.

'Rivers'* has classified red-green blinds into two distinct classes—(a) Deuteranopes and (b) Protanopes.

(a) **Deuteranopes:** Deuteranopes are those persons who can only experience the blue and yellow colour sensations, but whose spectrum is of normal length.

(b) **Protanopes:** Protanopes are those persons whose colour system again consists of blue and yellow, but who, in addition, have the spectrum shortened and cut off at the red end. Yellow forms the maximal point of brightness in the former (deuteranopes) and green in the case of the latter (protanopes).

However, all such cases are not so extreme. General findings suggest that there are different degrees of colourblindness extending from extreme cases of blue-yellow blindness to milder cases of those in whom red and green is not complete.

Blue-yellow blindness: Such weaknesses refer to defect in differentiating between blue and yellow wavelengths, congenital factors (genetic) could not have yet been definitely established. Such colour-blinds are also called **'tritanopes'**. However, some cases of lack of blue receptors and weaknesses of yellow receptors have been reported. But, by and large, the defect is thought to be acquired that accompany pathological changes in the retina. **Richardson** describes tritanopia as a defect of confusing the yellow and blue hues.

Tetranopes: Tetranopes are also a kind of colour blindness in which all colours are experienced either as red or green. An ordinary individual experiences a wavelength below 470 mμ as violet, whereas tetranopes experience 'red' and all wavelengths ranging between 470 mμ and 580 mμ are experienced as green while a normal person experiences all hues—red, blue, yellow that fall in this range of wavelength.

Total colourblindness: Total colour-blinds have monochromatic vision. Though, total colourblindness is a rare phenomenon, its occurrence cannot be disputed. The spectrum of total colour-blinds resembles a colourless band whose parts differ only in luminosity. Such persons are unable to experience any colour whatsoever.

Total colourblindness also takes two distinct forms. In one form, the point of maximal brightness lies in the region of the yellow while in the other form, it lies in the region of green—

* Article on vision in Schaffer's *Textbook of Psychology* cited in *Experimental Psychology*—Mary Collins and James Drever (1949) (Methuen & Co. London).

a condition that resembles to dark adapted eyes (achromatopia)*. In a number of cases, the 'achromatopia' has been found to be accompanied by an 'absolute central scotoma'. This refers to a condition in which the central point of vision—fovea—is not only blind to colour but can also experience no light of any kind. It is totally blind. Although, beyond fovea, vision may be practically normal.

Acquired colourblindness: In some cases, instances of acquired colour blindness may also be noted which are generally of temporary nature. One of the predisposing causes of this phenomenon is excessive use of tobacco. In some cases use of certain drugs such as santonin may also cause acquired colour blindness. The defect is progressive in nature. However, such defects can be improved.

7.4.3 Contrast Effect

Earlier, we have described the phenomenon of negative after-image or after-effect. This after-effect is in fact, the contrast effect known as **successive contrast** in which the removal of the original colour stimulus is followed by the appearence of its complementary colour. Such as if red is projected on a grey background, the after-image that it is likely to yield will be green (complementary to red).

In the same manner, the phenomenon of **simultaneous contrast** is also noticed, *i.e.* the contrast effect occurs simultaneously when the stimulus is still present, not withdrawn (contrast effect after withdrawal of original stimulus is called **successive contrast effect**). Simultaneous contrast occurs while visualizing a coloured object, because each area that stimulates the retina is modified by the surrounding areas. Hence, if a yellow patch of colour is placed against a colourless background, it will be observed that round the edge of the yellow, the background will assume a bluish tinge. The contrast effect is enhanced when the whole is covered with tissue paper because it serves to make the colour-edge defined and the consequential contrast effect is strengthened. However, when the tissue paper is removed, the contrast often disappears because the strong edges of the coloured patch cause the contrast to be subjectively destroyed. Similarly, if a colourless patch (black, white or grey) is placed on a coloured square, it assumes the complementary of its background, *viz.* a grey patch on a red square acquires greenish tinge, a grey patch on green also assumes the complementary colour of the patch. This is what we call **simultaneous contrast effect**. The colour that causes change in colourless patch is called **inducing colour** and the colour that it assumes is called **induced colour**. On prolonged fixation, these contrast effects disappear and the stimulus colour induces its own colour on the colourless surface. This is known as **simultaneous induction.**

Brightness contrast effect

Contrast effects are also influenced by the brightness of the colour. It is strongest when the two surfaces are of equal brightness. This can be easily demonstrated. If a strip of green paper is placed on a black background and a strip of similar brightness and hue is placed on a white background, the difference in the visibility of the two backgrounds may be noticed. The green on black would appear deeper and more saturated, the green on white would however appear lighter. This change in colour field follows the fundamental law of opposites—**a dark background**

* Achromatopia: Complete colour blindness, only monochromatic grey is visible.

makes neighbouring colour brighter while a light background makes it darker. The same law holds good with a colourless surface on a colourless background. A grey patch looks brighter or darker according to the background which is either black or white. Such effects are called **brightness contrast**.

The contrasting effect does not require the surfaces to be one on the top of the other, what is needed is that the two surfaces are adjacent to one another. Nearer the fields, greater is the contrast. Further, the contrast effects are not uniform throughout. It is strongest round the edges where the two surfaces adjoin. This is termed **marginal contrast** (Randkontrast) which is distinguishable from the contrast effect of the remainder of the area which is termed as **surface contrast** (Flachenkontrast). Similarly, the size of the area also affects contrast. If a small piece of white paper on a large black square and a larger white piece of paper is placed on a similar background will not appear similar as the smaller area is more conducive to stronger contrast as compared to larger area.

7.5 THEORIES OF COLOUR VISION

Till now we have been dealing with some of the wonderful complexities of colour vision. However, the question remains that how and what processes take place that can be applied to explain these kinds of experiences. To answer this, researchers have attempted to understand the nature of neural input (the afferent code) that enables us to experience hues, brightness, form etc. which are the characteristic features of colour vision. In this context, some theories of colour vision have been propounded. Some of the most important theories are as follows:

7.5.1 The Young-Helmholtz Theory

'The Young-Helmholtz' theory was first propounded in 1801 by '**Thomas Young**' and subsequently in the year 1860 by **Helmholtz**.

Basically, this theory is based on three elementary colours—carmine red (a red-bluish than the extreme red of the spectrum), yellowish-green and ultramarine blue which are sufficient to produce all colour and colourless sensations. The theory assumes that human eyes contain three types of cones, each one of which is sensitive or responsive to one of the three elementary colours named above. When all the three types of cones are equally stimulated, the resultant sensation is white. Hence, there are **trichromatic cones** (tri = three, chromatic = colours), each responsive to one chrome (colour). Thus they could demonstrate in their experiments and found that perception of any colour can be produced by proper addition of light at short, medium and long wavelengths within the visual spectrum. More simply, the action of long wavelength of the spectrum affects the first, of the middle wavelength the second and the short wavelength affects the third, but lights of all kinds excite all the three fibres in varying degrees. In modern terms, the theory states that these three nerve fibres are replaced by three photo-chemical substances and when all three chemical substances are stimulated, the colourless or achromatic sensation occurs. When they are stimulated in varying proportions, all colours of the spectrum are produced. In absence of any stimulation, we experience the sensation of black.

Although, the theory very well accounts for the fact that different mixtures of wavelengths yield different colour sensations and also that mixture of complementary colours produce the sensation of white, many other facts are not supported by this theory. For instance, research studies reveal the fact that different mixtures of wavelengths yield different colour sensations. Similarly, the existence of three kinds of cone systems are also supported by colour mixing experiments. However, the notion of existence of different regions for specific wavelengths in the cortex is not supported. Similarly, some other facts such as 'after-image' simultaneous contrast and similar other facts are not well understood or explained by this theory.

7.5.2 The Hering's Theory

Another 19th century researcher **Ewald Hering** in 1878 proposed another theory based on six elementary colours—red, green, yellow, blue, white and black. This theory is known as **Opponent Process Theory** or simply **The Hering's Theory**. Hering proposes that the six elementary colours can be paired into 3 as—'red-green', 'blue-yellow' and 'white-black'. The components of each pair are complementary to each other and at the same time, opposed or antagonistic to one another.

Hering is of the view that colour vision depends on two-receptor system—one processes **red-green** pair while another processes **yellow-blue pair.** Since Hering Theory rests on only two kinds of receptor system, this theory is often called as **Hering's Dichromatic (two colour) Theory.** Hering has also proposed a third channel for achromatic experience of **white-black pair.**

In essence, Hering proposed that colour receptors are like **stop-and-go traffic signal**. A red-green receptor is able to signal either only red or green. Similarly, a yellow-blue receptor is able to signal only either yellow or blue. The signal transmitted by the receptor depends on the stimulus. But, unlike traffic signals, it also depends on the state of the receptors. For instance, if a receptor has been signalling for red, for a while the receptor would first continue to signal red, a phenomenon of **positive after-image** and then it would signal green (negative after-image) as it is recovered. Thus, in each receptor the two colours act like opponents. When one is suddenly stopped, the opponent colour takes over. For this reason, this theory is also called as **opponent process theory**. The opponent process of the receptor is due to building (anabolic) and breaking down (katobolic) processes which make perception of different colours through dichromatic receptors as is shown in **Table 7.3**.

TABLE 7.3 Perception of different colours through dichromatic receptors

Colours	*Building up/Breaking down processes*	*Receptor system or approaches*
Red	is caused by katabolism	In the red-green apparatus
Orange	is caused by katabolism	In the red-green apparatus
Yellow	is caused by katabolism is caused by katabolism	In the yellow-blue apparatus In the yellow-blue apparatus
Green	is caused by anabolism	In the red-green apparatus
Blue	is caused by anabolism	In the yellow-blue apparatus
Violet	is caused by katabolism is caused by anabolism	In the red-green apparatus In the yellow-blue apparatus
White	is caused by katabolism	In the white-black apparatus
Black	is caused by anabolism	In the white-black apparatus

According to Hering, black is a sensation: the intrinsic light of the retina (*i.e.* what is experienced when retina has been for a short time, devoid of any stimulation which by some is termed as sensation of black)—a **mean grey**. Brightness is accounted partly to the activity in the black-white apparatus and partly to their own specific brightness. The warm colours (red and yellow), possess an inherent darkness.

Recent developments suggest that both the theories are partially correct. **Mac Nichol** (1964) using **microspectrophotometry** procedure was able to gather information that provide evidences in support of Young-Helmholtz theory. At the same time, some recordings taken with micro-electrodes also lend support to opponent process theory (Devalois and Jacobs, 1958). Further worth mentioning support to Young-Helmholtz comes from research studies of Kimble (1977). Hence, both the theories seem tenable and call for further extensive research studies.

7.5.3 The Ladd-Franklin Theory

Ladd-Franklin's theory is known as **Molecular Dissociation theory** which is based on the developmental assumptions. The theory holds that colour vision is in the third stage of development. In the first stage only colourless sensations are experienced. These are produced by decomposition of the grey molecule which is found undifferentiated in the rods. The outer range of atoms of the molecule becomes **torn off** in decomposition and produces a chemical substance which stimulates the nerve endings of the retina.

In the second stage, the outer range of atom is affected by different vibration rates and the former single response get split into two classes that correspond to the sensation of yellow and blue. In the third stage, the yellow response is broken up again into two parts that produce the sensations of red and green. The red and green are not complementary. When the red and green are simultaneously decomposed, they revert to the sensation of yellow and when yellow and blue are decomposed together, it gives rise to sensation of white or grey. When all the three are stimulated, the original sensation of grey is produced.

Colourblindness is explained as being activistic condition. Total colourblindness is at the first stage of vision, red-green at the second stage where blue and yellow have remained undifferentiated. The rare instances of blue-yellow blindness indicates that **blue and yellow** were the **primitive forms** of colour vision and that red-green the last to be attained, which was lost earliest. This is well in tune with Franklin's theory, that the vibrating portions of the colour molecule that occasions 'red' and 'green' are developed out of the portion whose decomposition occasions 'yellow'.

7.5.4 Edridge-Green Theory

Edridge-Green theory lays emphasis on the presence of visual purple in the rods only. This is the only best known visual substance. According to this theory, the function of rod is to form visual purple but does not take part in visual sensations. Although the cones are devoid of visual purple, Edridge-Green claims to have seen four canals or depressions which conduct the visual purple into the fovea—the **centre of acutest vision**.

The theory assumes that colour vision has evolved. The spectrum first appears grey. The first differentiation causes the two extremes of red and violet to appear then green, yellow, blue and finally orange. Sometimes a seventh colour indigo can be perceived. Colour blindness is activistic, and all these six stages are represented in travelling from colour-blindness to normal vision.

This view has greatly been criticized as it is opposed to duplicity theory of vision which is almost an established theory. Further the proposed classification and the order of appearence of colours is also a matter of great dispute.

7.6 CURRENT TRENDS IN UNDERSTANDING COLOURS

In recent years, scientists have gathered ample evidences that support Young-Helmholtz's theory as well as Hering's theory of colour vision. For example, Mac Nichol (1964) using 'microspectro-photometry' procedure was able to identify three different kinds of light sensitive pigments in cone system. These were found sensitive to blue, green and the third one to yellow. The third pigment was sensitive even to yellowish red part of the spectrum (upto wavelength 650 mμ) and it was especially sensitive to yellow at 750 mμ. All these three cones also respond to wavelengths above and below the range of colour spectrum. Kimble has also collected evidences to support Young-Helmholtz's contentions.

Scientists have also gathered evidences in support of Hering's views. For example, Jacobs (1958) and Devolois et al. (1966) have gathered evidences that support stop-go-hypothesis of Hering.

As for Ladd-Franklin's view, not much evidences could have been gathered because of the complexity of the developmental stage postulation of Franklin.

In fact, the present day scientists have proposed two-stage theory of colour vision. This incorporates the views of both—Young-Helmholtz's and Hering's views. To them, colour vision is a matter of two stage processing. In the first stage, the retina with different light sensitive pigments get excited (Young-Helmholtz's view) and convey the colour signals to the visual cortex. In the second stage, the nerve cells in the visual system through opponent processing (Hering's view) encodes the signals which are conveyed to the visual cortex and thus, colour sensation is produced.

The scientists, however, are vigorously engaged in collecting more and more information so that a new theory may be formulated that could explain all related phenomena adequately.

7.7 THE AUDITORY SENSATION

Next to vision, audition is the secondmost important sensory channel which provides knowledge about the world around. Through this channel of information, one may become aware, learn about and appreciate the world. Hearing also enables us to understand speech which is the chief medium of communication and interpersonal interaction. Through sensing a sound, we receive great many signals and cues such as, the warning horns of automobiles, chime (rhythmic sound) of the clock, fire engine's siren, footsteps of approaching persons from behind etc. All such knowledge are important for our adjustment with the environment. In addition, hearing also provides great aesthetic pleasures through listening to music.

We shall now examine in some detail the sense of hearing (audition) which follows hereafter.

7.7.1 Stimulus for Hearing

Stimuli for hearing are sound waves. Sound waves are longitudinal mechanical waves that are produced by vibration of a physical objects (such as when one strikes a steel bar or a tuning fork).

We all know that air contain very minute particles (we often notice these particles dancing in the beam of light that enters to our rooms through a whole in the window). When sound is produced, the object vibrates, *i.e.* it makes a back and forth movement and forms longitudinal waves in the medium (such as solid, liquid and gas) through which it passes. It alternatively compresses and ratifies the air in the surrounding. This generates a pressure wave that is transmitted outward in all directions and moves through air much in the same way as ripples move on the water. These waves of vibrating particles serve as stimuli for audition.

Sound waves have frequencies and wavelengths, both. But it is measured in frequencies—the number of waves peak, arrive at a point (mechanoreceptors in the ears), and are expressed in cycles per second (CPS). The preferred unit of this measurement is Hertz (Hz), named after German physicist **Heinrich Rudolf Hertz**. Sound waves are primary sources of knowledge of time (in categories like now and then, before and after etc.). At the same time, it is the secondary source of knowledge of space also because it enables us to apprehend an object's position and distance from the sensing organism.

7.7.2 Characteristic Features of Sound Waves

Sine waves' are pure tone. It is the simplest variety of sound waves. It is simple, because it can be used in different ways to duplicate or analyse any other kind of wave. It can be mathematically expressed by the sine function of trigonometry. Hence, called sine wave. It is produced when a single vibrating object moves back and forth freely and causes change in the pressure of air as in a tuning fork. This back and forth movement forms a wave as shown in **Figure 7.8**.

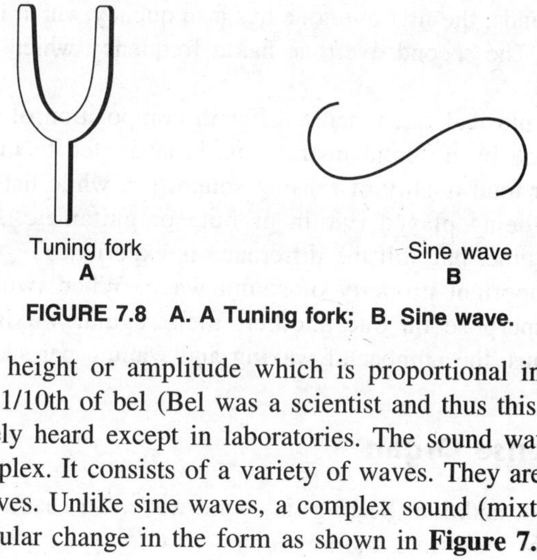

FIGURE 7.8 A. A Tuning fork; B. Sine wave.

Sound waves have height or amplitude which is proportional intensity and expressed in decibels (db) units. db is 1/10th of bel (Bel was a scientist and thus this unit is named after him).

Sine waves are rarely heard except in laboratories. The sound waves that we usually sense are not simple rather complex. It consists of a variety of waves. They are produced by the mixture of different frequency waves. Unlike sine waves, a complex sound (mixture of different frequency waves) wave shows a regular change in the form as shown in **Figure 7.9.**

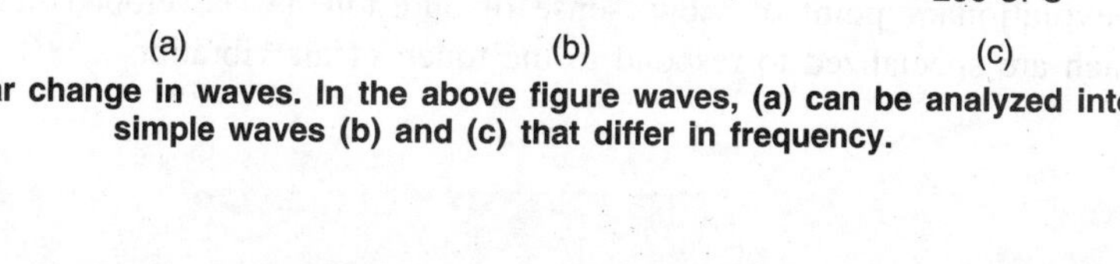

FIGURE 7.9 Regular change in waves. In the above figure waves, (a) can be analyzed into two sets of simple waves (b) and (c) that differ in frequency.

Sound waves are also classified as periodic and aperiodic. **Periodic** wave is one which has regular form and if there be any change, it changes at regular interval such as musical sound produced by a piano and other instruments. **Aperiodic** sound waves are irregular, *viz.* a noisy sound.

Thus, we notice that what we hear is a physical energy. Sound waves which have frequencies and amplitude, may be simple (pure) or mixed and periodic or aperiodic. These properties bear a relationship to the attributes of auditory sensation. For example, difference in frequencies of sound waves is related to the experience of **pitch**. Sound waves of low frequencies produce low pitch. Human mechanoreceptors usually respond to frequencies between 20 to 20,000 CPS. Suppose one hears two different waves—one vibrating at a rate of 250 CPS and another at a rate of 300 CPS. The difference in experience of these two waves will be the difference in pitch caused by number of cycles (frequencies) of two waves.

Experience of **loudness** is related to the amplitude or height of the waves. Greater the amplitude, louder is the experience of sound. However, loudness to an extent also depends on the frequencies of waves. Equally intense waves of lower frequencies are not as loud as those of higher frequencies. Thus, the threshold of intensity of sound lowers with increase in frequency. Human ear is most sensitive to frequencies between 512–2048 CPS. Sound waves of much lower intensities within this range can produce sensation of hearing.

Timbre is another attribute of audition which is related to the complexity of sound waves. Tone waves produced by a tuning fork is a pure (sine) while tone produced by a musical instrument (violin etc.) is complex as they can be analysed into sound waves of different frequencies. The tone of a lowest frequency is a **fundamental tone** and other tones are called **overtones**. In musical sounds, the first overtone has a frequency which is two times the frequency of the fundamental tone. The second overtone has a frequency which is three times that of the fundamental and so on.

However, different musical instruments differ in composition of overtones. The difference in total sensation produced by different instruments is attributed to these differences. The total effect is called **timbre** or total quality of sensing sound, *viz.* while listening to radio, one senses the type of instruments being played (violin or flute or guitar etc.). Each of these might be producing same musical tune, but still the difference is experienced.

Beat is also an important property of sound wave. When two sound waves of slightly different frequencies superpose on one another, then regular waxing and waning of sound intensity is produced. Thus, the number of waxing and waning per second is called **beat**.

7.7.3 Auditory Sense Organ

We know that stimulus for audition (hearing) is sound wave. To enable us to hear, it is necessary that our nervous system is set into motion. Physical energy of sound must be converted or transduced into electrical energy (nerve impulse) by the auditory receptors. This function is done by mechanical structure of ear within which the mechanoreceptors are found. Each mechanoreceptor cell ends in a brush of hairs projecting into a liquid substance which fills in the inner ear. These hair cells are the essential parts of the organ of hearing.

From evolutionary point of view, sense of audition has developed out of primitive sense of touch which are specialized to respond to the touch of air vibrations.

7.7.4 Anatomy of Human Ear

Figure. 7.10 shows the major structural parts of the ear which has three major parts—outer or external ear, middle ear and the inner ear. The outer or external ear collects the physical energy that passes onto middle ear and transmits the same to the inner ear where the physical energy is transduced into neural energy and conveyed to the auditory cortex in the brain and thus, the sense of audition takes place.

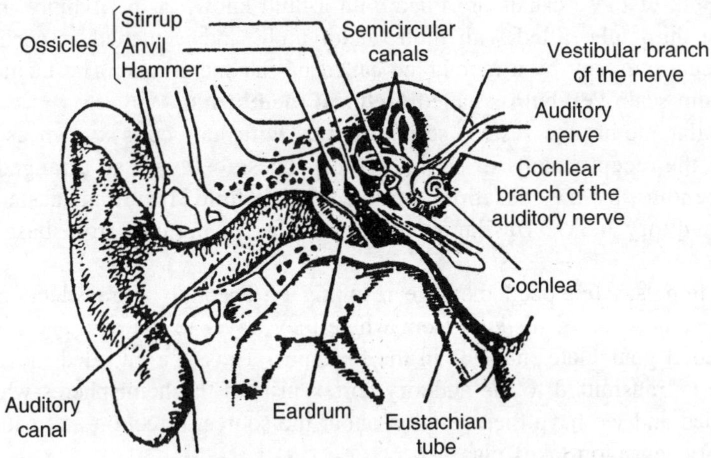

FIGURE 7.10 Structure of human ear.

The outer or external ear

The outermost part of the external ear is **pinna** that collects the energy (sound waves coming through the medium-air) and travels through a small air-filled duct called **auditory canal** or **scalmeatus** to the **eardrum** across the inner end of the canal (scalmeatus). It is a thin membranous structure, also called **tympanic membrane**. Alterations or vibrations due to the pressure of sound wave make this small membrane to move back and forth.

The middle ear

The middle ear begins from where the auditory canal ends. Eardrum is the enter-periphery of middle ear. Oscillations of eardrum, in turn, move the three small bones—the **ossicles**, so that the vibration is conducted through the middle ear to the entrance of cochlea in the ear. The ossicles or bones of the middle ear are connected like a series of levers causing mechanical transmission of energy by amplifying the energy. The bone closest to tympanic membrane is called **malleus** or **hammer**. This strikes the next bone **incus** or **anvil** and finally the **stirrup** or **stapes**. The flat side of **stapes** connects with the membrane called **oval window** from where the inner ear begins. The successive vibrations of these bones amplify the physical energy and transmit the concentrated energy to the primary organ of hearing, *i.e.* **cochlea** which is located in the inner ear.

The inner ear

The inner ear is contained in a bony structure spiralled like a snail and called **cochlea** (from Latin word meaning snail shell). The cochlea has three fluid-filled canals spiralling around together and separated from one another by membranes. These canals are **vertibular canal**, the **cochlear canal** and **tympanic canal**.

The complex structure of cochlea is the main organ of hearing. One of the three tubes—vertibular canal (the scala vertibuli) starts from oval window. Through it the vibrations are carried from base to the apex of the cochlea. At the apex, vibrations pass into the second tube the tympanic canal (scala tympany) which carries the vibrations from apex to the base and terminates at the round window. Both of these canals are filled with a fluid known a 'perilymph'. In between these two canals is the third tube filled with fluid 'endolymph' and is named as cochlear canal. It is separated from scala tympany by a membrane called basilar membrane. The membrane separating scale tympany from scala vertibuli is called **tactorial membrane**.

On the basilar membrane rests a series of rods with hair cells known as **organ of corti** (cilia) which are the receptor cells of sound stimuli. These cells are so arranged as to be set in a blowing and bending by the vibrations of surrounding fluid, resulting in starting of a nerve impulse in the auditory nerve. Basilar membrane varies in breadth from base to apex of the cochlea.

The nerve impulses (encoded message resulting on account of transduction process) reach first in the cochlear muscles of medulla from where they travel to the auditory cortex in temporal lobe through 'medial geniculate' nucleus in the thalamus. Thus, the encoded message in the form of nerve impulse is transmitted to the auditory cortex in both the hemispheres where the encoded message is decoded and we have the sensation about the source, direction and nature or quality of sound, *i.e.* auditory sensation takes place.

7.7.5 How Does Auditory Sensation Take Place?

As we have seen, sound wave is the appropriate stimulus for hearing. The air around us is not a vacuum but a collection of molecules that continuously move about at random exerting pressure and colliding with one another. Thus these molecules disturb the outer surrounding medium air and pushes the molecules of air to oscillate back and forth that spreads through air in the form of waves. These waves strike our ears and initiate a set of further mechanical pressure changes that trigger the auditory receptors located inside the internal parts of ear (cochlea). These receptor structures are called organs of corti (cilia). These receptors, on being excited, result in encoding of the sound waves, *i.e.* producing neural energy (auditory nerve impulse) that are transmitted to the auditory area of the cortex (temporal lobe) where the encoded message is 'decoded' and provides the sense of audition.

7.8 THEORIES OF HEARING (AUDITION)

Auditory experiences are complex and varied. It is amazing indeed, as to how does such a tiny subtle structure enables us to differentiate thousands of different kinds of tones? To find an answer to this question is very difficult because of the difficulties involved in investigating such a complex phenomenon. However, some physiologists, psychologists and physicists have made efforts to know many aspects and related facts about auditory experiences. These scientists have tried to gather physiological and physical aspects of audition and fit them together with the consequential aspects of auditory experiences. Such endeavours have resulted in the formulation of certain theories of audition that explains some of the important facts associated with auditory experiences. Some of the important such theories are as follows:

7.8.1 The Place or Resonance Theory

On the basis of excessive data made available by several research studies on 'audition' towards the turn of 19th century, **Herman von Helmholtz** propounded a theory of audition in the year 1863 which is known as 'Place or Resonance Theory of Audition'. In essence, the theory presumes that the fibres of 'basilar membrane' are series of resonating strings as we find strings arranged in a series in 'piano'. Since it resembles with 'piano'—sometimes it is also called **'Piano Theory'**. Each string of basilar membrane is attuned to a particular frequency of sound wave—narrow where high tones stimulate it, and wider where low tones stimulate it as is found in piano.

Helmholtz's analogy is like this—when one blow 'A' on a pitch pipe, 'A' string of piano vibrates. Similarly, when tone of certain frequency enters the ear the 'place' on the cochlea maximally sensitive to that frequency tone is activated. Thus, the theory assumes that each region of the basilar membrane is especially attuned to certain frequency of vibration. Since 'place' is so important in the theory, it is widely known as **'Place Theory'**.

Experience of **'pitch'**, according to this theory, depends upon the part of basilar membrane which is maximally responsive to the vibrating frequency. For this reason, sometimes the theory is also called—**'Pitch is Which'** theory, *i.e.* pitch is determined by which fibre is excited. It so happens because the afferent codes of different regions (places) or fibres on the basilar membrane go to different regions of the auditory area in the cortex and thus the different points of the cortex are the immediate correlates of a particular pitch experience.

Loudness, according to this theory, depends upon how much area or places of basilar membrane area excited. Greater the number of fibres activated, greater will be the experience of intensity. Thus, experience of loudness depends upon the spread or extensity of disturbance in either direction of the basilar membrane, whereas pitch experience depends upon the place which is maximally activated.

As for the other characteristics such as timbre, beat, mask etc. are concerned not much is known.

The theory of Helmholtz is supported by the cases of deafness. It is often found that some people are deaf to particular tones only and not for other tones.

Such instances are explained in terms of failure of the particular fibre to respond to the particular sound tone. Consequently deafness to a selective tone occurs—**'Mayers'** has reported the findings of an experiment done on dogs. It was found that when the lowest whorl of the cochlea was destroyed, the dog became deaf to low tones. This lends support to Helmholtz's assumption of 'pitch is which'. As he assumes, the fibres of the basilar membrane go on increasing series of length from its base to apex with shorter fibres at the base that respond to high notes and longer fibres towards the apex that respond to low notes. Hence, the instances of tone deafness lend support to Helmholtz's theory.

'Wever' and **'Smith'** (1944) have also in an experiment on animals found that different frequencies of vibrations are related to different fibres.

'Von Berkesy' (1957, 1961) also tested this theory in a series of experiements for which he was also awarded Nobel Prize. He performed one such experiment on guinea pigs. He made a small cut hole in the cochlea and observed with a microscope. He found that the narrower end of the basilar membrane was sensitive to high tones, while the intermediate tone frequencies caused displacement further towards the wider end. However, high tone frequencies were able to activate the entire membrane with equal displacement.

'Berkesy' further demonstrated that there are combinations of facilitations and inhibitions within the brain that sharpen the transmission and thus, it makes the theory tenable.

Limitations: But, Place Theory meets with certain difficulties with low tones. Some psychologists also opine that it is difficult to imagine as to how the fibres which range from decimal 04 to decimal 49 mm in length respond to tones ranging from 16 to 22000 vibrations.

'Ewald' while testing the Place theory suggests that physical principles other than response can explain how different regions of basilar membrane maximally respond to different frequencies.

Despite the above difficulties, the theory is significant as it is able to explain most of the phenomenon of auditory experiences satisfactorily.

7.8.2 The Frequency Theory

'Ernest Rutherford', a British physicist, has proposed the **'Frequency Theory'** or **'Telephone Theory'** of audition. This theory accounts for the entire range of hearing. According to him, frequencies of neural energies (impulses) are directly correlated with the frequency of sound wave. He believes that the 'cochlea' acts like a microphone and auditory nerve works like a telephone wire. Accordingly, 'pitch' depends upon the frequency of impulses travelling up to the auditory nerve. Therefore, greater the frequency, higher is the pitch. Thus, a tone of 10,000 Hz produces 10,000 evoked responses per second in the nerve, 500 Hz produces 500 responses and so on.

Loudness according to this theory is determined by the number of fibres activated.

Criticism: It is well known that an individual neuron can conduct only about 1000 impulses per second. Then how is it possible for the auditory nerves to transmit frequencies above this point? (because, a nerve takes an interval of at least 1000th part of a second for being reactivated). Hence, the ability of a neuron to produce neural impulses is limited. Therefore, it is difficult to assume the experience of pitch above the limited capacity. Hence, most scientists consider telephone theory as untenable.

7.8.3 The Volley Theory

Volley Theory was propounded by **Wever** and **Bray** (1930) that supplements the **Telephone Theory of Rutherford**. It is more commonly known as **Wever-Bray effect**. To explain the fact that we can experience frequencies much higher than the maximum frequency of nerve impulse a fibre is able to discharge, the theory suggests that the nerve fibres operate in groups and therefore, various fibres of the group react or discharge their volleys of impulses at different times. Thus, different groups of fibres fire up in a squad-like system. Thus, for instance, for a tone of 4000 CPS, there would be a spurt of activity in the auditory nerve every four thousandth of a second or once for every peak in sound wave but different groups of fibres would be responsible for the spurt each time.

To substantiate the above assumptions of the theory, **Wever** and **Bray** conducted an experiment on cat. The cochlea and auditory nerve of the cat were artificially desensitized and the cat was placed in a sound-proof room. The experimenters placed electrodes on the desensitized cochlea and nerve fibres connected with a radio amplifying system and a telephone receiver was also connected. Then sound vibrations of different frequencies were produced through the electrodes and it was found that the effects of such sound vibrations on the cochlea and nerve fibres were corresponding to the vibrating frequencies of sound which could be heard through the telephone receiver. This evidences the fact that the physical energy of sound has corresponding impact on auditory nerves.

Subsequently, **Davis** and his associates (1951) also found evidences in support of Wever and Bray's effect (Volley Theory). These researchers have explained this kind of effects in terms of **cochlear effect** which is mechanical in nature because the sound waves make corresponding exciting effect on the cochlea which is mechanical organ of hearing. Another effect is **neural effect** in which the vibrating tones activate the neural mechanisms correspondingly. The experimental observations done on these two kinds of effect shows high correlations between the vibrating frequencies of tones and their corresponding mechanical as well as neural effects on the auditory apparatus.

Though, the Volley Theory supplements the doubts raised by Telephone Theory, Volley Theory or its effect is also subjected to certain limitations and the efforts are in the offing to find an amicable answer to the raised questions.

7.9 CURRENT TRENDS

On the basis of ample research studies done by neuroscientists, physiologists and psychologists, it has currently been agreed that a combination of the Place Theory and Volley Theory would probably be more clear in explaining the phenomenon of audition. The Place Theory holds good for high frequencies (above 4000 Hz) while the Volley Theory does hold good for lower ranges of frequencies. Further, attempts are being done to formulate a general theory by taking into account the nerve coding patterns in the auditory pathways, cortex including various synaptic functions. In the present time, various scientists are actively engaged in researching on these aspects and gathering information that may explain the various complexities associated with and sensation of audition.

7.10 OTHER SENSES

The senses of vision and audition bring in most of the information we need to adjust to an ever-changing environment because they provide almost full picture of the things and other people of the world we live in. Other senses are, therefore, not considered relatively as significant as the senses of vision and audition. However, the other senses too are potentially important for survival and adaptation to the environment. For example, the senses of smell and taste may provide warning of dangerous gases and contaminated food that may endanger our lives. Further, they also produce pleasant or unpleasant affective feelings which in turn may initiate either approach or avoidant behaviours needed for adequate adaptation. Several receptors of skin are sensitive to touch, temperature, pain, quality of surface etc. and give signals to the brain about the dangers ranging from mosquitoes bite to hot plates. Similarly, the two proprioceptive senses provide information about postural positions of the body and movement of motion organs. These signals are in no way less significant for survival and adaptation.

Hence, a brief description of these senses is being presented herein below:

7.10.1 Smell

The sense for smell (olfaction from Latin word for smell) is a chemical sense and nose is the sense organ. The stimuli for olfaction are the various components which produce pleasant or unpleasant experiences ranging from the scent of perfume, and aromas of cookies to stinking of stench matters.

The nose is the receptive organ for smell. The smallest unit of a substance (a single molecule often composed of a few atoms) in the form of gas enters the nose and affects the **olfactory epitheliums**. The olfactory epithelium is located in the upper reaches of nose. The receptor structures in the epithelium are called **olfactory rods** (long and thin like a rod). At the tip of each rod are about half a dozen of **cilia**. The particles of chemicals interacting with cilia cause the signal. The axons from these cells join in two bundles—olfactory nerves and transmit the impulse to two structures. These structures are called the olfactory bulbs which extend out of the underside of the front brain (it is called bulbs because each ends is a bulb-like shape). From the bulbs, signals (impulses) move on into many areas of the cerebral cortex.

The scattering of signals is an unique feature of smell. Unlike other sense receptors, it does not travel through the thalamus (gateway or reception centre at the base of the brain from where the impulses are relayed to the specific areas). Rather the olfactory information is relayed by the comparatively odd network of neurons.

Another important aspect of olfactory sense system is that it was perhaps the first sense to develop in our most primitive ancestors (according to the theory of evolution as stated by **Ludel,** 1978).

Sensory experiences of smell vary widely from individual to individual and from time to time. Such variations are also attributed to psychophysiological states of the individuals in a given period of time.

7.10.2 Taste

Taste is the second sensation of chemical substances. Technically it is called gustation (from Latin word gust for smell and root word gusto).

The receptors for taste are specialized cells and grouped together in little clusters, called **taste buds**. These buds are located mostly on the top and sides of the tongue surface. A few of them are also found at the back of the mouth and in the throat. If you closely watch your tongue in front of a mirror, a number of large and small bumps are seen. These bumps are called **papillae** which are richly populated with taste buds. The walls of each of these bumps contain 200 or more taste buds (egg-shaped clusters of cells). Each of the taste cells in a taste bud has a kind of **antenna** (a hair-like cilium) which are similar to **cilia** extending from olfactory receptors. The taste cilia are bunched together forming a small tuft and extend into hole or taste pore in the walls of the **papillae**.

When substances enter our mouth, a portion of it dissolves in saliva and the solution bathes papillae. The dissolved molecules of substances flow over the cilia which triggers taste cells inside the bud.

Some variations in sensitivity to taste among individuals as well as the locations of the taste buds have been noted by the researchers. However, it is not clear how receptors are able to distinguish between different flavours. Current researchers have tried to construct a kind of spectrum for taste (gustation). Current theory assumes four basic tastes—sweet, sour, bitter and salty. Studies indicate that different portions on the tongue surface are sensitive to these four tastes. For example, honey and other sweet substances are tested at the tip of the tongue and bitter at the back. The middle area of the top of the tongue has fewer taste buds than other areas. Receptor cells of this portion transmit little sense impulses.

7.10.3 Skin Sensation

Skin sensations are called **cutaneous sensation**. These are four in number—pain, pressure (touch), warmth and cold. For all these sensations, there are four types of receptors.

The stimuli for pain are all those objects and forces that cause injury to the skin (pin, fire, chemicals etc.). The stimuli for pressure are all those objects and forces that depress the skin. These may be solids, liquids or gases (as strong wind). The stimuli for warmth and cold are the objects which are warmer or cooler than the skin itself. Skin temperature continually adapts to the environment. Hence, an object in a given temperature may be experienced as warm or cold only when the object's temperature differs from that of the skin.

The sense organs for the cutaneous senses are very small nerve endings in the skin. The pressure or touch system has four different types of receptors. Skin on hand's palm contains **Meissner corpuscles** to sense delicate touches. Skin with hairs has **basket nerves endings**. These are complex groupings around the base of the hair and do the same thing. In addition, there are **free nerve endings** throughout the skin which appear sensitive to gentle pressure. The small capsules called **Pacinian corpuscles** sense the deep pressures.

There are two **free nerve endings** which respond to temperature and are called **thermal receptors**. These receptors have not clearly been identified. However, on mapping the skin, cold and hot fibres have been plotted which respond to thermal variations.

Sensitivity of the skin senses vary from region to region. For example, lips and finger tips are found more acute than upper arms, upper thighs and back regions (Schmidt, 1978).

Failure to sense skin sensations are generally due to the effects of analgesic, aspirin, morphine and codein. In some cases, sound stimuli mask pain sensation called **acedio analgesia**. Some recent researches in 1980s (reported by Sobel, et al., 1982) suggest that music can heighten the production of **endorphins**—natural pain killing substance—produced by the body.

Skin sensations also fail when tissue damage occurs. Some people are born with inability to sense painful stimuli. This we call **congenital indifference to pain**. Its causes are unknown. Another reason for failure of skin sensation is tissue damage, such as in-burn injuries.

Kinesthetic sensation

Kinesthesis derives its origin from Greek word for motion. **Kinema** (which is also the root of cinema), which gives information to the brain (CNS) about the movements of joints, tendons and muscles. Though, we are seldom aware of the fact of any such signal transmitted to our CNS. However, such signals are of great significance for the brain to make various kinds of movements. If there be no kinesthetic impulse, it would not be possible for us to perform any coordinated actions or movements. Coordinated movements call for **feedback system** which is provided by kinesthesis. For example, if a muscle moves, it reports in, so to speak, that it has moved. Unless CNS has this feedback information, it cannot monitor the movement of the muscle.

Stimulus for kinesthesis

The source of stimulation for kinesthesis comes from the body itself. Everytime when one flexes an arm, make a fist or turn head suddenly, knitter or knits, there is a movement in the muscles, joints or tendons which stimulate a set of sense receptors in the body. These receptors are known as proprioceptors (the word proprio comes from Latin word **proprius** meaning one's own).

Receptors

Kinesthetic receptors are scattered throughout body under the skin in the walls of blood vessels, in coverings of bones and at other locations. Their signals indicate movement of body parts relative to each other.

Sensitivity to relative motion varies throughout the body. Many experiments show that the larger joints such as the hip and the shoulder are more sensitive than smaller parts, *viz.* Geldard (1972) suggests that no people are better equipped to sense raising of arms than pointing of fingers.

The sense of balance

'The sense of balance' is also called **labyrinthine sense** because cues of body position comes from the receptors located in the 'labyrinth' or inner ear called **vestibular receptors**. The term **vestibular** comes from Latin word meaning **entrance**. These receptors are not related to the sense of hearing, but helps us to adjust the forces on our bodies during tilting, bending and turning.

These sensors are located in three covered bony tubes called **semicircular canals**. These canals carry a fluid which moves whenever we turn or rotate our head. At the base of each canal, these fluids bathe a small jelly-like mass which act-like a soft plug in the tube. Sticking into this plug are **cilia** (similar to hair-like cells in cochlea). These respond with a nerve impulse when the fluid pushes against them and transmitted to the central nervous system (CNS). In this way, the CNS participates in maintaining equilibrium. In addition to these canals, the sense organs also include the other cavities in the bone near cochlea. These cavities are filled with small crystals that respond to gravity (static sense). These respond to the position or tilt of the head.

Just as kinesthesis, we are seldom aware of our sense of balance. It is automatic.

Researchers are of the opinion that damage to these canals leads to a crippling disability (Hueller, 1965). In humans, damage to any one of the canals leads to dizziness, vomiting, changes in heart rate and perspiration and difficulty in maintaining normal body posture.

Organic sensitivity

Free nerve endings are also found throughout our bodies, wherever blood vessels go. Some of these nerve endings are for pain reception and others for various other kinds of sensations such as feeling of being upset stomach, heaviness or congestion in chest, bowel tension, flatulence etc. In fact, there are quite a good number of other feelings that come from inside our body. All these are grouped together and called organic sensitivity, however, not much is known either about the receptors or about the way they make connections with the CNS to produce organic sensations.

SUMMARY

- As information gathering system, sensations are of various kinds. Of these, the senses of vision and audition are most important because through these senses, we become aware of most of the things of the world around us. Moreover, with every changes in the environment, we make adjustive behaviours on the basis of information received through visual and auditory senses.
- Visual sensation is the most important sensory experience. The stimulus for vision is the radiant energy received from light sources, and the sense organ for vision is our eyes.
- The structure of eye is very complex. It is a very small apparatus consisting of three layers, namely the sclera, choroid and retina.
- The receptors for light stimuli are found on the retina. These are of two kinds—rods and cones. These structures differ in size and shape as well as responsiveness. Rods give achromatic vision while cones produce chromatic vision. These receptor structures are not uniformly distributed on the retina, rather evenly distributed.
- There is a small depressed point on the retina which is called fovea—the point of clearest vision as larger number of cones are densely found around this region.
- The receptors transduce the light energies into neural energy which is transmitted to the visual area of the cortex through optic nerves. The visual cortex decodes the neural energy and thus we sense the visual objects.
- Colour vision is an important characteristic visual experience. Colours have the characteristics of hue, brightness and saturation.
- Various theories of colour vision have been proposed such as Young-Helmholtz theory, Hering's theory, Ladd-Franklin's theory, Edridge-Green theory etc.
- Next to vision, audition is the secondmost important sensation.
- The stimuli for audition are sound waves and the receptors (mechanoreceptors) are located inside the ear.
- Ear has three major parts—external ear, middle ear and the inner ear.
- The auditory receptors—organ of corti are found inside cochlea—the most sensitive organ of audition. These receptors transduce the vibrating sound waves into neural energy which are transmitted to the auditory area through auditory nerves and then we have the sensation of audition with characteristic features of sound such as pitch, loudness, timbre etc.
- Scientists have propounded various theories to explain and describe auditory sensation. Among these, the theory of Helmholtz (Place theory), Rutherford's Telephone theory and Wever and Bray's Volley theory are important.
- Besides, we also have sensations of smell, touch or cutaneous sensation, thermal sensation, taste or gustation sense, kinesthetic sensation, sense of balance and organic sensations.
- From the point of view of adjustment with the external and internal environment, these sensory experiences are also of great value as through these senses, we get signals of danger and thus central nervous system (CNS) prepares to cope with the situation.

CHAPTER 8

Perceptual Processes

8.1 INTRODUCTION

While introducing psychology in Chapter 1 of this book, psychology has been defined as a study of adjustive human behaviours. As we have seen in preceding chapters, the organism or an individual is constantly surrounded by various kinds of objects, persons, situations and different kinds of events occuring every now and then. All these forces of the environment exert impacts in our interactions with these varied forces. These interactions involve becoming aware of the diverse forces, sensing them sensibly and meaningfully and responding to them understandably. Merely becoming aware of the environmental forces is what we call sensation which is the primary and simplest mental process of cognition. However, for making adjustment or responding with a sense, mere awareness is not enough. We need to organize the information in a meaningful whole, identify the objects by abstracting it from the other objects, anticipating their effects. All these aspects of mental experiences are perceptions. Without perceiving the world, adjustive behaviour is not possible. Thus, perceiving is an important aspect of our mental cognition. The present chapter is therefore devoted to this important aspect of mental experience—*i.e.* knowing the world with a sense.

8.2 NATURE AND DEFINITION OF PERCEPTION

In Chapters 6 and 7, we have discussed the nature and various kinds of sensory processes that are used for gathering information about the external and internal world. Through these processes, we become aware of the present stimuli in the environment. This awareness involves elementary form of mental cognitions about certain features of the present stimuli such as size, shape, colour, intensity, brightness etc. Thus, sensory experiences are the mental images of the objects which are present in the immediate environment that impinges on our sense organs. However, sensory experiences do not provide cognition of the object's reality. Experiencing the objects's reality involves identifying the object that makes a **sensible sense** of the present stimulus. This is what we call **perception** or **perceptual experience**. **It is a cognition in reality**. Thus, perception is a mental process of identifying the object in its real form and assigning a meaning to the sensory details collected through sensory channels. In this sense, perception is both a presentative and representative process. For example, through sensory channel, we come to know that there is an object which is round in shape. But through perception, we identify this particular object as a 'ball' which is used for playing. Thus, the round-shaped characteristic sensory experience is assigned an identifying name that clarifies the nature, kind and use of the object. This involves two levels of processings. At the first level, an internal (mental) representation of the object is formed, *i.e.* an object which is round in shape. At the second level, the process of identification and recognition is carried out (*e.g.* the round-shaped object is a ball). This identification and recognition is possible by abstracting the object from other kinds of objects such as round table, a circle etc. and generalizing the present object with the concept of a 'ball'. While abstracting and generalizing, the brain is actively engaged in mental processings involving retrieval of past experiences, concepts or categories of objects stored in our long-term memory and organizing the various sensory details of the object in a frame of form that could convey the meaning of the object. Thus, it is both—**presentative and representative**.

Perception is an experience of the objects or persons which are present before the experiencing individual (the perceiver). An individual lives in a constantly changing world of experiences. He sees things, hears sounds, feels tastes and smells. All these senses produce **'sensible experience'** about the things and the sounds that he looks, hears, feels, tastes and smells. Thus, perception refers to the way the world looks, sounds, or felt and this perceived world is one's **immediate experience**.

Perception is an **active process**. It is not merely a mirror whereby one becomes aware of **what is out there**. It is a mental process by which sensory data and relevant past experiences are organized into an united whole, generalized and discriminated so as to give the most structured, meaningful picture of the sensed object or things. In this sense, it is representative in nature (because the perceptual experiences represent the object that are sensed). However, it is not just a point to point representation of the stimulus field. The perceptual experiences include objects, relationships and points of spatial focus. Often, some elements of the stimulus field are ignored, distorted, exaggerated or even changed to make a **more meaningful whole**. In this process of organizing, the clear patterns of the stimuli and relevant past experiences are not only useful but also play important role. These serve as vital aids. It is the function on the part of the brain that actively processes the input to provide a stable and meaningful pattern of the object, things or persons before us. Thus, perception is an active process.

Perception is also **selective** in nature. We perceive only those objects or persons that come in our focus of attention and do not perceive those which are out in the margin. Here, the question is what factors operate in selecting an object to be perceived? These factors are of two types. Certain characteristic features of the stimulus field such as size, novelty, intensity, attractiveness etc. determine an object to be taken into focus of attention. Besides, certain characteristics of the perceiver also form the basis of selecting a particular object to perceive and ignoring others. These factors include the motives, interests, needs, desires etc. These personal factors play significant role in exercising selection. For this reason, it is often said—**"We perceive a thing as we are and not as they are."** Thus, what we perceive are selectively brought into the focus of attention on some basis. In other words, we perceive our world by exercising a process of **selection** or **choosing**?

To make the process of perception more clear, perception may be viewed as standing midway along a continuum from direct sensing to thinking. At the one end of the continuum is the purest form of sensation which does not involve learning based on past experience. At the other end is thinking which is independent of stimuli (object) in the form of physical presence. But, perception uses both—sensory data from present stimulus and learning on the basis of past experience. Hence, perception is regarded as both—presentative and representative. However, this representation is not point to point as we have seen.

To summarize, perception is an active mental process of organizing and interpreting the sensory input into an united pattern of wholeness involving the process of selection and assigning a meaning to the organized whole, *i.e.* assigning an identifying name to the object or event being sensed. More precisely, perception may be defined as **the set of mental experiences arising from processing of the sensory data by the brain**.

8.3 CHARACTERISTICS OF PERCEPTION

Perception as we have just defined and described is an active mental process by which the sensory input is organized and interpreted through mental processings done by the cortex—the higher centre of brain. This processing involves operation of a set of variables that intervene between sensory stimulation and cognition in reality. This kind of experience has certain characteristic features which are as follows:

8.3.1 Perception is a Complex Mental Process

Perception involves several processes, *viz.* receptor process, symbolic process, affective and aesthetic processes and organizational processes (unification). It also involves retrieval of past memories, and recognizing in a meaningful way. Thus, it is a process of sensing the object in reality that involves several processes, and therefore, a complex process of mental cognition.

8.3.2 Perception is Immediate in Nature

Perception in fact, is in itself not a knowledge about the object. It is a mental process of acquiring knowledge about the object in the environment which is present here and now. In this process, the sensory input to the cortex is interpreted. Sensory input is a raw, undigested information about the stimulus. The cortex processes this information in the light of relevant memory (past experience). Thus, disorganized bundle of sensations are interpreted into meaningful information of the immediate environment. Thus, perception is a knowledge about the object or person which is present before the perceiver (here and now), *i.e.* it is a knowledge about the stimulating condition which is immediately present and impinges on the sense organs. This indicates the characteristic of immediateness of perceptual experiences. To make it clear, take for instance—an individual meets a friend in his office. Here he perceives his friend who is immediately present before him. After sometimes he leaves the office and goes. On returning home after the office hour, he reports to his family about the friend he has met in the office. While informing about the person to his family members, he may have an image of the person in his mind. But, this will not be called perception because, at the moment the person is not immediately present before him. None of his sensory organs is gathering information about him. He is simply describing about his friend on the basis of his memory which he is recalling in his absence.

8.3.3 Perception is an Active Mental Process

Perception is not merely sensory impression. Certain activities go on in the cortex as soon as the sensory data are transmitted. These activities involve organizing the sensory data, relating them to relevant past experiences, generalizing the organized information that resemble close to the past images stored in the long term memory and abstracting them from those which seem dissimilar and finally assigning meaning to the organized pattern by which it is identified as a 'form'. In so doing, certain details are ignored, or the missing details are filled up to provide sensible meaning to the object. For example, when we look at a sofa in the room, the entire elements of the objects are not looked such as only two legs are sensed, still we perceive it as a sofa which has four legs.

8.3.4 Perception is Selective in Nature

At a given moment, multitude of stimuli stimulate our sense organs but we do not perceive each and every stimuli. We take in only a few of them into our focus and perceive them clearly. Other stimuli are filtered out in the margin which are either not perceived or perceived dimly. This process of selection is determined by several factors. Some of these relate to the stimulus characteristics while some relate to personal factors of the perceiver.

8.3.5 Perception Involves Complex Receptor and Neural Processes

We perceive what we 'sense'. Sensing of objects follows a sensory channel consisting of receptor organs and afferent nerve fibres that transmit the neural energy to the sensory area in the cortex by establishing synaptic associations. The receptors encode the physical energy into a pattern of activity in the nerve fibres. This refers to the process of transduction and transmission. The neural structures in the cortex process the encoded information, *i.e.* translates the encoded impressions and with the help of past experiences and other mental operations, organize them in a structured pattern and identify the same by a definite meaning. Hence, perception involves complex receptor and neural processes in the sensory channels and central nervous system.

8.3.6 Perception is Organization of Stimuli

We perceive an object as united whole and not as scattered sensory elements. For example, when we perceive a rose flower, we do not perceive its elements separately, rather the entire elements are organized or unified together and identified as a single object **rose flower**. Thus, perception follows the principle of organization.

8.3.7 Perceptual Experience has the Attribute of Constancy

Constancy or stability in perceptual experiences is one of the significant attributes. This is an attribute according to which we tend to perceive an object in its original form even if the object is altered or varied. For example, if we move around in a room or see an object from different positions, the falling retinal images are variant (changed). Despite this, we tend to perceive the objects in their original form. Thus, the perceptual experiences are invariant (unchanged), *viz.* take a piece of coal and visualize the same in a corner of the room where the illuminating condition is low. Despite this, we perceive the coal as black without losing its shade of blackness. Next, if the same piece of coal is visualized in open sunlight, there would be no change in perceptual experience. Similarly, if a person is seen from a distance of 5 feet and again from a distance of 15 or 20 feet, the perceptual experience of the person will be invariant. If perceptual constancy does not operate, there would be a chaos and confusion for all of us because the same object would appear different each time we look at them. This constancy is found in size, shape, brightness, colour and location.

8.3.8 Perceptual Experiences are also Flexible

Though, constancy in perceptual experience is an important attribute, it is also flexible. For example, some pictures appear different at different times. Similarly, some cloths are so designed that their shades appear changing moment by moment. Thus, under certain varying conditons, perceptual experiences do vary which is known as the attribute of flexibility.

In the light of the above descriptions about the nature and various characteristics of perception, it can be more appropriately defined as follows:

> **Perception is a complex mental cognitive process through which we have immediate and meaningful knowledge of the present stimulus in the environment.**

8.4 PROCESSES INVOLVED IN PERCEPTION

Perception is not an unitary process. It involves several complex processes. Though, receptor process or functions play a necessary and predominant role, it also involves other processes. These have a variety of titles, however, may be grouped under four major heads which are as follows:

8.4.1 Receptor Process

In perceiving, receptor process is necessarily and predominantly involved. The object that we perceive is a stimulus received by our sense organs which are specialized to receive it. Thus, we speak of visual, auditory, olfactory, gustatory, kinesthetic, tactile, static or organic perceptions. In most of our daily life situations, when a stimulus appears, several receptor processes are simultaneously activated. We not only see an object, but also often hear or smell it at the same time.

The object present before us activates the sensory mechanism attuned to that stimulus. This evokes the receptor cells and initiates signal/impulses which are conducted through afferent nerves to the particular sensory area in the cortex and then the sensory experiences of the stimulus present in the environment takes place. This whole process in the sensory channel is called **receptor process**.

The reception does not involve only receiving and transducing the stimulus but also sets off a complicated pattern of events that represents the earlier stimulation. For example, when we look at a picture event (visual stimulation) it may remind us (symbolic process) about some other events associated with the present picture such as the contextual references (date, time place of occurrence, image of some kind of incidence fields, persons and other similar situations etc.), eventhough these are not present at the moment. Thus, the process of reception itself is a complex patterning of the physical energy received by the responding cells.

8.4.2 Symbolic Process

As has just been stated, symbolic process is reminding of something or having an image of it. Simulation on some earlier occassion leaves its engramed impressions in the nervous system which are stored in memory. When we sense a stimulus in present time, this stimulates several activities in the associative neurons of the cortex resulting in retreiving the stored engrams. This is called **symbolic process**. Hence, any present stimulation does not only arouse receptive functions but also serves to activate symbolic processes with the help of which the received information are categorized and recognized with a particular identifying name. These are called symbolic because, they represent the objects, situations or events of the past.

8.4.3 Affective Processes

Each perceptual experience has its affective aspects. Perception is not only sensing the present stimulus and imaging the former stimulation. But, the object being sensed also impresses us as pleasant or unpleasant or perhaps as neither. For example, while perceiving a rose flower, the affective feelings of pleasure and displeasure associated with the rose is also automatically aroused. Not only the affective feelings, often we also evaluate the object as good or bad to taste, beautiful or ugly in appearence, soothing or irritating or even none of these. These are termed as aesthetic experiences. Hence, the process of perception also involves affective and/ or aesthetic experiences.

8.4.4 Unifying Process

Perception is always in united form. Unification involves organization of sensory elements that provides a shape or form to the object. This shape gives the experience of 'whole'. Ancient philosophers and psychologists hold the view that percept is nothing more than a group of sensory elements—**the bundle hypothesis**. But, evidences brought forward by **Gestalt** psychologists is conclusive. According to them, perception is always of organized whole. This means that what we perceive is the object as a whole and not merely the sum total of sensory elements of the object.

The above processes can be summarized by taking an example of a particular perceptual experience. Let us take for example, **perception of a rose flower**. At least two receptor processes—vision and smell, are involved. Radiant energies reflected by the object stimulate our visual receptors in the visual apparatus and aroma particles of the stimulus (rose flower) stimulate the receptors in our nostrils. Related neural processes are aroused and thus we have two kinds of sensory experiences of the stimulus. But usually, we are unaware of the two sensations separately. These are aroused simultaneouly and are so interrelated that the experience is usually of **unitary**. It is analogous to water with its hydrogen and oxygen particles which are not immediately evident.

In addition to receptive process symbolic process is also involved. The sight and smell remind us of a previous occasion when we had seen the rose (in a nursery visited last winter or the rose garden in our own native place or in the neighbour etc.). These symbols appear as an image that represents the present stimulating object.

There are also affective or related processes. Seeing rose may arouse pleasant or unpleasant feelings or neither of the two. It may appear affectionate or arouse disgust depending upon the associated feelings with the object being perceived at the moment.

Aesthetic and evaluative experience may also be involved in our perception of the situation. It may be perceived as beautiful or ugly or indifferent. Such evaluations depend upon affective feelings, one's interests and likings as well as recall of past experiences of pleasurable or displeasurable events associated with the object being perceived. In this way, the affective and symbolic processes overlap.

Finally, the process of organization or unification takes place. The sensory inputs reacting the cortex from two different sense modalities with several sensory details—colour, size, shape, nature of aroma etc. are organized together and the representative symbols are retrieved to help in abstracting and generalizing the object along with assigning a particular identifying name of recognition (*i.e.* categorizing the object into a particular concept or scheme) etc. are done. Such mental processes enable us to perceive the object as an organized whole in the form of a **rose flower**.

Different processes involved in perception that have been described above may be represented in a summary of sequences as shown in **Table 8.1**.

TABLE 8.1 Processes involved in perceiving an object

Environment	*Sensory channels of the organism*			*Central process*	*Output*
1	2	3	4	5	6
Stimuli present in the environment, *i.e.* the objects or events	Physical energies act on the sense receptors	Generation of afferent code (neural energy). This is called the process of transduction and is the 'input' of the information	Neural energies travel to brain (conduction or transmission of neural energy)	Decoding and interpretative processes of the input. It includes organization, abstraction and generalization	Perceiving the object as united whole

8.5 DIFFERENCE BETWEEN PERCEPTION AND SENSATION

Sensations and perceptions, both are cognitive processes and serve useful purposes in knowing the world around us. For perceptual experiences to occur, sensory experience is a must. We cannot perceive any object or event unless we sense them. Hence, the two processes are inter-related to one another. However, the two processes are never alike. They differ very minutely from each other. These differences are as follows:

(a) Sensation is a simple mental process of sensing the stimuli present in the environment whereas, perception is a complex mental process. Sensation provides only a signal or cu about the object patterns. It does not give any complete or meaningful information or knowledge about what we are sensing at the moment. Meanings are assigned through the interpretative functions of the brain that involve several processes and then the sensed objects are perceived. Hence, perception is a complex process which provides an organized and well-defined knowledge or meaning to the object (stimuli) that produces sensory experiences.

(b) Sensation is mere apprehension or awareness of the object. What we sense is the various properties or characteristic features of the present stimulus (object or event) such as the size, the shape, the colour, the taste, the odour etc. In other words, sensation is merely the sensory details about the object. But, perception is not mere apprehension rather it provides a concrete meaning to the object.

(c) Sensation is only presentative but perception is presentative as well as representative besides being rational. The actual sense data at the moment are designated as presentative. On reaching the sensory data in the cortex, the symbolic process, *i.e.* retrieval of past experiences representing the object being sensed occurs. Symbolic processes are additions of the same order to the present sense data, but these are in fact, not presented rather reproduced. Then, there are rational factors which produce perceptual experience. These factors are determined by the relations of the object which is perceived in its sensory, ideational and affective contexts.

(d) Perception follows sensory stimulation while sensation is a primary process of cognition.

(e) Sensory experiences are almost uniform or similar for all individuals but perceptions may differ from individual to individual.

(f) Pure sensation is thought by many psychologists merely as 'myth'—particularly in the case of adults because it is almost difficult to abstract the two processes. However, pure sensation is a fact whereas perception is a concrete organized whole experience of the sensory datum and hence, not a myth rather a reality.

Thus, sensations and perceptions both are cognitive processes of the mind and bear the similarity in respect of the involved channels of the two processes, they very minutely differ from each other in many respects.

8.6 DIFFERENCE BETWEEN PERCEPTION AND ATTENTION

While describing the nature of perception, it has been stated that perception is a selective process. The moment one perceives an object or person, there may be several other objects or persons before him. All these may impinge on sense organs simultaneously. But he does not perceive them all. What we perceive is determined to a cosiderable extent by our attentive set, *i.e.* preparedness to attend and perceive. Therefore, attention is a basic factor in perception and therefore, perception is selective in nature and so is the attention. Owing to this, most often we say—**perceiving is attending**. However, though attention is a basic factor for perception, the two processes differ from each other in many respects. The main differences are as follows:

(a) Attention precedes perception. Attention in fact, anticipates perceptual experiences. Attention is a mental set that predisposes to perceive. For this reason, attention is called

perceptual attitude (**Peiron**, 1929), *i.e.* a **reaction of expectancy and exploration**. This kind of attitude makes one ready to perceive. **Paschal** (1941) calls this attitude as **anticipatory perceptual adjustment**. This refers to attention as readiness to perceive. Thus, attention precedes perception.

(b) Though, attention anticipates perception, but every anticipated object is not susceptible to perception. For example, one is expecting (anticipitating) the visit of an important guest on a day. Being prompted by this expectation, he is attentively anticipating the arrival of the expected guest, but for certain reasons, the expectation fails. In this example, though, pre-perceptual attitude or readiness to perceive exists, but perception does not occur because the expected guest does not arrive. Hence, perception is always of the reality whereas an attentive set may be imaginary.

(c) Our perceptual experiences involve the organizing and interpretative processes. These processes are not determined by attention, rather by personal factors and past experiences of the perceiver. As such, perceptions of different persons paying attention to the same object may vary. This is amply demonstrated in perceiving ambiguous pictures (such as in Rorsarch's ink blot test pictures).

(d) Attention and perception also differ in their physiological bases. Experimental data prove that attention is the resultant activity of reticulation formation in the brain stem while perception depends upon the activities of the association and projection areas of the cerebral cortex.

(e) Attention is usually classified into categories of voluntary and involuntary. There is no such classificatory category of perceptual experiences.

(f) Attention is a mental activity of attending to that involves receptor-neural and postural adjustments. In perception, however, no such adjustments are necessarily required.

Despite the above-stated differences, attention is a basic factor in perception. Attentional sets bring the perceptual objects into our focus for which one is mentally set. This makes the perception more and more clear. The other objects in the surrounding remain either in the peripheries or margin of focal point. As such, these other objects are either dimly perceived or not perceived at all. Thus, the two processes are closely related to each other.

Secondly, as we know, attention is a sort of mental set to attend, even the weaker stimuli are likely to be perceived more vividly as we often notice in a classroom situation. The attentive students in the class are found apprehending or perceiving the instructional lectures of even complicated or complex nature of concepts, equations, formulae etc. more clearly than those who are relatively less attentive or not attentive at all. Thus, attention **facilitates** perception. But, a given set does not always aid perception. Some sets actually interfere. For example, a teacher is so preoccupied with preparing a lecture note to be delivered in the class, that he fails to hear what is being announced on T.V. His set for preparing lecture note is synonymous with attending to writing which interferes with listening the important announcement on T.V. Thus, attention often inhibits our perceptions and sometimes puts the perceiver to disadvantage. Hence, the attentive sets function in both ways—as facilitating as well as inhibiting in perceiving an object.

8.7 ROLE OF PAST EXPERIENCE IN PERCEPTION

In perception, previous experience, has a very significant role to play. What we perceive is encoded, *i.e.* the input is put into a definite category. For example, when we look at an automobile, we tend to encode it, *i.e.* put it into a category of 'bus' or a 'car' or a 'scooter' or a 'motor bike'. Similarly when we see some people shouting and struggling, we encode the event as 'fight'. Encoding makes us economical as it spares from the painstaking task of analysing the details of the input. Encoding also makes the perceptual organization easier and thereby prepares us to deal with the demands of the situation. In the process of encoding, previous experience plays an important role. It helps in determining meaning of an object that we perceive. Assigning a meaning to the object or situation being perceived at the moment depends much upon how it has stimulated us in the past and how we have reacted to it. For example, a student whose father is very strict, perceives his teacher also as strict when he first comes near him. He becomes timid before him. Similarly, when a person has caused harm to someone in the past, he is likely to perceive him as his enemy and suspects him even if he shows generosity or kindness in the present. He thinks, the person is showing kindness to befool him. Thus, the present input of kindness is judged or pereived in the context of his past experience of harm received from the person.

Let us now consider how the past experience provides meaning to the sensing object? When there is a sensory input to the brain, vast amount of previous experiences recur and build up a set of concepts. These concepts are like **templates** (sancha) or stored patterns. The sensory inputs arriving at the cortex are successively compared with the recurring stored templates and matched with one another untill it finally matches sufficiently well with a particular concept (template). When the sensory input matches well with a particular pattern (template), it is assimilated into the pattern and thus the information is encoded under a category of identifying name (meaning).

Past experiences not only encode the sensory input or determine the meaning, they also guide our perceptions. We do not perceive our world with a blank mind, but with an expectancy or a hypothesis about what we are going to perceive. In other words, previous experience makes one prepared or mentally set to see things or events as he expects. Such expectancies are based on previous experiences, that predisposes one to encode a particular sensory input in a particular category.

8.7.1 Experimental Evidence

Some experimental studies also lend support to the fact that previous experiences play an important role in perception. One such evidence comes from the study done by Thouless (1931). He showed a chair to the subjects (S_S) in such a way that its image on the retina would arouse the sensation of a reversed order chair. But, it was found that the subjects perceived the chair in its normal right position. This shows a tendency on the part of subjects to react in a way similar to previous experience of perceiving the object in its normal and usual position.

Another evidence comes from studies done on bornblind people who were suffering from inborn cataracts. Such people sometimes gain their vision during childhood or later by surgical treatment.*

Such blinds when gained normal vision were presented two geometrical figures—a triangle (Δ) and a circle (O) owing to their blindness, they were deprived of any previous experience of such figures and thus, were unable to discriminate the two figures by assigning any label name. However, they sensed the structural differences between the two figures.*

---

* For critical discussion of such findings and relevant references, see Werthiemer, M., Hebb, D.O. and Sendon, M.—'Role of learning in perception'—Amer. Jl Psychology 1951, 64, pp. 133–137.

There are some more illustrations of the fact that in perceiving the new object, we utilize our background of previous experience. A boy who is taught in a school building with clock tower may interpret every building with clock tower as school. However, upon further contacts with the object and situations, our primitive interpretations may be modified or altered.

Some experimental studies have also shown that previous experiences biases our perceptions. For example, Bruner, Postman and Rodrigues (1951), Haire (1955), Clenn (1965) could obtain data that supports the inhibiting or biased modes of perceptions based on previous experiences.

With regard to the role of past experience and learning, there are two opposite views—the empiricist's view and the nativist's view. The former holds that past experiences play a key role in determining what and how we perceive the world today. The latter view holds that our perceptual abilities are largely innate or inborn and hence, past experience or learning has no important role to play.

It is in fact, difficult to resolve the controversy and therefore, the debate is still going on. In fact, ample evidences are available in support of both the views. In some cases, it is found that ability to organize sensory input into patterns to perceive in a definite shape and form are inborn. But, at the same time, there are evidences that show that perceptial organizations develop probably because of maturational processes and thus, the primary organizations, conceptual templates of different stimuli patterns are moulded due to maturation and learning (Fantz, 1967). These experimental studies lend support to the empiricist's views according to which past experiences have a key role to play in perception.

In fact, potentials to perceive and organize input are inborn, however, our past experiences and learning experiences are also important in the sense that they provide us with opportunities to utilize our inborn potentialities in a way that we can perceive our world in a meaningful way.

8.8 ORGANIZATIONAL PROCESSING IN PERCEPTION

How an individual groups and organizes the sensory inputs to form a meaningful precept? This has always been a puzzling question before psychologists. In this context, the psychologists seem to agree that perception in fact is a 'product' which is a function of stimulus factors as well as the subjective or personal factors. Both of these interact and the meaningful whole *i.e.* percept is the consequence of this interactional process. These two processes are named as **bottom-up processing** and **top-down processing** respectively.

(a) **Bottom-up processing:** It refers to the process of taking data from sensory receptors (bottom) into the system and sending them upward for extraction and analysis of relevant information. This process is also known as **stimulus driven** or **data driven**. It is so called because the perceptual processes are driven by the input from the receptors.

(b) **Top-down processing:** It refers to taking into account the perceiver's past experiences, knowledge, expectations, memory, motivations, socio-cultural background, beliefs, and attitudes etc. in the process of object perception. The implication is that one will take advantage of all these factors in order to deal with the incoming stimuli. This aspect of organizational processing is also known as **'conceptually driven'**.

Thus, the bottom-up processing leads to mental construction of external world and top-down processing helps in identification and recognition of the stimuli. Both the processes togehter make it possible to perceive the world around us.

8.9 THEORIES OF PERCEPTION OR POINTS OF VIEWS TOWARDS PERCEPTUAL PHENOMENON

Perceptual experience is a key cognitive process. Hence, it occupies a very important place in psychology. Quite a good number of psychologists have been actively engaged in studying various aspects of perception and thus, have contributed much to the area of perception.

There are four basic approaches of perception. These are 'Physiological approach', 'Structuralist's point of view', 'The Gestalt approach' and 'The Behaviouristic approach'. These approaches are merely attitudes, they are not theories in strict sense, nor are they mutually exclusive. The physiological attitude is **'parsimonious'** one which reduces all perceptual phenomena to the neurophysiological mechanism. The structuralist view is **'analytical'** that describes perceptual events in simple terms of elemental analysis and views perception as merely an addition or sum total of elementary details of sensory experiences. The **Gestaltist's view** covers a wide range of perceptual phenomena. The **behaviouristic approach** stresses the learnt nature of percepted behaviour.

The physiological viewpoint need not be discussed here as the major contents of this view have already been discussed in course of describing the nature of perception. The three remaining views or approaches are described hereunder:

8.9.1 The Structuralist's View

This is the initial psychological point of view which has been proposed by **'Wundt'** and his associate **'Titchner'**. 'Wundt' has taken the analytical view to explain the phenomenon of perceptual experiences.

The structuralists have made distinctions between **mind** and **consciousness**. To them, **mind** consists of the sum total of an individual's experiences ranging from birth to death whereas **consciousness** consists of the sum total of individual's **experiences at any given time**. Since, psychology is the study of consciousness, the perceptual experiences are the elements of our consciousness.

The structuralists also analyzed the consciousness and hold that consciousness can be analyzed into three basic elements—sensations, images and affects. Sensation is an element of perception and psychology primarily deals with sensory materials or sensations as elements of our perceptual experiences.

Titchner further talks of some basic attributes of 'consciousness' (consisting of perceptual experiences). The basic attributes include the **quality** and **intensity**, **clarity** and **duration**.

According to structuralists, conscious experience is the elementary form of cognition which involves sensations. Sensations are the basic elements of apparent knowledge which is known as apperception. In this process of apperception, the sense organs are activated and the resultant nerve impulses are conveyed to the relevant area in the brain and thus the conscious experience, *i.e.* apperception of the outerworld occurs. The conscious experience includes sensation, feelings and images that can be analyzed. Sensation is the most elementary form of conscious experience that provides apperceptive knowledge about the stimuli. This apperceptive experience is followed by a secondary process in the brain in which the associative cells of the sensory region along with the neighbouring areas are activated. These activities include the stored memories of our past experiences. These activities provide meaning to the apperceptive knowledge (sensory experiences). Thus, meaning to the sensations are added which we call 'perception'. In this sense, perception is the result of secondary processes that takes in the brain by dint of which a meaning is added to the sensory details. Hence, perception is sensation added with a meaning (sensation + meaning = perception). In other words, perception is summation of meaning to sensation.

Criticism: Gestalists have very bitterly criticized structuralist's view. Gestaltists hold that structualist's view is a combination of associationism and atomism which is not acceptable because, this view has utterly failed in explaining percepts adequately.

'Wertheimer' is considered as the founding pillar of Gestaltism who considers perception as the primary process of cognition whereas structuralists consider it as secondary process (sansation being the primary process in which meaning is added by secondary activities of the sensory contex). Gestaltis do not seem agreeable in differentiating apperception and perception. They hold that percepts are unified whole that cannot be broken down to elements.

8.9.2 Gestaltist's Approach

'Gestalt' comes from German word **'Gestalten'** for 'whole'. Gestalt psychologists consist of a group of psychologists who have extensively searched for what and how do we experience the world around us. These psychologists include **'Max Wertheimer'** (1912), **'Kurt Koffka'** (1935), **'Wolfgang Kohler'** (1938, 1940) and **'Brown and Voth'** (1937).

According to Gestaltists, sensation is the most elementary form of cognition (indeed of experience). It is merely an aspect and not the 'whole' of experience. Bare sensation does not exist in concrete. What we experience is an organized pattern rather than the elements of which patterns are made. Thus, the theory stands out in opposition to the structuralist's notion that percept is nothing more than a group of sensations—**'a bundle hypothesis'**. The Gestaltists have brought forth abundant evidences against this notion.

To answer the question—What do we perceive? The gestaltists hold that we perceive the **'whole'**, *i.e.* organized pattern or a form or a figure out of the sensory data. The physical energies of the stimulus field stimulate our sensory mechanism and neural impulses when reach to the brain, the brain becomes active to organize the sensory input and give an experience of the 'whole'. Thus, we perceive a book, a toy, a pen etc. as a whole and not the colour, pages, size, or any other sensory characteristics of the objects separately.

They further emphasize that perceptual experiences cannot be analyzed into elements or components, because the organized pattern or whole is more than the sum of its parts. The moment, sensory input are organized, it acquires a new property, called **gestalt quality**. Acquisition of this new property is explained on the principle of **isomorphism**. Literally, isomorphism refers to 'equality of form'. This principle can be made clear from an illustration of **'Boring'** (1942).

'If a system of points is marked on a flat rubber membrane and the membrane is then stretched tightly over some irregular surface, then the points in the stretched membrane are isomorphic with the points in the flat membrane.'*

Here, it should be made clear that there is no requirement that distances be identical in magnitude. Only the points correspond in their order—spatial as well as temporal. For example, suppose we look at rectangle. It is accompanied by a (roughly) rectangle like excitation. In other words, there is a parallel projection of the sensory surface of the stimulus field in the cortex, *i.e.*

* Boring, E.G., *Sensation and Perception in the History of Experimental Psychology*, N.Y.: Appleton-Century-Crofts, 1942, p. 84.

parallelism of molar mental events with molar physiological chart (1 : 1 relationship). Hence, it holds that if a rectangle is consciously perceived having four points, must be paralleled by corresponding four points excitation at some place in the brain (visual area).

Gestaltists have tried to answer another question, 'how does the organization take place?' To answer this, they talk of the 'field forces', *i.e.* the forces of the stimulus field that operate. These forces are of two types—**'cohesive'** and **'restraining'** forces. 'The cohesive force' attracts one another and are central in origin, integrative in function and perceptual in nature. The restraining forces, on the other hand, are peripheral in origin, segregative (disintegrative, autonomous) in function and sensory in nature. The former (cohesive) force assimilates the dynamically distributed energies together and form an organized pattern, resulting in perception of a figure against a background. The latter, on the other hand, gives experience of dis-crimination.

The Gestaltists, further elaborating their views, talk of the relative strengths of these two forces. **'Brown and Voth'** (1937) suggest that the basis of perception is the relative strength of cohesive and restraining forces. They hold that if the sum total of cohesive and restraining forces are equal ($E_C = E_R$), there would be no perception and if the $E_C > E_R$, then the perceptual work is predicted. However, if the $E_C < E_R$, it represents instability in the visual field. Hence, the stability of perceptual experience depends upon the balance in the relative strength of the cohesive and restraining forces. In this context, Gestaltists have brought forward various principles or laws of organization such as similarity, proximity, closure, inclusiveness etc. (These are discussed separately in the section—Perceptual Organization.)

In essence, Gestalt approach to perception is phenomenological and presumes that perceptual experiences are not just sum of sensations but perception is of the 'whole'.

Critical comments

The Gestalt approach, in fact is based purely on hypothetical constructs—isomorphism, visual field, field forces etc. The scientific reliabilities and validities of these constructs are yet to be established.

However, the approach has been successful in explaining most of the facts of our perceptual world very efficiently. As such, Gestalt approach is even today regarded as a landmark approach in the field of perception. But, the theory suffers from certain important shortcomings. The Gestaltists have outrightly ignored the role of personal factors such as meaning, value, motivation etc.

8.9.3 The Behaviouristic Approach

The 'Behaviourist' school of psychologists are well-known for their valuable and significant contributions in the areas of learning and motivation. In the area of perception, their contributions are relatively not so significant. In behavioural text, perceptual phenomena are more descriptive than interpretative or integrative. It describes the phenomenon in terms of mediating mental processes between stimulus and response (S–R). The behaviourists assume that perceptions are learned behaviours and, therefore, they do follow the principles as other responses follow—such as habit formation, generalization, discrimination, inhibition and so on.

Perhaps the most comprehensive attempt to explain perception in behaviouristic model may be found in Hull's systematic theory. Hull's system is based on interactive functions in the nervous system. According to him, afferent neural interactions in the nervous system is the basis of perceptual experience. They hold that all afferent neural impulses active in nervous system at any given time interact and change each other into something partially different in the manner that produce the perception of a pattern. Thus, the experience of pattern does not correspond to the physical stimuli in toto, rather it is modified or changed in such a manner that the perceived pattern possesses some features that are not found (traceable) in the original stimulation. To substantiate this, examples of 'after-images and simultaneous contrast' are cited as evidences.

After-image is a phenomenon of 'stimulus trace' which assumes that after-effects of receptor stimulation continues in the central nervous system (CNS) for a while after termination of the physical stimulus. These after-effects interact with other traces in the nervous system in two ways—spatial interaction and temporal interaction. When the after-effects of different afferent impulses interact simultaneously, it is called spatial interaction. The phenomenon of simultaneous contrast may be given as illustration. Suppose, we look at a grey paper in a blue surrounding. The afferent nerve impulses arising from grey paper interact with the afferent nerve impulses arising from blue surrounding in such a way that changes their quality (grey patch now appears yellowish). Here is an example of 'spatial interaction' because the traces of the two stimuli (grey and blue) are simultaneously present in the nervous system and interact with each other. Similarly, instances of 'temporal interaction' may also be noticed. For example, when a speech sound is modified by the preceding verbal context, we find the example of 'temporal interaction'.

In order to substantiate the above facts, behaviourists cite a few experimental evidences. **Woodbury** (1943) performed an experiment on a dog named **Dick**. The dog was trained to nose a bar in a wooden cage in order to get pellets of food. Conditions were so arranged that food would be forthcoming following simultaneous sounding of high and low pitch buzzer sounds and the dog reacted to either one of the sounds, *i.e.* the simultaneous sounding of the two pitches initiated a response to nose the cage bar. However, when the two pitches were presented individually with out following any reward, it was found that after sometime, the dog did not react. This supports the spatial interaction. This indicates that every stimulating condition forms a pattern of its own which determines a particular response.

Another experiment on another dog named **Chuk** was performed to demonstrate temporal interaction. In this experiment, the high and lower buzzer tones were presented in temporal sequence at an interval of one second and was either reinforced or non-reinforced. This arrangement led to the dog to form a pattern of discrimination between reinforced and non-reinforced stimuli. But when the ordering was changed, the dog was found not making any response. It so happened because owing to the change in temporal order of the same stimulus, the previously learnt patterning also changed.

However, one should remember that the above experimental facts throw light on discrimination learning and not on perception. Perception is said to be a mediating process in between the sensory and motor neural activities which cannot be sufficiently explained in terms of S–R formulae.

Critical comments

Hardcore behaviourists look upon Hull's 'interaction hypothesis' as imaginative concept. It has thrown wide gates to mysterious and unquantifiable field forces of Gestaltists. The Gestaltists, on the other hand, consider Hull as moleculist and thus, has presented his contentions in a silly manner. Hence, neither the behaviourists nor the gestaltists are pleased with him.

Yet, Hull's notion cannot be rejected outrightly. Enough evidences on both—neurological and behavioural levels—are available to prove that interactions of exceedingly complex nature take place—not only occasionally but also regularly. However, the difficulty is that Hull has not been able to explain the facts of perception sufficiently. The formulation is gross enough.

Moreover, the laws governing the degrees of such interaction and the effects (perceptual as well as behavioural) should have been explained. Even Hull is also aware of the insufficiency and suggested a method for quantitative investigation of interactions. As **'Osgood'** (1953) feels, "If studies on the suggested line are carried on in future, Hull's approach may prove an useful principle."

8.10 COMPARISON BETWEEN GESTALTIST AND BEHAVIOURISTIC APPROACHES TO PERCEPTION

The Gestaltist's and Behaviourists, though are opposed to each other in their views (approach), and methology, the two also bear certain similarities in explaining and describing perceptual experiences. At the same time, the two approaches also differ from each other in many respects. The important aspects of similarities and differences between them are briefly enumerated below:

8.10.1 Points of Similarities

1. The Gestalt psychologists hold that what we perceive is the 'whole' of the stimulus situation. The experience of wholeness involves organization of various aspects of stimulus situations. The behaviourists too believe that perception is the outcome of the interactive functions of the afferent neural activities in the CNS that provides a pattern of the stimulus situation and we perceive the objects in terms of the interactive patternings. The organization of stimulus field and patterning of the sensory neural impulses—both are similar because what we perceive as organized whole is the pattern—organizing is patterning. However, there exists a basic difference between the two in respect of the emphasis that they lay. The Gestaltists lay emphasis on stimulus factors that lead to organized pattern of the stimulus situation while the behaviourists lay emphasis on spatial and temporal orders of interactions that provide patterning of the stimulus situation.
2. Gestaltists hold the view that perceptual experience of the 'whole' is not exactly the same as sensory details. Experience of 'wholeness' may not correspond point to point similarity with the sensory details of the stimulus, rather it may be even something more. Similarly, the behaviourists do agree that the interactive patterns may be a changed pattern from the independent afferent neural impulses. In this way, the two approaches show similarity.

However, the two approaches sharply differ from each other. The main differences are as follows:

8.10.2 Points of Differences

(i) The behaviourists are strongly opposed to Wundt's and Titchner's notion of studying the experiential aspects of mind and instead propose that psychology is the study of behaviour and not conscious experience. Therefore, the behaviourists consider 'percepts' also as a learnt behaviour much like the other forms of learnt behaviours.

However, the Gestaltists consider perceptions as a part of concious experience and thus maintain the continuity with the Wundtian or structuralist's notion while ignore the behaviourists thought that 'percepts' are the aspects of behaviour. As such, the behaviourists and Gestaltists differ from each other in their notional views of perceptions.

(ii) Though, the Gestaltists seem to stand in opposition to the Wundt's and Titchner's views of 'elementalism' they also tend to agree that precepts are experiential aspects. Behaviourists do not agree with Gestaltists and state that 'percepts' are not expriences rather an aspect of behaviour that can be acquired, moulded or modified in the manner other behaviours are amenable to modifications and moulding or acquiring. Thus, perceptual behaviours are also governed and controlled by the principles applicable to other sets of behaviour modifications.

(iii) The behaviouristic approach to perception is more descriptive than explanatory. On the other hand, the Gestaltist's view is both descriptive as well as interpretative (explanatory).

(iv) Behaviourist's view on perceptions is ambiguous and vague. Moreover, behaviourists have taken help of facts to explain their views that are concerned with discrimination learning and not perceptions. But, Gestalt's approach to perception is vivid and not confusing. Gestaltists have been successful in clearly explaining the facts of perceptual experiences on the basis of field forces, reversible figures, laws of organization and the principle of isomorphism. These are considered important areas of scientific explorations even today.

(v) Behaviouristic approach is molecular while Gestalt's approach is phenomenological.

In consideration of the above similarities and differences in the approaches of the behaviouristic thinkers and that of the Gestaltists, the most tenable conclusion that can be drawn is that though the Gestaltists have been able to explain the phenomenon of perception more elaborately and clearly, the contentions of behaviouristic thoughts also can not be outrightly ignored. If further research is carried out in tune with Osgood's suggessions, the behaviouristic thought may also prove effective in explaining the phenomenon in a more better way and in an objective terms.

8.11 PERCEPTUAL ORGANIZATION (GROUPING)

All perceptions consist of an attempt to organize the sensory input received via sensory channel. Thus, what we perceive is not simply the patches of colours, sizes, or shapes, various degrees of brightness or low or high pitch of sounds. We perceive the objects in their concrete real form such as we perceive a table, a chair, a book, a house. All these may vary in diverse sensory characteristics, but we perceive them as a composite or grouped unit classified under different conceptual catagories with a label of identifying name.

How does this organization occur? Some of this is a matter of learning. But, much of it is probably an unlearned property of our sense organs and central nervous system (CNS). These tend to organize the sensory datum into form and thus, provide perception of 'form'—a grouped or organized pattern in its real form.

The tendency to organize depends upon several factors. This tendency has much been studied by Gestalt psychologists. They have figured out certain factors of organization which are classified into two broad categories—(i) **the peripheral laws** and (ii) **the central laws**. The peripheral laws or principles refer to the factors relating to the stimulus situation, *i.e.* those which operate in the peripheries of the stimulating conditions. On the other hand, the central laws or factors refer to the factors that are related to the individual or the perceiver. The former factors are inborn or innate while the latter are learned or acquired. Let us consider these factors.

8.11.1 The Peripheral Laws or Principles of Organization

Law of similarity

Similar elements tend to be grouped together and perceived as one pattern or whole than the dissimilar ones. For example, look at **Figure 8.1**.

OO × × Δ Δ
OO × × Δ Δ
OO × × Δ Δ

FIGURE 8.1 Perception of similar elements.

In this figure, all the elements are equally spaced, yet, they seem to organize themselves in three different patterns on the basis of similarity—a set of circles (O), set of × and a set of triangles.

Law of proximity

The elements or stimuli which are physically near to each other are perceived as parts of a pattern and make as one whole. On the other hand, the elements that stand out distant are perceived as another pattern. Thus, the proximity makes the elements grouped together. For example, look at **Figure 8.2**.

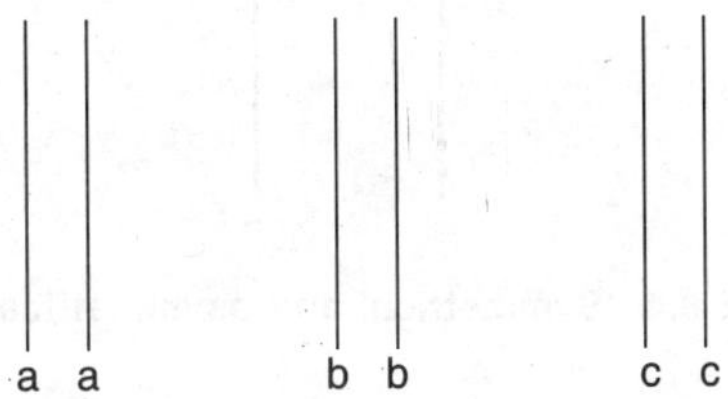

FIGURE 8.2 Proximity of elements.

Figure 8.2 perceived as three pairs of vertical lines more easily and not as 6 vertical lines. Introspectively, the nearness (proximity) produces the experience of belongingness. As such, Koffka (1935) holds the view that in effect, we feel 'things' and not the spaces between them.

Continuity

This is also known as common direction or common fate. The elements of a stimulus having common direction are grouped together and perceived as a separate object from those that have a different direction. This refers to a tendency in which the objects that appear to form a continuous pattern are perceived as belonging together. For example, look at **Figure 8.3**.

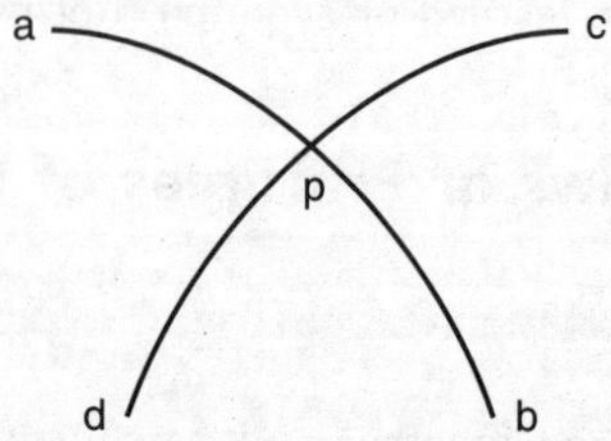

FIGURE 8.3 Elements of common direction.

In Figure 8.3, we are likely to identify two lines ab and cd crossing each other rather than to identify four lines a, b, c and d, meeting at point p. This is because of the continuity factor.

Good figure or symmetry

This principle suggests that symmetrical areas tend to be seen as figures against asymmetrical backgrounds. For example, in **Figure 8.4**, there are two arrow-headed lines 'a' and 'b'. Figure 'a' is symmetrical and as such perceived as good figure. It gives an experience of completeness. Figure 'b' is not symmetrical and therefore not experienced as good figure. It gives an experience of incompleteness. The symmetrical figures maintain the balance of set and as such tend to be perceived as good figures as well as well organized pattern than those which are not symmetrical.

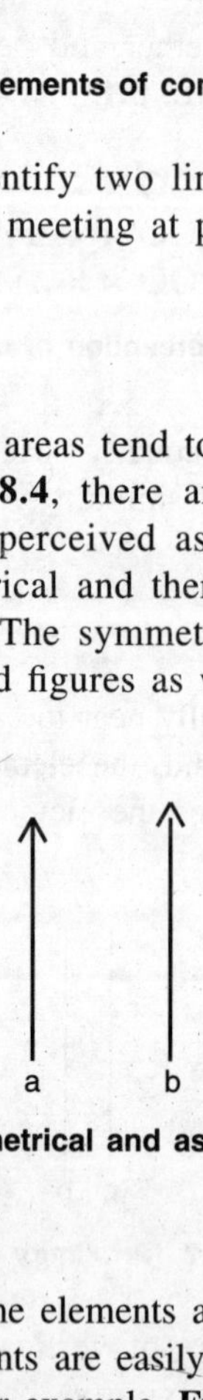

FIGURE 8.4 Symmetrical and asymmetrical figures.

Inclusiveness

The form or pattern which 'uses up' all the elements are more readily perceived than the others. The patterns which include in it all elements are easily grouped together and as such these kinds of patterns are more clear and distinct. For example, **Figure 8.5** is perceived as hexagonal object formed by all the elements (dots) rather than square formed by the four middle dots with single dot at either end.

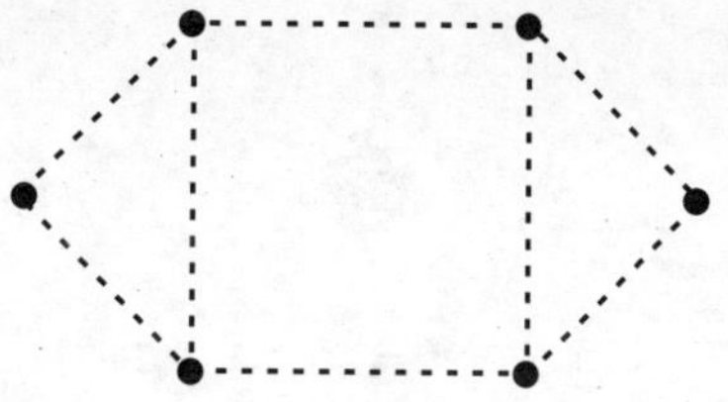

FIGURE 8.5 Inclusiveness of the elements.

Closure

While perceiving an object, we not only tend to include all the elements, rather intentionally supply the elements which are not present and thus perceive a meaningful whole. For this reason, the word shown in **Figure 8.6** can easily be read eventhough, the letters are incomplete. Thus, filling up the gaps in our perception is known as clousure.

FIGURE 8.6 Closure perception.

Context

Perception of an object is also determined by the context. We tend to perceive a thing with refrence to the context. Context enables us to perceive the details of a situation in relation to whole of which they are a part. Context helps learning concepts. Suppose, we do not know the exact meaning of a word, but the word is most often used in different contexts. Owing to its repeated use in some contextual references, we usually develop fairly well-defined idea of its meaning. For example, even an illiterate person is usually found using 'thanks', when he gets an occasion to express his feelings of obligation. Another example of context determining our perception is while driving an automobile on road, traffic light signals and/or hand signals given by vehicle drivers in the front are perceived and interpreted in reference to the context. Similarly our perceptions of the cloudy or bright days, discrimination of dark and light shadows etc. are all determined by the contextual clues.

8.11.2 Central Laws or Principles

Mental set

Perceiving the elements of the stimulus field grouped together forming an organized pattern is to a large extent determined by 'the mental set' of the perceiver. Usually, it is observed that even when the stimulus factors of organization do not operate in a particular situation, the object is perceived as a patterned form. For example the following is a picture taken from **Rorscharch Test of Ink Blot** (see **Figure 8.7**).

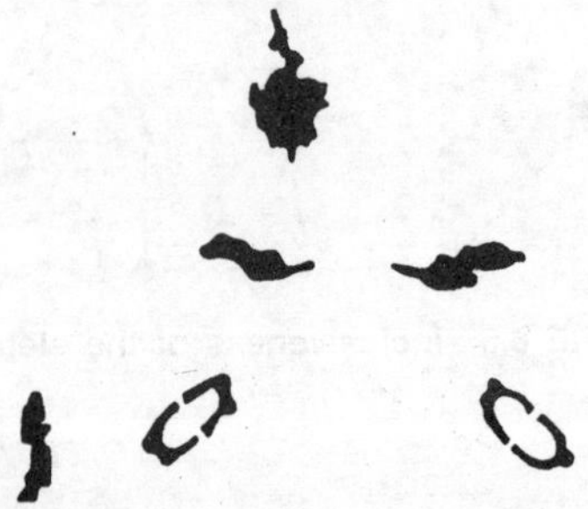

FIGURE 8.7 Rorscharch test of Ink Blot.

Figure 8.7 is unstructured or has no form. However, different persons may perceive some structured pattern that may represent some kind of objects such as butterfly, clouds, or similar other things. Though, the perceived pattern varies widely from person to person and also from time to time in the case of same person. However, people tend to perceive something. This tendency is determined by the mental set of the person. Most often we find mental set so strongly influencing that a person may tend to perceive the same object he has perceived on earlier occasion even if the previous picture on the second occasion has been presented with certain modifications.

Leeper has demonstrated this in one of his experiments in which he presented a picture to his subjects (S_S) who reported to have visualized some objects. On second occasion, the same picture with some modifications in the arrangements of the elements was presented. It was found that the subjects tended to repeat the earlier response. This shows the strong impact of mental set in determining perception.

Meaningfulness

Man lives in the realm of meanings. He is continuously in search of meanings of a wide variety of things, objects, situations, events of the surrounding world. The purpose of stimulus factors of organization is also to search meanings. Meanings provide interrelationships among the elements of stimulus field. Below are the two sets of words:

(i) AUTHORITY, PLUMBING, CARPET, SCHOLAR
(ii) CHILD, LAKE, BALL, DROWNED

The second set of words are interrelated. The four words together give a cue about a child whose ball is drowned in a lake. Hence, easily perceived as a meaningful event. The former set of four words are not interrelated. Hence, the four words are not patterned together, rather perceived as independent units. Relatedness among the elements of the object determine a stable meaning and therefore perceived as one organized unit.

Past experience

Our past experiences and familiarity with the objects of the world also detrmine our perceptual experiences. The following are 13 letters, each letter is close to each other. But, when we read them we read as a full sentence. This is because of our previous experience which tend us to perceive them as meaningful sentence.

(i) RAMISAGOODBOY : RAM IS A GOOD BOY
(ii) THEDOGATEMEAT : THE DOG ATE MEAT.

Motivation

The needs and desires of a perceiver strongly influence our perception. People want to fulfil their needs and desires through various means. One way to do this is to perceive objects in a picture as something that will satisfy their needs. Experiments have been done to examine the influence of hunger on perception. When hungry persons are shown ambiguous pictures, they tend to perceive food objects in the picture more often than those who are not hungry.

8.12 FIGURE AND GROUND PERCEPTION

Perceiving a figure against a background is perhaps the fundamental organizational tendency. Figures of objects are perceived as standing out from the general background of our experience. The Gestaltists opine that perception is always relative to figure and ground—a primitive form of organization. Thus, perception of a form or figure is never absolute or free from its background. For example, when we see words on a page, or a painting on a wall or birds flying in the sky, the words, the paintings and the birds stand out from the background and are perceived as figures; while the page, wall and sky stay behind the figure and are perceived as background. To test this, look at **Figure 8.8**.

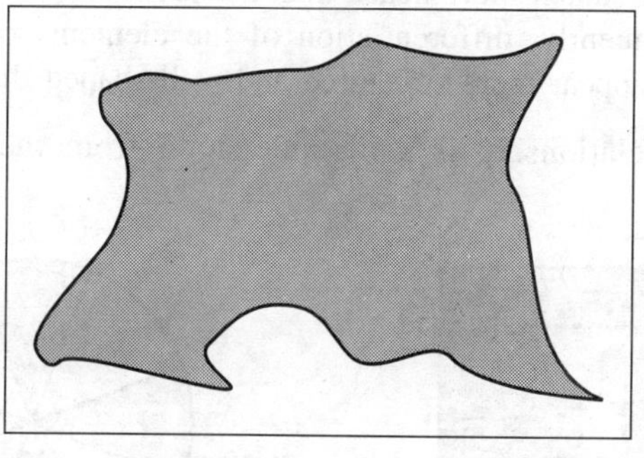

FIGURE 8.8 Perceiving a figure against a background.

While visualizing this picture, the dark area is experienced as figure and the rest of the white space within the boundary lines is experienced as background. Though the dark area does not resemble any familiar object of figure, still it is experienced as figure standing out against a background.

Rubin (1921) has attempted to analyze perceptional experiences and explain figure and ground relationships. According to him, perceptual experiences follows a sequence as follows:

- On stimulation by a stimulus, a state of awareness is aroused.
- It is followed by finding out the interrelations among several stimuli in the stimulus field.
- It again follows the differentiation of the immediately present stimulating conditions from other stimuli.
- Finally as a result of the above sequences the object stands out as clear and structured figure against the remaining elements that form ground.

Rubin has further elaborated this relationship between figure and background and mentioned certain salient characteristics of figures that appear distinguished from the ground. These are as follows:

(i) Ground forms the base of a figure on which a figure appears as standing out.
(ii) The figures have some sort of shape or form that possesses the 'object quality' *i.e.* the character of the object or thing. But, the ground is relatively formless (*i.e.* possesses no object quality).
(iii) Figures appear nearer to the perceiver while ground appears distant.
(iv) Figure is more impressive and meaningful than ground.
(v) Figure appears in the front and ground behind the figure.
(vi) Ground appears extended behind the figure. Koffka terms it as double representation, *i.e.* a geographical field of figure is represented doubly in the psychological field—once as a figure surface and once as (inferred) ground surface.
(vii) The area of figure being limited, can be more easily and definitely localized than the extended ground. Moreover, figures have surface texture while ground has a filmy texture.
(viii) The contours separating figures from ground belong to the figures and not to the ground. Hence, contours are perceived in figure.
(ix) Figures remain in the centre of consciousness and therefore more stable than the ground which falls in the peripheries and not in the centre of consciousness.
(x) As Koffka believes, figural organization is a dynamic process. The physical energies within the figure is much more dense than the ground and therefore, the cohesive forces dominate. Consequently, differentiation of the elements of a figure is difficult. This makes the figure appear more structured and well-shaped than the ground.

Figure and ground relationship is well understood from the reversible **Figures 8.9(a)** and **(b)**:

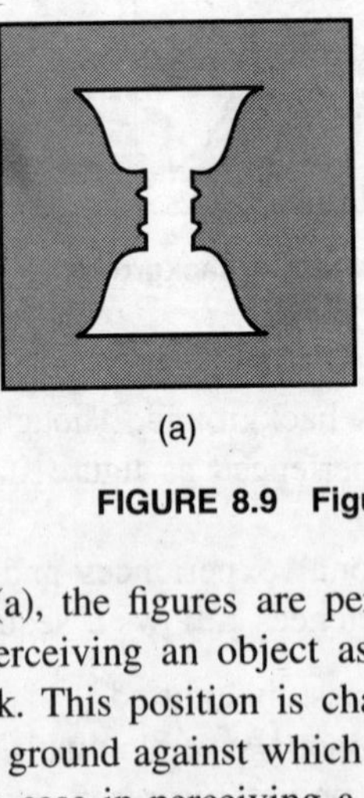

(a)

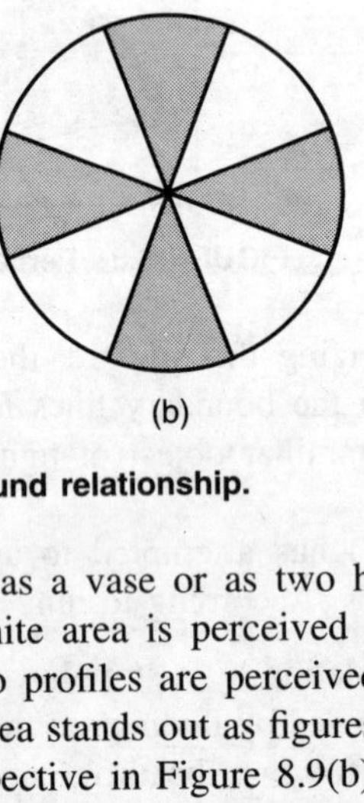

(b)

FIGURE 8.9 Figure and background relationship.

In Figure 8.9(a), the figures are perceptible either as a vase or as two human faces facing each other while perceiving an object as 'vase', the white area is perceived as figure against a background of black. This position is changed when two profiles are perceived as figure and the white area becomes ground against which the darkened area stands out as figures of the two human faces. Similar is the case in perceiving a reversible perspective in Figure 8.9(b).

In perceiving Figure 8.9(b), often the principle of smallness is also found operating. According to this principle, smaller areas tend to be seen as figures against a larger background.

In Figure 8.9(b), we are more likely to see a black cross rather than a white cross within the circle because of this principle.

Figure and ground relationship is also found in auditory perceptions. A melody sound is perceived as figure against the background of chords.

8.13 CONTOUR

In visual perception, perception of 'contour' is an important factor. Experience of contours makes us able to separate objects from the general ground. Contours are formed when marked difference in the brightness or colour of the background occurs. If the background is homogeneous and unfilled with any shade or light, no contour will be perceived. But, if the background is heterogeneous and shaded with colours or there are shades of markedly varying brightness, contour is perceived.

Contours give shape to the object in our visual field because they separate or mark off an object from other objects or general ground. However, contours in themselves are not the shapes. In **Figure 8.10**, two faces are formed by a single contour, but obviously, the shapes are different. Hence, though, contours determine shapes but they are shapeless by themselves.

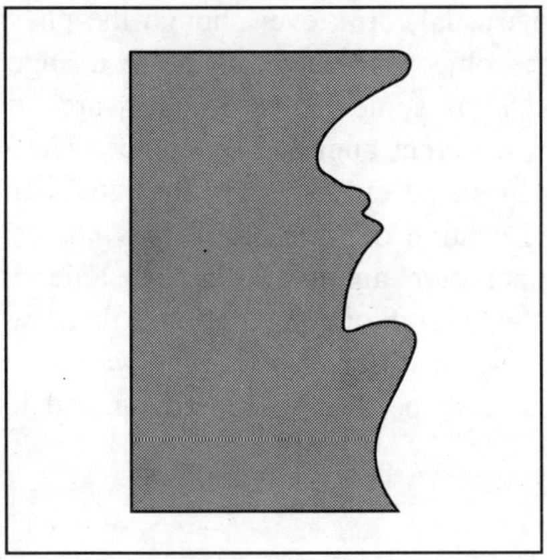

FIGURE 8.10 Contour in visual perception.

However, sometimes contours may be seen even though no difference in brightness of the stimulus field exists. Such contours are referred to as subjective contours. This is evident in **Figure 8.11**.

In Figure 8.11, one can perceive contours of the upright triangle, even though, there is no marked energy change across its boarder except at its corners. Phenomenon like this suggests involvement of some factors other than the changes in brightness of the stimulus field.

Another important feature of contour is that its formation is not simple rather complex. Experimental studies done in this field show that contour formation is an elaborate process and at the same time, it takes some time (at least 150 millisecond). Hence, it is not an immediate phenomenon (Werner, 1938, Ratliff, 1965).

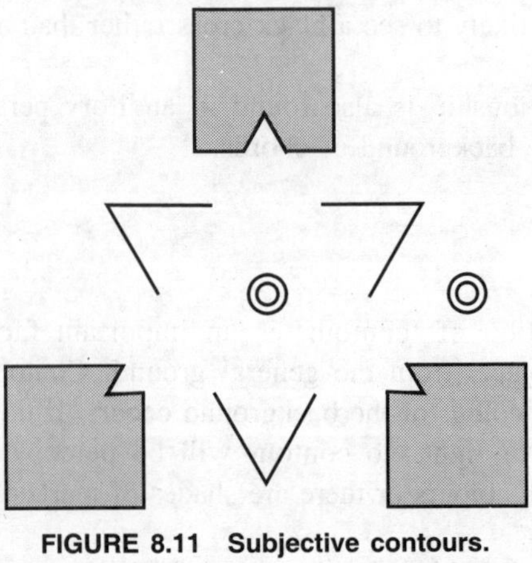

FIGURE 8.11 Subjective contours.

8.14 PERCEPTUAL CONSTANCY (STABILITY)

The world we perceive is relatively a stable world because what we perceive is stable. We tend to perceive familiar objects in its usual form, even though the physical stimuli from an object are not constant or the image of the object size and shape are changed when viewed from different positions. For example, the size of someone coming towards us does not appear to change significantly when viewed from different angles. The dinner plate on viewing from two different angles or sides does not differ in shape even though, the retinal images are different on viewing from different angles or sides. Location of sound also does not change when we turn our heads. It is so because, we tend to perceive an object as the same. In absence of such constancy phenomenon or characteristic feature of our perceptions, there would be chaos and confusion, because, the same object would appear different each time we look at them. This constancy feature is found in the perception of size, shape, brightness, colour and location. Let us discuss each of these constancies briefly:

8.14.1 Size Constancy

Size constancy refers to the tendency to perceive a familiar object approximately in its original experience of size irrespective of viewing from distance. If an object is viewed from distance its image on our retina is different than when viewed from near (a shorter distance). However, our perceptions of its size does not change. Thus, **while the retinal image of an object is variant, the perceptual size is constant**. This ability, however, increases with increase in age (Bower, 1966, Turnbull, 1961)

Size constancy is attributed to two major factors. Firstly, our brain is capable of interpreting the retinal image with respect to perceived distance. Therefore, it depends on our ability to perceive distance accurately. Another contributing factor is our familarity with the object. Our previous experience of size stored in the brain (LTM) helps us in perceiving the object in its known size irrespective of variant retinal images. How familiarity as cue helps in size perception has been described in some detail in the section on Space Perception later in this chapter.

8.14.2 Shape Constancy

If we look at the window directly in front, the image projected on retina is rectangular. But, when we see the same window from one side of it, the image becomes trapezoid, *i.e.* a rectangle without parallel sides. Similarly, when the door swings open towards us, the projected image of its shape goes through a series of distortions. Its rectangular shape become trapezoid—the edge towards us looks wider than the hinged edge. Despite these changes in the retinal image of the object's shape, our perceptions remain the same, *i.e.* we tend to perceive the windows and doors in their original rectangular shapes. This is what we call **shape constancy**. To illustrate this phenomenon of visual perception, let us examine the figure of some objects as shown in **Figure 8.12a, b** and **c.**

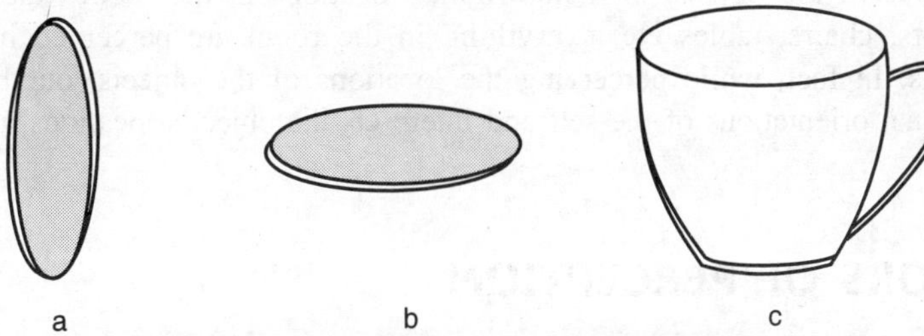

FIGURE 8.12 Shape constancy phenomenon.

The possible reason as has been stated in respect of size constancy is the automatic function of brain which preserves the perspective size and shape* of the previously experienced objects. The operation of size constancy depends partly upon the presence of distance cues and partly upon familiarity. Similarly, shape constancy is also achieved by our familiarity with the object as well as experience.

8.14.3 Colour and Brightness Constancy

Familiar objects retain their original colour despite variations in illuminating conditions. This accounts for colour constancy. For example, a green grassed lawn appear green whether we look in the broad daylight or twilight dimness. Similarly, if one enters into a party hall decorated with yellow light, initially for a while, the walls would appear a bit yellowish, but after a short while, everything becomes normal and walls appear white. In this case, the observer takes into account the nature of light and thus, colour constancy is achieved.

As in the case of colour, if you look at a piece of white paper in your dark room and again in the sunlight, the piece of paper will appear white in both the conditions even though, the illuminating conditions are variant. Here again we take into account the prevailing illumination while interpreting the retinal images of the objects that varies in different illuminating conditions.

'Wallach' (1963) in an experiment found that the perceived brightness of an object depends upon the ratio between illumination of the object and its background. Therefore, for perceptible change in brightness, a change in the ratio of intensity between object and surrounding is necessary. But, so long this ratio in the intensity of object and its brightness does not vary,

* Perspective size and shape: Judging the size according to the geometry of perspective—farther the object, smaller it is viewed. This size corresponds to the size of the image on retina.

perceived brightness remains constant or stable. However, this rule has certain limitations as has been suggested by 'Jamson' and 'Hurvich' (1964). They suggest that this rule does not hold good for all ranges of intensity. Despite this, the rule serves as unuseful explanation for brightness constancy.

8.14.4 Location Constancy

In general, we become habituated towards the location of objects around us which causes contancy of location. For example, when we are in lying down position in a room, the retinal images of the walls and other things of the room get transformed in a significant manner. Despite this, we are able to perceive the objects in their original locations in the room—the hinging walls, clocks, refrigerators, chairs, tables etc. everything in the room are perceived in their original locational positions. In fact, while perceiving the locations of the objects, our brain takes into account the positional orientations of the self and interprets the object's locations in relation to the orientations.

8.15 FACTORS OF PERCEPTION

As we have seen, perception has a physiological base with psychological concomitants. These have been described in the earlier section discussing the basic processes involved in percepts. However, some factors operate in producing the psychological experiences of the physical energies received through biological processes—sensory channels. Some of these factors are as mentioned below:

8.15.1 Redundancy of Sensory Cues

Our ability to identify or recognize objects, persons, events is enhanced by redundant sensory input. Redundancy refers to additional or some superfluous information through different types of cues picked up by a single sense organ or sometimes more than one sense organ. For example, an individual has to recognize three different geometrical figures—a triangle, a circle, and a rectangle as given in **Figure 8.13**.

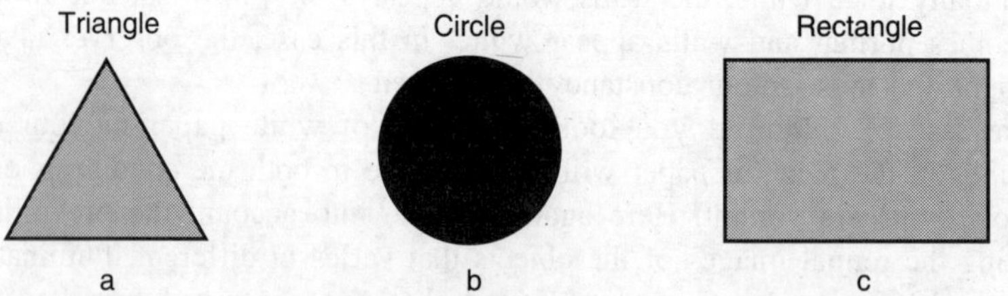

FIGURE 8.13 Redundant sensory input.

In Figure 8.13, we have two kinds of redundant cues—colour and form—as any one of them would be sufficient for discriminating the three stimuli. However, the two types of information provide double information and thus, help in distinguishing the three figures more accurately and dependably. Obviously, the redundancy of information makes our perceptions more dependable, more particularly in situations when several irrelevant or distracting stimuli are present in our perceptual field.

Redundancy of sensory cues favours correct recognition and identificaiton of objects and persons (perceptions). For example, we see a flower. There are several inputs of a flower—its colour, smell, shape, aesthetic sense etc. All these cues together help in correct recognition of the kind of flower. Similarly, the profile of a face, complexion, voice, body built and many other sensory characteristics of the man help in correctly recognizing him as old friend to whom someone has met after a long gap.

8.15.2 Context

Already discussed under Section 8.11.

8.15.3 Transposition

Transposition refers to learning to discriminate two stimuli on the basis of their relative relationships. For perceiving an object, interrelationship is of key importance. This has clearly been shown by experiments done on discrimination learning. One such experiment can be performed, using the stimuli as shown in **Figure 8.14**.

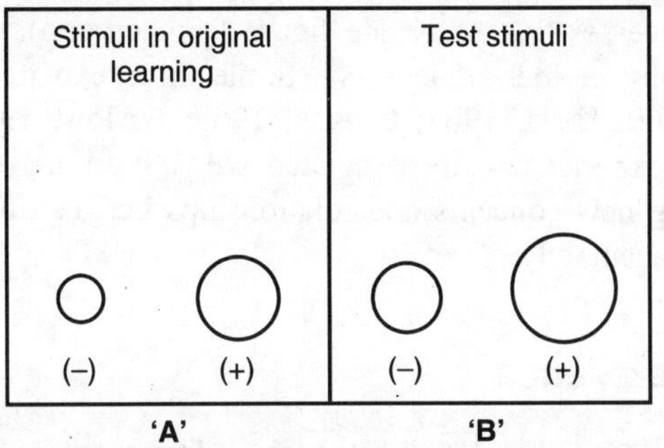

FIGURE 8.14 Relative relationships of stimuli.

In original learning condition, the learner's task is to find out which one of the two circles is correct. If he is reinforced for his choice of the larger of the two circles, (A) and choice of the smaller, is never reinforced, he will learn that the larger *i.e.* (positive circle) circle is correct. Now suppose we present before him two stimuli of which one is the old positive stimulus and the other is a new larger one. (B) Now in this test situation, the subject ('s') is asked to discriminate the correct one, he will probably choose the new larger one despite the fact the new smaller stimulus in the new pair is the one which was reinforced in the original learning period. The reason is that the 's' has learnt to respond in terms of perceived relationship—**larger of the two**. This is known as transposition. Similarly discriminating between—**darker of the two** has been subjected to experimentation in classical conditioning experiments using rats/hens (Thompson and Soloman, 1954).

8.15.4 Factors of Organization

Already discussed under Section 8.11.

8.15.5 Effect of Learning

Perception is also determined by learning. Knowledge of meaning of any stimulus depends upon learning. Everyday we learn many new things, objects, events and situations, to form concepts, learn similarities and differences etc. Learning all these serve as medium to experience the objects of the world meaningfully. Learning provides perceiving the object's properties.

The extent to which perceptual experiences are modified by learning has been under debate since very ancient times. There were two approaches—the **nativist** and the **empiricist** approach. Nativists argue that perceptual abilities are largely inborn while the empiricists opine that learning play an important role in determining our perceptions. The debate is still continuing and ample of evidences are available in support of both of these approaches. But, our purpose here is not to enter into the controversy. At this point, we shall consider certain pertinent facts as to how does learning determine and modify our perceptions.

Experiments done on this aspect evidently show that the experiences gained through learning enable us to organize the immediate sensory input into a pattern—a form and helps us in identifying the similarities among the elements of an object or discriminating them. Learning experiences also enable us to experience the interrelations among the elements forming an original pattern. Such experiences are essential aspects of our perceptions. To cite an example:

'Hebb' (1949) on the basis of evidences gathered from the studies of 'Senden' (1932) 'Riesen' (1947) concluded that though certain characteristics of perceptual organization are determined innately (especially the processes that segregate figure from ground), other characteristics can be shown as resulting from long periods of learning. Some more experiemental data (Leeper, 1935; Sendon, 1960; Landon, 1960; Ueda, 1967; Gibson, 1969; Barlow, 1972; Annis and Frost, 1973 etc.) support that learning experiences are associated with modifying the previous perceptions as well as enable us informing new concepts and relationships between the elements and identifying or recognizing the objects accurately.

8.15.6 Frame of Reference

Frame of reference is a system of related categories. These categories are used to categorize standards in judging and/or locating objects. For example, someone asks—**'where are you now?'** or **'who are you?'** To answer these questions we employ some frame of reference such as for the first question we give the address of the locality, direction and distance from some reference point which has meaning employing some system of dimension. For the second question our answer may be 'I am a student'. Here, the academic status is being employed as frame of reference.

Thus, frame of reference is also an important factor dertermining our perceptions of the objects, situations or events. This frame of reference is acquired through learning or experience.

In addition to these, there are some personal and social factors such as—(i) need, (ii) value, (iii) effect of symbolic meaning of the object, (iv) perceptual defence, (v) social norm, (vi) cultural determinants and (vii) social suggestion.

8.16 THE PERCEIVER'S (PERSONAL) FACTORS

Human beings are not just mechanical and passive recipients of stimuli from the external world. They are creative beings and try to understand the external world in their own ways. Thus, our perceptual experiences are not only the matter of varying complexities within the stimulus field nor these have only neurological basis, but are also a matter of perceiver's personal charac-teristics. These include the factors of motivations, expectations, values, attitudes, meanings, beliefs etc. These play an important role in giving meaning to the external world. Some of these factors are described herein below:

8.16.1 Needs

The momentary needs and desires of the perceiver strongly influence his or her perceptions. In fact, we perceive what we want to perceive, *i.e.* we tend to focus our attention selectively only on those objeects or events of the environment which appear to satisfy our current needs. Other objects or stimuli remain out of focus. For example, two friends enter into a restaurant together. One of them is hungry while another one is thirsty. The hungry one will choose to look for the menu while the thirsty one first asks for a glass of water. Obviously, in this instance the difference in selective attentiveness is influenced by the current needs of the two individuals and accordingly they tend to perceive the objects that have the potentiality to satisfy their current motivational states.

Several examples of our daily life situations also illustrate the selective role that the needs play in perceiving an object. For example, **'Osgood'** (1953)* cites his personal experiences. Two of his citations mentioned below are important:

(a) An office that I pass each day is numbered 400D, inevitably when the hour is near meal time, I perceive this as food.
(b) The car I used to drive had the euphemistic label SILVER STREAK (keel of a wheel) on its dashboard, inevitably when the hour is near meal time, I would read this as SILVER STEAK (fried piece of mutton).

The above-quoted experience of 'Osgood' obviously shows that sensory input of the objects are easily moulded to fit in the perceiver's current need states.

The need states influence our perceptions is also confirmed by several experimental studies. Sanford (1936, 1937) studied the effects of hunger need upon Word Association and the perception of ambiguous pictures. The results indicated that 'food habits' and physiological needs—both contributed to the effect of hunger upon perception. **Levonchain** and **Murphy** (1942) also obtained similar results for the hunger needs upon perception of ambiguous pictures.

MeClelland and **Atkinson** measured the effect of hunger need upon productions in subliminal (sub-conscious) visual perceptions test applied on naval trainees and found that food-related responses increased progressively with periods of deprivation.

Schafer and **Murphy** (1943) in their study on the effects of reward and punishment upon perception found that individuals on the whole, tend to perceive rewarded profiles more frequently than unrewarded profiles. The ratio was 54:13.

Postman and **Bruner** (1948) in a study of motivational situation involving frustration, found that word recognition threshold in the case of experimental group showed a significant increase as compared to non-frustrated group.

The above-mentioned experimental studies clearly show that need and other motivating conditions bear a significant influence upon our perceptual experiences.

---

* Osgood, C.E., *Method and Theory in Experimental Psychology*, N.Y., Oxford University Press, 1968, p. 286.

8.16.2 Value

Value is also an important determinant of perception. Every object has a value of its own. However, the value of an object varies from person to person. Some objects may appear valuable to some persons while not valuable to the others. For example, for a rich person, one rupee coin may have no value while the same coin may be highly valuable for a poor person.

Object value has three aspects of perceptual experiences—**selection**, **fixation** and **accentuation**. 'Selection' is a tendency to select the object for perception from among the several objects. 'Fixation' refers to a perceptual response tendency, *i.e.* the experience of selected perceptual object get fixated. **Accentuation** means paying emphasis on certain aspects or the property of the stimulus.

According to **Bruner** and **Goodman** (1947), the **value system** of an individual is an important behavioural determinant of perception. Behavioural determinant refers to the 'active adaptability function' of the organism. Accordingly, they proposed a hypothesis—"**greater the value of an object for the individual, the more it will be susceptible to organization**" and tested this hypothesis in a well-planned experiment. A group of school children, aged around ten years each was drawn from rich families of a progressive school in the Boston area and were served as subjects. An equal number of students from settlement house were chosen from Boston slum area. 10 children were of unspecified status and served as control group. Each of them saw a circular light spot on a ground glass screen set in a panel. The panel had a knob for controlling the size of the light areas on the screen. Before the experiment began, children were encouraged to explore the manipulation of this light. Subjects' (S_S) first task was to estimate from memory the size of a penny, a nickel, a dime, a quarter and a half dollar in that order and then in reversed order (*i.e.* from smaller coin to larger and again back from larger to the smaller coin). Two judgements were made each time. Following this, estimates were made with actual coins present (held in S_S palm about the same distance as the light and same order of presentation being used).

The results indicated that all children significantly overestimated their sizes. The amount of overestimation increased regularly with their value and not with their actual size. This indicates that socially valued objects are proportionally susceptible to behavioural determinants.

Another significant finding of this study was that children coming from poor families tended to reproduce the size of coins much larger than the actual sizes while the children coming from richer families tended to reproduce the sizes smaller than the actual. This kind of finding suggests that the poor children have greater 'subjective need' for money than the richer children and as such, showed grater overestimation of coin sizes. They value even the smallest coins greater because the coins have **objective value** as a medium of exchange for real need reducing objects.

Later on **Schooler** (1949) replicated this experiment with some difference in procedure. The findings though inconsistent with the findings of Bruner and Goodman, do suggest significance of **value system** as one of the determining factors of perceptual experience. However, much remains to be worked out by further research.

8.16.3 Symbolic Meaning

Any object, person or event is identified by its 'meaning'. Meaning is a symbolic representation of an object.

Every object possesses 'explicit' and 'implicit' meanings. Explicit meanings are objective symbols of recognizing or identifying an object. Such meanings are universal as people generally do not differ in their explicit meanings. Implicit meanings are 'subjective' (*i.e.* personal). People may have different subjective meanings for the same object.

Symbolic subjective meanings serve as sign value to what is received. Such meanings evoke reactions to stimulus pattern **which are relevant to something other than itself**.

Bruner and **Postman** (1948) in an experiment studied the effects of negative as well as positive sign values upon perceived size. They used same apparatus as was used by Bruner and Goodman to study need factor.

Three signs of equal sizes—a dollar sign, a swastik sign and an abstract geometrical design—were drawn on a plastic disc. The **dollar** is a positive sign because it is the largest American coin. **Swastik** sign is a negative sign because it represents Hitler's national sign and evokes fear of danger and its sight is presumed inauspicious. The geometrical designs are neutral, because it evokes neither a positive nor a negative response. The subjects (S_S) were asked to reproduce the size of three signs by manipulating the light on the ground glass of the panel just in front of them. The findings indicated that there was a significant variation in the sizes of the signs reproduced with manipulatable spot of light. Both the positive and negative signs were overestimated than the neutral signs. Bruner interprets this finding in terms of symbolic meanings of the symbols used. 'Dollar' is symbolized as having special significance as it is the largest American coin. Hence, reproduced larger than its actual size. 'Swastik' has a negative sign value that leads to accentuation of apparent size by alerting the individual to danger or threat.

8.16.4 Cognitive Style

Cognitive style refers to a consistent way of dealing with our environment. It significantly affects the way we perceive the environment. There are several cognitive styles that people use in perceiving their environment. One such style that is most extensively studied is 'field dependent' and 'field independent' cognitive style. Field dependent people perceive the external world in its totality (*i.e.* in a global or holistic manner). On the other hand, the field independent people perceive the world by breaking it into smaller units (*i.e.* in an analytic or differentiated manner).

For example, look at **Figure 8.15**. The figure presents the task to find out the hidden triangles in the picture. The 'field independents' would be able to find out the triangles quickly while the field dependents would take longer time.

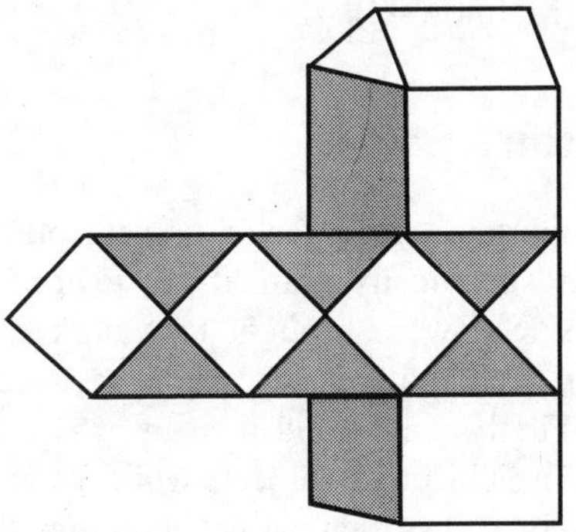

FIGURE 8.15 Field dependent and field independent style.

8.16.5 Expectations or Perceptual Sets

The expectations about what we might perceive in a given situation also influence our perception. The phenomenon of perceptual familiarisation or perceptual generalization reflects a strong tendency to see what we expect to see even when the results do not accurately reflect external reality. For example, suppose your milkman delivers you milk everyday at about 6 a.m., any knocking at the door around that time may be perceived as the presence of milkman, even if it may be someone else.

8.16.6 Other Personal Factors

Often in times of crisis, and influence of anxiety or emotions, attitudes, beliefs etc. also influence our perceptions. Suppose, two persons who were good friends, have had a quarrel and, therefore, are not in good terms. Consequently, they are not sure of their attitudes towards each other. The meaning of each one's acts become uncertain to the other. Under the circumstances, hostile feelings, anxiety or reassurance, desires etc. may influence their mutual perceptions. Similarly, when one foresees threats of danger (such as a soldier in a battlefield) one is in acute state of anxiety, stress or tension, his perceptions are likely to be influenced. Thus, personal emotional feelings, attitudes, mental status etc. are also important determinants of our perceptions and behavioural trends.

8.17 SOCIAL FACTORS

8.17.1 Social Norms

Man is a social being and therefore many of his perceptions are directly or indirectly shaped by his social experience. We tend to perceive an object, person or event in social frame of reference, *viz.* number 13 is considered as inauspicious in some societies. The sign *swastik* is considered as symbol of danger in certain societies while in Indian society it is an auspicious symbol. Consequently our perceptions of number 13 and swastik signs vary across societies. Similarly, resemblance in face cut of the offsprings with their biological parents are perceived by people of Trobrinder tribes as indicative of some kind of misfortune in future. Therefore, they usually ignore to perceive such resemblances (Malinowski).

8.17.2 Social Suggestion

Social suggestion is also an important social factor of perception. In general, it is observed that people tend to perceive what is specifically pointed out to them. **Sheriff** (1953) has shown this in an experiment. The subjects (S_S) were brought to a dark room and told to look at a small stationary spot of light that appeared moving. The subjects were required to estimate the rate of movements in two conditions. Firstly singly and then in group. In individual testing the estimate of movement greatly varied from subject to subject, while in group, the estimate was very close to group average. This obviously shows that while in group, the judgement or evaluations are influenced by interpersonal suggestion. Manufacturers of different products use this technique of suggestion by advertising the desirable properties of their products. The advertised qualities of products suggest the consumer to perceive the product having certain desirable qualities such as taste, aroma, economy, fragrance, soothing effect etc. (Husband and Godfrey, 1934; Pronko and Herman, 1960).

8.17.3 Cultural Influences

Different experiences and learning opportunities available to people in different cutural settings also influence their perceptions. People tend to perceive objects in their cultural perspectives. This is the reason that primitive tribes develop powers of observing distant wildlife that we cannot. This difference is due to culture. Cultural references are reflected in a variety of perceptions and large many studies lend support to the presupposition that **culture influences perception**.

In the year 1966, **Segall**, **Campbell** and **Herkovits** reported a series of studies on differences in perceptions due to cultural variations which they found in a comparative study of remote African villagers and western urban people. They were compared in their responses using vertical-horizontal illusions and Muller-Lyer illusions. It was found that the two groups reflected their illusory effects in accordance with their cultural backgrounds. The Africans living in dense jungles displayed greater illusion in the vertical-horizontal figures and western urbans in the Muller-Lyer illusion. This difference has been explained in terms of their experiences in the carpented and non-carpented environments.

In another study conducted in India, **Broota** and **Ganguli** (1975) found that in course of perceptual learning, Indians (Hindus and Muslims) perceived those aspects in the ambiguous figures more significantly which were associated with punishment (monotony) than the white American sample. The White Americans perceived the monetary aspects in the ambiguous pictures more significantly. These differences were attributed to cultural differences in child-rearing practices of the two groups.

From the aforementioned discussion of factors of perception, it is obvious that in addition to stimulus factors, the factors associated with the perceiver and his socio-cultural contexts play a key role in the process of perception. People process and interpret stimuli in their own ways depending on their personal, social and cultural conditions. Due to these reasons, our perceptions are tuned as well as modified in accordance with the personal and socio-cultural perspectives. Hence, **"We perceive a thing as we are and not as they are"**—seems quite convincing.

8.18 PERCEPTUAL DEFENCE

Perceptual defence is a phenomenon which is specifically related to the perceiver. Sometimes, it is found that people either ignore or fail to perceive certain stimuli, particularly those which are unpleasant, dissatisfying or cause anxiety as being dangerous or poses threat to the self-esteem. Such stimuli are generally 'edited-out' or certain elements in the set of stimuli are changed because of internal subjective factors such as needs or motivations, attitudes, value systems. The phenomenon like this is termed as **'perceptual defence'**. This refers to selective tendency of the perceiver either to ignore or make error in perceiving, judging or evaluating the stimulus event that are unpleasant or dissatisfying or not good in taste. In other words, perceptual defence may be defined **as an instant defence for an experience, one may have difficulty in accepting.**

Postman, **Bruner** and **McGinnies** (1948) have conducted experimental studies by exposing the subjects (S_S). 36 words one by one for a very brief period through a modified form of

Dodge's techistoscope. The words chosen represented 6 values on Allport-Vernon Lindsey Scale (theoretical, economic, aesthetic, social, political and religious). The presentation order was random and standard procedure was used to obtain **recognition threshold**. The results showed that the recognition threshold for 'covaluant' words (*i.e.* those which are resonant with the value system of the individual) was higher than the 'non-covaluant words'.

McGinnies (1949) also found that threat situations accentuate perceptual reactions as well as inhibit recognition. Inhibition delays and lowers recognition threshold.

However, there are some contradictions also. For example, **'Howes'** and **'Solomon'** (1950) have rejected 'McGinnies' hypothesis. According to them, the threshold for recognition depends upon the previous acquaintances and the frequency of use.

In view of the contradictions, it would be erroneous to come to any definite conclusion. However, it is clear that our perceptions get influenced by personal factors like motivations, cognitive styles as well as defensive attitude to recognize unwanted objects or events.

8.19 PERCEPTUAL VIGILANCE

Sometimes, people display readiness to perceive some stimuli eventhough the stimuli is distant or weak enough to arouse perceptual experience. This phenomenon is called 'perceptual vigilance'. In other words, perceptual vigilance is experiencing more than what the sensory data warrant. Such instances are due to perceiver's motivations, expectations, anxiety and other personal factors. For example, suppose a man vigilantly clings to the preconception that 'women are inferior drivers'. He suddenly witnesses an accident half a mile down the road and perceives the driver of the car as a woman who was on the wrong side of the road, although the sense data from the distance are relatively low.

A glaring example of perceptual vigilance was recently* witnessed when lacs of people throughout the country and even in some parts of the world reportedly experienced the **idol of lord Ganesha** drinking milk through spoon on a particular day and time. This news widely spread all over the country as 'chamatkar'. This perception was of course, influenced by the strong religious belief' **Astha** that weaved the external stimuli into the fabric of their beliefs ignoring the details that do not fit. Such phenomenon occurs due to the frame of reference which induces a person to perceive the objects or events in a pattern that fits the frame. Evidently, the recognition threshold of perceptual vigilence is very low because threatening or strong beliefs tend us to recognise even very weak stimuli very soon.

8.20 VISUAL SPACE PERCEPTION

We perceive an object in relation to its spatial characteristics. Hence, when we see an object or hear a sound, we not only experience the object in its concrete form, but also perceive the size, distance, spatial position (right/left, upward/downword etc.), magnitude etc. Perceiving thickness or depth—third dimension, is also an important aspect of our visual space perception. Here, the puzzling question arises as to how do we perceive 'third dimension' in view of the fact that our retina is able to register two-dimensional images only.

Owing to advances made in studying different psychological processes and environment of knowledge, answer to such puzzling questions is not hard to find today. While sensing to

* This incident occurred sometimes in early months of 1996.

perceive an object in the environment, we get several cues or signals such as—difference in shadows, vividness, size of the images, etc. These cues provide much information that enables us to perceive third dimension even though the physical images are only two dimensional, visual cues for tridimensional perceptions are generally classified into 'monocular' and 'binocular' cues.

8.20.1 Monocular Cues

Monocular cues are those which operate when only one eye is viewing the object. These cues were first recognized by Greek painters. They used these cues to represent distance in their pictures. These cues are as follows:

Linear perspective

The distant objects project a smaller image on the retina than the nearer objects. In addition, the distance separating the images of far objects also appear to be smaller. Suppose, you are looking at a rail-road track edges of a highway. These appear to meet on the horizon. Similarly, uniformly spaced objects such as electric poles appear to be spaced more closely as they recede into distance.

Aerial perspective or clearness

In general, more clear an object, nearer it seems and vice versa. Hence, ambiguity of image provides a cue for depth perception or perception of distance. We often experience distant mountain appearing farther away on a hazy day than on a clear day. It so happens because the haze in the atmosphere blurs the fine details.

Interposition or superposition or covering

Interposition occurs when one thing covers another thing. Such coverings obstruct viewing another object. When one object is totally in sight and another object is partially covered by it, the former will appear nearer to the latter object, *i.e.* covered and partially visible object. The object that covers the another object is superpositioned over another. Hence, the superpositioning object comes in front and appears nearer to the superimposed object. For example, look at **Figure 8.16**.

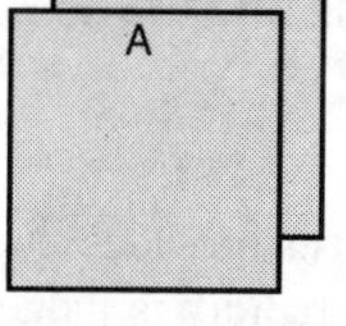

FIGURE 8.16 Interpositioning and superpositioning of an object.

In Figure 8.16, A superimposes B, resulting in A coming in front that appears nearer to B which looks behind and therefore relatively distant.

Light and shadow

The patterns of shadows and light also provide important monocular cues for depth perception. Usually, the shadowed objects are judged farther away than the unshadowed areas. Further, knowledge of source of light may also serve as a cue for depth perception. Our vast experiences of shadows cast by one object upon another give an indication of the farther object. Thus, patterns of light and shadows play important role in our perception thrust forward, depression, hollow etc. of the objects.

Familiar size

Vast amount of our experienced images of different objects' size remain stored in the form of memory images that provides useful cues about the distance of the object. For example, if you know the size of a man (or your friend) you can easily judge the distance at which he is standing. Similarly, while playing cards, we are able to judge the distance of card being presented. Thus familiarity of the size gives cues to judge distance from two-dimensional retinal images.

Gradients of texture

Gradient means progressive changes in something while texture denotes structure. Thus, progressive or continuous changes (not abrupt changes) provide cue for distance perception. The regions closest to the observer have a coarse texture and many details. But, as the distance increases, texture becomes finer and finer. Continuous changes of texture also provide information regarding depth to the CNS.

The texture gradient cue involves both the linear and size. **'Gibson'**, in his experiments, has demonstrated that the size and density of texture elements serve as important cue for the experience of distance. The objects lying on surface that looks finer in texture are perceived farther than those lying on visibly rough texture surface. Look at **Figure 8.18**.

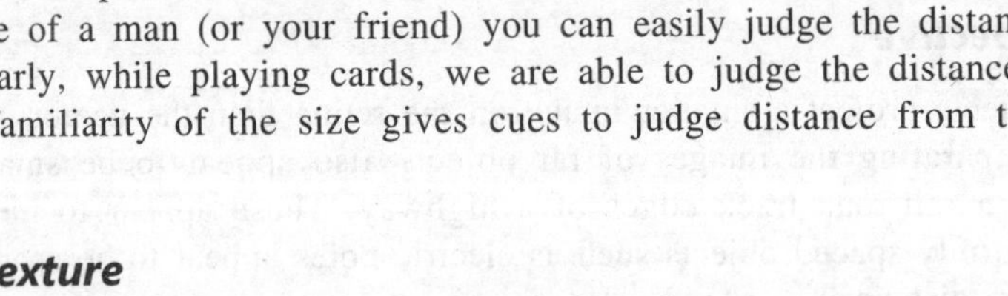

a b

FIGURE 8.17 Texture gradient.

Movement

The relative movement of the object also provides cue for judging distance. Other things being equal, the object which appears moving rapidly is judged as nearer or closer to that which appears moving slowly. While travelling in a train, the nearby objects are seen going apart in opposite direction while the distant objects appear to move with us, *i.e.* in direction the train is moving. Such cues account for perceiving distance.

In addition to the relative movements in the environment, evidences are also available to show that cues to perceive distances are also derived when an individual moves his head and eyes.

This is particularly found in judging near and distant objects. The relative amount of movement is usually less for distant objects than for near ones.

8.20.2 Binocular Cues

Binocular cues are those which give cues to visual perception by viewing an object with two eyes. These are as follows:

Retinal disparity

Ordinarily, we view objects of the world with both the eyes which are separated from each other by 65 mm. Because of this distance the images of the object on the retina of the two eyes are not exactly the same. Hence, the two images differ which we call retinal disparity. The fovea in the centre of each of the retina is much more sensitive than rest of the retina. While looking at an object, eyes are fixated in such a manner that the images fall most on each fovea. But, due to spatial differences of the two eyes, the images projected on each retina get slightly different. Moreover, the images are most different when the object is very close. Thus, gradient of disparities is established which give information about depth.

Convergence

This is a kinesthetic cue from muscles that turn and point the eyes. When we look at a nearby object, *i.e.* reading a book, we need to converge our eyes. This is done with the help of 6 extra ocular muscles located outside each eye so that the image of seen objects or lines of reading materials may fall on the fovea of each eye for fusion and clarity of vision. The degree or extent of convergence is signalled to the brain that functions as cue to distance. The angle of convergence differs with the distance of the object from eye. For near objects, the convergence is large that decreases as the object is farther away. For objects farther than 30 feet, the lines of sight of the eyes are parallel beyond which convergence has little value as a cue for depth perception.

Accommodation

Accommodation refers to increase or decrease of muscular tensions of the lens. It is like focusing in a camera. In camera, lens is adjusted to focus the image of the object or person in camera. This focusing is called adjustment or accommodation. The lens in the eye accommodates itself with the help of ciliary muscles to bring an image into focus on the ratina. The ciliary muscles attached to the lens make the lens to change its shape from concave to convex or from convex to concave depending upon the distance of the visible object. For the near objects, the muscles contract and the lens bulges out while for distant objects, the muscles relax and make the lens thinner. Thus, lens accommodates by changing its shape or curvature for near and distant objects. The strain on account of contracting and relaxing functions of the ciliary muscles in helping the lens to accommodate, provides cues to the brain to interpret the distance or any other third dimensional features of the objects. Thus, the accommodative signals of the two eyes provide cues for three-dimensional experiences in vision.

However, the research studies have shown that accommodation is a weak cue for the perception of distance.

Size of the rational images

The images projected on the retina may be big or small in size. This variation of size depends upon the distance of the object from sight. Nearer objects project bigger or larger images than the distant objects. Thus, the size of the images on retina also provides cues for tridimensional perceptions of the visual field.

8.21 STEREOSCOPIC VISION

To verify and establish the accuracy of binocular cues of tridimensional vision, stereoscopic studies have been done. **Wheatstone's study** (1833) in this context is considered as the pioneering study. On the basis of his studies, he has opined that human vision is **stereoscopic** and he invented an equipment, known as stereoscope. As has been stated earlier, the two eyes are at a distance of about 65 mm. This distance is called **interocular distance**. As such, they receive slightly different views of the object. The right retinal image has more of the right side of the object and hence, a little different image of the object than the left eye. Similarly, the left eye has more of the left side—a little different from the right eye. The two images get combined by the process of fusion in the brain that gives vivid depth effect of the binocular vision.

In stereoscope, two different stereograms (pictures of an object taken separately from two sides of the object) are presented with the help of stereoscope in both eyes (right side stereogram in the right eye and left side stereogram in the left eye). The stereograms are presented in such a way that one may visualize the corresponding sides with corresponding eyes only. It was observed that the subjects view single object due to fusion of the two images in the brain with vivid tridimensional features. Thus, it is evident that stereoscopic vision provides information about depth.

8.22 PERCEPTION OF MOTION

In physical sciences, **motion** means change in object's position in space. It denotes successive activity of change in position. When an object moves, it successively stimulates different areas of retina which is perceived as motion or movement. This is called **real motion**. But, in psychology, we are more concerned with **illusory motion** which is termed as **apparent motion**. Apparent motion means **perceiving a stationary object as moving**. Thus, experiencing change in the object's position in the space without any such change in reality is called apparent motion (see **Figure 8.18**). More simply, it can be said that **perceiving motion or movement without any real movement is what we call apparent motion**—as we experience while viewing movies. It is so experienced because of successive and rapid presentation of stationary object. **Thus, apparent motion refers to the perceptual experience of movement in the object which in fact, do not move rather are still or stationary.** Obviously, in apparent movement, there occurs no successive stimulation of different receptors in the ratina as happens in real motion. Even then we experience the motion, *i.e.* perceive the object moving. Such an event of perceptual experience has been called as **phi-phenomenon** (Wertheimer, 1912).

There are some other forms of apparent motions such as **stroboscopic motion**, **induced motion** and **autokinetic motion**.

Stroboscopic motion is also called **optical** or **beta movement**. The kind of movement seen in movies is a very common example of 'stroboscopic apparent motion'. A movie simply projects or throws very rapidly the successive pictures of moving scenes onto screen and different receptors in the retina are successively and rapidly stimulated. This rapid and successive order of stimulation is conveyed as afferent code to the visual cortex which interpret as movement of the stationary or still pictorial scenes on the screen.

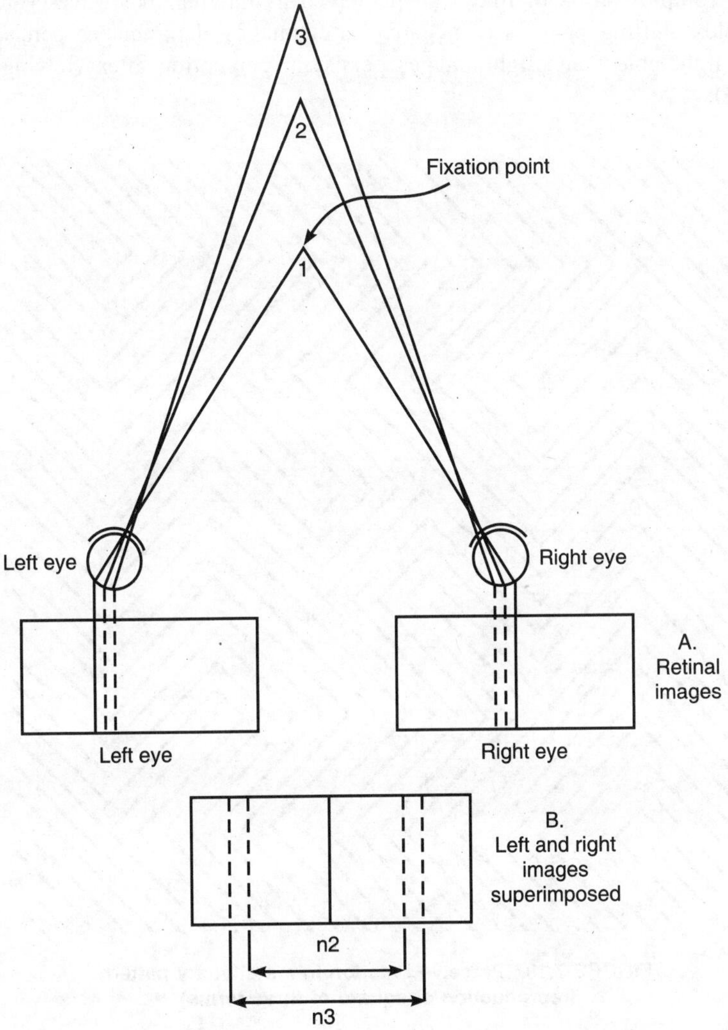

FIGURE 8.18 Two retinal images falling on two eyes differ from each other.

Induced movement: Induced movement occurs when a stationary spot or object is perceived as moving because its background or frame moves. For example, moon is perceived as moving or racing through a thin layer of clouds. Thus, the movement of the moving frame of clouds induces **induced movement** in the stationary moon.

Autokinetic movement: When a person stares or fixates on a small spot of light projected on wall, it would appear wandering (moving) without any logical pattern. This is an example of **autokinetic movement** (autokinetic—a Greek term meaning self-moving). It is presumed that kinesthetic stimulation of muscles due to eye movement accounts for such an experience of apparent motion.

Stationary patterns: Some stationary patterns are so made that appear to be moving. Such patterns contain complex shifts of lines and perceived as moving like waves (undulation). It is caused by complex shifting patterns of negative after-image—dark images persist in perception after viewing a light object and light images persist in perception after viewing a dark object (see **Figure 8.19**).

FIGURE 7.19 Perceived motion in a stationary pattern (reproduction of square of three forms).

8.23 SPACE PERCEPTION OF SOUND

While perceiving auditory signals, we are able to locate the position of sounding objects in space in terms of distance and direction. This ability is of considerable value in making adjustment in life. For example, while crossing a busy street, our life depends on locating accurately the position from which an unseen automobile is drawn on us.

8.23.1 Perceiving the Direction of Sound

Our ability to locate the direction of sound is due to our ears located at two different points in space. Sound waves stimulate the two ears differently for some distinct reasons such as:

(a) Difference in the time of arrival of the sound wave from same source at the two ears. A sound coming from an object at the left of the head strikes the left ear first before the right one. Though, the difference of arrival time may be very short, it tells us from which direction the sound is coming.
(b) Sound waves which strike the side of the ear first, strikes more strongly than they strike another side ear. Hence, the intensity with which the two ears are stimulated differs on the basis of which we come to know about the direction of sound.
(c) Sound waves, as we know, consist of areas of high and low pressure. The two ears at the different points in space will be stimulated in different phase of cycles.
(d) Usually we turn our heads in the direction from which sound waves arrive at the ears. By turning our heads in the direction of sound source, the direction of sound becomes identifiable.

The above cues of direction are useful only if the sounds come from one side or the other. Sounds coming directly in front and those above and behind us, are not easily distinguishable because the stimulation reaching the two ears is identical.

8.23.2 Perceiving the Distance of Sound

In perceiving the distance (how far away the source of sound) of sound, two clues help us—**loudness** and **timbre**. Farther away the source, weaker is the sound. Similarly, farther the source, purer it will be and conversely, nearer the sound more composite it is. This difference in composition results from loss of irregular sound waves (or noise) and from the loss of certain piercing overtones which lack sufficient energy to carry very far.

8.24 PERCEPTION OF TIME

Perception of time (temporal perception) takes many forms. Often we experience the time spent in doing a work. We also experience the exposure period of some kind of stimulus, *i.e.* duration of time. We also have the experience of temporal sequences and intervals. It also involves the memories of the past, events of the present and orientation towards future.

8.24.1 Factors Affecting Perception of Time

Time like space is perceived differently according to a variety of conditions within the perceiver. The important such factors within the individual are as follows:

Age and experience of the perceiver

Though, there exists wide individual differences in the speed with which specific time concepts are acquired, the ability to perceive time also depends on age and experience of the perceiver.

S. Pringer (1952) conducted an experiment to study children's knowledge of clocktime on 89 children in the age group of 4–6 years. They were instructed to set different timings in a clock and also to understand why the clock has two hands. It was observed that the errors in setting time varied with age and also experience of the children. One interesting error by a few children of both the age levels was to mistake 12:30 for 6:00. Their comments revealed that a favourite radio programme comes on at 6:00 and they had learned to watch for the two hands to be **straight up and down**.

In another study, **Cohen** (1964) found that perception of apparent duration of weeks, months and years also varies with the age of the subject.

Motivation

Usually time spent in monotonous work is overestimated while time spent in interesting work is underestimated. **Wyatt**, **Frober** and **Stock** (1929) in an early experiment found that errors in estimating time varied with the degree of boredom which is evident from the data shown in **Table 8.2**.

Table 8.2 Variations in estimating time

Actual time in minutes	*Estimation when slightly bored*	*Estimation when completely bored*
30 minutes	25 min.	30 min.
50 minutes	50 min.	55 min.
70 minutes	75 min.	85 min.
90 minutes	100 min.	110 min.
100 minutes	110 min.	120 min.

The judgement of time has also been found to be related to feelings of success and failure. As given interval of time is judged longer by the subjects experiencing failures than the subjects experiencing success. (Harton, 1939).

There is a popular proverbial saying—**Watched pot never boils**. This saying has experimentally been confirmed by **Filer** and **Meals** (1949). He found that subjects trying to get through a task to reach the desired goal estimates a given interval of time as longer than those working without any such motivation.

Drugs

Some drugs such as **amphetamine** and **secobarbitol** have been found to influence perception of time interval (Goldstone, Boardman and Lahman, 1958). They found that under the influence of amphetamine, an interval shorter than a second is perceived as a second. Secobarbitol has the opposite effect.

In some cultures, particular drug is believed to be associated with the sense of time and rhythm. For example, among Jazz musicians, there is fairly general belief that marijuana improves the sense of time and rhythm. Though, this is not supported by experimental studies (Aldrich, 1944).

Some Other Factors

Length of time intervals

Some studies have demonstrated that the accuracy of time perception is influenced by the length of time intervals. **Vierordt** (1968) in one study found that shorter duration of time intervals are overestimated while the longer ones are underestimated. **Woodrow** (1930) has concluded that shorter temporal intervals are more accurately perceived than longer intervals of time. However, some of the studies do not lend support to such conclusions rather the findings run contrary. Such contradictions are probably due to the variations in subjective characteristics of the individuals as well as differences associated with the characteristic features of the stimulus.

Stimulus characteristics

These are concerned with nature of time. The time may be continuous or discontinuous. It may be filled or unfilled. **Woodrow** (1928) in one of his studies found that empty intervals of 0.50 and 0.60 are not distinguishable. Further, a filled time interval is usually underestimated than the unfilled time interval. Similarly, the nature of task with which the time intervals are filled also have significant bearing on the perception of time.

8.24.2 Methods Employed for Studying Time Perception

Scientists usually employ three methods for experimental studies on time perception. These are as follows: (i) Reproduction method, (ii) Comparison method and (iii) Estimation method.

(i) **Reproduction method:** In this method, subjects are required to reproduce the given time intervals. The time interval produced by the experimenter is called the stimulus time interval while the time interval reproduced by the subjects (S_S) are called response time interval. A comparison of the two tells about the accuracy with which the subjects judge the given time intervals.

(ii) **Comparison method:** In this method, the two time intervals differing in length are presented before the subjects (S_S). who are required to judge which of the two is longer or shorter.

(iii) **Estimation method:** In this method, subjects (S_S) are asked to estimate the time elapsed between appearance and disappearance of a stimulus which are varied randomly in various trials.

8.25 ILLUSIONS

In our everyday life situations, we very frequently experience a form of perception which are misleading or inaccurate. For example, in dimlight, a rope is perceived as a snake. Sometimes, an unfamiliar face is perceived from distance as a face of a familiar friend, a rail track appears to meet on the horizon etc. Such forms of perceptions are called as **illusions** which are loosely defined as incorrect or false perceptions. But, psychologically, illusions cannot be said as **incorrect or false perception**. Illusions, in fact, possess all the characteristics of perceptions. Like perceptual experiences, illusions do provide knowledge or information about the objects of the world. This information is about the present stimulus and follow the same sensory channel and related processes as in perception, *i.e.* encoding of sensory input, organizing and interpreting the information, asigning an identifying name etc. However, in illusion, the experience as organized pattern of the stimulus does not agree or match with other more trustworthy perceptions of the same object. Illusions demonstrate that what we perceive depends upon processes which go far beyond the sensory input. Hence, **unusual perception**. For example, look at Figure 8.20 (A and B). In both of these two figures, a straight line is divided in two parts. In figure A, the part on the right is perceived as longer than the part on the left, *i.e.* they are unequally divided. But, the same line in figure B is perceived as equally divided. Psychologically, both the perceptions are the facts of perceptual experiences. But, the difference in perceiving the two figures is due to the difference in the pattern of structure that the two figures present. We do not get the same total stimulation from **Figures 8.20**. Hence, two different perceptions.

FIGURE 8.20 Unusual perceptual experience.

In both the cases, perceptions are determined by the characteristics of the stimuli. Therefore, geometrically, the two lines have equally been divided, but psychologically, their patterns produce different perceptions—line 'A' as unequally divided while line 'B' equally divided.

The above illustration of illusion is more or less permanent or 'stable' as well as universal because, the perceptions of the above figures do not change overtime. Moreover, almost each one of us is likely to perceive this kind of unusual perception (illusion). There are many more examples of permanent or universal illusions, *viz.* perceiving a railtrack or edges of a highway as meeting on the horizon or becoming less wider, while travelling in a running train, perceiving the stationary objects along outside the windows as moving etc. Some of the geometrical illusions of permanent or universal nature are shown in **Figure 8.21**.

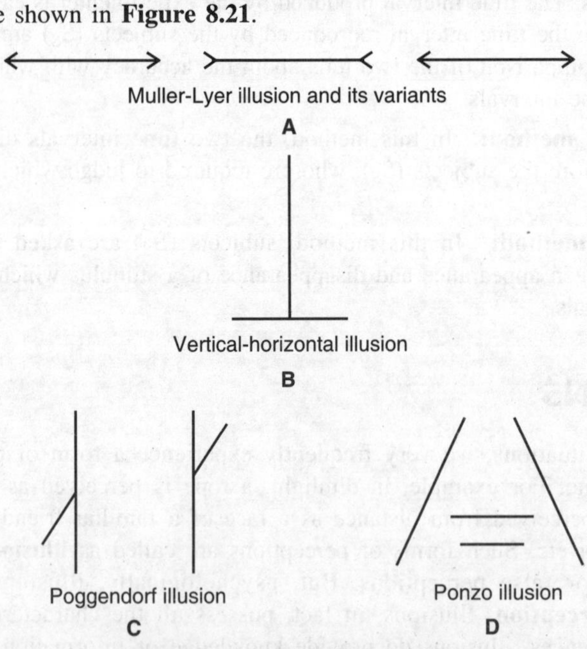

FIGURE 8.21 Geometical illusions.

Moon illusion: Moon illusion is also an universal nature of illusion because it is experienced by all of us. When the moon is in the horizon, it looks bigger than when it is in the zenith. Though the retinal image of moon in both the situations is constant because, the distance of moon from earth is same, however, its perceived size differs. This difference is attributed to the **size-distance relationships** as postulated by **Helmholtz**. 'Helmholtz' opines that our judgement of size is related to the judgement of distance. Accordingly, if we judge the distance of an object more than its real distance, the perceived size will be larger than the actual and vice versa. This means that for a given visual angle, the ratio of perceived size to perceived distance is fixed. This is called **size distance invariance hypothesis** and moon illusion is explained in terms of this hypothesis. According to this hypothesis, when the moon is in the horizon, the depth and distance cues such as interposition and linear perspectives provide the experience of moon as far distant and thus, perceived larger than actual. But, when the moon is high in the sky, no intervening object (cue) is available and the moon is perceived closer to us than the moon is at the horizon.

In addition to permanent and universal illusions, there are other illusions which are neither permanent nor universal. These are transitory (temporary) and personal. For example, in a dim twilight a rope is perceived as a snake, perceiving an unfamiliar person as a familiar friend etc. Such experiences occur under unusual or extraordinary situations—hastiness, defects in the sense organs, mental set, anxiety, emotional upsets and similar other personal factors which induces one to perceive a particular pattern in a manner, usually not perceived.

Thus, **illusions demonstrate unusual perceptions** and such illusory experiences may be related to any of the sense modalities.

8.26 HALLUCINATIONS

Another form of perception is hallucinatory experiences or simply hallucinations. Hallucinations refer to the psychological experience of an object which is not actually present. For example, while passing through solitary place in the darkness of night one may have haunting experience as if someone is following him, but when he looks behind and focusses torchlight, he finds nothing. Such haunting experiences are known as **hallucinations that provide information of our surroundings in absence of the experienced stimuli**.

In certain respect, illusions and hallucinations are alike. Both of these experiences are unusual and provide information about the world that are either unusual (illusion) or non-existent (hallucination). Like some of the illusory experiences that are temporary and personal, hallucinations are also transitory and personal or subjective experiences. However, the two experiences are distinct to each other in many ways. The main differences are as follows:

(i) Illusion is an unusual perception of the stimuli present in the environment while hallucinatory experiences are of those stimuli which are not immediately present in the environment.
(ii) Illusion is a normal phenomenon. Any normal person is susceptible to illusory experiences. But, hallucinatory experiences are generally associated with abnormal persons. For example, hallucination is a predominating symptom in schizophrenics or drug addicts.
(iii) Among normal individuals, illusions are classified as permanent or temporary, universal or personal. But, hallucinatory experiences in normal individuals are only temporary.

(iv) Illusions are produced by the characteristics of the external stimuli but hallucinatory experiences are purely subjective. Such experiences are not induced by any external factor.

(v) Illusory experiences are more vivid or clear (because the stimulus is present) while hallucinatory experiences are relatively ambiguous or hazy, because the stimuli are non-existent.

8.27 EXTRA SENSORY PERCEPTION (ESP)

Recent developments in the field of parapsychology has brought forth many facts relating to our perceptual experiences without involving physical stimulation of sensory organs. Phenomenon like this is known as **extrasensory perception (ESP)**. This includes the following phenomenon:

Telepathy: This refers to transfer of thoughts from one person to another at different places.

Clairvoyance: It refers to the perception of objects or events without involving sense organs such as stating the number and suit of a playingcard that is in a sealed envelope.

Pre-recognition: Pre-recognition is perceiving the future events such as some of the fortune-tellers often close their eyes, thinks for a while and says—what event is in the offing.

Psychokinesis (PK): It refers to controlling objects without touching them. This makes material body or energy system move on, such as bending of keys, moving the stationary coins on the surface, broken watches begin to function, making pencil to move on the table etc.

In a typical study of ESP, the subjects are asked to determine the symbols on the cards hidden from them. In such studies, pack of 24 cards containing five different symbols have generally been used. The responses are checked statistically to rule out the possibilities of guessing.

The phenomenon of ESP is still a subject of debate for the psychologists. Some psychologists believe that certain form of ESP are incontrovertible. For example, **Rhine** and **Brier** (1968), **McConneld** (1969), **van de Castle** (1969) argue that human beings have abilities to visualize and acknowledge certain events beyond sensory stimulations. However, many are not convinced because, such dramatic events are not replicable. Moreover, a few studies that have been done by parapsychologists do not provide any substantive evidence to work out any conclusive theory to explain the phenomenon of ESP (Hensel, C.G.M. 1966).*

In essence, ESP seems nothing more than a figment of people's imagination. At present, evidences for ESP is weak. However, extensive research on large scale is required to come to any conclusion.

* Hensel, C.G.M., A British psychologist in his famous book ESPA—Scientific Evaluation (1996). N.Y. Charles Scribner's Sons, points out that though a great deal of time, efforts and money have been spent but have brought forth no tenable finding. *

SUMMARY

- Perception refers to meaningful sensory experiences of the world around us. It is presentative as well as representative and rational process of cognition.
- Perception involves several processes like receptor, symbolic, affective and aesthetic and organizational or unifying processes.
- Perceptual experiences are characterized by certain characteristics such as—an active mental process, selective in nature, a complex process, immediateness, involves complex receptor and neural processes, has the attribute of constancy with flexibility and is an organized process of knowing the world meaningfully.
- Though, perception bears similarity with sensation and attentional processes, it also differs with these processes in many respects.
- Perception is an organizational process that involves botom-up and up-down levels of processing.
- There are various approaches to perception. Important such processes are structuralist's, Gestalt views and behaviouristic views.
- The organization of perceptual events are governed by certain principles of grouping. These are peripheral laws and central laws.
- The peripheral laws include—similarity, proximity, continuity, inclusiveness etc. There are innate tendencies that relate to stimulus situation.
- The central laws relate to personal factors and are learnt or acquired. These include need, values and meanings.
- We tend to perceive stimuli as a figure against a background. The two are intricately related and produce distinct experiences but are interrelated.
- Whatever we perceive, we tend to perceive the environment as stable. This is called perceptual constancy. For example, we tend to perceive the objects as constant in size, shape, form or brightness. Constancy in perception is influenced by our familiarity and also a tendency to take into account the spatial positions of viewing the objects.
- Perceptual experiences are influenced by several factors. Among these, the personal and socio-cultural contexts play important role in determining what we perceive.
- Certain phenomenon of perceptions such as perceptual defence and perceptual vigilance are important which has extensively been researched.
- Illusions are unusual perceptions. Illusions may be permanent and universal as well as temporary or personal.
- Hallucinations are perception of a non-existent stimulus. It is indicative of abnormal states of mind.
- ESP is a phenomenon which is a subject of debate and extensive research is required to substantiate it.

CHAPTER 9

Attentional Process

9.1 INTRODUCTION

Human beings live in a vast environment. Every moment of human life is in contact with a vast number of stimuli which have the potentiality to stimulate the sense organs and thus, human beings are capable of receiving a huge amount of information from the environment. This process of receiving information from the vast environment is a sensory process of 'sensing' the environment. Human beings also organize whatever they sense. This leads to organized experience of the sensed data—called 'perception'. But, human beings take in and use only a very small portion of the available stimuli in the environment. This refers to a mechanism that operates in selecting and processing of stimuli which are of great interest and highly valuable to us for adjustment. This mechanism is called the **attentional process**. It is a sort of **selective perception**. The present chapter is devoted to this important mechanism that enables us to selectively perceive the objects, persons or events from a wide range of stimuli and process the selected stimuli for the sake of adjustment with the environment.

9.2 NATURE AND DEFINITION

Attention is a very common term of our everyday language. We often use the term like—giving our attention to this or that thing or situation, concentrating attention on something, shifting of attention from one thing to another etc. All such usages of the term lead us to think of attention as a faculty or power that can be manipulated in any direction we wish to. However, this assumption is very simple. Attention indeed is a behaviour, an act, a process of attending and not a power or faculty. Therefore, it is more preferable to call it attending than attention.

Attending is a motivational process. Out of a wide range of stimuli (which are within physiological range), we tend to select only those which are related to our present need states or interests. For example, when an individual is deeply involved in study, he is not aware of other things placed on his reading table or the stimuli around him in the reading room—the temperature, different books on the table, alarm clock, conversations going on by others in a room attached to the reading room, furnishings in the room, etc. Sometimes the acts like somebody's entry to the reading room and placing a cup of tea on the reading table also go unnoticed. This means that the reader is selectively focusing on a single activity (reading) and the other stimuli of the surrounding are not being noticed. Thus, the mechanism of attentional process is a process of selective perception which is called attending.

What follows from the above description about the nature of the process of attending, is that it is a selective process of perceiving certain stimuli and either ignoring or not taking into cognizance (mental awareness) of other stimuli present in the environment. Accordingly, the process of attending may be defined as follows:

> **Attention is a term given to a perceptual process that selects certain input for inclusion into our conscious experience or awareness in a given period of time'.**

From the above definition, it is obvious that attention is 'to attend' and 'to attend' is a state of readiness to selectively bring certain stimuli of the environment into the focus of consciousness or attention. Thus, the attentional process is characterized by:

(a) **Attention is to attend:** This refers to a process of attentional act and, therefore, it is not a mental faculty or power.

(b) **To attend:** This denotes a state of readiness to take in or bring in certain stimuli or aspects of the environment into one's centre of consciousness or focus of attention. Thus, the attending person is mentally set to bring into his consciousness—a kind of inclination to attend.

(c) It is a **selective process** to take in certain stimuli into one's focus (centre) of consciousness. While attending, we do not respond indiscriminately to every stimuli or aspect of environment, rather we respond selectively in terms of our need states, interests, attitudes etc.

(d) **The process of attention divides our field of consciousness (or experience) into focus (centre) and margin.** The events that are attended to are clearly perceived because such events are taken into our focus field of consciousness while others are either dimly perceived or not perceived at all because these are in the margin or peripheries of the focal consciousness.

To understand the nature of attentional process, let us describe the process with an analogy of dish antenna on the roof. As we have seen earlier, our sense organs are the 'windows' to the external world. These windows are capable of picking up any amount of available information. But, there is a mechanism of regularity that filters or partially blocks out some inputs and allows others to get through. In this sense, our sense organs are like dish antenna on the roof that can pick up all available signals. But, tuner in our television system selects only the signal for which it has been tuned by the viewer and the remaining other signals are filtered out. In the same manner, the **'attentional processes'** limit or block out the reception of stimuli in a selective manner. In this sense, the attentional process serves the function of tuning by filtering out the information selectively for being processed. This selective function or filtering function is governed by the centre (directed by brain). These processes serve various functions in the organization of our perceptions and other cognitive functions. Some of these functions will be described in later sections of this chapter.

9.3 SOME ASPECTS OF ATTENTION

Psychologists have attempted to analyse the attentional process and have found three basic interrelated aspects of attention. These are as follows:

9.3.1 Attention as a Postural Adjustment

While attending, we usually tend to adjust our body positions and the related sense organs in such a way as to receive the particular stimuli most readily. In other words, we tend to select the significant or valuable stimuli from among a wide range of stimuli and situate the same into our focus of attention. For example, a physician in course of clinical examination of a patient with a stethoscope, we often notice that he bends a little towards the patients' heart and chest, often closes his eyes to shut out other distracting stimuli. This he does with a view to allow even the faint beats of heart sounds or respiratory irregularities. While taking records of pulse rate, he places the three fingers on the site of pulse beating and watches the wrist watch for a minute and mentally counts, judges the number of beats as well as the irregularities. Thus, he makes all possible postural adjustments of his body positions to take in the selected information into focus of attention. Similarly we find athletes taking a particular posture on the starting point of the race-track to take in the signal to start racing.

9.3.2 Attention as a Clearness in Consciousness

While attending the objects which are attended to, are relatively much more vivid or clear than those which are not attended to. At any given time, something is filtered out and taken into the focus or centre of consciousness while others remain in the periphery or margin and, therefore, do not provide any awareness of their presence or give only a dim or hazy awareness. For example, when one is grossly involved in reading an interesting novel, the contexts of the novel will be in his focus while other things such as ticking sounds of watch in the room, soft playing of radio sounds, though potentially intense, remain in the margin and therefore do not give any vivid or clear experience.

9.3.3 Attention as a Set Towards Action

Attention is a readiness to respond in a particular way to some stimuli situation. For example, in military, the order 'March' is responded to by armymen in a particular way—either they march forward or backward—depending upon the prior command to get them ready to march on command. The leader of the squad gives the command—'*squad forward march karega*'—'march'. Here the prior command is '*forward march karega*'—this command is given to get the squad ready to march in a particular direction and then the final command 'march' is given. The prior command induces readiness or make the squad mentally set to act upon the final command without losing any time.

Thus, the attentional process has three interconnected aspects. All these aspects are the parts of a single complex act, **Attention**.

9.4 SPAN OF ATTENTION

As we have seen, of the wide range of stimuli around us, we attend to only a few. We have also noted that attention divides our field of conscious experience into 'focus' and 'margin'. The objects, things, or events that enter into focus stand out distinctly clear and the rest in the margin are either out of our consciousness or if at all, they give a very dim or hazy apprehension.

At this point, an important question arises as to what number of objects can simultaneously exist in the focus? This question has been subjected to extensive experimental research. In general, the research studies have revealed that the capacity of attention is limited. As such, in a single act of attention, one can attend to only one object. Therefore, different tasks requiring attentional resources cannot be carried out simultaneously, because we have limited capacity to process the incoming information. In situations requiring to pay attention on two different sets of tasks, our attentional process follows the principle of 'serial processing', *i.e.* attending to one set of input and then to another. For example, you can probably not listen to music and read simultaneously because reading requires attentional resources for comprehension. Listening too requires attentional resources to comprehend the aesthetic pleasure as well as many details inherent in music. Thus, both of these tasks require simultaneous or 'parallel processing' which is not possible in view of the limited capacity of attentional mechanism or process. However, if the task is highly learned or routinized, then it is possible to attend to two different tasks simultaneously. For example, an efficient and perfect driver can drive the vehicle and also talk to the person sitting by his side. This condition is called **automacity** and in that case, **parallel processing** of attentional process may be possible.

Thus, when the two tasks requiring complex processing cannot be processed in parallel (simultaneously). Therefore, such tasks are processed in serial order one after another. This is a **central bottleneck** in information processing which is caused by the limits imposed by attention when the tasks are complex.

In order to ascertain the range of limitations of attentional process, psychologists have made attempts to investigate the number of objects one can attend to at a brief exposure, *i.e.* a fraction of a second (usually 1/10th of a second). This is what we call **span of attention** or **perceptual span. Hence, the span of attention refers to the amount of information an observer can take into his focus of attention from among a complex array of stimuli at a single momentary exposure**. This span is determined by using an instrument called **Techistoscope**. On the basis of several experiments, **Miller** has reported that our span of attention varies within the limit of seven plus or minus two (7 ± 2). This is also commonly known as **magic number**. It means that in a given period of time we can simultaneously attend to a set of five to seven numbers that can be extended to nine or more under special circumstances. Perhaps this is the reason that motorbikes or other automobiles are given a number plate that contains only four to five digit numbers. Our landline phone numbers also range from six to eight while the mobile numbers contain a maximum of ten digits. Such limits of numbering are done keeping in view the limited span of attention so that we may grasp such numbers more conveniently.

However, this span of attention varies in accordance with certain subjective and objective or internal or external (stimulus) factors such as organization of the stimulus material, heterogeneity or homogeneity of stimulus material, knowledge of result, mental fatigue, defects of sensory organ, presence of distracting stimuli etc.

9.5 FLUCTUATION OF ATTENTION

Fluctuation of attention is another phenomenon of attention. This refers to the length of time an individual can continuously focus his attention to a single object. Attention is not steady or concentrated throughout. At one time an object comes into focus at another time it goes out in the fringe. For example, if we give our attention to a very mild stimulus say, ticking of a timepiece heard from a distance or a very dimlight from a distant point, the ticking sound or the light may appear for a moment into our attention and at the next moment, it may pass out of attention. This is what we call **'fluctuation of attention'**. In other words, fluctuation is **'waxing and waning'** of attention in which at one moment the attended object or stimulus comes within one's attention, while at another moment it disappears. Thus the same object is sometimes attended to while at another moment it becomes out of attention.

Closely related to fluctuation is **shift of attention**. In shift of attention, our attention passes from one stimulus to another stimulus or from one aspect of the stimulus to another aspect of the stimulus. As we have seen in Chapter 8 that, when a reversible picture is presented, our attention (perception) shifts from vase to human face and from face to vase.

Shift of attention is an usual phenomenon found in children. Children generally lack the ability of concentration. Therefore, shift is most frequent. In adults also, attention shifts from one part of the object to another part. For example, while reading a book, our attention shifts from word to word, sentence to sentence, para to para and from page to page. Similarly while playing card-game, our attention shifts from one card to another.

Basic difference between fluctuation and shift of attention is that in the former case, the same object appears or disappears from our focus of attention while in the latter case, our attention shifts from one part or aspect to another part or aspect.

9.6 DIVISION OF ATTENTION OR DIVIDED ATTENTION

Sometimes we claim doing two things simultaneously. For example, one may copy from a page and also listen to radio. Under such situations the question is—whether there is any division of attention? It is still an open question. Studies done on this aspect have revealed that if one of the two tasks is of automatic nature, it is possible to attend to both the tasks simultaneously with approximately equal efficiency. Automatic tasks generally require no conscious effort of attending. Only one of the tasks may require greater degree of conscious attentive effort. For example, a driver while driving a car may also talk to a friend or attend to a phone call on a mobile set or listen to a music. However, if you watch closely, you will notice that they are still making relatively more attentive effort to driving than other activities. It indicates that on certain occassions, attention can be allocated to more than one thing at the same time. However, this is possible only with highly practised activities because they become almost automatic and require less attention to perform than new or slightly practised activities. This involves *automatic processing*. Automatic processing has three main characteristics: (i) it occurs without intention, (ii) it takes place unconsciously and (iii) it involves very little (or no) thought processes (*e.g.* we can read words or tie shoelaces without giving any thought to these activities.

But, when both the tasks require conscious efforts to attend and think, the attention is divided between them and the tasks cannot be performed so efficiently as those which are given attention separately. Thus, attention has the attribute of being divided when two stimuli require simultaneous focus.

This phenomenon is subjected to experimental studies which reveal many interesting facts.

9.7 DISTRACTION OF ATTENTION

The phenomenon of distraction is of considerable interest. There are some stimuli in the environment which act as destructor and our attention is distracted. Effect of noise as a destructor to attention has widely been studied experimentally. Studies on distraction is also important for psychologists working in organizations and industries.

Studies have revealed that distraction of attention is not only caused by environmental factors but also by individual (subjective) factors such as lack of ability to concentrate, impinging motivational states, habits etc.

9.8 KINDS OF ATTENTION

Attentional process is classified into three types—voluntary, involuntary and habitual.

9.8.1 Voluntary Attention

Voluntary attention is of intended nature. Whenever we intentionally or deliberately look or listen, the process of attention is voluntary. It involves conscious effort to select and situate a particular stimuli into the focus of attention. For example, if someone says—look here, listen what is being said, and if we respond to these commands accordingly, we are attending voluntarily.

9.8.2 Involuntary Attention

Sometimes certain stimulus force become so powerful that our attention is drawn to that stimulus without any conscious effort to attend. For such attention, we are generally not mentally prepared but our attention is abruptly and necessarily drawn. For example, a pistol shot, an intense flash of light, alarming siren sound, sudden cry of a child etc. have a force in themselves to draw our attention without any deliberate effort. Since involuntary attention is drawn because of the potential force of the stimulus—it is often termed as **stimulus based or dominated attention**. On the other hand, the voluntary attention is also **organism based** because it depends upon the conscious will of the attending person (organism).

9.8.3 Habitual Attention

Most often we attend to those objects more readily for which we have a mental set of habitual nature. For example, a young boy's readiness to notice a beautiful girl and a girl's readiness to notice a handsome boy, our readiness to perceive positive aspect in the activities of our friends and evils in the action of enemies, showing recurring interest in particular kind of food and drink etc. are indicative of our mental readiness to attend which is almost habitual in nature. Under the influence of such habitual readiness to attend, our attention is automatically drawn, *viz.* a chain-smoker is seen suddenly attracted towards an advertisement of cigarette, betel chewer suddenly stops near a betel shop. All these intances of our everyday life are the examples of habitual attention.

9.9 SELECTIVE ATTENTION

Attention is selective in nature. This aspect of attention has long been one of the central topics of interest for the psychologists.

Selective attention is in fact, a process that operates somewhat like a **gateway** to the focus of attention that **let in** certain inputs to the focus by a process of **filtering**. This is done by selecting the permeable inputs by voluntary process of brain and blocking others **out of the gate** that remain in the fringe (margin). This is called **filtering model process** in which the brain filters out or partially **'blocks out'** while some inputs are **let in**. Thus, selective attention refers to the phenomenon of concentrating over one activity at a time. The other activities (blocked out) are either not noticed or at best vaguely noticed. The 'let in' inputs are situated into the focus that is perceived as distinct and clear in form and shape.

To understand the selective functions of attentional process, imagine yourself in a party where you are engaged in chatting with a group of your friends. Out of many other kinds of voices and noises, you turn yourself to the voice of one of your friends with whom you are in dialogue. In the meanwhile, you listen someone referring your name in a corner of the party hall, your attention is diverted from your friend to the direction of sound where your name is being mentioned. Your friend is still talking to you but your attention is now diverted to the other side—what someone is saying about you. Apparently, you may pose that you are listening to your friend but in fact, you are unable to register anything.

Cherry, in the year 1953, studied the process of selectivity in 'dichotic listening' which is considered as an important experimental study. He presented two messages to the subjects—one to each ear with the help of earphones. They were instructed to **Shadow** (listen to the message and repeat out the same loudly) one of them fed to one ear. A different message was presented to each ear and the subjects were instructed to listen to one only. They were then questioned to find out how much of each message they had retained.

The experiment showed that very little content was picked up from the **unshadowed message**. The subjects did not notice if the speaker was using foreign language or if the speech was reversed. Processing of the unshadowed message was found to be minimal. They could notice the change in voice when switched from the male voice to the female.

One of the salient features of selective functions of attention is that concentration on the selected activity is not interfered by the blocked out activity or activities. However, at times, selective attention is felt disgusting particularly when we feel the need to concentrate on more than one activity simultaneously.

Selective attention has very extensively been studied to explain how does this work? and various views or models have been proposed. Important among such studies are the studies done by **Deutish** and **Deutish** (1963), **Triesman** (1969), **Lindsay** and **Norman** (1977). These studies state that since it is not possible to process all the information in the sensory channel, some inputs are filtered or partially **blocked out** while others **let in** to the focus. In the process, two kinds of events are noticed, *i.e.* (i) **parallel processing** and (ii) **serial processing**. These two processes can be explained through an example. Suppose, someone at a party is standing between two groups of people who are talking something on two different topics simultaneously. In the situation, he is likely to pick up something of both at the same time. In this case, **parallel processing** is taking place. But, when he finds that at a given time either one of the two is in the focus of attention because it is difficult to attend to more than one set of information at a time, it is termed as **serial processing**, *i.e.* attending to one set of information and then switching over to another. Thus, preferring to one and then to another is an example of **serial processing**. In both the kinds of processing, the unattended input is filtered out and sent to the margin or fringe resulting in dim or hazy awareness of the unattended information because he does not register most of the information.

Sometimes shifting of information from fringe to focus is also seen. This happens when some potential factors of attention such as intensity, novelty etc. are present in the blocked out beats of information. For example, if someone is still between the two conversations at the same stage, he is likely to switch his focus on the filtered-out conversation if the voice in this conversation is increased.

As regards the point or location in the sensory channel where blocking in filter model occurs, views of different scientists differ. **Broadbent** (1959) holds that the input blockage occurs at the sense organ or in the very early stages of the input processing. This is known as **Bottleneck Theory**. This resembles a bottle with very tiny opening that results in very small quantity or amount of water to enter inside the bottle. Similarly, when our sense organs have biological bottlenecks due to which it is unable to permit much of information to get through to the focus. Thus, only a few of information get through and much of it are filtered out.

Shiffrin and **Schneider** (1977), on the contrary, say that filtering takes place at the later stage of the information flow, *viz.* at the stage where input is interpreted as meaningful. Thus, cortex is the location where valuable inputs are selected and then situated into the focus while others are blocked out.

Still others link filtering process to the limitations of resources to focus (**Kahneman**, 1973). Such views lay emphasis on limited mental capacity for processing the incoming information. This limits our capacity to deal with all sensory inputs at a time. Therefore, we allocate limited resources and as such the limited capacity permits only one set of information at a time to **let in**.

Thus, we see that as regards the location of blockage in the sensory channel, there are various views or models and therefore it is not possible to draw any conclusion about it. However, selectivity in attentional process is a fact that is indicative of the limited capacity of the attentional process.

9.9.1 Factors of Selective Attention

Several factors influence selective attention. These generally relate to the characteristics of stimuli and the characteristics of individuals. They are generally classified as **external** and **internal** factors.

External factors: These are related to the features of stimuli. Other things held constant, the size, intensity, and motion of stimuli appear to be important.

Internal factors: These factors lie within the individual. These may be divided into two broad categories—motivational factors and cognitive factors. Motivational factors relate to our biological and social needs. The cognitive factors include the factors like interest, attitude, mental set etc.

All these factors have been described in some detail in a separate section on **factors of attention** later in this chapter.

9.9.2 Theories of Selective Attention

Several theories of selective attention have been developed to explain the process involved in selective attention. Three of such theories are considered important about which a brief description is being presented just to acquaint the students. These are as follows:

Filter theory

This theory was developed by **Broadbent** (1956). According to this theory, many stimuli simultaneously impinge upon our receptors creating a kind of **bottleneck** situation. Moving through the short term memory (STM) they enter the selective filter which permits only one stimulus to get through for further processing at the higher level. Other impinging stimuli are thus filtered out or screened out at that moment of time. Thus, we become aware of only that particular stimulus which gets through the selective filter while the others remain out of our conscious awareness.

Filter-attenuation theory

This is a modified form of Broadbent's theory which has been developed by **Triesman** (1962). This theory states that the stimuli that do not get access to the selective filter at a given moment of time are not blocked completely. The purpose of selective filtration is only to **attenuate**, *i.e.* weakening the strength of other stimuli. Thus, some of the stimuli manage to clear away or escape from selective filter and reach the higher levels of processing. This is the reason that often some stimuli which are particularly relevant to the person are noticeable even at a very low level of intensity. For example, when one is attentively engaged in talking with a friend in a party and somebody makes a reference of his name at some distance, even if it is fairly weak, it is capable of drawing his attention by escaping through the filter.

Multimode theory

This theory has been proposed by **Johnston** and **Heinz** (1978). This is a three-tier system theory. According to this theory, attentional process is a flexible system in which selective functions are done at three levels. The first level or stage of selective filtration occurs at the stage of sensory representation where visual images of stimuli are constructed. The second level or stage is called semantic level of representation where the object is categorized into a semantic category (*e.g.* names of objects). The third stage is conscious representation of the sensory and semantic constructs. Thus, selective functions of attention occur at different modes of stimuli representation. The theory also suggests that higher the processing, more mental efforts are required. Thus, at the stage or level one of selective processing (the earliest level), lesser degree of effort is required while at the third stage (last level of selection) much greater mental effort is needed.

9.10 SUSTAINED ATTENTION

Sustained attention is a wakeful concentration. Hence, also termed as **vigilance**. This refers to **maintaining attention on a task continuously for some longer duration—a state of heightened concentration on the task**.

This phenomenon was first noticed during the World War-II when the radar operating soldiers were required to watch vigilantly the incoming signals of enemy's aircrafts. The heightened concentration was found to be resulting in frequent failures to detect the signals. **MacWorth** (1950) devised **'stimulated display technique'** to study the phenomenon. He used **clock test** for the purpose. It was a clock-like apparatus with a black clockwise moving pointer over the plain dial of the clock. The rate of pointer's movement was 3" per second, with intermittent increase in rate by 6″ per second, *i.e.* just double the original rate. The subjects were instructed (stimulated) to wakefully concentrate on the speed of movement and respond by pressing an attached key whenever increase in the rate (speed) is noticed. The subjects were engaged on the task continuously for two hours and the data relating to number of press and response time (R.T.) were recorded. It was found that after half an hour of concentration, the performance decreased. On an average, the subjects missed to notice the increase in speed after every fourth signals of change in speed.

The pioneering study prompted many more experimenters to study the phenomenon of sustained attention. These studies throw some more light on the nature of sustained attention. The studies indicate that paying concentrated attention on external stimulus is an intense activity and requires much of mental efforts. In the tasks requiring vigilance or continuous active concentration, the state of arousal is heightened on central target and, therefore, other informations, in the fringe are ignored. This causes decrement in performance output. The law that governs it is termed as **Yerk's-Dodson law**. When the data in this situation are represented on a graph, the shape of the curve formed is that of an inverted shaped curve as shown in **Figure 9.1**.

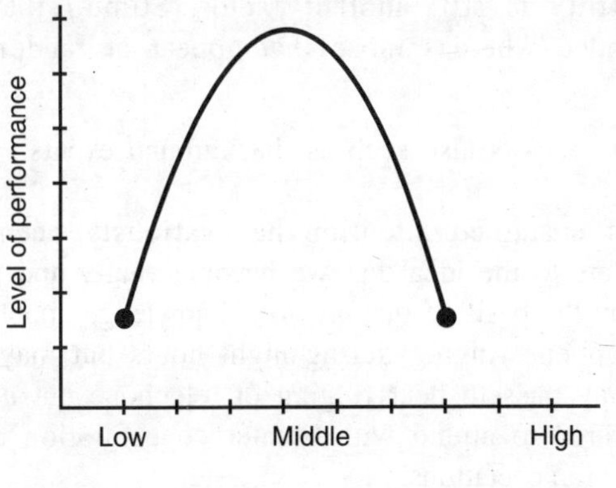

FIGURE 9.1 Showing inverted ∩ shape curve.

Figure 9.1 clearly shows that in sustained or vigilant attentive tasks, performance is at its peak (the best) when the degree of concentration is neither low nor high enough.

The students can conduct an experiment to demonstrate the impact of sustained attention on performance in their own college laboratory by using the following cancellation sheets.

Following is an illustrative example of cancellation sheet

z x b y a b c n d c e
f g a g c y r s i o u
i h n m o i a b e n p
p e r t t u e o l q m

The subject may be asked to cancel all vowel letters (a, e, i, o, u) wherever they occur in the sheet. This experiment will be done in two conditions. In condition I, after every trial, the subject is given a rest for 10 seconds. In condition II, the subject is required to perform continuously for 12 trials. (Each one sheet is designated as one trial.) After this, the performance of the two conditions are compared.

(**Note:** The second condition is a condition of sustained attention as it requires vigilant concentration on the task continuously for 12 trials.)

9.10.1 Factors Influencing Sustained Attention

Several factors can either facilitate or inhibit an individual's performance on a task of sustained attention. Some of these are as follows:

(a) **Sensory modality** is one of these factors. Performance is found to be superior when they are visual.
(b) **Clarity of stimuli** is another important factor influencing performance on sustained attention. Intense and long lasting stimuli facilitates sustained or vigilant concentration and consequently, performance is relatively better than when the stimuli is weak or the stimuli persists for a very brief period.
(c) **Temporal uncertainty** is again a third important influencer. When stimuli appear at regular intervals, they are better attended to than when they appear at irregular intervals.
(d) **Spatial uncertainty** is still another factor. Stimuli that appear at fixed place are readily attended whereas those that appear at random locations are difficult to attend.

There are several other factors also such as 'background events', 'knowledge of resources', 'expectancy' etc.

The phenomenon of sustained attention has variously been explained in terms of expectancy. Expectancy refers to the idea that we become **ready** and **prepared** for certain type of input for concentration on the basis of our previous knowledge about the stimuli. For example, a doctor may hear the telephone ringing during night hours but may miss the baby's cry, on the other hand, his wife may miss to hear ringing of telephone but not the baby's cry. In this instance, the two are prepared to attend with greater concentration the referent object of the environment as per their own expectations.

Thus, in essence the sustained attention is a deep concentration on a particular object of the environment which substantially affects the process of attention. The factors that determine facilitation or inhibition of sustained attention are largely psychophysical in nature and therefore their impacts are measured in psychophysical terms.

9.11 DIRECTION OF ATTENTION OR DETERMINANTS OF ATTENTION OR CONDITIONS (FACTORS) OF ATTENTION

Though our attention has the property of being shifted from one object to another or from one part of the object to another, it has certain orderliness too. Had there been no orderliness, it could not have been possible to carry out any concentrated activity. There are certain principles that determine the direction of our attention. These principles are called **Principles of attention getting**.

These principles govern what will be perceived and what will not be perceived or will be dimly or vaguely perceived. Such principles are of great practical significance. In education, a teacher's foremost task is to win pupil's attention, in advertising or selling, the attention of prospective buyers need to be attracted before the product is sold. Similarly, in most of our everyday situation, one need to bring into his focus the significant objects.

Many factors influence the direction of our attention. These factors are generally classified as external and internal factors. External factors are also termed as stimulus or objective factors while the internal factors are also termed as subjective (personal) or organismic factors.

9.11.1 External Factors

External or stimulus (objective) factors that govern attention getting may be considered under five major heads—prepotency, change, size, repetition and movement.

Prepotency

Some stimuli are prepotent, *i.e.* intense enough to draw our attention more readily than those which are relatively weak or less potent. For example, a loud sound, brighter light, strong smell etc. are prepotent over low sound, dimlight, very thin smell etc. Similarly, saturated colours over pastel shades, deep pressure over smooth pressure are prepotent to draw our attention.

Such prepotencies do not necessarily depend upon relative strength of competing stimulus nor does it depend upon past experience. Prepotency is a stimulus characteristic.

However, if two stimuli are competing for drawing attention, the one that is more potent, will draw our attention first than the other.

Change

Living beings are usually sensitive to change. Change in stimulus may take any form—from one place to another or one colour to another or sudden increase or decrease in intensity, atmospheric changes, appearance to disappearance of the stimuli, high to low or stationary to moving and so on. Such changes in the stimuli attract our attention. For example, if two persons are whispering together in a quiet atmosphere and in the middle, someone suddenly shouts, the shouting man draws the attention of whispering persons and they **sit-up to take notice**.

Size

Size of the stimulus too has the potency to draw our attention. This is the reason, some advertisers favour full page advertisement. However, there are some other interrelated factors also which determine attention. Even a full page size may suffer by its neatness, clumsiness, lack of dexterity etc. The main principle is that the size of the stimuli which appeals more to the perceiver's interests and needs or has more striking use of colours, are more pronouncing determinants of attention.

Repetition

Repetition is also an important determinant of attracting attention. For example, if a misspelled word repeatedly occurs in a page, it is likely to be noticed more readily than if it occurs seldom.

A weak stimulus also becomes effective if it is repeated time and again. Manufacturers and politicians repeat their advertisements again and again so as to catch the attention of the people.

Repetition is advantageous in two ways. Firstly, the repeated stimulus has a better chance of catching our attention at least once when we are inattentive. Secondly, repetition increases our sensitivity or alertness to the stimulus.

However, repetition has certain limitations too. Overrepetition sometimes leads to monotony. But, if the stimulus is repeated at regular interval with some variations or changes in style, design, colour etc., it makes the stimulus more prominent and acquires the quality of drawing attention.

Movement

Living beings are also sensitive to movement or motion and as such moving object acquires the property of catching our attention. Our visual mechanisms are involuntarily attracted to moving objects. It is the movement of their enemies that catches the attention of our soldiers during the night patrolling but it becomes difficult for them if the enemies are stationary or not making any movement.

In the field of advertising, the most effective signs are those that involve movement.

9.11.2 Internal or Organismic or Subjective Determinants

Besides external or stimulus factors, internal factors too are equally and in some cases even more important determinants of attention. These factors are cognitive factors that include motives, interest, set or expectancy etc.

Motives and interests

Motives and interests are most important factors in attracting attention. Motives and interests predispose a person not only to be attracted to but in holding the object. It is usually observed that when a teacher announces that he is now going to discuss **sex practices in our Indian society**, even the sleepiest student in the class becomes alert to listen the lecture because it appeals to the sex drive which despite being a dominant need among the adolescents remain traditionally suppressed. Advertisers use shapely girls in bathing suits as models even though the advertised product such as cigar, two wheelers etc. are nowhere related to them. Not only the basic needs or motives, any of the great variety of human motives and interests are important in directing our attention, *viz.* an unemployed youth first opens the page of newspaper where vacancies appear. A person interested in sports events, selectively pays his attention on the page where sport event news appear.

Set or expectancy

Set or expectancy also plays an important role in determining the direction of attention. An anxiously waiting mother get attracted to the sound of footsteps of passers-by, presuming the arrival of her son. A doctor is usually found to hear the sounding of bell expecting the arrival of a patient, ringing of telephone during night expecting a call but he may fail to hear the sound of his baby. A zoologist if knows before hand that he would be asked some questions on bird's life, while walking, he would be attentively gathering information about birds. When the drawing as shown below is included in a series of two digit numbers, subjects may report to have seen number 13. If the same drawing is exposed to the subject with a series of alphabets, subjects may report to have seen letter B. In the former case, the subject has the set or expectancy of numbers while in the latter case, subject has a set of letters (see **Figure 9.2**).

FIGURE 9.2 What a person sees depends upon what he is set to see.

Social suggestion

In general, we tend to attend what is pointed out directly and indirectly by the others. This is so because we have had enjoyed many satisfactions and avoided discomforts or injuries in the past acting on suggestions by the others. For example, if you go to a shop to buy something and watch that another person has just rejected a piece of the item you intended to buy and has asked to show him different piece, you too ask the salesman to do the same and reject the piece that was already rejected by the other buyer. Here the action of the previous customer contains implicit suggestion and accordingly determines your reaction to perceive the piece rejectable.

Thus, we find that our attention is determined by several external and internal factors. Among these the set and expectancy are perhaps the most important psychological factors because these are the cognitive factors of the individual concerned that direct and order the succession of our perceptual experience.

9.12 ATTENTION DEFICIT HYPER-ACTIVITY DISORDER (ADHD)

Attentional process denotes the process that selects some input for the conscious experience of the world around. This process occupies significance for observing our world in an orderly manner that leads to the perceptual organization and then to action, *i.e.* to respond to the environment and adjust with its demands. Hence, for adequate and healthy adjustive responses, the mechanism of attentional process is important. But, in certain cases the mechanisms get dysfunctional causing behavioural disorder.

One of the most common behavioural disorders found among children of primary school age is **Attention Deficit Hyper-activity Disorder (ADHD)**. It is characterized by impassivity, excessive motor activity and inability to attend. The boys are found more prone to this than the girls. If it is not detected earlier and managed properly, it may persist among adolescents as well as the adults. The central feature of this disorder is difficulty in sustaining attention, *i.e.* concentrating. This disorder is reflected in various ways of child's behaviours such as higher degree of distractions in attention, failure to follow instructions, difficulty in getting along with parents and negative approach by the peers and friends. Such children score poorly in school performances and exhibit their inability in reading or learning basic subjects in schools. Such inefficiencies are found despite the fact that they are good in intellectual abilities.

Studies done in this regard do not evidence any biological basis for this kind of disorder. However, some evidences of its association with certain kinds of dietary factors, more particularly with food colouring have been detected.

Socio-psychological factors such as home environment or family pathology seem to be a potent factor of this disorder. The current studies reveal that this disorder is associated with multiple environmental (sociocultural as well as physical environment) and psychological factors and that the disorder has also a wide range of effects.

9.12.1 Treatment

Psychologists seem to maintain disagreement with regard to most effective treatment of the disorder. Some psychiatrists prescribe a drug **Ritalin**. This drug is widely used and has been found effective in curing overactivity and distraction and enhancing the ability of attentiveness and power of concentration. However, this does not cure the disorder. Moreover, it has some side-effects also such as suppression of normal growth in height and weight.

Behaviour therapists favour behavioural management programmes to deal with such disorders. These programmes include positive reinforcement and structuring of learning materials in such a way that may minimize errors and maximize immediate feedback and success. This technique has been found most useful.

Cognitive therapists claim cognitive behavioural training programme to be of greater value for dealing with ADHD. In this technique, rewards for desired behaviours are combined with training in the use of verbal self-instructions, *e.g.* stop, think and then do. With this kind of training, children learn to stay in attention and exercise control over frequent shifts of attention from one object to another or from one aspect of the object to another aspect as well as reflective behaviours. Thus, through cognitive training programme, children are able to learn the kind of learning that is relatively stable over time.

SUMMARY

- Attention is a process that selects some of the sensory inputs to provide conscious experience. It selectively brings certain limited number of inputs into the focus of conscious experience.
- Attention has three interrelated aspects—postural adjustment, clearness in consciousness and it is a set towards action.
- Span of attention is the number of objects one can 'take in' to the focus in a very brief period of time. In general, this magic number has been found to be 7 ± 2.

- There are some other phenomena of attention such as fluctuation of attention, shift of attention and distraction of attention. These events of attentional process are the major areas of experimental research and many interesting findings are obtained.
- Attention is usually classified into three main types—voluntary, involuntary and habitual attention.
- Attention is selective in nature. Many external and internal factors influence the selective functions of attention. Many psychologists have proposed several theories to explain selective functions. Three such theories—Filter theory, Filter-attenuation theory and Multimode theory are important.
- Sustained attention is also an important area of research. It refers to vigilant nature of attention with heightened degree of concentration continuously for a longer duration. Several factors facilitate or inhibit our ability of sustained attention.
- There are several external and internal factors of attention that direct our attention. External factors include prepotency, change, size, repetition and movement. The internal factors include motivation, interest, expectancy and other cognitive factors.
- ADHD is a very common disorder of attentional process found mostly among pre-school children. Early detection and management of ADHD is important.

PART IV

Modification of Behaviour

CHAPTER 10

Learning

10.1 INTRODUCTION

Every organism is endowed with a fund of inborn capabilities to respond to the environmental situations and demands. But, biologically inherited inborn modes are not sufficient to make effective adjustment with the complex and dynamic environment. Therefore, in order to adapt ourselves to the environment, we must learn a staggering number of things. All our special skills, modification of older inherited patterns of biological responses, attitudes and beliefs, prejudices etc. are the products of learning.

Learning is the core of human understanding and adjustment. To clarify it, let us presuppose that a reputed pharmaceutical company launches a capsule product with molecules that may lead to unlearning of all acquired or learned responses but has no harmful effects on life. If someone takes this capsule, he would lose all that he has learned and would be reduced to a neonate with simple reflexive responses only. He would not be able to stand, walk and would be totally dependent on others even for the personal needs such as clothing, feeding etc. Thus, he would virtually become a living organism with no lifelike activities—a crippled living man. This hypothetical presupposition clearly speaks about the importance of learning for human life.

All responses of human beings can be classified into learned and unlearned categories. Unlearnt responses are hereditary inborn simple reflexes or instinctual tendencies. Beyond these simple responses, all our activities are learned or modified either through experience or some sort of training. But how one learns these varieties of activities and responses, what principles or laws govern learning, what are the processes of learning, etc. are some of the issues that are the main concerns of this chapter.

10.2 NATURE AND DEFINITION OF LEARNING

Learning is a pervasive term. It is a complex behavioural process. Therefore, to give a precise definition of learning is not an easy task. It begins with birth and continues till death. In the very beginning (primary stage of life), an infant is able to respond to a few immediate aspects of his environment, *viz.* when hungry, he sucks mother's breast or the nipple of a feeding bottle. He cries for lifting into lap or turns backward when faced with painful stimuli. However, these simple responses too undergo modifications on the basis of experiences. These modifications or changes are simple forms of learning. Psychologists call such learnings as **'conditioned responses'**.

During early childhood, we learn or acquire several motor skills followed by verbal skills resulting in the development of the ability of interpersonal communication skills. In course of acquiring these skills, we also learn to solve simple problems such as finding out the correct path, locations, defending oneself from frustrating situations, acquiring the standards of living, how to walk and talk with others etc. Gradually, we also learn the skills needed to solve complex problems involving logical reasoning and cognitions—thinking, memorising and similar other higher level mental abilities.

Thus, learning is a multifarious process and we learn a variety of things. Hence, learning is difficult to define. However, attempts have been made not only to define it but also to explain its nature.

Learning has variously been defined. Some define it as a relatively permanent change in behaviour occurring as a result of experience or practice (**Morgan** and **King**, 1956), some consider it as a process of acquiring new skills, some others feel learning as a process of change in one's way of responding resulting from environmental contacts (**Ruch**, 1958). Still others hold that any measurable change in behaviour—good or bad, adaptive or nonadaptive—is learning and this change is more or less permanent which satisfies the current motivating conditions of the individual (**McGeoh**, 1952).

Thus, learning has variously been defined. But in all such definitions, one thing—'change in behaviour' (or some kind of modification in behaviour) is a common ground for characterising or defining learning.

Learning, in fact, involves acquisition of a new behaviour—new ways of responding to the situation. Acquisition of a new behaviour is possible only when one gets some sort of training or makes efforts (practice) to get spared from older unprofitable modes of responses. The practice induces a change in behaviour and this change rules out the changes brought about by natural process of maturation or by injury or due to the effects of some kind of drugs. Such changes are not learned changes. For example, let us examine what happens when one learns typing? Before learning to type, the person was unable to set his fingers on the keyboard and make free movement of his fingers from one key to another to reproduce the spoken or written verbal materials on the type-writer machine. But, when he acquires this skill as a result of practice for a fairly long time, there occurs change in his finger setting patterns on the keyboard as well as movement of his fingers from one key to another. He now is able to do these in an orderly and systematic manner with fairly increased speed of typing. Thus, acquisition of this new skill implies some sort of change in behaviour pattern due to practice.

Change in behaviour may be in any of the several forms such as, acquiring a new skill, improvement in speed and accuracy of performance, increment in output or decrement in undesirable activities, bringing modifications in the behaviour pattern or unlearning of unprofitable behaviour patterns etc. In this sense, **'learning to unlearn'** is also learning.

Learning has concern with adjustment. Usually, situation to learn arises when one faces a new situation or problem. Under the situation, an individual finds his older behaviour patterns or unlearnt instinctive or simple reflexive activities either in sufficient or unworkable. Therefore, in order to cope with the given situation, he must learn some new mode(s) of behaviour with which he can more profitably adapt to the situation, *i.e.* he must learn a correct response and unlearn the incorrect ones. A correct response is defined in terms of the organism's motivation. For example, digging into a garbage heap may be correct for a rat if it is hungry and diving into a narrow hole by the rat may be a correct response if it is frightened. Hence, a correct response is that which leads to the attainment of the goal or target that satisfies the current motivation state of the organism or an individual.

Further, to merit learning, change in learning must be relatively permanent or stable. Any transitory change in behaviour does not qualify to be called learning. Thus, the change or modification in behaviour caused by some sort of training or experience or practice and if the change brought about is of stable nature (enduring), such changes or modifications are termed as learning. Changes in behaviour is usually measured in terms of accuracy (number of correct/incorrect responses), rate of performance, units of output, time consumed in performing a task or solving a problem etc. Hence, **any measurable change in behaviour of the organism can be termed as learning insofar as it is relatively permanent and the change has been caused by some sort of training or experience**. In this definition, the salient characteristic feature of learning is that the change in behaviour or response pattern due to practice is a 'measurable change.' This measurable change may be either qualitative or quantitative or both. If such changes are measured along the progress in practice trials, the change would indicate a successive order of improvement or progression and ultimately it reaches the criterion of stability, *i.e.* the change becomes relatively stable or permanent. Therefore, the above definition may be put in other way also, *i.e.*

> **Learning is acquisition of new responses or skills as a result of training and which results in relatively permanent change to the order of gradual or successive improvement or progression.**

10.3 LEARNING AND PERFORMANCE

Often learning and performance are used interchangeably. But, the two are typically distinct. Any act done by an individual is performance which serves as a basis to infer learning. Hence, the two are not alike but different.

The other way in which the two differ is that performance can be directly measured whereas learning can only be inferred in terms of performance. For this reason, performance is assumed as inferential signal of learning. For example, when you remember a poem by repeating or reciting it for several times (practice trials) and ultimately a point comes when you are able to recall the poem correctly, your recall of the poem will be called your performance that signals to infer that you have learnt the poem correctly. Thus, the quality and quantity of your recall (performance) is indicative of your learning.

The efficiency of performance depends on learning but learning does not depend upon performance. Performance is merely an inferential signal to learning. Moreover, performance may serve as means to end *i.e.* we may learn certain act (end) by means of performing the act (means).

Thus, it is obvious that performance and learning, though often used interchangeably, are distinct from each other.

10.4 LEARNING AND MATURATION

Maturation is a natural process of growth. In normal conditions, it follows its own cycle and phase independently. Certain important changes in behaviour of the living beings are also noticed that results from maturation. Moreover, certain level of maturation is necessarily required for skill acquisition or learning to occur. However, the two processes are distinct from each other. The broad differences between them are as follows:

(i) Maturation is a natural process of growth. It is a growth of the structure in response to the diffused stimulation received from surroundings. On the other hand, learning is a growth in response relating to the functioning of that structure.
(ii) Maturation is an inborn process of growth and development whereas learning is an acquired process of modification, improvement and acquisition of new ways of responding to the environment.
(iii) Maturation follows a definite and similar pattern of growth among all members of a species whereas learning does not follow any similarity and definite pattern among all the members of the same species.
(iv) The process of maturation does not vary from individual to individual. But learning varies from individual to individual.
(v) Maturation is a continuous process of growth till it is complete. Learning is not a continuous process. It is rather intermittent.
(vi) Maturational growth has a fixed and almost definite point of completion or accomplishment beyond which the process of growth ceases, it becomes stable followed by gradual decrement in biological capabilities. However, learning is an evergoing process throughout one's life span. It never ceases.
(vii) Since certain level of maturity is a prerequisite for any type of learning or skill acquisition, it can be said that learning depends on maturation. But this is not the case with maturation.
(viii) Maturation causes some sort of chemical changes in our inner world (internal organs of the body) and provides strength to the different organs of response. For example, sexual developments depend upon maturation rather than upon learning. Learning can bring changes in the external world and not in the internal world.
(ix) Learning is influenced by practice whereas practice has no influence over maturation.

Despite the above-mentioned differences, the two processes bear a close relationship. In fact, the two are complementary to each other [Shirley (1933), Stone (1934), (1935) and (1904), Cruze (1935)]. Their studies provide ample material to substantiate the view that the two processes **maturation and learning go side by side like a married couple, each facilitating the process of the other**. Hence, the two processes bear a very close interrelationship with each other.

10.5 KINDS OF LEARNING

As has been stated earlier, learning is a pervasive and very complex process. It is so pervasive that the whole of psychology can be regarded as the 'psychology of learning'. So, what we learn can neither be listed nor classified. We learn innumerable things. First we learn very **simple responses** such as, during infancy locating and sucking the nipple of mother's breast when hungry, cry in order to be picked up and withdraw from painful stimuli before they reach us. These are **orienting reflexes** which need to be modified through experience.

Later on during the early childhood, we learn **motor skills** such as, reaching to grasp objects, standing up unaided, putting on our cloths and buttoning or zipping them up etc. Similarly, as we grow and come in contact with the wider world around us, many more complex motor skills are added to our repertoire. In addition, we also begin to acquire **verbal skills** involving language—meaning of words and gestures (non-verbal or body language) pronouncing words, combining them to form meaningful sentences. These learnings serve very useful purpose in interpersonal communication and thus learn **communication skills** as well as comprehending the various concepts.

In course of learning motor, verbal and communication skills, we also learn **sensory-motor coordination skills** and gain efficiencies in **problem solving**. We begin with simple problems such as, finding our ways around, extricating ourselves from dangers, frustrations, threats, resolving conflicts, seeking and giving cooperation etc. Gradually, we learn more advanced cognitive, motor and operational skills.

We also acquire information about ourselves and the world around us. This is called **perceptual learning** or 'stimulus learning.' Our learning about the stimulus often requires us to respond and explore. Thus, we also learn responding to the stimuli called **response learning** and also learn to explore the environment—**exploration learning**.

Thus, we find that there is a gradual transition from simple forms of learning to the higher level complex forms of problem solving and in course of adding to our repertoire of different kinds of skills, we also **learn how to learn**. All these forms of learning are interwoven and interdependent. Hence, to assume various forms of learning as different kinds or reduce them to a common principle is still an unresolved question.

However, the different forms of learning stretching from simple responses to problem solving are classified in several ways by different psychologists to suit their theoretical contexts. Two ways of classifications are most common. These are—(i) verbal and motor learning and (ii) stimulus and response learning.

10.5.1 Verbal Learning

One of the forms of learning is verbal learning. Verbal learning refers to acquisition of verbal skills. It covers a wide range of learning. Words are the symbols that represent the various aspects—objects and things of our world. We learn facts of historical events, geographical contexts of the world around us, physical matters and principles, chemical elements and their various combinations through written words in books and journals, we also learn verbal skills of communication through spoken words or numbers. Thus, learning by using words, sentences, numbers or coded languages are called verbal learning. Verbal materials are used for associating our ideas with the objects of the world and also for learning how to solve complex problems presented in language form. Thus, learning by using verbal materials are called verbal learning.

10.5.2 Motor Learning

We also learn several activities that require movement of our motor organs such as arms, legs, fingers, heads etc. With the help of these motor organs we learn simple responses like eating, putting on cloths, dancing, playing various types of games. Gradually, we also learn various kinds of fine movements and combinations of movements involved in driving, complex forms of dancing, flying of aeroplanes, and even solving complicated problems by doing or performing, operating machines and tools etc. Thus, learning of activities that involve body movements and postures is called motor learning.

Sensory-motor learning

No motor learning is purely 'motor' in strict sense. Every motor skill requires in some way sensory information and one learns or acquires motor skills by co-ordinating sensory information and motor movements. Hence, most of the motor skills are 'sensory-motor'. But, in some of the motor tasks, sensory input is of not much significance while in others, sensory inputs are equally important. The task in which sensory and motor organs are of equal importance, is called 'sensory-motor' task learning. For example, learning painting by viewing, composing of written matters, typing of letters by seeing the handwritten scripts, etc. are some of the examples of sensory-motor task learning. Thus, the tasks that essentially require co-ordination between sensory and motor organs are called sensory motor task and accomplishing proficiencies in such tasks are called sensory-motor learning.

10.5.3 Stimulus Learning

It is a kind of 'perceptual learning' in which we learn various stimuli of the world which impinge upon our sense organs arousing sensory input. It involves sensing and organising, finding out the interrelationships between different informations coming from the physical stimuli, interpreting, judging and evaluating the stimuli. These are the cognitive functions that involve mental operations and no overt response. Thus, learning something about a stimulus or relationship between several stimuli and making no overt response is called 'stimulus' or 'perceptual learning'.

10.5.4 Response Learning

It is a learning to make a particular kind of response to a particular kind of stimuli, *i.e.* learning to associate specific response to specific stimuli—(SR association) is what we call **response learning**.

Response learning is further classified into two types—(a) single response learning and (b) multiple response learning. In single response learning, we learn a specific response to a specific stimulus or stimulus situation. This type of learning is called **conditioning learning**. Hence, conditioning is a restricted form of learning because, single response is acquired. This single response learning is further classified into three types of conditioning phenomenon—(a) **Classical conditioning**, (b) **Operant** or **Instrumental conditioning** and (c) **Aversive conditioning**.

Multiple response learning is mostly concerned with human learning that includes **conditioning**, **motor learning**, **discrimination learning**, **verbal learning**, **problem solving** and **concept learning**.

10.6 LEARNING CURVE

How acquisition of a skill or habit progresses may be graphically represented which is known as **learning curve**. The shape of a learning curve depends upon behaviour being learned and the criterion employed to measure (i.e. the term in which learning is measured). The learning curves in general shows the direction of progress and the rate at which performance is changed. Besides, learning curves also display many more characteristic features of learning process which we shall try to understand with the help of an imaginary curve of learning. But, before we discuss the characteristics of learning curve, let us first describe how a learning curve is plotted?

Usually, three major indices of learning are employed as measures of learning. These are: (a) quantity of performance or output, (b) time taken on the task and (c) correct or incorrect responses. Accordingly, the learning curves are named respectively as **output curve**, **time curve**, and **response curve—correct/incorrect response curves.**

10.6.1 Plotting a Learning Curve

Take a graph paper and draw a horizontal line at the base of the graph sheet. This line is called 'base line' or 'abscissa' (O-X axis). Learning trials are shown on this axis and written at equal distance from O to X (from left to right). A perpendicular line is drawn at the point of origin (O) which is called as 'ordinate' or O-Y axis. On this axis equal units of indices of learning (output, time or correct/incorrect responses) are written again at equal distances.

Now, plot the trialwise record of the chosen index of learning at the point where the trial and corresponding unit of learning index intersect each other. In this way, when the entire data of all the trials are plotted, each plotted dots are interconnected by a simple straight line with the help of a scale. The graphical representation is now ready and the formed shape of the graph gives the appearance of a curve. For this reason, this is called learning curve. For example, look at the curve as shown in **Figure 10.1**. It has been prepared on the basis of an imaginary data.

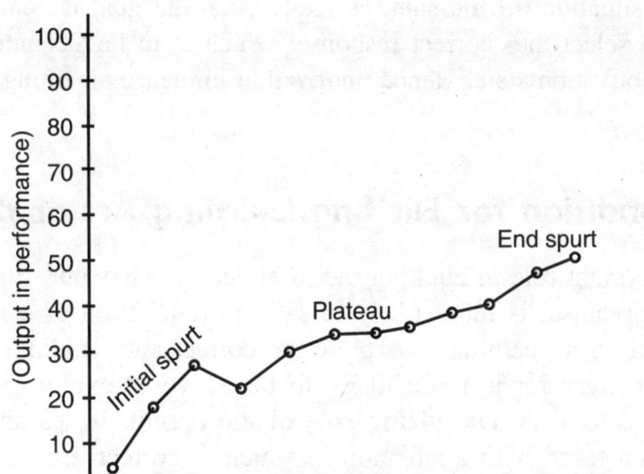

FIGURE 10.1 Learning curve.

10.6.2 Characteristics of Learning Curve

On perusal of the learning curve, certain salient features of progression in learning is very much clear. Just a glance of the curve shows that acquisition of skill is a gradual increase in the percentage of output, keeping pace with gradual increase in performance trials. Thus, progress in learning follows a **gradual process**.

Secondly, in the beginning two or three trials, the progress or increment is faster than the subsequent trials. This phenomenon is called **initial spurt** in learning or performance.

Thirdly, in the middle four trials (trial numbers 5, 6, 7 and 8) the curve is **flattened**—showing no further progress or improvement beyond 40% of output. This forms **plateau**—a state of stillness in progress of learning. This **stillness phenomenon** in learning is important for the experimenter to note. Fatigue or loss of interest or reduction of motivation is generally attributed to this phenomenon. Generally, it is observed that if additional incentive is added, the graph may again show upward trend—we call **rerise**. In learning situations, often more than one incidence of plateu may be seen.

Finally, there is the **end spurt** in the graph which perhaps is the physiological limit of the progress in learning because beyond this level, no further increase or improvement occurs even when additional incentive or rest is given.

Thus, learning curve is useful in understanding the gradual processes of improvement in acquiring a verbal or motor skill at a glance.

10.7 ROLE OF MOTIVATION IN LEARNING

Motivation plays a central or key role in learning. It is a fundamental condition of learning. Motivation arouses the organism to respond to the environmental stimuli. Hence, for learning to proceed efficiently, the organism must be sufficiently motivated to learn or acquire the required response. Motivation, in fact, initiates an activity (response), sustains the organisms to continue the correct response in the situation till the same is fixated, *i.e.* the goal is achieved. Motivation also enables the organism to select the 'correct response' which is to be sustained. 'Correct response' is defined in terms of motivation state. Hence, motivation influences learning in at least three ways which are as follows:

10.7.1 It is a Condition for Eliciting Learning Act or Behaviour

Motivation plays an important role in eliciting the to be learnt behaviour. For example, when food is presented, a hungry organism is more likely to salivate (elicitation of a response) than the not hungry organism. Similarly, in learning to explore the correct path leading to the goal in a maze learning situation, the hungry rat is more likely to be active to explore it than when it is not hungry. **Melton** (1941) calls it an **energizing role of motivation** in learning. He found that the motivated organism when faced with a situation in which a 'correct response' is not immediately available, shows variable behaviour, *i.e.* becomes overactive. This is a direct index of strength with which the organism is motivated. In learning situations, the organism is aroused to discover the correct response for which greater number of responses are tried. This enhances the probability of hitting on the correct response.

Thus, increased level of arousal is an important factor in learning. It is so because the increased energy level increases the likelihood of correct response to be found.

Melton has examined several studies done by quite a good number of researchers on animals as well as on human beings (such as, Bousfield and Mote, 1943; Richter, 1946; Wang, 1923; Young, 1936; Stroud, 1931; 1940, Courts, 1942; Davis, 1942; Reed, 1946). Though the findings are not much consistent however, the findings do suggest in general that motivating state increases the level of energy and thus, the probability of correct response to be elicited also increases. Hence, motivation conditions correct responses to occur.

10.7.2 Motivation is Necessary for Reinforcing the Response being Learnt

Reinforcement is an essential condition of learning. Reinforcement refers to those objects or events which either maintain or strengthen a response. To cite example, in 'Pavlov's classical conditioning experiment, the reinforcement strengthens the conditioned response. Similarly, punishment reinforces avoidance behaviour. Thus, motivation reinforces learning activity.

10.7.3 Motivation Controls the Variability of Behaviour

In learning a new mode of response or modifying the older pattern of response, a motivated person runs through a wide variety of responses as he is energized or fully activated. Hence, fully aroused. Out of these wide range of various kinds of responses, only one or two may be correct. The correct response provides reinforcement which is quickly distinguished and picked up. Thus, gradually, the non-reinforced response continues to decrease while the reinforcing response occurs repeatedly. Hence, the frequency of correct responses goes on increasing and the other responses in the repertory decrease. In simpler terms, motivation permits to learn the correct responses and unlearning of the incorrect responses. Thus, it controls the variousness or variability of responses.

Further, motivation also creates a mental set or preparedness to learn correct responses and unlearn those which are either incorrect or unprofitable. This mental set induces expectancy as to when and how to respond and distinguishing between reinforced and non-reinforced responses. This enables the learner to be mentally prepared what, when and how to respond in the learning situation.

The influence of motive in learning can be substantiated on the basis of experimental findings obtained by several researchers. The experiments by **Pavlov** on classical conditioning and **Thorndike's** famous experiment on cats in the cage are good examples (details of these experiments have been described later in the section that concerns with the discussion of their respective theories or approaches of learning). Pavlov in his experiment found that the hungry dog could be conditioned to salivate to the neutral stimulus (CS) only because the response was reinforced by the presence of food immediately after ringing of bell (CS) that served as signal for the food (reinforcement) to follow. This created a sort of mental set or preparedness in the dog to respond by salivating as the reinforcement is expected to follow the bell ringing sound. Similarly, Thorndike found that the correct response could be stamped in and the incorrect responses tended to be gradually stamped out only because the correct response had a reinforcing value—known as **law of effect**.

Young and **Richter** also found in their studies that the period of deprivation and level of activity were directly correlated. This means that greater the motivation, greater is the probability of repeating the correct response (defined in terms of motivating condition).

10.7.4 Some Examples of Role of Motivation on Human Beings

Some studies done on human subjects also lend support to the important role of motivation in learning. Experimental studies done on human subjects have shown that the strength and nature of rewards and punishments administered by a teacher or experimenter influence the rate of learning. Even the knowledge of step-by-step improvement in performance has also been found as exerting rewarding impacts on performance. **Abels** (1938) selected 60 young children who were divided in three groups of 20 each. The subjects were matched in age, sex, educational level and intelligence. The first served as non-rewarded group (controlled group), the second group was given verbal reward, *i.e.* they were verbally appreciated for their better performances in each trial (continuous verbal reward for the performance in each trial). The third group of children was given a penny (smaller unit of coin), *i.e.* were given material reward. It was found that the performance of the first group was poor as compared to rest of the two rewarded groups of children (two experimental groups). The performance of the third group (second experimental group which was monetarily rewarded) was the best. In further study, it was found that the rate of learning increased when children were rewarded with coins of greater values. Numerous other studies, such as those of **Gates** and **Rosenland** (1923), **Sears** (1936) have also shown that learners usually respond better to encouragement rather than discouragement.

Sarson and **Sarson** (1957) in a comprehensive study on the combined effects of encouragement or discouragement and high or low levels of motivation found that on the whole, the group of highly motivated subjects did somewhat better than others.

Murata (1959) in one of the studies found that reward is more effective in the beginning of a series of learning trials while punishment is more effective during the final phase of learning. In explanation, it is argued that the stress caused by punishment tends to interfere with new—unstable habits, but is less disruptive to the older and better established habits.

Experimentally, it has also been observed that punishment as an aid to learning, is most effective when it is combined with reward. For example, **Commins** and **Fagin** (1954) found that if an undesirable response is suppressed because of punishment, the subjects attempt to try for more desirable response if the same is reinforced by a reward. Thus, reward and punishment together act as 'cue' to discriminate correct and incorrect responses. Punishment alone cannot do this. Therefore, punishment should always be given in such a way that the learner can distinguish clearly what specific response is correct or incorrect.

10.7.5 Knowledge of Result

Knowledge of result functions as reinforcer in learning. Considerably, a good number of experimental evidences indicate that with knowledge of progress in performing a learning task, one learns to perform more rapidly than a person who is equally motivated with comparable ability, but is provided no knowledge about the progress, *i.e.* he works **in the dark** (Ammons, 1956).

Knowledge of result influences the learner in two ways—firstly, the knowledge of good performance accelerates the level of aspiration to do much better. Hence, it intrinsically impels or pushes the learner toward more better accomplishment. Similarly, in the event of knowledge about poor performance also impels one (intrinsically) to evaluate or explore the shortcomings and try to remove the shortcomings to improve the performance.

However, sometimes, knowledge of result may exert negative influence as well. Knowledge about success may arouse undesirable extent of superiority which may interfere with his accomplishment to attain the aspiration level. Similarly, knowledge about failure may induce feeling of inferiority which may lead to frustration and lower down interest in the task.

Despite these possibilities of negative effects most of the experimental evidences lend support to the positive effect of knowledge of result. In recent years this positive effect is called as 'Psychological feedback' (Bwon, 1949). **Psychological feedback** is a process whereby the learner gains information about the 'corrections' of his previous response so that he can adjust his behaviour to compensate for errors. **Elwell** and **Grindley** (1938) has long ago demonstrated in one of their experiments that learning improves under the knowledge of result condition as compared to without knowledge of result condition.

Bray (1959) conducted a study on gunner trainees. The trainees were required to **track** targets with 40 mm guns. This task involved continuous sighting of the gun on a moving object. Tracking with this gun required to follow horizontal movement of the target as well as to follow the vertical movement. Standard army method to provide training in this skill was employed, *i.e.* giving verbal instructions and coaching before, during and after each session of gunnery practice. Three experimental conditions—(i) standard army method for group A, (ii) each man coached his partner—group B, and (iii) for group C, a special telescope sight mounted on the gun was used to check the accuracy of aim and giving a buzzer sound signal to the group C. Whenever the gun was off the target, *i.e.* providing knowledge of result. The men in group 'C' were also informed of their scores at the end of each session.

The results clearly evidenced that the trainees in group C (knowledge of result group) improved much more rapidly than the other two groups. The group 'C' also achieved the greatest proficiency. The standard army method proved least effective of the three groups.

The above finding has been verified in many other situations, *viz.* **Bilodeau** and **Schumsky** (1959) in a well-designed experiment found that knowledge of result is a decisive factor in learning lever positioning task by army trainees irrespective of the fact that knowledge of result is given early or late in the training. Similarly, **Greenspoon** and **Foreman** (1956) studied the influence of delay in knowledge of result. Though, lengthening of knowledge reduced the rate of learning, even the longest delay gave better results than when no knowledge of result was given.

The above-mentioned experimental findings show the role of extrinsic motivation in learning. However, the intrinsic motivation such as, self-instructions, interests, need to achieve, higher level of aspiration etc. also motivate human beings to learn at faster rates with maximum level of proficiency. This is the reason that teachers in school today rely less on extrinsic rewards and punishments and try to create interest among the pupils so that learning becomes a reward in itself. When one is keenly interested and feels the 'need to learn' he learns better than those who are not otherwise keenly interested or feel the **need to learn**.

Among the intrinsic motivating factors, need for achievement (**n** Ach) and stress has very extensively been studied. In one study by **Mishra** (1974) it was found that greater the **n** Ach, better the performance and vice versa. Similarly, **Lazarus** and **Erickson** (1952) found that working under pressure of time or any other distracting conditions induces stress in the learner. But often, such stresses help in performance with greater efficiency. This happens particularly in conditions in which a particular response is strengthened. But, when a new response is to be substituted for older one, it exerts impeding effect (Palermo, 1957). However, the influence of stress on learning depends upon the degree of frustration, personality factors and the level of motivation.

Thus, what we notice is that motivation plays a highly significant role in learning and, therefore, we can conclude **that learning is not possible unless one is motivated to learn.**

10.8 HOW DO WE LEARN?

Learning takes place in many ways. There are some methods that are used in the acquisition of simple responses while other methods are used in the acquisition of complex responses. In this section, we shall be describing the simplest kind of learning that is known as **conditioning**. Two types of conditioning phenomenon have been identified. These are: (i) **classical conditioning** and **operant** or **Instrumental conditioning.**

In addition, there are also some other ways of learning about which we shall discuss in the next chapter. For the present, we restrict our discussion of these two types of conditioning learning only—the **classical** and **operant** conditioning.

10.9 CLASSICAL CONDITIONING

Behaviourists hold the view that learning is a behaviour which takes place when the organism forms an internal connection or association between two observable and measurable events. These are termed as stimulus and response connection (S-R association). In other words, the organism learns to associate a specific stimulus with a specific response. This model suggests to explain learning in terms of S-R (stimulus and response) relationship. A stimulus is that which an organism can sense and evoke or elicit a response in the organism. A response is a behaviour which is systematically related to the stimulus. Hence, all kinds of learning may be supposed to consist of S-R connections. This is also known as 'associative learning' because learning is possible by underlying S-R associations. 'Classical conditioning' is a form of 'associative learning'. The name it gets from the fact that this kind of learning was studied in 'classical' experiments of 'Pavlov' (1839–1936).

Pavlov was primarily interested in the study of **physiology of digestion**. In course of his studies, he noticed that the dog (on which he was doing his experiment) started secreting saliva merely on sighting the empty plate in which food was served. Pavlov was amazed over this simple fact and started to study the phenomenon extensively.

As we know, saliva secretion is a natural reflexive response to food or anything put into the mouth. Hence, this kind of reflexive response has a natural association with the kind of stimulus that elicits salivatory response. In this sense, food is an **unconditioned stimulus** (UCS) while salivation—a naturally associated reflexive response is an **unconditioned response** (UCR). The empty food plate is a **neutral stimulus**. But when the salivatory response gets associated with this neutral stimulus, the response would be called **conditioned response** (CR) while the associated neutral stimulus (empty food plate) would be called **conditioned stimulus (CS)**, because this is a new association between the two and such association is not natural rather acquired or learned association.

To establish the above-mentioned fact experimentally, Pavlov conducted an experiment on his dog on which he was studying the physiological process of digestion. The experiment was carried out in two phases. In the first phase, the dog was harnessed in a soundproof room. This was repeated several times for several days. It was so done with a view to let the dog adapt in the new situation of the room. In the meantime, a simple surgery was done and an end of the tube was inserted in dog's jaw while the another end of the tube was put in a measuring glass jar. The experimental set-up is illustrated as shown in **Figure 10.2**.

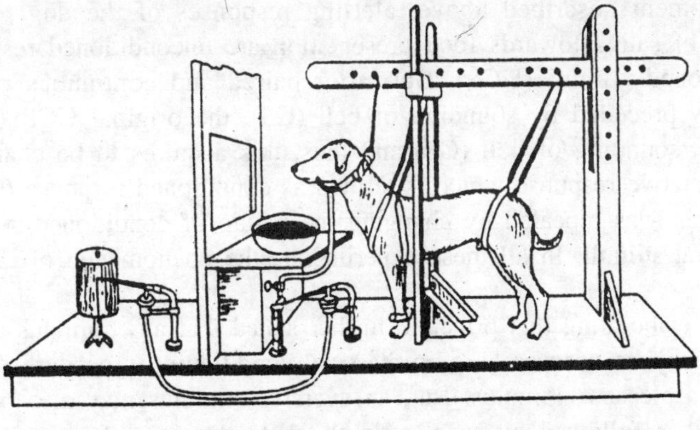

FIGURE 10.2 Classical conditioning experiment on dog.

The above preliminary phase was followed by the second phase of the experiment. In this phase, the dog was kept hungry and was placed in the harness with fitted tube. A bell was sounded which was immediately followed by meat powder (food). The dog was allowed to eat it. This procedure was repeated continuously for a few days. After a number of such practice trials, a test trial was introduced in which everything was the same except food presentation which was delayed a bit after sounding of bell (it was delayed by over 30 seconds). It was observed that the dog began to secrete saliva in response to the bell itself which earlier used to be secreted on presentation of food. Thus, the UCR (salivation response) which was originally associated with UCS (food) shifted its association from UCS to CS (bell). This new association is called stimulus—stimulus association (S–S association) and the resultant response is called **conditioned response**–(CR).

This phenomenon of conditioning (also known as **respondent conditioning**) is shown in **Table 10.1**.

TABLE 10.1 Procedural operations and terminologies used in classical conditioning experiments.

Stages of conditioning	*Operations*
1. Before conditioning (Before experiment)	Dog in harness on several trials (habituation) Exposure to bell sound—Neutral stimulus/Alerting responses observed
2. During conditioning (Experimental trials)	Sounding of bell (CS) followed by food (UCS) secretion of saliva—UCR
3. After conditioning (Test trial)	Sounding of bell (CS)—secretion of saliva (CR), the two becomes associated

Pavlov terms the natural stimulus as UCS and the natural response to it as UCR. But when any natural response to a natural stimulus (UCR or simply UR) gets associated with a neutral stimulus, the neutral stimulus is called conditioned stimulus (CS) and the newly associated response is termed as conditioned response (CR). These abbreviations are explained below:

UCS or US	Unconditioned stimulus	(*e.g.* food)
UCR or UR	Unconditioned response	(*e.g.* secretion of saliva on presentation of food)
CS	Conditioned stimulus	(*e.g.* sounding of bell)
CR	Conditioned response	(*e.g.* secretion of saliva on sounding of bell)

In the experiment described above, alerting responses of the dog towards sounding of bell and secretion of saliva towards food presentation are unconditioned responses (UCR) made towards unconditioned stimuli (UCS). But, after paired and continuous presentation of food (UCS) immediately preceded by sounding of bell (CS), the original UCR (salivation response) got associated with sounding of bell (CS) and thus, this acquires to be characterised as learned association or associative response which is termed as conditioned response (CR).

The experiment was repeated by changing the nature of conditioned stimulus (CS) such as light or other neutral stimuli. In all these experiments, the phenomenon of conditioning could be observed.

Pavlov while elaborating this principle further stated that any stimulus that elicits an inborn reflexive response may be used as UCS in classical conditioning procedure. The meat powder in this experiment is a pleasent stimulus. But, an aversive stimulus may also be used as UCS. For example, if the bell is followed by an electric shock to the paw of an animal, the UCR to the stimulus (flexion of the paw) soon comes to be associated with bell (**Bechterve**, 1954). Here, electric shock is UCS because it automatically evokes flexive response in the animal. It is evoked without any learning. But this response becomes conditioned to the bell (CS) due to repeated paired presentation with UCS. Bechterve calls it **associative reflex** but others use Pavlovian terminology—**conditioning**.

Watson also conducted an experiment on an infant named Albert by using unpleasant aversive stimulus—pistol shot sound that aroused fear—a natural or unconditioned response (UCR) in the infant towards brusting shot sound of the pistol. He found that this reflexive sound became so strongly conditioned that the infant began to fear of even his mother when she approached to him dressed in white fur coat. It was because the infant has learnt conditioned act of withdrawal from white furry rat that signalled the production of bursting pistol shot-sound as the two were continuously presented in pair form before the infant for several days whenever the child made orientation reflective response of approaching towards the white furry rat.

10.9.1 Some Salient Features of Classical Conditioning Procedure

The Pavlovian procedure of conditioning phenomenon has certain essential characteristic features. These are as follows:

(a) Pairing and sequential interval of paired stimulus presentation is first salient necessity in classical conditioning procedure. The UCS and CS are presented in pair form with a very brief sequential interval in which the UCS follows the CS or CS precedes the UCS with a very brief temporal interval between them (say 2 seconds).

(b) Another important notable point is continuity of paired presentation of CS and UCS. In the above experiment, the CS (bell) and UCS (food) were presented in paired form continuously for several days. By virtue of which the association between CS and CR could be acquired.

(c) Still another important feature of classical conditioning is that in this kind of conditioning we learn S–S association and not S–R association. Hence, it is also called S–S learning in which one stimulus (*e.g.* sound of bell) becomes a signal of another stimulus (e.g. food). In other words, **one stimulus signifies the possible occurrence of another stimulus**.

Examples of classical conditioning are abundant in everyday life. Suppose you have just taken your lunch and feel satisfied. However, immediately you are exposed to some delicious sweet dish on the table. This signals its taste in your mouth and triggers the secretion of saliva. You feel like eating it. This is a conditioned response (CR). Let us take another example of children. In early childhood one is naturally afraid of loud noise. Suppose, you present a white teddy bear to a child and almost simultaneously, a loud noise occurs. If this situation occurs repeatedly for several times, the child in due course will take the white teddy as signal for the unpleasant loud sound and thus, he would begin to elicit fear response merely on sighting the teddy bear.

In the similar manner, most of the emotions of fear, attractions, hatred etc. develop due to conditioning. Even the development of attitudinal dispositions, certain kinds of beliefs, prejudices, language etc. are also conditioned in some way. Suppose, a person has the previous experience of getting sick whenever he eats banana. He feels nauseated when he is exposed to a banana. Feeling nauseated merely by seeing a banana is an example of conditioning. Similarly, on many occasions we may notice the phenomenon of conditioning in our day-to-day life situations.

Pavlov's work had a widespread influence on the development of psychological thought in general and on the psychology of learning in particular. Since then, countless number of experiments have been done to demonstrate conditioning procedures on both human and animal subjects and thus, conditioning has now become a fundamental concept in psychology.

10.9.2 Determinants (Factors) of Classical Conditioning

Any response is said to be conditioned when a stimulus other than natural or original evokes the natural or original response (UCR). Such responses are called **conditioned response** (CR) or **conditioned reflex** (C Reflex). However, conditioning depends on certain factors or conditions. If the necessary conditions are not present, the phenomenon of conditioning is unlikely to occur. These factors are: (a) contiguity, (b) practice, (c) types of conditioned stimulus and (d) intensity of stimuli.

Contiguity

Contiguity means simultaneous presentation of neutral (CS) and natural (UCS) stimulus. In Pavlovian procedure, the bell was a neutral stimulus (CS) and meat powder—a natural stimulus (UCS) for eliciting unconditioned response (UCR), *i.e.* salivation response. These two stimuli were presented in pair form by virtue of which, the neutral stimulus bell had become conditioned stimulus (CS). Had these not been paired, the neutral stimulus could not have acquired the potential to evoke CR.

In this context, temporal relation between these two stimuli is also an important factor. Each paired presentation of CS and UCS is called trial and the period during which association between CS and UCS occurs is called 'interstimulus interval.'*

In Pavlovian conditioning, it is observed that **the stage of acquisition** on account of such pairing with maintaining the temporal contiguity (interstimulus interval) of the two stimuli began by third trial with 7 drops of saliva and by seventh trial, saliva secretion levelled off and continued with minor fluctuations at about the same strength for remaining trials. This is called **stable level of responding** (asymptote† of learning curve). Beyond this level, further acquisition

* The time that elapses between onset of conditioned stimulus (CS) and onset of unconditioned stimulus (UCS).

† Strength of response that becomes stable in the learning curve which shows neither any increase nor any decrease of curve line.

trials do not strengthen the response anymore. Hence, the stage of acquisition in Pavlov's experiment began from 3rd trial and continued upto 7th trial.

In a series of experiments, time intervals between CS and UCS were varied to observe various phenomena like **simultaneous conditioning, delayed conditioning**, **trace conditioning** and **backward conditioning**. These phenomena are shown in **Figure 10.3**.

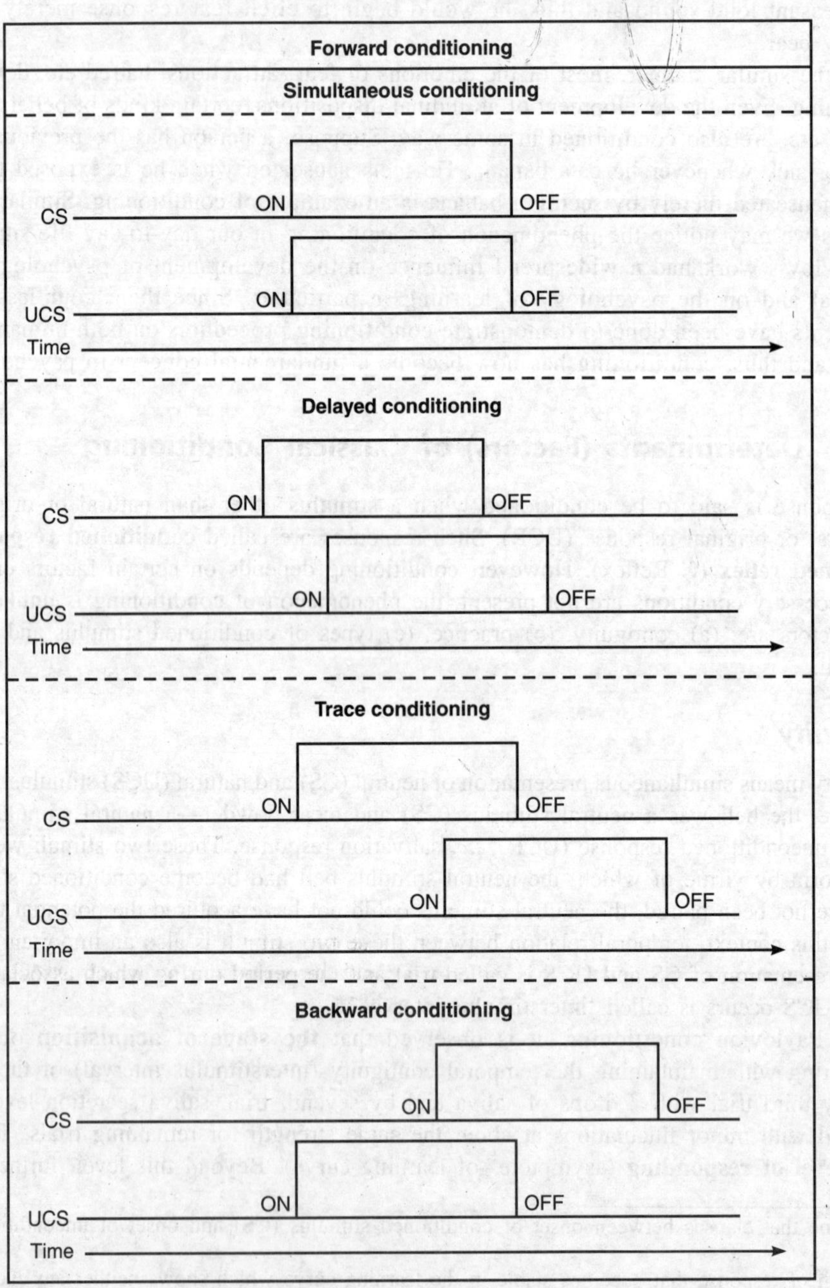

FIGURE 10.3 Temporal relations between CS and UCS in Pavlovian conditioning.

(i) **Simultaneous conditioning:** In simultaneous conditioning the time interval between CS and UCS is kept too short, *i.e.* fraction of a second (1/2 of a second). This temporal gap is kept constant in all the trials until response occurs.

(ii) **Delayed conditioning:** In delayed conditioning, the time gap between CS and UCS is increased by a few seconds (usually 1 to 2 seconds).

(iii) **Trace or sign conditioning:** In trace conditioning experiments, CS is presented first and then removed just before UCS appears. Thus, only a neural trace is allowed to remain for being conditioned.

(iv) **Backward conditioning:** In backward conditioning, the temporal location of CS and UCS is reversed. UCS is presented before the onset of CS.

Thus, it is clear that temporal relations in pairing of CS and UCS is an important factor of conditioning in Pavlov's procedure. Interstimulus pairing must be 'optimal' for better conditioning. Usually when UCS follows a CS by a definite interval of brief duration produces better conditioning because it better permits anticipatory responses. The optimal interstimulus interval depends upon the situation and the kind of response employed as UCR. However, in general, short intervals (approx. 2 seconds) is optimal as Kimble (1967) suggests.

Practice

It is another necessary condition for conditioning to occur. CS and UCS must be repeated in pair form over a considerable period of times. In Pavlov's experiment, salivation responses to sounding of bell became stronger with increasing number of paired trials. However, the amount of practice necessary for CR to occur, depends upon the strength of the response to the UCS.

The above factors relate to conditioning procedures of the experimental studies. In addition to these, certain other factors relating to stimulus being chosen are also important for conditioning behaviours. These are: (i) types of stimulus and (ii) intensity of CS.

(i) **Types of unconditioned stimuli (UCS):** In classical conditioning experiments, usually two types of UCS are used. These are either 'appetitive' or 'aversive'. The **appetitive stimuli** are such which automatically elicit approaching responses, *i.e.* preparatory to consume the presented stimuli such as eating, drinking, caressing etc. These stimuli give satisfaction and pleasure. The **aversive UCR**, on the other hand, is such that elicit avoiding or escaping responses because, these are noisy, bitter in taste, painful or shocking (as in electric shocks) and harmful.

It has been found that when appetitive UCS is used, CR acquisition is slower and requires greater number of trials whereas aversive UCR is established in one or two or three trials depending on the intensity of the aversive stimuli.

(ii) **Intensity of conditioned stimuli (CS):** This influences the course of both appetitive and aversive classical conditioning. The more intense CS, more effective it would be in accelerating the acquisition of CR. It means that stronger the CS, fewer number of acquisition trials are required for conditioning.

10.9.3 Theories about Classical Conditioning

Theories of classical conditioning are the products of many experimental studies done on conditioning phenomenon applying Pavlovian procedure. These theories describe and provide the findings of these studies in an orderly manner. These theories are also concerned with the processes involved in conditioning acquisition.

Two of such theories are relevant and important. These are: (i) Stimulus Substitution Theory and (ii) Information and Expectation Theory.

Stimulus Substitution Theory

This is the classical theory of conditioning that originated with Pavlov and remained influential for many years. It is a very simple theory that relies upon the idea of pairing of CS and UCS in acquiring conditioned response. According to this theory, the pairing results in the acquisition of capacity to substitute for UCS in evoking a response. To put it in other words, an association, *i.e.* a link or a bond is formed between CS and UCS as a result of which the CS becomes the equivalent to UCS in evoking a response. Pavlov believed that this association or link-up occurs in two areas of brain (cerebral cortex). One area is activated by CS while another one is activated by UCS. The activation of the UCS area in the brain results in a 'reflex' (automatic response). Thus, during conditioning procedure, due to pairing of CS and UCS with a very short temporal interval, the CS acquires the ability to excite or activate the UCS area in the brain that leads to the elicitation of reflex response.

Though this theory appears appealing and simple, it is not acceptable to more recent theorists of learning. The major difficulty in this theory is that CR and UCR must be the same or at least bear maximum similarity. However, the researchers have noted in their observations that the CR may not always be same as UCR has been found in some studies done on animals in which UCR is found to intensify the level of activity while CR is found to slow down.

Information and Expectation Theory

This theory states that CS serves as signal for the UCS to occur. Thus presentation of CS arouses an expectation for the UCS to be presented and therefore the learner makes a response with this expectation.

The question arises here as to how does the CS become a signal for UCS? A number of studies have been done. These studies show that this happens because UCS is a surprising or novel event (Kamin, 1969; Terry and Wagner, 1975). This novel or surprising UCS event induces the learner to look retrogressively by utilizing the memory traces of the recent past event in which CS was presented. Since in every trial, CS precedes UCS, the learner while looks back to the recent memory traces, he consistently finds the traces of CS each time (in each trial) before UCS. Thus, an association or link or bond between CS and UCS is formed. Therefore, whenever the CS is presented, UCS is expected and CR is made in anticipation of the UCS.

Thus, the theory assumes that CR is not an automatic event on account of CS–UCS pairing rather conditioned responses are behaviours or actions and the learner engages in such behaviours in expectation of future event—occurrence of UCS.

10.9.4 Some Important Phenomenon of Classical Conditioning

Extinction

In various experimental studies, it has been observed that if unconditioned stimulus (UCS) is omitted, *i.e.* not presented, the conditioned response (CR) gradually diminishes. This is called **extinction**. It so happens because in conditioning procedure, the reinforcement is automatic by pairing of CS with UCS. The UCS here serves as 'reinforcer' for the CS to occur. In the event of removal of UCS (unpaired presentation of CS), the reinforcement is no longer available. Hence, the acquired CR cease or get extincted. In 'Pavlov's' experiment, after the acquisition of CR (salivation response) associated with bell sound (CS), only CS was repeatedly presented without following the UCS (reinforcement). It was found that salivation response to bell sound (CR) gradually weakened. In 'Bechterve's' experiment also a decrease in the frequency of flexion responses (CR) was noticed. Hence, repeated presence of CS singly (without pairing with UCS) results in extinction of conditioned response.

However, cessation of CR is not forgetting or erasing of what has been learnt. Extinction is rather a process of learning to 'inhibit' the acquired CR during conditioning. It is a kind of new learning which superimposes the old one without destroying the conditioned response acquired earlier. This fact is substantiated by two related phenomena—**spontaneous recovery** and **reconditioning**.

Spontaneous recovery

Pavlov found evidences that in extinction phenomenon, the conditioned response (CR) is not completely or entirely erased. Thus, all is not forgotten because the extinguished CR reappears spontaneously after a brief rest of extinction. Although, the reappearance of the extincted response may not be in its original strength, but it does evidence the fact that the animals tend to retain at least some of the learning association formed by original pairing of CS with UCS. Therefore, the extinguished CR after rest of extinction spontaneously recovers when CS alone is presented. This is shown in **Figure 10.4**.

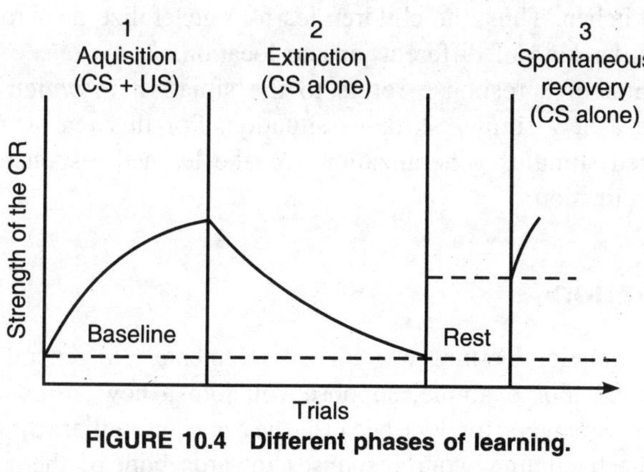

FIGURE 10.4 Different phases of learning.

However, the amount of spontaneous recovery depends on the duration of lapsed time after the extinction session. The longer the duration of lapsed time, the greater is the recovery of acquired CR. Such recovery occurs spontaneously.

Thus, it is obvious that experimental extinction does not cause forgetting rather, it only inhibits the response which is weared off during rest and as such, the CR reappears spontaneously.

Reconditioning

Another evidence regarding extinction as a process of inhibition is obtained from reconditioning phenomenon. After extinction, on reinstatement of the reinforcement, *i.e.* pairing of CS with UCS (as given in original conditioning trials), Pavlov found that reconditioning occurred more rapidly than before. Experimentally, if the experimenter continues the procedure—conditioning–extinguishing–reconditioning–reextinction and so on up to a certain point, it would be observed that conditioning reoccurs each time a little faster and extinction also takes place more rapidly than before. Thus, extinction does not mean cessation of original conditioning, rather it paves the way to learn both kinds of responses—to respond and not to respond. In other words, one learns when to do (to respond) and when not to do (not to respond).

Stimulus generalization

Generalization means responding similarly to similar set of another stimuli. It is generally observed that we tend to respond similarly to the objects and events which are different but resemble the one to which we have become conditioned. This means that once CR has been acquired, situations or objects similar to the original CS evoke the same reaction. Best example of this phenomenon is the case of Albert, a 11-month old baby. Albert became conditioned to white-furred rat (CS) and showed frightened reactions. Subsequently, the fear response was generalized to other white furry animals and objects. He even became afraid of a wad of cotton. Similarly, **Hovland** (1937) also conducted an experiment using galvanic skin response (GSR) as CR. And an electric shock as UCS and sound of a pure tone of a particular frequency as CS. The findings suggest that **the greater the similarity between stimuli, the greater is the generalization between them**. Sometimes response generalization is also noticed.

In our everyday life situations also, we notice that children locate the sweets in absence of their mothers when they hide it in a different jar and at different location. It happens because the children had earlier been conditioned to find out the sweets used to be kept in another jar and at another location in the kitchen. Thus, the children learn to generalize their responses of finding out the sweets kept in a similar kind of different jar and location.

Thus, generalization of a response refers to the situation in which the learned response is elicited (occurred) in a new similar stimulus situation. For this reason (similarity in stimulus situation) it is also called stimulus generalization, *i.e.* the learned response is generalized to the similarity of a stimulus situation.

10.9.5 Discrimination

Another process is discrimination learning which is complementary to generalization. Discrimination is a response to difference. For example, suppose you join a new group. Two members of the group—‘A’ and ‘B’—are strangers for you because they are unfamiliar. Since both (A and B) are unfamiliar to you, in the beginning, your responses towards both of them will be a generalized response (here, unfamiliarity with both is an aspect of similarity for you). But, in due course, whenever you happen to meet ‘A’, you feel pleasure and whenever you meet ‘B’ you feel neither any pleasure nor displeasure. Hence, there is no any element of attraction towards ‘B’ because the response of being attracted is not reinforced. But, your response of being attracted towards A is always reinforced because of pleasure experience whenever you happen to meet him.

Therefore, your response towards 'A' will be different from that of 'B' as the former had the opportunities of being reinforced.

Similarly, suppose a child is conditioned to be afraid of a person wearing black dress and has a bushy moustache. Now whenever he meets with any stranger in black dress with a beard, the child shows signs of fear. This is an example of generalization. But, when the same child meets a stranger in grey dress with cleanly shaved face, he shows no sign of fear. This is an example of discrimination. Thus, it is obvious that generalization occurs when discrimination fails. Discrimination depends on the discriminating ability or discrimination learning.

Humans and animals, both can learn to discriminate. It is through discrimination learning that children learn to differentiate between alphabets. Discriminating between different geo-graphical figures also exemplifies discrimination learning. The fact that human beings as well as animals both can learn fine discriminations is supported by the experimental studies done by Fields (1954) and Slucki and Porter (1965).

To demonstrate discrimination learning, the particular response is reinforced positively while the others are negatively reinforced. Thus, the organism learns differential patterns of res-ponses towards two different stimuli which are reinforced differently (positively and negatively). One such experiment was done on hens which were trained to pick up grains scattered on two discs—black and grey. The hens were given electric shocks whenever they approached to peck on the grey disc. However, they were allowed to peck on black disc. This procedure was repeated for several days. When the hens learnt to approach for pecking on the black disc, the black disc was replaced by a white disc. It was found that the hens now used to peck on grey disc in place of white disc (that replaced the black disc). Thus, they learnt to discriminate in pecking response. They learnt the darker of the two discs which yielded positive reinforcement and, therefore, learnt to avoid the lighter, of the two which yielded negative reinforcement.

Here, it is important to note that generalization occurs even when one learns to discriminate the stimuli. For example, in different sessions of experimental situations, the brightness of light may be varied in discriminable steps by increasing and decreasing in equal number of steps (say 4 steps in each series of manipulation of stimulus situation). The organism is placed in one of the brighter conditions and the frequency of occurrence of learned responses to various degrees of brightness are recorded. It has been found that the frequencies of responces to various degrees of increasing and decreasing orders occur in the manner as shown in **Figure 10.5**.

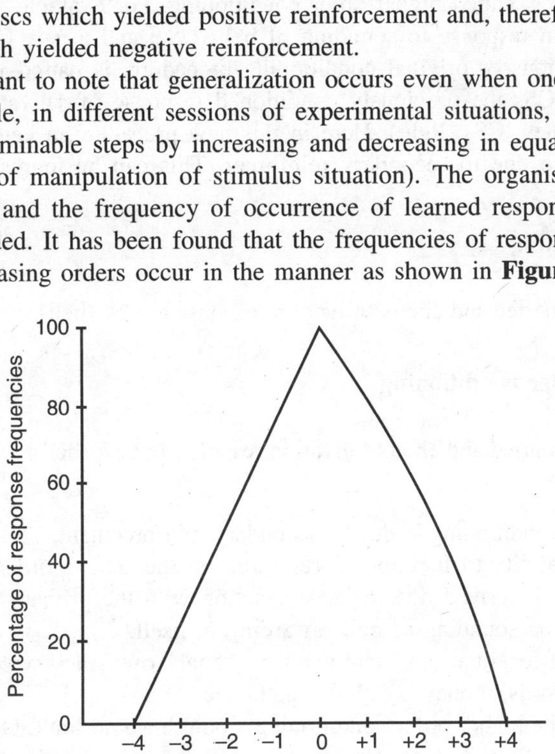

FIGURE 10.5 Generalization stimuli and percentage of operants on their presentation.

From Figure 10.5, it is evident that maximum responses have occurred when the light is brighter at the training level. However, due to changes in brightness level, by increasing or decreasing the brightness on either side, shows reduction in pecking rates. It shows that with maximal change in brightness, the rate of pecking response decreases appreciably. At this point, the reduction is almost hundred per cent. Curves like these are indicative of **generalization gradients** meaning that **generalization is a function of graded stimulus similarity**.

10.9.6 Reinforcement

Reinforcement is that event or stimulus which increases or maintains the strength of response (CR in classical conditioning). In classical conditioning the UCS serves as reinforcement because in pair with CS it evokes and strengthens the to be learnt response (salivation in response to conditioned stimulus—CS, *i.e.* sounding of bell). It is known as **primary reinforcement**. When this reinforcer is terminated, extinction of CR occurs. Another kind of reinforcement is also possible in classical conditioning. This is known as **secondary reinforcement** and the consequent elicitation of response is called **higher order conditioning.**

10.9.7 Higher Order Conditioning

When a new CS (CS_2) is paired with previous CS (CS_1) and acquires the ability to elicit a specific response, it is called 'secondary reinforcement' and the kind of conditioning that occurs due to secondary reinforcement is called higher-order conditioning. For example, once the dog has been conditioned to salivate in response to sounding of bell (CS_1) and a new CS (CS_2), suppose light instead of food, in previous or original conditioning procedure, is paired with CS_1 (bell) serving as UCS which follows CS_2 the previously conditioned response of salivation to bell is likely to be associated with this new CS_2 (light). Here in this new procedure, a new order of conditioning to a new CS takes place due to secondary reinforcer. This can be represented in the following paradigm:

Original conditioning

$$\left.\begin{array}{l}\text{CS} - \text{Bell}\\ \text{US} - \text{Food}\end{array}\right\}\text{paried and elicits salivation response to } CS_1 \text{ (bell).}$$

In the second order conditioning

$$\left.\begin{array}{l}\text{CS} - \text{Light}\\ \text{US} - \text{Bell}\end{array}\right\}\text{paried and elicits salivation response to } CS_2 \text{ (bell).}$$

The second order conditioning is due to secondary reinforcement. This is also called 'derived reinforcement' because ability to function as reinforcer in the second order is not inherent in the stimulus but this ability is derived due to its association with the primary reinforcement of food. This association makes the sounding of bell rewarding in itself.

In our everyday life situations, many of our goals owe their value to their secondary reinforcement such as words, money, symbols, status etc.

'Pavlov' believes the higher order conditioning would have no limit. One may pair the second CS with still a new CS_3, CS_4 and so on. However, in experimental situation, Pavlov failed to obtain higher order conditioning beyond second order. The reason being absence of primary reinforcement causing extinction, and thus further order of conditioning is inhibited. Though, Pavlov with some procedural changes could obtain third order conditioning also, but with great difficulty. Second order conditioning is relatively easy to obtain.

10.9.8 Experimental Neurosis

Sometimes the differences between stimuli are so slight that it becomes very difficult to discriminate them. When this happens, an experimental neurosis may develop. In experimental situation, a dog is made to discriminate between a circle and an oval. After the dog has learnt to discriminate, the oval is gradually made more circular. At least, there exists only a slight difference between the two shapes. At this point, the dog becomes upset, appears fearful, barks and struggles. The discrimination is very hard as well as stressful. Development of this phenomenon is known as 'experimental neurosis'. This phenomenon is more probable when negative (aversive) rather than positive (rewarding) reinforcer is used. It is likely that children (or even adults) may also exhibit similar behaviour when they are pressed to discriminate beyond their capabilities. Very often, this is noticed with the students in examination situation when they are pressed to answer two similar types of questions with a slightly different approach.

10.9.9 Counter Conditioning

Watson and **Rayner** (1920) conditioned fear reaction in a baby by pairing the sight of a white rat (CS) with a loud ringing sound (UCS). This fear was generalized to similar stimuli such as other furry objects, a fur coat and cotton, white beard etc. In another session, the baby was given food while white rat was at some distance (thus, fear was aroused weakly). The procedure was repeated several times and gradually, fear was extinguished. In this case, fear reduction may be accounted for two possible reasons. The fear was reduced partly because it was non-reinforced. Another possible reason might be that a response stronger than fear and incompatible with it was elicited in presence of fear stimulus—**the positive emotional reaction to food**. This latter reaction was conditioned to the white rat and since it was incompatible with fear, fear was replaced. Thus, fear in this case has been eliminated by **counter conditioning**—another response which was dominant over fear.

However, counter conditioning depends on relative strength of competing responses. This technique is widely used by psychotherapists in the treatment of psychological disorders of behaviour known as **behaviour modification technique**.

10.9.10 Pseudo-conditioning

Sometimes it is noticed that in experimental situations, the subject or the organism elicits a response similar to conditioned response (CR) without being conditioned (*i.e.* without typical pairing of CS with UCS). Such a phenomenon is called **pseudo-conditioning**. For example, the dog is brought to the experimental condition and as soon as the dog enters the experimental room, it begins to salivate without presenting CS with UCS in pair form. Similarly, suppose a teacher calls a particular student shoutingly and the student begins to display fear response anticipating punishment. Such responses occur on the basis of past experience. The student's past experience tells that whenever the teacher calls a student shoutingly, he awards punishment and as such begins to show fear reactions.

10.9.11 Significance of Classical Conditioning

Till now we have been primarily discussing about salivary and flexion responses because the classical conditioning researchers used these reflexes in their studies and established several principles of classical conditioning. But, such reflexive responses are of little use for human beings in their day-to-day adjustive behaviours with the situations of the environment. Instead, the emotional responses that become conditioned to certain stimuli are for more important for day-to-day international transactions in human life.

Most of our subjective feelings ranging from violent emotional reactions to the very subtle changes of mood are by and large conditioned reactions. The stimulus for conditioning our emotional reactions may be a particular face, a scene or a voice. For example, phobic reactions, depressive moods on sighting a particular scene or face profile, hatred feelings towards particular persons etc. are the examples of conditioned emotional feelings which play significant role in our adjustive behaviours and interpersonal relations. We often find it difficult to trace when such feelings and emotions got conditioned to and to what particular kind of conditioned stimulus it could be conditioned. It becomes difficult because such reactions take a generalized pattern.

Since, most of such emotional reactions are learned through conditioning, it is also possible to unlearn them by applying counter conditioning procedures or desensitising. Based on these assumptions, psychologists have developed various behaviour modification techniques or behaviour therapies which have the base in conditioning principles and related phenomenon.

Thus, the principles of conditioning have practical implications and significance.

Critical comments

Though classical conditioning principles have had a widespread influence on the development of psychological thought and the phenomenon has been demonstrated in countless experimental works done on human beings as well as on animals, this principle has severely been criticized by many researchers on some important grounds. These are as follows:

(i) The theory suffers from limited scope of applicability to a wider range of learning situations. It is applicable in simple forms of learning only because in a given situation we can condition only a single response with a single stimulus only. Thus, conditioning principle is unable to describe and explain the **multi-response learning situations**. This is supported by a series of experimental works of Bazren (1939a, 1939b, 1940, 1949). As the findings indicate, conditioning principle seem to hold good in learning simple responses, particularly the reflexive behaviour. Other kinds of complex learning, learning of language and other symbols become important which are acquired later in life and the conditioning ability gradually reduces its force. Therefore, learning of complex problems cannot be successfully explained in terms of classical conditioning alone.

(ii) Conditioning procedure is mechanical in nature. Therefore, it does not explain well the responses learnt under natural conditions because the same cannot be mechanically reproduced or created.

(iii) Conditioning is a temporary phenomenon. Pavlov himself has noticed that after conditioning has been acquired and not repeatedly reinforced, it diminishes.

(iv) Conditioning principle lays emphasis on practice and reflex repetition. Conditioning occurs when CS is repeatedly followed by UCS. But, most of the learning, particularly the incidental learning and cognitive or insightful learning does not require practice over longer period of time. Hence, this principle does not cover all kinds of learning.

(v) Thorndike (1931), Hilgard (1940), Skinner (1953) and Marquis (1961) hold the view that though reflex is key to some kinds of conditioning, but more often, conditioning occurs through organism's own non-reflexive behaviours and their consequences. These behaviours are more important for learning to take place because they become instrumental in forming an association between stimulus and to be learned behaviour. Classical conditioning does not recognize significance of such non-reflexive behaviours and their consequences.

In view of the above shortcomings, researchers have proposed some other principles. Important among them is operant or instrumental conditioning which is being described hereunder.

Operant (instrumental) conditioning

B.F. Skinner (1938) talks of a different type of conditioning principle which is a modified procedure of Pavlovian classical conditioning procedure. Building up on Thorndike's work, Skinner began to publish a series of papers around 1930s exploring such voluntary responses which he calls **'operants'**. An 'operant' is a response or group of responses that acts upon the environment each time in the same way.

According to Skinner, the operants are those responses which are emitted, *i.e.* elicited spontaneously without any immediately identifiable stimuli. For example, to understand it, a comparison of Pavlov's dog and Thorndike's cat seems plausible. Pavlov's dog first responds to the meat powder (UCS) and later to sound of bell (CS). The salivation response in either case is brought forth by an identifiable stimulus. But, Thorndike's cat emits any number of responses that are not prompted by any particular stimulus (for details of Thorndike's experiment, see Section 11.2 of Chpater 11).

The essence of the theory is that the strength of response (*i.e.* frequency, rate, probability of occurrence) increases as a result of being followed by a reinforcer. Thus, for example, suppose a member of a group is non-talkative. But, he might increase his frequency of talk as a result of getting interested or approving reactions of other members of the group. Hence, getting interested and approving the reactions of others become **'instrumental'** in learning to increase the frequency of talking responses and thus, the non-talkative member may become a good orator of the group. From this example, it becomes evident that the reinforcer follows the response and not that it precedes the response (as is noticed in classical conditioning) which is instrumental in learning or strengthening of the response.

To clarify the instrumental or operant conditioning, let us look back to classical conditioning procedure. In classical conditioning procedure, presentation of two stimuli—CS and UCS—in close temporal contiguity is essentially involved. These two stimuli occur quite independently of anything that the subject has done, *viz.* dog sits or barks for cookie. In instrumental conditioning procedure, however, UCS does not occur unless the animal first makes a specific response that the experimenter defines. Such conditioning is called 'instrumental' because the organism's behaviour is instrumental in making the UCS to occur.

In instrumental or operant conditioning, the UCS that is produced by subject's efforts, is called 'reinforcer' when it becomes effective in increasing the probability of repeating the response again and again.

Instrumental conditioning is also called operant conditioning. Operant means that when a response operates on the environment, it may have the consequence that can affect the likelihood that the response will occur again and again. Thus, operants are those responses or behaviours that are voluntarily emitted by the learner to operate on the environment. Since these are voluntarily emitted responses, these are under the control of the learner. In this sense, Skinner's instrumental conditioning is concerned with the acquisition of voluntary responses of the organism which are not reflexive as we find in classical conditioning.

Skinner conducted his experiments on rats and pigeons in a specialky made boxes known as 'Skinner Box' as shown in **Figure 10.6**.

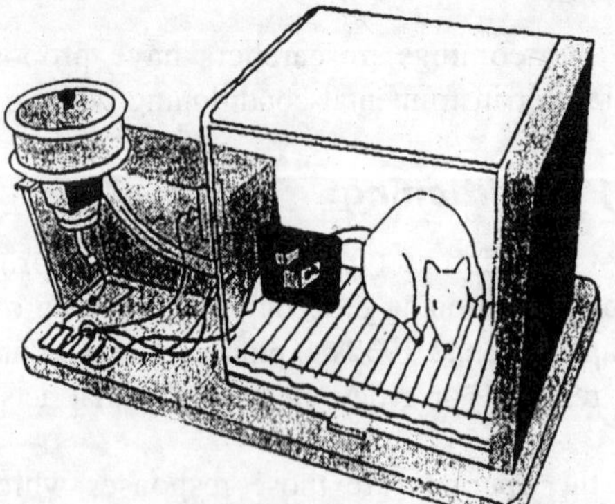

FIGURE 10.6 Skinner box.

Skinner placed a hungry rat in the box. Initially, the rat was inactive inside the box, but soon it adapted to the environment and being hungry, began to explore the box. In course of this exploratory behaviour eventually it pressed the lever and a pallet of food is released, i.e. reinforcement is contingent upon pressing the lever. After eating, the rat continued to explore the environment and after a while, it pressed the lever second time and a pallet of food was released again. In this way, the rat kept on pressing the lever. After the 4th press, the rat pressed the lever rapidly again and again and thus, the operant or instrumental act was in its full swing.

What follows from the above experiment is that in instrumental conditioning, the learner is first motivated to emit a response to achieve a goal. Being motivated, the learner makes some general kind of exploratory behaviour, *i.e.* the organism becomes active to make a response. In course of such exploratory behaviour, he makes a response that becomes an instrument or means to attain goal. This exploratory behaviour operates on the environment as it is rewarding for the organism (because such operants provide reinforcement). Therefore, the probability of occurring such operant behaviours (responses) again and again increases and thus, the behaviour is finally learned or the instrumental behaviour (operant) becomes learned response.

In our daily life situations also, we notice the examples of instrumental conditioning in abundant. Children often locate their desired sweets in absence of their mothers who had kept the sweets safely. We often become polite to get favour from others. We learn many operations of equipments such as T.V., camera, radio etc. on the basis of conditioning of this kind. In fact, we learn many shortcuts to obtain our desired goals through instrumental conditioning.

In order to better understand the operant or instrumental conditioning, let us see the major points that distinguishes it from Pavlovian classical conditioning.

Comparison between instrumental (operant) conditioning and Pavlovian classical conditioning

The classical and operant conditioning principles are similar to one another in certain respects, however, the two principles have some differences too on certain counts. The basic similarities and differences are as follows:

Similarities

(i) The classical and instrumental—both the principles use the concepts of conditioned stimulus (CS), reinforcement and conditioned response (CR). In classical conditioning, CS is considered as signal for the presence UCS because the CS and UCS, both are contiguous in time and space as the two are presented in pair form with a very little temporal interval in which CS precedes while UCS follows. In operant conditioning as in **Skinner box**, a new stimulus situation is present in which the learner has to learn to press the lever. The action leads to dropping of food pallets (**reinforcement**). The stimuli in the box and sight of the lever are CS while lever pressing act is CR which is followed by reinforcement (food pallets). Thus, in operant or instrumental procedures of conditioning also some elements of classical conditioning are present.

(ii) Another similarity in the two forms of conditioning is that both kinds of conditioning are the examples of simple learning.

(iii) In both of the conditioning procedures, same kinds of processes such as extinction, generalization, discrimination, spontaneous recovery are observed. These processes in the light of operant conditioning have been discussed in a later section of this chapter.

Differences

(i) In classical conditioning, the conditioned response (CR) is mechanically produced by pairing the CS with UCS. Hence, it is an **elicited response**. But in operant conditioning, responses are **emitted**, *i.e.* spontaneously produced.

(ii) The elicited responses are relatively fixed—reflex-like responses (which are almost automatic) such as salivation or limb flexion. But, in operant conditioning, the responses are variable responses (not fixed) such as running, walking, pushing etc. These responses are under the voluntary control of the organism and before training, these are unlearnt behaviours to the UCS. These acts operate on the environment and, therefore, termed as operant behaviour. Classical conditioning, on the other hand, are called respondent conditioning or reflex conditioning.

(iii) In Pavlovian conditioning, the CS is a specific stimulus which is presented intermittently by the experimenter for a brief period by associating it with UCS. But in operant conditoning the CS is unspecified. The whole situation inside the 'Skinner box' is CS and remains present throughout the learning period. For example, a box with a lever is the situation in which the animal is kept for learning. This whole situation is CS and remains present throughout the period of learning. Under this situation, the animal is free to emit any number of responses. Hence, CS is neither specified or fixed by the experimenter nor it is presented intermittently with temporal gap. It happens to occur.

(iv) In operant conditioning reinforcement is contingent upon what the subject does in a situation. Hence, the emitted response of the learner in operant conditioning is instrumental in securing reinforcement (for this reason it is called instrumental conditioning or learning). However, in classical learning, there is no contingency of reinforcement on any response. It is predetermined and metaphoric that CS is paired with UCS reinforcers to elicit the—**to be learnt behaviour**.

(v) In classical conditioning, reinforcement precedes the **to be learnt behaviour** whereas in operant conditioning reinforcement follows the **to be learnt behaviour**.

(vi) In classical conditioning, for eliciting conditioned behaviour (CR) elaborate mechanical and apparatus arrangements are needed. But in operant conditioning, no such elaborate arrangements are needed. It goes around us all the time. The only essential feature is that reinforcement follows the response **Green Spoon** (1955), **Hildum** and **Brown** (1956) in their studies could succeed in getting CR achieved by their subject without any elaborate experimental arrangements of apparatus and equipments. The only required arrangement was the judicious use of reinforcement that followed conditioned response (CR).

The major differences between classical and operant conditioning can be illustrated with the help of following paradigm:

Classical conditioning $S_1 - S_2 - R$
Operant conditioning $S_1 - R_1, S_2 - R_2, S_3 - R_3 ...$

From the above paradigm, it is clear that in classical conditioning, the unconditioned stimulus (S_2) follows the conditioned stimulus (S_1) which in turn reinforces and a response (R) is elicited. Hence, reinforcement precedes the conditioned response—CR. But, in operant condition-ing as soon as S_1 is presented, it arouses any number of response (R) out of which one response (correct response) produces reinforcing stimulus (S_2) and strengthens the emitted response. Hence, reinforcement is contingent upon response and not on pairing of CS with UCS. Moreover, in operant conditioning, reinforcement follows the response which becomes instrumental for the conditioning to occur.

The basic underlying principle in instrumental (operant) conditioning may also be understood with a pictorial paradigmatic representation as shown in **Figure 10.7**.

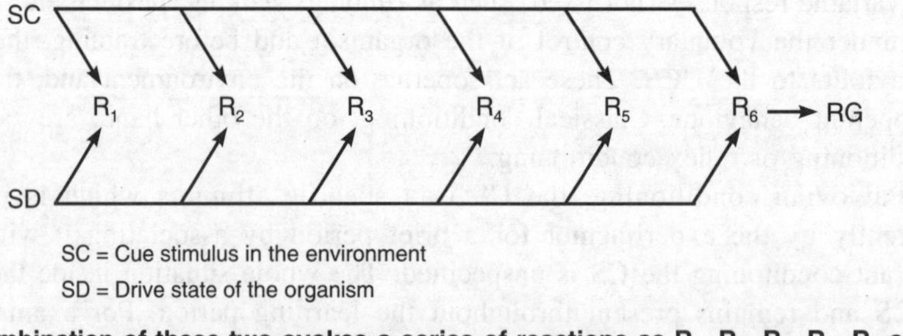

FIGURE 10.7 Combination of these two evokes a series of reactions as R_1, R_2, R_3, R_4, R_5 and finally R_6 which is correct response as it reinforces the attainment of the goal RG.

In the above paradigm, the cue stimulus (SC) make up the situation which in combination with the drive state of the organism (SD) evokes a series of responses (R_1, R_2 ... R_6). Most of these responses are errors except R_6 which is essential and followed by reinforcement (RG–goal response).

10.9.12 Shaping of Behaviour

In operant conditioning, there is freedom on the part of the learner to emit responses. This makes it possible for the experimenter to shape behaviour through appropriate use of reinforcement. For example, in Skinner's experiment, the experimenter would shape the behaviour without waiting for the animal to emit the first response. This shaping may involve the following steps.

(a) First, the hungry rat would be allowed to habituate to the environment in the operant chamber (Skinner box).
(b) Next, the rat would be given pallets of food from food magazine until it ate promptly, *i.e.* **magazine trained.**
(c) Then the shaping of lever pressing behaviour would begin as in the following manner:

Whenever, the rat would wander into the front part of the box near the bar, the experi-menter would release the food pallet by pressing a switch fitted externally. Thus, the experimenter would reinforce this behaviour. This provides a clue to the rat about the location (place or point in the box) from where food pallet is delivered and the clicking sound produced by the depression of lever provides a clue about how the food pallets are made to be released. These sensory clues are picked up (learnt) by the rat. The rate would then come closer to the desired response of pressing the lever. This may again be reinforced perhaps on putting the paws on the lever and then for actually pressing it. Thus, in shaping the behaviour, the learner is led to the final behaviour through learning a chain of simpler responses leading to the final response. To put it in other words, the learner comes to approximate the final response through a series of successive steps and, therefore, the technique is known as **successive approximation.**

The principle of shaping is general one which applies to the instrumental learning of humans as well as lower animals, Wolf, et al. (1964) has made a report of shaping the behaviour of a seriously disturbed child which may be cited as an example of shaping human behaviour by applying successive approximation technique through instrumental learning procedure.

'The boy had numerous difficulty. Over and above, the boy was practically blind after a series of cataract operations when he was only 24 years old. It was extremely important for him to wear glasses. This behaviour was shaped by successive approximation technique to the desired response of continuously wearing of the glasses'.

Most of our behaviours may be thought as having been shaped if not deliberately, at least in the process of child rearing. Many attitudes, beliefs, customs, learned goals and certain aspects of language use etc. are the results of shaping by means of reinforcement.

10.9.13 Some Important Phenomena of Instrumental (Operant) Conditioning

Extinction

Just as in classical conditioning procedure in operant conditioning procedure also it is possible to extinguish the conditioned response (CR) by withholding reinforcement. For instance, in Skinner box, if the rat no longer gets food pallets on pressing the lever, the rate of responding gradually slows down and ultimately, the rat makes no more response than before. Thus, the learned behaviour is 'extincted'. Like classical conditioning, the phenomenon of **spontaneous recovery** in operant conditioning is also seen when after an interval of time (post-extinction rest), the animal is reinforced again.

Primary and secondary reinforcement

In operant conditioning, reinforcement is considered as essential for learning to occur. According to this theory, anything that strengthens a response is reinforcer.

As in classical conditioning procedure, we may distinguish between primary and secondary reinforcement in operant conditioning procedure also. In this procedure, a primary reinforcement is caused by a stimulus or reinforcer that is effective for untrained subject. However, in classical conditioning, primary reinforcer elicits the natural reflex responses (salivation or flexion of limb), whereas in operant conditioning, primary reinforcer shapes the responses by causing the subject to do more frequently and rapidly than before.

As for secondary reinforcement, both are comparable. Operant conditioning theorists also hold that the pairing of a second stimulus with the primary reinforcer over a series of trials results in second order conditioning, *i.e.* the second reinforcer acquires the ability to call forth the response which was previously conditioned to the primary reinforcement. When this happens, it becomes a secondary reinforcement. **The second order learning in fact, is a new learning.**

In addition, secondary reinforcement is also useful in maintaining the behaviour learnt through primary reinforcement when it is not forthcoming after a response. This has been demonstrated by **Fox** and **King** (1951) and **Bugelaki** (1938).

The importance of secondary reinforcer can be evidenced from our everyday life situations. Its significance is particularly noticed in socialising children and making them adapt to social norms, value, traditions etc. In such situations, the use of second reinforcer is more prominent than primary reinforcement. Usually, the praise words, encouragement, threats of punishment etc. are more frequently used which are secondary reinforcers and these not only make the child to learn new responses but also help in maintaining whatever the primary reinforcer has led them to learn.

Schedule of reinforcement

Schedule of reinforcement refers to the arrangements of reinforcement delivery during the course of conditioning trials. There are several ways of scheduling reinforcement delivery and each way of scheduling influences the conditioning in its own ways. This results in occurrences of conditioned response (CR) with differential characteristic features. Since in instrumental (or operant) conditioning, reinforcement follows the desired response, either every instrumental response may be followed by reinforcement or it may be delivered intermittently such as after every 2nd, 3rd or 5th trial. Thus, reinforcement schedule may either be continuous or partial (intermittent).

(a) **Continuous reinforcement:** In this schedule of reinforcement delivery, each and every trial is followed (continuously) by delivery of reinforcement provided, the response is conditioned one (*i.e.* the desired or to be learnt response). For example, every press of lever by the rat in Skinner box is followed by pallets of food.

(b) **Intermittent or partial reinforcement:** In this kind of scheduling, reinforcement is not delivered for each desired response trial, *i.e.* every conditioned response is not continuously reinforced, rather the reinforcement is delivered intermittently or partially, *i.e.* some desired responses are reinforced while others are not reinforced.

Partial or intermittent reinforcement is ordinarily delivered or administered according to some plan or schedule. This schedule may be planned either as **fixed ratio of schedule** or it may be an **interval schedule**. In fixed ratio scheduling the reinforcement is delivered in terms of a fixed number of trial to be reinforced, *i.e.* every third or fourth trial of instrumental response may be fixed for the delivery of reinforcement.

In the latter plan of scheduling (interval schedule) temporal interval in place of number of trial is planned for the delivery of reinforcement such as, reinforcement may be delivered once every minute provided, the learner makes the desired response during the interval. Obviously, interval schedule is not a fixed schedule because it depends on occurrence of the conditioned response (CR) during the interval.

Experimental studies evidence the fact that partial reinforcement schedule has greater **resistance to extinction** and hence, the conditioned response (CR) persists longer than in continuous schedule of reinforcement.

Delayed reinforcement

Delayed reinforcement means reinforcing the desired response after a pause, *i.e.* the desired response is not immediately followed by a reinforcer rather it is delivered by giving some pause (delaying). It has been found that delay in the delivery of reinforcement leads to poorer level of performance. If you ask your fellowmen which reward (immediate or delayed) they would prefer after doing certain task, they would probably show their preference for immediate reward over the delayed reward.

As discussed above, the fixed ratio or the interval schedules of reinforcement may again be either fixed or varied. In varied delivery schedules, the delivery of reinforcement is not kept constant but varied randomly. Owing to random order of variations in the delivery of reinforcement in either terms (in terms of number of trials or temporal intervals), the learners are unable to discover when the reward (or reinforcement) would be coming and hence, the rate of response is relatively steady.

Thus, the partial or intermittent schedules of reinforcement may be of four kinds—fixed ratio (FR) variable ratio (VR), fixed interval (FI) and variable interval (VI).

Generalization and discrimination

(a) **Generalization:** As in classical conditioning, principle of 'generalization' has been noticed in operant conditioning also. For example, the response in operant conditioning has been learnt in a particular situation (say in Skinner box) with certain types of light and the situation is changed but contain major similarities, the similar response in this changed stimulus situation also occurs. But, the rate is relatively lower than the rate in the original stimulus situation (Olson and King, 1962).

(b) **Discrimination learning:** To demonstrate discrimination learning, particular response is reinforced by a positive stimulus (s+) and other responses are not reinforced, *i.e.* they are made to extinguish. Responses to these other stimuli are called negative stimuli (s–). Thus, discrimination learning is dependent upon positive reinforcements that follow the response.

Escape conditioning

Sometimes unpleasant stimulus is removed to make the situation pleasing. The unpleasant stimulus is a negative reinforcer. To avoid such noxious producing stimuli, the organism tends to escape, we call escape conditioning. For example, one may learn to fasten seat belt to shut off the buzzing sound in the car. This is escape conditioning. The unpleasant stimulus cannot be prevented unless one make certain alterations in the car but it can be escaped by giving an operant response.

Similarly many other phenomena like avoidance conditioning (active avoidance), conditioned emotional responses etc. are also explained in terms of operant behaviour.

Kinds of instrumental or operant conditioning

Instrumental conditioning is classified into two types: (1) reward conditioning and (2) aversive conditioning. These two types of operant conditonings have resemblance with Pavlov's pleasant and unpleasant stimuli.

(a) **Reward conditioning:** This refers to such kind of association or bond of a response with the stimulus that arouses pleasant experiences in the organism or the learner. For example, in Skinner box the rat's lever pressing act is associated with a rewarding stimulus—release of food pallets. As such it gives pleasure to the animal and hence, the probability of such operant behaviour is increased.

(b) **Aversive conditioning:** It is just opposite of reward conditioning. This refers to association of an operant response with the kind of stimulus that the organism avoids or tends to unlearn these responses because such responses are noxious or unpleasant.

In the former case, the organism tends to repeat the response frequently. Hence, there is increase in responding while in the latter case, the probability of occurrence decreases. Escape conditioning as described above is also a kind of aversive conditioning—a kind of passive avoidance.

10.9.14 Significance of Instrumental (Operant) Conditioning

Instrumental (Operant) conditioning is not merely a game played between experimenter and the animals in Skinner box. Such experiments have demonstrated certain principles which are significant for human life. Instrumental conditioning principle is of greatest value in socialising a child, *i.e.* shaping the child's behaviour into our social norms and values. This fact has been pointed out by Skinner in his famous book **'Science and Human Behaviour'** (1953). Skinner in this book has also described some of the ways in which the various agents of our social life, *viz.* the government schools which use reinforcers to shape behaviour. However, the parents or other socializing agents of the society do not make deliberate efforts to shape behaviour but the society is so arranged that reinforcements are contingent upon behaviour.

Often, instrumental or operant conditioning is also used deliberately to shape our desired behaviour. Programmed learning, personalized system of instructions, applying the reinforcement principles in business operations, and certain types of therapies for psychologically disordered personalities are the examples of such deliberate use of instrumental conditioning in shaping our desired behaviours.

Thus, instrumental conditioning has significant application value.

Critical comments

(i) The propounders of instrumental conditioning hold the view that all learning can be explained in terms of operant conditioning procedure. But, this is not true. Particularly, the logical learning or other higher learning processes cannot be explained in terms of operant conditioning.

(ii) This principle of learning also suffers from some procedural errors. For example, the behaviour of the animal in Skinner box is a narrow selection in the context of animal's potentialities which are varied. It is so because the nature of physical situation available to the rat in the box restricts the animal's freedom to act or behave.

(iii) **'Osgood'** has mentioned several pitfalls of the instrumental conditioning procedure which are of major considerations.

However, the theory is a landmark in the sense that it explains many of the phenomena of everyday life situation learnings which classical conditioning fails to explain.

10.10 CURRENT THOUGHTS REGARDING LEARNING ACTIVITIES

From what has been described till now, it is apparent that there is no point of agreement among the psychologists with regard to the processes involved in acquiring or learning a response. In this context, most of the classical behaviourist thinkers think of learning processes in terms of conditioning. Two such conditioning procedures—Pavlovian classical conditioning and Skinner's operant (instrumental) conditioning—are of much significance.

The classical conditoning procedure is mechanical in nature in which fixed conditioned stimulus is presented in pair form with UCS. This procedure explains that repeated presentation of CS with UCS in close temporal contiguity makes one to shift his UR towards the CS and thus on association, a new kind of response to a new stimulus is acquired or learned. On the contrary, in instrumental conditioning, some voluntary behaviour or response of the organism is operant in a learning situation and this operant response is subsequently reinforced and thus the operant behaviour is conditioned.

In fact, the two procedures differ only in procedure and not in their approach. However, none of the two procedures is sufficient to explain the wide variety of learnings. Conditioning seems important in respect of simple forms of learning only. But, human beings learn a wide variety of things ranging from the simplest to very high level of complex forms of learning.

In view of the insufficiency of conditioning principles to describe all kinds of learning, many other psychologists have proposed various other theories. These other principles or theories have been described in Chapter 11—some other principles (theories) and various aspects of learning. These other principles deal with both the behavioural as well as cognitive aspects of learning and discuss various kinds of learning such as verbal learning, skill learning, observational learning etc.

SUMMARY

- Learning is a relatively measurable permanent change in behaviour of the organism as a result of experience, practice or training.
- Learning can be inferred whereas performance is directly observable event which depends on learning to a great extent.
- Learning and maturation are two distinct processes. Learning is acquired whereas maturation is an innate natural process of growth. However, the two processes are closely interrelated because learning, to a great extent, depends upon certain level of maturity.
- We learn innumerable things which can conveniently be grouped as verbal learning, motor learning, sensory-motor learning, perceptual learning and conditioning.
- The phenomenon of learning represented on a graph paper is called learning curve. Learning curves display certain characteristics such as gradual progress, initial spurt, plateau and end spurt.
- Motivation is a key factor in determining learning. It elicits a response, functions as reinforcer, controls variations in behaviour.
- Knowledge of result is also a motivating factor in learning. It provides feedback to the learner.
- We can learn or acquire a response in many ways. One such way of acquisition is conditioning.
- Two types of conditioning principles are of greater significance. These are classical conditioning and operant or instrumental conditioning.
- Classical conditioning procedure has been studied by Pavlov while he was working on physiological systems involved in digestion.
- Classical conditioning procedure states that when a conditioned stimulus (CS) precedes an unconditioned stimulus (UCS) in close temporal contiguity, the unconditioned response (UCR) to UCS shifts to CS and thus, a new association is formed. This kind of association is S-S (stimulus-stimulus) association, resulting due to pairing of CS and UCS.
- Instrumental or operant conditioning principle has been advocated by B.F. Skinner. According to him, the response is operant for learning as it serves instrumental of the reinforcement to occur and as such, the response is emitted and not elicited by mechanical pairing of CS with UCS.
- The two conditioning procedures bear certain similarities and differences both. The major difference is that classical conditioning is concerned with reflexive behaviours while operant conditioning procedure is used to study voluntary behaviour.
- Through both procedures of conditioning, certain phenomenon such as reinforcement, extinction, higher order conditioning, spontaneous recovery, generalization, discrimination etc. are explained in terms of their specific procedures of conditioning.
- Classical as well as operant or instrumental conditioning do not have only experimental value but are significant to explain much of our human life acquisitions, such as emotional reactions, shaping of behaviours and modifying disordered behaviours.

CHAPTER 11

Some Other Principles (Theories) and Aspects of Learning

11.1 INTRODUCTION

In Chapter 10, learning has been described as a change or modification of behaviour that is an outcome of some kind of experience, practice or training and that such resultant changes are relatively of permanent or enduring nature. Thus, learning is a key process of human behaviour. In everyday life situations, we acquire a wide varieties of things such as the process of communication, learning of social traditions and customs, interacting with others, formation of attitudes, development of beliefs, recognizing the goals, acquisition of traits of personality, learning to perceive wide varieties of environmental stimuli etc. In all these abilities, learning plays a central role.

How do we learn has always been a fundamental question before the thinkers of all ages and areas. So is the case with psychologists. In Chapter 10, we discussed two fundamental principles of conditioning that are involved in learning some simple forms of learning by associating our responses to the stimulus situations—a kind of associative learning. But, in view of wider range of learning activities, these principles have limited applicability. We do not only learn simply to associate specific response with specific stimulus but also learn a varieties of complex motor as well as cognitive skills. Most of our learnings are incidental while others intentional. We also learn verbal skills of using symbols (language). Besides, development of habits, operational skills, using the cognitive structures etc. are all learnt. Hence, in order to understand a wide variety of learnings that takes place, it is important for the students to get acquainted with many other principles of learning as well as the various aspects related to behaviour modification (learning).

The main thrust of this chapter is to familiarize the students with some of these other principles and aspects of learning.

11.2 SOME MAJOR PRINCIPLES OF LEARNING

Several psychologists have conducted extensive experimental research on learning and proposed various principles. Some of such major principles are described hereunder:

11.2.1 Thorndike's Connectionism

Connectionism is also a form of associative learning. This refers to connection or bond between stimulus and correct response which is formed by **trial and error**, *i.e.* **try out** method. This theory is variously called as **connectionism** or **trial and error theory** or **stimulus-response (S-R) theory**. This theory was propounded by **E.L. Thorndike** in the year 1898 and again in 1913 on the basis of his experimental works to study the behaviour of cats.

According to **Thorndike**, learning behaviour arises when the organism faces a new and difficult situation—a problem. In order to solve the problem or problematic situation, the organism (the learner) tries all sorts of movements one by one in a random manner (frisker movements). Most of these are erroneous or incorrect movements. In course of trying out all sorts of possible movements, the correct movement is eventually made, *i.e.* the activity required to solve the given problem is accidentally performed—a sort of **lucky mistake** that ultimately changes the future behaviour as this 'luckily mistaken' behaviour proves correct one which is learnt by practice and the erroneously performed behaviours are gradually unlearnt or extinguished. In this way, a connection between learning situation (stimulus—'S') and the correct response—(R) is made. Thus, the correct response gradually gets bonded with the learning situation which is termed as **S-R bond**.

Experimental evidence

Thorndike's 'trial and error' or 'connectionism' is based on several experiments performed by him. Two of such experiments mentioned below are most popular.

Puzzle box experiment: Thorndike housed a hungry cat in a puzzle box (cage) and presented fried fish in a tray outside the cage which the cat could view from inside the cage. The cage was made of vertical slate (a thin strip of wood) through which the fried fish could be viewed and also smelt. Inside the box, a loop of string hanged which if pulled, could open the door and let the hungry cat through to eat the fish (reward). When the cat was first placed inside the cage and since it was hungry, it struggled energetically to get out of the box. It did many different things such as, trying to squeeze between the slate, scratching at the box, clawing at the door etc. but all these were without any effect. To quote Thorndike:

> **At first the cat is ineffective in attempts to escape, the cat tries to squeeze through any opening, it claws and bites, sits at the bars, it thrusts its paws out through any opening and claws at everything it reaches for eight to ten minutes it will claw, bite and squeeze incessantly.**
>
> —THORNDIKE*, 1898

But then, in course of these random activities, eventually the cat pulls the string, the door

* Thorndike (1898), Animal Intelligence: An experimental study of the associative process in animals, *Psycholo. Monographs*, 2 (Whole No. 8).

comes to open, it goes through and eats the fish (reward) (see **Figure 11.1**). This eventual pulling of string is the **'lucky mistake'** because it proves successful and changes future behaviour of the cat. This procedure was repeated for several days. Each day, much of the same thing happened, although the lucky mistake response gradually began to occur a bit sooner. Gradually, as the number of trials (days) increased, the ineffective modes of responses were extinguished and the correct response used to occur more rapidly. To quote Thorndike again:

> **Gradually all other non-successful impulses will be stamped out and the particular impulse leading to successful act will be stamped in by the resultant pleasure, until after many trials the cat will when put in a box, immediately claw button or loop in a definite way.***

FIGURE 11.1 Problem box.

Maze experiment: Thorndike performed another experiment on rats using maze as a problem. The rat was deprived of food for 24 hours and was brought to entry of the maze. Food was available in the goal box of the maze which could be obtained by going through the maze pathways from entry door to the goal box. It could be reached expeditiously by avoiding the blind alleys. When the rat enters the door, being hungry, it sensed the smell of the food and began its exploratory behaviour. In the beginning, the rat explored the maze after putting in some efforts. It tried to reach the goal by following almost each and every blind paths. It entered and rentered. In course of these exploratory activities, eventually, the rat entered the correct path leading directly to the goal. When the food is reached, the trial ends. The procedure was repeated regularly for several days until the maze is run from entrance to the goal box without error, *i.e.* without entering into the blind alleys. The criterion of learning in this experiment was three consecutive errorless trial, *i.e.* the habit to follow only the correct path was thought to be the part of index of learning when rat was able to make errorless run into the maze continuously for three consecutive days.

From the two experiments of Thorndike, one may assume that at the outset of learning, each response has some initial probability of occurrence. However, the probability is different for different responses. For example, in cage problem, the squeezing response of the cat has higher probability than the correct response of the cat pulling the string. Thus, there is initial hierachy of response probabilities and the effect of training trials is to increase selectively the probability of one of the responses in the repertory. The correct response here is one which brings reward and by way of satisfying the drive of the organism which is acquired through **trial and error** and strengthened by repeated practice.

* Thorndike, E.L., 1898, *ibid.*

The theory makes clear some fundamental characteristics of learning process which are as follows:

(i) Learning is a gradual process
(ii) Practice is important for holding the connection strongly.
(iii) Motivation (drive state) is an important condition for learning behaviour to occur.
(iv) Success of a response is rewarding and therefore such responses are learnt while those which are unsuccessful are unlearnt.
(v) Learning involves the process of trial and error.

Laws of learning

Basing on the material facts obtained in course of series of studies, Thorndike formulated three basic 'laws' that govern the process of learning. These laws are as follows:

(i) **Law of effect:** This is the most important law of learning. According to this law, the strengthening or weakening of S-R connections depend upon the effect that a response produces on the organism (learner). This law states that a response which has satisfying effect, such as satisfaction of a drive, escape from punishment, or relief from fear will be learned while the response which has an unpleasent effect, such as frustration of a motive, punishment or fear, will not be learned. This law is based on formal philosophical principle of 'hedonism' (pleasure principle). The law states that satisfying effect of a response strengthens the connection between the response and the stimulus that arouses the responses. On the other hand, the annoying effect of a response weakens the connection. In other words, the satisfying activities are **stamped in** and the annoying ones are **stamped out**. In the case of puzzle box problem, the connection between the stimulus—**the string** and the response of pulling the string was strengthened because it made the cat through to the fish outside the cage. The connections between other movements that the cat made in response to the other stimuli within the cage, were gradually weakened and eliminated as they produced annoying effect.

(ii) **Law of exercise:** The law of exercise is another important law of learning. According to this law, more often repeated responses are assumed to be established. In this sense, the law is often referred to as 'Law of frequency'. Accordingly, less repeated responses die out. Thus, this law consists of two sublaws—**the law of use** and the **law of disuse**. The law of effect which has just been described, explains the repetition of correct response and the law of use explains the establishment of correct response. Similarly, the law of effect also explains why the incorrect responses are not repeated while the law of disuse explains why incorrect responses are eliminated.

The law of exercise is a well established principle. This is the reason that the part of the body which is more exercised become stronger than less exercised part of the body. Thus, the responses that are most frequently repeated (kept in use) are likely to be established in future than the less frequently repeated (disuse) responses.

(iii) **Law of readiness:** Sometimes a reference is made to a third law of learning called **law of readiness**. This law is a corollary of the 'law of effect'. It refers to the state of the organism which makes him ready to respond. Under the law of readiness, the organism experiences satisfaction in responding to the situation. But, when he is not ready or set to respond, it causes annoyance. Thus, this law is not an independent law of learning rather just a corollary of law of effect. Thus law is important in inducing a tendency to learn and hence, applies to every intent learning situation.

Critical comments

Thorndike's theory of connectionism (S-R association) is considered as a landmark theory of learning for two basic reasons—firstly, Thorndike in fact, laid the foundation stone for founding of difficult theories of learning. Secondly, his works on cats and rats inspired many researchers to work extensively on how and what one learns and how learned behaviours are strengthened.

Thorndike's theory is based on well established fact of 'Practice'. Practice makes our learned responses perfect, *i.e.* practice establishes S-R connections perfectly. Though, this notion of Thorndike has met with severe criticism due to exaggerated emphasis on it, however, as we find in most learning occasions, more particularly in motor learning, considerable amount of practice is indispensable. Moreover, Thorndike is supposed to be the first psychologist to recognize the significance of motivation in learning which led to the formulation of **law of effect**. **Hill** (1977)* has rightly stated "he (Thorndike) incorporated within his objective psychology of learning, **the law of effect and thus, became the first real reinforcement theorist**.

However, the theory suffers from certain pertinent shortcomings. The major shortcomings are as follows:

(i) Gestalt psychologists have raised severe critical comments describing the theory far from reality. According to the Gestaltists, the emphasis on practice in the theory is undue because, practice alone is not important. Moreover, the theory is analytical in nature whereas what we learn is the pattern of the whole learning situation for which **insight** and not the **practice** is important.

(ii) Behaviourists have also criticized Thorndike's concept of **law of effect**. According to them, the concepts of **satisfaction** and **annoyance** are subjective. Therefore, to explain learning behaviour on the basis of subjective aspects would be misleading.

(iii) According to this theory, the repetition of a response is dependent upon the effect that it produces. Satisfying responses are repeated while annoying ones are not repeated. Hence, learning of a response is effected backwardly. This analogy is not understandable to many learning theorists as how the consequence of the response can influence the response which occurs first and its consequence follows.

(iv) The theory is mechanistic. It assumes that satisfying responses get fixated automatically while the annoying responses drop out. Thus, it does not recognize the importance of insight or intelligence at all. Thorndike has himself accepted that **he failed to notice even a single activity being aroused on any rationale**. He believes, the effect of reward and punishment are mechanistic and autonomic. However, **Knafer** (1968) found that for higher level conditioning, concentrations and awareness is a must. Hence, 'insight' instead of mechanical repetition is more important.

Thus, it is clear that Thorndike's theory suffers from several criticisms. However, the theory is important in the sense that building upon Thorndike's work, further theories of learning were propounded and thus, it paved the way for progressive research in the area of learning.

---

* Hill, W.F. (1977), *Learning: A Survey of Psychological Interpretations*, 3rd ed., San Francisco Chandler.

11.3 INSIGHT THEORY

Kohler and Koffka, pregnant with the principle of 'Gestalt' severely criticized analytical approach of behaviourists on learning and advocated **Insight theory** of learning based on cognitive principles. This theory has been built up on the facts gathered in course of works done on **perceptual learning**, a phenomenon that involves the formation of S-S (stimulus-stimulus) association instead of S-R association.

The theory holds that learning is neither a gradual process nor does it involve any observable trial and error procedure to come to solution of a problem. Solutions come suddenly. Most often there would be no apparent progress, followed by sudden visualization of the solution. Visualization of this sudden solution is called **insight**.

Gestaltists argue that the phenomena such as learning must be treated as a **whole**. In learning, whole is greater than sum of its parts. Learning comes in **sudden flashes** (or **insight**) only when the learner puts the parts together in such a way that the **complete whole** becomes an organized pattern and that exceeds the mere sum or total of those parts (Wittings and Williams-III, 1984).

Gestaltists suggested this theory on the basis of some experiments done on chimpanzees. One such experiment is described hereinbelow:

A chimpanzee, named 'Sultan' was kept isolated in a cage, hence, it was prevented from being acquainted with other animals. After a considerable deprivation of food, a few bananas were kept outside the cage at a distance which was beyond the reach of Sultan. Sultan was given two sticks of different lengths. The sticks were hollow but firm bamboo rods. The bananas were kept at such a distance that it could not even be reached with the help of either of the sticks independently. The chimpanzee took much pains to try to reach the bananas with one or the other stick, even through pushing the shoulders from the bars. But, all efforts proved futile. He then stopped making efforts and began to play with the two sticks in despair. Eventually, the narrow end of one stick got fitted into the broad hollow end of the other stick. Thus, when the two sticks joined together, it became relatively a longer stick. The chimpanzee gazed at this change in the situation and felt delighted (see **Figure 11.2**). This sort of delight is usually expressed in human beings as **Aha Experience**! This insight which the **chimp** (Sultan) invented from perceiving the two sticks, the objects and the distance as one related unit forming one united pattern leading to the solution of the problem. Sultan immediately pulled the banana and thus, the problem was solved. Kohler (1925) explains it as follows:

> **Solving the problem required the chimp to put several pieces together into a meaningful whole. The solution in this experiment resulted from insight, a sudden realization following a period of mental wrestling with a problem without reward*.**

FIGURE 11.2 Two-stick problem to show insight learning by chimpanzee.

* Kohler, W. (1925), *The Mentality of Apes*, N.Y. Harcourt, Bruce.

11.3.1 Another Experiment

In another experiment, Kohler hanged a basket of fruits with the ceiling in a room. The basket was hanged at a height so that Sultan could not reach the fruit even by jumping. There were three tool boxes kept in the room hither and thither. The hungry Sultan was brought into the room. At the beginning, the chimp (Sultan) attempted to reach the basket by jumping from the floor—**a routine response**, but failed. Then the chimp looked the situation inside the room. He saw the boxes, went near one box and tried to catch the basket by standing on the box but failed again. Then he brought another box and finally the third box, piled each box on one another and then the chimp was able to reach the basket. In future, it was observed that the chimp used the three boxes without wasting time to reach the target. Here again the three boxes piled one another and the suspended basket of fruits became interrelated elements of perception of the whole (see **Figure 11.3**).

FIGURE 11.3 A fruit basket hanging with the roof; and a monkey is trying to reach it by standing on the boxes.

The above two experiments obviously show how insight or perception of relations (cognitive awareness or map) between the different elements of a situation and goal get organized together forming a pattern that enables the organism to achieve the goal, *i.e.* solving the problem.

Insight is defined **as sudden perception of relationships between the elements of a situation and goal which suddenly comes and goes on without any break till one reaches the goal.**

Insightful learning is characterized as follows:

(i) Insight depends upon arrangement of the problem situation. Insight comes easily provided the essentials for solutions are so arranged that their relationship can be perceived, *viz.* the required tools are present, and that these can easily be putt together to form a whole pattern etc.

(ii) Once solution occurs with insight, it can be promptly repeated. For trial and error, gradual solution is the rule while for insightful learning, sudden solution is the rule and, therefore, on next similar occasion, previous mode of solution is repeated without any trial and error.

(iii) A solution achieved with insight can be applied in a new situation also. What is learnt through insight is not an S-R sequence rather a cognitive relationship between **means and end**.

An effective learner is rich in resources and able to adapt himself to new situation. He is capable enough to use what he knows in new situation. He should be successful to discover the situations he has never faced before. Emphasis on insightful learning in place of mechanical rote learning encourages problem solving behaviour. Hence, problem solving behaviour can be better explained in terms of insight rather than trial and error or conditioning.

Critical comments

Insight has a very important place in learning—particularly higher level learning among developed organisms. This fact cannot be denied. It rather plays a key role in solving complex problem of higher order with which human beings mostly confront. However, this theory is not a fully perfect theory of learning. It suffers from following shortcomings:

(i) One of the salient characteristics of insight is **suddenness**. Insight comes dramatically. But, all kinds of learnings are not sudden. Even insight according to 'Dunker' is gradual and graduated.

(ii) Insight theory does not agree with trial and error notion. But, if we minutely consider the experiments of Kohler, we would find that Sultan also tried different movements and then found solution eventually. Hence, the elements of trial and error is found in insight experiments also.

(iii) The learning situation selected by Kohler was biased. The situation cannot be regarded as representative of all kinds of learning situations. Particularly, the acquisition of motor skill is possible by mechanical trial and error, these skills cannot be acquired dramatically.

11.4 C.L. HULL'S REINFORCEMENT THEORY

C.L. Hull occupies a very significant position among 'neo-behaviourist' psychologists. It was Hull who could turn Darwinian-Thorndikian approach into a refined systematic theory of learning.

Hull was influenced by both—the Watsonian S-R (stimulus-response) and Woodworth's S-O-R (stimulus-organism-response) formulae of behaviour events. The S-O-R formula of behaviour is much like a PC computer, where 'S' stands for the **stimulus input** which the 'O', *i.e.* organism receives and processes the information to determine the kind of response (R), *i.e.* output. Likewise, in a PC computer, the information is fed by operating the keyboard, the central process unit (CPU) of the computer system processes the fed information and the output is displayed on the visual disc screen of the computer.

Hull having understood the significance of S-O-R formulae, incorporated the same to explain learnt behaviour. Hull calls the organism related variables as the **intervening variables** which are internal states of the organism such as the 'drivestate' that can be inferred. To explain learning phenomenon alongs S-O-R paradigm, Hull envisaged **hypothetico-deductive** method which in fact, has three steps. At the first step, a system of definition or concept is set in order. At the second step, some postulates (tentative hypothetical statements about the behaviour) are formulated on the basis of definitions or concepts in the first step. At the final third step, several theorems or corrolaries are deduced. Thus, on the basis of the entire set of definitions, postulates and corollaries or theorems, a formal systematic and integrated scientific theory emerged which is known as **Mathematico-deductive theory** or **model of learning**. This model is based on vast number of empirical data and use of mathematical constructs which has the characteristic of being tested and verified. Hence, a scientific model of learning could be advanced.

Hull's mathematical model is also known by some other names. One such name is 'neobehaviouristic theory' because it follows the footstep of behaviourism in a new form. It is also known as 'association theory' because he believes that during learning the twin elements S and R (stimulus and response) combine together to form a 'new association'. 'S' or the stimulus is the physical 'energy' (light, sound and so forth) while 'R' (response) is the 'effector mechanism' (muscular movement or glandular secretions and the like) and learning is the connection or association of these two events in such a way that produce the effect of change or modification of response that can better adapt to the environmental stimulation.

Sometimes, this theory is also called as Hull-Spencer Theory (Logan, 1959), because Hull was the founder of this theory while 'Spencer' (younger colleague of Hull) had refined the theory considerably and gave more rigid experimental tests to the outline proposed by Hull.

Hull's theory is **probabilistic** in nature because, it is possible for an experimenter to assign a probability of a response to occur on the basis of number of reinforced trials. This is what we intend to predict in a model of learning. In **Hull-Spencer theory**, the probability of a response is the product of two general factors:

(i) drive motivation and other features of learning situation
(ii) habit strength, *i.e.* the degree of association built up or extinguished in previous trial. **Hull-Spencer's** notion of learning is expressed in a simple equation as mentioned below:

$$F \text{ (tendency/respond)} = D \text{ (drive)} \times H \text{ (habitt strength)} - (F = D \times H)$$

This equation means that in a particular learning or extinction situation, the probability of tendency to respond is the product of motivational level and strength of habit. For measuring motivational or drive state level, hours of deprivation is used as parameter. Hence, a rat that has learned a reinforced or rewarded response, will be more likely to perform the response if it is hungry for 22 hours compared to 3 hours. In order to predict habit strength, the number of previously experienced reinforced trials is an important factor. Assuming this, a law of habit formation was framed which is expressed as follows:

$$H = 1 - 10^{0.03}N^{*}$$

In this equation, N is the number of reinforced trials and .03 is empirically determined constant. This expression was determined by fitting a curve to some data obtained by **Williams** (1938) and **Perin** (1942). In these experiments, hungry rats were placed in a bar pressing situation. Different rats were given varying number of reinforcement trials ranging from very few trials 5 to as many as 95. Later on, rats were placed in a box and subjected to extinction procedure and number of responses made during extinction trials were recorded. In this phase of experiment, some of the rats were kept hungry for 3 hours while others were for 22 hours. Applying statistical procedures, estimate value was made and the parameter of the equation was applied. The value of D (drive level) at 22 hours turned out to be 66 and for 3 hours, 25. The rate of learning was estimated to be 0.02.[†]

Thus, the mathematical models are used to predict the outcomes of experiments. By tesing the models in this way and modifying the same as needed, increased sophisticated models are developed to cover all sorts of learning situations.

11.4.1 Some Definitions of Key Concepts in Hull's System

Some key concepts used by Hull are the 'Habit strength' ($_SH_R$), 'Reaction potential' ($_SE_R$) and 'Reinforcement'. These key concepts are explained hereinbelow:

---

* Deese and Hulse, *The Psychology of Learning*, 3rd ed., McGraw Hills, Koga Kasha, 1959, p. 83.
† Analysis of data by Hull, 1951, *Essentials of Behaviour*.

Habit strengh ($_SH_R$)

Hull assumes that the elements that combine during learning to form new association are the stimuli (S) and response (R). A stimulus is the **physical energy** (light, sound and so forth). A response is an **effector mechanism** (muscular movements, glandular secretions and the like). Hull in his postulate says, 'the tendency for a particular stimulus to evoke a particular response increases in strength as a function of number of times the stimulus and response occurres together and so long as each pairing of S and R is reinforced. Hence, $_SH_R$ is related to the number of reinforced trials as expressed in mathematical terms—$_SH_R = 1 - 10^{0.03}N$. Thus, according to Hull, the things that combine to form new learning and the conditions under which this combination takes place, determine the strength of habit ($_SH_R$). Here, the things that combine are the elements of association (S and R) while the conditions of learning are the number of reinforced trials and drive levels.

Reaction potential ($_SE_R$)

This is the output variable in Hull's system which is directly correlated with response strength measures such as reaction latency or amplitude of response. The magnitude of RP (reaction potential) is determined by a number of variables, but chief among these is habit strength and drive level (D), more particularly the primary drives like hunger and thirst. These are intervening variables. These are tied to the length of deprivation time. The greater the time of deprivation, greater is the strength of D. Hull assumes that RP is related to habit strength ($_SH_R$) and to drive according to multiplicative function—$_SE_R = {_SH_R} \times D$. This means to say that habits are displayed in overt behaviour with measurable response strength when they are activated by drives and the relationship between $_SH_R$ and D is assumed to be multiplicative.

The concept of $_SE_R$, as stated above, *i.e.* $_SH_R \times D$ is in simple form only so as to understand the concept in a simple way. In its complete form, it is expressed as

$$_SE_R = {_SH_R} \times D \times V \times K$$

where

$_SH_R$ = habit strength
D = drive
V = stimulus intensity, *i.e.* valency and
K = incentive-motivation.

All these are intervening variables tied with mathematical functions, respectively to the drive state, intensity of the stimulus that evokes a reaction and to the amount of reinforcement that is used. In Hull's system, V and K are like D in that they are performance variables which directly influence reaction potential ($_SE_R$). We also note from the equation that these variables multiply with $_SH_R$ to produce the response latency or response amplitude that the experimenter measures when a stimulus evokes a response on a particular occasion.

Reinforcement

According to Hull, reinforcement is necessary for learning or to say for habit strength to develop. Though, Spencer does not consider it necessary. However, Hull assumes that $_SH_R$ depends upon the number of reinforced trials and also assumes that reinforcers gain their effectiveness by reducing the level of existing drive. Thus his theory sometimes is also called as **drive reduction theory**.

Hull holds that $_SH_R$ is assumed to increase in magnitude gradually and continuously as a function of reinforced practice and lead to a relatively permanent change in behaviour. Hence, Hull's theory is more popularly called **'Reinforcement theory'**.

Inhibitory potential (I)

Hull in one of his postulates, has also dealt with inhibition or inhibitory potential. He has divided inhibitions in two kinds—**reactive inhibition** (I_R) and **conditioned inhibition** ($_SI_R$) Reactive inhibition refers to the tendency of not repeating the immediately preceding response. This is analogous to fatigue which often disappears after a brief period of rest. However, if the rest is not enough, I_R continues to built up from response to response. This is indicative of negtive motivational state. Conditioned inhibition ($_SI_R$) is a kind of habit of not responding produced by negative inhibition (I_R). Hence, it is a sort of failure to respond.

Since both kinds of inhibitions tend to cancel the effects of reaction potential ($_SE_R$) or excitatory potential, they are subtracted from $_SE_R$ to arrive at net value of $_SE_R$.

Hull has also used some other constructs such as oscillation principle, behavioural threshold, indexing functions, incompatible responses etc. Within the limited scope of this book, it is not possible to go into the details of all the constructs and postulates. Interested readers are, however, suggested to consult 'Theories of Learning' by Hilgard and Bowler (1981). However, a very brief account of postulates are being presented hereunder that gives an overall view of the basic constructs and postulates in Hull's principle of learning (see **Table 11.1**).

TABLE 11.1 Numerical values in postulates

Postulate numbers	*Contents*
Postulate nos. 1 and 2	Deals with neural activities in the brain following a sensory input.
Postulate no. 3	Deals with the role of reinforcement in learning.
Postulate no. 4	Deals with habit formation ($_SH_R$), *i.e.* tendency for a stimulus trace to produce an associated response that depends upon several factors: drive, delay in reinforcement, time gap between S and R.
Postulate no. 5	Deals with primary drive.
Postulate nos. 6 and 7	Deals with stimulus intensity (V) and incentive motivation (K) respectively.
Postulate no. 8	Deals with reaction potential ($_SE_R$), *i.e.* $_SE_R = {_SH_R} \times D \times K \times V$
Postulate no. 9	Deals with two kinds of inhibitions I_R and $_SI_R$, i.e. reactive inhibitions and conditioned inhibitions.
Postulate no. 10	Deals with stimulus generalization.
Postulate no. 11	Deals with stimulus interaction.
Postulate no. 12	Deals with behavioural oscillations ($_SL_R$).
Postulate no. 13	Deals with reaction potential as it is related to reaction threshold.
Postulate no. 14	Deals again with reaction potential in relation to reaction latency.
Postulate no. 15	Deals yet with reaction potential in relation to reaction amplitude.
Postulate no. 16	Deals with reaction potential in relation to total response to extinction.
Postulate no. 17	Deals with the problem of individual differences.

Note: Major symbols used in Hull's Model

$_SH_R$	:	Habit strength	$_SE_R$	:	Reaction potential
I	:	Inhibitions	D	:	Drive
I_R	:	Reactive inhibitions	V	:	Stimulus intensity (valency)
$_SI_R$	:	Conditioned inhibitions	K	:	Incentive motivation

The final, *i.e.* seventeenth postulate states that the constant numerical values appearing in different equations in various postulates and corollaries tend to vary from individual to individual and also from one physiological state to another in the same individual at different times. This accounts for individual differences and situational differences in learning abilities.

To sum up, Hull's system or theory comprises a series of postulates and corollaries that centre around drive, reinforcement and response strength. For Hull, reinforcement is significant because it reduces drive. Repetition of stimulus response sequence produces inhibition. The core theme of Hull's theory is that learning increases gradually with increase in reinforced trials. For this reason, his theory is also known as **increment theory of learning**.

Critical comments

(i) Hull has severely been criticised for introducing mathematics to explain the key points and concepts of his theory. This has made the explanation complex enough and obscure to comprehend. It seems, he was obsessed with mathematics, otherwise his theory could have been nicely explained.

(ii) Some critics have charged Hull with dualism of thought. On the one hand, he claims himself as behaviourist while, on the other, he has explained his theory with the help of intervening variables of the organism. His dependence upon inferred organismic state and wider use of intervening variables are subjective and hence, not amenable to objective demonstration.

(iii) Though Hull claims that his system is highly logical, it suffers from many logical flaws. Kock (1959) observes several difficulties owing to which, he finds himself at a loss to arrive at a particular conclusion in a logical way.

(iv) According to Osgood, Hull's theory suffers from backward effect. Hull assumues that reinforcement reduces drive level and therefore one learns the reinforced trials. But, the truth is otherwise. The organism emits a response which subsequently is reinforced. Then how can reinforcement work backward in time?

(v) Hull has laid emphasis on response learning only and ignored place learning. For this reason, Woodworth considers Hull's theory only partially correct.

11.4.2 Evaluation of Hull's System

Despite the criticisms as stated above, Hull occupies a very significant position among the learning theorists for some salient features of his system which are distinct and unique in itself. The distinct characteristics are as follows:

(i) The attribute of quantification is one such characteristic feature that distinguishes his theory from all other theories of learning. The concepts of intervening variables such as response latency, response probability, response intensity, reactive inhibitions, conditioned inhibitions etc. are all relevant as well as quantitatively measurable.

(ii) From the scientific point of view, the testability and verifiability of this theory are two most distinct features that meet the scientific criteria. **Osgood** opines—**Hull's theory is most explicitly worked-out position and hence, the most testable**.

(iii) In addition, Hull's theory contains heuristic value and the attributes of objectivity. To quote Osgood, **much of the experimental literature in the field during the recent years has been aimed either in criticism or in support of some aspects of Hull's**

theory. This remark amply proves that Hull's constructs have heuristic value and hence, is an important contribution to the area of learning.

In essence, though the theory suffers from certain limitations and criticisms, the scientific orientations, mathematical interpretations and heuristic values that it contains, are some important features of this theory and hence, its contributions cannot be ignored. These, along with some other salient features of Hull's system have in fact, influenced the contemporary psychology of learning in many ways. This explicitly speaks of the strength and potentiality of Hull's system in the area of learning.

11.5 TOLMAN'S COGNITIVE THEORY

E.C. Tolman is considered as a later behaviourist psychologist. However, he has also included in his system the subjective intervening variables. Hence, before we go into the details of his theory of learning, let us first examine his position as a behaviourist. Who belongs to what school of thought is determined by his beliefs and expressions about the different aspects of a discipline in question. **Spence** (1951) has classified all learning theories into two broader categories—**S-R theories** and **S-S theories** (stimulus-response association theory and stimulus-stimulus association theory respectively). S-S theory is also called sign theory. In the former category are included the theories of Thorndike, Skinner, Hull, Miller, Dolard and Spence. The latter category includes the theories of Pavlov, Kohler and Koffka, Tolman, Adams and Zener. S-R theories strictly adhere to objectively observable behaviouristic approach and explain learning phenomenon in terms of association between stimulus and response (S-R bond). The S-S theorists on the other hand, have explained learning by associating it with perception which is mentalistic.

Tolman has tried to take and combine the best of both the approaches. His theoretical formulations closely resemble S-R views but at the same time he has tried to explain it by incorporating the non-observable set of intervening variables such as 'demand', 'appetite', 'differentiation', 'motor skill', 'hypotheses' and 'biases'. However, his explanation bears the behaviouristic bend of mind and he considers behaviour in terms of **means-end-relationship**.

In other words, for him behaviour is 'goal-directed', *i.e.* 'purposive'. For this reason, he is characterized as 'purposive behaviourist' and his system is called 'purposive behaviourism'.

This bend of **Tolman's** mind is explicitly expressed in his theory of learning which is variously known as **sign-Gestalt** or **sign-significate** or **cognitive** or **expectancy theory**.

Tolman's purposive theory of learning lays emphasis on development of **cognition** rather than **S-R bonds**. His theory is also known as 'sign-Gestalt' which means that the organism usually learns the succession of stimuli or sign in the environment that 'leads to' or 'signifies' the goal or end. Gradually, a relationship between stimuli or cues in the environment and one's own expectations is established. To cite an example, in maze learning a rat has several choice points (many stimuli). At each choice point, certain expectancy is built up. If the rat takes an appropriate and correct choice, expectancy is strengthened. In this way, by strengthening or confirming choices it develops a 'cognitive map' of the whole maze situation. The development of cognition owes mainly to the 'processing of input' received by the senses about the stimuli present in the environment of learning situation. Therefore, in essence, learning is nothing but developing cognition or a 'mental picture' of the whole learning situation—a kind of perceptual learning. 'Cognition' involves intellectual grasping of meaning or significance of a given event or stimulus situation. In this sense, cognitive learning is a sort of 'place learning' with the help of 'sign or significate' that leads to the goal.

Tolman (1932) elaborating his theory states that while learning, we acquire a large body of information from the environment (sensory input) which changes our perception of the situation depending upon the way, an individual views the situation when he is exposed to it. New information is stored and old experiences come to associate. This helps in developing an integrated cognitive map of the situation and determines—'what leads to what' and thus the 'means-end relationship' develops.

Tolman further holds that this kind of development takes place even without any explicit manipulation of reinforcement. Development of cognitive map or means to end relationship is in fact, implicit which is caused by sensory information processing of stimuli in the environment. Past experience, however, has a significant role to play. This information processing and past experience enable the rat to locate food along with the shortest or the correct path that leads to the goal.

Thus, in essence, the cognitive learning theory proposes that the learner forms a cognitive structure in mind, it preserves and organize information about the various aspects of learning situation.

Tolman later on in the year 1949 added some new learning or connections in his earlier version of the theory. These are six in number and explained them on the lines formally stated by Freud and Lewin.

These new connections or associations are as follows:

(i) **Cathexis:** This refers to the attachment of specific types of goal object (both attractive and disturbing) to basic drive. This concept has been used by Freud and is equivalent to **Lewin's** conception of **valency**. Here 'Tolman' means that whenever a particular goal object satisfies a particular drive, a cathexis of that particular drive on that particular goal object is formed or associated (learnt). For this reason, perhaps a child in his early stage learns a relationship (cathexis) between his hunger and biscuit.

(ii) **Equivalence beliefs:** In a particular situation of reward and punishment, the situation itself is believed as equivalent to that reward and punishment. Here, the situation acquires some of the properties of goal object (reward and punishment). This obviously refers to a kind of secondary reinforcement, *viz.* a student receiving gold medal for his excellence at the university examination may consider it equivalent to special honour and prestige for his merit.

(iii) **Field expectancies:** 'Field expectancies' are what Tolman earlier called **sign-Gestalt expectancies**. When the animals learn route from one place to another, or the kind of tool used for a particular purpose, a cognitive map of the field expectancy is said to be formed.

(iv) **Field cognition mode:** This refers to a higher order needs of expectancies and means an inclination to learn certain things more readily than the others. Such inclinations are partly innate and partly learnt. Our ability to use language in a variety of situations is perhaps one of the examples of **field cognition mode**. However, what Tolman means by this is not much clear.

(v) **Drive discrimination:** This refers to our ability to discriminate among various types of drives. This ability is found in animals as well as men. However, this is not a very important kind of learning. This concept seems to have been derived from **Hull** (1933) and **Leeper** (1936).

(vi) **Motor patterns:** Following **Guthrian** model, **Tolman** here refers to the development of instrumental skill sequences and recognizes this as one of the important aspects of learning. As he holds, such sensory-motor associations are learned in a single trial on the basis of sheer **contiguity**.

11.5.1 Some Experimental Evidences (or Support)

Tolman's theory has been important in the sense that it could provocate and generate several researches done either by him or some of the fellowmen. Three kinds of experimental works are often cited in support of Tolman's earlier version of 1932. These, however, do not contradict the revised version of his theory. Two of these experiments are described here. One more experiment is concerned with 'latent learning' which will be described separately in Section 11.9 of this chapter.

Reward expectancy experiment

In Tolman's system, expectancy is one of the important intervening variables. As he holds, in a learning situation, building up of expectations and their confirmation or strengthening functions are 'basic' for 'cognitive map' to develop. Though, he does not give any emphasis on reinforcement for the development of cognition, however, he does recognize the significance of value and valency of goal objects. A goal has a positive value if that satisfies the driving state of the organism because, it is required to repair internal deficits due to deprivation. In addition to this, the goal object has also a valency. Valency reflects **goodness** or **badness** of a goal object. Valency arises expectations. For example, a hungry animal is rewarded on a number of occasions in the past with the positively valued object, the animal expects something of the particular 'goodness' associated with that goal object (food) in the goal box when it begins to run the maze on a new occasion. This expectancy constitutes the valency of the goal object on that particular trial.

To substantiate this expectancy learning, **Trinkle Paugh** conducted an experiment on monkeys. He placed bananas under one of the two containers while monkey was watching. After the deprivation hour, monkey was let loose and it was found that the monkey readily chose the container with bananas. Later, lettuce leaf in place of banana was placed in the same container (lettuce leaf is a less preferred food for monkey, hence of bad valency). It was found that monkey rejected this and showed disruption of behaviour because he had expected banana (positive value with positive valency) whereas lettuce leaf, though positive in value but negative in valency. This lends support to Tolman's view that expectancy learning takes place when goal object is positive in value and valency, both.

Place or goal learning experiment

Tolman's theory lays emphasis on 'cognition' rather than learning the fixed sequence of movements as has been claimed by Hull. To prove it, Tolman and Honzik (1930) conducted an experiment. For this purpose, a special maze was constructed as shown in **Figure 11.4**.

The maze had 3 paths from starting box to the goal box (paths 1, 2 and 3). Path one was the shortest, path three was longest one while path two was of intermediate length. There were 2 blocks—A and B—which the experimenter could manipulate by making them active as per planning. When block A is imposed, path 1 is blocked and when block B is made active, paths 1 and 2 both are blocked as these had common segments leading to the goal box. After a preliminary acquaintance trials, experimental trials began and rats established a preference for paths in order 1, 2 and 3.

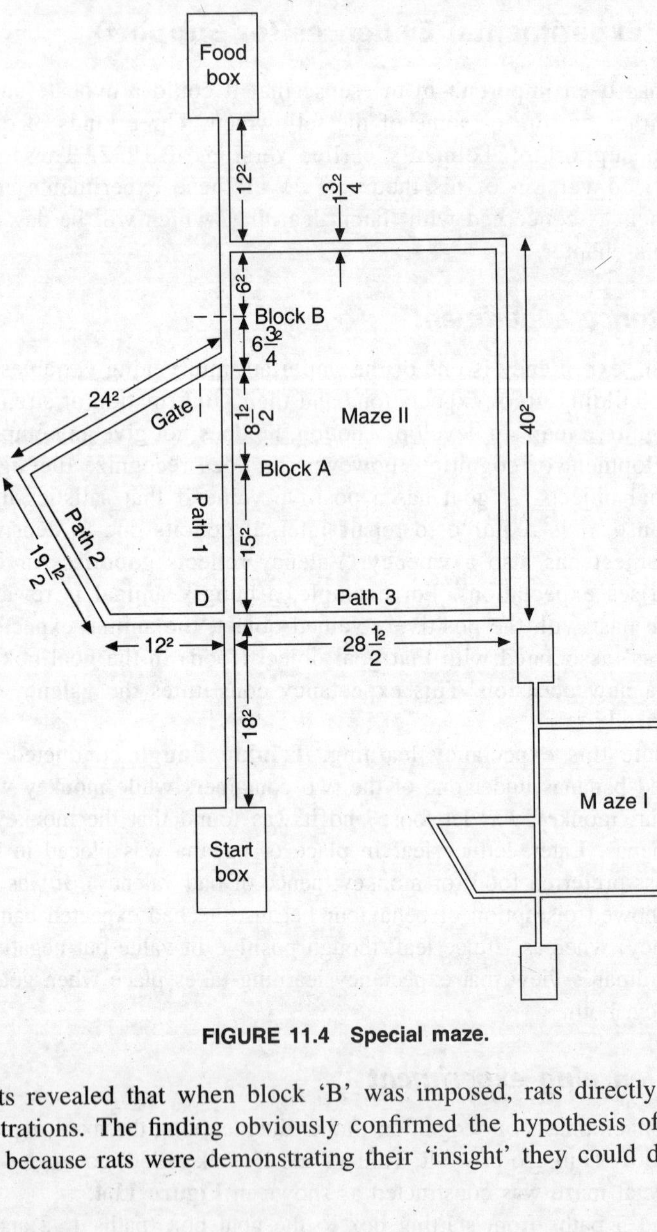

FIGURE 11.4 Special maze.

Final results revealed that when block 'B' was imposed, rats directly ran through path 3 and secured frustrations. The finding obviously confirmed the hypothesis of 'cognitive map' of Tolman's theory because rats were demonstrating their 'insight' they could develop of the whole situation.

Critical comments

(i) Though, Tolman claims to be a behaviourist, his system has several intervening variables which are hardly observable in a scientific objective fashion. These variables are expectancy, cognitive map etc. These are subjective aspects. Hence, the system represents dualism which is not amenable to science.

(ii) Max and Hillix (1963) have remarked that Tolman has markedly failed in proposing any logical and integrated theory. He has introduced too many variables with many unanswerable questions. On the whole, the theory suffers from fragmentation as there is very little coherence within it.

(iii) Osgood opines that though Tolman talks about sign significate, expectancy, however, he does not lament upon temporal factors that exert many influences in developing sign significate expectations.

Despite these criticisms, Tolman's system had a tremendous impact in the field of learning. Use of intervening variables by him has in fact, greatly prompted Hull who also has used intervening variables very extensively in his theory.

11.6 COMPARISON BETWEEN HULL AND TOLMAN'S THEORIES OF LEARNING

Among the later behaviourists, Hull and Tolman are considered as the most prominent personalities of strong determination of their respective views. Though, the two personalities have presented two distinct views of learning, they also bear some similarity in their approach. Hence, it seems important to examine the basic points of similarities and differences between their approaches to learning.

Similarities

(i) Hull and Tolman, both show their agreement in their views that whenever the learner (rats) in maze learning situation is encountered by a block (inhibition) in the main route leading to the goal, they opt for or choose the alternative route or course to reach the goal.

(ii) Hull and Tolman both have made distinction in learning and performance. Hull could make clear this difference in his revised form of the theory (1952 revision). Hence, the two bear similarity on this point.

(iii) Hull and Tolman, both in their respective theories, have talked about three major kinds of variables—the independent variable (learning situation or task), the dependent variable (the event of learning) and the intervening variables that mediate in between. In fact, Hull has borrowed this concept of intervening variable from being influenced by Tolman.

Differences

(i) While learning—what do we learn? On this point Hull and Tolman have different opinions. Hull lays emphasis on 'response learning' in which the organism learns to associate specific response with specific stimulus situation.

Tolman, on the other hand, is of the view that the organism learns the place, goal or relationship between different elements of stimulus situation that serves the purpose of achieving the goal—'means-end relationship'. Hence, it is a purposive lerning—to develop insight and acquire the principles involved between means and end.

(ii) Hull and Tolman also differ on the issue of significance of reinforcement in learning According to Hull, reinforcement strengthens the association between stimulus and response (S-R association). Moreover, the organism learns only those responses that are reinforced in each learning trial. For this reason, Hull's theory is popularly known as 'reinforcement theory'.

Tolman, on the other hand, assumes the role of reinforcement in performanc and not in learning. He holds the view that when learned acts need to be expressed in performance terms, reinforcement becomes significant.

(iii) In the context of problem solving also, the two theorists stand apart. Hull is of the view that in problem solving situation, the learner (or the problem solver) relies upon trial and error procedure instead of insight. However, Tolman assumes the significanc of 'cognition' about the problem in which insight and expectation are of paramoun significance.

(iv) According to Hull, the learner when encounters a problem situation of learning, i mentally a clean slate (blank mind), *i.e.* he is inactive or passive. However, in cours of learning, the sensory impressions of the acquired habits are imprinted onto the blan mind. On the other hand, according to Tolman, the organism's mind is never blank as h possesses the ability to think and hence, mentally active. Owing to these activities, th organism in a learning situation or problem solving situation is able to construct variou hypotheses and through mental processing, he is able to select the hypothesis that be fits in and thus, learns to solve the problem.

(v) Hull and Tolman also differ in their views about the unit of learning behaviour. Accordin to Hull, in a learning situation, the learning behaviours can be understood by analysin the pattern of behaviour into smaller units or elements. Hence, Hull lays emphasis o elemental analysis of learning behaviour. Tolman, however, does not agree with element analysis of learning behaviour rather emphasizes on the pattern of behaviour as a whol Hence, Tolman's view is molar while Hull's view is molecular.

From the above description, it is obvious that though Hull and Tolman bear some similariti in their systems, the two views have some differences too.

11.7 GUTHRIE'S CONTIGUITY THEORY

E.R. Guthrie is one of the neo-behaviourists who followed the track setforth by early behaviouris with some distinction in the sense that he demphasized motivation and reinforcement to be any significance in modifying our behaviour. He rather emphasized on **'contiguity'** in learning. seems, he owes to **Aristotle's** notion that **two events would be associated together if they occ together closely**.

In learning theories of Pavlov, Thorndike, Hull etc. the principal idea is that learning is S-R affair. For Guthrie, this association between a stimulus and a response is a matter of tempo contiguity, *i.e.* the association to occur between a stimulus and a response is simply a matter contiguity (closeness) in time and reinforcement is not necessary. Reinforcement is secondary. quote Guthrie (1935, 1952)—**'A combination of stimuli which has accompanied a moveme will on its recurrence tend to be followed by that movement.'***

* Guthrie, E.R., 1935, *The Psychology of Learning*, New York, Harper.

Strictly speaking, contiguity theory of learning is a single principal theory and employs few assumptions than others. This is a great scientific advantage of this theory.

It is also a mechanistic theory in the sense that according to this theory, for learning, all that is required is to contract one's muscles in some order and pattern. Development of this new pattern or order depends upon proper signal or stimulus and as soon as the two (proper signal or stimulus and response) occur in close association of time, learning is complete. Thus, Guthrie neither considers the importance of practice nor reinforcement as necessary factors for learning.

While lamenting upon the theory, Guthrie has used constructs, similar to Hull but he has applied fewer of them. $_SH_R$, $_SE_R$, inhibitions etc. have not been used by Guthrie. The major unobservable fact in Guthrie's theory are the implicit muscular movements and the distinctive proprioceptive cues produced by these muscular movements, Guthrie has also used the notion of **'maintaining stimuli'** which are akin to drive and set. These remain relatively constant throughout the learning situation.

The entire system of Guthrie can be seen in reference to his one of the postulates which states that **a response becomes maximally associated with a stimulus when the two particular events (S-R) occur contiguously**. This statement obviously means that learning is a single trial association merely by contiguity. Undoubtedly, such an utterance is highly valuable for being simple and generality of application in a number of everyday illustrations. But, it also raises some questions such as:

(i) If learning is a single trial phenomenon, why does the learning curve in general show gradual improvement?
(ii) If contiguity is essential for association between S and R, what explanation can be offered for the common phenomenon of **trace conditioning**?

Guthrie has tried to answer the above two queries. As for the former, he has distinguished between 'movements' and 'acts'. According to him, the movement is a pattern of muscular or glandular response while act is a series of such movements culminating in the **end result**. Guthrie while making his assertions, that learning is complete in a single trial by association being formed on the basis of contiguity, he refers to the movements and not to the acts. Since acts involve many movements, it may take many trials to perfect a pattern of many movements that is eventually successful in performing the act (such as lever pressing or escape from puzzle box).

With regard to the second question, Guthrie says that in such cases (*i.e.* **trace conditioning**) the true conditioner is not the physical stimulus (such as bell) rather the proprioceptive stimuli which results from movements elicited by the physical stimulus (bell) and these are contiguous with the desired response. For example, in classical conditioning experiment of Pavlov, when the bell rings, the dog responds by **listening**. This involves a series of movements such as **postural changes, turning of head, picking the ears** etc. When the salivation begins, the accompanying stimuli are not furnished by bell but by these responses to the bell.

In still another postulate, Guthrie talks about incompatible responses which results in complete elimination of the previous association. This notion seems similar to **Voeks** (1949)—**The Principle of Posterity**. But, Guthrie himself is not very clear about it.

Guthrie's notion of contiguity principle is associated with his dissatisfaction with 'instrumental conditioning' experiments. He asserts, that in Skinner box experiment, ordinarily we count the number of times per minute rat presses the lever. He objects to this approach. He believes that the association of a particular movement with the stimuli is important. The counting of number of acts, *i.e.* result of movement is only secondary. **Guthrie** and **Horton** (1946) studied the puzzle box problem of Thorndike. They were interested in shedding the way in which cats learned to escape from puzzle. They arranged motion pictures from puzzle box and displayed a greater degree of behavioural stereotypes. In most cases, movements were identical from trial to trial. This was taken as good indicator of association between cues and movement.

Thus, in essence, contiguity theory lays emphasis on contiguity as the single condition for forming association and that it is complete in one single trial. However, while making distinction between movement and act, Guthrie too agrees with the significance of practice or repetition in perfecting the learning of an act, involving complex functions that consist of several movements.

Critical comments

Guthrie has been subjected to criticisms which are mentioned hereinbelow:

(i) Several psychologists such as Skinner, Thorndike, Hull etc. show their disagreement with Guthrie for laying no emphasis on reinforcement. Role of reinforcement, in fact, gets support from a vast number of experimental studies which cannot be sidetracked or ignored.

(ii) Guthrie has also been severely criticized for ignoring the role of individual differences. He states that in learning situations animals exhibit stereotyped behaviour (refer to Guthrie and Horton's study on puzzle box problem). However, this is not correct. Individual differences and not the stereotyping is the correct assumption. The experimental evidences cited by Guthrie and Horton are very scanty to substantiate stereotyping reactions and ignoring individual differences.

(iii) Guthrie has utterly failed to be clear and explicit on many basic issues (**Mueller** and **Schoenford,** 1964). To cite an example, Guthrie is not very clear about the postulate regarding elimination, forgetting, reward etc.

(iv) Lack of ample experimental support to the theory is still another point of criticism.

Despite these criticisms, Guthrie occupies the position of a major learning theorist. His theory in fact, is a gem in simplicity and generality. It is very difficult to disprove the principle of contiguity. Hence, his theory occupies a significant position.

11.8 OBSERVATIONAL LEARNING

As has been stated earlier, learning is a very pervasive and complex process. Besides, it is also a key process of behaviour modification—whether innate, unlearnt, adaptive or maladaptive. All sorts of behaviours bear the stamp of learning in some way or the other. We have already discussed quite a good many theories and principles of learning which are widely applied by psychologists in understanding about the nature of man (also of the animals). One such wider area of application is personality. Psychologists take keen interest in knowing the role of learning in the formation, development and shaping of personality.

In this context, 'cognitive learning' is also an important kind of learning in which the perceptual experiences have dominating role to play. Such learnings include **'sign learning'**, **'insight learning'** etc. These types of learnings have earlier been discussed while describing Kohler, Kaffka's theory of learning (insight) and Tolman's theory of contiguity (sign learning).

One more type of cognitive learning is the 'observational learning' which is also called as **imitative learning**. This type of learning has been much emphasized by **'Albert Bandura'** and **'Richard Walters'** (1963). They consider this type of learning much more important than the theories of **John Dollard** and **Meal Miller's** (1950) theory of **early social learning theory** and B.F. Skinner's (1953) **radical behaviourism** etc.

Observational learning generally takes place in social situation involving a model and an imitator. When the observer (imitator) observes another individual (the model) solving a problem one or more times and then the observer applies the observed tricks (imitates the mode of response of the model) and solves the problem with similar success, he is said to have learnt the correct mode of responding through passive observtaion. The examples of observational learning in our everyday life situations are abundant. Many criminals learn the criminal tips by observing models in T.V. or movies. We learn many styles of speech, skills of advertising, attracting audiences, impressing others, aggressive behaviours, gambling, tricks, addictions to drugs and alcohols etc. by means of observational learning. While describing observational learning, psychologists have identified three kinds of modelling. These are:

11.8.1 Imitation

Students who copy mannerism of a favoured teacher, a cricket player while watching a cricket game match, the observer tends to observe very minutely the style in which his favoured player gives a shot and copies the same when he actually plays. In both of the above examples, learning by imitation is exhibited. Similarly, the fashion designers employ the models to popularize their dress designs showing it through T.V., advertise the various designs through attractive models in magazines or newspapers. People, in general, observe these and imitate the models. We also observe our superiors and other people behaving in a novel social situation and emulate them. Such kinds of observational learning is a common experience of all of us. In fact, in observational learning, we consider our superiors, favoured persons or other likable individuals as our 'ideal persons' (models) and attempt to emulate their patterns of behaviour or imitate them exactly in the same manner. Thus, it is also called **model learning** or **imitative learning**.

11.8.2 Vicarious Learning

Often observation of behaviour includes an awareness of the consequences of behaviour. This may be both—reinforcing or avoiding. However, the imitator or the observer blindly imitates (without caring for the consequences) and is reinforced. This leads him to anticipate the reinforcement again and then repeats the behaviour next time also. For example, someone is watching a tennis game on T.V. and notices that one player bends the knee and follows through with each stroke consistently and wins the points. So, the observer when himself begins to play tennis, he repeats the same actions more deeply, anticipating a similar anticipating stroke. Thus, the imitator or the observer observes the model and experiences the model's behaviour and its consequences vicariously. Therefore, the process is called **vicarious reinforcement**.

11.8.3 Live versus Symbolic Modelling

Studies have revealed that imitation can be inspired by either a live or symbolic (representational) model. For example, a young boy learns to imitate the laughing face, speech and styles of a hero to attract the attention of others, a sad face to attract parent's sympathy etc. In general, greater the similarity between the model and the learner, greater will be the learning. Further, higher the status of the model, more the observer will tend to imitate the behaviour.

We also tend to imitate a symbolic or representative models. For example, assembling the stereo set by reading the instructions given in the manual pages, learning customs and religious traditions by reading religious books or watching others while observing prayers etc.

Bandura, while elaborating the concept of observational learning maintains that four processes govern such types of model learning. These processes are as follows:

(i) **Attentional process:** Observational learning cannot take place unless one pays attention to the model. Paying attention depends upon several factors such as sensory capabilities of the observer, characteristics of the model, needs and motivations of the observer etc.

(ii) **Retentional process:** The learner organises and retains what he has observed in the model. Then he makes a cognitive map of all that he has observed by imagining and mentally rehearsing future experiences. This is a sort of representational blueprint which is stored and as soon as the signal to reproduce the imagined blueprint is received, the same is reproduced as outcome.

(iii) **Motor reproduction process:** Depending upon the capabilities, the learner then transforms the cognitive map into action.

(iv) **Motivational process:** The actual or imagined rewards of the imitated behaviour determine either persistence or extinguishness of the model behaviour.

Thus, observational learning is learning of a mode of response in a social situation. Hence, it is also called **'social learning'** because we tend to emulate the behaviours of others around us—a social situation that involves observations of behaviours of others and copying the same.

In order to understand the nature of observational learning, 'Bandura' and his colleagues conducted several research studies. In one of his well-known studies, Bandura showed a film of 5 minutes duration to children. The film shows that in a room there were large many toys including a large sized 'bobo doll'. A grown-up boy enters the room and looks around. The boy begins to show aggressive behaviours towards the toys in general and towards the bobo doll in particular, *viz.* hitting, throwing on the floor, kicking and sitting on the doll.

Next time, the film had 3 different versions. In one version, a group of children saw the boy (model) being rewarded and praised by an adult for being aggressive to the doll. In the second version, another group of children saw the boy being punished by the adult for being aggressive to the doll. In the third version, the model boy was shown neither being rewarded nor being punished for the aggressive reactions.

After showing the three versions of the film to the two groups of children, they were again brought to the experimental room in which similar toys were placed around. The children were allowed to play with them and were secretly observed by the experimenter. It was found that those who viewed the first version of the film were most aggressive. (These children viewed the boy being rewarded for being aggressive to the doll). On the other hand, those who viewed the second version in which the boy was given punishment for being aggressive to the doll, were found least aggressive.

In this experiment, all children observed and acquired the knowledge of aggressive behaviour. But, their performance was influenced by model's behaviour being either rewarded or punished.

Hence, it is concluded that **in observational learning though the observer acquires the knowledge by observing the behaviour of the model, his performance is influenced by model's behaviour being either rewarded or punished.**

We, including children learn most of the social or interpersonal behaviours by observing and emulating the behaviour of others. We acquire most of the features of personality such as aggressiveness, impulsiveness, politeness, industriousness, indolence, pro-social behaviours, pro-environmental behaviours etc. are the examples of daily life learnings through observation of others around us.

Thus, observational learning is also an important mode of learning that brings change or modification in our behaviour.

11.9 LATENT LEARNING

Latent learning is again a kind of cognitive or perceptual learning. Latent learning refers to the kind of learning that is not manifested during the course of learning but as soon as the opportunities (such as reward or reinforcement) occur, such learnings are manifested. Latent learning phenomenon usually occurs in low level drive conditions or when the apparent reward is not available.

We have earlier discussed that when S-S associations are formed, it also includes learning of spatial relationships or cognitive maps. However, the question is whether S-S associations necessarily depend upon reinforcement or reward? *i.e.* whether such associations (S-S association) are related to drive reduction? In this context, let us examine an experiment by **Seward** (1949). The experiment was carried on rats. After adaptation in a simple straight alley maze, the rats were allowed to explore T maze with distinctive end boxes at the ends of the cross arm. On the test day, each rat was allowed to explore the T maze for 3 minutes and then were placed in a detention box at distance for about 25 minutes. Next, each rat was taken from the detention box and put into a distinctive box where food was available. After eating food, rats were placed in the starting box at the base stem of the maze and were allowed to choose between the empty goal boxes. Food odour was controlled by putting food outside the goal boxes. It was found that of the 32 rats, 28 (87.5%) went to the goal box in which they had been fed. One controlled experiment, in which no exploration was allowed before feeding in the goal box, indicated that prior exploration of the T maze was necessary for this result. 27 of the 55 rats (49%) chose the end box in which they had been fed in this control experiment. This is very close to chance expectation—50%. Other controlled experiments strengthened the case for latent learning and learning without reinforcement.

The experimenter offered very simple interpretation of the results. According to the researcher, the rats were making S-S association, *i.e.* were building cognitive maps while they were exploring the T maze. Therefore, when food was introduced, the latent S-S associations enabled most of the animals to locate the route to the goal box (in which they were fed). Thus, it is obvious that latent learning does not necessarily depend upon any drive or need state nor does it depend on reinforcement stimulus that reduces drive state.

The above-mentioned experiments clearly demonstrate the fact that stimulus-stimulus association or cognitive learning may occur even without reinforcement.

However, in such latent learning also, reward or reinforcement seems important in the sense that reinforcement works as activating our latent learning, *i.e.* when reinforced, the S-S association is put to use. Reinforcement allows to stamp in the correct associations (S-S association) and stamp out the incorrect ones. In other words, reinforcement permits to perform correctly whatever has been learnt latently. Tolman in his system has also made distinctions between learning and performing in the context of reinforcement.

Thus, S-S association or perceptual learning may be possible without reinforcement, however, such learnings can be put to use only when reward or reinforcement is made available.

11.10 SKILL LEARNING

Performing a complex task smoothly and efficiently is called 'skill learning', *viz.* car driving, aeroplane piloting, ship navigating, shorthand writing. Writing and reading are some of the examples of skills. **Skills are learned** by practice and exercise. Technically speaking, **a skill is a chain of perceptual motor responses, i.e. a sequence of stimulus-response associations (S-R associations)**. In performing a skill-based task, we make a number of movements of response organs such as movement of legs, feet, toes, arms, fingers, head turnings, bending etc. All these movements involve getting them associated with a chain of elements in the stimuli and getting these associations organized in order or sequence. Therefore, **skill acquisition is learning to organize the series of S-R associations in a larger response pattern**.

11.10.1 Phases of Skill Acquisition

According to **'Fitts'**, skill learning passes through three phases—the cognitive phase, associative phase and autonomous phase. Each phase is characterized by different types of mental processes.

The cognitive phase

This is the beginning phase of skill learning. It is characterized by taking of the input and processing in the manner so as to develop better understanding of the task demands and response outcomes. It is the conscious phase in which the learner becomes consciously aware of the entire task situation. In other words, in this phase, the learner draws a cognitive map of the relevant features of the task situation into his consciousness. The learner understands and memorises the instructions. He also understands the **modus operandi** of performance, *i.e.* how the task is to be performed? The available external cues, instructional demands, response outcomes etc. everything is kept alive into the consciousness. Thus, it is the phase of **cognitive awareness**.

The associative phase

This is the phase of establishing associations between stimulus and response. In this phase, various sensory inputs are linked with appropriate responses. As the practice trials increase, there is gradual decrease in error, and level of performance goes up. The time taken also decreases which shows smoothness in performance. With continued errorless practice, the performance gradually advances towards automation in performance and thus, the learner transits to the third and final phase of skill learning. The associative phase, however, demands higher order **attentiveness** to the sensory inputs that he receives in different practice trials and maintaining of the concentration on the task.

The autonomous phase

This is the final phase of skill learning. In this phase, two kinds of changes in performance occur—(a) the attentional demands of second phase (associative phase) decrease and (b) the interferences by the external factors reduce. With these two types of changes, the performance attains **automaticity** as the demand of conscious efforts to perform is minimal.

The transitions from one phase to another clearly show the significance of practice in performance. Practice brings efficiency and perfection, *i.e.* more and more we practice, better and better is our performance. Thus, **practice brings perfection**.

11.11 INTENTIONAL AND INCIDENTAL LEARNING

11.11.1 Intentional Learning

Intentional learning refers to intended learning, *i.e.* the learner intends to learn. This involves conscious efforts to learn. Intent to learn is one of the most important motivational factors that determines or influences our learning. For example, a student of history intends to learn the facts of history, associates the dates or periods of different historical events while the students of geography intends to learn the geographical features more consciously than a student of history.

The significance of intended learning in human beings has been demonstrated in some of the earliest studies. For example **Mayers** (1913) instructed his subjects to count the number of O's distributed randomly among other letters printed in a colour on coloured paper. Later, they were asked what other letters were present, what colours they were, and on what colour papers they were printed. Their incorrect answers showed that they could learn very little other than for what they were instructed, *i.e.* they had intent to learn.

In a more systematic study on intentional learning, **Postman and Senders** (1946) and **Postman and Adams** (1957) found that the nature and amount of learning were clearly influenced by the kind of instructions used.

Intentional learning is also called **'purposive learning'**, because we intend to learn those things that serve some kind of purpose. Such learnings are intended to achieve some goal and hence, intentional learning is motivational learning. The achievement of intended goal is reinforcing and hence, such learnings are concerned with some purpose.

11.11.2 Incidental Learning

Incidental learning is a sort of **chance learning** in which the organism acquires many cues and distinct features of the situation. Such acquisitions are neither reinforced nor the learner intends to satisfy any driving or need state. For example, when one visits a new city, he acquires many distinct features of the city—the distance, conditions of road, traffic signals, electric poles, turnings, the language used by the people of the city, and many other similar things. None of such acquistions is reinforced or intended, *i.e.* consciously wanted to learn.

Incidental learning despite being unintended, serves some useful purpose in life, more particularly, incidental learning is found much useful in discriminating the stimulus situation on the basis of multiple cues that we learn incidentally. Perhaps, due to this reason, most of the reinforcement theorists of learning advance arguments that how can we say with certainty that incidental learning has no reinforcement?

Though, whether incidental learning has reinforcement or not is a matter of debate, but incidental learning is a fact which has experimentally been supported (Postman 1964, Buxton 1940, Mechanic 1962).

Thus, incidental learning is also a fact that serves many useful purposes.

11.12 VERBAL LEARNING

One of the important aspects of human behaviour is verbal behaviour that distinguishes human beings from other animals. Humans converse with one another, listen, speak, read books and even think with the help of verbal symbols. If we minutely observe the daily life situation transactions of human beings, we would hardly find any aspects of human behaviour that bear no stamp of verbal learning.

Verbal learning involves words. Words are the symbols that represent something. Numbers, code words etc. are also verbal symbols. All these symbols stand for objects, events, situations and attributes or properties of these objects and events. Hence, verbal learning involves development of abilities to manipulate the symbols—words, numbers, verbal cues, codes etc. Abilities to manipulate these symbols make it possible for humans to learn many responses and acquire various skills such as message communication, formation of concepts, gaining proficiency in solving verbal problems, and similar various abilities that enable them to adapt with the environment effectively.

11.12.1 Materials Used to Study Verbal Learning

Verbal learning materials include all the cases of learning by using words—responding to or with. In addition, numbers, nonsense syllables, code languages, verbal signs, verbal problems, forming concepts by using verbal symbols etc. all constitute material for verbal learning.

A German psychologist, **Herman Ebbinghaus** in 1880, was the first to develop nonsense syllables for experimental studies on verbal learning. Even today, nonsense syllables consisting of consonant-vowel-consonant (CVS) letters of English* alphabets or consonant-consonant-consonant (CCC) of the alphabets are used as verbal materials for experimental studies. However, meaningful words, codes, stories or poems are also often used. But, the use of CVC or CCC trigrams are most preferred materials because of certain advantages over the meaningful words or other materials.

A sample of such varied materials (meaningful and nonsense syllables) used for experimental works are given in **Table 11.2**.

TABLE 11.2 Sample of verbal materials used in verbal learning experiments

	Nonsense syllables*		Meaningful words	
	CVC trigrams	*CCC trigrams*	*Unfamiliar words*	*Familiar words*
1.	XOY	KTE	VERVE	GOOD
2.	JIR	ZNA	THILL	BACK
3.	DUZ	XPM	SCOFF	ABET
4.	KAC	RVN	MANSE	SCAR
5.	LEB	DCL	DEVEN	BOOK
6.	ZIX	FNX	TENOR	MOON

* It is more convenient to prepare nonsense syllables using English alphabets. It is also convenient to standardize it. However, efforts to make nonsense syllables using Hindi alphabets need to be initiated.

11.12.2 Methods for Measuring Verbal Learning

To measure verbal learning, psychologists have evolved certain dependable methods or techniques. These techniques are important in two ways—firstly it enables the experimenter to compare results and secondly, it calls forth from the learner particular kind of learning, memory, strategies and processes. All these methods involve recall as the basic procedure with certain procedural modifications that intend to measure different processes involved in learning verbal meterials. Following are the major methods used for measuring verbal learning.

Free recall

In free recall, each item of learning material is presented before the subject (learner) one by one in serial order with a very short spacing of interval in between (usually 2 seconds) each item. After the exposure of each item of the learning task, the subject or learner is asked to spell-out, i.e. recall each item that he remembers irrespective of their serial order of exposure. Thus, the subject is free to recall correctly any item of the list without caring for the order of presentation. Here, only the correct recall in each exposure (trial) is taken as the measure of learning in a trial. Hence, it is called free recall. It is also called simple recall because of two reasons: firstly, the subject is required simply to recall the items correctly and not the serial order or position of the items in the list. Secondly, the subject learns only the items to be recalled and not their vertical orderly associations with other items in the list. Thus, there is single event of learning—'the items to be learnt' (recalled correctly). This is unitary learning, hence simple. It has been observed that generally learning by free recall is easier than the other methods, *i.e.* serial recall, paired associate or prompting and anticipation. In this method, usually the subjects require lesser number of trials to reach the criterion of learning as compared to the other methods. To measure the process of verbal learning, the learning trials are continued till the learner reaches the criterion and thus, the number of trials is taken as the measure of learning.

This method is used to measure how subjects organize words or other materials for storage in memory. Studies show that the items in the beginning and at the end of the list are learned more easily than the middle items. This feature of learning is explained in terms of laws of **'primacy'** and **'finality'** that seem to operate and, therefore, the first one or two items and the items at the final end are learnt more quickly than the other items of the learning material.

Serial recall

In serial recall method, the items are exposed just in the manner the items are presented in free recall method. But, unlike free recall, the learner is required to recall what he remembers in serial order, *i.e.* the order of exposure. Obviously, the process of learning becomes relatively complicated. In serial learning, one has to learn not only the words or syllables, but also the serial position in which the items are vertically related to one another, *i.e.* which word or syllable precedes or follows the particular word or syllable being learnt. This method is useful to study the process of relatively more active search and retrieval from memory store. The process of exposure is repeated continuously again and again till the learner reaches the criterion of learning.

On comparison of the two methods, it is observed that learning by free recall is comparatively easier than the serial recall because of the fact that in the former, there is single act of learning event (unitary learning), *i.e.* learning only the units of words or syllables and not their relative positions in the list. On the other hand, serial learning involves multiple process of learning, *i.e.* learning the unitary items in relation to their relative positions. Hence, it is a bit difficult process of learning and hence, requires more number of trials to reach the criterion. However, the experimental studies using this method also show that memory of serially learnt materials is stronger than free recall. Probably, this is due to the fact of overlearning of most of the items. For example, suppose a learner is given two different but comparable lists of CVC trigrams in two different sessions—list A and B. List A is allowed to be learnt by free recall method while list B is allowed to be learnt by serial recall. Suppose the subject learns list A (free recall) in 10 trials while he learns list B (serial recall) in 15 trials. Thus, the subject takes 5 more trials in learning the similar list and therefore most of the items of the list are overpractised or learnt by 50% due to which the memory of second list will be relatively stronger—**the more we learn, stronger is our learning and better is our memory**.

In serial learning, we learn to associate the different items in vertical order. Hence, this method is used to measure the vertical associations, *i.e.* how each of the items is vertically associated in position with one another.

Prompting and anticipation method

This method is also called **serial anticipation** method. It is similar to serial learning. But the procedure is different. The items are presented one at a time for a brief period (say 2 seconds) as for free or serial recall. After exposing the whole list once, the subject is shown item No. 1 for two seconds within which the subject (learner) is required to anticipate the next (immediately that follows) item. Then he is presented the 2nd item and the subject is again required to anticipate the third item of the list. The same procedure is followed till the end of the list and hence the completion of this anticipatory trial is counted as trial No. 1. In the same way the list is presented again and again until the learner reaches the predetermined criterion of learning. Note that after the first run, the learner has to anticipate the response item by being prompted to anticipate when a stimulus item (prompter) is exposed. The subject is required to anticipate the response item before it is presented as stimulus item (prompter) for the anticipation of the next response item again before it is presented as stimulus item (prompter for the still next). Thus, each item in the list functions as both—stimulus (prompter) and response item except the first one which has no stimulus item. In experiments, a neutral item is added in symbolical form to the first item of the list to serve as the stimulus item for the first item of the original list. The symbolic form of the added item may be like OOO, ΔΔΔ, XXX etc. This neutral item serves only as a cue item and is not reckoned while determining the learners score in a trial. The score is total number of correct anticipations in each trial.

This method is called anticipation method because in each trial, the learner anticipates what follows next on being prompted by the appearance of the stimulus item.

One of the advantages of this method is that the effect of knowledge of result operates automatically in the procedure because in every anticipation, the correct item is exposed as stimulus item to the subject that provides knowledge to the learner whether his anticipation was correct or incorrect or whether he has failed in anticipating the response item. This kind of automatic feedback is of great motivational value in learning.

This method again used to measure vertical spatial relationships of different items in the list to be learnt.

Paired associate method

In this method, each learning item is presented before the subject (learner) in pair form of nonsense syllables with numbers or other symbols (*e.g.* meaningful words, signs or codes). Like conditioning, here also a response word or item in learning is learnt by associating it with stimulus word or item (S-S association). To put in other words, in pair associate, each stimulus item has a paired response item and thus, the learner learns to associate the two stimuli together. A sample of such associated pairs of items is given in **Table 11.3**.

TABLE 11.3 Sample of learning material for paired associate method of verbal learning

Stimulus item		*Response item*
ZKQ	→	MAN
RMS	→	EGG
LFK	→	FAN
XQD	→	DOG
CCB	→	EYE
JHB	→	MAT
SPW	→	RAT
JFN	→	GOD

For conducting experiments, a list of paired items is prepared. The first member of the pairs is CCC trigrams which bear no meaning (nonsense). The second member of the pairs is meaningful words of the comparable length and size. The former is called **stimulus item** while the latter is called **response item.** The learner is first exposed each paired item serially with instructions to remember the response item of the pair through associating the same with the stimulus item (first member of the pair). Thus, in this case, the association is **horizontal** and not vertical as in serial learning. Each pair is exposed for 4 seconds (2 seconds for each member of the pair). After first exposure, only stimulus item is exposed for 2 seconds during which the subject has to recall by anticipating the response item (2nd member of the pair). This is the beginning of the trial of learning process. The subject tries to recall the correct associated member of the pair. However, it is possible that subject may either fail or recall incorrectly or partially. In all these possible correct or incorrect responses, the associated pair is shown and then the experimenter switches on to the next stimulus member of the pair in order. The procedure is followed till the end of the list. Next, second learning trial is started in the same manner as in the first trial. In this way, learning trials are continued till the learner reaches the criterion of learning (usually two consecutive trials of correct recall of the whole list). Then the experiment ends and the number of correct associations in each trial and the total number of trials required to reach the criterion are considerd as measures of learning.

The data obtained in all these methods can be represented in a graph that may show many features of verbal learning process such as, gradual improvement or progression, plateau, steep rise, slowness, rerising and finally the end spurt.

11.12.3 Methods of Verbal Learning

Following are the three ways in which one can learn verbal materials.

Whole and part method

One may learn the whole learning material by breaking them into several parts of equal units and learning each part separately. For example, a learner is given a 4-stanza poem to learn and memorize. He memorizes the first stanza by repeatedly reading it. Then he repeatedly reads second stanza, then the third and finally the fourth stanza. In this way, he learns the whole poem by dividing it into parts. Conversely, one may read and re-read the entire poem as a whole and continue to repeat till the whole poem is fully learned. This is called **whole method** while the former is called **part method**.

Now the question is as to which one method is economical and better. Some argue that in part method, the learner has not to wait for long for being rewarded for his efforts. He repeats each part one by one and as soon as he is able to reproduce a part successfully, he is immediately rewarded by the success for that part. Similarly, when he learns the second part, again reward comes to him for his success in the next part and so on. Thus, every part is reinforced by part of reward in the form of feeling of success in the part. On the other hand, in whole method, one is required to repeat the whole materials several times till the attainment of the criterion for learning. Thus, the reward is not only delayed, but less in frequency as in part method, in which the reward comes relatively more frequently. As a rule, prompt reinforcement or quick reward rather than delayed reinforcement or belated reward keeps the motivation at the optimal level throughout the period of learning.

But, whole learning has also an advantage of its own. The entire material is learned as an integrated whole, while the part learning requires additional efforts to integrate the parts because each part stands as an isolated unit. Hence, to answer as to which one method is more economical is difficult. The answer is not conclusive. It depends upon several variables such as, nature of material (difficult or easy), length of material (long or short), relatedness of the items, certain characteristics of the learner (old or young, intelligent or dull, previous learning habits etc.).

Massed and distributed learning

Another procedure of learning is massed or distributed. One may learn a maze or memorize a list of new words by continuous practice or may take rest in between the trials distributed in some units. For example, a child may learn a list of 100 new words continuously for several hours or he may learn the entire list by distributing the whole period of learning in several units of time with an intermittent rest, *viz.* 2 hours of continuous reading may be distributed or spaced in four units of 30 minutes each with a break of 5 minutes after each 30 minutes (total numbers of rest intervals being 3).

It has generally been found that in psycho-motor tasks spaced method makes learning easier than massed practice. However, each interval of rest may not be beneficial. For different tasks, there is optimal duration of interval to produce optimal results.

Moreover, the location of interval is also an important variable to produce better results of spacing the duration of learning.

Why the distributed or spaced learning is economical? There are several reasons for why the spaced learning is generally found better than the massed learning. In the first place, continuous learning for a prolonged period induces fatigue and thus, the effectiveness of learner's effort is upset. When fatigued, we often experience 'loss of motion' while trying to study or trying to accomplish anything. A short-working unit usually better motivates us to work rather than a longer one. When the working unit is short, 'extra effort' is induced while a longer working unit induces a tendency to save ourselves from **longpull** ahead.

Further, a rest period in between, reduces fatigue and leads to improved motivation. In addition, intermittent periods of rest are also useful for neural traces of learnt materials for better preservation or consolidation. Owing to spacing and rest intervals, intense external stimulation eases and allows interval consolidation to occur (Woodworth and Scholsberg, 1954).

Active and passive learning

Active learning refers to recitation with conscious efforts while passive learning is just reading the material for several times without giving any conscious effort. Conscious recitation is reading with understanding the contents. For example, after every reading one may test by rehearsing or mentally reciting the material from memory. In doing so, he takes strain to recapitulate as much as possible and finds out the mistakes. Moreover, he learns the task with due care to understand the interrelations, conceptual cues and associated meanings. But in passive learning one goes on simply reading the material without caring for the interconnections, associations etc. He just gives readings for several times, stops for a while and finds out the amount he is able to reproduce.

Usually, active method is supposed to be better than the passive as active method takes little time than passive learning.

11.13 FACTORS IN HUMAN LEARNING

Learning may be rapid, slow or there may be no learning at all. These facts of learning depends upon several factors governing the process of learning. These factors may be divided into following main groups:

11.13.1 Methods of Learning

We have just described various methods of learning and how they influence learning. Therefore, these need not be repeated. In the present section, the subjective factors and factors associated with learning tasks are described below:

Subjective or personal factors

Factors under this group are those which lie within the learner and include the intelligence, chronological age, motivation, previous learning, anxiety states and readiness to learn. These are briefly described in separate sections mentioned below:

(a) **Intelligence:** Intelligence, as we measure and express, is in the form of intelligence quotient (IQ) value. IQ describes one's intellectual level in relation to other persons of the similar category (age group, class group, occupational group, professional status group etc.) in the general population. IQ is generally found to be positively related to the ability to learn. Thus, a person, high in intelligence is supposed to learn more rapidly and effectively. However, it is not the case always. Some research studies done in this area reveal that intelligence is not always related to learning ability (Woodrow, 1946). For this reason, intelligence is not defined solely in terms of learning ability. It is rather a global capacity.

(b) **Chronological age:** Learning is a matter of age as has been postulated by **Thorndike et al.** (1938). Age level is an index of maturity level. All kinds of learnings require a minimum level of maturity. For example, first accurate measurement of verbal learning is possible approximately at the age of 5 and then after the verbal learning ability steadily increases up to approximately 17–20 years of age. Thereafter, the ability remains constant up to approximately 50 years of age with slight droppings. Beyond 50 years, a sharp drop in the ability to learn new materials or skills is noticed. Such kind of data have been used in the construction of intelligence tests.

Moreover, some studies have also demonstrated that acquisition of verbal abilities in children is easy and spontaneous during certain age of development. This is known as **critical period or stage**. Thus, age is an important determinant of learning more particularly, the verbal learning.

(c) **Motivation:** Learner's motivation arouses desire to learn or intent to learn. This is a very importnt factor in determining learning. Postman (1964) has cited several examples of intentional versus incidental learning and has come to the conclusion that for efficient learning, individuals must intent to learn. More details about the role of motivation in learning has been described in Section 10.7 of Chapter 10.

(d) **Previous learning:** Our past learning experiences are another important individual factor of learning. Previous learning experiences influence our present learning in two ways—it facilitates the present learning (positive transfer phenomenon) and sometimes it interferes with the present learning (negative transfer phenomenon). Most often, we find that previous learning has a relevance to the present learning and, therefore, the past experience becomes an important tool either in facilitating or inhibiting or interfering with the new learning. For example, when we put questions—Has the individual learned how to learn? We find here the case of positive transfer. On the other hand, when we see that learner's past habits interfere with new learning, we notice negative transfer. Thus, previous learning has an importnat role to play.

(e) **Anxiety state:** Anxiety is also an important determinant factor of our ability to learn. In our everyday life situations, most of us carry some amount of anxiety, which we often find mounting, while preparing and taking examinations or facing an interview or encountering a problematic situation. But, some people are more anxious than others. We can score the level of anxiety by administering appropriate anxiety scales and classify people on high or low anxiety dimensions.

How anxiety levels of individuals bear on his ability to learn is an intricate question to answer. It depends upon learning task. **Spence** (1964) has found that in simple eyelid conditioning experiments, high anxious subjects respond more rapidly than the low anxious subjects. Simple discrimination learning generally remains uninfluenced by anxiety. However, for complicated tasks as in school learning, anxiety is a hinderance. This has been demonstrated by **Spielberger** (1962) and many more researchers.

(f) **Preparedness or readiness to learn:** The members of different species are very different from one another in their capabilities, both sensory as well as response abilities. The mechanism necessary to learn or form any sort of associations—S-S or S-R associations also vary from species to species. To put it in another way, we may say that different species are biologically constrained in their capabilities of learning. What kind of association (whether S-S or S-R) an organism can easily form or acquire depends upon the **associative mechanism** which is a genetic endowment and accordingly, the organisms are prepared or ready to learn. Thus, a particular type of associative learning is easy for apes or human beings while the same may be either most difficult or often impossible for cats or rats.

This means that one can learn only those for which one is prepared or ready to learn.

This concept of preparedness or readiness can be easily understood as a continuum along a dimension. On the one end of the continuum, are those learning tasks which are easy for the members of some species and on the other end, there are those tasks for which those members are not prepared and, therefore, cannot learn at all. In the middle of the continuum are those tasks for which the members are neither prepared nor unprepared. Therefore, they can learn such tasks with great difficulty.

Thus, preparedness refers to the genetical endowment of range of skills that one can learn and hence, those skills or abilities which are not coverable in the range, are either not learnt or are difficult to learn. This concept of preparedness equally applies in verbal skills also.

11.13.2 Nature of Learning Materials

The kind of learning material considerably influences the rate of learning. The task may be meaningful or meaningless. It may be easy or difficult or hard. The task may be longer or shorter. It may be interesting or monotonous. All these variables are of considerable significance and bearing not only the rate of learning but also the efficiency with which it may be learned. Learning involves organization of learning materials, categorization and semantic conceptualization. Hence, these characteristics or properties of learning materials become important. Generally, meaningful material is learnt more easily than meaningless materials. Longer materials are relatively learnt slowly as it requires more number of trials while shorter one is quickly learnt in few trials. Similarly, the hard or complex tasks require more efforts than the simple ones.

In addition to the above-mentioned factors, environment of learning is also important. This factor includes fatigue, interpolation by previous learning, pleasantness of learning environment, chunking etc. These factors are discussed in some detail in the next Chapter 12 of the book—Memory Process.

11.14 TRANSFER OF LEARNING

Transfer is a general phenomenon. Learning one skill or task often influences the acquisition of another skill or task. For example, a child when learns cycling, the gained ability is transferred to the process of learning any other two-wheeler vehicle such as scooter or bike. Similarly when we learn to drive a particular make of car, we also become able to drive other makes of cars with certain modifications or changes in the system such as right-hand driving to left-hand driving etc. The proficiency gained in additions and subtractions while learning in schools enables the pupils correctly calculate the price he should pay in buying an object. In school learning situations also, the abilities gained in additions and subtractions, enable children to learn other mathematical operations such as multiplication and division. Similarly, on many other situations also, we find the phenomenon of transfer in operation. Thus, transfer refers to the impact of earlier acquired habit or ability in the acquisition of a new habit or a task.

Transfer effects are of two types—**positive** and **negative**. In **positive transfer**, the acquisition of one type of skill facilitates the acquisition of another. On the other hand, when the acquisition of earlier habit or skill interferes in the acquisition of a new skill or task, it is known as **negative transfer**. In technical terms, positive transfer is also referred to as **transfer of training** while the negative transfer is referred to as **habit interference**. It is so called because earlier acquired habits are interfering in nature to the acquisition of new habit or skill. However, sometimes the effect of earlier learning or acquisition on later task is neither facilitative nor inhibitive. Such effects are called zero effect or **no transfer effect**. Thus, zero effect shows absence of any effect of earlier learning on new (later) learning.

The positive, negative and zero transfer effects are shown in **Table 11.4**.

TABLE 11.4 The phenomenon of transfer effect: transfer in learning

	Nature of transfer	*Original (previous) learning*	*Later (news) learning*	*(Kind of effect)*
A.	Positive transfer	Task-A	Taks-B	(Facilitating)
B.	Negative transfer	Task-C	Task-D	(Interfering)
C.	Zero transfer	Task-E	Task-F	(No effect)

11.14.1 Kinds of Transfer in Learning

In the area of learning, psychologists have recognized two types of transfer phenomenon. These are **nonspecific (general)** or **generic transfer** and **specific transfer**. The effect of former type of transfer is always positive while the effect of latter type may be both—positive and negative.

Nonspecific (general) or generic transfer

This type of transfer is quite general in nature and is neither conceptualized nor described in detail. Despite ambiguity in conceptualization, it has been observed in general that previous learning serves as predisposing effect to learn another task in a better way. Its effect is a sort of **warming up** in which prior knowledge or learning predisposes one to learn another task more conveniently. Thus, in course of performing an original task, such kinds of warming up effects of its knowledge prepare or make the learner ready to perform next task with some convenience. Such a phenomenon is witnessed by all of us in our daily life situations. An athlete or a cricket player before going to play or take part in sports activities makes a light preparatory exercises just to get himself 'warmed up' for final demonstration in the competition. Children's initial practice in drawing irregular lines on the board or moving pencil on a sheet of paper warms them up to draw lines smoothly to learn alphabet writings, drawing symmetrical lines, sketching figures etc. All these are examples of nonspecific or generic transfer.

Similarly, we find the examinees in the examination hall that in the beginning, their rate of writing answers is slow which gradually increases. This also exemplifies the nonspecific or generic transfer. Thus, **warming up is a kind of establishing adjustment with the items situations, equipments etc. which are used in learning or performing a task**. This adjustment results from initial practice.

Another important element of non-specific transfer is **learning to learn**. 'Learning to learn' means learning or acquiring the basic skills and best methods to learn or perform an original task which too is acquired or developed through previous practice. Such practices or trials bring almost permanent change in the individual and transfer effects of such learnings facilitate in learning a task. For example, adequate knowledge of vocabulary, rules of grammar, previous habits of recitation, previous knowledge of a subject etc. facilitate in further structure of sentences, use of appropriate words and rules of grammar, rapid reading of books, higher level concepts of a subject etc. Thus, learning to learn serves as a base or foundation over which learning or acquisition of some skill depends and facilitates in acquiring a new skill. To put it another way, **learning to learn** provides convenience in further or future learning and thus, learning to learn is also a form of non-specific transfer effect in future learning.

It is important to remember here that the transfer effect of 'warming up' is of temporary nature while the effect of 'learning to learn' is relatively permanent.

Specific transfer

While learning something, it consists of a series of stimulus-response associations (S-R associations). Thus, learning involves a chain of discriminable stimuli, each of which has to be associated with a specific response. Specific transfer, therefore, means effect of learning of a task on the other task. The learning of one task may either facilitate the learning of another task or make it more difficult or may have no such effect. This kind of transfer effect depends upon similarity or dissimilarity between the initial learning task and the second task. The possible relationship between stimuli and responses are shown in **Table 11.5**.

TABLE 11.5 Transfer effect on the basis of stimulus-response similarities and differences

	Initial task	*Second task*	*Comments*	*Nature of transfer*
1.	SA-RA	SC-RD	Stimulus and response both are different	Zero effect
2.	SA-RA	SA-RA	Both are similar	Positive transfer
3.	SA-RA	SA-RD	Stimuli are similar but responses differ	Some amount of positive transfer may occur
4.	SA-RA	SC-RA	Stimulus is different but responses are similar	Positive transfer is obtained
5.	SA-RA	SA-RA	Both are similar but association pairs are interchanged	Negative transfer will occur

From Table 11.5, it is evident that five distinct possibilities of stimulus-stimulus (S-S) or stimulus-response (S-R) associations and the resultant transfer effects are possible. All such **transfer effects are specific because these effects are caused by certain specific factors that operate in forming S-S or S-R associations such as similarity in stimulus situation, response similarity, stimulus differences or response differences.** Due to operation of these factors, the transfer effect is either positive or negative and if none of these specific factors is operative, no transfer effect (zero effect) occurs.

Thus, specific transfer effect is an effect that can be attributed to some specific factor involved in learning tasks.

On the basis of several experimental studies, the following conclusions have been drawn about specific transfer.

(i) In the first situation, in both the learning conditions the stimuli and responses are different and hence, will have no transfer effect, *i.e.* zero transfer will occur.
(ii) In the second condition, in both the learning conditions, stimuli and responses are similar that causes positive transfer effect of the initial learning on learning of second task.
(iii) In the third condition, the stimulus situations in the two conditions of learning are similar but the response to the stimuli in the two conditions differs. Here due to stimulus similarity, some amount of positive transfer effect will occur.
(iv) In the fourth condition, stimulus situations are different but demand similar patterns of response. Hence, here again some amount of positive transfer will occur.
(v) In the fifth condition, the stimulus and response both are similar, however, S-R associations are altered. This will cause negative transfer effect of the initial learning on the learning of second task.

11.14.2 Bases of Transfer

The phenomenon of transfer occurs on account of the following factors:

Similarity of contents

Parts of old habits 'runoff' as a response to new situation more easily when the contents of the two stimulus situations with some minor modifications are the same. For example, suppose, a pupil learns about the national movement in his political science class. He again learns about the events of national movement in the history class. Since, the contents of the two class situations are the same, what has been learnt through lectures in the former is more amenable to be transferred to another. Similarly, one learns the alphabets QQSTNIPJFA. In another session, he is given to learn QSTNHPLAR. Here, the learning of the second series of alphabets will be easier because, most of the items are already learned in the former set. A person familiar with one card game finds it easier to learn other games. Many similar examples may be cited.

Similarity of technique

Most tasks or problems involve similar techniques to be followed in performing or solving a problem. Hence, techniques learned in one situation are transferred to another situation. For example, one learns a scientific approach to the problem in one subject and applies the same scientific procedure in the other fields is an example of transfer of technique. Likewise, if a student takes a course in formal logic and thereafter thinks more logically, test his thinking in terms of logic. The procedures of formal logic are transferred here.

Similarity of principle

Transfer of technique and principle are akin to each other. Roberts (1932) in his study found that the principles learned in one situation were applied in another situation and thus, the similarity of principle made new learning easier. Similarly Katona (1908) in a study of puzzle solving problem in human adults, showed that when subjects were taught the principle involved in solution of one kind of problem, they solved new problems also as this too involved the similar principles. On the other hand, those who did not learn the principle, failed to show such transfer.

Combination of all these

When the two tasks or problems are similar in contents, techniques and principles, the amount of transfer is supposed to be maximum. This has been shown in a number of studies involving motor as well as verbal learning situations. For example, **Judid** (1908) and **Harlow** (1949) observed that the combined similarities (contents, techniques and principles) favour transfer of previous experience more readily because these together organize in such a manner that induces a sort of **learning set**. Cues received from each elements of similarities are organized together and thus, give a more vivid picture of the intricacies involved in a situation and make the solution easier.

From the above descriptions, it is obvious that transfer of learning is an important phenomenon of learning event and thus, an important aspect of behaviour modification or learning behaviour.

SUMMARY

- The field or area of learning is not only pervasive but also varied and extensive. This has resulted in deep and innumerable studies done by scholars and hence, quite a large number of theories or principles could be formulated in this area.
- Thorndike, on the basis of his extensive experimental works on cats and rats, formulated S-R theory of learning emphasizing that in learning situations, an organism forms bond or association between a specific stimulus to a specific response through trial and error procedure. Hence, his theory is known as **connectionism**.
- The Gestalt psychologists proposed insight theory of learning and stated that what we learn is a pattern of the situation as a whole and the solution to the problem comes suddenly—insight.
- Hull being influenced by both—Watsonian S-R formulae and Woodworth's S-O-R formulae of behaviour proposed **drive reduction theory** or **reinforcement** theory of learning. In essence, he holds that learning is a drive reduction behaviour and emphasized various concepts of ${}_SH_R$. In equation form his theory is ${}_SE_R$ (reaction potential) $= {}_SH_R \times D \times V \times K$.
- Tolman distinguishes himself from Hull on the ground that Hull followed the associationist bent of mind in his theory whereas learning involves understanding (cognitive process). Hence, his theory is known as cognitive theory. He assumes learning as a means-end relationship and therefore learning is purposive in nature.
- Guthrie is a well-known neo-behaviourist with some distinction. He has emphasized the significance of reinforcement and motivations and has laid emphasis on temporal contiguity between stimulus and response. His theory is a single principled theory.
- Bandura and Wallers have recently described a new approach of learning, we call—**observational learning**. It is a sort of imitative learning. It is also called social learning because learning occurs in social contexts of interpersonal relations.
- There are various other kinds of cognitive learnings. One such type is known as latent learning which is not exhibited during the course of learning but is put to use when reinforcement is available.
- Skill learning is another kind of learning in which we acquire performance skills of a task by practice and exercise. Skill learning involves three phases—cognitive phase, associative phase and autonomous phase.

- We learn things in either ways—intentionally or incidentally. The former is called intent learning, while the latter is incidental learning. The examples of incidental learning are most commonly found in our daily life learning of various events.
- Verbal learning is learnt through the use of symbols—words, numbers, virtual cues etc.
- For experimental studies, we use mostly CVC or CCC trigrams as material for verbal learning.
- There are various ways of measuring verbal learning. These include—free recall, serial recall, prompting and anticipation and paired recall methods.
- There are various methods that are employed in learning. These are whole versus part, massed versus distributed, active versus passive methods of learning.
- Human learning is influenced by several factors. Chief among them is methods of learning, subjective factors such as motivation, age, intelligence, previous learning, anxiety states and preparedness for learning. In addition, nature of learning task and environment of learning are also associated with learning as important determinants.
- Transfer of training is an effect of earlier learning on new learning. Such transfer effects may be positive or negative.
- Transfer phenomenon is classified as generic or general (nonspecific) and specific transfer.
- Transfer of training based on similarity in content, similarity of technique, similarity of principle and combination of all these.

Part V

Memory Process

CHAPTER 12

Remembering and Forgetting

12.1 INTRODUCTION

In the preceding chapter, learning has been defined as relatively enduring change in behaviour due to practice or training or past experience. This implies that there must be some retention from trial to trial and after completion of learning trials, it is said that the process of learning has been completed. Obviously then, all learning implies retaining. If nothing is left from previous experience nothing would be learned.

Remembering and forgetting are common and practical eventual aspects of every human being. In our everyday life situations, we often use the term memory or remembering as we say—he is sharp in memory or his memory is poor, often I forget things, my memory is good etc. All these utterances mean that every human being has a system or mechanism in which life experiences are stored and he is able to use them as and when the occasion arises. Hence, the ability to use the stored information becomes the basis that signals about good or bad (poor) memory. If one is able to use past events in the present, we assume that memory is good. Conversely, the inability to use the past in the present is indicative of bad or weak memory (forgetting).

In fact memory is the centre of all our cognitive processes such as perceptions, thinking communication processes, language comprehension, problem solving, reasoning, decision-making etc. Memory also provides the sense of continuity in life because it establishes a link between past and present, it helps in aquiring one's identity as a person and it enables us to store a large amount of information. Such capacity of storing enables a man to remember large many things. However, with the lapse of time, we also forget. It so happens due to many factors and forgetting has effects—good and bad, both.

After learning, memory is second important aspect of human life. In absence of this mechanism, learning would be of no use to human beings. Memory is a higher level mental (cognitive) process. There are various organs of memory such as short term memory, long term memory, semantic memory, retrieval process etc. The present chapter is devoted to the description of all these various organs of memory and processing processes involved in memorizing an event, what is the nature of forgetting, the factors that cause forgetting and we shall also discuss the ways to improve our memory.

12.2 WHAT IS MEMORY?

Most of us usually think of memory as an event or act. But in fact, it is a mental process much as other processes. This is the reason, we prefer to call remembering rather than to remember.

The word memory derives its origin from Latin term 'memoria' which means historical account or remembrance. In this sense, 'memory' is remembering the past events or experiences. This refers to the fact that remembering is retaining the past events or experiences with or without awareness. Many of our learned acts are performed automatically, *i.e.* without being aware of what we are doing. This is especially true of motor activities. In these instances, there is memory but without awareness. This is to say that in such cases of memory, neural retentive activities do not involve symbolic processes and probably for this reason such memories are often referred to as **'biological memory'**.

Remembering is a process through which the earlier experiences are reintegrated or reestablished on the basis of some partial cues. This is called the process of recollection or reintegration. For example, one may reintegrate or recollect his own marriage day ceremony when something in the present reminds him, such as seeing a **barat**, hearing the orchestra sound etc. These reminders serve as stimuli (cue) for the total past experience of one's marriage which is revived.

'Reintegration' may also occur in retrieval of factual information. For example, when a student of history writes down the answer to questions on a historical event or a person describes the salient features of a tourist place he had once visited in the past. In all these instances of memories, the person recalls one or two isolated parts of the facts present in the form of cues that lead him to retrieve or search for more and more details of the information he had once acquired and this searching (or the process of retrieving) ultimately leads to **reintegration**.

Memory is usually measured in terms of either **recall** or **recognition**. These two are the indices of what we remember and what we have forgotten. Hence, the organs of remembering are (i) previous learning and (ii) retention. While the recall and recognitions are the indices of our retention. Thus these two are also the integral parts of memory.

Remembering is often measured in terms of relearning. The difference in the number of trials required for original learning and the number of trials required to relearn the same (if some part of the previous learning has been forgotten), gives an index of memory.

From the above description, it is evident that memory is a mental process which is basic to all our cognitive processes—thinking, problem solving, perceiving, imagining, decision-making abilities etc. Further, memory has three interrelated components. These are: **encoding**, of sensory input or stimulus information, **storage** or retention of encoded information and **retrieval** of information whenever required. It also includes the various indices of memory such as recall, recognition, reintegration, relearning etc. which provide evidence of memory.

12.3 INFORMATION PROCESSING MODEL OF MEMORY

Quite an increasing number of psychologists today view human beings (and also other animals) as **information processors**. Our brain is like a digital computer device that takes in information **process** it and then produces the **output**. This view is called 'information-processing view' of mental activity which stresses the flow of information from input to output. According to this view, we acquire information from external and internal environment (input), mental or cognitive activities select, transform and store the input (processing) and ultimately the person does a behaviour (output). Memory is an outcome of these information processes. A schematic representation of the information-process model is shown in **Figure 12.1**.

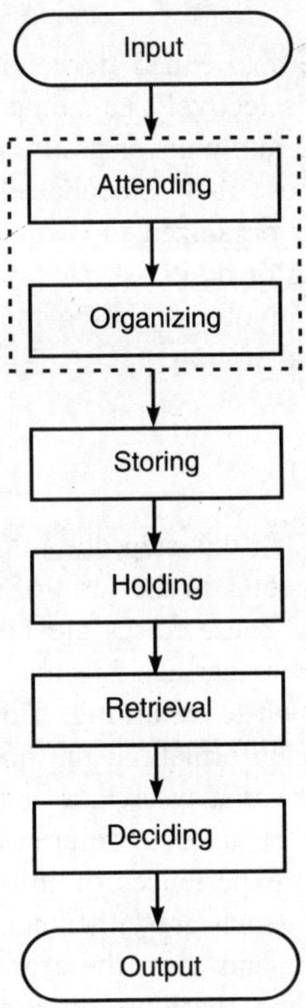

FIGURE 12.1 Schematic representation of information processing model.

12.3.1 Input

Input comes through the sensory channel from external and internal environment. Objects and events of the environment act on the sense organs (receptors) causing neural impulses which are conducted through sensory fibres to the concerned areas in the brain. This is **sensory input**—an undigested form of information about any behavioural event. Thus, it is obvious that the inputs are the sensory images of the stimuli which is the primary step in the process of memory. In this process, the information is represented in **coded** form. This coding occurs by a physiological process of neural activity called **transaction** and its product is called the **nerve impulse**.

This contains the entire characteristic feature of the information in coded form and hence, it is called **encoding**. The encoded messages of the information are in fact **electro-chemical energy** which travel through neural pathways and thus, pass on to the centre for processing. Therefore, it is known as central processor (CP), where the encoded information is processed and stored. Encoding is also used for rehearsing (i.e. practising and repeating) the input (information), organizing the input in groups or clusters and also relating it to the previously stored information. Thus, **encoding is an active process by which the information is put into memory**.

12.3.2 Attending and Organizing

Attending and organizing together are also called **perceiving**. Perceiving is interpretation of the encoded sensory input. This involves selectively attending to certain aspects of information and organizing or clustering the information into units or groups or fitting the information in a particular frame of reference; for example, suppose that someone tells you his phone number—23205314. This phone number can be grouped or organized in two ways—(2320), (5314) or (23) (20) (53) (14). The parentheses indicate grouping of digits.

The process of organizing also involves relating the information to the previously stored information, collating, interpretating and storing.

12.3.3 Storing and Holding

Storing of information is the third step. In this step, the information or some part of it is stored in the cerebral cortex in various memory stores in the form of some kind of neuro-physiological trace usually referred to as **memory traces**. These traces are hold or stored for sometimes depending upon the surface or elaborate levels of rehearsals. In other words, it is a process of laying down of memory traces. Thus, it is also known as **retaining**. This is most important aspect of memory because unless we hold in (retain) the information, the question of memory does not arise. We memorize the information or experience that we retain or that are stored in the memory system. Once an information is stored, it can be used in future as and when required. Students in the examination hall reproduce the learnt experiences or information which are retained or stored and fail to reproduce the information which are either not stored or poorly stored. Some of the encoded information is used only once and thus, these are stored or retained for a brief period only (temporarily) and after using it once, these are discarded. However, most of the information is important to be stored for longer period which is frequently used as and when required.

Storing of memory traces also depend upon prior organizing processes. Therefore, according to the model, learning may be regarded as an **organizing and storing process**. As a rule, more active and resourceful organization is, better is the final level of mastery (learning) followed by retention. In other words, **the better we learn the better becomes our memory**.

12.3.4 Retrieving

This is the fourth stage of memory processing. In this stage, a process of searching out (retrieving) the relevant information from memory store occurs. Thus, through the process of retrieving, the stored information is brought on the surface (consciousness). In this sense, it is a process of recovering the stored information from memory. It involves recalling and recognizing—a measure of retention. Suppose, you were in some other city during your early school age. Now you are pursuing your studies in a new city. One fine morning, you notice a man in your street and immediately recognize him as your bosom friend of your early school days from where you completed your study upto standard VII. Now you are pursuing some technical course after completing standard XII. But, you are able to recognize him even after a gap of over 6 years. You are also able to recall his name. This evidences that the past experiences of your friend's name and appearance were stored in your memory system and you are able to retrieve this information from your memory storage system that enabled you to bring the information into your consciousness which is reflected in recalling his name and recognizing his appearance as one of your bosom friends. Thus, **retrieving is a process of searching out the stored information from memory store to bring into consciousness for use**.

12.3.5 Deciding

The process of retrieving includes the mental process of decision-making or deciding. While we search out a particular poet of past experience from among a vast number of other sets of information or expriences, we also decide which of the stored information best fits the present available 'cue' of wanted information. This leads to correct recall or recognition. Similarly, decision-making behaviour is also found in other cognitive processes such as thinking, problem solving etc.

12.3.6 Output

This is the final behaviour which results from the above-stated stages of processing. Whatever we reproduce, or recall the past experiences are the **output**—the outcome of above-stated stages of central processing.

The above-described information processing model is a simple and general model. In the present times, different psychologists have presented **multiple memory system**. In this system, psychologists usually talk of 2 to 4 store chambers in the system. These store chambers differ mainly in the rate of decay (deterioration) of information. Here, **Atkinson** and **Shiffrin** (1971) model of memory is being presented. This is a **'stage model'** of memory and considered as most representative model of memory.

12.4 ATKINSON–SHIFFRIN MODEL OF MEMORY

According to **stage model** (Atkinson and Shiffrin, 1971), there are three memory stores with a buffer or central processor (CP). Each of the systems has different functions with respect to sensory inputs as shown in **Figure 12.2**.

Let us examine these three-stage memory systems separately.

12.4.1 Sensory Memory

Sensory input, *i.e.* the incoming information first enters the sensory memory (SM), where the

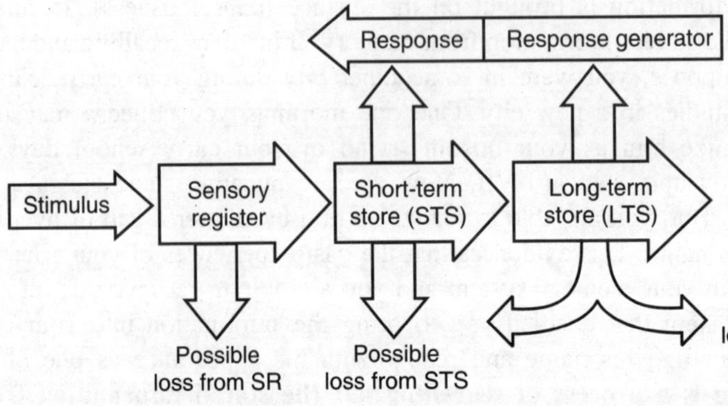

FIGURE 12.2 A version of the Atkinson–Shiffrin model of memory.

information is registered. Sensory memory has a large capacity. This level retains the unprocessed signal images of the physical energies received from sensory channel. Though, this system has a large capacity, but it is of very short duration, *i.e.* less than a second. This system registers information from each of the senses with reasonable accuracy. Often this system is referred to as sensory memories or sensory registers, because informations from all the senses are registered here as exact replica of the stimulus. For example, the transitory visual images (such as trail of light that stays after the bulb is switched off), flash of letters on the screen or a momentary auditory images of first spoken words etc. are retained in for a brief period (for a fraction of a second). These visual and auditory memories are also called **iconic memory*** and **echoic memory**† respectively. Let us describe these two types of memories briefly.

Iconic memory or visual sensory memory (VSM)

This kind of memory is most widely known as **pictorial memory**. When a visual stimulus impinges on retina, an image of the stimulus is formed which we call **retinal image**. This image persists on the retina for a fraction of seconds even after removal of the visual stimulus.

Visual sensory memory (VSM) is stored for a very brief time (approximately .30 of a second) only. This period of iconic or visual memory (VSM) is useful for **apparent motion** as we experience on a movie screen. This sensory lag also applies in the case of reading words or sentences where the letters and words get integrated within the period of sensory lag.

Echoic or auditory sensory memory (ASM)

This is widely known as **echoic memory**. It refers to persistence or lingering of sound impressions for sometimes even when the sound ceases. It does persist or linger on for a very brief period. It is the echoic memory that accounts for listening the sounds in organized form of words or sentences. The duration of echoic memory in sensory memory (SM) is approximately 2 to 3 seconds (longer than iconic memory). The sounds are stored in raw form. Its storage capacity is large.

---

* Iconic memory—brief retention of visual data.

† Echoic memory—brief retention of sound data.

12.4.2 Short-term Memory (STM)

This is the second level store of memory. It is limited in capacity and storage time. The central process (CP) controls the information processing. It selects some parts of ever-changing information in sensory memory (SM) and transfers the same to short-term memory (STM). STM is also called as **working memory** because it holds the information received from SM for a shorter period of time and further processing of the information takes place. It is an active system of memory because it constantly handles, combines and transforms the materials drawn from long-term memory (LTM) as well as sensory memory (SM). Since, information in STM lasts for a brief period only, it is usually known as **immediate memory chamber**. This means that the period of retaining information in this chamber is limited. However, the duration of its retention may be increased, provided the information is continuously rehearsed. But, if rehearsing is prevented on any account, the retention drops off rapidly. **Peterson** and **Peterson** (1959), **Murdock** (1961), **Hellyer** (1962) in their three different experiments have shown that the level of retention declines to a fairly low level within 15 to 17 seconds. However, whether such decay is caused by a spontaneous deterioration of memory traces or by interference from or displacement by new input, is not clear. But, some kind of interference does occur owing to which most of the part, particularly the unrehearsed portion of the information get lost.

The capacity or storage limit of STM is also limited. In experiments, it has been found that STM can hold a very small amount of information. Experiments on memory span for numbers have shown that the numerical span of memory (*e.g.* telephone number and similar other kinds of digits) of STM is roughly 7 ± 2.

Let us examine an example to understand how is information in STM processed? Suppose, you ask someone to listen a series of following digits and immediately recall the exposed (listened) digits. The digits are—194719501984. These digits are read out rapidly and the subject is required to recall them immediately after echoic exposure. Possibly, the subject may fail to recall the digits correctly because, informations reaching the sensory memory (SM) are very rapidly replaced by subsequent sound of other digits. This results in non-transference of the input into STM. But, when it is read out a bit slowly, the listener gets an opportunity to organize the material and mentally rehearse the digits. This results in transfer of the materials into STM. In short-term memory (STM), with the help of relevant information already stored in long-term memory (LTM), the listener is able to organize the materials into three units—1947, 1950, and 1984 and with the help of LTM, the listener is able to associate these three units of years with relevant historical events—1947 being the independence day, 1950 when India was declared as republican country, and 1984 when the iron lady Mrs. Indira Gandhi was assassinated. Owing to clustering of these 12 digits into three clusters and processing with the help of LTM to associate the clustered units with relevant historical events, it is possible to increase the capacity as well as remember (store) them for some longer duration.

In experimental studies, it has been found that in the absence of opportunities to rehearse, the materials in STM do not last for more than 18 seconds. Such rehearsal trials are called **'maintenance trials'** because rehearsing helps in maintaining the materials in STM for some longer duration. For example, suppose someone is asked to dial on mobile phone a particular number—9835331394. It is possible that this number may persist in STM till it is dialled. However, after dialling once, the number may be forgotten as it could not be rehearsed, *i.e.* no maintenance trial could be done.

Experimental studies have also shown that in STM, the sensory information is maintained in **acoustic codes**, i.e. in terms of sound codes. It has also been found that quite often, the items are retained in terms of **visual codes** or sometimes **semantic codes**. The **visual code** relates to how the items appear while **semantic code** refers to the meaning of the item.

The concept of working memory

In recent years, psychologists seem to hold that STM is not unitary rather it consists of many components. This is known as multi-component view of short-term memory (STM). **Baddeley** (1986) was the first to propose this view of STM. **Baddeley** holds that STM is not a passive chamber of storage rather it is a **workbench** that holds a wider variety of memory materials that are constantly handled, manipulated and transformed as people perform various cognitive tasks. This **workbench** is called **working memory**.

Working memory has three levels or components which are mentioned as below:

(i) The first component is **phonological loop** which holds a limited number of sounds and unless rehearsed, they decay within 2 seconds.
(ii) Second component is **visio-spatial sketch pad**. It stores visual and spatial information and like phonological loop, the capacity of this sketch pad too is limited.
(iii) The third component is called the **central executive**. It organizes information from phonological loop, visio-spatial sketch pad as well as from the long-term memory (LTM). Like a truê executive, it allocates attentional resources to be distributed to various informations needed to perform a given cognitive operation and monitors, plans, and controls behaviour.

Thus, STM is also an active memory chamber involved in processing of input to yield viable immediate memory. It also functions as doorstep to LTM.

12.4.3 Long-term Memory (LTM)

Some portion of materials that survive the capacity and duration limitations of short-term memory (STM) finally gets entry into the long-term memory (LTM). Experiments provide evidence to the fact that more often an item in STM is rehearsed or repeated, the more it is likely to be retained in LTM. Rehearsing perhaps increases the likelihood of organizing the information and relating it to prior existing other information in the LTM.

Unlike STM, the capacity of storing at LTM level is virtually unlimited and relatively permanent. Many of the materials remain stored in LTM lifelong. It has been found that many informations and experiences gathered during primary school stage also remain stored in LTM for a pretty longer duration. At the same time, it is also found that some of the remote past experiences decay in strength and are not readily available for retrieval especially for recalling and if recalled, these may not be always accurate or some of the informations are altered, some are condensed or shortened and some may include new additions at the time of recall.

The storage capacity of LTM is practically infinite. It has in its store various kinds of experiences, learnt abilities, memories of historical events, social interactional experiences, various kinds of scientific laws, principles, rules, various kinds of concepts, etc. For example, names and physical appearances of large number of persons, visual images of different places (where we had visited earlier), large number of vocabularies, scientific facts and concepts etc. all remain stored in LTM for pretty longer duration.

It has been shown that once any information enters the long term memory (LTM) store, it is never forgotten because it gets **encoded semantically**, *i.e.* in terms of their meaning that an information carries. What we experience as forgetting is in fact retrieval failure i.e. for various reasons we cannot retrieve the stored information. Retrieval related forgetting has been described later in this chapter.

So far we have discussed only the structural features of the **stage model**. Questions which still remain to be addressed are—how does information move from one store to another and by what mechanisms, it continues to stay in any particular memory store? Let us examine the answers to these questions.

How does information travel from one store to another? To answer this question, **Atkinson** and **Shiffrin** have proposed the notion of **control processes** that function to monitor the flow of information through various memory stores (SM, STM and LTM). As has been stated earlier, all informations which our senses receive are not registered. Only those informations which are attended to; enter into the STM from sensory memory (SM). Thus, the **selective attention** (see Section 9.9 of Chapter 9) is the first control process that decides what will travel from sensory memory (SM) to short-term memory (STM). The sense impressions which do not receive attention, fade out quickly. The STM then sets into motion another control process of **maintenance rehearsal** to retain the material for as much time as required. As is clear from its name, such rehearsals only maintain the information in the STM through repetition and when such repetitions are discontinued, the information is lost.

Another control process which operates in STM to expand its capacity, is **chunking**. Through chunking it is possible to expand the capacity of STM which otherwise is 7 ± 2. For example, the following digits may be chunked together as shown in the parenthesis—194719492004 (1947, 1949, 2004) and remember these digits by relating the years when India became an independent country, the year when Indian constitution was adopted and the year when the tsunami hit the coastal regions of India and South East Asian countries.

From the STM information moves to the long-term memory through **elaborative rehearsals.** In elaborative rehearsals, attempts are made to connect the **to be retained information** to the already existing information in the LTM. For example, to remember the meaning of the word **humanity** becomes easier when the meanings of concepts such as **compassion**, **truth**, and **benevolence** are already in place. The number of associations that we create around the new information determines its permanence. In elaborative rehearsals, we attempt to analyze the information in terms of various associations that it arouses. It involves organizations of **'input'** in as many ways as possible. The information can also be expanded in some kind of logical framework, it can be linked to similar memories or one can create mental images.

Waught and **Norman** (1965) hold the view that transfer from STM to LTM is a random process. So, through rehearsal and repetition, longer an item is in STM, the greater is its probability of getting into LTM.

In addition, reinforcement, emotional arousal, or motivational relevance of the information also affect the probability of information to be stored in LTM.

Experimental studies carried out to test the stage model of memory have produced mixed results. Some experiments evidence the fact that STM and LTM are the separate memory chambers while others doubt their separate distinctiveness.

As for the location of storage of encoded structures, in LTM, clinical and neurological investigations have suggested that the memory traces are stored in the hippocampi (hippocampus is a part of temporal lobe in each side of brain). This part is especially responsible for storage of verbal information (Miller 1970).

So far consolidation of encoded memory traces, evidences show that LTM requires time for storing information ranging from a few minutes to hours after completion of original learning or experience.

However, the question of location and form in which information stored in LTM is still not fully known. Researches are on and mounting evidences are likely to be obtained in years to come. The evidences available till date indicate that the information is encoded by several neural structures called memory traces and are widely distributed in cortical and subcortical structures.

Experimental evidences have also been obtained showing that in STM as well as in LTM, information can be encoded both acoustically as well as semantically. Earlier, it was believed that in STM information is encoded acoustically while in LTM, it is encoded semantically.

Shallace and **Warrington** (1970) have cited an example of a man that stand contrary to the stage model propositions. The man was known as KF who met with an accident and damaged the portion of the left side of cerebral hemisphere. Subsequently, it was found that his LTM was intact while STM was seriously affected. According to stage model, information moves to LTM via STM and if KF's STM was affected how can his LTM be normal? Several other studies have also shown that memory processes are similar irrespective of whether an information is retained temporarily or relatively permanently. Besides, memory process can be adequately understood without positioning into separate memory stores. All such evidences led to the development of **levels of processing model** of memory which is being described separately hereinbelow:

Levels of processing model

Psychologists have tried to describe and explain the nature of memory on the basis of computer system. Psychologists consider human beings and other animals as computer processor. Just like a computer, human beings also select, convert, classify or categorize and analyze information by specific processing. Through processing one organizes the information (input) and the inputs are processed to various systems of memory, retrieved and the outcome of all these processings is what we call memory. Thus, memory is a system of **information processing**. Psychologists have proposed various models of information processing. One such processing model is **stage model** which has been described above. In view of certain contrary evidences in respect of stage model. **Craik** and **Lockhart** (1972) have put forward another model which is known as the **level of processing model**.

In general, the information processing theories (models) of memory view memory process in terms of discrete stages each with its own characteristics. Further, information is transferred from one stage to another till some of it is finally stored in long-term memory (LTM). **Craik** and **Lockhart** in contrast to this general view have proposed a new model. They proposed that it is possible to analyze the **input** (incoming information) at more than one level. Following are the three levels of processing:

First level (shallowest): The first level of processing is shallowest. It is simply a sensory level of processing through which we merely become aware of the incoming information. It is the level in which input is registered into our sensory memory and the physical structural aspects of information are processed. For example, one might attend only to the shape of letters in a word say **'rat'** inspite of whether the word is written in capital or small letters or colour of the ink in which it is written. This is the first and superficial or shallowest level of processing.

Second level—intermediate (phonetic): Second level is intermediate level in which one might consider and attend to the phonetic sounds that are attached to the input, say the letters in the above example. In this second level, the structural features are transferred into at least one meaningful word—the word **rat** which has three specific letters.

Analysing information at these two levels produces fragile memory and therefore is likely to decay quickly.

Third level—deepest (semantic): The third level of processing is the deepest level. In order to ensure that the input is retained for a longer period, it is important that it gets analyzed and understood in terms of meaning that it carries. Therefore, it is called **semantic level of processing**. It this level, an elaborate knowledge or cognition of the stimulus situation is obtained such as what is the meaning of the stimulus? What are its example? What does it denote and connote? How does it relate to some specific object or subject and how does it differ from others etc. are some of the questions which arise and answers are tried to obtain. Analysis at the deepest level gives the best memory because **deeper is the processing, better is the consolidation of memory traces and deeper is the memory traces, lesser is the chance of decaying**.

It has been observed that when the meaning of input is related to one's own self, deepest level of processing occurs. For example, you read a biography which contains certain instances of events which resemble much with your (reader's) life events. Under the situation, the read biographical records are likely to be stored deeply because the described events are semantically processed in reference to one's own self. The consequent memory traces are deep enough which can hardly be decayed.

At this point, it is important to note that mere rehearsal trials at the first level (sensory or perpetual level) of processing is not enough. Rather, the quality of rehearsal is much more important. Rehearsal trials are of many types. However, two types of rehearsals are mostly used. These are **maintenance rehearsal** and **elaborate rehearsal**. The former is also known as type-I rehearsal while the latter one is called type-II rehearsal. Let us understand these two types with the help of an example. Suppose, you are told to dial a number 033-23205314 and pass on a particular message. The phone is kept in the next room. After getting the instruction, you go to the room to dial and convey the message. In the meanwhile, you keep on repeating (rehearsing) the telephone number. Thus, it remains live in your memory. You dial the number, and get the response and convey the message as instructed. After completion of the job, you forget the dialled number. This is the example of **maintenance or type one rehearsal** in which you kept on mentally rehearsing the instructed message and phone number till the completion of the job.

On the other hand, in **'elaborate rehearsal' (type two rehearsal)**, the input is analyzed in detail, *i.e.* one tries to analyze the input in terms of different kinds of associations that it arouses. In so doing, the information may be broken down into **chunks** and attempts are made to recognize them. For example, the mobile number 9835331394 may be broken down in several ways, such as (98353), (31394) or (98), (35), (33), (13), (94). These may also be associated with certain other numbers such as one's own car number, mobile numbers, bank account numbers or roll numbers of close classmates etc. Thus, **rehearsing the input by clustering them in groups or associating them with more familiar traces already in the LTM is called elaborate processing**. The inputs which are elaborately processed, relatively last longer in LTM.

12.5 TYPES OF LONG-TERM MEMORY

As we have seen while discussing **working memory**, it is obvious that STM is now being viewed as consisting of more than one component. In the same way, it is suggested that long-term memory (LTM) too is not unitary because it contains a wide variety of informations. In view of this, LTM is also viewed as consisting of various types. Psychologists have attempted to classify the various stored items of LTM into certain categories in several ways. However, the classification proposed by **Tulving** (1972) is quite comprehensive. According to him, there are three types of long-term memories—**episodic**, **semantic** and **procedural**. The episodic and semantic memories taken together are also called **declarative memory**. The salient features of these three types of LTM are described below:

12.5.1 Episodic Memory

In this type of memories, the personal experiences of the individual are stored. It is called **episodic** because it stores not only the experiences but also the relevant contextual references of the experiences. These contextual aspects or references include the temporal (e.g. references of time and date or days etc.), the spatial references (i.e. what, where and for whom the event concern). We can better understand the nature of episodic memory on the basis of some reminiscents as mentioned below:

(a) I remember, during my childhood, I very easily used to get sick.
(b) On the very first day of my college life, a teacher treated me with great love and affection. As a result, even today, I think very high of him and have great respect for him.
(c) I happened to meet a stranger in train yesterday. He looked very peculiar.
(d) The tragic scenes of 1975 flood is unforgettable.

From the above examples, it is obvious that the episodic memory contains the references of the contexts of previous experiences or events. It is called 'episodic' because they concern with the life episodes that had occurred during the past. It may also be called **autographic memory** because in this category of memory, personal life experiences of various events or episodes remain stored.

The episodic memories have certain important characteristics. One such characteristic is that such memories are affective (emotional) in nature. It has been observed that usually the pleasant and unpleasant kinds of life events are remembered for longer period than the neutral or non-emotional events. For example, the gallantry awards given to a soldier for his bravery shown in combats is hard to forget as it gives high sense of pleasure. Similarly, failures in examinations despite hard studies are unforgettable for a student and remain stored in his memory for long. Though, it is also true that we experience quite a large number of pleasure and displeasure but we do not remember all such experiences too long. Most of these events are forgotton in due course and only a few important ones are retained for long and retrieved easily.

Another important feature of episodic memory is that remote distant past events take relatively longer time to retrieve and recall.

Further, most of the events are recalled with certain modifications in the original text of the event. Thus, older past experiences are **reconstructed**. Hence, the reproduced contents are distorted and condensed. For this reason, the episodic memories are often considered as not much reliable or dependable.

12.5.2 Semantic Memory

Semantic means, meaning with connotations. Hence, it is not merely meaning rather more than that. In psychological terminology in the context of memory, it refers to organized set of acquired knowledge which we store in our memory system. Hence, semantic memory stores all kinds of knowledge held by a person in different forms. It is not merely a mental dictionary rather, it also invokes comprehension and understanding which are stored in units of concepts, facts, ideas, applicability of facts or concepts etc. Thus, semantic memory is organization of knowledge. Some of the examples of this type of memory are mentioned below:

(a) I know that the earth revolves on its axis and around the sun.
(b) I know that one billion is 1,000,000,000.
(c) I know that illusion is an unusual perception.
(d) I know that on multiplying any number with zero (0), the product will be zero (0).
(e) I know that the sun does not move.

Obviously, the semantic memory is different from episodic memory. It is not related to time and place. Further, semantic memory is not emotional in nature and such memories are relatively less forgotten. Semantic memory is also easily retrievable and recallable. Semantic memories are tested and measured in terms of testing one's general knowledge. For example, if you are asked—Are tigers carnivorous? Your answer to this question will exemplify your knowledge about carnivorous animals. If you know, your answer will be very quick as it is stored in your semantic memory.

In laboratory settings, psychologists use some special methods to measure semantic memory experimentally. Usually the following four types of methods are used frequently:

(a) **Laxical decisions:** In this method, a series of letters are presented and the subjects are asked to decide whether that is a word. Correctness of the answer and response time are noted. For example, the letter C, O, W, D, O, G, S, U, N, E, A, R, T, H, S, K, Y are presented one by one and the subject is asked to say whether these are words or no words.

(b) **Categorical tasks:** Words or pictures of different conceptual objects are presented and the subjects are required to say which belong to what kind of conceptual category. Such as pictures of apples, mangoes, carrots, little fingers, animals etc. are presented and asked to classify them into their relevant conceptual categories (fruits/vegetables/animals etc.).

(c) **Symbolic comparison:** In such tasks, subjects are required to decide about abstract properties in relative comparisons. For example, he may be asked to tell which one is greater heinous crime—murder or manslaughter? Which one is a greater disaster—drought or flood? Here again the response and response time is noted.

(d) **Sentence verification task:** In this method, the subjects are given sentences to check whether the sentences are true or false? Such as—'cow is a four-footed animal, it gives milk, has two horns, but cannot climb on trees'. The subject gives his/her response as true or false and response time is taken together that indicates semantic memory.

12.5.3 Procedural Memory

This type of memory refers to memorizing how things are done, *i.e.* the procedural steps involved in performing a task. Thus, it is more related to skill acquisition or experiences involving S-R associations and skill patterns. Generally, we recall procedural memories in the early phases of performing a skill-based task such as driving a car, operating a machine, working on computers, correcting faults in machines, building houses, writing, steps involved in solving mathematical problems etc. As the number of practice trials in performing a task increases, the skill becomes spontaneous or automatic. The stored sequence of various procedural steps of a skill are retrieved and put to use with very little effort.

A summary of comparative characteristics of sensory, short-term and long-term memories is presented in Table 12.1.

TABLE 12.1 A comparison of features of SM, STM and LTM

Characteristics	*Sensory memory (SM)*	*Short-term memory (STM)*	*Long-term memory (LTM)*
Duration	• Iconic—1/2 second • Echoic—2 seconds	20 Seconds	Life long
Capacity	Large	7 ± 2	Unlimited
Retrieval	Parallel search	Serial/exhaustive exploration	Parallel distributed search
Encoding	Sensory (visual and auditory)	Phonological or acoustic, visual, semantic	Semantic and sensory
Forgetting	Trace decay	Decay interference and displacement	Interference, decay and lack of cues

12.6 RETENTION

We have defined remembering as retention. Retention is storing or holding the information into memory stores in the form of a structure—we call **traces** or **memory traces**. These structures are neural etches (carved engrams). Thus, the output of remembering process **memory** is nothing but unearthing or retrieving of encoded information held in or retained in the form of memory traces in LTM.

Retention is a very important aspect of remembering because memory depends upon how much and how well (organized) the previous experiences are retained. For this reason, it is believed **the better we retain, better is our memory** and **poorer we retain, poorer is our memory**. Hence, remembering is what we retain.

12.6.1 Measurement of Retention

How much do we remember? The answer to this question would mean what we have retained. This can be known by employing some measures. Usually three principal methods are used. These are **recall**, **recognition** and **relearning** or **saving method.**

Recall or reproduction method

Recall means 'calling back again'. Thus, bringing into consciousness and producing the same in absence of the original material which one has learnt or experienced in the past is called **recall** or **reproduction**. In the process of recall, an individual revives his earlier experiences or original learning. In Chapter 10, various methods of recalling (e.g. free recall, serial recall, prompting and anticipation, paired associate) have been described, However, the nature of recall in the context of learning and memory differ. In the context of learning, materials are recalled immediately after each exposure. Hence, it called **immediate recall** which is a measure of learning process. But, in the context of memory, there is **delayed recall**, i.e. recall occurs after some interval of completion of original learning trial. The lapse of time that intervenes between completion of original learning and recall of the same is called **retention interval**. Thus, **delayed recall is a test of retention (or storage) of original learning while immediate recall is a test of learning.**

To test memory employing recall method, a model design of experiment is given in Table 12.2.

TABLE 12.2 Design to measure memory using recall method

Original learning (OL)	*Methods of learning*	*Criteria of learning*	*Retention interval*	*Test of retention*
A list of 12 CVC trigrams	Serial recall	Correct immediate recall of each item of original learning list in two consecutive trials in serial order of exposure	15 minutes	Serial recall of the originally learnt list of CVC trigrams

In the above design, immediate recall has been used for learning the original task while delayed recall has been used for testing retention (memory) after allowing 15 minutes of retention interval on completion of original learning (*i.e.* after reaching the criteria of learning determined by the experimenter).

Thus, the number of correct delayed recalled items would indicate the amount of retention and the amount of forgetting or poor retention.

Similar to recall, method of **reproduction** is also used to test memory explicitly. In reproduction method, subjects are required to reproduce the learnt material in written form (as is done in examination hall) or drawing a learnt design, solving mathematical problems by working out on the problem by reproducing the learnt solutions. Often, the term reproduction is used interchangeably with recall. However, the two subtly differ but roughly refer to the same process—recall as a measure of retention.

Recognition

Recognition refers to identification of the past images of familiar objects. In other words, it is a process of acknowledging our familiarities with persons, objects, events or situations. Correct recognition of familiar and unfamiliar object reflects the storage or retention of the past images and thus, measures memory (retention of visual images of the experienced objects). In this method, originally learnt or familiar materials are mixed with unfamiliar or unlearnt materials and subjects are asked to identify correctly (or sort out) the familiar ones from amongst the unfamiliar materials. In this way, the correct recognitions indicate the amount of memory. Recognition score is obtained by applying the following formulae:

$$\text{Recognition score} = \frac{R - W}{N_1 + N_2} \times 100$$

Here, R = number of correct recognition, W = number of incorrect or wrong recognition, N_1 = number of items in original learning or familiar objects, N_2 = number of unlearnt or unfamiliar materials. Number 100 is used to obtain the percentage score of recognition.

Correct recognition: Number of correct recognition as familiar and number of correct recognition as not familiar taken together gives the total number of correct recognition (R).

Incorrect or wrong recognition: Failure to recognize correctly as familiar and also the number of items recognized as familiar from the set of unfamiliar or unexperienced items taken together is the total number of wrong recognition (W).

Forced choice procedure of recognition

This is one of the varied forms of recognition. In this procedure, three times more than old (familiar) items are selected as unfamiliar set or items. In course of testing the recognition, the experimenter presents one old (familiar) item mixed with three new items (unfamiliar) and thus, the subject is forced to indicate the old item with which he is familiar. The total number of correctly recognized old item is the recognition score.

Relearning or saving method

In relearning method, the subject is required to relearn the task to the level of original learning. The difference in the number of trials required to achieve the criterion of learning in relearning from the number of trials taken in original learning, gives an indication of the extent of residue from the past. For example, if original learning required 30 trials to reach a certain level of proficiency and 10 trials in relearning, then 20 trials (or 66.67 of the original 30 trials) are saved in relearning and therefore it is also called **saving method**. The saving score is obtained by applying the following formulae:

$$\text{Saving score} = \frac{\text{Original trial} - \text{Relearning trial}}{\text{Original trial}} \times 100$$

Reconstruction method

Sometimes, psychologists also use reconstruction method. This method is more particularly used to test the memory of skill performance. Here, subject is tested for the reproduction of the order or arrangement of stimuli presented to him in a certain order or arranged in a certain manner—temporal or spatial. After the stimuli are presented, their original arrangement is disturbed. Subject is required to set them in the presented order. Subject's score will be the number of presentation needed to reproduce the correct order.

12.6.2 Some Implicit Measures of Memory

Psychologists have also evolved certain indirect or implicit measures of memory or retention. Indirect or implicit measures refer to such procedures in which 'S' is not consciously aware of retention being measured. Subjects are assigned certain tasks to perform and in course of performing the tasks, his memory is reflected indirectly or implicitly (without conscious awareness of the subject. Following are the two most widely used implicit measures:

Word completion test (WCT)

This kind of test involves incomplete words or fragmented words and subjects are required to complete the words by supplying the missing letters in between (for example M-r-o-). Such a word is completed by supplying or adding the necessary missing letters. If the subject is able to supply or add the necessary missing letter to make it a complete word, it would mean that the correct spelling of the word is stored in his memory. In this technique of testing, subject is free to add any letter that completes the fragmented letters into a word (*i.e.* a word that carries sense of meaning). For example, a fragmented word may be --T-AL. It can be completed in too ways—'RITUAL' or 'HUTUAL'. Thus, in such procedures, any set of letters may complete the word or any set of letters may be missing. If the subject completes the word by adding any set of letters, it would mean that the word he knows is stored in his memory.

Repetition priming task (RPT)

This kind of task uses the priming technique. We store many kinds of information that we cannot report verbally. For instance, information necessary to ride a bicycle or play a sitar. Besides, we also store information that we are not aware of which is described as implicit memory. In RPT method, subjects are shown a list of words such as garden, playground, house etc. and then they are shown parts of these words like gar, pla, ho etc. along with parts of other words they had not seen. Subjects complete the parts of seen words more quickly than parts of words they had not seen. When asked, they are often unaware of this and report that they have only guessed.

12.7 THE PROCESS OF RETRIEVAL IN MEMORY

In recent years, psychologists have adopted a cognitive view of memory, so that certain elements that act between **input** and **output** may be isolated. The cognitive view of memory divides memory into three stages—encoding, storage and retrieval.

Encoding implies transformation of sensory input into a form that can be processed by memory system. The encoded information is transferred into the memory store for **storage**. Finally, through the process of **retrieval** the memorized information is located when needed. These three stages can be linked to the filing system in an office. The boss in the office sends a message telephonically to his PA. The PA receives the message and encodes it into a typed document suitable for filing. The document then is stored in a file using date, the name of the sender or the subject of the message to determine where it is to be placed. When an information is needed at a later time, it must be retrieved by searching the files. Failure to remember would mean faulty encoding, failure to store or inability to retrieve.

Individuals are found so efficient in their ability to retrieve a word or name from memory that they usually become hardly aware of the processes involved. Sometimes we fail to retrieve an item immediately although we feel sure that it is in our memory. For example, one may not recall offhand the name of a friend or city. But, if he thinks for a while and tries out various possibilities, he would probably recall the name. Sometimes, the name suddenly comes long after one stops thinking. Events such as these evidence the fact that active search of memory store goes on even though one may not be consciously aware of the same.

12.7.1 Tip of the Tongue Phenomenon

Often we find a situation in which one feels certain that he knows a specific name, word, meaning etc. yet, he is unable to reproduce the same immediately. In other words, one feels the item lying just beneath awareness and hence, unable to recall immediately. This is called **tip of tongue (TOT)** phenomenon. The word or name seems to be on the tip of our tongue, but one feels unable to recall or express. Situation like this often makes one feel quite tormented until an active search reveals the correct word.

12.8 ORGANIZATION IN MEMORY

Memory is a system of storage. When we talk of memory, we mean long-term memory (LTM) which is a storehouse of innumerable experiences that happened yesterday, a day before yesterday and so on back to our earliest years of life. It contains or holds vast amount of information, events, knowledge, experiences etc. of the past. These materials are stored either as episodic or semantic or procedural forms of memory. If such a vast amount of contents are not stored in organized order or sequence, quick retrieval and subsequent recall of the stored contents would be difficult and would be indicative of poor memory. Hence, our long-term memory is not an untidy jumble of unrelated information rather, we store them in order. We organize, categorize and classify them in a number of ways. It is like a library with a good cross-indexing system. This indexing system includes concepts or categories, images, cognitive maps, schema and script. Let us examine briefly these various units in which experiences are organized and stored in LTM.

12.8.1 Concepts and Categories

The most important unit of representation of knowledge in LTM is a concept. **Concepts** are mental categories for objects and events, which are similar to each other in one or in more than one way.

Concepts once formed, get organized in categories—a category itself is a concept, but it also functions to organize similarities among other concepts based on common features. For example, the word 'mango' is a category because different varieties of mangoes can be subsumed within it and it is also a concept within the category of fruit.

Organization in terms of concepts and categories are arranged in hierarchical order. For example, we organize and form concepts of names of animals, vegetables and fruits in order. The various animals may be divided into several categories such as four-footed, reptiles, birds, insects, parasites etc. These categories are again divided into various categories. Similarly, vegetables are also divided into various categories in terms of inherent properties. Such organized categories and concepts enable us to retrieve them quickly. Suppose, you are asked to name five four-footed animals and you become immediately able to name cows, buffaloes, horses, elephants and tigers as belonging to four-footed category of animals. This is possible only because you had stored the names of these various animals organized into a particular conceptual category—**four-footed animals.**

The concepts and categories are often organized in hierarchical order ranging from subordinate to superordinate categories.

12.8.2 Schema

Schemas are the outline sketches of classificatory or categorization of objects. These are the units or pockets of categorizing and storing of knowledge or information. Therefore, schemas are pockets of information—a cognitive structure with network of associations that guide our behaviour. **Schemas** are used to classify or categorize our concepts of objects and experiences on the basis of certain dominant characteristics. For example, think of a schema of a drawing room. It will have different objects/things like a sofa set, centre table, paintings etc. which are found in a drawing room.

So far we have examined the concept as the basic end at which knowledge is represented in LTM and the notion of category and schema as the first level at which concepts are organized. Let us now look at a higher level of organization that concepts acquire in the long-term memory (LTM).

In the year 1969, **Allan Collins** and **Ross Quillian** published a landmark research paper in which they suggested that knowledge in long-term memory (LTM) is organized hierarchically and assumes a network structure. Elements of this structure are called **'nodes'**. Nodes are the concepts while connections between nodes are **labelled relationships** which indicate category membership or concept attributes. In order to verify the proposed network structure of long-term knowledge, the subjects of the experiments were asked to verify, the truth of the statements such as **canary is a bird or a canary is an animal**. Answer was in yes/no categories. These were generally class-inclusion statements in which the subject word was **canary** (perhaps we know, it is a bird) and the predicate took the form **is a**. A critical finding of such experiment was that as the predicate became hierarchically more remote from the subject in a sentence, the subjects took longer time to verify that it is true or false. Thus, subjects took longer time to verify that a canary is an animal than to the statement that canary is a bird because bird is an immediate subordinate category in which canary is subsumed while animal is a superordinate category which is more distant and remote from the concept **canary**. According to this view, we can store all knowledge at a certain level that **applies to all the members of a category without having to repeat that information at the lower levels in the hierarchy**. This ensures a high degree of **cognitive economy**. This means maximal efficient use of the capacity of long-term memory with minimum redundancy.

How the information in semantic memory is organized in logical hierarchies is shown in **Figure 12.3**.

Images

Memories are not only organized in the form of concepts or schemas. Knowledges are also represented or encoded in perceptual form in terms of images. An image is a concrete form of representation which directly conveys the perceptual attributes of an object. For example, if you come across the word **school**, an image of your own school is likely to be generated. In fact, almost all concrete objects or even concepts generate images and knowledge related to them is encoded both verbally as well as visually. Thus, informations or experiences acquired in the past are encoded **semantically** (in terms of verbal words) as well as **visual-spatial terms**. This is known as **dual coding hypothesis** originally proposed by **Paivio** (1965, 1971). The hypothesis suggests that concrete nouns and concrete objects related information are encoded and stored in the form of concrete images while abstract concepts related informations assume verbal and

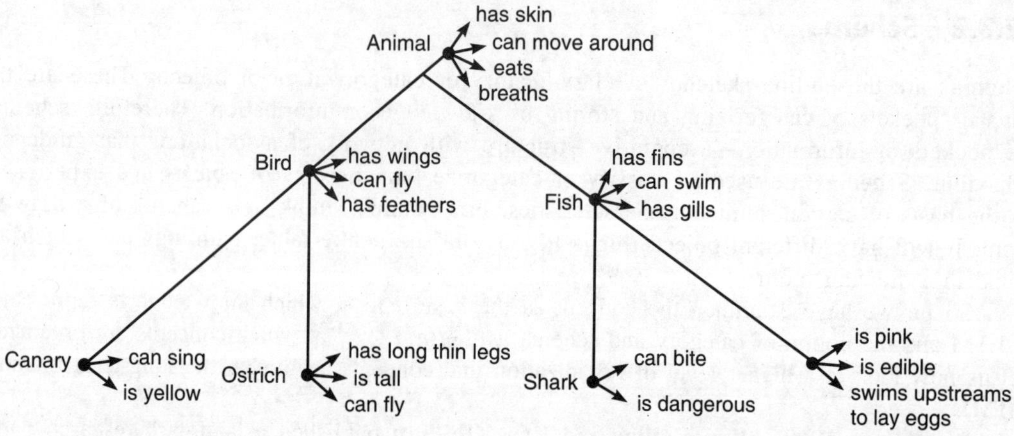

FIGURE 12.3 In semantic memory, information may be organized in logical hierarchies.

descriptive code. For example, if you are asked to describe a bird, the first thing that happens is that an image of a bird is generated and your descriptions about the bird bases on this image. On the other hand, the meanings of concepts like truth, justice, honesty etc. will have no accompanying images. Hence, any information that has been encoded are in the verbal as well as imagery form that enables us to recall with greater ease.

Basing on **dual code hypothesis**, children are made to learn alphabets by associating them with visual images of objects such as 'A for apple', 'B for ball', etc. with pictures of the objects along with the alphabets appearing on the pages of alphabets books.

Cognitive map

We all live in a spatial environment. The streets or roads through which we pass, the surrounding streets, crossings, other buildings, trees etc. exist all around us and we become familiar with them. All such informations or knowledges are encoded and stored in the form of images that leads to the development of **mental models**, *i.e.* **cognitive map** of spatial environment.

For example, suppose you are standing at a crossing in a city where you reside. A friend meets you and expresses his desire to let him know the location of your house as he intends to meet you a day after. While describing the location of your house you give him the house number and street name/number and also describe quite a good number of locational signs with map of roads, turnings, significant crossing, landmark signs, parks, trees, electric poles etc. These details represent the mental models or cognitive maps of the space which are stored in LTM and help in retrieving the exact location of your house with salient environmental structures. Such cognitive maps develop out of visual images as well as verbal descriptions.

Script

Script is also a special kind of schema (unit of organization) into which certain routine activities in sequential orders are organized. Such schematic arrangements are largely concerned with social interactional activities. For example, you have to attend a **reception party** of your friend. You have learnt certain **manners**, **etiquettes** of attending such social functions which are stored in your memory in a schema of script, i.e. sequential order of doing or performing behaviours such as, deciding to buy a worthy gift that fits well with the occasion and closeness of inter-relationship, going to the market to buy the gift, getting it packed nicely and subscribing your good wishes over the gift pack, dressing yourself smartly and then going to the ceremonial place meeting the couple and so on. All these sequences of activities to be performed are stored in the memory in an organized way under a schema which we call **script**. Thus, script is a schema of procedural activities and on getting a brief account of activities, it is possible to infer the detailed procedural sequences involved in performing a task such as, arranging marriage ceremonies, anniversaries etc.

In addition to ceremonial or social interactional activities, there are many routine tasks of daily life which require procedural organizations in script form. For example, assembling a bicycle, following road directions, preparing to cook an exotic dish from instructions given in cookery book. These scripts refer to the belief about the manner in which environment is structured. Such beliefs are formed with the help of concrete images as well as verbal descriptions.

12.9 TWO PIONEERING RESEARCH STUDIES DONE ON MEMORY

12.9.1 Herman Ebbinghaus' Study (1985)

A German psychologist **Herman Ebbinghaus** (1985) is considered as the father of modern experimental studies in the field of memory. He experimentally studied on memorizing verbal materials to know as to how associations between items are formed and retained. He hold the view that in memorizing meaningful materials, the effects of previous associations, meaningfulness and difficulties in preparing comparable verbal materials for comparative studies etc. are inherent. So, in order to avoid these difficulties and control the possible effects of inherent properties in meaningful verbal materials, he devised a new kind of verbal material for experimental studies. He prepared a long list of nonsense syllables usually consisting of three letters called CVC trigrams (combination of consonant-vowel-consonant letters, i.e. trigrams). These materials are free from possible errors of meaningful verbal items as these are nonsense syllables. However, it is better to call them CVC trigrams to avoid the effect of negative feelings of the subjects attached with pronouncing an experimental material as nonsense. Examples of CVC trigrams are CEF, LOZ, BAF etc. Using these materials in experiments (in which Ebbinghaus himself served as subject), he discovered some important factors that influence **rote memory**. He assumed that **memories are associative which are formed on the basis of contiguous presentation of verbal items**. In this context, he also described the phenomenon of **remote associations** which according to him, are weaker in strength. **Ebbinghaus** also studied the effects of time intervals using different units of intervals and plotted a **curve of forgetting** which is valid even today for explaining data obtained through experimental works on memory. The curve of forgetting is presented in **Figure 12.4** which shows that initially, forgetting is rapid, followed by a slow decline. On the basis of his extensive studies, he also came to the conclusion that forgetting is a **passive process** which is caused by lapse of time in an automatic manner. This means that **older the experiences, poorer is the memory**.

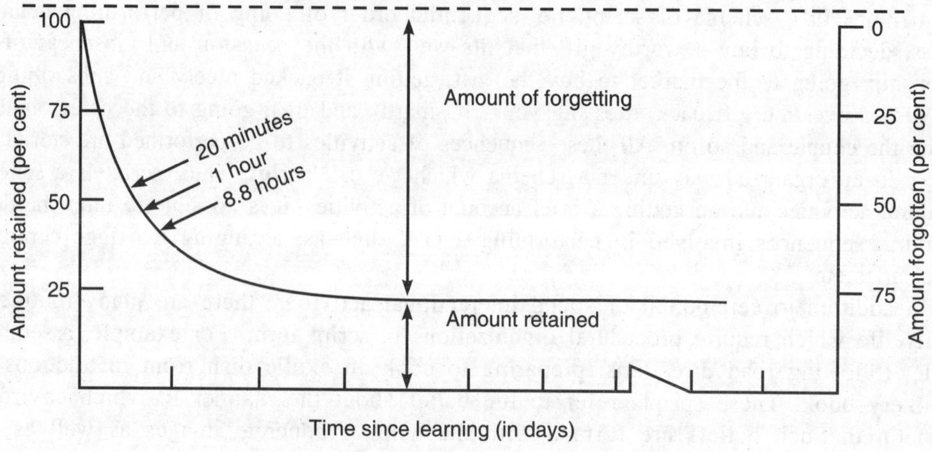

FIGURE 12.4 Ebbinghaus' curve of forgetting.

12.9.2 Fredrick Bartlett (1932)

Another pioneer study in the area of memory research was done by **Fredrick Bartlett** (1932), a British psychologist. He states that Ebbinghaus' study is unnatural because he has used verbal materials which were meaningless or the words which had meanings but had no relevance to daily life events with which we are mostly concerned. In our daily life situations, we learn descriptive events, experience the events described in stories, prose excerpts and extracts, poems etc. In course of memorizing and storing such materials, these are constructed and reconstructed. He used serial reproduction method to study how these materials are constructed and reconstructed. He narrated story of ghosts to the subjects and obtained several reproductions. On analysing the reproduced materials, he found that reproduced materials were not exact reproductions of the original text, rather were reconstructed. He concluded that memory in fact, is an active process of interpretation and reconstruction. Individuals store the information in coded form but in course of retrieval and subsequent reproduction, these codes undergo construction and reconstruction. As a result, many of the elements of the original text are omitted, some new elements are added, the original lessons are condensed or elaborated. Thus, the reproduced materials vary widely from the original one as the uncritical aspects are modified, *i.e.* the reproduced materials though contain the central meaning or ideas, their forms are changed from the original text. As such, the original text is presented in a new modified form.

The pioneering studies of Ebbinghaus and Bartlett have had significant impacts on experimental researches being done on memory. Their studies are in fact the founding pillars of experimental studies in the area of remembering and forgetting. Hence, the contributions of these two psychologists are highly valued by researchers even today.

12.10 CONSTRUCTION AND RECONSTRUCTION IN MEMORY

If we carefully examine the contentions held by **Ebbinghaus**, it would be evident that memory primarily consists of reproduction of stored materials. He and his followers have emphasized the quantity of information that can be stored in the memory and judged its accuracy by matching the contents of storage and reproduction. If the reproduced version of the stored material showed any deviation, it was seen as an error and a case of memory failure. This storage metaphor of memory implied that the memory was a passive occurrence of learnt material that has been transported to its long-term storehouse. This position was challenged by **Bartlett** in the early thirties who contended that memory is an active process and all that we have stored undergoe continuous change and modification. What we memorize is influenced by meanings we assign to the stimulus material and once it is committed to our memory system, it cannot remain in isolation from other cognitive processes. In essence, therefore, Bartlett saw memory as a constructive and not a reproductive process. Elaborating his views, he opines:

The sensory inputs (information) about the world around us are processed at deep level and then stored in long-term memory (LTM). Processing at deep level means **semantic** and **interpretative processing**. Interpretation is a constructive and reconstructive process. This process involves modifications in the original text of information. This modification occurs at the encoding stage of information and, therefore, what we retrieve at the time of recalling or reproducing is a modified form of the experienced event. For example, suppose you alongwith a friend witness a car accident that occurred while both of you were together at the accident sight. After sometimes, both of you come back to respective homes and narrate the incident to the family members. While narrating the incident, your friend says—'a speedy car hit another car causing grevious injury to the drivers of the two cars'. On the other hand, you describe the incident like this—'two cars collided with each other and both the driving persons sustained injuries'. Though, both of you witnessed the same incident but the descriptive details of the incident varies widely. Your friend made the incident a bit more serious and attributed it to speedy driving whereas you described the incident in simpler terms without any attributions. Thus, while encoding the input, the two individuals interpreted the event differently that accounts for differential versions of the incident. Hence, the event has been reconstructed on the basis of subjective factors of perceiving the event.

Take another example. Suppose, you read a short story with great interest. After having completed the reading, you write down the story in your own words, based on your memory. You keep your story safely. Next day, you again rewrite the same story and keep safe this second script also. Similarly you prepare a third script and subsequently the fourth script. Now you compare all these four scripts about the same story with one another. You will find wide variations in each of the successively produced version of the same story. In each reproductions, certain elements have been omitted while some new elements have been added. Thus, each reproduced version of the original story presents something new (novel in form, compactness, precision etc.). Hence, what we encode and store in LTM is not a **true print** of the original text rather a **modified form** which happens due to active process of construction and reconstruction. Therefore, **memory is not a passive rather a constructive and reconstructive process**. The process of **construction** occurs during encoding of the information, *i.e.* **to be remembered** information before it is stored in LTM. On the other hand, **reconstruction** is a process of modification of already stored input. But, the distinction between construction and reconstruction process is often **blurred** because, it often becomes difficult to say whether the modification of input occurred at encoding stage or later. Reconstruction is sometimes called **confabulation** which applies in the case of persons with memory disorders. Such persons store very little of information and try to fill the gaps during retrieval process.

The constructive and reconstructive processes of memory have certain essential features which are as follows:

12.10.1 Memory is Not a Passive Rather an Active Process

Memory is not passive. What we store in our LTM is interpretation of the events experienced by us. The experiences are given a semantic code in the form of schema or pocket. Thus, we retain the **semantic codes** and **visual spatial schema** which are not the exact true copy of the original text rather a modification of the experienced event. Therefore, memory is an active process of construction and reconstruction.

12.10.2 The Construction Occurs at the Time of Encoding the Experience before it is Stored in LTM

Modification of sensory input involves construction and reconstruction of the experienced event. Construction occurs during encoding before storage in LTM. How we encode the sensory input depends on several factors such as, the **context**, **mood**, **mental set** and the factors that affects **analysis** or **interpretation** of the experience. The aspects of encoding has been described in Chapter 6.

The process of reconstruction occurs during retrieval of the stored codes when we try to interpret the event and corresponding **visio-spatial images.**

12.10.3 Human Memory is an Active System

It is not only an organized system of concepts, images, cognitive map, schema and scripts but, it is also an **active system**. Therefore, while retrieving the event, the organizational interpretation is **transformed**. The order or sequence and form of reproduction depend upon the objective of retrieval. Besides, individual's interests, motivations, desires, contexts, etc. also influence and determine the nature and order of reproduction. This causes some inconsistencies between what has been experienced and what is being reproduced. As a result, the nature of original interpretative construction is transformed. Thus, it is evident that memory is an active process which involves distortions, constructions and reconstructions in the original text of past experiences.

12.10.4 Sensory Inputs are Perceptually Analysed and Interpreted before these Enter in LTM

These inputs enter the LTM after being analyzed and interpreted. Consequently, certain inputs may be considered as irrelevant and insignificant. Memory of such materials are weak and forgotten quickly. This is one of the reasons of forgetting. Whatever enters the LTM has to be integrated with the overall memory system. The incoherent elements do not have sense. Memory of such elements are poor and are, therefore, dropped (forgotten).

Thus, human memory is both—**constructive** and **reconstructive**.

12.11 SOME IMPORTANT PHENOMENA OF MEMORY

12.11.1 Eyewitness Memory

From practical point of view, eyewitness memory is considered important. In all kinds of criminal cases, the police and judiciary consider eyewitness memory as significant because conviction of criminals depends much on eyewitnesses. An eyewitness oathfully describes the crime events that had occurred in his presence and solemnly affirms his statement of the incident that it is exactly what he has witnessed. Therefore, the police and judiciary assume that eyewitness' account is true and reliable or dependable because the detailed account of the crime occurrence is stored in his memory which is being reproduced in the court. No doubt, normally the eyewitness account should be a true account of the event. But, since the memory is constructive and reconstructive, the possibilities of errors cannot outrightly be ruled out.

To test the accuracy of eyewitness, **Elizabeth Loftus** (1979) conducted a study.

Subjects were shown a short film of a car accident. Immediately after, the subjects were asked to describe what they had viewed? They were asked to provide an estimate of the speed of cars when collision occurred. The experimenter phrased some questions differently to two groups of subjects to fill out the questionnaire. Among the questions, three questions were critical as mentioned below:

(a) How fast were the cars going when they smashed into each other?
(b) How fast were the cars going when they hit each other?
(c) How fast were the cars going when they bumped each other?

It was found that the group of subjects who were given the **smashed** question estimated the speed of cars twice more than the estimate given by another group who were asked about **bumping together**. This experiment clearly shows the alterations or distortions in reporting the eyewitnessed events. In a subsequent experiment after a gap of one week with some additional questions an additional critical question was added—'Did you see broken glasses at the sight of the accident? (there was no broken glasses in the film). The smashed group again were twice as likely to report that they remembered seeing broken glasses as were those who had been given 'hit' question.

The experiment shows eyewitnessed events are misrepresented while retrieving and reporting. The probability of misrepresentation increases with lapse of time as has been evidenced in the above experiment in which, after a week the smashed group says twice more than hit group that they had seen broken glasses.

Though, eyewitness is considered important in legal matters and judiciary relies upon memories of eyewitnesses and eyewitness statements are also tested to determine the extent of objectivity in reporting the seen incident of criminal acts. However, since the nature of memory is constructive and reconstructive, the eyewitness accounts are likely to be misrepresented and possibilities of distortions exist. Therefore, it becomes an important point of considerations for the judiciary and police to examine the extent of accuracy and dependability on eyewitness' accounts.

12.11.2 Implicit Memory

Implicit memory refers to the memories about which the person is not aware. It is automatically retrieved. This fact has recently been revealed in studies on memory. The study indicates that individuals are often able to retrieve such events which are not in the conscious awareness of the individual. For example, a typist knows all the letters on the keyboard, but can hardly recall verbally the blank keys. However, while drawing the typing, his fingers presses only the correct keys as these keys are in his implicit memory. Similarly, if a person who has sustained brain injuries and are exposed to certain common words. On testing the recall of the exposed words, it is likely that he may not recall them. But, when they are given cues by exposing the letters with which the shown words are made, he is likely to recall the exposed words correctly.

Implicit memory though lies outside the boundary of conscious awareness, it influences our behaviour in important ways. The phenomenon of implicit memory is also found in normal individuals.

12.11.3 False or Illusory Memory Syndrome

It refers to a pattern of thoughts and actions which are distorted and mistaken form of memory. The person claims such memories as true which has previously been repressed. This is a sort of syndrome which arouse questions or doubts about the accuracy of the recollected memories in which the individual reports about the memories of early traumatic experiences. Owing to distortion, people not only report false memory but also believe them as complete. However, it does not mean that traumatic experiences are not repressed. The traumatic experiences do get repressed. However, one needs to be cautious in accepting the claim of repressed experiences and for this reason, psychotherapists use memory recovery techniques to sort out the illusory memories.

12.11.4 Autobiographical Memories

These are personal (subjective) memories as these are concerned with individual's own life events of the past. Such memories are not evenly distributed throughout our lives. Some periods of life produce more memories than others. For example, early childhood memories (upto first 4 to 5 years of life) are hardly retrievable and recallable. This is called **childhood amnesia**. However, our memories of later childhood years till adulthood increase perhaps because developments during these years give amazing experiences. The emotional experiences, novelty and importance of developmental events contribute in making these memories permanent. After the age of 30, new memories begin to decrease. During old age, we forget most of the past events and remember only the events of the recent past.

12.11.5 Flash Bulb Memories

These are memories of events that are very arousing or surprizing. Such memories are very detailed. They are like a photograph taken with an advanced model camera. You can push the button and after a minute you have a recreation of the scene. You can look at the photograph whenever you want. Flash bulb memories are like images frozen in memories and tied to particular places, dates and times. Perhaps people put in greater efforts in the formation of these memories and highlighting details might lead to deeper levels of processing as well as offer more cues for retrieval.

12.11.6 Inducing False Memories

False memory can be induced and implanted through imagination inflation. **Garry, Manning** and **Loftus** in the year 1996 carried out an experimental study to understand the features of false memory.

Initially, the experimenters presented a list of events before the subjects that could be supposed to have occurred in their lives. It was followed by experimental studies in three phases.

In the first phase of the experiment, the subjects rated the likelihood that each of these events actually occurred in their lives to the best of their childhood memories. Two weeks later, the subjects were again asked to imagine those events and visualize as if they actually occurred in their lives. For visualizing the events as actually occurring, the events that were initially rated as low likelihood of occurrence, were chosen in particular. It was the **second phase** of the experiment. Finally, in the third phase, the experimenters pretended that they had misplaced the event likelihood ratings which they had obtained during the first phase and therefore requested the subjects to respond to the list once again, *i.e.* re-rate the likelihood of occurrence of those events in their lives. It was found that the events which were rated low on likelihood during the first phase but were visualized and imagined as real in the second phase were now rated high. It was an interesting finding in which the subjects rated those events as actually occurred in their lives. Such findings clearly suggest that memory can be induced and implanted through imagination inflation. Such kind of finding provides useful insight into memory processes.

12.12 FORGETTING

Like memory or remembering, forgetting is also an important cognitive function of mind that influences our behaviour in a significant way. Forgetting refers to failure either to recall or to retain, i.e. it is a failure to revive the learnt or acquired information into present consciousness. Though, it is correct that our memory system has a very wide scope of retaining vast number of informations of various kinds for considerably longer period of time, it is also true that for certain reasons, it is not possible to keep on remembering each and every bit of information. We forget many of the acquired experiences or information. Many of these are forgotten because of infrequent use owing to which the memory traces lose their strength and become weak and gradually fade out. This causes forgetting. Sometimes, new information invades or intrudes causing displacement or superimposition over the older traces by the newer ones. Further, often we voluntarily forget some experiences which are unpleasant and cause distress. Thus, the past experiences do not always remain fresh. Therefore, forgetting is a common event of life.

As regards the nature of forgetting, there seems no agreement in the views held by different psychologists. There are at least four different ways in which the phenomenon of forgetting has been explained. These are called the theories of forgetting. These theories are described separately hereinbelow:

12.12.1 Decay or Disuse Theory

This theory is the outcome of extensive experimental work of Ebbinghaus (1885). This theory can be better understood with the help of a curve called **retention curve** or **forgetting curve**. A retention curve graphically shows the amount we remember as a function of passage of time (see **Figure 12.5**). In experimental studies, particularly in the memory of verbal materials, it has been found that as a function of time elapsed between learning and test of retention (i.e. retention interval) the memory traces stored in LTM undergo certain changes, *i.e.* some part of the total information is destroyed or forgotten.

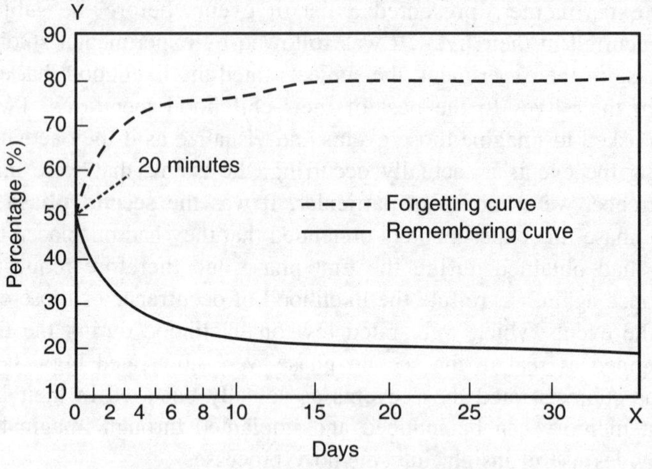

FIGURE 12.5 Ebbinghaus' forgetting curve.

The first attempt to measure and graphically represent the amount of retention was made by German psychologist **Ebbinghaus** (1885). He himself served as a subject and used the method of saving. He did many experiments on memory. In one of his experiments he memorized a list of nonsense syllables such as BEZ, XES, JEK, VAM, PUW etc. He waited for various lengths of retention intervals (RI) ranging from 20 minutes to 31 days and then relearned the same syllables. In this way, he was able to obtain saving scores for different intervals between original learning and relearning. Ebbinghaus' results are shown in **Figure 12.5**.

On the horizontal axis (0–X line) of the curve are the units of time representing learning. The number 0 (zero) represents the time of completing the original learning. The perpendicular (vertical) axis (0–Y line) represents the degree of retention in terms of percentage (evidenced by recall of the originally learnt items). This curve is known as Ebbinghaus' curve of forgetting.

The curve shows a rapid initial drop in retention followed by progressively smaller losses as the time passes. This fact indicates that the loss or fading out of retention is not at a steady rate. This fact has repeatedly been verified by Ebbinghaus (1885) and Cain and Willey (1939). This implies that as the retention interval increases the originally learnt material get consolidated due to implicit rehearsal as well as non-interference by any new information.

The Ebbinghaus' curve further shows that forgetting is a passive process which is caused by the time factor. **The longer the experiences, the poorer is the memory**. This hypothesis assumes that learning leaves a **trace** in the brain. This trace is a kind of physical change which was not present before learning. With the passage of time, the normal metabolic process of brain causes fading or decaying of the memory traces formed in course of learning. Consequently, the traces begin to disintegrate gradually which eventually lead to disappearance of the traces from memory stores. How does the lapse of time cause decaying of the retained material? Lapse of time causes disuse of past learning, *i.e.* after acquisition. If the learnt material is not kept in practice for long, the traces fade out due to lack of rehearsal. Besides, new learning experiences superimpose the older one. Thus, **older the experiences, poorer is the memory**.

However, although the above explanation seems plausible, no direct evidence supports the theory of decay due to disuse or mere lapse of time. In many instances, most of the earlier experiences or learnings are retained over a longer period of time even without intervening practice. For example, many of our motor skills such as swimming, driving, bicycling etc. are not forgotten, even though these skills are not kept in use for many years. Similarly, many of our verbal materials are also retained for longer duration. We may be able to recall quite accurately a poem we memorized during early school days, while we may be unable to recall or remember some parts learned during high school years. Here, the question is why the decay process did not operate on earlier experience (school days memory of the early school days poem) while it appears to operate on learning of later years which is relatively recent than the earlier one? These facts reveal that the unavailable memories are not necessarily **decayed** due to passage of time rather most forgettings occur due to the interfering effects of some new learnings that **interpolate** during interval or some **motivating factors** play a role.

12.12.2 Interference Theory

Some other psychologists such as **Pilzecker**, **Muller**, **Woodworth** and others maintain that forgetting is not a passive or effortless activity. It is rather an active process. These psychologists cite two kinds of evidences gathered in course of research.

These are as follows:

(i) What we do during retention interval (*i.e.* between the period of completion of original learning and test of retention) determines the course of forgetting; new learning may interfere with the previous learning. This is called **interference effect**. Such effects are of two types (a) **retroactive** and **proactive** inhibitions.

In **retroactive inhibition**, it is found that a new learning after original learning, interferes with the consolidation of the original learning traces. As such, if a learning is immediately followed by a new activity, forgetting is more greater as compared to the original learning followed by rest. This phenomenon can be easily demonstrated by doing an experiment as shown in **Table 12.3**.

TABLE 12.3 Comparative study of results of retention test

	Step I	Step II	Step III	
Conditions of experiment	*Original learning (OL)*	*Retention interval (10 minutes)*	*Test of retention*	
			Recall	*Relearning*
Control condition	List of CVC trigrams (List A)	Rest with time filling passive activity	List A	List A
		Rest for 5 minutes		
Experimental condition	List of CVC trigrams (List B)	Learning an interpolated task (List C) comparable to List B	List B	List B

A comparison of the results obtained in retention tests of the two conditions would show that forgetting is greater in experimental condition than in controlled condition. It so happens due to the interfering effects of the interpolated task during retention interval. The interpolation affects consolidation of original learning traces and the two responses come in competing situation and in most cases greater number of intrusions may be found.

In the same manner, prior learning also interferes with the later learning if no rest interval intervenes between the two learning activities. This is called **pro-active inhibition (PI)**. Here, the prior learning materials compete with learning material that follows and thus the prior learning traces are inhibited from being consolidated adequately. To demonstrate pro-active inhibition, the following experimental design, shown in **Table 12.4,** may be followed.

TABLE 12.4 Demonstrating pro-active inhibition

	Conditions of experiment	*Engagement*		*Test of retention*		
1	Controlled condition	Relaxation with time filling engagement	Original learning of List A	Retention interval 15 minutes	Recall List A	Relearning List A
			Interconditional rest for 5 minutes			
2	Experimental condition	Learning List C (Interpolated task)	Original learning of List B	–do–	List A	Relearning List A

Lower scores in the experimental condition as compared to controlled condition are taken as evidence that learning of List B is interfered pro-actively with learning of List 'C' that occurs prior to original learning of List B.

The phenomena of **retroactive** and **proactive** have variously been explained and accordingly, different researchers have put forward different views. These views explain as to how does the proactive or retroactive inhibitions cause interference to the consolidation of original learning materials. These views are known as theories of retro/proactive inhibitions.

It has in general been observed that the retroactive interfering effects are relatively more than the proactive interfering effects. Moreover, the effect of retroactive inhibition is minimal or almost nil if the time interval between original learning and interpolated learning is increased.

Theories of retro/proactive inhibitions

Retro or proactive inhibitions are in fact, negative transfer effects of the interpolated tasks (of the subsequent learning on the previous original learning or the previous task on the subsequent original learning). Such inhibiting effects cause interferences in the fixation or consolidation of original learning materials and thus cause suffering to their memories.

How and under what circumstances such interfering effects take place? To answer this, psychologists have proposed different theories which are given hereinbelow:

The anti-consolidation or perseveration: Anti-consolidation is just opposite of consolida-tion or fixation. According to this theory, the after-effects of the activity of learning persists even when learning trials have stopped. The persistence or perseveration of the after-effects or traces lead to their consolidation or stabilization and thus, the traces are fixated. Being stabilized, they are likely to be retained longer and better remembered. However, when the original learning is immediately followed by different kinds of learning activity (interpolated activity) then it creates obstruction in the process of stabilization. It destabilises the process of consolidation of the after-effects (traces) of the original learning. In other words, the interpolated learning materials function as anti-consolidation of the original learning traces or we may say, it prevents the consolidation of the original learning. Hence, the traces of the original learning are weakened and results in poor recall or loss of memory. This does not happen when original learning is followed by relaxation that permits the persistence and thereby consolidation of the original learning traces occurs.

The theory of perseveration is based on the fundamental principle of **mental inertia**. According to this principle, any nervous activity persists for sometimes even when the stimulus that has aroused the neural activity is removed. Technically, this is called **terminal lag** of a neural process. Such a phenomenon is evidenced from the occurrence of after-sensation. For example, if you keep looking at a stimulus, say a green patch and turn your eyes to a white surface, you may experience a dim patch of green on the white surface. This is called after-sensation which happens due to persistence of the effect of original sensation even when the same ceases. In this context, we should also understand the difference between **terminal lag** and **initial lag**. 'Initial lag' is also a neural process which is different from **terminal lag**. Initial lag refers to a neural process that takes some time to build up after the application of the stimulus. Experiments on response time (RT) presents an example of **initial lag** in which sometimes elapses between onset of a stimulus and responding to the stimulus.

This law of 'mental inertia' is also called the law of perseveration of mental energy. This fundamental law along with the assumptions about memory traces, supply the basis for anti-consolidation theory of RI in which RI is supposed to be caused due to obstructions by an interpolated activity that prevents or inhibits the consolidation of after-effects (traces) of original learning.

Response-competition or interference theory: **McGeoh** and his associates (1942) have proposed response-competition theory of retro/pro-active inhibition. It is also known as transfer theory. It is an extension of interference theory of forgetting discussed earlier. The theory assumes that when the learner recalls what he has learned earlier, his responses are interfered with by the responses that he acquires while engaging in the interpolated activity. Thus, a competition of response takes place that produces the failure in recall. This fact is evidenced in experiments on retroactive and proactive inhibitions where we notice a good number of intrusions of the interpolated learning materials in the recalled items of the original learning materials. McKinney and McGeoh (1935) in one study estimated approximately 25 per cent of the total retroaction might be due to overt intrusion and remainder presumably is attributable to implicit response competition.

Two-factor theory: **Melton** and **Irwin** (1940) and **Underwood** (1945) have combined the two theories—anti-consolidation or unlearning and response competition or interference theories and thus, it is referred to as two-factor theory. In fact, it is a modification of **transfer** (response competition) theory. According to this theory, the total interference is attributed to (a) competition between the original and interpolated response at the point of recall and (b) unlearning or anti-consolidation of the originally hold responses during interpolation. **Underwood** holds that unlearning of original response reduces the effectiveness with which it can compete at the time of recall. Hence, the total retroactive inhibition (RI) is due to the interference of the interpolated responses during attempted recall of the original materials and thus, it is still an interference theory of forgetting. This theory further makes it clear that proactive inhibition involves only the competition factor whereas retroactive inhibition includes unlearning as well as competition of response. Therefore, the magnitude of decrement for the same material should be more in RI than in PI.

Which of the above three theories is good, is difficult to answer. The reason is that none of the theories covers all aspects of forgetting such as inter and intra list similarities, reminiscence, motivated forgetting etc. However, abundant experimental evidences favour each theory in different contexts. Hence, no theory can be discarded.

12.12.3 Bartlett's View Regarding Remembering and Forgetting

Bartlett (1932) holds that the learned materials are vulnerable to change at two stages at the encoding stage and at the retrieval stage. Thus, **to be remembered** items are modified by construction and reconstruction processes. These two processes have already been discussed earlier in Section 12.9. At this moment, let us describe the methods that Bartlett employed to study the phenomenon of construction and reconstruction processes of memory.

Bartlett conducted an experiment in which a group of subjects were narrated a story—**The War of Ghosts**. Bartlett asked his subjects to recall the story and carefully marked the changes that come with time. He found and concluded that the entire personality of the individual—his emotions, his attitudes, his cultural frame of reference contribute to what he remembers.

Bartlett used three different methods to test how forgetting proceeds. These methods are mentioned hereinbelow:

Serial reproduction method: In serial reproduction, one subject narrates a story once or twice. Then he is asked to narrate it to another who in turn narrates it to still another and so on. In this way, changes introduced from one mouth to another, is marked.

Successive reproduction method: In this method, one subject is told the story once or twice. Then he is asked to reproduce the story several times successively at different time intervals. Hence, changes in the original story in successive reproductions are marked.

Single reproduction: In this method, more than one subject (matched in all respects) are used. All the subjects are told the original story once or twice and asked to reproduce the story separately only once. Changes introduced by different subjects in their single reproductions are compared.

In all the methods, it was found that though the central theme of the story was retained, a marked distortion of details occurred in the reproductions in different time intervals or from one mouth to another.

Similar distortions have been tested in figure drawings, spread of rumours, patterns of forms etc. Bartlett's study has further been supported by the studies of Wolf (1964), Allport (1930) and Gibson (1929).

Thus, according to Bartlett, recall is a reconstructive process in which most of the details of the original experiences are changed according to one's own personality and emotional reactions.

12.12.4 Motivated Forgetting

The essence of Bartlett's view was that the core of memory in lifelike situation is an emotional attitude which at the time of recall or reproduction, organize and transmute that which is recalled.

Rappaport (1942, 1943) has cited many examples of motivated forgetting such as selective forgetting commonly known as 'fugue'. This state involves loss of all memories that may bring back an individual into a pain-producing situation. He forgets his name, his address, his associates and so on. Everyday forgettings such as forgetting of a particular name, place, motivated slips of pen and tongue, accidental breaking of unwanted gifts etc. also richly substantiate motivated forgettings as has been observed by **Sigmund Freud** (1914). In all such instances, forgetting is neither caused by loss of memory traces in a passive manner due to lapse of time nor by any kind of interference by an interpolated activity rather by an unconscious motive or will to forget.

Repression is the core concept in Freudian theory. Repression is pushing back into unconscious, all the ideas and behaviours that produce ego anxiety. Accordingly, the memories of such events which may cause ego anxiety are repressed and hence, these events are forgotten. Otherwise these may activate guilt or cause anxiety.

Freud calls all such forgettings as repressed memories in which the traumatic experiences are repressed into the unconscious because such experience hurts a person. As such, these repressed experiences are not available for retrieval from memory. The painful, threatening and embarrassing memories are held out of consciousness.

In some persons, traumatic experiences may give rise to **psychological amnesia**. Some experience crisis, and are utterly incapable of coping with such events. They close their eyes, ears and mind to such harsh realities of life and take **mental flight** from them. This state results in highly generalized amnesia which often is reflected in a kind of disorder known as **fugue**. The person forgets his personal identity and assumes a new identity—name, address etc. Such persons often reflect double independent personality.

Forgetfulness or loss of memory under stress and heightened state of anxiety is not uncommon. Many of us aspire and work hard to achieve our determined goal. But, often we meet with frustrations and become extremely nervous or disturbed. Situations like this may cause forgetting.

Thus, the motivated forgetting theory stresses on repression of experiences more particularly the painful or distressful experiences. Hence, forgetting is not loss of memory rather is repression of memory.

12.12.5 Reminiscence

Reminiscence is an antithesis of forgetting refers to a continued increase in skill after practice ceases. It occurs occasionally when learning is partial. This phenomenon has been observed in various kinds of learning including verbal learning (McClelland, 1943), pursuit motor learning (Leavitt, 1945) and mirror tracing experiments (Snoddy, 1935). Reminiscence phenomenon has also been observed in children's learning of geometrical designs but only after a minimum delay of 4 hours from practice. In this case, more reminiscence was found among duller children (Lele, Bhatt and Patel, 1956).

Reminiscence in fact, means a temporary improvement in performance without practice appearing over short intervals between 2 and 5 minutes. This is known as **Ward-Hovland Phenomenon** (1937, 1938). Another phenomenon known as **Ballard Williams** (1913, 1928) **phenomenon**. The main difference between the two is that in the latter case, the improvement in performance appears at much longer interval as great as 2 or more days.

The gross fact is that reminiscence refers to continued improvement in performance which is caused by improvement carried over from trial to trial—a sort of facilitating effects of the preceding trial. Hence, performance in trial number 4 is better than in trial number 3, trial 8 is better than trial 7 and so on. This obviously means that some facilitating effect is carried over from trial to trial. Experimentation on this phenomenon aims at plotting the temporal course of the facilitating effect and to determine the interval at which it is maximum.

The possible cause for such objective facts of improvement may be simple positive growth (Snoddy, 1935), dissipation of inhibition during rest (Hull et al., 1940), differential weakening of remote association (McGeoh, 1942), consolidation of memory traces (Muller and Pilzecker, 1900), or recovery from performance decrement (McClelland, 1942).

The degree of reminiscence depends upon many factors such as meaningfulness of the material, determination to recall, degree of mastery and length of time involved. Usually the degree of reminiscence is greater with meaningful material. Individuals who show greater efforts to recall show greater reminiscence. Martin (1940) and Boxton (1943) have observed that the degree of reminiscence increases up to a certain point of mastery beyond which there is no improvement. Leavitt (1945) observed that fast learners show more reminiscence over longer intervals.

Thus, 'reminiscence as a phenomenon refers to improvement in performance as evidenced by some measure of ability to recall at some time after the original practice without any intervening practice'—an antithesis of forgetting that strengthens retention in place of weakening due to lack of practice.

12.13 CAUSES OF FORGETTING

Remembering or forgetting is a matter of strength of learning, strength of retention and factors operative in retrieving the stored materials to reproduce or recall the stored materials from memory system. Hence, the major causes of forgetting can be classified under three major heads:

12.13.1 Factors Relating to Poor Learning

Generally, it is believed that better we learn, better will be our memory and conversely, poorer is the learning, poorer is our memory. Thus, it is clear that learning and memory are inseparable units and, therefore, memory depends upon how better or poor we learn and acquire various experiences.

There are several factors which influence the strength of learning such as:

Meaningfulness of the learning materials

It is our everyday experience that memory of meaningful materials is better than meaningless materials. It is so because, meaningful materials are easily associated and are better organized. Comparison of **Ebbinghaus** (1985) and **Bartlett's** (1932) experimental works lend support to this notion. **Ebbinghaus** used nonsense syllables that make no 'sense'. Consequently, as his curve of forgetting shows, after an interval of 20 minutes only, 41.8% materials were forgotten and as the interval time increased the amount of forgetting too steadily increased to 78% by the 31st day. On the other hand, **Bartlett** used meaningful materials in which no such steep fall in memory could be found.

Lyon (1914), in his experiment, gave to a group of subjects, 4 different types of materials to learn and memorize. The material included 200 nonsense syllables, 200 single digits, 200 meaningful words taken from a prose and 200 meaningful words taken from a poem. The procedure was to compare the rates of learning for equal amounts of materials with varying degrees of meaningfulness. The findings indicated that with decreasing degrees of meaningfulness, more and more trials were needed to learn and memory for meaningless material (nonsense syllables and digits) was poorer as compared to words taken from prose and poem. Similarly, Kingsley and Carry (1957), Sheffield (1946a–1946b), Doweling and Braun (1957), Carroll and Bruke (1965) and others also show that retention for meaningful is organized materials is easier than meaningless materials. Such findings can be linked to popular notion—**it is much easier to learn 'sense' than 'nonsense'**. Similarly, **'it is much easier to retain sense than nonsense'**. The reason for poor memory for nonsense materials is that it is never learned well (Underwood, 1964). So, the traces formed for being retained are relatively less vivid and hence, not well retained.

Degree of learning

It is a very common presumption that more complete mastery of the original material lead to better memory. **Krueger** (1929) in a very early experimental study made his subjects to learn list of single syllable/nouns to three different degrees—100 per cent learning, 150 per cent learning and 200 per cent learning. 100 per cent learning meant learning of the material up to the criterion of single correct reproduction. This is simple learning. 150 per cent learning meant that the subject overlearnt the material for half again as many trials needed for simple 100 per cent learning. 200 per cent learning meant overlearning twice more the trials needed for simple 100 per cent learning. The results showed that the amount of retention depended upon the amount of overlearning. The amount of difference between 100 per cent and 150 per cent learning was greater than the difference between 150 per cent and 200 per cent. This proves that overlearning beyond moderate level is not much effective because, beyond moderate degree of overlearning, a point of diminishing return is reached. Thus, for good retention, there is probably an optimum level or degree of overlearning and this optimum degree depends upon the nature of learning task as well as learner's ability.

Learning methods

There are several ways of learning such as massed vs spaced learning, whole vs part learning, active vs passive learning, learning with understanding or simply rote learning etc. These methods have been described in Chapter 11.

Other factors relating to learning

There are some other factors of learning such as the difficulty level of learning task, amount of learning material, environment of learning, motivational determinants, mental states of the learner etc. All these factors contribute in a significant way—how well the material is organized and learnt. A well-organized material is likely to be better retained than poorly organized materials and consequently, the memory is also influenced accordingly.

12.13.2 Factors Relating to Retention or Encoding Errors

Retention takes place between learning and recall. During this period, *i.e.* retention intervals, certain factors operate in the process of consolidation of learned materials. Such factors influence encoding processes.

As information flows in from the senses, much of it is lost in the sensory memory (SM) itself within a fraction of a second. It so happens because immediately following information displaces the earlier one. Hence, they are lost in less than a second before being further processed and encoded in short-term memory (STM). Even the materials that survive longer to move into STM, are subjected to distortion under the influence of interfering effects of another competing materials or sometimes due to misleading influence of long term-memory (LTM).

Interfering effects

Interfering effects have already been described in Section 12.12.2 of this Chapter-which occur either in retroactive or proactive directions. These interferences may be due to either anticonsolidation (perseverance) or response competitions or the two factors may jointly operate and exert negative influences in getting the original experiences retained better. Interfering effects have extensively been studied by many psychologists such as Dallenbach (1924), Woodworth (1938), McGeoh (1942), Foster and Crowley (1948), Irwin (1948) and others.

Waking vs sleeping

From perusal of interfering theory, it is plausible to think that forgetting is a matter of how the retention interval is spent? Accordingly, if the interval following original learning is spent in ordinary waking activities, there is usually more forgetting than if the retention interval is spent in relaxation like sleeping. Ormer (1932) has found that during waking state, other activities (even if these are unrelated to original learning) disrupt consolidation of the memory traces, while during sleep, the engrams carved by original learning get consolidated more easily as the same is not easily disrupted by any other activity.

The interference in retention or consolidation of encoded information is often referred to forgetting after encoding.

12.13.3 Retrieval Related Forgetting

Forgetting is indicated when we fail to recall or reproduce the past learning. This implies that certain factors interfere with retrieval and subsequent reproduction. Among such factors are blocking by memorization of similar material, lack of intention to retrieve and recall, wrong mental set, non-availability or insufficiency of available retrieval cues etc.

Retrieval of similar material

Often we encounter situations in which memorizing similar materials interfere with the recall of desired material. For example, suppose you are trying to recall the names of an author of a book whose name is 'Braun' but you are unable to recall it accurately. While retrieving, you are memorizing some similar name such as Crown, Broadbent, Bruce etc. Owing to some similarity in phonetic sounds of these names, correct recall is hampered.

Lack of intention

Lack of intention to recall also interferes with correct retrieving and recall. For example, Bower (1981) in his study found that the mood, emotional states and motivation at the time of learning and recall provide a good cue in the retrieval process. Thus, lack of proper mood, intention and emotional states affect retrieval and subsequent recall.

Non-availability of right cues

Retrieval depends upon right cues which help in bringing back the early learning experiences into consciousness. This fact has been studied more recently by Rovee-Collier et al. (1989) and accordingly conclude that some forgettings are cue dependent. Therefore, if the cues used to encode material are either not available or are not vivid or are insufficient during retrieval, memory is likely to suffer.

Some additional factors

In addition, some more factors such as prolonged illness, injury to brain, shock amnesia, wrong mental set, fatigue etc. also incapacitate a person from retrieving previous learning. Consequently, memory suffers.

Thus, we find that forgetting is caused by multitude of factors that influence either proper learning, encoding or cause failure to retrieve the stored materials.

12.14 DO MEMORY TRACES FADE OUT COMPLETELY?

While discussing the theories of forgetting, we have considered the 'decay theory', 'interference theory' and 'motivated forgetting' which have different implications in formulating the hypothesis as to whether memory traces fade out completely or whether memories are permanent? The 'decay theory' emphasizes physical erosion or loss of memory with passage of time. The motivated forgetting notion suggests that the information is permanently stored, but certain emotionally toned events make it inaccessible to retrieve because these are repressed or pushed back to unconscious state of mind. The interference theory can be interpreted as supporting the either position. The interfering elements can either destroy the traces or prevent the same from retrieval, keeping the traces intact. Hence, there are two basic approaches—one favouring the loss of memory, another approach believes forgetting due to inability to retrieve the information codes. The former approach is said to be **trace dependent approach** while the latter approach is said to be **cue dependent approach** (Tulving and Madigan, 1970). Trace dependent forgetting is caused by actual loss or decay of memory traces. In cue dependent forgetting, the informations remain stored, but the cue that allows retrieval is lacking. Cue dependent forgetting is most obvious in the instances of 'tip of the tongue' phenomenon (see Section 12.7) when a cue suddenly permits access to recall what was previously not recalled. Further, instances of cue dependent forgettings are also seen in psycho-analytic sessions from interpretations of free association ideas, dream interpretation, hypnosis and other sources employed in diagnosing the abnormal cases.

However, in some situations failure to recall represents a combination of both—the trace dependent as well as cue dependent forgettings. At the moment, we have no conclusive answer to the question whether some memories are permanent?

Our everyday experience provides strong evidence to suggest that memory traces are permanently carved in our brains. Sometimes we find ourselves amazed when we recall most of such details of an event which we had never thought possible. The recovery of childhood memories under hypnosis, sudden revival of images experienced in remote past years etc. are some of the examples of permanent nature of memories.

Some startling evidences have come from direct electrical stimulation of the brain of epileptic patients, undergoing surgery. The surgeon, while performing surgery, carefully maps the surrounding area by electrical stimulation (under local anaesthesia). In this procedure, the patient is conscious and can describe the sensations he experiences during electrical stimulation. Under the condition, vivid memories can be elicited. The patient reports a sudden flash of some previous event complete with all the sensations experienced on that earlier occasion. These experiences appear to be real events from the past.

Interestingly enough, surgical removal of the area from which recollection has been evoked does not destroy the individual's memory of that event. Perhaps the information has been stored in multiple representation (various copies of remembered events). Therefore, removal of a certain brain tissue destroys simply one copy while other copies remain intact. Or, the memory event is stored elsewhere in the brain and electrically stimulated area activates the remote location only.

Though, electrical stimulation provides strong evidence in support of the hypothesis that memories are permanent, however, some more authenticated evidences are needed and till then the controversy would remain unresolved.

12.15 MEMORY SPAN

Span of memory refers to the amount of materials that an individual can recall from his memory store usually from his sensory memory. This amount varies depending upon the nature of material and also upon individual's own characteristics. However, the experimenters have tried vigorously to determine an average level for different kinds of materials—digits, letters, words, complexities of materials etc.

Miller (1956) of Harvard University discussed his personal problem with a clinical psychologists. His 'problem' was that he had the feeling that number was following him. He outlined some substantial and serious research on immediate memory using words, numbers, letters etc. He found that subjects remembered between 5 and 9 when tested immediately. The average comes to 7 ± 2 which he called the 'magic number' as it resembled closely to 'seven wonders', 'seven seas', 'seven deadly sins' and so forth. However, Miller seems to have either misunderstood or misestimated the span limit.

Usually, span of memory is determined by recall or recognition output of verbal tasks in a single presentation for a very brief period (1/10th of a second). The span for average college students is 7 to 8. On oral presentation, however, it may go up to 9 to 10. For this reason, perhaps the telephone numbers in large cities have 7 to 8 digits. The span for letters is slightly less than numbers.

Experiments done on this topic have revealed certain important facts. One such fact is when the amount of material greater than span of memory is given to a subject to learn, the total length of learning time as well as per unit average time has been found to increase. But, this increase is limited to a point of difficulty in material. Beyond that increase difficulty level has little effect unless the material is lengthened considerably (Shurrager 1940). Thus, for shorter lists, increase in difficulty is disproportionately greater than the increase in length while opposite is the case when the list is longer.

Similarly, differences in nature of material such as, meaningfulness and meaninglessness, words vs digits, instructions as to what to learn (only the essential ideas or the entire text) etc. also influence our memory span significantly.

Thus, it is clear that though our memory span is limited, it depends on several factors associated with the material.

In addition, memory span is also a matter of subjective or personal characteristics. There are individuals whose span of memory for certain types of materials such as digits, words, letters, geometrical figures, symbols etc. is tremendously long enough. Some of the important subjective factors are intellectual abilities, power of concentration, age, sex, aptitude etc.

12.16 AMNESIA

Amnesia is a very common word of everyday usage. It refers to partial or complete loss of memory. It may involve dysfunctioning of memory system either at the encoding level, storage or retrieval. Its severity varies from individual to individual. Individual differences in post-treatment recovery is also noticed. Some recover from amnesia partially while others recover fully. But, some patients do not respond to the treatment at all. Some of the major types of **amnesia** are discussed below:

12.16.1 Transient Amnesia

It is a transient state of loss of capacity to retrieve the stored information due to several factors such as exposure to carbon monoxide poisoning emitted from automobile exhaust, epileptic fits, effects of electroconvulsive therapy (ECT), hypoglycaemia (a decreased level of glucose in blood), internal injury to brain, emotional traumatic experiences etc.

12.16.2 Organic Amnesia

This kind of amnesia usually results from neurological damages caused by accidental injuries or brain tumours. Tumours when grow beyond certain limit, cause loss of memory profoundly. It is often termed as **global amnesia** because it causes massive loss of memory. Further, in certain cases, brain surgery also has been found resulting in amnesia (loss of memory).

Organic amnesias are of different types. These vary in terms of time of onset as well as manifested symptoms. For example, brain injury received during the childhood may be mani-fested during the adolescence or adulthood stage.

Neuropsychologists usually classify organic amnesia in two types as mentioned below:

Retrograde amnesia

Retrograde amnesia refers to the impairment of memory for past events, *i.e.* the experiences which were stored prior to sustaining injury. In such cases, present encoding is not impaired rather, whatever could be encoded and stored prior to injury are impaired. Such cases of memory loss may range from recent past to remote past events. Such patients are able to maintain exact knowledge about the present world, preserve perceptual and social skills and maintain the level of intellectual competency. Hence, they are able to carryout their daily life successfully.

Anterograde amnesia

It refers to the inability to encode and store new information, *i.e.* after having sustained the amnesia producing trauma or injury. In this kind of amnesia the long-term memory (LTM) is impaired in a massive way. However, the short-term memory (STM) remains as effective as before. Some patients are able to process the information received from different sources (visual, auditory, tactile, gustatory, olfactory) but are unable to transfer them into long-term memory (LTM).

In anterograde amnesia, the materials of the past stored experiences or knowledge are not impaired (*i.e.* the events that occurred prior to the onset of amnesia) but they are unable to learn and remember new facts and events.

Thus, amnesia refers to the loss of memory due to psychological or organic injuries to brain.

12.17 IMPROVING MEMORY

Almost each one of us ardently desires to possess an excellent memory system that is robust and dependable. After having learnt about various memory related processes, you would certainly like to know how to enhance your memory. There are several strategies to improve memory. These strategies are called **mnemonics** (pronounced as ni-mo-nicks). Some of these mnemonics involve use of images while others emphasize self-induced organization of learned information.

12.17.1 Mnemonics Using Images

Mnemonics using images require creating of vivid and interacting images of and around the 'to be remembered' materials. Two of such devices are most important. These are as follows:

Keyword method

This is a most common mnemonic device. Suppose you want to learn words of a foreign language. In keyword method, an English word (assumption here is that you know the English language) that sounds similar to the word of the foreign language (the word to be remembered) is identified. This English word will function as a keyword. For example, if one wants to learn a Spanish word 'pato' for duck, you may choose 'pot' as a keyword in English and the 'to be remembered' Spanish word is imagined as interacting with it. You may imagine a duck in a pot full of water. This method of learning words of a foreign language is much superior as compared to any kind of rote memorizing. Similarly if you learn BODMAS as a keyword you may easily remember the sequence to be followed in simplifying problems of arithmetic.

Method of loci

'Loci' is a plural of latin word Locus for 'place'. It is a sort of imagery walk that one is required to make or construct a mental scene or picture that contains very familiar objects and put the items to be remembered in strategic locations. Then as we picture the scene in our imagination, the items to be remembered will standout among the more familiar items. With practice, this works very well. For example, a child is taught if they associate the word 'spring' with water falling from the tap in the bathroom from the roof during rainy season and thus, receives a cue to put spring in the appropriate location of the imagined picture and recall becomes easier. Thus, in the method of loci, 'to be remembered' objects are arranged in a physical space in the form of visual images.

12.17.2 Mnemonics Using Organization

Organization refers to imposing certain order on the material one wants to remember. Mnemonics of this kind are helpful because the framework that he creates while organization makes the retrieval fairly easy. This involves the following strategies.

Chunking: While describing the features of short-term memory, we have described how chunking increases the capacity of STM. In chunking, several smaller units are combined to form large chunks. For creating chunks, it is important to discover some organization principles which can link smaller units. Therefore, chunking in addition to serving as mechanism to enhance STM capacity, can also be used to improve our memory.

First letter technique: In this strategy, we need to pick up the first letter of each word and arrange them to form another word or a sentence. For example CBI, ICU, LIC etc. are the initial letters of larger words such as Central Bureau of Investigation (CBI), Intensive Care Unit (ICU), Life Insurance Corporation (LIC) etc. By using the first letter of larger words, we are able to recall the larger words with ease.

Engaging in deep level processing: If you want to memorize any information well, engage in deep level processing. Craik and Lockhart have demonstrated that processing information in terms of meaning that they carry leads to better memory as compared to attending to their surface features. Deep level processing involves asking many questions related to the information, considering its meaning, its relationships to the facts one already knows etc. Thus, new information becomes part of our pre-existing knowledge framework that increases the chances of inspiring memory.

Minimising the interference: Interference as we have seen earlier is a major factor of forgetting. Therefore, one should try to avoid it as far as possible. For this intermittent relaxation intervals should be allowed after learning so that after-effects of learnt material may be well consolidated before trying to learn another subject or material. This means to say that one should try to avoid interpolation of any other material.

Give yourself enough retrieval cues: While we learn something, we should think of retrieval cues inherent in the learning material. We should try to identify them and link the parts of the learning material to these cues. Cues will be easier to remember than the larger contents and the links that are created between cues and contents of learning material facilitate us in retrieving the learnt materials.

PQRST technique: Thomas and **Robinson** (1962) have developed this technique which is particularly useful for students to remember the contents of their textbooks. It involves five stages:

P = Purview
Q = Questions
R = Read
S = Self-recitation
T = Test

To make this technique effective, one is required to follow three basic steps—organizing, elaborating and retrieving the material—to be remembered.

Purview (P): This refers to observing the main titles, pictures, and going through the summary of the chapter or sections therein and thus forming first-hand idea of the main contents.

Qucstion (Q): In this stage, each section of the reading material is put in to question form and an attempt is made to anticipate the kind of information each section is likely to provide.

Read (R): Now reading of the concerned section is done. Reading will provide answers to the questions raised during the second stage. Attempt should also be made to write down what one has read in the section. This helps retrieval process because writing also involves subvocal practice and identification of retrieval cues becomes easy.

Self-recitation (S): This is a kind of rehearsing the obtained information through reading. Recitation within the self helps in deeper processing of the sensory input.

Test (T): After completing all the above steps, test your comprehension and knowledge about the material.

PQRST is a very useful and effective technique as it helps in organizing, elaborating and retrieval of the read materials. Thus deeper level of processing is possible.

12.17.3 Use of Multiple Methods and Strategies

No doubt, the above strategies of enhancing memory are useful, however, different strategies have limited applications and do not provide solutions to all kinds of memory disorders. For overall improvement in memory, multiple techniques are suggested. Besides, for improving memory, optimal level of physical and mental health is also important because memory much depends upon mental and physical hygiene. To maintain good mental and physical health, we should be ready to be active to make effort we should have strong determination, hygienic daily routine, exercise and should also inculcate habits of study with regularity, collection of large amount of information and develop the habit of elaborate processing.

SUMMARY

- Memory is an important system of storing past experiences and retrieving the stored materials as and when required.
- As a process, memory involves three basic processes—encoding, storing and retrieving—as reflected in recognizing and recalling of the learnt materials.
- Memory system prepares a ground or framework for all cognitive processes such as decision-making, thinking, problem solving etc.

- Memory system consists of three major components, namely the sensory memory (SM), short term memory (STM) and long-term memory (LTM).
- Sensory memory registers the sensory input which is transferred to STM for further processing. The average capacity of STM is 7 ± 2 and the information can remain stored in STM for a brief period only. However, rehearsing attempts may increase its storage duration.
- The capacity of LTM is very vast and information in this store can last longer—relatively permanent.
- Retrieval from LTM is a result of parallel-distributed search.
- There are different levels of processing which can be classified into three basic levels—shallow or surface level processing in STM, intermediacy level of processing and finally deepest level of processing.
- The deepest level of processing permits the information to be stored in LTM for longer duration.
- To encode the information, usually two kinds of rehearsals are done. One is called maintenance rehearsal that can allow the input to remain in STM till completion of the task. Another is elaborate rehearsal that allows the input to be permanently encoded and stored in STM.
- Memory is measured explicitly in terms of recall, recognition and relearning. Besides, the implicit measures include word completion and Repetition Priming Task (RPT).
- Long-term memories are of three basic types—episodic, semantic and procedural memories.
- Human memory is a well-organized system. It is organized in terms of concepts, schema, images, cognitive maps and scripts. While organizing the input, we apply economy of cognition.
- Memory is not a passive process. It is an active process in which inputs are constructed during encoding stage and reconstructed while retrieving.
- The pioneering studies by Ebbinghaus and Bartlett are considered important contributions in the area of memory research.
- Forgetting is loss of memory which is caused either by failure to encode, failure to retain the encoded information or failure to retrieve.
- Various theories of forgetting have been developed to explain the phenomenon of forgetting. Among these, the decay theory, interference theory and motivated theory are important.
- There are various factors of forgetting such as poor learning, retroactive and pro-active inhibitions, lack of retrieval cues etc. Within these major factors several other factors are also included.
- Amnesia is a morbid kind of forgetting which is either transitory or organic. Organic amnesia is classified as anterograde and retrograde.
- Memory can be enhanced by applying certain mnemonic devices such as keyword method, method of loci, chunking, use of images, deeper levels of processing, minimizing interferences, PQRST technique etc.

PART VI

Symbolic Processes

PART VI

Symbolic Processes

CHAPTER 13

Thinking

13.1 INTRODUCTION

Passing through learning to retention and then to 'thinking' is a logical sequence. A logical sequence indeed, because for what we think of, must be learned and retained. We think with symbols, which represent past experience—may be in the form of words, gestures or images. All these are the tools of our thought processes. Till now in the preceding chapters of this book, man has been characterized as **doer**, i.e. he does something. Man senses the objects of the world around him, organizes and interprets the sensory input in a meaningful **whole** (perceives), learns to manipulate and develops abilities to respond effectively and correctly to the environment (learns), stores and retains the learned abilities or acquired experiences so that he may use them in future whenever required. But over and above, man also thinks and reasons. Owing to this ability, man is sharply differentiated from the other lower animals in the hierarchy. Man is primarily characterized not only as 'doer' but also as 'thinker'. **Aristotle** defines man as a 'rational being'. **Descart** while differentiating mind with matter, holds that **mind is that which thinks**.

The present chapter is concerned with various aspects of this process—**thinking** which is most important symbolic process of cognition and of the mankind indeed.

13.2 NATURE OF THINKING

Thinking is a most important and complex process of cognition. In fact, thinking in some way or the other is the main determinant of all our behaviours. It is a behavioural process much like perception, learning and remembering. It is not only much like other processes (named above) but also closely interrelated. Its similarity to learning and other processes lies in the fact that a thoughtful person attempts to solve a problem to which he confronts with and finds that the usual patterns of behaviours do not work well in solving the problem effectively because of certain kinds of changes in the situation. He then becomes overtly inactive, quiet and calm and begins to manipulate various symbols implicitly. This is what we call thinking. His thinking leads him to the senses of his personal identity, provides context for his perceptions and helps in representing his experiences. Thus, thinking is closely related to perception, though not predominantly perceptual. When a person 'perceives' the world around him, he also **'thinks'** and when he thinks, he also **perceives**. Similarly, the emotion, motivation, learning, and other aspects of cognitive processes including behaviours enter into thinking. In fact, the subdivisions of behaviours into categories are more artificial than real. All behaviours are interrelated because the organism (or the man) is an 'integrated whole'. Therefore, each process is dynamically related to each other—sometimes directly and sometimes indirectly. Usually, the process of thinking starts when a person faces a problem. Whenever a person finds himself in a novel situation in which he is motivated to achieve a goal, but progress towards the goal is blocked by some obstacles and for which he has no readymade response, he is said to be confronted with a problem. Under the situation, he begins to 'think'. Thinking enables him to solve the problem. He begins to sort out mentally the various possibilities. When one is deeply involved in thinking, he overtly appears idle and inactive. But, in reality, he is not idle rather actively engaged in thinking. This activity proceeds 'inside the person'. Hence, it is an implicit behaviour directed towards arriving at a solution to the problem, which triggers off the thought process and this process continues till an acceptable solution is found (i.e. goal is achieved).

Thinking is a symbolic activity. A symbol represents something. For example, name of a person is a symbol. The name is a word—either spoken or written. It is not a person in itself, rather it stands for the person who may be of a particular size, colour, status etc. When the name is uttered, it reminds one of the particular persons with specific characteristics. Thus, naming word is a symbol which represents the persons. All words are thus symbols because they represent objects, persons, or situations. Similarly, many other symbols—ideas, images etc.—are all symbols. While thinking, these symbols are implicitly manipulated in various ways. These are arranged and disarranged. Some of the symbols that appear close to the solution are tried out. If trying out appears successful, a decision is taken and finally implemented, i.e. acted upon. If it seems unprofitable, another symbol is tried. This process of trying out continues till appropriate solution of the problem is obtained and as soon as solution is arrived at, 'thought process' in reference to the problem that initiated it, terminates.

In this sense, thinking is a covert higher level mental activity, initiated by a problem or problematic situation and ends as soon as solution of the problem is arrived at.

13.3 DEFINING THINKING

Since, thinking is a covert higher level mental activity, it is difficult to give a brief definition of this process.

The common sense view is that thinking is some kind of activity, mediation or a fancy. But, this common sense view does not provide any definite meaning to the term. It is in view of the fact that thinking is elusive and apparently incapable of direct observation. Hence, lacks precise and objective meaning. Further, everybody thinks but, relatively very few of us ever think about thinking.

Apart from common parlance, psychologists too have used this term variously. To some, it is a wishful thinking—'fantasy' or 'day dreaming', the 'idle fitting' from one half formed notion to another. This sort of activity is an imaginative expression of underlying wishes, needs, or wants. Others consider it synonymous with remembering. An attempt to recall what one has had perceived or learned in the past. This is reflected in our everyday phrases like—'I am trying to think when I last visited the Kashmir valley'. Similarly, the term is also used in terms of 'imaginative thinking' to find out feasible or possible solution to the problem, or as a command to be attentive to execute some kind of task, usually expressed in phrases as—'think what you are doing'? In addition, sometimes the term is used in reference to what we believe. For example, someone asks—'what do you think about it'? Here the word 'think' means believe. But all beliefs are not capable of being labelled as thinking because they lack 'rationality'.

Thus, what we find is that the term 'thinking' is used in various ways. But all these usages are misleading or confusing. There are evidences available for and against each usage of the term. Thinking instead is a very complex mental activity. It is disjunctive as well as polymorphous. Thinking in fact is churning into polymorphous symbolic activities of the mind, ideational, non-percepted and symbolic in character. Hence, a precise objective definition is difficult to give. However, to define, 'thinking' is important because, definition makes clear the intrinsic quality of a thing, concept, premise or a process. More particularly, since thinking is considered as defining characteristics of mankind and it is most complex form of human behaviour (highest mental activity), to give a precise and objective definition of this process is much more important.

Thinking, as we have seen, is a polymorphous process. It includes organization of information and knowledge, evaluation, manipulation of symbols, decision-making, judgments, comparison, reasoning and the like. In modern terminology, it is called a **cognitive process** in which various symbols such as ideas, images, meanings etc. are implicitly manipulated with a view to arrive at a solution to the problem. Considering the involvement of such a large number of processes in one 'act of thinking', a workable definition may be given as follows:

> **Thinking is a higher order covert mental process of cognition characterized by the use of symbols as representation of objects and events and which is directed towards solution of the problem that initiates this higher order process of cognition.**

From the above definition, it is clear that: Thinking is a higher order mental activity. It is a covert or implicit activity. Thought processes are characterized by the use of symbols, which represent objects and events. Thought process aims at arriving at a solution to the problem and is a cognitive symbolical process which is initiated by a problem.

13.4 KINDS OF THINKING

Thoughts are basically of two types—'Autistic' and 'Realistic'. 'Autistic' thinking is determined by one's own needs, desires and feelings. 'Realistic' thinking is largely determined by requirements of objective situation. Autistic thinking is concerned with self-gratification. It does not give any regard to reality. Realistic thinking is productive. It is directed towards solution of a real problem. However, both kinds of thinking serve some purpose to the 'thinker' and hence, both are motivated. Let us now discuss these two kinds of thinking in some greater detail.

13.4.1 Autistic Thinking

Autistic thinking is a sort of wishful thinking, the person is found grossly involved in personalised thinking. He is completely detached from reality. It is a state of fantasy or daydreaming. His imaginative activities are evoked primarily by internal stimuli, i.e. from within the thinking individuals. For example, daydreaming is a form of 'autistic thinking' in which the dreamer roams in his fantasies only and seeks no real achievement, such as—'building castles in the air'.

To some extent, everybody dreams or fantasizes. To an extent, such autistic thinking is not considered harmful rather helpful. Some artists and inventors report that a significant idea first came to their minds in a dream, which they subsequently evaluated and elaborated during waking state. However, it is not a matter of rule that every idea of dream may lead to rich inventions. Often, it is found 'hat a person who is dissatisfied with his everyday routine life, has daydreams of success and gratification. But if it becomes a regular phenomenon of recurring nature, it is harmful. Such regular features are usually characterized as abnormal and the extreme forms of fantasies are known as 'delusion' which is a common symptom found in psychotic patients.

Thus, autistic thinking is thinking for self-gratification without caring for the reality.

13.4.2 Realistic Thinking

In contrast to autistic thinking, is 'realistic thinking'. This kind of thinking helps one to adjust with the real world because, it is deeply rooted in an individual's immediate reality. Usually, in realistic thinking, the reasoning is motivated by the need to reach solutions to problems related to individual's livelihood or his very survival. But, a realistic thinker often may also engage himself for sheer pleasure that may be derived from solving difficult and complicated problems such as by engaging in chess playing or crossword puzzle activities.

Such kinds of thinking have much significance in exploratory or inventive activities. Barring a few simple everyday life activities, 'exploration' is required almost in all real problems of life—simple or complex. Hence, through realistic thinking, we make an attempt to explore mentally, the ways and means to solve real problems of life.

Realistic thinking involves three processes, namely (a) deductive thinking (b) inductive thinking and (c) evaluative thinking.

Deductive thinking

Deductive thinking involves 'reasoning' to deduce conclusions on the basis of observed fact. Deducing a conclusion involves certain assumptions based on previous experience or knowledge. For example, your past experience tells that people run on the platform to catch a train. Now if you find a person desperately running on the railway platform, you may assume and conclude that the person is getting late and is running to catch the train. This is what we call deductive reasoning or thinking. Thus, deductive reasoning begins with a general assumption that you know and believe to be true and then draw a specific conclusion based on that assumption. In other words, it is a reasoning from general to particular. In the above-mentioned example, the general assumption is that people run on the platform when they get late to catch train. Therefore, the person who is seen running on the platform is also getting late for the train. However, this kind of conclusion is likely to be invalid because this conclusion is based on general assumption and not on the knowledge that this assumption is always true. People do not always run on the platform only when they get late for the train. They may run for some other reasons also. To avoid such possible mistakes in deducing conclusion, people make large number of observations, gather much of information, compare and analyze all information and then deduce the conclusion.

Inductive thinking

Some problems are such that cannot be solved by deducing ideas on the basis of available evidences. Thinker must add something new and more than one solution. Such a situation calls for reasoning to be induced from known to the unknown. From known, he makes an intuitive jump (or leap), formulates a new hypothesis or suggests further line of exploration. Such kind of thinking is the essence of creative thinking in science and art. This involves general conclusion based on particular or specific observation i.e. from specific to general. In the earlier example, if one observes the other person's subsequent action or actions such as the running person enters into the train and returns with a bag. Based on this observation, he may conclude that the person had left his bag in the train.

For example, take another example of syllogism:

Man is mortal	—	Premise I
Naresh is a man	—	Premise II
So, Naresh is mortal	—	Valid conclusion.

Sometimes inductive reasoning is also likely to be invalid or unsound when one induces a conclusion without knowing all possible facts. For example:

All politicians are men	—	Premise I
All men are mortal	—	Premise II
So, all mortals are politicians	—	Invalid conclusion.

Thus, it is obvious that in inductive thinking to conclude, we proceed from specific observations to infer general law. First we examine a number of specific observations and then some general principles by which people can be tried to use those principles to generate specific hypothesis. However, sometimes we also make a jump to a conclusion without knowing all possible facts.

Evaluative thinking

Evaluative thinking is a kind of critical thinking. The thinker evaluates and judges about the appropriateness or soundness of an idea or solution. The validity of the outcome here depends on reasoning as well as standard of norm used by the thinker. If the standard is faulty, the solution also becomes faulty. Hence, evaluative thinking aims at judging the appropriateness or suitability or goodness or effectiveness of an idea or representation.

Thus, with the help of above-mentioned forms of thinking, a person makes mental exploration to solve his problems.

13.5 TOOLS OF THINKING

All kinds or forms of thinking are not tiresome or difficult. For example, in daydreaming, there is a flow of pleasurable and gratifying ideas, which flow without any check or rein. Nothing would be more easy for a man than to wander into the world of pleasurable dreams. However, there are occasions when we find that 'to think' is rather a rigorous job. Ideas tend to run without any sequence. Therefore, to explore thoughtful ideas which may solve the problem poses difficulty. Besides, certain stumbling blocks also come in the way of an orderly thought processes. Thinker solves those stumbling blocks by using symbols. Symbols represent objects and events or situations. For example, a person while describing an incident uses verbal symbols—words, pictorial symbols to describe the direction, place etc. related to the occurrence of the incident. Similarly while thinking to solve a problem, one uses various symbols, orders them and interconnects them in such a way that is directed towards the desired solutions. In so doing, various tools are put to use. These are discussed below:

13.5.1 Role of Images in Thinking

Images are necessary for thinking. Suppose, you are asked to imagine a cat sitting on a tree with its tail slightly raised and curved. You would most likely try to form a visual image of the whole situation. Take another example. Think yourself standing in front of Taj Mahal and describe what you visualize. While doing this, you are actually forming a visual image of the situation. You are probably trying to see through your mind's eye just in the way you see a picture.

Thus, images are representations (a symbol) of the sensory experiences of the past and we know that thinking consists of symbolic mediation. Mediation fills the gap. Thinking being symbolic mediation, fills the gap between stimulus situation (problem) and the response the person makes to it. This mediation is symbolic because thinking is done with processes inside us which are symbols. Symbols are representations of our past experiences of the world.

Structuralists hold the view that thinking is a process of combining and recombining of images according to requirement. To quote Titchner*—'thought is the verbal counterpart of active imagination. Active imagination is thinking in images, carried on in words'.

The images are derived from past sensations and constitute the elements of which ideas are composed. This forms the basic form of thought. Thus, images are basic tools of thinking. For example, '**Beethoven**' was a famous singer. It is believed that when he became deaf, he was able to create most of his magnificent symphonic works on the basis of auditory images. Images help thinking in two ways:

(i) In the first place, images serve as abstractions of certain features of past experiences. These are stored in our long-term memory (LTM) which if retrieved while thinking on a problem, provide cue to the solution.

(ii) Secondly, it gives direction to think. For example, someone asks you the road to a particular place. What happens while giving direction? First you recollect your memories in which the images of the road are revived into your consciousness. These images contain the features of the road—shape, length, breadth, trees along the sides, turnings, traffic signals etc. These serve as a landmark cue in giving direction of the road and place. Thus, images represent the objects of your past experience and provide a cue from the present on the one hand and directs our thought processes on the other.

13.5.2 Kinds of Images

Images are of various kinds. **English** (1934), **Boring**, **Langfield** and **Weld** (1936) mention five main kinds of images:

* Titchner, E.B., *A Primer of Psychology* (Revised Edition), New York, McMillan, 1914, p. 213.

After-image

In real sense, after-image is not an image rather an effect of sensation after the sensation producing stimuli ceases. It refers to the persistence of activity in the sense organ for a brief period.

Memory image

To recall a previous sensory experience of perceptions in approximately exact form is memory image. Sense of familiarity is one of the outstanding features of this kind of image. However, such images are less clear and detailed than the original.

Eidetic image

Eidetic images are vivid memory images. It is also called 'photographic imagery'. People with the help of eidetic images are able to recreate entire visual experiences. They may have almost perfect visual image (Haber, 1969). Eidetic images are also seen in other sense modalities. People with eidetic images are often able to tell the exact position of formula or fact on a printed page of a book. They can give a glance for a fraction of seconds at an object and can describe the complete details (including the subtle details) of the object. **Luria** (1968) found that the subject was shown 4 lines of 12 digits for about 3 minutes and the subject was able to reproduce the whole set of digits in exactly the same position within 40 seconds. **Gummerman** and **Gray** (1971) report a 19-year young girl who was able to effectively reproduce the minute details of paintings of a picture after having a glance for 30 seconds.

Imaginative image

Imaginative images are similar to memory images, but these are not recalled items of the previous experiences. Rather, it is a typical combination of the previous experiences. Often they appear quite unusual in nature as in dreams. For example, images of ghosts, angels, horse with wings, mental picture of 'Ardhnareshwar' etc. Such images do not represent experience of any real object rather of imagined objects which are mentally structured by combining various imaginary images. A story writer or a novelist constructs characters in the story with the help of imaginations, and determines their specific roles. The characters and their roles are never real but imaginative. However, through the use of those imaginary images, the story writer is able to focus on reader's mind a real situation. Similarly, in experiments on 'reaction time' (RT) subject responds to an imaginary situation created by the experimenter. The subject is hardly required to respond to any similar experimental situation in real life. However, imaginary images do occur particularly more dominantly in abnormal cases.

Hypnogogic and hypnopomptic images

'Hypnogogic' images occur during drowsy state—between waking and sleeping, i.e. just before one falls into deep sleep. On the other hand, 'hypnopomptic' images occur between sleeping and waking. These are memory images of vivid nature. These may be visual, auditory and kinesthetic. Such images are very frequently found in those who are drug addicts and suffer from other kinds of abnormalities and hallucinations. In normal cases, however, such images provide with a good source for creative works. For example, **Lewis Carrol** is believed to have derived so much hypnogogic images that he invented a peculiar instrument called 'Nyctograph' to enable to record ideas without making one to be fully waking up.

Robert Thomson (1969) cites some more examples of creativity based on images occurring during just falling into sleep or just before awakening. William Blake was a renowned poet-cum-painter who has painted some of his famous visionary pictures which were the products of his hallucinatory images (hypnogogic and hypnopomptic images). He used to see angels and demons, which he portrayed. An American mathematician who mainly struggled with a typical geometrical problem woke up suddenly one morning and found the problem solved on the walls of his bedroom that presented the solution diagrammatically. Thus, images are one of the important symbolic tools of thought processes.

13.5.3 Are Images Essential for Thinking?

For thinking, whether images or consciousness of sensations are essential or not—is a controversial issue. Some hold the view that thinking involves images. Structuralists (Titchner, Wundt etc.) consider thinking as a mediating process which essentially use images as symbols for mediation. Others do not favour this. To them, thinking is 'abstract' and therefore, images are not essential.

According to structuralists, analysis of mental contents by introspection method reveal that all mental processes are composed of simple, irreducible elements—sensation, affection (feeling) and images. Images are derived from sensations. They constitute the elements of which ideas are composed and form the basic content of thought. However, images are never the true photocopy of sensation. It stands distinct from sensation in the properties of intensity, clarity and duration. In images, these properties of sensations are relatively lesser in degree or strength.

Role of images has been substantiated by some experimental evidences. For example, **Hutten Locher** (1973) in one study asked his subjects to imagine that they are standing on a street corner in a section of the city (to which the subjects were familiar) and think—how would they walk from that point to a target point (goal) they know. They were also asked to narrate the images that they experienced while thinking their walk to the target point (imaginery journey). The introspective reports of the subjects revealed that all subjects had made a visual map containing the trees along roadsides, turnings, houses, colours of houses, drains in the streets, electric poles etc. But, these kinds of images lacked clarity and most of the images were incomplete too. Some of the details such as, the length of the road, number of turnings, number of poles, exact colour of the houses etc. were missing. This shows that mental map is only abstraction of certain features of the experience and not vivid or complete picture of the experience. However, this evidences the use of images as a tool in thinking.

Clarifying the stand about the role of images in thinking **Berkeley** (1710) has clearly stated—'Whether others have this wonderful faculty of abstracting their ideas, they best can tell. For myself, I find I have indeed a faculty of imagining or representing to myself, the ideas of those particular things I have perceived, and of variously compounding and dividing them... the ideas of man that I frame to myself must be either of a white or a black or a tawny, a straight or a crooked, a tall or a low or a middle sized man. I cannot by any effort of thought conceive the abstract idea.*

* Berkeley, G.A., *A treatise concerning the principles of human knowledge*, Dublin (1710) cited in Method and Theory in Experimental Psychology—Osgood, p. 646.

Till about 1900, the general view was that all images, ideas and feelings are compounds of elemental sensations. Hence, no thought could be present without such conscious content. However, this notion was refuted by members of 'Wüzberg School'. The rift of Wüzberg School psychologists began due to discovery of **Galton** (1883) who reported that vast majority of scientific thinkers had no apparent images.

Kulpe, a disciple of **Wundt** also gathered evidences contrary to structuralists' view and found imageless components of thought.

In one experiment, **Marbe** (1901) found that his subjects were able to judge the relative heaviness of two different weights without any image content in mind. He advocated the notion of **conscious attitude** (Bewusstseinslagen) to account for the mental process.

According to Marbe, conscious attitude is a state of mind which mediates between problem and its solutions and this state is more than mere counterparts of perceptions as the term image implies.

Orth, another **Wüzberg** School psychologist considers conscious attitude as imageless state and not analysable in structuralist's term. **Watt** and **Ach** elaborating the discovery of 'Marbe', explains the imageless state as a state of 'mental set' (einstelling) and determining tendencies which prepares the thinker to think without manipulating images. Thus, in a situation of judgment, no images are required. The only requirement is the occurrence of a stimulus and subject's preparedness to respond.

Wüzberg School of psychologists indeed do not deny the existence of 'image', but they contend that thinking does not necessarily involve images. Imageless thought may also occur. However, the significance of Wüzberg School studies lies in the following statements:

(i) The facts gathered from studies on imageless thought demonstrate that thought processes consist not merely of images, but something more than that.

(ii) Thought often seems to be determined by a 'set' or other determining tendencies. A set is a readiness to respond (think) in a predetermined way. It seems, the moment a thought provoking stimulus is present, thought process begins to run off automatically as if one has already thought to think and the process starts. For example, a problem is given $\frac{8}{\underline{6}}$. Answer to this may be very quickly given without any image. But, there are three possible answers—2, 14 and 48. Any one of these possible answers will depend upon the 'set', whether one is set to subtract, add or multiply. Set can also be induced by appropriate instructions. If, however, there is no instructional set, set is likely to be self-induced. But, in this situation, set will vary from individual to individual and solutions to the problem will accordingly be determined.

(iii) Many of the important events in thinking may not be conscious. Hence, like a bird or butterfly we cannot catch or inspect an idea or a thought. This suggests that idea is more a process than an object.

Titchner has also accepted the facts gathered by Wüzberg School but disagrees with the explanations given by them. According to Titchner, the subject of Wüzberg School had in their introspections, incorporated meaning rather than sensory experiences. Therefore, if meanings are ruled out as non-existent and non-concurrent, then no imageless thought would be found.

Huxley (1959) once in a letter wrote—'I have always been poor in imageries even the meaningful words of poets fail to cast any image in my mind, not even while going to sleep or even at the time of recall'. The contents of Huxley's letter obviously refuse Titchner's claim that owing to descriptions of 'meaning' images were washed out and lend support to Wüzberg psychologists' views about imageless thought.

The issue of imageless thought is still an unresolved issue. Evidences are for both—for and against. Hence, an insoluble issue. However, we may take a compromising stand that though images are significant tools of thought, however, something may also occur without any concrete image. Instead, some other activity may mediate in the process.

13.5.4 Cognitive Map and Thinking

The process of thought and cognition is closely interrelated. Often the two are used interchangeably as synonyms.

The process of thought begins when a problem or problematic situation arises. In this sense, problem is the 'stimulus' and 'to think' over the problem is a response to the problem. Knowing includes comprehending, i.e. becoming fully aware of the problem as a whole. This is called 'cognition', i.e. to comprehend or to know about the whole aspect of the problem. This involves many processes taking into cognition of the problem, searching of the possible 'strategy' or 'images' acquired during the past that are stored into mental structure, conserving, applying the law of reversibility and so on. If all these fail, the thinker makes a minute observation over the problem and searches out the distinctive characteristics of the problem that may give some new direction, i.e. new information is gathered and assimilated into mental structure (schema). Thus, a thinking person creates a map of the entire aspects of the problem, all possible ways of strategies of solutions and also the ability to apply the needed operations or to change the mental structure. This respectively is called assimilation and accommodation.

In this context, **Piaget** while studying the thinking process of children has described the sequential changes or developments that take place in course of ongoing thought processes of children and proposed a theory about mental activity called—'cognitive theory'.

Piaget has used certain key ideas in his theory. These include biological nature of intelligence, adaptation, mental organization (schemas), assimilation, accommodation and equilibration.

Piaget in fact started his career as a biologist, so he stressed on the biological nature of intelligence. This means that organizing thought process is a part of biological nature which permits 'adaptation' to the environment around us. A child adopts two ways of adaptation. Firstly, depending upon the level of mental organization existing at a particular time—he assimilates (takes in) all possible information to modify his environment so that it fits into his already developed ways of thinking and acting. Secondly, if the available mental structure is not rich enough to take in information (assimilate), the individual modifies his own mental structure so as to fit in with existing characteristics of the environment. For example, suppose a child is encircled by various objects in a large sized hall. The child tries to reach out and pick up certain things of his environment that he can and thus, assimilates them into the grasping scheme of his mental organization. But, some of the things are too big, heavy, hot or slippery to be grasped. Hence, not assimilable into the primitive grasping scheme. In this case, the primitive grasping scheme will gradually change to differentiate between graspable objects from ungraspable ones. This is called 'accommodation'. By accommodation a sort of balance is arrived at between assimilation of new information and accommodation or change of scheme. This balance is termed as 'equilibration'. This is a regulatory process that keeps the mental scheme changing as and when needed.

In order to make it more clear, let us take an example of a formal group—say a political party that has certain rules as an organization. The rules are the tools of its operation while the organization is the mental structure (scheme) existing at a particular time of its development.

The political party can take in (assimilable) new members who fit into its existing rules and structure. But, suppose the party intends to enrol certain people as its members but they do not quite fit into the existing organization (scheme) but may prove valuable for the party (as is often noticed during hung assembly or parliament situation). In such situations, the political group (party) may make exceptions. It may change its rules and ideologies (of course within the rules provided for such changes) and thus, brings about a balance in the group. It changed from one balanced structure to another one (with slightly amending the rules or ideologies). This illustrates the concept of equilibration—a process existing in the social organization as well as biological ones.

Thus, it is obvious that while we think, we use our mental structure (scheme) and also accommodate with the situation to bring balance in the existing mental structure (scheme). This is the essence of cognitive map which is very close to thinking process.

13.5.5 Role of Language

Thought and language are closely related. Considering its close association, many psychologists often call thinking as 'restrained speaking', 'sub-vocal talking' or 'implicit language activity' or 'submerged talking'. What caused the car stop suddenly? The probable answers to this question (that haunts the driver's mind implicitly) also occur in language form—Let us see what happened?—has the fuel exhausted?—'no'—may be the battery is dead—'no' and so on. Each of the alternative answer to the problem is tried and ultimately it is detected that small sand particles have entered into the crankshaft and possibly made the engine dead stop. Solution of the problem has been found. Thus, right from perception of the thought problem to its solution, language as a symbol is an important tool of thinking. Similarly, if one tries to analyse everyday thinking on various problems and situations, it would be found that words are evident everywhere.

While thinking, it appears that somebody is talking to himself. Thus, thinking is closely tied up with inner speech. It is often associated with activities of speech mechanism, especially of the tongue and throat in those who cannot hear and speak, and of fingers in deaf and dumbs. **Jacobson** (1932) and **Max** (1937) attempted to obtain patterns of action currents from subjects who were given instructions to imagine, mentally multiply numbers, thinking about eternity etc. It was found that these patterns resembled much with the patterns obtained while one actually speaks something. This provide evidences that thinking involves language as a tool.

Using language as tool in thinking is also found in children. However, their use of language is relatively louder to adults—until they learn that it is customary as well as worthwhile to keep one's thought to oneself.

As regards the role of language in thinking, some theories have been proposed. Some of the popular such theories are as mentioned below:

(i) Language as determinant of thought
(ii) Thought as determinant of language
(iii) Language and thought have different origins and the two proceed along parallel lines during the stages of development with overlapping functions.

Let us examine these theories one by one.

Language as determinant of thought

In Hindi and other Indian languages we use a number of different words for various kinships.

We have different terms for mother's brother, father's elder brother, father's younger brother, mother's sister's husband, father's sister's husband and so on. An English person uses just one word 'uncle' to describe all these relationships. In the English language, there are dozens of words for colours whereas some tribal languages have only 2 to 4 colour terms. Do such differences matter for how we think? Does an Indian child find it easier to think about and differentiate between different relationships compared to her English-speaking counterpart? Does our thinking process depend on how we describe it in our language?

Benjamin Lee Whorf (1956) was of the view that language determines the contents of thought. This view is known as **linguistic relativity hypothesis**. In its strong version, this hypothesis holds what and how individuals can possibly think is determined by the language and linguistic categories they use (linguistic determinism). Experimental evidence, however, maintains that it is possible to have the same level or quality of thoughts in all languages depending upon the availability of linguistic categories and structures. Some thoughts may be easier in one language as compared to another.

Thought as determinant of language

The noted Swiss psychologist **Jean Piaget** believed that thought not only determines language but also precedes it. Piaget argued that children form an internal representation of the world through thinking. For example, when children see something and later copy it (a process of imitation) thinking does take place. It happens without involving any language. A child's observation of other's behaviour no doubt, involves thinking but not language. Language is just one of the vehicles of thinking. As actions become internalized, language may affect children's range of symbolic thinking but is not necessary for the origin of thought. Piaget believed that though language can be taught to children, understanding of the words requires knowledge of the underlying concepts i.e. thinking. Thus, thought is basic and necessary if language is to be understood.

Different origins of language and thought

The Russian psychologist, **Lev Vyogotsky** argued that thoughts and languages develop in a child separately till he attains the age of two. Before two years, thought is preverbal and is experienced more in action (Piaget's sensory-motor stage). The child's utterances are more automatic reflexes—crying when uncomfortable—than becoming sad. Around two years of age, the child expresses thought verbally and his/her speech reflects rationality. Now children are able to manipulate thoughts using soundless speech. During this period the development of thought and language become interdependent. The development of conceptual thinking depends upon the quality of 'inner speech' and vice versa. Thought is used without language when the process of thinking is non-verbal such as visual or movement related. Language is used without thought when expressing feelings or exchanging pleasantries, for example, 'Good Morning! How are you? Very well, I am fine'. When the two functions overlap, they can be used together to produce verbal thought and rational speech. To clarity, let us consider the different stages of thought and language development as conceived by Vygotsky.

Vygotsky considers thought and language to develop in three parallel stages as mentioned below:

First stage: In the first stage of thinking, the objects or things are organized into categories or heaps, which are based on perceived similarities and differences in the objects and not on the basis of logic or rule.

Second stage: The second stage of thought processes is concerned with the perception of its structured aspects. In this stage, children perceive unchangeable concrete and factual bounds between individual components of objects.

Third stage (final stage): This stage is called the stage of conceptual thinking. In this stage children are able to make abstract links between components and also analyse them.

The language development follows the following sequences:

First stage: First, the non-intellectual or thoughtless speech develops into a 'naive stage'. In this stage, symbolic functions of words are acquired.

Second stage: This is 'egocentric stage' of language development. In this stage, they happily talk about what they are doing even though no one is listening to them.

Third stage: The egocentric stage is followed by the third stage of inner speech. In this stage, children manipulate thoughts using soundless speech.

Vygostsky believes that the three stages of the two processes occur in sequential orders one by one. During the transition from one to another stage, the original structures are destroyed and new structures are constructed. Vygotsky also believes that during the 3rd and final stage of thought and language development, the two become interdependent and when these two overlap, both can be used together to produce verbal thought and rational speech.

Despite these controversial issues, experimental studies in general demonstrate that thought and language are inseparable aspects of cognitive processes. For example **Slobin** (1971) has opined that while thinking, precisions of a language enable us to make different types of associations. Grammar of a language also affects our thinking patterns. Grammatical rules predispose selectivity of things. Rules of grammar specify the ways to symbolize the world.

The relationship of language to thought can also be illustrated from our everyday observation. Suppose you are driving a car on a national highway. It suddenly goes wrong and stops. This situation is perceived as a problem in languages form—'what happened'?

Among human beings some evidences have been obtained which do not demonstrate the use of words or language as essential for thinking. For example, many skills of thought processes can be acquired and developed without involving language. Secondly, very often we find it difficult to express in words what and how our thought processes proceed and what has been grasped in thinking. Even if we try and find some word or words, it may not satisfactorily explain our implicit mental behaviour of thinking. Besides often we notice that while describing our thinking, some such words are uttered which did not actually occur in course of thinking. Again, the study of speech disorders due to brain injury or disease suggests that patients can think even without adequate control over their language.

Wüzberg School psychologists, on the basis of records obtained in their studies, have also shown that intelligent adaptive responses can occur in problem-solving situation without using either words or any kind of image. Set and determining tendencies operate without the actual use of language in purposeful and intelligent thoughts.

Thus, we see that the relation of language to thought is a subject of interest and controversy, both. We may therefore, conclude that although words or language may be important in shaping our thinking, they are probably not essential to thought and sometimes may also hinder the process. Thinking is in fact, more like struggling, striving or searching for something than it is like talking or reading. The controversy may come to an end only if further studies throw some light on the entire question of relationship between language pattern and thought.

13.6 ROLE OF SET AND DIRECTION

One group of mechanism that operates during thinking is called **set** which functions as organizing, controlling and directing roles in thinking.

Gibson (1941) has analyzed the term 'set' in at least eight distinctive meanings, each describing different functions such as,

(i) Pre-aroused expectations of certain stimulus features
(ii) Readiness to discriminate
(iii) Readiness to select some particular kind of object from a perceptual field
(iv) Readiness to react to a stimulus in a certain way
(v) Intention to perform a particular operation
(vi) Transfer of previous effects of learning in a new situation
(vii) A tendency to complete a begun task and
(viii) Fixity or overpersistence in a given direction.

Though, different meanings describe different functions, they contain certain similar mechanism at work and are known as 'tendencies', 'readiness' and 'intentions'. In short, 'set' refers to a frame of mind to perform a particular operation to solve a problem'. When this set becomes stable, it becomes attitudes or habits. This set or mental frame of readiness is **einstelling** in German or **'direction'** in English vocabulary. This set or readiness is induced either by past experience or by instructions given by the experimenter while performing an experiment. For example, a series of pair of number is presented and the subject is 'forewarned' (instructed) to add or multiply or subtract. Sometimes, set also emerges by picking up while solving a problem by trial and error or through operation of positive or negative transfer and generalization.

Since, thinking process begins with a problem, therefore thinker's thoughts are directed towards solution of the problem—'the thinker is set to think' for arriving at a solution. This set brings forth the ideas which are relevant to the different aspects of the problem and gives directions to approach towards solution of the problem. For example, while driving a car stops midway, a number of ideas relating to the possible reasons for sudden stoppage of car comes in mind, which are also tried, one by one and in this way, one arrives at a solution. From this example, it is obvious that 'set' guides thinking to proceed in a particular direction.

A mental set may either help or hinder thinking. It depends on whether it directs our thinking towards the goal or makes us 'blind' to the key elements. Suppose a subject is given the following anagrams to unscramble them

List A	*Solution*	*List B*	*Solution*
HGNTI	NIGHT	NARTI	TRAIN
ETWRA	WATER	RVOEC	COVER
LBTEA	TABLE	TGIHE	EIGHT
HGLTI	LIGHT	KALCB	BLACK
MAFER	FRAME	RVOEL	LOVER

To unscramble the anagrams of List A, subject is required to arrange the letters in the sequence of 3, 5, 2, 1, 4, i.e. putting third letter, then fifth letter, then second letter, then first letter and finally the fourth letter of the anagrams. Subject is required to follow the same rule to unscramble all the anagrams of List A. The operations of same rule thus facilitate the solution. But, operation of the same rule to unscramble the anagrams of List B will hinder the solution, because here different operation is required. To unscramble them, the sequence will be 5, 3, 2, 1, 4, putting the 5th, 3rd, 2nd, 1st, and then finally the 4th letter in order.

The way in which set hinders problem solving has extensively been studied by **Luchins** and **Luchins** (1954, 1959). The researchers have shown how a particular set is fixated which hinders the solution of a problem requiring attack by a method other than previous one. In Table 13.1, there are total 11 problems. For each problem, there are 3 empty jars—A, B and C—with known capacities. The subject is required to obtain the desired quantity of water with the help of these three jars (A, B and C). Problem number 1 is an example or demonstration problem. This problem can be solved in two ways:

(i) By filling 13 unit jar (B), then from it filling 5 unit jar (A) twice and then 2 unit jar once (C). Thus, leaving 1 unit—'The desired unit of water, or

(ii) Another way would be filling 5 unit jar (A), and then emptying with 2 unit jar twice (C). The remaining unit of water will be the desired unit (i.e. 1 unit). Problem numbers 2 to 6 are 'set problems' which could be solved by the method which can be expressed in algebraic equtionb–a–2c. That is, first fill in the largest jar (B) to its full capacity (viz. Problem no. 2–127 units). Then empty 21 units by jar (A) and then 6 units of water from jar (B) will be emptied twice (–3 × 2 units). Thus, the remaining units of water in jar (B) will be 100 units.

Problem numbers 7 and 8 are also solvable by the operation of algebraic equation b–a–2c. But these two problems are also solvable in a more convenient manner, i.e. by not using jar (B) at all. For example, take Problem no. 7. Fill in jar (A) to its capacity, i.e. 23 units and use jar (C) to empty 3 units from it to obtain 20 units of water. Similarly in Problem no. 8, fill in jar (A) (15 units) and also jar (C) 3 units. The two jars together will give 18 units of water. But, Problem no. '9' can be solved by only one method, i.e. 'A–C'. Problem numbers 10 and 11 again can be solved in the 'set way' if the subject is persistent in repetitive subtraction as well as manipulation of only two smaller jars. The problems used by Luchins and Lunchins are shown in **Table 13.1**.

TABLE 13.1 Set hindering problem solving

	Problem	*Given the following jars*			*To obtain the amount of water*
		A	*B*	*C*	
1	Demonstration problem	5	13	2	1
2	Set problem	21	127	3	100
3		14	163	25	99
4		18	43	10	5
5		9	42	6	21
6		20	59	4	31
7	Alternative method problem	23	49	3	20
8		15	39	3	18
9	Critical problem	28	76	3	25
10		18	48	4	22
11	Test problem	14	36	8	6

With the help of above problems, the experimenter wanted to determine if successful use of a given method served to fixate the subject and blind to other approaches?

Luchins' hypothesis was confirmed. Even graduate students were found following the 'set' mechanically like a plodder in problems 7 and 8 when they were shown the direct alternative method at the conclusion of the experiment. Subjects exclaimed—'How stupid of me' and the like.

In another session of the experiment, the hypothesis was retested by bringing some procedural variation. Some subjects were taken aside and were asked to write down the word 'Don't be blind' on paper and finish the problem number 6. This served as a cue for the subjects to apply some other possible way of solving the problems. It was found that this increased the number of intelligent solutions to problems 7 and 8. Interestingly, in some younger public school children, the instruction 'don't be blind' proved ineffective. Here also set induced in schools—'to do as they were taught' led them 'to do as they did it before'. When the subjects were asked to explain what 'don't be blind' meant, some answered—just do what you did before or 'don't be blind to the rules which serves all the problems'.

The findings are interpreted by **Gestaltists** as **rigidity of organization** established by rote mechanical practice. Behaviourists explain it in terms of **habit family hierarchy**. According to this concept, a particular mediating reaction or response becomes variably associated with system skill sequence. Hence, the particular operational mode becomes strongly associated with the problem sequence and thus, cause hindrance in solving the problem by any other operation. Luchins tried a number of variations in the procedure and obtained results that fit well in either of the two theories.

Many of the studies such as those of **Watt** (1905), **Maier** (1930), **Weaver** and **Madden** (1949), **Birch** and **Rabinowtz** (1951), **Kendler**, **Greenberg** and **Richman** (1952), **Adamson** (1952) etc. also show the effect of mental set in solving a problem which is positive as well as negative, i.e. facilitating as well as inhibiting or hindering.

The effect of set is also seen in our day-to-day tricks. For example, if you spell the words and ask a person how he pronounces them, you use the words beginning with Mac like Mac Donald, Mac Tavish, Mac Millan and then slip in machinery. With the set of names, he may fall in your trap and may pronounce the Machinery as Mac Hinry.

Green (1966) has also shown the effect of set on the direction of thought. He used anagram problem such as ELCAM, TYPAR, DSLEA, and LSFEE etc. These anagrams can be unscrambled by rearranging the letters in sequence of 3, 4, 5, 1, 2, Thus, the anagrams would stand for CAMEL, PARTY, LEADS and FEELS. Now before solving further, the subject is given to unscramble APCHE. Two words can be made by unscrambling the anagram—PEACH and CHEAP. The subject is more likely to make CHEAP rather than PEACH by following the previous operation (3, 4, 5, 2, 1) whereas in order to make PEACH, the required operation would be 2, 5, 1, 3, 4.

Set may be induced by immediate past experience or long established practices or by instructions which receive old habits. Set biases the thinker at the start of his problem, directs him away from certain thoughts and towards others. It acts like implied assumptions as in positive and negative transfer effects.

The hindering effects of set can be reduced to an extent by (1) Cautioning the subject (e.g. don't be blind) just before the critical problem and encouraging to find out alternative. (2) Reducing the number as practice trials with an operation and (3). By separating practice and critical trials (i.e. in which another operation is required) by sufficient time intervals, i.e. days or weeks.

However, it is generally observed that 'set' induced by practice is usually so strong that any warning against it may fail to make any effect.

Thus it is obvious that set is an important determinant of implicit mental behaviour—Thinking which guides and directs the process of thought.

13.7 TRIAL AND ERROR IN THINKING

We know that thinking begins with a problem and the 'thinker' makes implicit search to solve the problem. Implicit searching behaviour is directed towards finding out an appropriate response to unravel the 'knot' (perplexities or obstacles or blockages) for which he has no readymade response. To achieve this goal, while thinking one manipulates different ideas, images, or other symbols, formulates certain hypothesis and implicitly tests the hypotheses. This is **implicit trial and error**. For example, a student is financially vacuous and need some money to clear off college dues for which the last date is just tomorrow. This is a problem for him and begins to think how to arrange money within such a short time. He looks through the pockets of his other suits (error, change in stimulus situation), he may visualize his passbook (again error, change in stimulus situation), he may think about borrowing money from a distant relation residing in the same town and then recalls that he already owes him (again error, change in stimulus situation) and he may finally stumble into thinking about his girlfriend who is daughter of a wealthy man and is generous to help the needy one—and thus **the problem facing student is on his way**, i.e. he has found the solution to his problem. In this illustration, most of the trial and error has been implicit.

In thinking, implicit trial and error may be both random and planned. In the above illustration, financially vacuous student made some random exploration of possible solutions and eventually got the clue which he tested and became successful. But, all trial and error are not random. **Edison's discovery** of filament for incandescent light was not an outcome of random search. He systematically tested each substance (one after another) in a planned manner. Scientific discoveries involve careful testing of hypothesis—a controlled and well-planned trial and error. In our everyday life situations also while dealing with various problems, we make a planned trial and error to test the possibilities rather than random trial and error.

Thus, thinking process involves implicit trial and error.

13.8 INSIGHT IN THINKING

Very often, solution to a problem through mechanical trial and error is not possible. Such problems require quite a novel approach to the problem which comes to the mind all on a sudden—**a sudden flash**. When sudden flash comes, the individual feels delighted and is usually expressed in **Aha! Experience**. For example, he says—'Aha!' I have found. To illustrate, let us think of a student of mathematics who has been working hard on an intricate mathematical problem. He finds the problem much complicated because all his efforts proved erroneous (trial and error). He leaves the job (trying to solve) and begins to think. He mentally tries to interconnect the relationship of different elements in the problem and organize the scattered elements into a particular form. But, he is still unsuccessful to find any positive clue. Ultimately, he leaves thinking. After a few seconds or minutes (sometimes hours and days) suddenly an idea flashes in his mind which appear close to the solution of the problem. This **sudden flash is insight**. He works according to the flash and finds the problem solved. The sudden flashed idea is new one—something like invention and he feels delighted. Such feelings of delight is usually expressed as Aha! I have found, 'how stupid I am', why such a simple idea did not occur to my mind earlier etc.

Campbell (1960) holds that insight emerges from mediational process of unconscious level of mind.

Many scientists, mathematicians or creative thinkers report that new relationships and meanings of objects and events are suddenly seen when a problem arises, they are new symbolic arrangements until one of them solves it. We often have the experience of suddenly seeing a correct solution after a period of unsuccessful trial and error.

According to Gestalt psychologists, insight results from cognitive processes which restructures the problem in the mind. This helps in sudden flash of new idea. However, one should note that all insights do not always lead to correct solutions. Sometimes a wrong insight may emerge. This can be determined only when the suddenly flashed idea is put to use and tested.

From the above-mentioned study, it is obvious that problem solving behaviours in addition to mechanical trial and error also involve insight as a tool of thinking. Insight is particularly important in solution of complex nature of problems requiring higher order cognition.

13.9 PROBLEM SOLVING

Starting a section on problem solving is a problem in itself. Right from explaining the nature of thinking, through to the mediating processes, the word has most frequently been occurring. But 'problem solving as a thinking behaviour is something different from earlier options. What we mean by problem solving behaviour is the use of thought process to overcome obstacles and work toward goal.

All attempts to solve problems are not 'thinking'. There are problems, which are solved by overt trial and error or a new relationship is established because of conditioning. Such problem solving behaviours are externally observable. These involve mechanical manipulation of responses to the situation in either random or systematic manner. Though, in this case also the association between the observable situation and observable response is mediated by a symbolic process, the mediation is objectively observable. Hence, easy to trace. But, most of the symbolic processes in the humans are implicit and therefore difficult to trace. The necessary components of solutions are hidden. The implicit process of solving the problem may involve implicit trial and error as well as insight using images or words or other symbols as tools and thus, solutions are deduced.

Thus, problem solving behaviour is implicit symbolic mediation which is directed toward deducing a correct solution to the problem, i.e. using of thought processes to overcome the obstacles and working towards goals. The obstacles can be trivial or burdensome. Accordingly, some solutions may be very simple such as using simple rules to add a set, a number or the solution may break the traditional rules to 'explore new'.

Whether the solution is simple or not, all problem solving behaviours require passing through several steps as discussed below:

13.9.1 Steps in Problem Solving

Many researchers have worked on problem solving behaviour. Important of them are **Wallas** (1926), **Dewey** (1933), **Patrick** (1937), **Vinake** (1952), **Coffer** (1957), etc. On the basis of findings of these researchers, a few formulations about the steps involved may be made as follows:

Conceiving the problem

It is the characteristic of a problem solver how he conceives or formulates a problem. The same problem is conceived differently by different individuals, which bear significance in determining the approach with which he may try to arrive at the solution. This is well illustrated in the problem used by **Haier** (1936) in an experiment popularly known as **'string problem'**. The problem was to construct two pendulums with the help of given materials in such a way that each would swing over a designated point on the floor. The materials available to the subjects were coils of wire, two kinds of clamps, chalk and lengths of wood. The subjects displayed six different types of solutions. Five of these were unsuccessful. Difference in approach to solve the problem was attributed to the difference in perceiving the problem. Some perceived the difficulty being simply the fact that strings were not long enough. Therefore, they approached to search for increasing the length of the strings. But, since, appropriate materials were not available, the approach could not prove successful. Others perceived, they were not tall enough to bring the strings together. Similarly, those who could be successful, perceived the problem differently in the right direction. Thus, how one perceives or defines a problem, influences the approach to be adopted for thinking. Perceiving the problem is in fact, defining the problem and defining the problem makes clear the approach with which one may proceed to solve the problem. Hence, conceiving the problem is an important aspect of problem solving behaviour.

Becoming motivated or interested in a problem

To solve a problem, one must feel the need to solve it. Feeling of the need for solution makes one to be deeply concerned towards solving the problem. An unmotivated person hardly gets interested in the problem. The needs may vary. One may feel the urge to create something new, public acclaim or recognition, establishment of superiority by solving a complex problem etc. Such urges make the problem solver think eagerly and provide directions for exploring and also make him satiated for the success in the venture.

Assembling the materials with which to work

The thinker while thinking to solve a problem must examine minutely the situation with which he has to work to solve the problem. For example, if a scientist is thinking to invent a new medicine for a particular disease—say jaundice, he must examine in detail as to why other available drugs are inadequate? What and how the composite molecules function? Whether the new drug would be cost effective? The feasibilities of availability of the new molecules, their side-effect if any etc. A deep and minute exploration of the materials with which a thinker is concerned is in fact, a stage of preparation in creative thinking. It is a sort of search or exploration of the field within which the problem exists—**'Working out in one's head'** is the characteristic feature of this phase.

Determining a number of possible solutions

As a result of working out in one's head, various possible ways of solving the problem may occur. Sometimes these solutions come so suddenly, dramatically and adequately that the thinker thinks of them as internal inspiration or illumination which is a characteristic phase of creative thinking. The various possible solutions are then arranged in order for testing and evaluating.

Evaluation of the suggested solution

Systematic arrangement of various possible solutions that could be derived, are judged and evaluated in terms of certain criterion. For this, further information pertaining to the problem is recalled from LTM and used as standard against which hypotheses are checked. It is possible that the first hypothesis may prove unprofitable. Then the second hypothesis may be tested and evaluated and then the third one and so on till a particular hypothesis is considered as the most adequate.

Objective test and revision of the solution

The particular hypothesis considered adequate is put to objective test. If found good, the hypothesis is accepted and confirmed. If not, new facts may be sought and new observation may be made. The new facts may confirm the hypothesis or prove it fallacious or suggest for revision. In scientific, artistic and even everyday life, tentative solutions are subjected to careful tests before they are accepted for practical use. This is the stage of 'verification' in creative thinking.

Implementation of the solution

This is the final phase of problem solving behaviour in which the objectively validated solution is put to use and thus, solution to the problem is accomplished, i.e. the goal is reached and the thought process comes to an end.

From the above description, it is obvious that the problem solving behaviour is a sequential behaviour, which begins with a problem, the problem is conceived or defined, mental exploration is initiated, several possible solutions come out which are evaluated and put to objective validation and then finally it becomes usable. Almost in all problem solving behaviours, these steps are found operative.

13.9.2 Strategies of Problem Solving or Thinking

While solving a problem, the problem solver employs one or more strategies, core of any strategy is the hypothesis which is searched, retrieved, judged, tested and either accepted or rejected finally in the light of testing or validating the solution.

There are various strategies that a problem solver chooses to employ. According to Gestaltist, the basis of solution to any problem is the development of 'insight'—a 'sudden flash' and if once, the suddenly flashed solution works well, the solution occupies the highest order for solving similar nature of problem later on. Thus, when one is confronted with similar nature of problem in future, the probability of occurrence of the earlier insight increases.

Some of the important strategies are mentioned below under separate headings:

Algorithms

Some problem solving situations are such that they can be very easily solved by employing set rules or procedures that guarantee the solution. This strategy is most profitable in situations involving mechanical solution. For example, rules of multiplication, simplification, rules of syllogism in logical conclusions, rules of grammar involved in verbal problems etc. are solved by employing algorithms.

Heuristics

Heuristics is a strategy, trick or simplification procedure that limits the search for solution of different problems. These are shortcut rules of thumb that often lead to quicker solutions. These shortcut rules are based on past experiences with those problems and involve reasoning. However, heuristics do not guarantee solutions but if they work, search time is greatly reduced. Human beings generally use heuristics in playing chess or in solving geometrical problems.

Means-end analysis

This is a form of heuristics approach. In this approach, a problem is subdivided into a number of subproblems. So, efforts are made to search for the hypothesis which are closer to the solution of each subproblem separately and thus, the difference between current states and designated goal is reduced. Such strategies are very often employed while solving class problems working through mathematical complexities computer programming etc.

Backward search

This is often called 'sub-goal method'. We begin with the result to be proved and then attempt to work backward step-by-step to the given initial step state. This strategy is more profitable in the case of—

(a) Problems where goal has more information than the problem and
(b) The nature of problem is such that forward and backward operations may be done.

The problem solver sets the sub-goals and the problem is broken into smaller sections to make them easy to manage and then proceeds step by step. For example, you have to write down an essay on a very current topic to be presented in a competition. You first decide the goal—what approach to the topic would convey something new (goal determination). Then you break the body of the essay into several sections, such as—introduction, overview, objective, major theme, summary and finally the conclusive remarks. This kind of working on the problem is 'backward' because, first the end product (goal) is determined, the problem is subdivided and then, stepwise manipulation is done to arrive at the final solution.

There may be several other strategies, *viz.* applying the principle of logic or rules of reasoning, mechanical trial and error, gap filling, thinking by structure, determining the probabilities and desirability as a decision etc. A problem solver may use any or more of the strategies depending upon the nature of the problem and activity of the solver. But, here one should note that there is no fixed sequence of any strategy. There are possibilities of **fits and starts, regression and perseverance** (back and forth), **partial solutions and failures** and occasionally new problems may crop up enroute.

13.9.3 Factors Affecting Problem Solving or Obstacles or Barriers of Problem Solving

Problem solving behaviour involves mechanical processes such as trial and error (applying learnt rules of operations), solution through understanding, solving by logical reasoning and often by insight.

Our common experiences as well as fact-finding experiments on problem solving behaviours provide abundant evidences that like perception and learning, problem solving is also to some extent 'personalized'. This implies that one's background of motives, experiences, beliefs, and his state of preparedness provide unique frame of work to think and solve his problem.

The problem-solver while thinking to solve the problem employs certain strategies of his own. But, in course of applying the chosen strategies, certain factors intervene or operate which either facilitate or hinder the accomplishment of goal (solution), some of these factors have already been described in separate sections of this chapter. In the present section, these factors are collected together in abridged form for clear understanding to the readers. Such factors are discussed below under separate headings:

Mental set

Mental set is an important factor. It is a tendency of a person to solve problems by following already tried mental operation. Sometimes, the situation we are in a particular moment, gives us a 'set' that determines the manner in which we attack a problem. Usually, prior success with a particular strategy sometimes helps in solving a problem. However, this tendency also creates a mental rigidity that obstructs the problem solver to think of any new rules or strategies. Thus, mental set in certain situations enhances the quality and speed of problem solving while in other situations it hinders problems solving.

The effect of such personalized characteristics of attacking a problem has extensively been studied by researchers. Some of the findings of the study have been reported in Section 13.6 of this chapter.

Past experience

Our past experience is another contributing factor in problem solving behaviour. Concepts and generalizations formed in the past are very often used in solving a problem in the present. Most of the present problems have great resemblance with the past and the solvable tricks are stored in our memory stores. Being instigated by the recurrence of the past problem or a new problem with similarity to the past, the mediating symbols from memory stores are recalled and give clue to solve the problem. But, not all the problems are solved by recalling the past experiences. Some problems require working out new concepts and discrimination.

In general, however, greater the relevant experience in a given field, more concepts and generalizations one may have for use as potential tools in solving a new problem of that field. Thus, a mathematician, or an architect, will be more quick in solving the mathematical and architectural design related problems than those who have no background experience of those fields. Without relevant past experience, we fail to conceptualize a problem in right perspective. Hence, barring a few instances such as those requiring comparatively new orientations, past experience is likely to play a major role in solving a problem.

Personal context

Individual's personal context is also an important determinant of problem solving behaviour. **Hilton** (1958) has shown the influence of personal context in a study involving problems appropriate to male and female roles. Subjects for study comprised undergraduate level—24 males and 25 females. They were given a list of 20 problems. Half of the problems had content, appropriate to masculine roles while the other half to female roles. Clear-cut differences were found. When the problems were altered so as to make them less appropriate to either of the roles, sex difference was reduced.

Some experiments on problem solving ability and a general tendency towards conformity, emotional involvements as a defence of a controversial position also show that individual's personal context plays a significant role in search for solution to a problem.

Frustration and stress

Frustration and stress influence problem solving behaviour. There is evidence that stress strengthens problem-solving behaviours when it is of moderate degree and one is concerned or interested in solving the problem. But, when the stress is too much and a new response is to be substituted for old one, it usually impedes (Erickson, 1952; Palermo, 1957).

Reynolds (1960) in a study has found that in general, the effect of stress is more of a hindrance to problem-solving. Particularly when the solution requires a complex response, different from the old habits of response and action then simple isolated judgements are required and previous experience is directly applicable. Furthermore, it has also been found that when problem solver does not feel the need to defend himself from threat, he shows greater flexibility in exploring new solutions (Cowen, 1952).

Thus, stress and frustration do have influence in determining problem solving behaviour.

Freeing thoughts from rigid patterns

Often a problem solver is badly trapped in some kind of rigid or functional fixity of previous mode of response which hinders him from shifting or thinking to evolve a new formula. One way to overcome or lessen the tendency of rigidity or functional fixity is to allow time pass.

Another method to be free from rigid pattern is practising a good number of uncommon responses. Practice in this fashion would aid the individual in solving later problems even if the solutions were unrelated to any of the earlier responses. **Heyman** and **Anderson** (1965) has suggested the following eight rules, which may prevent the kind of rigidity, that leads to failure in solving a problem. These are:

(i) Running over the elements in a rapid succession several times till a pattern emerges which encompasses all these elements simultaneously.
(ii) Suspending the judgement and one should not jump to the conclusion.
(iii) Exploring the environment by varying temporal and spatial arrangements of the material.
(iv) Producing a second alternative solution after the first.
(v) Critical evaluation of one's own idea.
(vi) When struck, one should change his representational system. In case, concrete representation is not working, try an abstract one and vice versa.
(vii) Taking a break when one is struck.
(viii) Discussing the problem with someone.

Brainstorming

Problem solving is facilitated by **warming-up**. Advertising agencies and industrial or manufacturing organizations are widely using this technique of warming up to train individuals in making uncommon responses and associations. This technique helps them freeing their minds from any hindering rigidity. The technique uses the traditional modes of attacking a problem. This technique is known as 'brainstorming'. In this technique, an attempt is made to increase imaginative ideas by a division of the process into two stages:

The first stage is called **green light stage** in which the individual or group is presented with a problem or question and encouraged to try without any inhibition or reluctance. Thus, the subjects are encourged to free from any inhibition and entirely uncritical. They are free to think anything—profitable or unprofitable, practical or impractical. All hypotheses are written down, even the far-fetched ones. If several persons are working together, no person would criticize anybody's idea in this stage. Thus, people are free from the fear of any kind of threat as to criticism or being ridiculed for wrong idea. This, in fact, is very much similar to 'free association' technique of psycho-analysis (Freud). Under the situation, novel ideas are likely to be produced more readily.

The second stage is **red light stage**. The person is encouraged to be judicial. He considers each hypothesis very carefully and retains even those which he considers as unprofitable. He then further reconsiders them all and in the course, eventually selects the one which he considers as the most promising, and tries out. This way, more and more mental exercise helps an individual to be free from all kinds of inhibitions and free association of ideas storms the brain to dig out new modes more readily.

13.10 PROBLEM SOLVING BEHAVIOUR AS AN INFORMATION PROCESSING MODEL

It does not matter whether the problem is simple or difficult, thought processes are not easy to analyse. None of the traditional theories that attempts to explain thinking or problem solving process in terms of S-R association are adequate. Thinking or problem solving is not merely a chain of stimuli and response from initial cue to eventual solution. It is something more than that. Problem solving involves processes of sorting through and recognizing a great deal of information. Sorting and recognizing processes follow some rules and procedures to derive a solution, the processed information is stored into memory chambers. The nature of problem solving activity is very much similar to the way information is processed by a highly sophisticated computer system. These similarities have led to the psychologists of the day to some interesting efforts to formulate models of problem solving based on programming of a computer system.

The basis of any computer programming is registration of 'input'. In problem solving, the input is the 'task information', which is registered through sense modalities. The source of task information may be external or internal environment which is registered in sensory register (SR) through sensory channel. For example, in Haier's experiment as mentioned in Section 13.9 of this chapter the task information is both—the instructions to the subject, which specifies the required goal and the obstacles enroute to the goal. The discrepancy between the 'required' and 'current situation' is the 'objective problem'—the problem that an external observer can describe externally. This leads to 'focus of attention'.

The problem solver more or less transforms the task information into internal representation of the objective problem. This consists of symbols—images or words. In other words, the objective problem is perceived and thus, is transformed into 'subjective problem'—the problem as the solver perceives or conceives or structures. The conception of problem may or may not be adequate. It may require new input for clarity and understanding. Signal for 'new input' is received and the solver gives a fresh look or may ask to repeat the problem. For example, in the class, if a teacher puts a question, students raise their hands and request to repeat the question or to supplement the gaps if any or to make it more understandable. Thus, continual interplay of solving process begins at this level. This interplay involves valuable functioning as a result of which the irrelevant components are given up, ambiguity and gaps in the task information are sorted out and signal to reregister some new input is sent which follow the process as before and the problem is thus, well conceived and structured. In computer also, in the event of incomplete input (poorly fed data) or wrong, irrelevant, unmatching feeding of data, signals as 'errors' or demand for more richer data (new input) appear on the visual screen and the programmer gives a fresh look and refeed the data to make it rich enough for further processing.

The moment a problem is well-conceived (structured or defined) working on problem by Central Processor (CP) begins. Solutions are generated and evaluated or judged against the criteria of discrepancy between the goal and current situation. This criterion guides the problem solver to develop strategies for solving the problem. A well-defined problem provides retrieval cues from memory storage about the possible solutions, which are evaluated and judged, i.e. their relative potency in reducing the discrepancy between the goal, and the current situation is determined and those which appear unworkable are abandoned. If any one of the solutions appears adequate (workable) the process ends (terminates). If, however, any of the retrieved solution seems inadequate, signal to obtain more additional information (input) is sent. The additional information is registered and followed the original sequence. In other words, further study of the problem is initiated. Three important points should be noted here. First, presentation or sticking with unworkable hypothesis causes failure. Secondly, normally a problem solver works with one solution (hypothesis) at a time. Thirdly, information acquired while working on a problem, may suggest some new solution(s). These processes very much resemble with the process in the Central Processor Unit (CPU) of a computer.

Working on additional input and suggested hypothesis (solution) again involves retrieval from memory storage for evaluation and testing for the hypothesis. Actual testing can be through observing the consequences by recalling the outcome of former actions or by reasoning. Thus, finally an adequate solution is selected which generates response mechanism to produce "output (i.e. solution of the problem)" by making adequate response to the current situation.

The information processing model as described above is shown diagrammatically in **Figure 13.1**.

In the model (diagrammatic representation) the 'input' is the task information which is registered and filtered and then leads to focus of attention. The attended input is transferred to cognition (CPU) of the cortex where the problem is structured and thus transformed into subjective problem—the problem as conceived by the solver. This transformation is possible by means of evaluation of the cognition of the input and thus, the input is clarified. It leads to the solution (production) and its evaluation. If solution is found unworkable, additional input (task information) is demanded. If, however, solution is found workable, output is generated through various human actions.

The diagrammatic picture of information processing model, shown in **Figure 13.1**, exhibits many similarities with computer system of problem solving process.

The computer system is usually divided into threee main components—Input, CPU, and Output.

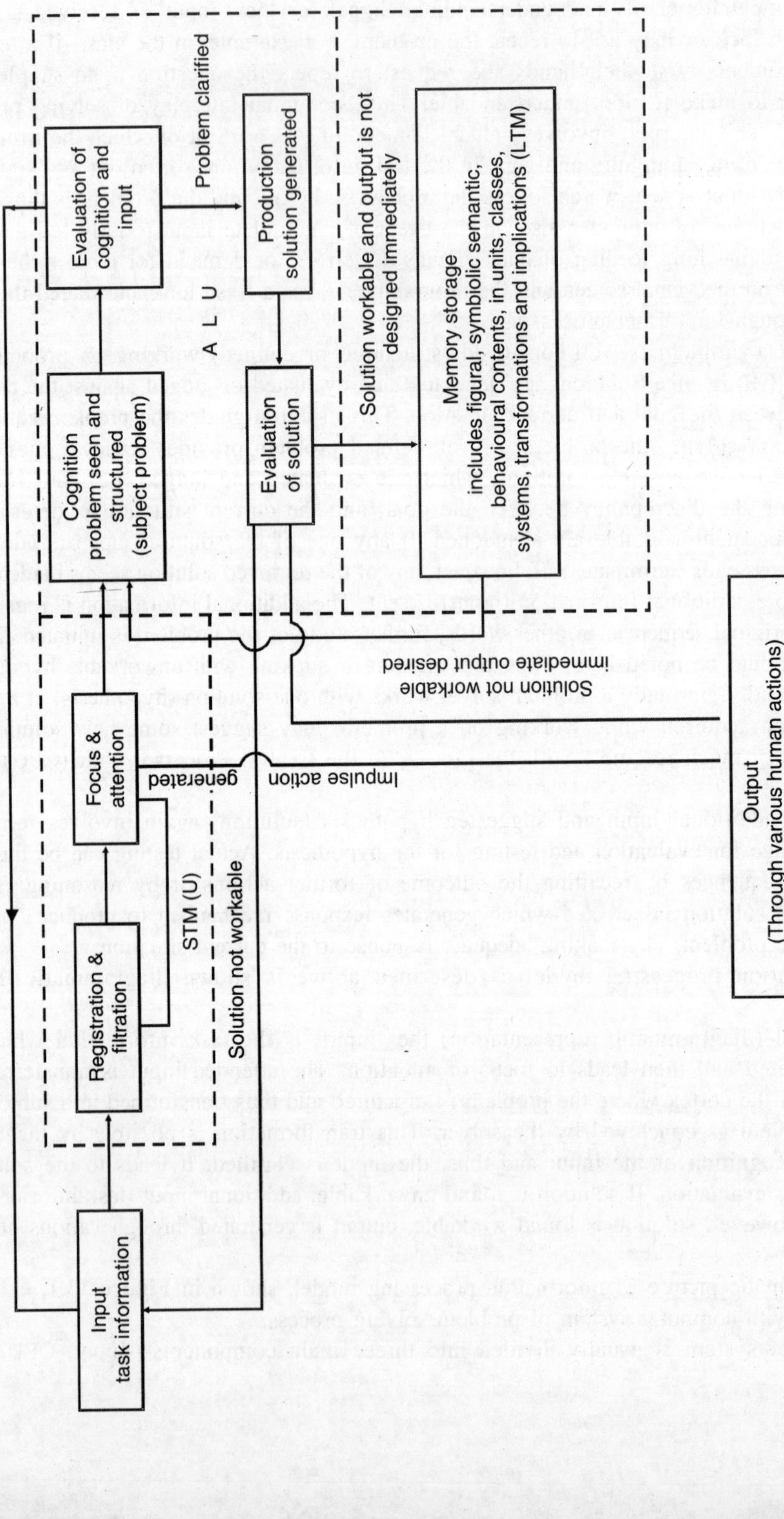

FIGURE 13.1 Schematic representation of information process model of problem solving behaviour.

13.10.1 Input

This is in the form of a keyboard in a computer through which information is fed. In human beings, while thinking, this input is fed through sensory channel.

Central process unit (CPU): This is the most important part of any computer system. The very name—'central processor unit' itself indicates that all processing of different kinds of information coming through input channels are done in CPU. Information is processed and transformed here. This unit is further subdivided into three parts—Control Unit (CU), Arithmetic Logic Unit (ALU) and Immediate Access Storage (IAS).

Control unit (CU): Control unit does initial scanning of the information and forms an objective problem. If the control function feels no need of any help to the prefed information or even if the logical calculations are not required, then it displays the final output. In human thinking, this function is done by sensory memory where initial information is registered and filtered. It also focuses the attention on the objective problem and if feels that no thinking is necessary, then directly changes into impulse action.

Arithmetic logic unit (ALU): This part of CPU does most of the logical calculations and creates logical solutions. Similarly in human beings, this part (cerebral cortex) does most of the logical thinking and calculations (cognition, evaluation, judgement, decision-making etc.). If it feels that action is required, then it sends the solutions as output through action (response). Otherwise, it records solution into LTM (Long Term Memory).

Immediate access storage (IAS): It is very helpful in performing logical solutions. In other words, it provides the computer with prerecorded information to see and evaluate a problem and also to record the eventual solution. In human thinking, the retrieval of past experiences stored in memory, function as immediate access storage. While processing information, the LTM provides with constant flow of similar type of problems and solutions available in its record as immediate access to help the control unit to arrive at a solution with their help.

13.11 THEORIES OF THINKING

Thinking as we have seen is an implicit symbolic process. It is a chain of symbolic processes which comprises figural, semantic, images, words, behavioural contents, gestural symbols etc. These are stored in memory storage in units, class, relationship systems, transformation systems and even implicative systems. Many psychologists on the basis of action current studies regard thinking as mental activity of the higher centres involving implicit muscular activities. But since, these activities are so minute and implicit that they can scarcely be observed through naked eye. These activities can only be inferred from graphs of action currents obtained by some special device. However, in general, almost we all agree that thought is a mediating process which occurs in between the problem of thought and its subsequent solution. But, the pertinent question is about the 'venue' of this mediating symbolic process. Where does this process occur? Gestaltists and behaviourists have offered two different explanations, which are known as two distinct theories as mentioned hereinbelow under separate headings.

13.11.1 Central Theory

According to this theory, the 'brain' or 'cerebral cortex' is the seat of all our cognitive functions—seat of 'mind'. Therefore, all interactions and interplays necessary and sufficient for 'thinking', occur in the higher centre of the brain called 'cerebral cortex'. Thus, cerebral cortex is the venue of thought operations except the stirring events of thinking (stimulus in problem form) and externally observable outcome (solution in the form of response) of thinking that occur outside the cortex, i.e. in the peripheries. In between these two events, the mediating process (thought process) occurs in the cortex. The 'input' (information) propagates ideas, images and the like in the cortex. These symbols are arranged, disarranged, rearranged or manipulated in a particular way to arrive at appropriate solutions, which are evaluated and judged by the centre and a decision to put to test by actually acting out is taken. This is an observable event and hence, the outcome of the thought. It is not only the output but also an objective test of the end product of thought process. Central theory of thought is diagrammatically represented in **Figure 13.2**.

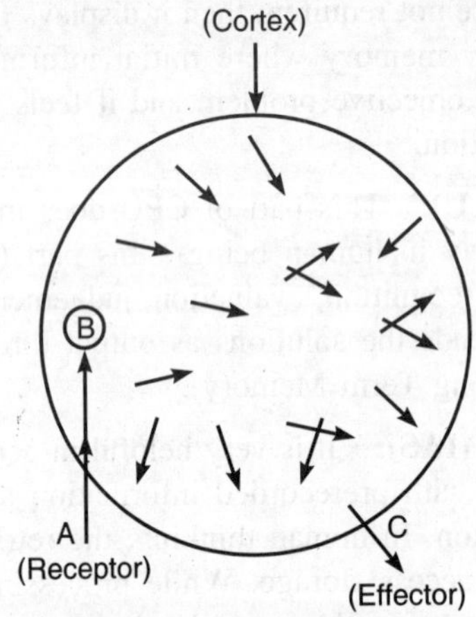

FIGURE 13.2 Schematic representation of central theory.

From Figure 13.2, it is clear that the incoming patterns of stimulation form receptors route to cerebral cortex and give rise to symbolic processes (arrows inside the cortex represent the cortical processes of mediation) such as transformation of objective problem into subjective problem, retrieval of possible solutions, evaluation of solutions, judgement, decision-making etc. All these interactions take place in the cortex and as soon as the adequate or workable solution is found, motor impulse to effector is transmitted and thus, the solution is put to test by actual muscular activity.

Critical comment

The central theory in fact expresses the common sense view that 'thinking goes on in the mind'. The facts of central theory cannot be substantiated by neuropsychological studies. However, there is no denying the fact that the architectural design of the brain is such that any kind of complex interaction may take place. Hence, everything is possible but little is precisely measurable and substantiable.

13.11.2 Peripheral-Central Theory

Contrary to central theory, the peripheral-central theory has been proposed. Often this theory is also referred to as peripheral theory only. But it is not proper to call this theory only as 'peripher because the theory does not rule out the significance of cortex in thinking. The theory undoubtedly lays emphasis on the peripheral activities but at the same time cortical functions are also considered important. Therefore, 'peripheral-central theory' is the appropriate name with which this theory ought to be called.

According to this theory, cortex has two functions

(a) 'as a relay station' and (b) 'as a locus of awareness'. As relay station, it transmits impulses from receptors to effectors (say muscles) and also movement produced reception (kinesthetic) to yet another effector. As a locus of awareness the awareness of thought occurs in the sensory area of the cortex.

Watson, the main propounder of this theory, is of the view that thinking is a purely stimulus-response affair (S-R affair), much similar to behaviours displayed in running a maze. The only difference between the two lies in the degree of skeletal movements. In thinking, this movement is implicit and hence minimal while in running a maze, skeletal movement is overt or explicit and much more. To elaborate further, this theory holds that problem of thought is the initiating stimulus which evokes certain implicit responses within the individual. The stimulation arises in the sensory cortex where an appropriate selection occurs and a motor impulse is initiated and transmitted to some effector. The activity of the effector arouses a sensory impulse (kinesthetic) which, in turn, goes to sensory cortex whereby means of association pathways the process is repeated. Thus, a chain or series of sensory and implicit muscular responses are generated and continued till the solution of the problem is accomplished, i.e. attainment of the goal. Thus, thinking is a series of perceptions of the sensory impulses and responses. The main theme of the theory can be diagrammatically represented as in **Figure 13.3**.

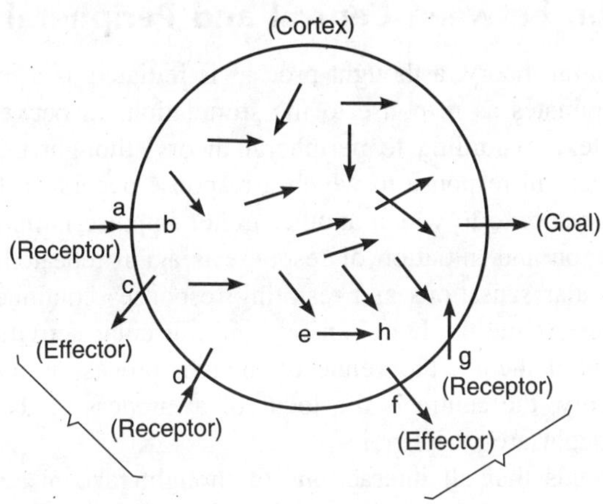

FIGURE 13.3 Schematic representation of peripheral.

a = Receptor activity of the initiating stimulus (thinking) giving rise to sensory experience of the problem
b = Generation of motor impulse in the cortex
c = Repsonse by the effector as a result of the motor impulse—(b)
d = Movement-produced sensation (kinesthetic) of the activity evoked in the effector—(c)
e = Generation of motor impulse in the corex in response to movement-produced sensation—(d)
f = Yet another activity of the effector as a result of motor impulse—(e)
g = Again sensation (kinesthetic) of the activity evoked by the (f)
h = Again generation of motor impulse in the cortex
Goal (G) = Final output (cortex response), i.e. accomplishment of the goal or 'G'.

From Figure 13.3, it is obvious that thinking involves a chain of sensory and motor implicit responses which continues till 'goal' (solution) is achieved. However, the patterns of sensations (proprioceptive and others) arising from the implicit responses are momentary states of awareness. Further, it is also clear that although the locus of awareness is central, the necessary conditions of thought are peripheral.

This theory is also called 'motor theory' because of the emphasis it lays on motor activities. The theory bears great resemblance to **William James** (1890)* view of habit formation. According to James, a habit is more or less a series of automatic actions as shown in **Figure 13.4**.

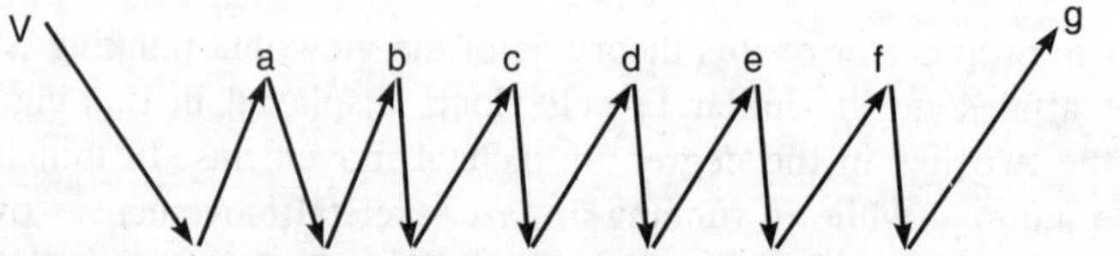

FIGURE 13.4 Diagram to show possible kinesthetic basis of habit.

Note here

V = 'Command to Start', i.e. whatever initially sets off the habitual chain of motor activities or muscular contractions—ABCDEFG.

a, b, c, d, e, f, g—Kinesthetic sensations.

'G'—final intellectual process which brings the series to end.

13.11.3 Comparison between Central and Peripheral Theories

1. According to central theory, a thought process is initiated as a result of stimulation by a problem and terminates as response to the stimulation. In between, all interactions take place in the cortex. According to peripheral theory, thought processes are initiated by sensing the problem in response to which a response occurs. In turn, there is kinesthetic sensation and in response to which another motor impulse is initiated. It again arouses a kinesthetic sensation and initiation of response is again repeated. Thus, through a series of repeated muscular sensations and resulting responses continue till a final response is made. Hence, there is multitude of sensory and muscular activities forming a chain.
2. According to central theory, the venue of thought process is cortex whereas according to peripheral theory, the centre is the locus of awareness of thought and the necessary conditions of thought are peripheral.
3. Central theory holds that all interactions of thought take place in the cortex whereas peripheral theory holds that whole body is found involved in thinking. Cortex only provides necessary engrams for thought, which are stored in it.
4. Central theory cannot be empirically tested. But peripheral theory provides some testable hypothesis.

Though, central theory lacks testable hypothesis, it does not mean that it is untenable. The lack of testable hypothesis is indicative of our ignorance. Science is progressive in nature. Therefore, future studies are likely to lend some reliable evidences and ultimately prove it to be correct by specifying how it works.

---

* James, W., *The Principles of Psychology*, New York: Holt, 1890, p. 116.

13.11.4 Some Experimental Evidences in Support of the Two Theories

Efforts have been made to gather empirical facts in support of the two theories. Some of these studies are briefly described here:

Clark (1922) made an attempt to obtain a variety of measures of what goes on while one thinks? She gave her subjects (10 graduate students), different kinds of problems in 5 successive sessions. Data at various sittings were obtained on imaginary, overt movement, effects of distraction, and physiological changes in respiration, arm volume, horizontal and vertical movements of larynx and tongue. She found that in addition to imagery, many other kinds of movements also accompany the solutions. These movements have been explained in terms of adaptive attitude of the body while thinking. Most of these movements aid the thinker to concentrate on problem with full calmness. Further, some minute movements were also observed, such as movement of the eye, lips and other muscles. She links these movements with changes occurring in the contents of the consciousness during the period of thinking. In regard to subvocal activities also, she found some minute movement of the larynx and tongue in many of the verbal elements of thought process.

However, in some of the seemingly verbal elements, no such movement could be detected. In the light of these contradictions, Clark opines that inner speech alone cannot account for all thoughts.

Osgood* also made an attempt to see if thought can occur without peripheral involvements, but could not succeed. Similarly, Thoroson (1925), Jacobson (1932), Max (1934), (1925a), (1935b), (1937) also found ample evidences to show that peripheral movements accompany thought processes.

On the other hand, **Smith et al.** (1947) in a medical experiment with d-tubocurarine (curara)—a drug which paralyses the muscles without affecting nervous system, lends support to the view that thinking can occur as a purely central process. Similarly, Sokolov (1960), Glickman and Fieldman (1961) have also demonstrated that peripheral receptors are probably not involved in thinking.

On the basis of available evidences, we are not in a position to take either of the theories as correct or incorrect. If we take an extreme peripheral position, the complex interactions of brain is left out and if we take the extreme central position, then economical role played by overflow of motor activities in organizing and evaluating the thought processes will be left out. Such a position will not yield any valid production about thinking. Therefore, it would be reasonable for us to take a compromising view as Osgood has suggested—'The development of symbolic processes may require peripheral mediation which becomes telescoped to a largely central representation in the mature individual'. This view may fit much of the evidences. Young people usually make more use of overt mediations than adults. Adults tend to regress to more overt levels under stress. Less intelligents use more motor potentials during thought and imagination than those who are more intelligent.

Hence, a compromised view seem to be important. Compromised view is also important in the sense that it is likely to encourage further research and make the knowledge about 'the psychology of thinking' richer and richer.

---

* Osgood, C.E., *Method and Theory in Experimental Psychology*, N.Y. Oxford University, 1968, p. 653.

13.11.5 Piaget's Cognitive Theory

Cognition is a process of knowing and understanding the world. It primarily refers not only to knowing but also reasoning, deciding, judging and even theorizing. But, in psychology, this term is used in a general way—a process by which knowledge of an object is obtained. This knowledge is partly obtained through perceptions and partly through remembering, imaginations, reasoning etc. Thus, the term cognition is synonyms for 'thinking'.

Jean Piaget, a famous Swiss psychologist and philosopher (however, basically he was a biologist) had very extensively studied intelligence of children since 1920. For him, intelligence is not only the mean score obtained on a test, rather it is a mental or cognitive process. This process enables a child to know about the world he lives in. Thus, knowledge or understanding about the world is the central idea of Piaget's conception of cognition.

Piaget terms his approach as 'genetic epistemology'. Epistemology is a science of knowledge through knowing. It studies about the nature and acquisition of knowledge. Piaget focuses on the development or genesis of cognition. Therefore, his approach is termed as 'genetic epistemology' and not that he makes any reference to the gene or heredity.

Piaget views the development of knowledge (cognition) as a form of adaptation which involves the interplay of two processes, namely, the 'assimilation' and 'accommodation'. Adaptation is an innate tendency of which assimilation and accommodation are the two sub- processes. Both these processes serve as strategies in obtaining knowledge about the objects around us. Assimilation refers to modifying one's environment so as to fit into one's already developed ways of thinking and acting. Memorization of the past helps in the process of assimilation or takes in information. For example, a shadowy form in a dark room is recognized by a child as a parent coming to deliver milk. This recognition is based on the past experience of the child, which he has incorporated in his existing mental structure and the ability to assimilate stimuli from environment. This is called assimilation. Therefore, assimilation is a process of taking in information as far as possible depending upon the level of mental organization (scheme)* at a particular time.

Another sub-process of adaptation is 'accommodation'. When the level of mental structure of a child is not advanced enough to assimilate (take in) information, the mental structure is gradually modified to fit in the aspects of the environment to the mental organization or 'scheme'. Such modifications permit grasping. Thus, through modification of mental organization (scheme) the primitive scheme changes to differentiate between graspable and ungraspable.

Biologically, assimilation and accommodation are constant functions of brain. However, cognitive development itself is not constant. In fact, cognitive development passes through four different stages. Normally, every individual passes through these stages in order. But, the rate of development is not the same in every individual. Some individuals reach the final stage of cognitive development at most early age (before teenage) while others never attain the final stage completely. Hence, assigning any age boundary to a stage is difficult. Despite this, a tentative age level is suggestible and accordingly the characteristic features of each stage are described hereinbelow:

Sensory-motor stage

This is the first stage of cognitive development in a child. This stage contains six sub-stages starting from zero month of birth to approximately 2 years after birth. In the beginning, the child

* Specific ways of knowing—An action sequence gained by thought.

is only a bundle of simple reflexes. He does not differentiate the self from the rest of the world, viz. turning towards the present, flinging of arms towards crib, grasping at ratling sounds of spoons etc. Within a few months after birth some of the reflex patterns gradually fade out as the child develops some control over movement. By the time the child starts walking, one can notice he can display curiosity by reaching blocks. Shaking them in the manner as if he is weighing or appraising weights, size and shape. As the baby grows, newer responses emerge and there is increase in intentional movements. Elementary memory also begins to appear and start anticipating the things. By the time of sensory-motor stage the child develops self-concept and symbolic manipulation of the world in terms of sensory-motor schemes (mental organization that has been internalized) appear.

Pre-operational stage

This is the second step of cognitive development in a child. As the child steps into the pre-operational stage, he acquires new tools that sharpen his knowledge. Use of language is one such tool. Language stands as symbol for things or people to understand about them. The child also becomes able to manipulate things mentally in place of performing physically as in the first phase (sensory-motor). But, still cognition is neither complete nor accurate. Pre-operational children are incapable of utilizing most of the operations with knowledge. This is the reason, 'Piaget' defines pre-operational children in terms of 'what they cannot do' and not in terms of 'what they can do'. This is evident from some classical experiments. In one experiment, a child is presented with two rows of toys with equal number of toys in each row. The toys of one row were spread two inches apart while the toys of second row were spread 4 inches apart thus, taking up more space. The child reports that the number of toys in the second row is more than the first row. The experiments like this demonstrate lack of understanding of the principle of **conservation** which states that the amount of substance remains unchanged even if the substance is modified. Thus, cognitive judgement in the pre-operational stage bases more on appearance rather than on knowledge of conservation principle. Similarly, children in this stage are also unable to **reverse logical operations**. Therefore, the child cannot think that the number of toys in the second row will be same as in the first row if the operating distances are reduced to the distance as in the first row.

Thus, it is evident that the organizational scheme of cognitive development in the pre-operational stage does not incorporate the principles of conservation and reversibility.

Concrete operational stage

The third stage of cognitive development begins at the age of approximately 7 to 8 years. By this time, children develop the ability to exchange conversations and manipulate concrete objects or situations. Egocentricism gradually begins to vanish and his thinking becomes more adult-like. They begin to recognize the opinions of their peers seeing things different from them. Thus, egocentricism becomes socialized.

The child at this stage is concrete-bound. He can understand conversation because he is capable of utilizing reverse concrete operations. For example, in toys experiment, the child in this stage is able to understand that the number of toys remains the same whether these are spread out or are closely clumped.

The ability to conserve depends upon the ability of reversibility. Thus, the child, while observing a box can imagine that the spread-out toys on the floor can be packed into the box. This he does by reversing his thought.

Though the child in concrete operational stage is endowed with these useful capabilities, these are still limited. Abstract thinking is still in its elementary phase. Therefore, he is able to manipulate only the concrete objects to which he has encountered and not the symbolic things.

Formal operational stage

This is the final stage of cognitive development among children, which begins around the age of adolescence, i.e. during teen ages. By this time, mental operations extend and include formalized and systematic logical operations such as—search for general principles, application of symbols, explorations, scientific thoughts, exploring hypotheses for themselves etc. In our everyday life, we can notice an adolescent thinking like this—'If I were a teacher, I would enjoy giving every student top grades. But, then I think of it—students will stop studying….' Such thoughts mean that the adolescent child has developed the ability to explore hypotheses for himself.

Thus, in formal operational stage, children with growing interaction with the world move to systematic logical reasoning and towards a search for general principle. Children, in fact, acquire genuine scientific methods of thinking and reasoning.

Critical comment

Though for decades Piaget's theory of 'cognitive development' better served the researchers, teachers and parents in understanding behaviour of children. However, some experimental evidences do not lend much support to Piaget's views. For example, egocentricism among children met with challenge when in one study a 4-year old child was found speaking with due care of listener's ability (Gellermann, 1939). The task for a 4-year child was to describe a toy to a 2-year child and then to a peer or adult. It was observed that the subjects used very short and simple sentences for the younger children while more complex descriptions were given to older persons. Thus, the researcher concluded—"These children were hardly egocentric".

In the light of some challenging facts as above, two other theories were propounded by James Bruner (1966) and Robert Gagne (1970, 1974). These researchers lay greater emphasis on the role of parents, teachers and school in the progression of skills to think from simpler to complex one.

Thus, cognitive development has variously been described. However, Piaget's contribution is of paramount significance.

13.12 CONCEPTS

While thinking, we use concepts. Use of concepts is almost essential for thinking. All noun words of a language (except personal nouns) are concepts, viz. animal, beauty, men, house, gold, length, water etc. are all noun words which represent a class of objects and hence, are all concepts. Concepts are mediating symbols of thought processes which represent a set of objects or events to which one reacts in the same way. Concepts represent the similarities in otherwise diverse objects, situations or events.

In a sense, concepts are condensations of our past experiences. This implies that concepts bring together the learned properties of many different things. For example, a patient approaches a doctor and spells out bits of information about his illness. The bit of information enters into doctor's mind as separate components. But, these bits of information did not remain separate for long. The different components soon began to coalesce (unite) into 'general idea'. This general idea is formed from different pieces of information—we call 'concepts'. The concept developed by the doctor is a condensation of different bits of information—the patient's look, pattern of symptoms, physio-chemical changes in the body etc. This concept is in the name or category of disease diagnosed by the doctor.

Similarly, suppose someone meets with a strange object. He reacts with this strange object by saying—'it looks like unusual vegetable' or fruit'. By saying this, he is trying to generalize the object to a category with which he is familiar (vegetable or fruit) on the basis of some property which is commonly found in a vegetable or a fruit, even though the present object (strange object) has many other diverse characteristics.

Concepts have variously been defined by different psychologists. For example, Osgood* defines—**'concepts as common response (usually verbal) made to a class of phenomena, the members of which display certain common property'.**

According to **Morgan** and **King**—'A concept is a symbolic construction that represents some common and general feature of attributes of object'.

'Vinacke', 'Morie' and 'Sanford' have also offered definitions in their own way. But, if we closely examine all these definitions, we would notice that two things are common in all the definitions—(a) generality of application and (b) differentiation among the cases to which concepts apply. These two are respectively referred to as the processes of 'generalization' and 'abstraction'. These two processes go together in which abstraction proceeds generalization. Abstracting is observing the essential feature of an object or event. For example, a child while acquiring the concept 'tree' must observe some such attribute, which are common to all trees regardless of how much different trees differ from one another (such as some trees bear fruits, some flowers, some are ornamental, some are large, some are very tiny plants etc.). But, certain feature of a tree is commonly found in all trees despite much diversity. Observing the common property in diverse object is called abstracting. The child's first experience with a tree may be hearing the word 'tree' associated with mango tree, but later on he hears the same word attached to Gulmohar—an object of quite different nature and kind. Still later he hears about teak (*Tactiona grandis*) tree. Thus the child observes some characteristics common to all these different kinds of trees, abstraction of which favours the formation of the concept of 'tree'. After a series of such experiences with varieties of trees, a child may see a 'willow', which has never been called a tree in his presence. If a child designates it as tree, it may be presumed that the child must have observed something of which this object has in common with other trees. In so doing, the child must have put aspects of his previous experience together with the present experience and found this object being like others in certain respects before reaching the conclusion and designating it as tree. This process is called 'generalization'. Hence, generalization is a process through which the present object is put into a category of certain aspects of previous experience on the basis of similarity of the property or attribute. It may be noted here that a person can abstract without generalization but generalization without abstraction is not possible. Hence, for concepts, both the processes are essential.

At this point, we should also bear clearly in mind that the process of abstracting and generalization is not necessarily deliberate or even carried out consciously. Most often, our equivalent reactions to a set of objects or events also provide evidences of a concept. For example, in a dinner party, we arrange two separate stalls—vegetarian and non-vegetarian.

* Osgood, C.E., *op cit.*

All items such as fishes, eggs, muttons, chickens are grouped together in one stall—'non-vegetarian'. The vegetable items of different varieties are grouped together in another stall—'vegetarian'. Here grouping of different varieties of food and eatables in the vegetarian and non-vegetarian categories involve reacting to the food items in equivalent manner on the basis of certain common properties. Thus, this equivalence of reactions or response depends upon something which despite diversity have something in common. Animals also react to certain situations in equivalent terms of which we can be sure to say whether they behave deliberately or are conscious of certain similarities.

Hence, it is clear that when one reacts to a set of objects or event in the same way—either verbally or non-verbally, we call to have a concept. That is, to react equivalently by calling each set of objects by the same name or by performing equivalent non-verbal response to them, viz. calling all printed papers bound together as 'book' and treating cash and cheques as functionally equivalent.

We may now define concepts as follows:

> **A concept is basically a category for classifying and responding in the same way to a set of objects, events, things or specific people or situations on the basis of some common defining characteristics.**

13.12.1 Concepts and Thinking

Concept is an important tool of thought process. While we think, we make use of concepts. Concepts are mediating symbols of thought processes. It is not only an essential tool but the basic ability for thinking. How do we know that a parrot, not the lion is a bird? Concepts usually fall into hierarchies or levels of understanding. The levels are classified as superordinate (the highest level), the basic (an intermediate level) and subordinate (the lowest level). While speaking, we mostly use the basic level concepts. For example, we most usually say 'I saw a dog'—intermediate or basic level concept. We hardly say—I saw a four-legged animal that barks and wags its tail (the lowest level—subordinate level) or animal (superordinate level). The basic level concept is far too specific than needed for conversation while the superordinate level is far too vague.

While thinking, most of the concepts that we use are neither clear nor unambiguous. They are fuzzy. They often overlap one another and are poorly defined. For example, under which category a stool can be put—chair or table? To answer this question, we need to construct a **'prototype'**. A prototype is the best representative member of the category. **Eleanor Rosch** argues that in considering how people think about concepts, prototypes are often involved in real life. In prototype matching, people decide whether an item is a member of a category by comparing it with the most typical item(s) of the category. Hence, if you compare a stool with a standard study chair (if you consider it as a typical example of a chair) and a small study table (if you consider it as the typical example of a table) and match the properties of the stool with these two concepts. If it matches with a chair, you would put it under the category of 'chair', otherwise it comes in the category of 'table'.

While thinking, concepts make the information processing economical and hence, aids in thinking. While forming concepts, we do not only learn to categorize or classify an object but also learn the laws that govern the concepts. For example, when we see the traffic signals, we not only learn to differentiate between red and green lights, but we also learn the meaning that it conveys, viz. red light conveys to 'stop' while the green signal conveys 'go'. It is really very surprising that we learn abundant of concepts. The governing laws which are stored in our memory system as symbols concepts help us in manipulating the problems of thought to arrive at an appropriate solution to the problem. Concepts also help us in our day-to-day interactions.

13.12.2 Characteristics of Concepts

Some of the important characteristics of concepts are mentioned hereinbelow:

1. Concepts are symbolic means of classifying the stimuli (object) on the basis of certain common property. For example, we put horses, oxen, dogs, cows etc. into a category of 'four-footed animals'; crows, parrots and others into category of 'birds'; mangoes, bananas, oranges, apples etc. into the category of 'fruits' and so on. All these diverse objects and organisms are classified into a specific category according to some common defining characteristics, which they possess.
2. Though sensory data are important in the formation of a concept, but concepts are not merely sensory details of an object. Concepts are combined and elaborated form of data, viz. examine the geometrical **Figure 13.5**.

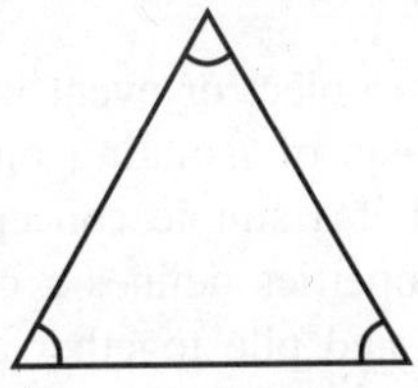

FIGURE 13.5 Conceptualization of data.

   The sensory details of the figure are three simple lines joining at three points—two at the extremes of the horizontal base and one at the apex. But, all those sensory data are combined and conceptualized as a 'triangle'. Triangles are of many diverse kinds differing in measures of angles, lengths of lines forming triangles, colour, shape etc. But, all varieties of triangles are conceptualized as triangles. Similarly, various forms of rectangles, circles, squares etc. are also conceptualized as rectangles, circles and so on.
3. Concepts depend on past experience. This is the reason that an inborn blind person may not conceptualize and differentiate between a circle and a triangle even when the vision is restored by surgical operation.
4. Concept is a selective system. This system is a byproduct of mental organization. Through selection, we are able to classify and categorize a wide variety of objects of the world in specific categories on the basis of observing something common in them.
5. Concepts are symbolical in nature. For this reason, we react to different stimuli in the same way. Human beings usually symbolize diverse objects through verbal responses while the animals symbolize in terms of space, time and order.

13.12.3 Kinds or Types of Concepts

The rules by which features are connected to form concepts may be either simple or complex. Psychologists have studied the types of concepts on the basis of rules employed to define a concept. These are known as artificial and natural concepts. Both of these concepts are mentioned hereinbelow:

Artificial concepts

These are well-defined concepts. The rules by which the features of these concepts are connected are pure and rigid. For example, take triangles or rectangles. Such geometrical figures are the examples of artificial concepts. These are well-defined concepts because the features that represent triangles or rectangles are essential features. These figures must possess all the essentially defined properties or features to become a concept. Let us take an example of a 'square'. A square is a well-defined concept. It must have four attributes, namely four sides, each side must have equal lengths and each angle should also be equal—90° along with equal lengths of diagonals. Thus, a square has four features which are connected by conjunctive rule and, therefore, every geometrical figure with these four features connected by conjunctive rules is conceptualized as 'square', distinct from figures of a rectangle or a triangle.

The artificial concepts can be divided into four different kinds on the basis of the governing rules. There are as follows:

(a) **Simple concepts:** When an object or event is categorized as belonging to a particular class or category on the basis of isolating only one set of common property, which defines the concept, we call it a simple concept. According to **Morgan** and **King**—'if only one set of common properties defines a concept, we call it as a 'simple concept'. For example, when we sort and pile together all cards having circle in one pile, while cards having triangles are sorted and piled separately despite the fact that different cards may have circles and triangle of different sizes and colours.

(b) **Conjunctive concepts:** Conjunctive concepts are defined by the presence of several characteristics. For example, the two teams of football players in a playground are categoriezed on the basis of several joint characteristics such as—the colour of their dress, relative position and direction of their runs with balls or the direction of passing the ball etc. The match viewers use conjunctive concepts while watching the game.

(c) **Disjunctive concepts:** Disjunctive concepts are generally very complex and difficult to attain. It is so because, a number of disjunctive concept classes contain at least one common element from a large class of element, viz., petrol, coal, electricity, kerosene oil, firewood etc. are diverse elements, each with distinctive concept class. But, one element in all these is common—all these 'burn' and on the basis of this one common element, these disjunctive concepts are classified under the concept—'fuel'. Similarly, scooter, bike, car, jeep, bus etc. are all put under the concept—'automobile'.

(d) **Relational concepts:** This kind of concept is defined in terms of relationship between the elements and not in terms of absolute property or properties of the elements, viz. the concepts of child and adults, long and short, youth and old etc. In such cases classification is done in terms of relative differences in age, length, or size and not in terms of any absolute property.

Natural concepts

Natural concepts are those which are neither well defined nor have any boundary or limits of features as numerous features may be found. For example, if we ask a question—Is hen an animal? Here, the word 'animal' is a natural concept. But, the defining features of animals are numerous and hence, has no definite limit of its features. Thus, it is obvious that a natural concept is ill-defined and may have numerous features. The basis of such concepts are **prototype** which are basic and are easily acquired (Mervis and Rosh, 1981). Natural concepts include the biological objects, real world products and human artifacts such as furnitures, tools, clothes, etc. The natural concepts to a degree reflect the way our brain processes and sorts information as we find in dividing colours—'red', 'green', 'blue', and so forth (Rosh, 1973). Thus, natural concepts are largely formed with the help of past experiences which appear in thinking very early in life.

Characteristics of natural concepts: All natural categories (concepts) share four important characteristics. These are as follows:

(a) **Natural concepts have fuzzy boundaries:** The different kinds of natural objects have no definite feature. On one occasion the object is categorized in one category while on another occasion, the same object is considered as belonging to another category. For example, 'dress' is a natural concept that includes a variety of dresses—shirts, paints or trousers, sarees, jumpers, wollen suits etc. If one is required to pack the dresses safely, we generally pack all these varieties of dresses in different wardrobes such as sarees are stocked in a particular wardrobe, trousers are stocked in another wardrobe and so on. Similarly, jack fruit (kathal) is a fruit as well as a vegetable on two different occasions. Again 'to fly' is the most salient feature found in all birds. But a peacock inside a cage cannot fly. Even then it is a categorized as bird.

(b) **Instances of all natural concepts are organized around prototypes:** A prototype refers to experientially imagined examples of a category—most similar to typical instances. While classifying an object into a category, we compare the object with the prototype and then decide the object whether the same resembles closer to the prototype. For example, suppose we see a man after a long gap of association and want to categorize him into a category of our schoolmate group. We hear him talking and when we find that the sound tone is very near to our prototype of a familiar friend, we immediately enquire of him in reference to the prototype of sound tone and finally identify him as our friend of school days.

(c) **Natural categories have family resemblance:** Categories of natural objects contain such features that indicate family resemblance. For example, take the category of birds. All birds have wings, lay eggs, fly, peck, perch on trees or top of the tall structures etc. Similarly, all human beings are mammalians. Vegetables, fruits etc. also have certain features of family resemblance despite certain unit differences within the category. For example, look at **Figure 13.6** showing family resemblances in seven faces.

(d) **Natural concepts organized at different levels of abstraction:** Natural concepts are organized at different levels of abstraction. Three of such levels of abstraction are important. These are as follows:

- Basic level
- Superordinate level and
- Subordinate level

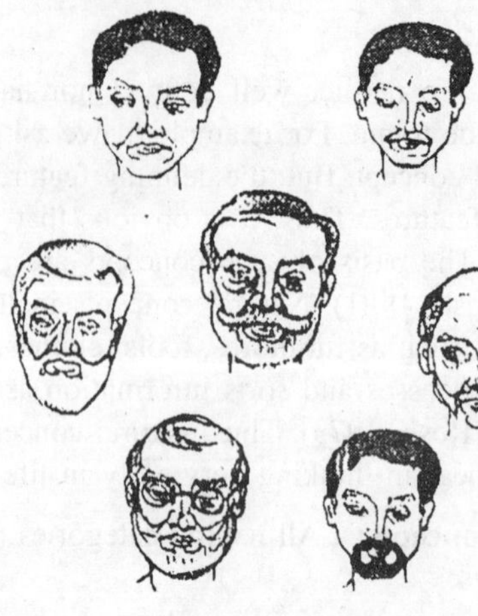

FIGURE 13.6 Family resemblances in faces.

The basic level concepts are abstracted on the basis of basic inherent features such as chairs and tables, apples and oranges, trousers and shirts are classified in terms of basic level.

Furniture, fruits and garments respectively are the superordinate levels of abstracting these basic level objects that include chairs, tables (as furniture), oranges and apples (as fruits), trousers and shirts (as garments). Similarly, the juicy, fleshy fruits are subordinate levels of abstracting concepts.

Basic level categories provide optimal level of specificity and thus, perceptual analysis becomes easier. Information processing is simple and facilitates in achieving accuracy of communication. It is found that children first learn the basic level categories while the superordinate and subordinate categories for further organization in semantic memory are learnt later in advance stages of cognitive development.

13.12.4 Differences between Artificial and Natural Concepts

Following are some of the differences between artificial and natural concepts:

1. Artificial concepts are those which are well defined and the rules connecting the features are precise and rigid. On the other hand, natural concepts are usually not well-defined.
2. Artificial concepts have no prototype whereas the basic of natural concepts are its prototype.
3. The artificial concepts, in addition to essential features connected by conjunctive rules, also have certain relevant features on the basis of which, the same categories of objects are conceptualized as different. To understand how similar objects are conceptualized differently on the basis of certain relevant features (which are not included in essential features) are shown in **Figure 13.7**, where the set of triangles and squares are conceptualized differently on the basis of their colour, + and dot signs appearing at the top or sides differently. In natural concepts, we form concepts basically on the basis of basic level predominant characteristics and ignore other relevant features.

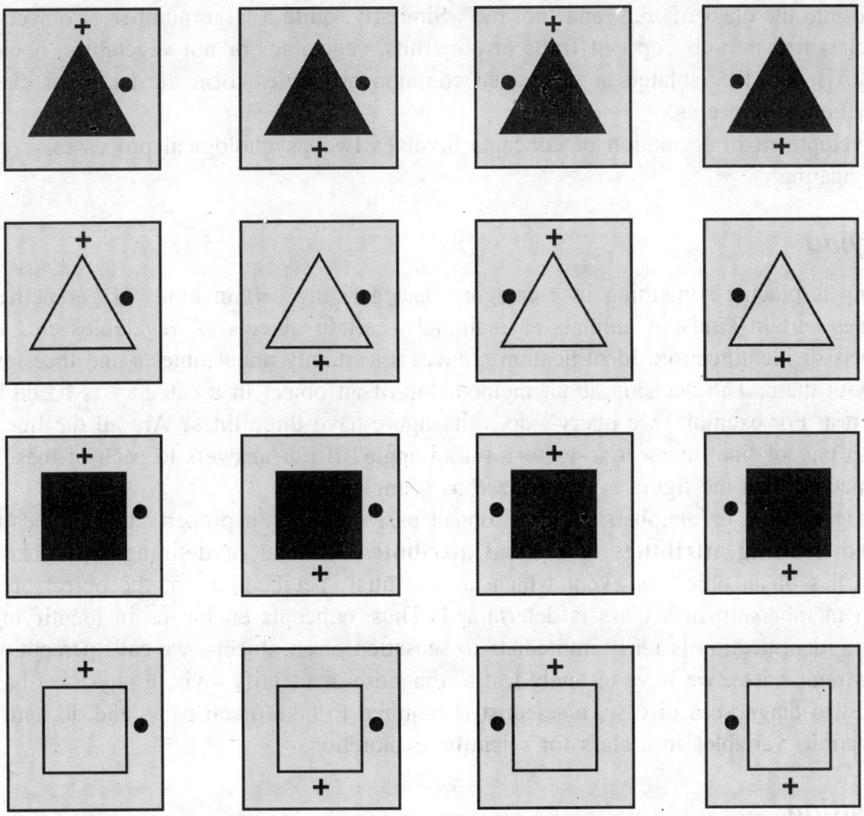

FIGURE 13.7 Samples of some artificial examples.

13.12.5 Formation or Determinant or Attainment of Concepts

Concepts are general symbolic mediators. A word of a language is a symbol that refers to something specific as well as something general. For example, the word 'mother' refers to the mother of a particular individual or a person and it also refers to mother in general. Similarly, the word 'house' when refers to a house in a particular street of the town with specific number or name applies to a specific house. But, when the word 'house' is referred in general, any house with critical attributes of a house—is called general concept. Hence, the concepts have the attributes of generality and applications.

Concept attainment or development is a process of 'isolating' common property or properties of an object or event. By common property we mean some such features or characteristics of an object which are the same in several otherwise situations. For example, the 'redness', 'triangularity', 'rectangularity', 'circleness' etc. may be the common property of a diverse number of objects and serve as identifiable or critical attribute for isolating the objects and categorizing them in some conceptual frame. This process of 'isolating' is also called 'abstracting' which later on are subjected to 'generalization', i.e. fitting into a category of a particular class of objects having similar property.

Concepts enable us to divide things into classes. Hence, with the concept of redness, objects are sorted into the class of 'red' and 'not red'. Similarly, quite a large number of objects or things may be classified into concepts of fruits or not fruits, vegetables or not vegetables, books and not books etc. Hence, the isolated or abstracted common properties form the basis for classification and formation of concepts.

Development or formation of concepts involves two psychological processes—'identifying' and 'anticipating'.

Identifying

Identifying is placing something in a category. Categorizing certain kinds of geometrical figures as triangles certain kinds of animals as mammals, certain objects as vegetables etc. are all the by-products of identification. Identification reduces uncertainty about objects and thus, prepares us to deal with them. The decision about membership of an object in a category is based on certain kinds of test. For example, we query—does the figure have three lines? Are all the lines straight? Does each pair of line intersect so as to form an angle? If our answers to each of these questions are affirmative, then the figure is categorized as triangle.

Categorization or membership of an object bases on certain property that defines the object and called **defining attributes** or **critical attributes**. Critical or defining attributes are those characteristics of an object or event which are essential specifications of the object or event and by which membership in a class is determined. Thus, concepts enable us in identifying objects. Sometimes identification is fairly immediate to sensation of an object—we call 'perception'. But in certain extreme cases, we have to apply test to diagnose or identify—viz. a physician has to apply certain test to diagnose a disease, a scientist is required to take much pains and do hard labour to include various variables in a class for scientific exploration.

Anticipating

Another aspect of concept is anticipation. When an object is classified or identified as a member of a particular class or category, it is expected that the object must have certain other characteristics of a member of that category, viz. if an animal is identified as dog, it is also anticipated that it will also bark, chase cats and subject to rabies. Similarly, when a physician identifies certain disease, he also anticipates (predicts the course of disease, the medicine to which it will respond and the period of recovery).

Thus, concepts involve identification and anticipation both, which together enable us to know about the world in an abstracted form.

13.12.6 Factors of Concept Formation

Concepts are infact learnt. In learning or attaining (or development or formation) a concept, certain factors operate. These factors either help or hinder the attainment of concepts. Hence, it is valuable to know something about how these factors operate.

Transfer

As in other kinds of learning, the phenomenon of transfer is also important in learning concepts. When one already knows the concept similar to the one he is learning, he will learn it more rapidly—phenomenon of 'positive transfer' will operate in this situation. Similarly, 'negative transfer' may also be found operating. Such situations arise when apparently the present new concept appears similar to the concept one has already learned but is quite different in some important respects. Thus, he may have difficulty in understanding them. **Smoke** (1932) in his experimental study has shown that transfer often hinders rapid development of concepts. Therefore, the teachers while capitalizing on transfer must point out the similarities and differences, both.

Distinctiveness

Distinctiveness refers to vividness of the isolated common property. More easily a common property is isolated, more better it stands out as aid in concept attainment and anything that obscures or imbeds it, retards the attainment of concept. This has amply been shown by **Hull** (1920) in an experiment on simple concept formation using Chinese characters as 'nonsense' materials. The common properties were embedded in a complex character and were presented in jumbled order. Had the characters with some property been grouped together, the concept attainment would have been easier.

Good organization

The prominence or vividness of common property of the stimuli much depend on how well the identical elements are organized. When the identical elements are well organized and appear as good figure, the abstraction of common properties becomes easy and thus, the attainment of concept is fastened. Hull in an experiment could demonstrate that isolating the common or equivalent attributes from a well-organized object situation is easier than from a poorly organized object situation.

13.12.7 Other Factors

Johnson (1955) mentions three other contributing factors of concept attainment. These are as follows:

(a) **Ability to manipulate materials:** If a person is allowed or given an opportunity to rearrange, redraw or reorganize the materials containing common properties, he is more likely to discover the appropriate concept. Hence, the ability to manipulate the objects is a favourable condition in the development of concepts.

(b) **Instructions or general purpose:** Instructions provide the proper direction and goal to accomplish something for doing. Hence, proper instructions to discover common property favours attainment or search for the concepts.

(c) **Relevant available information:** Concept learning is relatively faster if all the relevant information is available at the same time rather than in scattered form.

Over and above, the level of intelligence and richness of vocabulary are also important contributing factors in the attainment of concepts. Level of intelligence is closely and positively associated with the identification of common properties or attributes. A person of high level of intelligence identifies and isolates the common property more efficiently and hence, is able to attain the concept rapidly. **Welch** and **Long** (1948), (1942) in their studies of the development of concepts in children have found that chronological and mental age—both play significant role in concept attainment.

'Vocabulary' also influence the development of concepts in an important way. **Orden** (1945) has found high correlation between vocabulary and development of concepts. Though, since children and animals—which are poor in language, do form concepts by means of their motor activities, temporal, spatial and sequential order, one may argue that language or vocabulary is not essential. However, since language is one of the chief means of communication and verbal responses, the role of vocabulary cannot be undermined. Vocabulary brings effectiveness in concept formation.

Thus, concept attainment is influenced by several factors.

13.13 CREATIVE THINKING

Ceres is the name of Roman Goddess of agriculture. This name is closely related to the word 'creare' Latin word for 'create' that implies or suggests fruitfulness—making something of nothing. This creativity is simply the ability or power or potentiality to create something new and original or unique.

Creative thinking refers to higher order thought processes, which has characteristic feature of originality and is directed towards the productive solutions of the problem. It is concerned with creativity which is viewed in two distinct but related ways—one way is to consider it as special case of problem solving behaviour. Another view is to consider creative act in reference to the context, i.e. how do an individual's schemas (large units of knowledge) affect what he creates.

Creativity is viewed in terms of problem solving behaviour. The creative thinkers often create problems before they solve them. Researches done in the area have shown that more creative subjects pick up the unformulated problems and they themselves formulate them into integrative harmonious whole that leads to productive solutions, i.e. poems, pictures, experiments, new inventions, etc. Such people themselves make the task challenging and lead a creative life characterized by 'originality', 'uniqueness' and 'imaginativeness'.

Viewing from another point of view (context), creativity is a matter of learning and knowledge. The concepts and schemas provide a kind of filter in the mind. Such filtration enables the fine artists, the inventive scientists and creative scholars to organize sense data and other information into a novel creative product. Thus, creative thinking as a problem solving behaviour depend much on tremendous amount of previously acquired knowledge (Gagne, 1970).

By integrating the above two views of viewing the creativity, we may define creative thinking as—**a form of thought processes which are directed towards discovering something new, novel, unusual and characterized by originality**.

Thus, a creative thinker attempts to search for new relationship between unrelated elements of a situation, finds out new solutions of the problem, invents some new method or device to produce something original and unique whereby win public recognition.

Some psychologists believe that creative thinkers project an unique personality which is determined by their genes and culture into the development of a novel and useful effect, event, concept or thing.

Creative thinking is likely to involve 'inductive thinking'. Creative thinking in general is also free from rigid thought patterns. It is an ability to look at situations in a fresh way. But, creative thinkers also use 'evaluative thinking' to make the creative product effective. Creative thinkers are self-critics. They criticize their own ideas, make revisions and polish up the final product in order to obtain original idea. A creative thinker usually freely rambles in imaginations but systematic testing and evaluation of the idea is essential to provide final shape to the idea.

13.13.1 Some Characteristics of Creative Thinkers (People)

Psychologists in recent times have vigorously been studying the personality features of creative people of various ages. Some of these features are intelligence, sociability and aesthetic values.

Intelligence

Studies generally suggest that creative people are above normals in intelligence but, very intelligent people are not necessarily creative. Some brilliant individuals attack new ideas so vigorously and skilfully that they analyze them always and never go beyond existing traditions. Thus, their thinking process remains limited to convergent thinking. Creative thinking is in fact, divergent thought in which the mental work leads the thinker away from ordinary traditional path. Therefore, the teachers or educational administrators while 'singling out' the gifted children should not go by IQ alone.

Sociability

Most people have the notion that creative individuals are 'lone wolf', i.e. they prefer loneliness and do not mix with others (not sociable), They are introvert. But, recent studies have revealed that such notions are incorrect because **Green** (1957) and **Gagne** (1970) in their studies found that the creative students were higher on sociability measures than noncreative.

Aesthetic value

Creative people are also aesthetic. **Gumeson** (1963) in his study found that creative junior college students were higher in their aesthetic values than those who were less creative.

In general, creative people have enthusiasm for living and constantly engage in utilizing their creative power to significant productions, solving complicated problems and oriented towards well being of the society as a whole.

Other characteristic features

A dimension or **origence** (Welsh, 1975) has also been shown to be related to creativity. Such people resist conventional approaches and follow his own approach even if the same is non-reinforcing. Such people are more interested in artistic, literary and aesthetic matters. Such fields are more individualized in expression.

13.13.2 Stages of Creative Thinking

In recent years, more and more attention has been given to the way human mind operates while thinking creatively. The researchers in general agree that creative products in fact are spontaneous or sudden which it seems, results from a lot of preparations that had undergone at the unconscious level. This is called 'insight' that strikes only the prepared mind. In this context, the story of famous scientist 'Archimedes' is a good example.

"The king Hieros of Syracose decided to place a golden crown in a temple as a thank offering to God. He weighed the gold and gave it to a contractor to prepare a crown. The contractor prepared the crown—beautifully designed and delivered the same to the king within the stipulated timeframe. The king was glad to see the beautiful architectural finishings of the crown, it was weighed and it was found that the crown weighed exactly the original weight of the gold. Being delighted with the good work and hard labour, the crown-maker was highly rewarded with material and non-material (recognition) rewards. Later on, someone asked the king that the crown-maker has in fact cheated the king by replacing a good amount of gold with silver in its place.

*The king Hieros became furious enough for having been befooled and wanted to punish the crown-maker after substantiating the truth without melting the crown. So, he called a meeting of all the intellectuals of his kingdom and asked them to find out a device to detect the amount of gold that was replaced by silver without breaking or melting the original crown. It was a problem indeed to find out a suitable device to measure and differentiate the amount of gold and silver separately. Archimedes also became interested but he also found the problem as difficult as others. However, he was keeping this problem in his mind. One day, he happened to get into the bathing tub and noticed that when he got into the tub, exactly the same amount of water flowed over the sides as the volume of his body that was under the water. This gave him the clue to the problem and he promptly leapt from the tub in a rush of joy and ran home shouting loudly—**Eureka! Eureka!** meaning I have found, I have found. The cheating of crown-maker was detected. He dropped the silver-mixed crown into the water and the volume of the displaced water was measured. Then pure gold of the same weight was also dropped in the water and the displaced water volume was measured. Silver-mixed crown had larger volume than the equal weight of the pure gold crown. Thus, the theft of actual amount of gold was ascertained and the crown-maker was punished."*

It is evident that Archimedes could suddenly find the solution because he was seriously seized with the problem, he was prepared with various aspects of the problem and unconscious manipulation to find the ways and means to solve it, was undergoing that ultimately resulted in finding an appropriate solution of the problem as a **sudden flash**.

Studies have shown that creative thinking proceeds through five distinctive stages. These are as follows:

Preparatory phase

Preparation is the beginning of creative thought. This phase is characterized by exploratory and familiarizing behaviour. Preparation involves two kinds of preparations—general and specific. General preparation refers to some kind of background knowledge of the area of creativity. For example, medical education provides information to a doctor (symbolic process) which prepares himself for possible creativity in medicine. Einstein's concept of relativity could not have possibly occurred to him, had he not possessed some information about physics and mathematics.

Specific preparation refers to the preparations needed for specific problems. Thus, when a medical professional confronts a specific difficult medical problem (say how to control the dreaded disease—cancer), he may need to consult other authorities and discuss along the aspects of problem before coming to a conclusion.

The stage of preparation often includes much trial and error. For example, in creating a poem, making a scientific exploration, or inventing a new medicine of a dreaded disease, the concerned thinker searches out a wide variety of things, starts and restarts the poem or chemical elements of drug or exploratory tools, data are also destroyed and recollected. Some inventors often remark that much of their inspiration is in fact the outcome of preparation. Statements like this imply that before one advances toward a new discovery, he actively engages himself in preparation for a pretty long period. Preparation involves statement and description of the problem, collection of necessary facts, arranging and disarranging of facts considering each aspect of the problem very minutely, availability of the resources to solve the problem—the necessary tools, interrelationships etc. There are innumerable instances of great inventors such as Galileo, Einstein, Fleming, Galton, Bacquere etc. who did not make their discoveries overnight rather had to go for a long period of preparation.

Incubation

This is a phase of inactivity in the search for attaining productivity. Usually, creative problems are so intricate and complicated that immediate solution is hard to arrive at. It requires a great deal of perseverance and a strong orientation towards solution. Therefore, many psychologists feel that in between the period of preparation and actual solution, there comes a phase of 'incubation'—a period of 'lull' or absence of any conscious activity toward creativity or thinking to solve the problem. Conscious thinking on the problem is suspended and the creative thinker appears to be unconcerned with the problem. However, certain ideas concerning the problem recur. Hence incubation is a 'period of no obvious progress'. Some creative thinkers deliberately put all thoughts in the background after preparing themselves. Some go for walk leisurely, read light literature, engage in household affairs or perhaps even go for sleep.

Many psychologists assume that during the period of incubation, streams of unconscious become active and find out the solution of the problem. This would however be difficult either to prove or disprove. But, it is almost certain that some sort of associational activities continue in some degree—called 'perseveration' as we have seen in the story of Archimedes. This fact is also evidenced from instances in which solutions to some creative problems have been reported to have come during dreams.

Illumination

Generally, illumination is the final phase of creative thinking. Illumination is actually a 'flash', which comes suddenly and lights up every aspect of the problem. Most creative thinkers report that their creative ideas following a period of incubation come to them unexpectedly—all of a sudden. Such ideas may occur any time, sometimes when one is dreaming. Illumination resembles 'insight' or Aha! experience (Eureka! Eureka! as was experienced by Archimedes) which sometimes occurs when there is no obvious problem.

Scientists, poets, mathematicians, engineers etc. occasionally discover something new about which they were not looking for. 'Horace Walpole' has coined a word—'serendipity' to refer such kinds of events. Serendipidity is a word derived from the story **'the three princes of Serendip'**. This term denotes **the faculty of making lucky and unexpected finds**. In the story, the three princes were always making discoveries, by accident and sagacity of things they were not in quest of (Benet, 1943, p. 1012)*. The discovery of penicillin by Sir Alexander Fleming is also a good illustration of unexpected sudden flash of significant discovery.

---

* Cited in *Introduction to Psychology*—Munn, N.L., Fernald Jr. Fernald Carmichael (1973). Oxford and IBH Publishing Co., p. 308.

Evaluation

The suddenly flashed solution is followed by evaluating its appropriateness by rigorous testing procedures. Thus, in this stage, the found solutions are fully worked out and judged its tenability. If it is found untenable, the alternative solutions are judged and evaluated. Thus, the creative thinker reverts to original phase of preparation and proceeds accordingly to find out the alternative solution which may serve more satisfactorily.

Revision

In some cases, the found solution may need certain modifications or revision. Thus, to arrive at a really 'good new idea', the creative thinker enters into final fifth stage of revision.

Patric, in his experimental procedures, discusses only four stages. The stage of evaluation or testing and revision is combined together and is called verification and revision. In this phase, often the suggested solution is questioned—is it logical? Sometimes logical term is determined by costing it into syllogistc form and testing it by law of formal logic. But, very often, verification needs controlled observation to test the idea as correct or workable and revision, if necessary. This method (controlled observation) is followed by scientists and inventors of creative productions. Thus, verification is the finality of the inspired or illuminated idea.

13.13.3 Nature of Creative Thinking

Creative thinking is distinguished from other types of thinking by the fact that it involves the production of novel and original ideas or solutions to the problems. Sometimes creative thinking is understood just as a new way of thinking or thinking differently. However, it is important to note here that in creative thinking, originality in addition to novelty is also important. Creative thinking, in fact, refers to the originality and uniqueness of ideas or solutions that did not previous exist. According to **Bruner**, creative thinking is also characterized by **effective surprise**, *i.e.* if the product or idea is unusual, it would be experienced by most of us as **instant surprise**.

Another important characteristic feature of creative thinking is its appropriateness in a particular context. Simply thinking of being different without serving any purpose cannot be regarded as creative thinking. For example, many abnormal persons coin new scripts, words, fantastic things etc. which are not only new but also unique. But, such creations are irrelevant and do not serve any purpose either to the individual or to others. Hence, these are not creative products.

Researchers in general hold that a thinking is said to be creative when it is reality-oriented, appropriate, constructive and socially desirable.

J.P. Guilford, a pioneer in creativity research, has proposed two types of thinking—convergent and divergent.

Convergent thinking

Convergent thinking refers to the thinking that is required to solve problem which has only one correct answer. The mind converges to the correct solution. For example, look at the following question based on a number series where the thinker is supposed to find the next correct number. Here only the right answer is expected.

Question: 4, 8, 12, 16, ... What will come next?

Answer: 20

Now think of certain questions for which there is not one right answer but many answers. A few such questions are as mentioned below:

- What are the various uses of books?
- What improvements would you suggest in your reading room so that it is felt comfortable as well as aesthetically pleasing
- What will happen if examination system is abolished in universities?

To answer the above questions, we require to think in divergent way.

Divergent thinking

Divergent thinking is open-ended thinking where one may think of several answers to a question or different solutions of a problem in terms of one's own knowledge and experience.

Divergent thinking ability is characterized by four distinctive characteristics. These are—fluency, flexibility, originality and elaboration.

(a) **Fluency:** It is the ability to produce many ideas for a given task or a problem. The more ideas an individual is able to produce, higher is his/her ability of fluency, *viz.* more the number of uses of paper plate, more would be the fluency.

(b) **Flexibility:** It indicates variety in thinking such as thinking in terms of different uses of a thing, object or different ways of interpreting an idea or solution. Flexibility does not bind the creative thinker to stick to a particular idea or solution only, but to think of several alternatives to find the unique idea or solution.

(c) **Originality:** It is an ability to produce rare or unusual ideas or solutions to a problem. It provides new relationships between the elements and thinking becomes unique.

(d) **Elaboration:** It enables the thinker to go into the details and work out the impli-cations of novel ideas.

Divergent thinking facilitates generation of a variety of ideas which may not appear to be related. For example, what are the common ideas for enhancing national economy? The related answers may be related to greater quantity of production, checking of hoarding, restructuring of taxing system to discourage black money etc. However, if someone thinks of some novel measures of enhancing GDP by expanding market, converting the desert fields into cultivable fields, accelerating achievement, motivation etc. All such ideas are divergent in nature.

One should note here that for creative thinking, both the divergent and convergent thoughts are important. Divergent thinking enables us to generate wider range of ideas whereas convergent thinking is important in the sense that it allows to identify the most useful or appropriate idea.

13.13.4 Barriers to Creative Thinking

There are certain blocks that hinder creative thinking. These blocks are habitual, perceptual, motivational, emotional and cultural.

Habitual blocks

Although, much of habitual learning is important for smooth and efficient functioning, the tendency to be overpowered by habits in one's ways of thinking may prove detrimental in creative productions.

Habits compel us to think and perceive things in a familiar way and blinds the novel ways of thinking.

Perceptual blocks

The perceptual blocks prevent us from being open to new and original ideas. For example, see the following problem in **Figure 13.8(a)** and solution in **Figure 13.8(b)**.

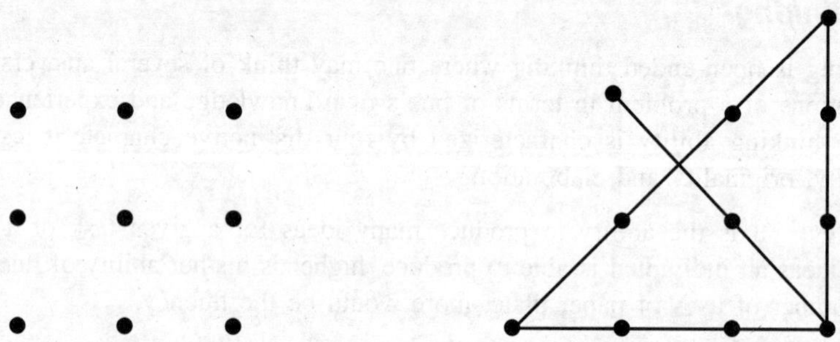

(a) Problem figure.

(b) Answer figure.

FIGURE 13.8

The problem here is to join the 9 dots together without lifting pencil from paper and join the dots by drawing only 4 straight lines going through each dot only once.

The solution of the above problem lies in going beyond the boundaries. Generally, we perceive the existence of boundary which in fact, does not exist. Thus, most often, our perceptions which are mostly assumed or self-imposed, blocks creative thinking.

Motivational and emotional blocks

These subjective factors also interfere with creative thinking which shows that this is not merely a cognitive process. Lack of motivation, fear of failure, or ridicules or rejection, one's poor self-concept, negativism etc. may hamper creative thinking.

Cultural barriers

Such barriers are related to excessive adherence to traditions, cultural expectations, conformity pressures and stereotypes. Conformity to an extent is essential for social existence but excessive conformity to cultural traditions, rituals, and procedures are likely to block creative thinking. Cultural blocks arise due to fear of being different or isolated, tendency to maintain status quo, willingness to accept mediocrity, preservation of personal security, social pressure over dependence on others etc.

13.13.5 Improving Creativity

The fact is that everyone has the potentiality to be creative. However, one may differ in the expression of creative thinking. Therefore, we require to tap our creative potentials and remove the barriers or blocks. For this, we need to be trained in utilizing our creative potentials by following certain strategies. Some of such important strategies are outlined hereinbelow:

- Become more aware and sensitive to be able to make and respond to feelings, sights, sounds, textures around you, spot problems, missing information, anomalies, gaps, deficiencies and so on. Try to notice contradictions and incompleteness in situations that others may not do. For this, cultivate the habit of wider reading, exposure to variety of information, develop the art of asking questions, pondering over the mysteries of situations and objects.
- Generate many ideas, responses, solutions on a given task. Try to be divergent, look the task situation from multiple angles.
- Try to use brainstorming technique (**Osburn's technique**) to increase fluency and flexibility of ideas.
- Think freely and keep your mind open.
- Originality can be developed by practising fluency, flexibility, habit of associative thinking, exploring linkages and fusing distinct or remote ideas.
- A creative thinker is said not to evolve a new idea but a new combination of ideas. Hence, try to combine and recombine divergent ideas in a new way.
- Engage yourself more in such activities which require imaginative ideas and original thinking rather than routine works.
- Never accept the first idea or solution. Try to explore successive ideas or solutions and then take a decision.
- Get a feedback on the solution you decide.
- Try to think, what solutions others offer to you.
- Allow time for incubation.
- Resist temptation for immediate reward and cope with the frustration.
- Beware of your own defences and think of the possible means of failure.
- Develop self-confidence, strengthen the self-concept.

There are many more strategies. The above few are only suggestive. Psychologists today are trying to train youths to be creative and imaginative in their approach.

SUMMARY

- Thinking is an implicit mental activity of higher order, symbolic in nature initiated by a problem, directed towards solution of the problem and terminates with accomplishment of the solution to the problem.
- Thought processes are of various types. Broadly, they are classified as autistic, realistic and evaluative.
- Realistic thinking involves deductive and inductive reasoning.
- Thinking involves various tools such as images, cognitive map, use of language, trial and error.

- Many psychologists consider that images are not necessary for thinking. Wüzberg School of psychologists have found evidences in favour of imageless thought. However, the controversy is still unresolved.
- Mental set is an important determinant of thinking. It exerts facilitative and inhibitive—both kinds of influences to our thinking. The inhibiting influences are due to functional fixidity.
- Problem solving is an important aspect of behaviour which is comparable to a computer device.
- Problem solving utilizes several strategies such as algorithms, heuristic means-end analyses, and backward search.
- Several factors affect solution of a problem such as mental set, past experience, personal context, frustration, strain etc.
- As for venue of thinking—there are two approaches. These are central theory and peripheral theory.
- Central theory assumes the cerebral cortex as the main venue of thought processes.
- Peripheral theory emphasizes that peripheral functions are the major area of thinking process. Cerebral cortex functions merely as locus of awareness. Thinking is a chain of sensory and muscular activities that take place in the peripheries.
- Piaget has advanced cognitive theory of thinking that develops through various stages in children. The major stages are—sensory-motor, pre-operational, concrete operational and finally the formal operational stage.
- Concepts are mediating symbols of thought which involves the process of identification and anticipation.
- Several factors such as transfer, distinctiveness, goal organization etc. influence concept formation.
- Concepts are broadly classified as artificial and natural.
- Artificial concepts are well-defined while natural concepts are ill-defined with no limit of boundaries.
- Creative thinking is higher order thinking. It involves convergent and divergent thinking.
- Creative thinking proceeds through five main stages—preparation, incubation, illumination, evaluation and revision.
- The major obstacles to creative thinking are habits, lack of motives, emotions and cultural barriers.
- One can improve creativity by adopting certain strategies. Several such strategies have been suggested.

Part VII

Conative Aspects of Behaviour

CHAPTER 14

Motivation

14.1 INTRODUCTION

Psychology, being a science of adjustive behaviour, is concerned not only with what and how of behaviour but also with 'why' of behaviour. 'Why we do, what we do' is a fundamental question. Man besides being knower and interpreter of various information, events and objects, is also characterized as 'doer', i.e. he does something. In fact, every organism—man as well as animal, being active, always found doing something. It is also observed that activities of organisms, particularly of human beings are not haphazard or random, rather their behaviours or activities are directed towards certain selected goals. This means to say that the organism selects certain goals and becomes active to achieve it. Selection of goal is determined by certain kinds of needs and the selected goal serves to satisfy the need state and as soon as the current need state is satisfied, the selective activity terminates, which can again be initiated if the need state rearouses the organism to be active.

However, the fundamental question—Why do we do, what we do—still remains unanswered. Psychologists in particular and other scientists in general have tried to find an answer to this question and the answer is that we are motivated to do what we want to do, i.e. some need conditions push us to do and at the same time the goal before us pulls us to do. Thus, **push and pull factors** operate behind all our activities which is known as **conative aspect of behaviour** or the impulsive aspect of mind that impels us or arouses us to move or act selectively in the direction of goal that pulls to behave as the goal can satisfy the current state of arousal.

This aspect is what we call 'motivation' which, in fact, is involved in all kinds of our behaviour and hence, occupy a very key position in explaining behaviour events. Hence, the main thrust of this chapter is the motivation that lies as inner force behind all our behaviours.

14.2 NATURE AND DEFINITION

Motive is a common word with which almost every common man is familiar. It refers to what one intends while displaying a particular kind of behaviour. The term is synonymical with 'wants', which means a driving force within the individual. In other words, it is a 'causative force' that impels an individual to act. This driving or causative force may be either positive or negative. The positive force 'impels' a person towards certain object or condition and, therefore, behaviour is of 'approach type'. On the other hand, the negative force 'repel' a person away from certain object or condition and therefore, the behaviour is of 'avoidant type'. Accordingly, the approach object is called positive goal (G+) while the avoidant object is called negative goal (G–). When the two forces operate within the individual, the behaviour that they initiate are distinguished on the basis of differences in their emotional accompaniments. However, in meaning, both bear similarity as both function as initiator and sustainer of behaviour.

The term motive derives from Latin word 'movere', i.e. that moves or arouses. In literal sense therefore, the motive means that force within the organism that impels to act or that drives or energises to perform an action. Hence, motive is the mover of the behaviour.

In common parlance, different persons use the term in different senses. Some use it as a noun and accordingly explain it as a 'drive'—a force that triggers off an action. Some use it as an adjective and refer it as an energizing force that initiates a response. Still others use it as verb and describe it as a force of an action or response. But to the psychologists, motive has altogether a different meaning. They assimilate all the three senses of common use and explain it as a state or condition which if aroused, makes the organism restless. In order to be relieved of the state of restlessness, the organism selects a particular course of action that leads to a goal, performs the selected course of action and sustains himself in that act till he attains the goal and satisfies the state, i.e. relieved of the state of arousal and thus, the state of equilibrium is reached (i.e. that state of restlessness ends). This state of the individual is internal which is aroused in the event of some kind of 'wantedness'. This state of wantedness moves the organism towards some selected course of action out of many alternative courses and thus, directs his response to a particular goal or object. The entire course of this behaviour event is called motivated behaviour. One of the salient features of motivated behaviour is that it is sustained (preserved), i.e. it continues till the goal is achieved and the motivating condition is satisfied.

From the above description about the nature of motivation, we can define it as—**'a set of one or more conditions which activate—turn-on behaviour, direct the behaviour towards some goal and maintain behaviour until the goal is reached'***.

To understand the nature of motivation more clearly, let us briefly outline some of the salient characteristics of motivation as mentioned below:

(i) Motivation is a particular state or condition of the organism.
(ii) This state is aroused out of need, want or drive.
(iii) In motivational state, the organism finds himself in a state of restlessness and tends to act.
(iv) Motivational state is selective in nature which is directed towards attainment of the goal.
(v) The aroused motivational behaviour persists in the organism till attainment of the goal.
(vi) The intensity of action and state of restlessness decrease in degree as he reaches toward the fulfilment of his goal and the activity comes to a halt as soon as the goal is attained.
(vii) The halted activity may be reinitiated only when the motivating conditions reappear.

* Witting, A.F. and Williams III G., *Psychology—An Introduction*, McGraw Hill Book Co., New York, 1984 p. 357.

From the overview of the above-cited definition and its characteristic features, motivation may be defined in more simpler terms as follows:

Motivation is an internal state of the organism which starts with a physiological or psychological feeling of wantedness or deficiency (need) that activates (drives) behaviour which is directed towards attainment of a goal (or incentive).

14.3 MOTIVATIONAL CYCLE

While describing the nature of motivation and defining the process, it has clearly been stated that motivation is a general term which refers to a state within the organism and which arouses a particular behaviour in the organism. This aroused behaviour is directed towards the goal or incentive and the behaviour in question is maintained or sustained till the motivating state is satisfied, i.e. goal is achieved. When the goal is achieved, the state which aroused the behaviour gradually decreases in intensity and ceases or comes to a halt on attaining the goal. Thus, the cycle ends until the state is aroused in some way again. This cycle can be represented in the following way (see **Figure 14.1**).

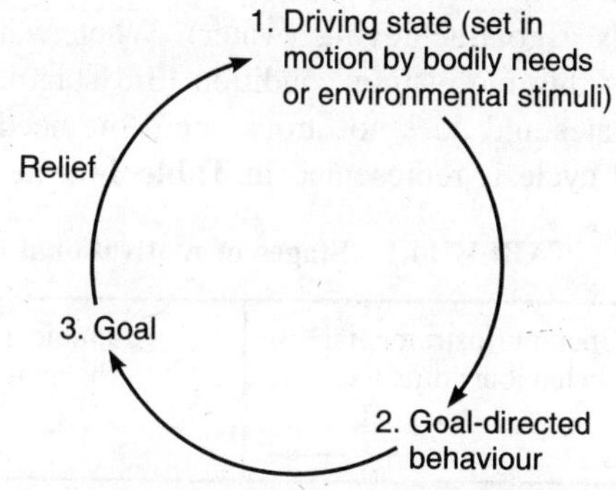

FIGURE 14.1 Motivational cycle.

The above cycle is explained as below:

14.3.1 A Motivating State within the Individual

This is the first stage of the cycle. It has various names with very fine distinctions depending upon whether one is describing about animal or human motivation. We use the term 'drive' to describe animal motivation, particularly the physiological state which impels an animal to action. 'Need' is another term frequently used to describe motivating conditions of human beings, particularly in reference to social motives, such as the need for gregariousness, curiosity, self- assertion etc. Motive is a general term which covers both the drive and need states often used interchangeably with motive.

14.3.2 Arousal and Directedness of Behaviour (Instrumental Behaviour)

This is the second stage of motivational cycle. The driving state within the organism incites an action or arouses the organism to motion (behaviour), which sooner or later become instrumental in reducing motive. Thus, behaviour is operant or instrumental. For example, hunger is a drive state. This state arouses food exploring behaviour which is instrumental in satisfying or reducing motive. But, this is only a 'means' towards the goal or satisfaction of the motivating condition and not the 'end'.

14.3.3 Attainment of the Goal

The third stage in motivational cycle is the reduction or satisfaction by attaining the goal. On reducing the drive in this third stage, the organism feels relieved from the state of disequilibrium caused by motivating state and the operant behaviour ends until the motivational state is aroused again.

For example, in thirst, lack of water in the body is a 'need' (1st stage) that motivates or impels the individual. This need arouses exploring behaviour to find out water (2nd stage). This behaviour is directed towards a goal-achieving (water). When water is obtained, the individual drinks it and thereby satisfies this motivating condition (3rd stage). On reaching this third stage, the motivational cycle terminates and does not arouse until the need for water builds up again.

The above motivational cycle is represented in **Table 14.1** in a precised manner.

TABLE 14.1 Stages of motivational cycle

Stimulating condition within the organism →	Operant (instrumental behaviour) directed towards the goal →	Attainment of the goal →	Termination of motivational cycle →
↓	↓	↓	↓
Thirst/need for water which is a drive	Exploratory behaviour to find out water	Drinking of water and satisfying the motive	End of the cycle till the need for water reappears

Obviously, the goal depends on the active motive. The goal may be positive or negative. Positive impels the person towards certain objects, i.e. induces approaching behaviour. For example, a hungry man approaches towards food items or objects. The negative goal repels a person away from certain object and thus he avoids it. For example, a person who escapes or avoids a dangerous and unpleasant situations have negative goals.

So far the physiological motives are concerned, goals are fixed and relatively unchangeable. If one is thirsty, water is generally the only goal, although, there are various forms in which water can be consumed. Similarly, if one is hungry, nothing but food or any eatable item would do. But, for more complex motives, there are usually many alternative goals. Attainment of any one of them may do. For example, one may satisfy his need for recognition by becoming a political leader, an eminent scientist, a good cricket player, taking up social reform work etc. Thus, although goals must be appropriate to one's motives, the study of goal itself is a complex aspect of motivation.

14.3.4 Some Terminologies Related to Motives

While describing the motivational cycle, references to some terminologies have been made which are often used interchangeably. These terminologies are need, drive, instinct, and incentive. All these come under the broad cluster of the term motivation. However, all these terminologies are subtly different in meaning. These terminologies are explained below:

Needs

Needs refer to lack or deficit of some necessity. It is a state of physiological imbalance. For example, needs exist when the organism is deprived of food or water. Similarly, when an individual is deprived of other people who may serve as friend or companion, he is in need of a companion. Thus, the needs for food, water and affiliation are indicative of deficit or state of wantedness. Although psychological needs may also be deficiency-based, but sometimes, they are not. For example, a student with consistent history of success may have strong need to excel (top) all others in the examination. Here, the need to top is not based on deficiency.

Drive

Needs lead to drive. A drive is a state of tension or arousal produced by need. It energises random activity when one of the random activities leads to the goal, it reduces the drive and the organism stops being active. The organism returns to a state of balance (homeostasis). Examples of drive are hunger, thirst, drive for affiliation, achievement, power etc. Thus, drive is action-oriented and energise the organism to alleviate needs.

Sometimes, needs and drives are used interchangeably. However, needs refer to a state of deprivation or deficiency while drives refer to the consequential state of being driven. Hence, the two terms are parallel but not identical.

Incentives

Incentive is the object of the environment that alleviates a need and reduce the drive. Thus, attainment of an incentive results in restoration of physiological or psychological balance and brings halt to the initiated behaviour. For example, eating food, drinking water, obtaining friends etc. are all incentives which tend to restore the balance and cut off the motivated behaviour as the aroused drives are reduced.

Instinct

The term instinct denotes inborn patterns of behaviour that are biologically determined rather than learned. For example, curiosity, flight, repulsion, reproduction, mating, parental care etc. are instincts. These are innate tendencies found in all the members of a species that direct behaviour in predictable ways. Instinct most approximately refers to **'an urge to do something'**. Thus, it has an **'impetus'** which drives the organism to do something.

Motives

Motive and drives are often used interchangeably. However, again the two terms are parallel but not identical. Drives refer to a state of arousal on account of certain need while motive is a general term which is a cluster of need, drive, incentive and instinct. Need and drive together selectively initiate, direct and maintain a behaviour till the attainment of goal (incentive) that satisfies the driving state. Thus, the term motive includes the following:

(i) Need: A state of deficiency and wantedness.
(ii) Drive: Resultant state of need that drives the organism to action.
(iii) Instinct: An urge to do something to satisfy or reduce drive.
(iv) Incentive (goal): The object attainment of which satisfies the need state and reduces drive.
(v) Selective behaviour: Goal directed behaviour is selected, i.e. it performs such actions that can satisfy need and reduce drive.
(vi) Maintenance of behaviour: Continuation of goal directed behaviour till goal is achieved.

14.3.5 Influences of Motives on Behaviour

As has been stated, motives lie behind all our actions. It influences our behaviour in at least three ways:

(i) In the first place, motivation is a condition for eliciting a response or behaviour. Motivating conditions 'triggers off' (or turn on) an action. For example, when food is presented before an organism which is satiated will not salivate as much as a hungry organism salivates.
(ii) Motivation is essential for reinforcement. Here, reinforcement refers to rewarding condition. A reward should be appropriate to the motive. For example, for a hungry organism, food is appropriate reward while for a thirsty organism, water is the appropriate reward. Thus, by motivating an individual some relevant object may be made as reinforcement which is an essential condition in the acquisition of a response (learning).
(iii) Motivation increases variability of behaviour. When one form of behaviour does not lead to the goal, i.e. reinforced, the person tries another form of behaviour. His goal remains the same but the mode of behaviour to achieve the goal may vary. This variability is one of the characteristics of motivated behaviour. Thus, motivation increases the variability of responses and thereby increases the probability of correct response to occur.

Hence, motivation influences our behaviour in three ways—it elicits a response, permits the reinforcement to occur and also increases the variability of behaviour.

14.4 HOMEOSTASIS

Physiologically-driven individual or organism comes in a state of physiological disequilibrium which is restored by consummatory behaviour, i.e. when the driven state is satisfied. Th physiological process of tending to maintain balance among internal physiological condition is called 'homeostasis' (Cannon, 1932). Such a balance has high survival value. For example, body temperature, blood pressure, chemical elements in blood etc. must be maintained near the normal value and should neither rise nor fall beyond normal range. If however, it so happens, the homeostatic mechanism gets involved to keep conditions within normal limits. In addition, body also makes use of 'regulatory behaviour' to maintain homeostatic balance (Richter, 1943). Such regulatory behaviour is instrumental in satisfying the physiological driving states and therefore, they are called 'operant responses'. For example, when the body becomes empty of food or water, the physiological homeostasis mechanism cannot maintain balance. Therefore, body demands more food and water from external world. It does this by motivating our behaviour to obtain more food and water from outside and on being successful, the disturbed balance is restored.

From the above, it is clear that physiological motives are parts of physiological mechanism to maintain homeostatic balance of the internal body.

14.5 TWO FUNDAMENTAL THEORIES OF MOTIVATION

Study of motivation has always been a central topic of research for the psychologists. To understand motives, psychologists have used different perspectives and approaches. In these efforts, human beings have been considered in different ways. Some view human beings as 'machine' which only operates on given command. Others view human as God like all knowing, a judge and a scientist. These views had led to the development of a varieties of theories of motivation. Of these, two such early theories are important. These are the **'instinct theory'** and the **'drive theory'** as mentioned below:

14.5.1 Instinct Theory

This is one of the earliest theories of motivation. The instinct theory assumes that in all members of a species, innate instinctual tendencies are found which are concerned primarily with psycho-physical dispositions that direct their behaviours in predictable ways. The biologists and the ethologists study these instinctual behaviours in animals in their natural settings. These studies have revealed that certain behaviours of different species such as 'building of nests', 'communication of direction of food by bees', 'spinning of webs by spiders' etc. are done exactly in the manner their parents did. Such behaviours have certain characteristics, such as:

(i) These behaviours occur in response to specific types of stimulation. Such specific responses are evoked by the environmental cues which are called 'releasers'.
(ii) Instinctual behaviours are fixed action patterns.
(iii) Instinctual behaviours are survival behaviours.
(iv) These behaviours are unlearnt and 'species-specific'.

In the context of instinctual behaviours, the works of **Lorenz** (1973) and **Tin Bergen** (1951) are famous. One of the best examples of instinctive behaviour is 'imprinting'. The baby geese follow the imprint to their mothers or have a tendency to follow her as soon as they are able to walk.

McDougall (1908) has used the term 'instinct' to denote as an inherited disposition. According to him, this disposition functions in three ways—energizing, action and goal direction. He has listed 12 human instincts which are: (a) curiosity, (b) pugnacity, (c) flight, (d) repulsion,

(e) self-abasement, (f) reproduction, (g) self-assertion, (h) acquisition, (i) creativity, (j) gregariousness, (k) parental care and (l) food exploration.

In modern times, the idea of instinct as explanation of human behaviour is not acceptable as most psychologists of the day consider human behaviour as product of interaction of genetic and environmental factors.

14.5.2 Drive Theory

Psychologists today prefer to use the concept of 'need' in place of 'instinct'. Need refers to a state of lack or deficit of some necessities and the state of need leads to drive. A drive is a state of tension or arousal produced by a need. Drive energises the organism. This means that the drive makes the organism to perform certain act (activates) to satisfy the need (goal) and the organism does a goal-directed behaviour. Thus, the drive provides energy and the organism is driven to act or behave to achieve the goal. As soon as the goal is achieved, the aroused state of tension and consequent driven act (or behaviour) comes to an end. In other words, the organism restores the state of homeostasis or equilibrium. Thus, the sequence of motivational events is as shown in **Table 14.2**.

TABLE 14.2 Sequence of motivational events

Need →	→	Drive →	→	Goal directed behaviour →	→	Attainment of the goal →	→	Reduction in driving state →	→	End of the motivational behaviour

Following the above sequence, this theory is also called **need-drive-incentive theory** or **drive reduction theory**. According to this theory, drive is stimulated by biological factors but the behaviour that reduces the drive may be learned or acquired. This is mainly concerned with maintaining balance or homeostasis. Drives are classified as primary and secondary.

'Primary drives' refer to basic physiological needs, such as hunger, thirst, sex etc. 'Secondary drives' include intense external as well as internal stimulation. For example, arousal of sexual drive by stimulating the sensuous body parts is secondary drive. Sometimes when a neutral stimulus is repeatedly presented in pair form with a potentially strong drive, the neutral stimulus acquires the motivational character which is known as conditioned or acquired drive (this kind of motive has been described in course of Pavlov's experiment on dog in the context of learning). Similarly, fear is also an example of acquired drive. It indicates the repulsive state of the organism which is aroused by stimuli that signal threatening effect. Some external stimuli may also 'push and pull' the organism.

14.6 NATURE OF EXPERIMENTAL STUDIES ON MOTIVATION

As has been stated earlier, study of motivational aspect of human beings has been a central topic of experimental research. Consequently, quite a good number of theories have also been propounded. To name a few such theories are Atkinson's theory, Attribution theory, Vector theory, Need hierarchy theory etc. A close scrutiny of motivational aspect of human behaviour would show that motivation has two facets—one emphasizes the goal-directed nature of behaviour while the other emphasizes the body's response to such internal factors as hunger and pain. The former is also known as purposive while the latter is called as regulatory. However, it is interesting to note here that both the aspects of motivation involve 'need'. One concerns with life threatening needs—either in the form of excess or deficit (e.g. hunger, thirst, excretions etc.) while the other involves psychosocial needs such as achievement, affiliation, power etc. which if not fulfilled, does not cause death but are important for our personal and social life. The reason is that human beings besides sharing with animals in respect of primary physiological needs, are also socio-cultural beings. As a socio-cultural being, he is free to be creative and grow and also deal with the social environment effectively. Hence, his personal needs of achievement and power along with affiliation with others become important aspects of human life. Hence, human beings are aroused by higher and higher levels of achievement and power needs in different areas of life.

Most of our behaviours are directed towards seeking pleasurable consequences and avoiding the unpleasant ones. For example, when we feel hungry, we want to seek food to eat. Eating food when hungry or drinking water when thirsty, are satisfying. Similarly, achieving excellence and success in our endeavours, gaining power to exercise control over others etc. are also pleasurable events and provide satisfaction on having been achieved such goals.

Hence, the psychologists are interested in experimental research of both kinds of our needs—primary biological needs as well as higher order psychological needs of human beings such as need for achievement, need for affiliation, need for power and many more similar needs.

14.7 KINDS OF MOTIVES

The motives that arouse and direct our responses are broadly classified into two groups—(i) Physiological drives and (ii) Acquired motives. Physiological drives are biological in nature as they usually result from basic tissue needs, such as—water, food, oxygen, sleep, warmth or coolness. Acquired motives result from needs for social approval, security, self-esteem, knowledge etc. These two groups of motives are further classified into several types. General typological classification of motives can be better understood by glancing over the schematic classification as shown in **Table 14.3**.

TABLE 14.3 Classification of motives

(i) Physiological motives or biological or primary motives

Hunger motive	Thirst motive	Sex motive	Maternal drive	Excretion motive	Other physiological motives

(ii) Unlearnt/General motives

Motive for activity	Curiosity motive	Manipulative motive	Contact comfort motive

(iii) Social/Personal/Acquired motives

Social motive	Achievement motive	Affiliative motive	Power motive	Cognitive motive	Approval motive

14.7.1 Physiological Motives

This is also called 'biological motives' or 'drives' because these arise out of basic needs. These are innate. Biologists adhering to the concept of adaptive act hold that organisms have needs (internal physiological imbalance) that produce drive, which stimulates behaviour leading to certain actions towards achieving certain goals which reduce the drive. Hence, physiological drives are innate but the way in which these drives get satisfied are greatly influenced by learning and cultural factors. Biological drives influence our behaviour from birth and are present even during foetus life during which such drives are automatically satisfied by the mother's body. Biological drives are inherited and found in every member of all the species. Therefore, they possess species resemblance or similarity. Some of the basic biological drives are discussed briefly below:

Hunger

Hunger is a powerful motivator. When someone is deprived of food for certain length of time, the need for food dominates everything else. It motivates us to obtain and consume food if someone goes without food for considerably longer duration, the body uses up the materials in growth, repair of tissues and storage of reserve supplies. This happens due to metabolism of food which is a continuous process in living beings and tissue need for food is created. This is the genesis of hunger motive.

When tissue need for food arises, chemical changes in blood stream take place and communicated to co-coordinating centre in the brain which instigates a wide variety of hunger behaviours. From introspection, we fed a mass of sensations coming from stomach region such as contractions. Experience of contractions in the stomach is felt as hunger pangs—source of hunger motive (Cannon, 1934). However, some physiologists have found contrary evidences. **Davis et al.** (1954) have found that feeling of stomach contractions are not regularly associated with hunger. Most often, contractions are felt after taking food rather than before. In some cases, introspective report of hunger has been noted even after removal of entire stomach (Wangensteen and Carlson, 1931). Sometimes, hunger is reflected in feelings of weakness and lightness. Hence, contraction in stomach is not the surest indication of hunger in an animal or a person. Therefore, 'wanting to eat something' is perhaps the most reliable indication of hunger.

Some researchers point out the changes in blood chemistry as the source of hunger. A low level of concentration of glucose in the blood, a low level of protein and the amount of fats stored in the body has more prominently been observed in hunger (Quiglec et al. 1929; Carlson, 1915).

The liver is also found to respond to the lack of body fuel by sending nerve impulses to the brain. The aroma, taste or even appearance of food may also result in desire to eat. It may be noted here that none of these alone gives the feeling that one is hungry, rather all those in combination act with external factors such as taste, colour, aroma, observing others eating etc. help in understanding that one is feeling hungry.

One of the important relevant questions regarding hunger relates to the localization of sensory experience of hunger in the nervous system. In this context, a pathbreaking experiment has been reported by **Heatherington** and **Ranson** (1940). The experiment suggests that a section of the hypothalamus appears to be involved in **satiety system** and hence, is closely tied with hunger drive. Some later experiments also lend support to this finding. On the basis of these studies, it is concluded that hypothalamus performs the regulatory behaviour in maintaining homeostasis. In other words, the hypothalamus receives the signal about need for food (nutrient) from body and controls the operant responses and thus, performs the regulatory function to maintain homeostasis.

Some more recent researches (Hulihan Giblin and Skolnick, 1982; Kolata, 1982) have found that 'amphetamine', a potentially dangerous diet drug stimulates the central nervous system and kills appetite. They have located areas or sites in the hypothalamus and brain stem where 'amphetamine binds', i.e. become attached to brain tissue. Though, the findings are not conclusive, yet, they suggest that the binding sites in the central nervous system are the control centres for appetite.

Research studies on 'hunger' have some more questions unanswered. For example, why do people sometimes feel hungry eventhough their body does not require any nutrition and why people stop feeling hungry after a few initial hours or days of fasting? Why people often feel the need to eat at the sight or smell coming from a fascinating food, even though, they have eaten enough of food just few moments before? etc.

The fact is that hunger is not entirely controlled internally. Some external stimulus and personal factors play an important role. Sight and smell of fascinating food is an external stimulus factor which may entice a person to eat even though he has taken enough of food just a moment before. Similarly, personal factors such a one's preferences, tastes, aversions etc. also determine hunger motive and behaviour. In most persons and animals, preferred food often becomes **specific food need** as is seen in children who crave for toffee. This kind of phenomenon has been demonstrated in experiments done on rats by surgically removing the adrenal glands. The surgery causes the rats losing salt constantly and therefore they need supply of salt from external sources for survival. This is termed as **specific food needs**. It is also observed that deprivation of a specific food substance leads to an increased preference for that substance. For example, when doctor advises a diabetic patient not to take sweets, after a few days or months, they make a run to eat sweets. Such increase in food preference is termed as **specific hunger**.

In eating behaviours, aversions have also been noticed. **Young** (1944) in one experiment found that aversions to a particular kind of food substances is the outcome of eating that substance most regularly. **Rozin** (1957) has noticed that aversions also develop for diets that are deficient in substances. For example, rats that are maintained on a diet deficient in 'thiamine' (vitamin B_1) develop aversions for that diet when opportunity is given. Similarly, hard diabeties that maintain glucose level on dietry control, develop aversions to high calorie food items. Aversions like this help the individual to find a balanced diet.

Eating behaviour is also culturally determined. Aversions or preferences to non-vegetarians or vegetarian diets, using spoons and forks while eating, etc. are most common examples of culturally determined food habits.

Thus, we find that though hunger is a physiological drive, internally controlled and regulated, much of our eating behaviour bears the stamp of learning and culture.

Thirst

Need for water is no less important to need for food. Its importance lies in the body's use of food itself and water being constantly lost through various internal organs, such as skin and kidneys. What causes us thirsty and thus, motivates us to drink water? To answer this, researchers have followed the same track of investigation as in the case of hunger. First, the researchers searched for the causes of thirst in the part of the body outside brain and then followed the trial to the brain and in the course, simple model could be elaborated.

Several decades ago, physiologists thought that thirst is seated in the tongue, throat and stomach. Even today, dryness of the throat is assumed to be the basis of thirst. Though, it is generally found that people drink water when they feel dryness in the mouth, however, it is almost proved that a dry mouth is not the sole factor involved in thirst. For example, Bernard (1949) found that animals continued to drink even when their mouths were soaked. In human beings also **Walf** (1958) had observed that they generally become thirsty when their mouths and throats were moist.

In recent researches, two sources of thirst have been identified (Epstein, 1973):

(i) loss of water from cells and (ii) reduction of blood volume. When water is lost from bodily fluids, water leaves the interior of the cells, thus dehydrating the cells. It is called cellular dehydration. The **'osmoreceptors'** found in hypothalamus, generate nerve impulses when cellular dehydration occurs. These impulses act as signals for thirst and drinking.

Secondly, loss of water from body also results from **hyporolemia**—a condition characterized by decrease in the volume of blood resulting in low blood pressure. This condition stimulates kidneys that responds by release of an enzyme called **renin** which through several step process produces a substance, known as **'angiotensin-II'*** that circulates in the blood and signals drinking.

The above two mechanisms taken together are called **double depletion hypothesis**.

But, what mechanism stops the drinking of water? Some psychologists assume that the mechanism that explains intake of water also accounts for stopping the intake also. However, others opine that the stimuli resulting from intake of water in the stomach play a role in stopping water drinking.

Despite the above-mentioned explanations precise physiological mechanisms involved in the thirst drive are yet not fully understood.

Sex

One of the most powerful drives both in animals and human beings is the sex drive. It is a strong biological drive in the sense that it is inborn, unlearnt, characteristic of all species and that it culminates in a physiological event (orgasm). Moreover, it is also a strong determinant of behaviour. But, this motive sharply differs from other physiological motives (hunger and thirst) in many respects, such as:

(i) Hunger and thirst are vital for survival of the organism whereas sex is not so. It is essential for the survival of the species.
(ii) The motivated behaviour in hunger and thirst serves to reduce tissue need (deficit) but there is no such deficit in sex.
(iii) The motivated behaviour in hunger and thirst restores the used-up body energy while sexual behaviour uses up the body energy itself. It does not restore or build up energy.
(iv) Unlike hunger and thirst, there is no evidence to show physiological process of building up which reduces sexual activity.

Sexual behaviour is in fact a combination of internal factors (hormones and brain mechanisms) and external factors—learning and environmental stimuli.

Internal mechanisms: There is sex gland that secretes sex hormones. In males, 'testes'

* An inactive substance formed by the action of renin on a protein in the blood plasma. In the lungs angiotensin I is converted into angiotensin II, a highly active substance which constricts blood vessels and causes release of aldosterone from adrenal cortex (hypertension).

get stimulation from pituitary hormones to manufacture and secrete sex hormone—'testosterone'. In females, the pituitary hormone stimulates 'ovaries' to manufacture and secrete sex hormone—'estrogen' and 'progesterone'. When these sex glands (testes and ovaries) mature at 'puberty', there is marked increase in these hormones. This increase in sex hormones brings certain characteristic changes in adolescents, such as—formation of masculine and feminine bodies, development of sex organs, changes in voice, hair distribution etc. At the same time, interest in opposite sex also develops. If the sex glands do not develop in a normal way or are removed, the development of typical sex characteristics is impaired.

One puzzling question, which has been vexing the scientists, is whether hormones play crucial role in sexual behaviour? The findings of studies present a very complicated picture. In general, however, among lower animals (e.g. rats) sex hormones are more crucial than higher animals such as chimpanzees and human beings (Beach, 1965). It was found that mating behaviour of spayed female rats disappears and becomes able to mate again only when hormones are artificially given. The males were found to continue mating after castration for a shortwhile but then become incapable till sex hormone is reinjected. But, similar surgical operation among human beings does not show such clear effects. In some cases, removal of sex glands ceases sexual motivation while in almost equal number of cases, it is unaffected due to castration or ovariotomy. Further, it has also been found that males or females may have normal supply of sex hormones even if they are impotent or frigid. Findings on monkeys or chimpanzees also indicate that sex hormones have no crucial role to play.

From the above descriptions and findings of studies, it is discerned that for all animals, hormones play an important role in the development of sex-related characteristics and sexual motivation. However, sexual behaviour is not uniformally dependent on sex hormones. Hormones play a crucial role among the lower animals than higher animals. Among higher animals, habits, learning and other environmental stimuli are of greater significance in sexual motivations. Some studies done by **Beach** (1947), **Yerks** (1943), **Harlow** (1962) etc. evidence the fact that sex hormone plays relatively smaller roles while habits and experience play a major role in higher animals. Thus, habit is much more important in sexual motivation of higher animals because it determines the way human beings express their sexual motivation.

Maternal drive

Maternal motive is another physiological motive which has hormonal basis. This motive is much similar to what has been stated about sex motive. Maternal behaviour is instinctive in nature because such behaviours are unlearnt (more particularly in lower animals such as rats), and also that these behaviours are characteristic of the species.

As has been said, the basis of maternal motive is secretion of hormone (prolactin). The foetus present in uterus stimulate pituitary gland to produce prolactin (during pregnancy) which in turn stimulates mammary glands. Stimulation of mammary glands serves double purpose—(a) it supplies milk for nursing the post-natal offsprings and (b) it is also important in maternal behaviour of lower animals. **Lehman** (1961) observed that when mammary gland hormone is injected into virgin female rat and is given young of another rat, the injected rat accepts and cares the young rat similar to natural mother rat.

Though, maternal motive has hormonal basis (a physiological process), it is also modifiable by psychological factors. **Campbell** and **Misanine** (1969) in their studies noted that rats and hamsters (a kind of rat) exhibit more maternal behaviour after they had experience with the young. Similarly, it has also been observed that such animals which are uninfluenced by harmones, also display maternal behaviour on being exposed to young and get an opportunity to co-exist with the young. Such observations evidence the fact that hormones make sure the maternal behaviour in the natural mothers. But, probability is great that experience with the young may also develop maternal behaviour. Hence, experience of maternal behaviour is also an important factor.

Here, it is important to note that although experience with the young may develop maternal behaviour, it cannot be termed as learning because, emergence of maternal behaviour on exposure is neither conditioning nor any kind of reinforcement in the same way as these two are found associated with the phenomenon of learning. Hence, it is obvious that experience may bring out the underneath, unlearned motives and it may have some additive value in hormonal arousal of the concerned drive.

As regards maternal behaviours in human beings, no scientific analysis and experimentation is practicable. The explanations are largely based on inferences from animal studies and from casual observations of human mothers. In fact, maternal motive in humans are universal and this is indicative of the physiological bases. However, exceptions do exist. Occasionally, some human mothers do not exhibit desire to nurture their infants. In some cases, legitimacy of the infants also determines the pattern of maternal behaviour. Such differences owe mainly to social and cultural norms. In conclusion, therefore, it is proper to assume human maternal motive to have physiological basis in hormones, but are also supported by socio-cultural context (social learning and pressure).

Excretion

Excretion is a physiological process to eliminate the internal wastes. It is concerned with bowel and bladder tensions. When the bladder and lower colon become distended due to accumulation of waste product and pressure builds up in these two regions resulting in the stimulation of the receptors found in their walls. This stimulation produces the drive to excrete that are satisfied by urination and defecation. Thus, this is a drive to empty the bowel and bladder.

This drive is usually of less significance in adult life because obstacles to their relief are rare. However, during the early stages of development they play a significant role. During early childhood (in the toilet training phase) some mothers overemphasize toilet habits and start toilet training too early. The muscles that control bowel and bladder movements are the last to come under child's control. Moreover, the child derives primitive enjoyment from relieving the tension caused by accumulated wastes. Hence, too early toilet training is frustrating to the child because he feels punished for soiling himself for what he is too young to control.

Psychologists hold the view that too early and too severe training makes the child to feel insecure. In some cases, the child also learns to use his excretory functions as a tool of dominance and deliberately withhold bowel movements or bed wets. Thus, the child gains a feeling of power. Such problems may be avoided if toilet training is initiated at appropriate time, *i.e.* by the time child is physically ready. Parents should not exert excessive pressure on him and should also reinforce the child by praising him for the success.

Other physiological drives

There are some more physiological drives that arise out of several other body needs essential for survival and physiological comfort. Such drives are 'air hunger', 'rest' and 'sleep' 'warmth and cold', 'pain' etc.

(a) **Air hunger:** Body essentially requires oxygen. However, usually we have no sensation of the need for oxygen. But, when carbon dioxide collects in the lungs and respiratory pathways are obstructed, we immediately feel discomfort and intense pain till the respiratory tract get rid of the carbon dioxide.

The need for oxygen or air hunger is typically demonstrated when we are gradually deprived of oxygen as when we climb a high mountain or ascend in an aeroplane or when we have asthmatic attack.

(b) **Rest and sleep:** Rest and sleep are also physiological needs to get rid of muscular fatigue and mental rest due to long hours of strenuous work. This situation arises due to excessive accumulation of lactic acid in the muscles which continuously and repeatedly contract and relax in continuous work. Rest allows the blood stream to remove the accumulated lactic acid and thus, restores the potentials of muscular movements.

(c) **Warmth and cold:** Senses of warmth and cold depend on receptors in the skin (thermo-receptors). Some receptors are sensitive to warm objects while some to cold. Temperature of body is also regulated by physiological mechanism. Whenever the balance is disturbed, body activity is stimulated and we tend to such behaviours that may bring back the balance and provide relief to the body. For example, we tend to wear warm clothes during winter and use air coolers or air conditioners during summer.

(d) **Pain:** We all share to avoid pain. Anything that destroys or tend to harm tissues can be a stimulus for pain. The moment we feel pain, we quickly withdraw the part of the body from the stimulus. This is termed as 'withdrawal reflex'. To this extent pain is not a drive. This is a simple reflex mechanism. However, if pain continues even after withdrawal or due to some organic condition, it serves as a drive which can be escaped only by some appropriate action. Under such circumstances, a number of operant responses are aroused and the consummatory responses are the pain relieving activities, such as massage, drug etc.

From what has been described about the physiological or the biogenic drives (motives), it is clear that these motives arise out of driving states. Biological drives are regulatory mechanisms to maintain physiological equilibrium of the individual. Many of the biological drives are internal and automatic while some are modifiable by external environment.

14.7.2 Unlearned/General Motives

In our everyday observations, we notice quite a large number of such behaviours which cannot be explained in terms of physiological drives in spite of the fact that these may have indirect linkage with biological processes. For example, we spend a good deal of time just looking at newspapers, viewing televisions, sports activities, hunting, touring etc. Most of these behaviours have no obvious connections with physiological motives or drive states. Yet, some of these may be indirectly connected to our physiological needs. For example, walking in the morning or yoga exercises may be related to our physiological need to **'keep fit'**, we work in the office to earn livelihood which can satisfy our hunger drive and so on. However, since these motives lack physiological base yet, not truly learned and are characterstics of all the members of a species. Hence, these motives are unlearned. But, scientists have not yet coined any appropriate category to classify these various kinds of motives. So, these are called 'general motives'.

General motives include motives for activity, explorative and manipulative motives, sensory stimulation, affectional motives, competance etc. In the present section, we shall be describing three of such motives which are most common.

Motives for activity

All species, both animals and humans, spend a good time moving about without any apparent reason. Thus, motive for bodily activity is characteristic of all the species. Such behaviours (moving about) satisfy the motive for activity. Though, in some cases, activity may accompany physiological motive such as when the animal is hungry or thirsty. But, some of the activities do not accompany any apparent physiological motive.

Some activities may have sensory arousal such as, in the presence of some annoying or disturbing stimulus (strong light, horns, foul smells, chilly winds etc). Presence of such stimulating conditions arouse an organism and makes them more active. Similarly, novel stimulating situations also arouse one's interest or curiosity to be active which is itself a motive.

But, motive for activity may not necessarily involve any physiological or sensory basis. In this context, some evidence has been obtained. One such evidence comes from an experimental study of **Hill** (1956). He made some rats confined in a maze with insufficient space to move about. The confined rats in the cage were the experimental group. Basing on the period of confinement, these rats were classified into three groups, i.e. three experimental groups. One group was confined for 5 hours, another for 24 hours and the third group was confined for $46^1/_2$ hours. A fourth group served as control group, i.e. these rats were also confined in a similar cage but with sufficient space to move about. It was found that the amount of activity varied with duration of confinement. The rats confined for longest time were most active while the control group was least active.

Another evidence came from experimental study of **Kagan** and **Berkun** (1954). They found that activity itself acts as reinforcer in acquiring habit.

The above evidences lend support to the fact that activity is also a motive. This is the reason that no organism can sit idle. Living beings are active by birth.

Curiosity

Curiosity is also referred to as **'exploratory motive'**. When an organism is placed in a novel or strange situation, the organism automatically tends to explore surroundings thoroughly. In fact, our ignorance about a number of things in the surrounding becomes a powerful motivator and prompts us to be curious and explorative. This motive has been observed in a variety of experiments done on animals and humans. Humans if allowed to explore, get internal satisfaction reflected in their smiles and babbling.

Romanes (1981) was the first to observe exploratory behaviours in monkeys. He observed that monkeys tirelessly investigate their surroundings and manipulate any object sheer for fun as no reward could be gained.

Thorndike (1901) also reported the case of a monkey who repeatedly struck a projecting wire with a view to make it vibrate. In some later studies, visual curiosity and exploration were observed in monkeys from the very beginning of their lives. **Butter** and **Harlow** (1954) found that visual curiosity and exploratory behaviours starting from the very beginning of life gradually increases with gradual maturity. Owing to such increase, ability to locate objects in the surrounding, and learning to discriminate develops which finally leads to building up of strong need to explore the world visually.

Curiosity can also be observed in infants and children. When children are shown simple patterns, such as squares and circles, they first look at them and then habituate. They examine complex patterns for a longer period.

Evidences gathered from systematic studies show that curiosity is unlearned as it appears early in human life and is also seen in simple animals. Though, curiosity is an adaptive motive yet, the ability to explore may increase as one comes in contact with larger number of objects around the world.

Manipulative motive

Though, there is no clear cut distinction between curiosity or exploratory motive and manipulative motive, some experimental evidences do show that a need to manipulate objects strongly motivate learning. One such evidence comes from the study of **Harlow** and **McClearn** (1954). The researchers found that monkeys were able to learn discrimination reasonably well only by tending to manipulate rather than any kind of reinforcement.

Contact comfort motive

Similarly, a motive called—**'contact comfort'** is also a general motive that has been experimentally studied by **Harlow** (1958) using baby monkeys who were led by surrogate mothers (artificial mothers). It was found that baby monkeys felt much more comfortable when the surrogate mothers resemble real mothers—cloth mothers in place of wire mothers. It evidently shows the significance of contact comfort as a general unlearned motive.

Thus, much of our behaviour is aroused by some kinds of motives which are not directly biological nor learned. These are general motives which determine most of our behaviours in a significant way.

14.7.3 Social/Personal/Acquired Motives (Psychosociogenic Motives)

In addition to biogenic and unlearned general motives, our behaviour is also aroused by even more complex motives that we acquire in our personal and socio-cultural lives. These are called acquired motives or psychosociogenic motives.

Psychologists have been searching for a definite classification of motives but have not yet found. The difficulty is in view of the fact that there can be no watertight distinction between so-called physiological, unlearned general motives and acquired psychosociogenic motives. Motives in fact, vary all the way from the most distinctively physiological to the most highly acquired motives. For example, drive to breath has a well-known physiological base which functions without awareness of the organism or even any sort of preplan. But, even this drive can be modified to some extent by learning. For example, a swimmer learns to breath in a way that allows him to travel through the water more effectively. Similar is the case with mountaineers, air travellers etc.

In the same way, the unlearned general motives (such as exploratory and manipulative motives) are not distinctively physiological or unlearned. These motives gain strength with increasing experiences of the surroundings around us. In addition, these motives themselves become a case of larger element of learning in social situations. For example, when we meet a stranger, our exploratory behaviour is aroused and curiosity to know more and more about the stranger is increased.

So far, classification of social motives is concerned, it is practically an unsolvable problem. Comprehensive listing of social or acquired motives is indeed a herculean task. The part of difficulty is attributable to our ignorance to devise any standard measure to separate each social motive independent to each other and also to analyse their sources and operation. We may make all sorts of lists for different purposes. Another difficulty concerns with the interconnected nature of social motives and goals. Two individuals may have same goal but their motives may be different and vice versa.

However, some of the social motives have very extensively been studied. A list of such motives with corresponding goals and effects is being presented in **Table 14.4**.

TABLE 14.4 A classification of major personal/social motives based on extensive tests and interviews of a large number of young people*

Sl. No.	*Motives*	*Goals and effects*
1.	Abasement	To submit passively to others. To seek and accept injury, blame and criticism.
2.	Achievement	To accomplish difficult tasks to rival and surpass others.
3.	Affiliation	To seek and enjoy co-operation with others. To make friends.
4.	Aggression	To overcome opposition forcefully. To fight and revenge injury. To be little curse and rescue others.
5.	Autonomy	To be free of restraints and obligations. To be independent and free to act according to impulse.
6.	Counteraction	To master or makeup for failure by renewed efforts. To overcome weaknesses and maintain pride and self-respect at high level.
7.	Deference	To admire and support superior persons. To yield eagerly to other people.
8.	Defend	To defend oneself against attack, criticism or blame. To justify and vindicate oneself.
9.	Dominance	To control and influence the behaviour of others.
10.	Exhibition	To make an impression. To be seen and heard by others. To show off.
11.	Harm avoidance	To avoid pain, physical injury, illness and death.
12.	Infavoidance	To avoid humiliation. To refrain from action because of fear of failure.
13.	Nurturance	To help and take care of sick or defenceless people. To assist others who are in trouble.
14.	Order	To put things in order. To achieve cleanliness, arrangement and organization.
15.	Play	To devote one's free time in sports, games and parties. To laugh and make a joke of everything. To be light-hearted and gay.
16.	Rejection	To remain aloof and indifferent to an inferior person. To jilt and stub others.
17.	Sentience	To seek and enjoy sensuous impressions and sensations to enjoy the art genuinely.

Classificatory Table 14.4 contains only a limited number of motives that operate in relation to other people around us. In fact, researchers have proposed a large number of such lists, each

* Murray, H.A., et al. (1938), *Explorations in Personality: A clinical and experimental study of fifty men of college age*, New York, Oxford University Press.

with a difference from one another. However, none of these lists has ever been given assent to as comprehensive list by the behavioural scientist. Moreover, attempt to devise such lists is still continuing, but owing to its complexities and certain limitations, no such list is likely to achieve finality. However, efforts must continue so that constant revisions and improvements in accuracy may be brought about.

Now let us examine acquired social motives in some greater detail. Among these, we shall include 'achievement', 'affiliation', 'power', 'aggression' and 'cognitive dissonance'.

Need for achievement (*n* Ach)

Humans learn to compete, to get ahead of others, to surpass their own standards and to succeed in difficult tasks. This tendency of human beings is termed as **achievement motive** or **need for achievement** (*n* Ach). This need has perhaps been studied more than any other social or personal need (McClelland et al. 1953; Atkinson and Feather, 1966). It is a motive for success in performing a task. 'McClelland' has defined this need as—**Achievement motive can be defined as a striving to increase or keep as high as possible one's own capabilities in which a standard of excellence is thought to apply and where the execution of such activities can, therefore be, either to succeed or fail.**

Thus, *n* Ach is a disposition which is manifested in overt striving for accomplishment in whatever one undertakes and performs his task with some degree of excellence. In this sense, it is a drive to overcome challenge, advance and grow. This motivation drives the individual to seek accomplishment for their own pride. They work for inner satisfaction of their desire to succeed and feel self-pride. This motive is similar to **competence motive** in which an individual is driven to do high quality work. He seeks mastery in job and tends towards professional growth. They tend to perform well for their inner satisfactions they feel from doing it.

n Ach energises direct behaviour and influences perception of situation. Though, it is not a biological motive but impacts human behaviour tremendously. People differ in the degree or level of *n* Ach. This motive is measured by 'Thematic Apperception Test' (TAT)—a projective method of assessment. In this technique, certain ambiguous pictures or pictures with multi meanings are presented before the testee who are asked to write down a short story. The stories are analysed in terms of **Achievement Imageries (AI)** which give an index of level of achievement motive. In the stories, the testees project their own achievement imageries. **Atkinson** has developed a theory of achievement motivation on the basis of the findings of the early studies done by McClelland.

McClelland (1961) and other researchers have correlated achievement motivation with high scholastic performances and success in business.

High *n* Ach persons usually opt for moderate risk tasks, they are future-oriented and persist more on the task. McClelland has found that in general the cultures which value independence and achievement are economically more advanced (*e.g.* the protestant countries) than the societies which value dependency and are not achievement-oriented. Similarly, the parents who socialize their children with greater independence and autonomy training, promote achievement motivation in their children by making them self-supportive and becoming upwardly mobile. Researchers have also found that females, particularly those who have accepted the traditional women's role in the society and are yet, placed in a competitive situation, develop fear of success. Thus, there is gender/individual difference in the fear of success motive. In recent years, however, the scenario has changed and if it continues, women too can be expected more alike men in respect of achievement motivation.

Achievement motivation develops during the formative periods of children through child rearing practices. During this period, they learn valuing achievement from their parent, other role models and social influences about the values of attaining good positions, social standing and distinguished status in the society. This kind of value learning promotes the development of 'achievement themas' and 'images'.

Need for affiliation (*n* Affil.)

Need for affiliation or affiliation motive is also called motive for gregariousness which is an important social motive as this motive is an integral part of our social lives. Affiliation refers to relating with others which is a major part of our social life and is almost universal in the sense that warmth and comfort of social contacts begin with feeding during infancy and is characteristic of all living beings (human beings and animals—both). In studies, it has been found that persons with moderate level of affiliation needs are more effective managers. Biological attachment, reduction of fear, assistance stimulation, information and self-evaluation are some of the important factors that cause us to be affiliative.

Schachter (1959) has also noted in his studies that anxiety is also an important determinant of affiliation motive because anxiety increases the tendency to affiliate. Hence, anxiety appears to be a learned cue for seeking companionship.

Like *n* Ach, need for affiliation is also measured by Thematic Apprehension Test (TAT) pictures in which the testee projects his own affiliative imageries in the themes of stories in response to the TAT picture situations. Studies have also revealed that like *n* Ach, people also differ in their strength of need to affiliate.

Need for power (*n* Pow.)

Power is the core concern of modern life. It is a concern over controlling the means of influencing the behaviour of another person (**Veroff**, 1957). Adler is supposed to be the pioneer advocate of this motive. Adler officially broke his ties with Freud and reposed an opposing theoretical position in which he overemphasized the drive for superiority or power.

Power need is the need to manipulate others or a drive for superiority over others. It refers to **'the ability or capacity of a person to produce (consciously or unconsciously) internal effect on the behaviour or emotions of another person'**. The goals of this motive (*n* pow.) are to influence, control, cajole, persuade, lead, charm others and thus, to enhance one's own reputation in the eyes of others. People with strong power motive derive satisfaction by achieving these goals. To achieve these goals, people usually strive for high political gains and positions, try to be at high positions in authority. Such people are found to indulge in lobbying, manipulating and managing to control the activities of others or masses in general. The acute form of power motive leads to autocratic behaviours. In this sense, power motive is a desire **'to-be-in-charge'** to gain status, prestige and influence others.

TAT stories are scored to measure power motive in terms of emphasis on strong vigorous. actions that express power and actions that cause strong arousal in others and indicate explicit concerns for reputation and prestige. Power imagery is focussed on concerns about one's impact about maintaining or restoring one's power or prestige. One important characteristic of this motive is that it is a latent motive until aroused. This motive has been found to be related to power related signals in the environment, competitiveness and aggression. Studies have shown that those who score high on *n* pow. usually engage in fighting, participation in competitive activities (sports, hot debates etc.), drinking and gambling. However, it is more true of men than women.

Another important feature of this motive is that those who are high on *n* pow. are relatively more assertive.

Machiavellianism

Niccolo Machiavelli (1469–1527) in his book, 'The Prince' offered some practical advice to rulers as to how to maintain power. In essence, he suggested that rulers should outwardly follow the rule of conventional morality but secretly they should use craft and deceitful practices to maintain themselves in power. Accordingly, the psychologists have coined the term 'Machiavellianism' (Christie and Geis, 1970) to refer to manifestation of power motive by exploiting and manipulating others in a deceitful and unscrupulous fashion.

Machiavellianism is not same as power motivation. Machiavellianism, in fact, refers to a strategy to express power motivation. Such persons are manipulators. In addition, they generally show little warmth in their personal relationships, poorly guided by conventional morality in their dealings with others. Machiavels are in fact, reality-oriented (interested in practical results) and have little interest in ideologies (Christie and Geis, 1970). Thus, the strategy of deceitful ways of expressing power motivation has been dubbed with Machiavels and called 'Machiavellianism'.

Some paper-pencil tests have been devised to identify Machaivels. Some experimental studies done by Geis (1978) have also revealed that those who are high on this measure indeed manipulate others, make to break interpersonal relations in opportunistic way, deny cheating and use lie in manipulating others. Such phenomenon is very frequently seen in political games now-a-days, more particularly democratic countries like India.

Aggression

Aggression is a motive to fight or aggress. It can be best defined as a tendency to make harm or hurt the aggressive stimuli. Aggressiveness appears as a common phenomenon (because in some form or the other, it is commonly found in all individuals or societies).

This tendency is also observed in animals. Since this tendency is omnipresent, most people consider aggressiveness as universal. But, it varies greatly from one society to another and also from one species to another. **Batesan** (1936) has long ago identified certain tribes (Itamul tribes) as extremely aggressive not only when they are on war path, but also in other aspects of tribal life. On the other hand, **Kaplon** and **Plout** (1956) observed that among 'Hutterites' (a religious sect) fighting or verbal abuse is not permitted. In the event of interpersonal disagreement a spirit of compromise or even giving in one's opponent is the accepted principle to maintain interpersonal relationships. They are expected not to be angry, swear or lose temper. Similar contrast in aggressiveness is found in many other societies and cultures. These instances obviously suggest that aggressiveness is not innate.

Many studies have shown that aggressive reactions are the consequences of frustration of a drive. Besides, aggressive behaviour is also a learnt behaviour which is acquired either through imitation of an aggressive model or through selective reinforcement or through combination of the two. Anthropologists interpret behaviours of Itamul tribal in terms of combined effects of imitation and reinforcement. Adolescent boys of the tribe are constantly surrounded by adult patterns of aggression on the one hand and are also rewarded or approved for these pattern and disapproved for behaving differently on the other.

Sometimes, a distinction is made between **hostile aggression** and **instrumental aggression**. The former has its goal—harming another person. In the later type of aggression, the aggressive individual uses aggression as a means to satisfy some other motive (Buss, 1961, 1966). For example, an individual may use threats to force others to comply with his or her wishes. Similarly, a child may use aggression for gaining attention of his or her parents.

In essence, aggression is a reaction or response to certain kinds of situations such as frustration, injury or insult or threats to self or deprivation. Such situations are common as well as frequent in our dailylife. Research studies show that when aggressive behaviours are reinforced, it becomes habitual way of reacting to satisfy other motives. Hence, this motive is socially learned.

Cognitive dissonance

Cognitive dissonance is an attempt to reduce discrepancy between an idea or belief and actual event. It is cognitive because motivation to reduce discrepancy is aroused when a person perceives disagreement (dissonance) between idea and real happenings. To make it more clear, example of strange behaviour of religious cult would be more appropriate. Suppose that a member of the cult group announces his prediction that on a certain date and time, the whole of the world would face massive destruction due to unprecedented natural calamities—earthquakes, floods, epidemics etc. A few of the faithful believers pick up and the prediction is widely spread. The cult group begins to gather and anxiously wait for the event to occur. Some of them begin to worship (anushthans) and offer prayers. However, as the predicted date and time approaches, it passes without any such happening. Thus, the faithful believers find themselves in a state of despair and experience dissonance due to contradictions in what had been predicated and what happened. Sometimes later some of the cult group rises up and announces that they have found the 'explanation' for the dissonance. The God had made his appearance and told that owing to what they had done, God being pleased, had saved the world from destruction. This announce-ment dramatically changes the behaviour of the cult group and despondence changes into joy. Thus, by creating an explanation they eliminated the dissonance between prediction and non-occurrence of the predicted event.

Approval motive

The desire to be socially approved is a very common desire found in every individual. This desire drives the individual to behave in a socially approved manner. Evidences of this desire can be found in revelations of any kind of personality tests such as projective tests, inventories or behaviour studies. Research findings on the topic suggest that strength of 'approval motive' like all other social motives varies from individual to individual.

Approval motive has more extensively been studied by applying **Marlowe–Crowne social desirability test**. This test depicts the picture of an 'approval dependent persons'. Such people are more socially conforming, can be easily persuaded and are favourable towards tasks set by others. At the same time, such persons are very cautious in risk-taking behaviours.

Those who are high on *n* Approval depend on such approval for feeling of self-esteem. This need is generally positioned in the middle of a continuum scale. At the one extreme of the scale is the need for affiliation while at the other extreme is the need for status or power as shown in **Figure 14.2**.

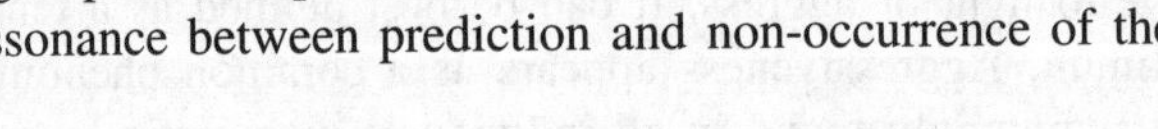

FIGURE 14.2 Scaling approval motive.

Level of aspiration

Aspiration level is also a personal motive. Every individual has some degree of aspirations to achieve the goal that he sets in life. It is personal because in choosing life goals and performing everyday activities, individuals differ widely in their levels of aspiration. Further, one's level of aspiration is also modified from time to time depending upon success and failure in attaining the goals. For example, one may aspire to become a physician while another may aspire to become an academician. Similarly, in performance situation, one may aspire to attain the highest order of performance while other may aspire at some lower level. Such levels of aspirations are in fact, what one expects to succeed or how accurately and/or quickly he can perform a given task.

As has been said earlier, the levels of aspirations are subject to modification depending upon the success or failure in accomplishing one's set goal. Laboratory investigations in general suggest that usually one sets his aspiration very close to his potentiality to achieve. However, sometimes an individual sets his aspiration level much higher to his actual ability to achieve. This discrepancy results in failure to attain the level aspired by him. Under such circumstances, he lowers his aspiration level close to his potentiality to achieve. Likewise, sometimes an individual fixes his level of aspiration at a point much lower to his ability and succeeds very easily. This prompts him to aspire at some higher level. Thus, success and failure to attain the aspired goal modifies one's level of aspiration.

Reinforcement

Reinforcement is one of the important motivating conditions of behaviour because it increases the probability of occurrence of a desired (reinforced) response. Reinforcement refers to an agent called reinforcer. A reinforcer is an event that maintains and increases the strength of a response. All sorts of rewards or incentives in this sense are reinforcers. For example, food reinforces food searching behaviours. Similarly, praise may be a reinforcer for the child to learn and strengthen the desired response. A reinforcer also changes the rate of behaviour as is evidenced from conditioning experiments (classical as well as operant).

Reinforcement may be either positive or negative. A positive reinforcer strengthens or increases the probability of a response to occur again and again. The negative reinforcer causes withdrawal or termination of a response as is noticed in aversive conditioning. When positive reinforcer is present, subject ordinarily approaches the object while in the event of negative reinforcer, the subject avoids to work for the object. Thus, in essence, reinforcement changes his rate and direction of behaviour.

Researches done on reinforcement have revealed a number of factors related to reinforcement in modifying behaviours. Among these factors, the amount of reinforcement and delay in reinforcement are important. The findings of these studies in general state that within limits, greater the amount of reinforcement, more rapid is the probability for correct response to occur and get strengthened. Some studies have demonstrated the quality of reinforcement also serve as important factor in learning. Delay in reinforcements refers to the time gap between response and reinforcement. When reinforcement follows the behaviour immediately, the likelihood of its being strengthened or frequency of its occurrence increases. Just opposite is the case when it follows the behaviour late.

In this context, scheduling of reinforcement has also been found as important determinant of response strengthening. (For more details, see Chapter 10 on Modification of Behaviour.)

14.8 INTRINSIC AND EXTRINSIC FRAMEWORK OF MOTIVATION

'Exploration need' is one of the important needs of the organism that **pushes** one to be active in dealing with the environment he lives in. This is the **intrinsic motivation**—a motivation to be effective while dealing with the objects of the world. This is also called **effectance motivation.** This refers to the 'need to know and to be effective' with the environment. This need persists throughout life and are also difficult to satisfy (though not impossible). This is 'intrinsic' because it pushes us from within. The individual by nature is not passive rather a purposeful agent who deals with his environment as effectively as he can. Hence, intrinsic motivation is 'person's need for feeling competent and self-determining in dealing with his environment'—(Deci, 1975). It is intrinsic because the goals are internal feelings of effectiveness, competence and self-determination. This is a sort of **self-motivation** in which the individual feels inner satisfaction—self-rewarded for his 'effectance'. In contrast, there is also extrinsic motivation. This motive 'pulls' the organism towards the goals which are not within the individual but in the environment, such as rewards, money, or grades in the school. Hence, the extrinsic motives are the forces or stimuli in the environment that induce and channel our behaviour towards the goals or incentives which are not within the individual rather external to him (in the external environment). Behaviours directed towards the external goals are conceived as a 'reaction' to the demands and pressures, rewards and punishment.

The intrinsic and extrinsic frameworks are also termed as **push and pull model** of motivation. The intrinsic need to feel competent pushes one to behave in such a way that he attains the internal feelings of competency by dealing with the environment effectively. This gives an impression of the individual as an active agent rather then passive one.

On the other hand is the extrinsic need to achieve a goal that is not within the individual rather in the environment. The environmental goals attract or 'pull' one to react or behave in a manner that he achieves the extrinsic rewards, viz. acquisition of wealth, power, money, gallantry awards etc.

Though, the extrinsic rewards are useful in guiding human behaviour in business, school or in office dealings and dealing with others in the society, but sometimes, it may suppress intrinsic motive resulting in impairment of effective performance (Condry, 1977; Lepper and Greene, 1978). It so happens because when a person is pulled by extrinsic rewards, he evolves a strategy of economical efforts in place of working hard for originality, creativity and for satisfaction that may come from mastery and deep understanding of a problem (intrinsic motive). Thus, extrinsic motive may reduce a powerful aspect of motivation—one's intrinsic motive to know and to be effective. The person perceives extrinsic reward only in terms of an instrument that controls his self. Intrinsically motivated people like challenge, surprise and complexity in real life. Research studies have shown that extrinsic rewards often interfere performance. Hence, students are encouraged to be more intrinsically motivated and suggest a lesser use of external reward.

14.9 MEASUREMENT OF MOTIVES

As we have seen, motives are internal forces or conditions of the organism that impels one to some kind of action. Therefore, motives cannot be directly observed. However, it can be inferred from behaviour.

Our knowledge of the biological drives comes from studying behaviour of the animals under experimental conditions. It is a well-established fact that measurement and quantification are the basic aims of any science. Psychologists too have devised ways of measuring the strength of drives by varying the drive stimulation and then observing the consequential effects on some aspects of behaviour. The stimuli which are varied or manipulated may be internal (such as varying the hours of food or water deprivation) or external (such as amount of electrical current applied on the skin). The effects of these stimulations can be measured by (i) gross motor activity, (ii) rate of responding, (iii) amount of obstruction needed to prevent the animal from reaching the goal, (iv) performance shown by the animal when choice is given, (v) force or amplitude of response, (vi) action of the autonomic nervous system and (vii) speed of learning.

Applying the above, some studies on biological drives have been done by psychologists and physiologists. Four basic methods have been used in these studies. These methods are as follows:

14.9.1 Activity Cage Method

Campbell and **Sheffield** (1953) designed a cage and studied the hunger motive on rats. The rat is in the right portion of the cage (see Figure 14.3). It runs in the revolving drum at the left. The revolution cycles of the drum in either direction are recorded by the cyclometer. There is a sliding door by which the rat may either be allowed or prevented to enter into it. A resliding tray under the apparatus collects the debris.

The researchers found that hunger increases the activity in the rats and this increase corresponds to the period of food deprivation. Thus, it clearly shows a positive and close relationship between the amount of food deprivation and the amount of activity (**Figure 14.3**).

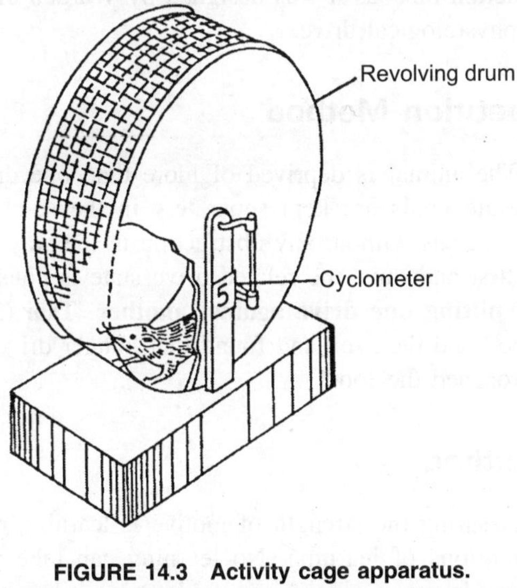

FIGURE 14.3 Activity cage apparatus.

In another study, rats were put on a diet that reduced weight and were given access to revolving drum for an hour daily. The amount of activity in rats was found to be a function of loss of body weight. The obtained correlationship was approximately .99, an extremely high correlationship (Moskowitz, 1959). In still another study done by Greene (1959), it was found that in course of gradual restoration of normal weight, there was a gradual decrease in activity level also. In both of these experiments the findings were obtained in which other relevant extraneous variables of such changes in the activity level were controlled. Thus, increase in activity or decrease when satisfied, is attributable to the hunger conditions only.

In yet another study, the rat during heat period was found to be very active. In the revolving drum it could run equivalent to 15 or more miles a day (Wang, 1923). In this case, sex drive seems to be responsible for excess activity. Similar evidences have also been obtained in the case of thirst, deprivation from offsprings, nest building drives etc.

14.9.2 Obstruction Method

This is another important method of studying the relative strength of physiological drives. In this method, a box with two compartments is used. The two compartments are connected with a narrow passage which is electrically charged. The hunger or thirst deprived animals are allowed to enter into the compartment. In another compartment, food or water (goal) is kept, which the animal in the first compartment can easily visualize. The door of the compartment is so made that it automatically opens. When the animal moves along the passage, it receives electric shock. Thus, the animal is obstructed in reaching the goal. It has been observed that in a state of mild hunger or thirst, the animal does not cross the obstruction. But when the need for food or water is relatively stronger, it crosses the obstruction (electric shock). The strength of sex motive has also been studied through this method. The female rat is placed in one compartment while the male rat is placed in another compartment. When the female rat is in 'heat' (i.e. the need for sex is aroused) it crosses the obstruction and reaches the male rat. These studies were long ago done by **Morgan** (1916, 1923), **Jenkins** and **Warner** (1926), and **Moss** (1974). Obstruction method is also known as 'Columbia obstruction box' as it was designed by Warden of Columbia University who made extensive studies of physiological drive.

14.9.3 Drive Competition Method

This is a simple method. The animal is deprived of more than one drive at a time, say hunger, thirst and sex and appropriate goals are kept separately in the same apparatus. The animal is allowed to choose any of the goals without any obstruction in the way. Observation is made as to which goal box is chosen first and thus, the related drive state is considered stronger than other. This method is also called **pitting one drive against another**. **Tsai** (1928) used this method by depriving the animal for food and then sex and found that hunger drive is relatively stronger than sex as the animal first approached the food.

14.9.4 Learning Method

Still another method for measuring the strength of motive is learning method. Motivation in fact, is one of the essential conditions of learning. No learning can take place unless the learner is adequately motivated to learn. In many experiments on learning it has been observed that 'stronger the motive, quicker and stronger is the learning'. The reason is that stronger motives release more energy in the organism to reach the goal in a better way. On the other hand, a weak motive neither releases much energy to learn nor does it impels the organism to learn the task proficiently. Thus, learning is slower and not concentrated.

The above methods have usefully been employed to study physiological motives of animals and inferences have been drawn in respect of human beings too. Human beings are not subjected to study about their physiological drives because it is difficult to apply proper controls over them. However, obstruction method and drive competition method could have successfully been applied in the study of children.

14.10 MEASUREMENT OF HUMAN SOCIO-PSYCHOGENIC (ACQUIRED) MOTIVES

To assess socio-psychogenic motives, usually three types of measures are employed. These are projective tests, situational test and inventories. The projective tests are indirect tests, while the situational tests involve drawing inferences from actions of the individuals in different situations and the inventories are self-report techniques, specially designed to seek verbal reports or responses on verbal questionnaires reflecting various need states.

14.10.1 Projective Tests

Projective tests are indirect measures of needs and motives. Various kinds of projective techniques to measure personality have been discussed in some greater detail in the chapter on Personality (Chapter 17). While assessing personality through projective tests, the dominant needs or motives operating within the individuals are also reflected. Hence, these tests are also employed to assess the dominant motives or needs. The major projective tests are—'Thematic Apperception Test (TAT)', 'Rorschach Ink Blot Test (RT or BT)', Word Association Test (WAT), 'Picture Frustration Test (PFT)' and 'McClelland's Achievement Imagery Test (AIT)'.

Thematic apperception test (TAT)

It consists of 20 picture cards of unfamiliar structured situations. The testees are shown each picture card for a brief period one by one for observing the situation details depicted in the picture and then write down a short story (or verbally narrate) on the depicted situation in the pictures. These stories are analysed in terms of number of themes which reflect the dominating needs and tendencies. This test has been developed by **Murray** (1943).

Rorschach test (RT or BT)

It consists of 10 ambiguous picture cards which resemble blots of ink. The testees are shown each picture one by one and asked to state the portions in the pictures and the kind of structured objects with which the specific portion(s) resemble with. The responses are recorded in terms of location, determinant, number and patterns of responses, popularity and originality. These scores do not only reflect the structural and functional aspects of personality but also the needs and motives that direct the behavioural tendencies or the dispositions. This test has been developed by **Rorschach** (1942).

Word association test

WAT is a verbal measure consisting of some words representing personality dispositions and motivating conditions randomly mixed with the neutral words which are spelled out by the investigator one by one to the testees who are supposed to express their verbal reactions that immediately occurs in mind. The verbally manifested reactions are recorded and response time is also measured which reflect the dominating needs or motives that arouses the person in responding in a specific manner.

Picture frustration test (PFT)

PFT was developed by **Rosenzweig**. It consists of series of cartoons in which one person frustrates another or calls attention to frustrating conditions. This test mainly focuses on frustration and aggression. The analysis of responses bases on type and direction of aggression which may be classified as obstacle dominance (emphasis on the frustrating object), ego defence (emphasis on protection of frustrated person) and need persistence (emphasis on constructive solution to the problem). The direction of aggression may be either towards the environment (extragressive), or towards oneself (intragressive) or inaggressive or tuned off in an attempt to show off or evade the situation. Udai Pareck and Rosenzweig have jointly adapted this test for Indian population.

McClelland's imagery achievement

McClelland has also devised a TAT test to measure the strength of *n* Ach through achievement imageries reflected in stories. This test is also used to assess need for affiliation and power need. This test collects data relating to the achievement imageries (AI) or affiliative images or power images and accordingly the concerned needs are inferred.

14.10.2 Situational Tests

These tests are used to draw inferences from actions. Behaviours are known as reflective of inner states of arousal. Hence, certain characteristic features or attributes of behaviours are reflective of inner motivational states. These characteristics include attention to specific objects, persistence in action, manifestation of satisfaction from goal achievement, consistent avoidance of an object in the situation the person acts. At this point, it is important to bear in mind that none of the behavioural attribute in isolation is reflective of any specific need or motive. In fact, behavioural criteria need to be supplemented by other methods so that the drawn inferences may be maximally correct.

Situational tests are also applied to measure variations in strength of a motive. For example, in order to study aggressiveness in small children, children are given dolls to play. They are observed that for how many times the child does something aggressive or destructive with the doll. In grown-up persons, aggression may be studied by insulting or abusing the person and observing his reactive responses.

Similarly, to study affiliation need, a person may be given a choice between waiting in a room under solitary condition and waiting with others. Such situational tests often prove most illuminating in researches on human motives.

14.10.3 Inventories or Self Report Techniques

Psychologists have developed quite a good number of inventories to measure personality and dominating motives. Inventories consist of verbal statements or questions and the subjects are required to respond to the items by checking in certain defined categories such as true/false, yes/no or doubtful, agree/disagree, checking or rating the statements along dimensions etc.

Quite a good number of such inventories are popular that include Edward's Personal Preference Record (EPPR), Sentence Competition Test (SCT), Valuing Achievement (*V* Ach), Taylor's Manifest Anxiety Scale, Mandler-Sarson Anxiety Test etc.

14.10.4 Experimental Studies

Psychologists have also employed experimental procedures to study about human motivation as a technique of basic research.

Many experimental studies in the area of learning, cognition, memory etc. have been done and some basic facts relating to motivational correlates of these processes have been gathered. Such studies relate to effects of reward and punishment, knowledge of result, deprivation of needs, social reinforcement, different schedules of reinforcement etc. Such studies are important not only as a basic research but have significant implications in the applied fields such as education, industry, administration etc.

Over and above, analysis of art and literature, clinical interviews, analysis of historical events etc. are also important tools for assessing motivational aspects of behaviour.

14.11 FRUSTRATION OF MOTIVES

As has been described, motivation is a goal-directed behaviour. The attainment of goal is satisfying and the motivating condition is allayed resulting in termination of goal-directed behaviour. However, in our dailylife situations, we very often come across the occasions when we fail to realize our goals due to blockage or obstacles. Such situations are painful, but common experience of all humans in different degrees. In addition, on many occasions we are faced with more than one motive or need at the same time.

These two circumstances—obstruction or blockage of motive (goal realization) and simultaneous operation of more than one motive—are the concerns that can be explained in the form of two important concepts—frustration and conflict.

14.11.1 Frustration

We come across many situations when the things go in an unexpected direction and we fail to realize our goal. This is referred to as **frustration of motive**. Frustration of motive occurs when an anticipated desirable goal is not attained and the motive is blocked. It is an aversive state that no one likes.

There are various situations which produce frustration. These can broadly be classified into two major categories—the environmental obstruction and inability of the individual to attain the goal. These are briefly discussed below:

Environmental obstruction or blockage

Sometimes obstruction in the environment of the person blocks goal attainment. For example, a child wants to play with a moving toy or doll. But the child finds the toy defunct or it is locked in the almirah. This hinders the child's need to play and thus, the motive to play is blocked. Our primary drives are also obstructed by the environmental circumstances. The sources of such blockages are nonavailability of money to obtain food, overload of work due to which one is unable to find time to take food, strike by grossary traders, death of someone in the family, curfew due to disturbed law and order situation etc. Prisoners in jails also experience frustration relating to many of their primary and derived motives such as sex, status, fraternity, affiliation with family members etc.

Inability of the individual to attain the goal

A motive is also frustrated when the person lacks the ability to attain the goal. This obstruction is not environmental but personal, i.e. the obstruction is inside (within) the individual. For example, a student's motive or desire to achieve excellence in the examination for which he labours hard. But, he may fail to achieve the desired level of excellency due to lack of adequate capabilities to achieve the goal (excellent performance). This frustrates the students *n* Ach. Similarly, our primary drives may also be frustrated due to subjective factors such as some sort of weakness or short-comings in the individual. For example, a young man's sex motive is frustrated when he desires to marry a beautiful girl of a very high status because his own status does not match her status. Inability to earn livelihood may block hunger drive.

Studies done on frustration of motives have demonstrated a variety of behavioural and emotional reactions. These include aggressive behaviour, flexion, escape, avoidance and crying. **Dollard** and **Hiller** (1939) have proposed a famous hypothesis which is known as frustration aggression hypothesis. This hypothesis states that frustration produces aggression which are often directed either towards the self or towards others (substitute), i.e. the blocking agent.

14.12 CONFLICT

Conflict of motives is also an important source of frustration. Conflict occurs when two motives pushes us from within simultaneously and the person must choose between the competing needs. Such conflicts are of various types which are mentioned herein below:

14.12.1 Approach–Approach Conflict

In this type of conflict, individuals are confronted with two positive force goals and as such, the person wants to achieve both the goals. But the demand of the situation is that the individual has to make a choice of any one of them. For example, making a choice between two equally worth-seeing movies, choosing a life partner between two equally attractive girls, two liked dishes, choosing for either an interesting book or going for sweets etc. are some of the examples of approach–approach conflict. In this type of conflicting situations, two alternative force fields are available. Hence, after a bit of deliberations choosing one of them is relatively easier and thus, the conflict is resolved easily.

14.12.2 Approach–Avoidance Conflict

When a goal has both—the positive and negative valence—the nature of conflict is approach–avoidance type. For example, a young girl wants to join film industry and play a role, but she also knows that such aspiring girls are subjected to sexual harassment (exploitation). Thus, aspiring to join film industry is attractive (positive valence) as well as it is associated with fear of being sexually exploited (negative valence). Such a position typically produces indecisiveness and makes the individual's behaviour vacillating. In such situations, **the individual is willing to strike but is afraid of wound**. Thus, in this type of conflict, the goals have both—the desirable (approaching) as well as undesirable (avoiding or aversive) features.

14.12.3 Avoidance–Avoidance Conflict

When a person is faced with equally undesirable cause of action, avoidance–avoidance conflict occurs. For example, a person is nominated as a member on a committee to work with a person he does not like to work with. But, he cannot say it as it may offend the person whom he dislikes. Similarly an honest man neither want to bribe a corrupt officer nor he would like to suffer delay in the execution of his work pending before him. In both the situations the twin actions are equally negative or undesirable but the person cannot avoid one without encountering the other. This kind of conflict is capsuled in popular saying—**caught between the devil and the deep blue sea**. For example, a boy must do his arithmetic work or get a spanking, a woman must work a job she intensely dislikes or take a chance of losing the job and her income. Thus, in this type of conflicting situations, we think of things that we do not want to do but must do even less desirable alternatives.

14.12.4 Double or Multiple Approach Avoidance Conflict

Many of life's major decisions involve multiple or double approach avoidance conflicts. It involves different goals with positive and negative questions. For example, suppose a woman is engaged to be married. The marriage has a 'positive valence' because marriage would provide stability and security and because she loves the man she will be marrying. On the another hand, suppose that the marriage is repellent to her because it will mean giving up an attractive job offer in another city. So far career is concerned, she is attracted to the new job offer but also repelled by the problem it will create for her marriage. What will she do? Partly the answer would depend on the relative strength of approach and avoidant tendencies. Similarly, suppose, you are interested to buy a colour TV. Now the point of consideration is to decide which brand of TV you would like to buy. One brand of TV is a product of a very popular manufacturing company, but the cost is high. Another one is most delicate and no good service centre is available on the local level. Thus, both the product brands have certain merits as well as demerits. This produces a situation of indecisiveness in our everyday life situations, we often come across such conflicting situations such as making a decision about the marriage of son/daughter deciding to select new job offers, purchasing etc. In all these situations, we resolve the conflict through a process of deliberation and weighing the relative strengths of the competing goals (positive and negative valences).

14.13 REACTIONS TO FRUSTRATIONS

Frustrations caused by non-satiation of motivating conditions lead to both successful and unsuccessful ways of adjusting. There are individuals who possess the power to tolerate frustrations and choose adaptive reactions. Others who lack the power to tolerate, react to it in diverse ways. Some adopt non-adaptive modes to resolve conflicts, while others defend themselves against undesirable consequences of the frustrations. These are called 'defense mechanisms' such as repression, sublimation, rationalization, projection, reaction formation, introjections, identification etc. These mechanisms are also called **ego defenses** because these mechanisms save the 'self' or 'ego' from being hurt by frustrations. Others get into the state of anxiety. Anxiety is a very common effect of frustration. When anxiety becomes intense and recurring in nature, the individuals become mentally sick. Still others become aggressive and emotionally disturbed. All these reactions are non-adaptive. Detailed descriptions of these modes of reactions are beyond the scope of this book. Interested readers are advised to consult books on 'Psychopathology'.

14.14 FUNCTIONS OF MOTIVATION OR ROLE OF MOTIVATION ON PERFORMANCE

Some general influences of motive on behaviour have been described earlier. In general, motives triggers an action, it functions as an essential condition of reinforcement and increases the variability of response. In the present section, we shall describe briefly how does these motives influence work?

As has been said, the term motive is concerned with 'why' of any behaviour. Psychologists in general hold that we behave because we feel motivated to behave, i.e. some inner force pushes from within to act and some goal object pulls toward to behave. Thus, all our action tendencies are impelled by inner state to act called motivation. Hence, our behaviours are initiated and directed by motivating conditions.

Role of motivation is primarily concerned with its influence on performance. **Melton** states three basic roles of motivation on performance. These are energizing role, the directing role and the emphasizing role.

14.14.1 The Energising Role

Motive energizes the organism, i.e. initiates general activity. The amount of general activity is a direct index of the strength of motivation. When the motivated organism faces a situation in which he must discover a correct response, shows variable behaviour and 'greater the number of responses, greater is the probability of hitting the correct response'. Thus, motivation provides increased level of energy to perform or behave.

14.14.2 The Directing Role

Motives not only provide energy for general activity, but also direct the behaviour in right direction. Thus, motives control the variability of response initiated due to energizing function of motives. Motives direct our activity towards the goal object. For example, a hungry animal when motivated (energized), is not the case of being simply motivated but it is motivated towards something. Its behaviour is therefore, likely to be directed towards such places where food had previously been found. Similarly, a student eager for knowledge is certain to go to the library and not to the house of a friend. Thus, the general principle is that in motivational state, we tend to make responses towards a goal which in the past has had the potentiality to reduce the motivationally aroused state. Hence, our past experiences or learnings establish a relationship between motivational state and goal object that has the potentiality to eliminate or reduce the strength of motive. Therefore, motives not only energize us to behave but also direct the behaviour towards the goal object.

14.14.3 The Emphasizing Role

When an organism is motivated, it gets activated, its activities are directed towards goal object (incentive) and finally the goal is achieved. Following the goal achievement, the preceding sequence is strengthened. This is called the **law of effect** (Thorndike). Thus, reduction or elimination of motivation through interaction with incentive (appropriate to the motivating condition) tends to strengthen or select the responses which brings about relief (satiates). In learning situation, such responses are **stamped in** and those which fail to satiate or provide relief are **stamped out**. In other words, such responses are rejected and, therefore, are not learnt. In fact, the emphasizing or selecting functions of motivation develop directive functions and by strengthening of responses, variability of aroused behaviour is controlled. This results in efficacy of behaviour. Furthermore, receipt of incentive affects the energy level of the organism (within certain limits). Thus, the three functions of motivation are closely interrelated.

In essence, motivation exerts its influence on behaviour in three important ways—by energizing the organism for activity, directing its activities towards the goal object and strengthening or emphasizing the sequence of responses preceding reward.

14.15 SOME BASIC APPROACHES OR THEORIES OF MOTIVATION

Motivation, being the central problem of psychology, has drawn the attention of many psychologists and extensive search in the area has been done. Owing to the keen interest of scientists, several approaches of viewing motivation have been proposed. To cover all these approaches would be beyond the scope of this book. Hence, the following five popular approaches are being described in this section.

14.15.1 Need Hierarchy Theory

The humanistic psychologist **Abraham Maslow** (1954) has proposed need hierarchy theory of motivation which is related to effectance motivation and intrinsic motivation. Need hierarchy theory includes both kinds of needs—the deficiency related as well as growth related needs. In the first, humans seek to restore the homeostatic state which is disturbed due to lack or deficiency of certain kinds of body needs essential for survival. The second motive is concerned with seeking to go beyond (grow more and more). The growth-oriented people welcome uncertainty, tension and pain and, therefore, such people are revolutionary.

He has arranged all human needs in **order of dominance** as represented in **Figure 14.4**. These needs are arranged in hierarchical order from primitive to higher order human needs. At the bottommost layer of the hierarchy are the primary physiological needs such as hunger, thirst, sex

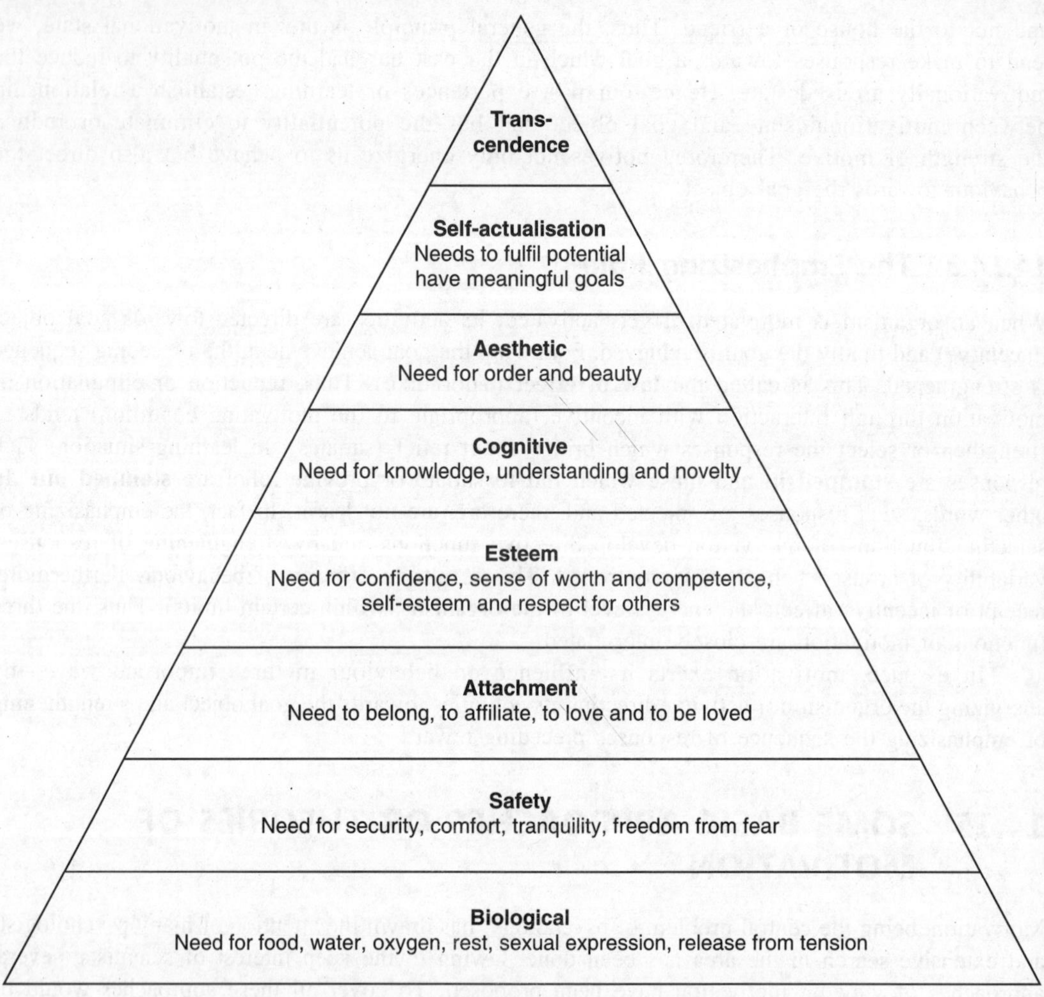

FIGURE 14.4 Maslow's hierarchy of needs.

etc. When these needs are satisfied, then the individuals move to the next ladder of hierarchy—the 'need for security'. This includes physiological as well as psychological—both kinds of security. Next is the social need of affiliation, *i.e.* 'need to love' and 'to be loved'. After meeting this need successfully, we move on to next higher order need—'self-esteem', *i.e.* to feel esteemed by ourselves and by others. Next in the hierarchy are the 'cognitive needs' which include the needs for knowledge, understanding and novelty. Then is the aesthetic need, *i.e.* desire for order and beauty. When all those needs are satisfied, people move on to 'self-actualization' need. This need drives the individual to fully utilize his potentials. Such persons are self-aware, socially responsive, spontaneous, creative, open to novelty and challenge. They have sense of humour and are capable of deep interpersonal relationship. Maslow's hierarchy goes further to include the 'need for transcendence'. This involves higher states of consciousness such as 'cosmic vision', experiencing oneself as the part of the 'universe'.

In the hierarchy of needs, the needs at the lower level dominate as long as they are not satisfied. For this reason, Maslow calls the needs as 'prepotent', i.e. every need is strong enough and unless one need is satisfied, another need is away from the focus. Thus, the individual moves on to next higher need only when the lower level needs are satisfied. For example, in a starving man, the physiological need—hunger is the most dominant need. He is preoccupied with obtaining food. Therefore, he does not aspire for social approval (belongingness and love needs). He may even not think of satisfying other day's meal (safety need), because for him only today's meal is important. But, once the most dominant need (for today's meal) is satisfied, he may begin to think for the future—whether his hunger need will always be met? Thus, he moves on to next in the hierarchy—the safety or security need appears and presses for satisfaction. Similarly, the other higher order of needs begin to appear when the lower order needs is satisfied.

The growth need in self-actualized people are expressed through **metaneeds**—'wholeness', 'perfection', 'completion', 'justice', 'richness', 'simplicity', 'aliveness', 'beauty', 'uniqueness', 'truth', 'meaningfulness', 'anatomy' etc. They are the persons who have the potentials of positive life enhancing forces for personal growth. It is important to note that such people are very few as most people remain overconcerned with lower level needs only. Self-actualization represents full development of personal potentials.

At the top of the hierarchy, lies the transcendence needs which represent spiritual needs. While the self-actualized people are rare, the transcendence need people are the rarest.

The various levels of needs are related to ecological conditions. Therefore, horizontal movement across different needs is also possible in place of vertical order of movement. For example, in Indian concept, human life has four goals—'Artha', 'Kama', 'Dharma', and 'Purushartha'. These goals are not vertically arranged, rather one has to pursue the desires and everyday concerns—Artha and Kama within the framework of 'Dharma'. These needs are not independent rather these operate in close relationship.

However, these hierarchies are not rigid. Individuals differ in strength of these complex motives. Some are found high in self-esteem (egoistic need) and low in need for belongingness and love need (social need) and vice versa. Thus, hierarchical order does not strictly apply to each person. But, it does represent the range of needs which have significance in many of our life situations. There are societies where people have to struggle for food, shelter and safety. As such, these societies are still poor in scientific and architectural endeavour.

14.15.2 Opponent–Process Theory

The opponent–process theory has been developed taking the 'hedonistic' view. This view states that we are motivated to seek goals which give positive emotional feelings and we tend to avoid those which results in displeasure. The opponent-process theory while taking hedonistic principle also goes to say what is pleasant and what is unpleasant (Solomon and Corbit, 1974). Since the theory states what is pleasant and unpleasant—the two opposing dimensions of emotional affects associated with motivated behaviour—the theory may also be classified as a theory of emotion. When the motivational state arouses us, it follows a general course of emotional states also. The peak point of this emotional-motivational state (we may call state A) occurs immediately after emotion provoking situation is encountered (note that this state A or peak of arousal state may be either pleasant or unpleasant). Next, when the emotion provoking stimulus is still present, the intensity of the emotional-motivational state adapts and a decline to a steady state may be noticed and when the emotion provoking situation terminates, an after reaction occurs which is opposite to state A, i.e. state B (an opponent state). In this stage the emotionally-motivationally aroused 'affects' gradually declines to normal state (base line). This decline (stage B) continues till the person reaches the base line (from where stage A began). Thus, the sequence of emotional-motivational changes take place in the following order:

Baseline → Peak of state A → Decline of state A to a steady state → State B → Decline of state B to baseline

To understand it let us take an example of an individual using heroin for the first time may have an initial feeling of rush of intense pleasure—peak of state A from baseline; it is followed by a less intense of good emotional feeling (decline of state A to a steady state) and then by a crave and displeasure before the emotional-provoking state returns to a normal—the baseline.

Now suppose, the same emotion provoking happens for many times repeatedly, i.e. the heroin user finds the rush pleasurable and get motivated (as it arouses an expectation of pleasure) to repeat the experience many times. With repeated usage the user develops drug tolerance. Hence, he will experience the pleasure lesser (less of state A) while the intensity of unpleasant after response (state B) increases. Initially, the heroin user was motivated by the expected pleasure of the rush, after having been become a habitual user of heroin, he is now motivated to use the drug to reduce the discomfort felt during the drug-free phase. In both the situations, the heroin user is hooked and is motivated to use heroin.

Thus, the theory provides us a way to think about the basis of some learned motives. For example, the heroin user in the above example is motivated to use the drug to avoid or prevent the discomfortable consequences of withdrawal, some people acquire the need to seek thrill to experience elation after danger is over.

Critical comments

Many critics hold that opponent process theory does not offer explanations of primary or biological needs.

Many psychologists also hold that all motivated behaviours do not involve necessarily the opponent process.

14.15.3 Optimal Level Theory

Like opponent process theory, optimal level theory is also based on hedonistic principles. This theory assumes that there is certain optimal (or best) level of arousal that is pleasurable (Friske and Maddi, 1961; Berlyne, 1971). This theory may also be called **just right theory**. The theory states that the individual is motivated to behave in such a way so that the optimal level of arousal is maintained. For example, if the arousal is too low, the person would seek a situation or stimulus that increases its level to the optimal and if it is too high, the behaviour will be directed towards lowering the level of arousal to the optimal level. To understand this, suppose, you on a particular day become busy enough and hence, highly aroused. To reduce the level of your arousal, you are likely to keep the telephone off so that you are not required to attend every call, or you may ask someone to ask the visitor if any, that you are not available. You take these steps with a view to reduce your over-arousal due to busy schedules. On the contrary, on some day you may find yourself quite in a state of inactivity—least arousal. To increase the level of your arousal, you make out a programme to go to movie or pay visits to some of your friends so that you may attain the optimal level of arousal. Thus, people seems to be motivated to maintain the optimal level of arousal and accordingly direct their behaviour in either ways—to reduce the arousal level or to increase the level of arousal.

The theory is supported by some experimental studies also *viz.* **Anderson Weiner** (1969) etc.

14.15.4 Valence–Vector Theory

'Valence–vector theory' is a dynamic concept of **Kurt Lewin** known as **valence psychology**. The concept valence is related to motivational aspects of human behaviour. This dynamic aspect of Lewin describes about 'how' an individual goes to behave in a situation. In this sense, valence-vector theory is different from topological or structural concepts.

Lewin's major dynamic concepts include energy, tension, need, valence and vector.

Lewin assumes a person as a complex energy system and the entire psychological systems are performed by psychic energy. When an individual experiences the state of disequilibrium, the psychic energy is initiated to restore the state of disequilibrium.

Tension, according to Lewin, is the outcome of the state of disequilibrium between inner personal regions or systems which he terms as the inter-force disturbance of the complex psychic systems which has two properties. The first property is that tension tends to be equalized. For example, suppose a psychic system has three components—x, y and z. Now suppose x component is highly tensed whereas the remaining y and z components are low tensed. In the situation, the high tension follows the y and z components till all the components become equally tensed. This equalization is achieved by several psychological processes such as thinking, remembering, perceptions etc.

Second property of tension is that it exerts pressure on the boundary system within which the different system components are found. If the boundary is weak, i.e. permeable, the tension will easily flow from one system to another. Such tension effects are observed in experimental studies on 'zigarnik effect' in which it is observed that memory for unfinished task is better than finished task. This evidences the fact that the need or motive produces tension in the psycho-logical system which persists so long the need is not satisfied. Fulfilment of need reduces tension.

Need refers to physiological or psychological condition that causes either decrease or increase in tension of a system. Lewin talks of two kinds of needs—current need and quasi need. Current need refers to deficit of any kind that is more important determinant of tension arousal. Quasi need refers to specific intentions which are shaped by social factors, viz. the need to take a particular kind of food only is a quasi need while need to take food to satisfy hunger need is current need.

Valence refers to positive or negative value or forces that a goal object contains. Accordingly, we either approach to the goal object or avoid it. It depends upon the positive or negative valence that the goal object contains for different energy systems of the psychological field within the individual. Thus approaching or repelling behaviours depend upon the attractiveness, i.e. valence of the goal object. Lewin has considered valence in quantitative terms and hence, it may be strong, moderate or weak.

Vector refers to those forces that influence an individual the extent to which he moves in a particular direction. Vector has three properties—direction, strength and a point of content.

Vector has a direction according to which it directs our behaviour either towards or away from the goal object.

Vector has also a strength because it is related to valence. When the valence is positive, we tend to approach (direction) and the extent or degree with which we approach the goal object depends upon the strength of attractiveness (positive valence). Similarly, our repelling behaviour also depends on the strength of negative valence of the goal object.

The vector has also a point of content, i.e. the point when the direction of behaviour terminates (i.e. the point at which the goal is achieved).

Valence-vector theory also assumes that when several vectors (both positive and negative) direct our behaviour simultaneously, the state of mental conflict is aroused. Lewin assumes human being's life space has several regions with several valences at the same time. Such situations are conflicting that may be of either approach–approach, approach–avoidant or avoidance–avoidance types, In this context, Lewin has also put forward a hypothesis—'With increasing distances between the individual and goal, the positive valence decreases'. **Fajans** (1933) in her experimental study confirmed this hypothesis.

Lewin also put forward another hypothesis—**The goal which is obstructed (person is not allowed to reach goal), results in increased (e.g. stronger) positive valence**. This hypothesis resembles with the popular saying—"Grass on the other side of the river looks greener". This hypothesis was also experimentally tested by 'Wright' (1943) and the findings lend support to the hypothesis.

Thus, Lewin in his theory has laid emphasis on several motivational concepts like energy, tension, need valence, and vector. All these concepts attempt to explain as to why does a person behave in a particular manner in a particular situation.

Critical comments

One of the major limitations of this theory is that Lewin has used several concepts such as energy, force, valence, vector etc. which have been taken from physics and mathematics that are not amenable to be objectively measured in psychological process and inferring the motivational states adequately. Hence, any generalized conclusion would not be dependable.

14.15.5 Psychoanalytic Approach

Psychoanalytic view of motivation has been proposed by **Sigmund Freud** who assumes that our actions or behaviours are determined by inner forces and impulses. These forces often operate beneath the conscious level of mind, i.e. in the unconscious. Thus, Freud talks of unconscious motives that play a most significant role not only in shaping and developing of personality, but also in motivating a person to choose a course of action in the direction of achieving a goal. Broad line of this theory is presented below:

Instinctual drives

Freud believes that human behaviour is instinctual. All our activities originate from two instinctual forces which are mutually antagonistic to each other. These two opposing forces are—**The life instinct (eros)** and **The death instinct (thantos)** which operate simultaneously and activate the individual. Life instinct produces constructive behaviours and therefore the initiated behaviour is integrated—logical and constructive in nature. It enhances the life and growth. Death instinct puses towards destruction. The energy of life instinct is 'libido' which involves several sex-related activities. Death instinct when directed inward, takes the form of suicide or destruction of the self. When directed outwardly, it takes the form of aggression toward others. Thus, for the psychoanalysts, the basic human motives are 'sex' and 'aggression'.

Freud also holds that these two basic motives are found early in child's life. Sex is expressed in the pleasure derived from stimulating erotic zones (sensitive zones) of the body. Aggression is expressed in biting or hitting. When prohibitions by parents are placed, the two motives are repressed and remain active as unconscious motives which are expressed in disguised form in dreams or mental ill health. The concept of unconscious is the corner stone of psycho-analytic theory.

14.16 CURRENT STATUS OF MOTIVATIONAL PSYCHOLOGY

Probably no other field of psychology has so extensively been studied as the field of motivation. The reason is obvious. Motivation is the key factor of 'why' of any behaviour event in all walks of life—home, school, industries, organizations or any aspect of human behaviour. Studies done so far in this area have shown that drive, reinforcement and incentives are of much use in determining our adaptive behaviours in different situations. In schools, industries, psychiatric clinics, social reform centres, business organizations, office, administration, governance management etc. different kinds of reinforcement programmes are planned and implemented with a view to motivate individuals towards determined goals. Some studies done during the recent past years also claim that social behaviour can be improved and even the economic development of the poor societies may be accelerated by enhancing the need for achievement (*n* Ach)- (McClelland, 1961).

Previous studies indicate that external reward like money, gifts etc. are positively and closely related to increased levels of motivation. But, the recent studies reveal that external rewards do not necessarily motivate every individual because some people are 'self-motivated'. For them, external reward does not count much. Therefore, in the present time, the idea of self-motivation is gaining ground. Realizing the significance of self-motivation, **Hertzberg** has developed a theory of **'work-motivation'**. This theory is known as **'two-factor theory'** of motivation (Hartzberg, 1966). He contends that in work situation, the events associated with high job attitudes are directly or indirectly related to the job activities. These are achievement, recognition, the work itself, responsibilities and advancement. These factors are job content factors as these are inherent in job itself. Job content factors are termed as **'motivators'**. Besides, there are events which are predominantly associated with low job attitudes. These are extrinsic to the work itself and are associated with job context rather than job activities. These are termed as hygienic factors. Hygienic factors merely prevent dissatisfaction. These are not satisfiers or motivators as these cannot contribute to positive satisfaction. Hertzberg asserts that in work situations, self-realization can be achieved only through the fulfilment of factors that are intrinsic to work itself, i.e. motivating factors.

In the field of organizations, quite a good number of research activities on motivational aspects are being done and broad-based theories of motivation are emerging. Two such theories—**'equity theory'** and **'attribution theory'**—have received greater attention.

Weight control and obesity are very common in the present time. This phenomenon is being globally experienced. Motivational studies concerning hunger, eating behaviour, sexual activities sleep etc. help us in understanding the problems of increasing weight and obesity. Attempts are afoot to provide solutions to these problems.

Studies on instinctive behaviours of animals such as, nest building, maternal care, mating etc. have demonstrated some interesting patterns. This has widened the scope of motivational research.

In the recent years, neuroscientists are also seen vigrously concerned with researching on the neurological bases of different motives and locating their seats in the brain.

Thus, we find that current emerging trends in the area of motivational research has not only furnished some new facts but have also widened the scope of study tremendously.

SUMMARY

- Motivation refers to internal driving or pushing states.
- Motivation effects to activate, direct and persist the individual to maintain its activity till goal is achieved.
- Motivation follows a cyclic order—initiation of the behaviour after being aroused by the driving force till the termination of the initiated behaviour after goal achievement that reduces the state of arousal.
- Motives are of several types. Some are physiological or biogenic—hunger, thirst, sex, maternal drive, sleep etc. while others are unlearned general motives such as activity, curiosity, exploration etc.
- There are also the acquired social needs such as *n* Ach., *n* Affil., *n* Pow., aggression and so on.
- Motives are difficult to measure. We can only draw inferences from observations.
- Usually, the physiological drives are measured by using Cage method, Obstruction method, Drive competition method etc. Through employing these methods on animals, inferences about humans are drawn.
- Psychologists use certain measures to study human motives. These include projective techniques, situational texts and inventories. These measures are useful for studying human motives of higher order such as *n* Ach., *n* Affil., *n* Pow. etc.
- Psychologists also use experimental studies in a variety of situations, more particularly, in the case of learning.
- Motives influence our behaviour at least in three ways—as energizing, directing and emphasizing functions.
- When an individual faces obstructions in achieving goals, motives are frustrated. The chief sources of frustrations are—environmental, subjective inhibitions and conflict of motives.
- Conflicts of motives take different forms, such as—approach–approach conflict, approach–avoidance conflict, avoidance–avoidance conflict and double or multiple approach–avoidance conflict.
- Different forms of conflicts require different modes of resolution. Those who fail to resolve their conflicts through desirable means are subjected to ill mental health and abnormal behaviours.
- There are different approaches to motivation. Some of the important approaches are need hierarchy, opponent–process theory, optimal level approach, valence vector approach and psychoanalytic views.
- Currently, the study of motivation occupies the central theme of scientific research and many new theories are emerging. These theories have more applied implications rather than simply describing the motivational aspects of behaviour. Hence, our knowledge about the motivational aspects in different areas of application is increasing day by day.

Part VIII

Affective Processes

CHAPTER 15

Emotion

15.1 INTRODUCTION

In the last chapter, man has been characterized as 'doer'. Though man is a rational being and as such, while doing or displaying the behaviour, he makes use of his rational thoughts, reasons and applies logic in doing for whatever he is motivated to do. But at the same time, man is also an emotional being. As an emotional being he often becomes angry and sometimes feel afraid of something. These are the emotions of anger and fear. Similarily, at times a man bursts into laughter or/gets involved in love. The fact is that in most situations of our live's affairs, we find ourselves tinged with feelings and emotions of joy and sorrow, excitement and disappointment, love, fear, hope and despair. These emotions and feelings have additive value to living. These add colour and spice to living. Emotions are like spice without which life would be dull. But, often these feelings and emotions become sour, because these put the man in trouble. For example, when a man is in intense emotion, his judgements are disturbed, friends become enemies and life turns miserable. Hence, emotions are both energising as well as enervating. To quote **Hebb Do**—'Emotion is both organizing (making behaviour more effective) and disorganizing. It is both energizing and debilitating.*

Thus, so far study of adjustive behaviour is concerned, the study of emotional aspect of behaviour is in no way less important to motivation or to any other aspect of behaviour. Hence, the present chapter is devoted to this important aspect of adjustive behaviour.

15.2 NATURE, MEANING AND DEFINITION

To give a precised definition of emotion is an arduous task. Like motivation, the affective states—emotions and associated feelings, cannot be observed directly. However, inferences by observing the overt behaviours accompanied by reflections on face, voice, gestures etc. can be drawn. But,

* Quoted in Morgan and King's, *Introduction to Psychology*, Tata McGraw-Hill, New Delhi, 1975.

since man is a dynamic person, such inferences sometimes go wrong. Despite these difficulties, the studies done so far indicate that emotions is **conscious experience** of joy, sorrow, hope, love, excitement, anger, hate and many other feelings.

The difficulties in defining emotions are four-fold. These are as follows:

(a) Emotional and non-emotional behaviours are not easily distinguishable.
(b) Human emotions mix up with one another like colours of the spectrum. Hence, different emotions are difficult to be differentiated.
(c) Some of the basic emotions such as gloom, delight, love, fear, anger etc. often combine together in varying degrees and produce complex emotional patterns. We observe such patterns in romantic love, religious ecstasy (enthusiasm), patriotism, zeal, shock, hatred, contempt etc. For example, a young man has got a very lucrative job in a foreign country and has achieved excellence in performance. But, he may be found torn between pride and success on the one hand and regret for being away from his parents and friends on the other.
(d) Emotional reactions are generalized in nature and involve the entire systems of the organism—physiologically as well as psychologically. It is at least difficult if not impossible to measure and observe all physiological and psychological changes in a particular emotional state.

The term emotion is often considered synonymous with the term 'feeling' and 'mood'. **Feeling** denotes the pleasure and pain dimensions of emotion which usually involve bodily functions. **Mood** is an affective state of long duration but relatively of lesser intensity than emotion. Both of these concepts (feeling and mood) are narrower than the concept of emotion. Emotions are a complex pattern of arousal, subjective feeling and cognitive interpretation. Emotions, as we experience, move us internally and this process involves physiological and psychological reactions.

Emotion is a subjective feeling which varies from individual to individual. When an emotion is produced, the stimulus situation is perceived and evaluated as significant. This obviously means that the present emotion arousing situation is related to past experience and is also seen as having implication for the future. For example, presence of a dangerous situation arouses fear or horror in us because, we perceive the situation as dangerous on the basis of past experience. Similarly, our emotions of anger is aroused because we perceive the situation as dangerous or insulting—threats of being attacked. The emotion of love is aroused because we perceive the love object as positively affectionate. Hence, it is clear that the arousal of emotion depends upon subjective perception of (experience) the stimulus situation as **emotion provoking** based on sensing and evaluation, the situation as emotional.

Emotions usually occur with great suddenness. We suddenly and almost automatically feel pride at the success of son, anger at the sight of fast approaching enemies, disgust at the sight of careless table manners, love at the sight of beloved etc. Such sudden reactions do not depend much upon the events themselves, but the way in which events are evaluated or judged. Thus, **emotion is a sudden reaction to stimuli perceived and evaluated as emotional**.

Emotions vary in their intensity (high, moderate or low) and quality (happiness, sadness, jealous, fear etc.). Subjective factors and situational contexts influence the experience of emotions. These factors are gender, personality, and psychopathological states of certain kinds. Evidences indicate that women generally experience all the emotions except anger more intensely than men. Men are prone to high intensity and frequency of anger. This gender difference is attributed to the social roles attached to men (competitiveness) and women (affiliation and caring).

15.3 DIFFERENCE BETWEEN EMOTION AND FEELING

In general, emotion and feeling are not differentiated because both of these are connected with the affective states of a person and the two processes are so intermixed that their separate entity is difficult to identify. However, there exists some subtle difference between them which are as follows:

(i) Feeling is a simple and primary affective process while emotion is a complex affective process.
(ii) Feeling precedes emotional experience and every emotional experience is accompanied by feeling. For example, the feeling of pleasure and pain are connected with emotional experiences of joy and sorrow. Thus, two affects (emotion and feeling) are closely and intimately interrelated to each other. What we mean to say is that emotional experiences are necessarily accompanied by feelings whereas in feeling, emotional experience is not necessary. Feeling of pleasure and displeasure may occur without any emotional experience. However, when feeling is expressed either in explicit or implicit behavioural form, it takes turn into emotion. Therefore, it can be said that feeling is relatively less active process of affect while emotion is an active affective process.
(iii) Feeling is always subjective or personal while emotion may be both subjective as well as objective. For example, it is not possible to observe feelings of pleasure and displeasure while emotions are objectively observable phenomenon as these are explicitly expressive.
(iv) Feelings are classified only as pleasure and pain while emotions are of several kinds—anger, fear, joy, love, jealousy, excitement etc.
(v) In feelings, usually no marked physiological changes are noticed while emotions have physiological bases of arousal and hence, physiological changes occur.
(vi) As compared to feeling, in emotional states persons are stirred up as a whole because emotions arouse the individual as a whole.

Thus, it is apparent that though feeling and emotion both are affective processes, the two processes differ from each other very finely.

15.4 MOTIVES AND EMOTIONS

There are some similarities between motive and emotion. Most often the two are described as two faces of the same coin. To an extent, it is true also. Motivation and emotion, both move the individual towards certain kinds of behaviour. It is generally said that **life without emotion would be life without motion**. This implies that emotions produce motions.

Motive and emotion, both of these terms derive their origin from Latin. Motive derives from the word 'movere' while emotion derives from the word 'emovere'. The former refers to a state that implies one to act while the latter refers to the state of **stirred-up** state, a condition in which an individual becomes 'stirred up' as a whole and get excited. In other words, this state may be called as behavioural arousal which varies from deep sleep to intense activity. This state of arousal is psychologically originated and depends upon experience of the emotion provoking situation. Such an arousal state of the organism (or person) brings disturbance in the entire physiological mechanism and is reflected in external and internal body changes.

Further, like motive, emotion is also a force which determines what we strive and what we try to avoid or evade.

Despite the above similarities, motives and emotions differ from each other in at least two ways:

(a) First, emotion is a cognitive reaction to external stimulus while motive is an internal pattern of stimulation which is associated with some kind of 'need'—biological or psychological.

(b) Second, emotions especially the negative ones arise in emergency situations where habitual or organized responses are not readily available. On the other hand, the arousal and satisfaction of motives, particularly the physiological drives follow automatic sequence.

In order to make these differences more clear, let us take an example. In thirst, one feels thirsty when water supply to body tissues are relatively low. This state can be easily alleviated by drinking water. Here, the behavioural sequence is habitual and automatic. But suppose, someone wakes up in the night and finds that a part of his house is in flames. Here, the situation is experienced as emergent. He has no habitual and automatic sequence of behaviour. He suddenly gets excited and moves on to devise an appropriate response hurriedly.

From the above description of emotion, we can precisely define it in the following terms:

"Emotion is a state of being moved, stirred up or behaviourally aroused on experiencing an emotional situation and which involves external and internal physiological changes as a whole".

Since, emotion has been defined as a reaction to some kind of external stimuli which are perceived and experienced as emotion provoking situations, it is obvious that emotion is a **subjective feeling** of excitement. Psychologists therefore use the term 'affect'* which is contrasted with **cognition or action.** Therefore, **emotion refers to affective state of the individual**.

15.5 SOME BASIC EMOTIONS

Emotions are of different kinds. Psychologists have attempted to identify basic emotions. It has been noted that at least six emotions are globally experienced and recognized. These are anger, disgust, fear, happiness, sadness and surprise. **Izard** has proposed a set of 10 basic emotions, i.e. joy, surprise, anger, disgust, contempt, fear, shame, guilt, interest and excitement with combinations of them resulting in other emotional blends. According to **Plutchik** there are 8 basic or primary emotions. All other emotions result from various mixtures of these basic emotions. He has arranged these basic emotions in four pairs of opposites, i.e. **joy-sadness, acceptance-disgust, fear-anger** and **surprise-anticipation**.

In the present section, some of the basic emotions are being described in some greater detail. These are 'anger', 'fear' and 'love'.

---

* Psychology is the only area in which 'affect' is used as noun, otherwise this word is used as verb which means to have influence on or to change.

15.5.1 Anger

Emotion of anger is the most noted anger. Studies done on this affective state show that any kind of interference in the goal directed activity makes one red with anger. Such situations are equally potential in provoking anger in children as well as in adults. When any want or any ongoing activity is thwarted, obstacles stand on the way or one is restrained from doing what he wants to do, are some of the situations which produce anger. For example, a bone is snatched away from the mouth of a hungry dog, it suddenly attacks or pounces upon. Similarly, when a person wants to do something and some obstacle or somebody stands in his way, he becomes angry.

Though, frustrations of motives can arouse anger in a person of any age, it undergoes considerable changes with age. This change is due to the fact that what frustrates a child may not necessarily frustrate an adult. That is, the kind of things people do and does not want to do, varies with age and therefore, frustration also varies. During infancy, simple restraints frustrate activity and exploratory motive. Such restraints are most common causes of anger among the infants. In children, imposed disciplines, restraints to certain activities, interference in autonomy frequently produce anger. For example, when a child is imposed for toilet-training, washing of faces, not allowed to go out, he becomes angry.

Among older children and adolescents, cause of anger again shifts. This shift is from physical restraints to frustration of social and personal motives. For example, an adolescent expresses his anger when need for achievement, recognition, ambitions etc. are frustrated. Adolescents also become angry when they are abused by others, social approval is thwarted or feel left alone.

Social frustrations are common for anger in adults also with a difference. Most adults through experience and learning become able to control outburst of their anger. They become intellectually and emotionally matured. As such, they are able to understand realities of life and take a balanced view of life. In other words, adults learn to control their anger and display only a milder feeling of anger. Such milder feelings of anger are known as **'annoyance'**.

Thus, it is obvious that the main source of anger is **frustration**. However, it much depends on how a person perceives frustrations. The experience varies from person to person. For example, a marketing executive with high *n* Ach. may perceive the arrival of another marketing executive in the company as a source of frustration because the new executive is perceived as an obstacle standing in his way of target achievement. Such perceptions may lead to **acts of war**—an anger compound. On the other hand, another executive with high *n* Affil. or sociability may perceive the new executive in positive direction and therefore, there would be no trace of any anger.

As a general rule, frustrations lead to anger and then to aggression. But, it is not always so. One researcher **David Funkenstein** (1955) in a study on students working on frustrating work found that these students were reacting in three different ways. Some were angry at the experimenter, some were angry at themselves and the third group was fearful. **Frankenstein** reported that different hormones were active in different groups. Those who were afraid and also those who were angry themselves had higher amount of **epinephrine** hormones. Those who were angry at the experimenter, secreted **norepinephrine** hormones. Both of these hormones tend to increase heart rate and blood pressure.

Anger does not always lead to direct attack or hitting the source of anger. It depends upon cognitive understanding of the situation. For example, a wife when becomes angry with her husband who is too strong for her, she ventilates her anger on her child. Similarly, a subordinate when abused or reproved by his boss in the office, may experience anger but he expresses his anger on returning home to his family. Such expression of anger are called **'displaced anger'**, i.e. expression of anger is on a substitute who is weak and not supposed to cause harm to the angry man.

Besides, there are some situations when we learn to contain anger. So, anger does not necessarily lead to aggression. For example, a boy when becomes angry with his sister may hesitate to hit her, because he knows through conditioning that he may be punished by his parents.

Expression of anger

As has been described above, anger leads to aggression which is expressed in various forms. The form varies from person to person and also from situation to situation. Expression of anger also varies with age. Preschool children usually express their anger in the form of 'temper tantrum', surliness, bad tempered, bullying and fighting. These are direct forms of expression which are directed towards the anger provoking objects and situations. Adolescents generally express their anger through 'sarcasm', 'abuses', 'scolds', verbal threats', 'gossiping' and even 'plotting'. Adults, however, seldom express their anger in these ways. By adulthood super-ego becomes strengthened which exert heavy social pressure. Owing to this, adults display their emotional maturity more than expressing their anger. However, milder forms of anger are expressed in some verbal remarks and intelligent ways of avoiding the work which he does not want to do.

15.5.2 Fear

Just as anger, fear arousing situations also change with age. During infancy and early childhood, fear is usually caused by sudden and/or unexpected strange situations. For example, sudden loud noise of some unusual nature may cause fear. Similarly, scary animals, masked faces and similar other strange objects when appear unexpectedly, produce fear. Thus, during very young age, stimulus for fear is usually a strange situation which one encounters suddenly or unexpectedly.

When the child grows older, the fear arousing stimulus shift. They fear of imaginary creatures, loneliness, darkness, and all those objects which can cause body harm. In later stage of childhood, social humiliations, ridicule, social threats etc. produce fear. Thus, during this phase of growth and development of an individual, we learn to be afraid of something and hence, fear is a learned emotion.

As we reach adulthood through adolescence, many social situations take an increase as a source of fear (Wake, 1950). During early adolescence phase, unlearned fears though continue to some lesser degree, such fears are never prominent. Rather, social fears become more prominent. Such fears include being left alone (out of group), of being ridiculed, criticism etc. These situations haunt the adolescents very much and thus, develop fear.

To the adults, such things which pose a threat of failure loss of money or property, status, feelings of insecurity, separation from dear ones or family, bad health etc. are the fear arousing situations.

Some fears are unlearned (innate), viz. fear of loud noise, sudden loss of support, pain etc. Such fears are prominent among infants. Other fears are learned mostly through classical conditioning. Scores of experimental studies have shown that fears can be developed through conditioning procedures. One such experiment on an infant named Albert is very famous. This experiment was done by **Watson** and **Raynor (1920)**. They picked up a boy of 11 months old whose name was Albert. In the beginning, the boy did not show any sign of fear of animals. He was shown a rabbit. The boy was delighted and made attempts to be close to the animal instead of getting away. Subsequently, a white furry rat was shown to him and almost simultaneously followed a sudden loud burst of sound. The boy shrunked back to get away from it. It was a natural response to a natural stimulus unconditioned response (UCR). The procedure was repeated several times continuously for several days. The repeated procedure developed fear of white furry rat in the child. This could be demonstrated when he was shown a white rabbit which formerly did not cause fear. Now, however, he has been afraid of not only at the sight of rabbit but also to any white furry object.

Another factor in learning to fear is discrimination learning. As we grow old, we begin to discriminate a wide varieties of objects, each giving a distinct perception. We learn to discriminate between usual and unusual, normal and strange. Such discrimination provides a prism of perceptual spectrum and when a situation is such that does not fit well in the spectrum, we become afraid of that situation or object. Discrimination learning also provides us with information as to what object is dangerous and what is delightful. As we see in the fear of snakes, children of less than 2 years old usually show no sign of fear while the older children behave as if they are afraid (James and James, 1928).

Besides, socialization, cultural values, social norms, etc. also greatly contribute towards learning to fear something.

15.5.3 Love and Affection

Love and affection are also very common emotions found in all species in different forms. Since, love and affection are so tied together that they can scarcely be separated from each other. In fact, the two terms are used interchangeably to cover entire empathetic aspects of affective feelings associated with pleasure.

Emotion of love and affection are most important in man's life. It is usually said 'Love is life' and vice versa.

Freud, the pioneer of psychoanalysis has used the term in a very wider perspective. He defines it as a **reciprocal state of attraction** so that when someone loves, there must be someone to receive love. Hence, it is a two-way affair.

Freud's concept of love is different from **passion** or **infatuation**. **Passion** is an emotional state so strong as to overrule good judgement while, **infatuation** is **erotic attraction** without reciprocity.

Love is akin to Greek word 'agape' which means that love goes between people. Love is never an one way affair, rather always a two-way affair. Therefore, one who loves somebody must also be loved in return.

Like anger and fear, love also undergoes change with age. The most primitive basis of love and affection is pleasure associated with stimulation of erotic zones—warmth of the mother's body and sucking at the breast. Infants need to be cuddled, fondled and petted. Failure to satisfy these needs leads to dire consequences both, physical and psychological.

Stimuli for love and affection in older children are too many. Someone may love a toy, a pet, a novel etc. Norman, L. Munn cites an example of his own son who had a toy rabbit which was soft and woolly. The boy took the toy to the bed with him for many years, used to hug and kiss like a person even when he grew old enough and became decrepit. This sort of things happen in almost every family. The basis of such love and affection for objects and persons is not very clear. However, it seems logical to assume that objects and persons become substitute for the original stimulus—mother whose warmth is a dominant need.

As a child grows and enters into adulthood through adolescence, stimuli to arouse affection is limited by cultural influences. Sexual attraction becomes a potent factor. However, in maternal and paternal affections, sex plays a minor role. Human love, in addition to sex, satisfies several motives in different individuals. For example, someone may want to be mothered by wife, a woman may want from her husband to take a parental attitude. These motives are satisfied by love and affection in which sex is secondary.

15.6 PHYSIOLOGICAL CORRELATES OF EMOTION

Mr. X is desperate to get a job. He has prepared well for the interview and feels confident. As he enters the room and interview begins he becomes extremely tense. His feet become cold, his heart starts pounding and he is unable to answer appropriately.

In the above example, why did this happen? Try to think about similar situation that most of us often face in our life. This happens because Mr. X is in a state of emotional stress that causes a number of physiological changes. While describing the nature of emotion, it has been stated that emotion is stirred-up state in which the individual is aroused as a whole. This obviously means that some changes in whole body mechanisms occur that distinguish emotional state from non-emotional state. Prominent among such changes are: (i) The changes in external body parts—facial, vocal, postural etc. and (ii) the changes in the internal automatic functions of the body (visceral changes). The external changes are, however, likely to be voluntarily inhibited by suppressing the awareness of the emotion in the conscious mind. The visceral changes on the other hand are not usually subjected to voluntary control. Therefore, measurement of physiological changes is considered most sensitive and objective indicators of emotion.

15.6.1 Internal Changes in Emotion

Some of the internal changes are being described below:

Heart rate and blood pressure: When we experience intense emotion such as anger or fear, we become aware of changes in the rate of heart beat. Heart rate usually goes up (increased). This increase is accompanied by more vigorous contraction of the body. This is caused by hyper functioning of the sympathetic nervous system. Consequently, the amount of blood pumped by the heart increases which is indicated in the increase of heart rate.

Hyper functioning of sympathetic nervous system also brings changes is blood pressure. However, the direction of change in blood pressure is not clearly predictable even in the same state of emotion. The change may be either 'hyper' or 'hypo', i.e. high or low. But, usually rise in BP is more frequent.

Changes in breathing: In a state of emotion, changes in breathing (respiration) also take place. Respiratory changes may take a variety of changes, such as rate of breathing may either speed up or slow down, breathing may be either deeper or shallow, dramatic changes in respiration (expiration ratio 1/E ratio) etc. For instance, in a state of fear one may inhale slowly, hold and then exhale rapidly.

Various respiratory changes during emotion is often interrupted by sneezing, yawning, coughing and sighing. Though, breathing phenomenon in emotion is very complex, yet, it does serve as a sensitive signal of even subtle emotion.

Changes in skin temperature: Occasional rise or drop in skin temperature during emotion has been reported. It is assumed that experience of emotional security results in the rise of skin temperature while emotional stress results in drop of the same. Unfortunately, since it is difficult to measure changes in skin temperature, it is not so much used as indicator of emotion as other changes.

Some other changes: Quite a large number of other bodily changes with some regularity occur in emotions. For example, changes occurring in secretary functions of the salivary glands are observed in the state of fear in the form of dryness of mouth, disruption in digestive functions, sweating or dryness of skin, hyper-excretion, tension of skeletal muscles resulting in tremor etc.

Changes in glandular responses: In the state of strong emotion (e.g. anger), adrenal gland gets excited and pours excessive amount of **adrenalin** as well as **noradrenalin** hormones into the blood. Under the influence of 'adrenalin' the liver releases stored sugar into the blood. This causes chemical changes in blood resulting in quick clotting of blood, rise in blood pressure, rapidity of pulse rate, enlarging of air passage into lungs to admit more air, enlargement of eyes' pupil to admit more light, rise in skin temperature and excessive sweating, particularly on the palms and hands.

Noradrenalin hormones bring about constriction of blood vesicles at the body surface. Besides thyroid and pituitary glands also have been found to be involved in emotional response.

Glandular responses help in emotionally charged individuals to cope physically with the emergency situation during emotion. However, if the emotion provoking situation is not met by direct action, the hyperglandular functioning has been found harmful to the individual.

The galvanic skin response (GSR): In a state of emotion, certain changes in the electrical properties of the skin take place. When a person perspires heavily, two important changes in electrical property of skin take place: (i) the tissues generate electromotive force (voltage) and (ii) the electrical resistance of the skin is changed. These changes are measured by a very sensitive electrical apparatus called galvanic skin response (GSR). In older texts, this response is named psychogalvanic response (PGR).

Sweat glands in fact, respond to a part of the nervous system which is not under conscious control of the organism. Therefore, GSR in combination with blood pressure and respiration is highly sensitive indicator of emotion. In lie detection, this is mostly used. Consciousness of guilt brings about a fear response. Therefore, a guilty individual responds emotionally to questions related to his crime. In lie detection, both critical and neutral questions are put and a comparison of degree of emotion to different questions is made by measuring the rate of respiration, blood pressure and GSR. A skilled lie detector can then determine with a fair certainty whether or not the individual is telling a lie.

In some studies, it has been found that a lie detector can detect guilty even when no lies are told and subject deliberately tries to **defeat the test** (Lykken, 1960). Therefore, lie detection sometimes proves erroneous.

Further, it has also been found that often it becomes difficult for the law enforcement officer to determine whether the suspect is telling lie about everything or is not telling lie at all

(Ellson, Davis, Saltzman and Burke, 1952). In addition, some persons are not well suited to testing. These include very intelligent persons,* mentally retarded, highly nervous individuals, psychopathic personalities and false confessors.

Despite these limitations, lie detector is an useful aid for crime investigating agencies. GSR has also been used in measuring the strength of emotion in social context (Cooper, 1959).

Pupliometrics: It has earlier been stated that during emotion, certain changes in pupils of the eyes take place. Generally, when there is favourable reaction towards the emotional situation, pupil of the eye dilates in response to that and contracts to distasteful stimuli. To measure such changes in the eyes, **Eckhard Hess** discovered a new device in the year 1960 which is known as **pupliometrics**.

The discoverer of this apparatus was one day just looking at some photographs of animals while relaxing to bed. As he came to a particular beautiful photograph, his pupils dilated. His wife noticed it and suggested that he must be using poor light. But Hess assured that he was not. He was immediately reminded of Charles Darwin who first spoke about widening and narrowing of eyes during emotion. This prompted him to conduct an off-hand experiment (without any pre-determined plan). He showed his male assistant a number of photographs including a magazine photo of nude-pin-up girl. Photographs were thoroughly shuffled in such a way that even Hess could not see which one he was showing. As the 7th picture was shown, assistant's pupil suddenly widened enough about three times more than the normal size. This seventh picture was of the nude-pin-up girl. Then he began systematic work and devised the apparatus to measure pupil reaction.

In **Figure 15.1**, Hess is shown demonstrating his device for measuring the change of pupil size. The image of the eye, greatly magnified, is shown on the television monitor. This apparatus is used in a variety of tests. This apparatus is also expected to be of great use in lie detection and psychotherapy.

FIGURE 15.1 Photo of pupilometric.

* Highly intelligent persons usually gain valuntary control over their visceral responses.

15.6.2 Overt Expression or External Changes in Emotion

Overt-responses of the body parts—face, vocal mechanisms, body postures and gestures (non-verbal responses or body language) are directly involved in manipulating the environment. So, while one is in a state of emotion, significant changes in overt body parts take place. Observing such external physical expressions serve as important indicators of emotional experiences. Some of these external signs are described below:

Facial expression

Face, in fact, is a barometer of emotion. Though to an extent, our hand and body movements also give significant clues of a particular emotion, yet most people pay more attention on face rather than body postures. Language of face is perhaps stronger communication than verbal words. Psychologists have extensively studied facial changes in various emotional states such as anger, fear, happiness, surprise etc. Thompson (1941) studied blind children and found that on the basis of facial expression in them, different emotions could be differentiated. Such children have no experience of seeing the patterns of changes in others even then different marks of different emotions could be found on their faces.

Undoubtedly, face is a barometer of communicating one's feelings and emotions, but the pattern of expressions differs from person to person and culture to culture. Each individual develops his unique ways of expressing emotions. Hence, it does not provide a reliable clue for judgement.

However, emotions are classified in dimensions of pleasantness and unpleasantness, some reliable differences in the pattern of facial expression can be observed. For example, usually it is observed that face rises up when the emotional experience is pleasant and turns down when there is unpleasant emotion.

Facial patterns are usually studied by using photographs of faces representing different emotions and subjects are asked to judge the kind of emotions that different photos indicate.

Engen et al. (1957, 1958) have shown that three dimensions of emotional expressions through facial patterns can be judged with reasonably fair reliability. These dimensions are as follows:

(a) **Pleasantness–unpleasantness:** In this dimension, the faces are judged in the degree to which the expressions represent feelings of pleasantness or unpleasantness. Different judges show fairly close agreement on this dimension.

(b) **Attention–rejection:** Wide open eyes, flared nostrils, openness of mouth etc. are some of the characteristic patterns of attention dimension. These seem as if to bring the sense organs close to the object. In rejection, the patterns are just the reverse. The eyes, nostrils, lips are highly shut as if keeping the object out of stimulation.

(c) **Sleep–tension:** It refers to the level of excitement or arousal as portrayed. It is the central dimension of emotion. At one extreme is the state of relaxation (sleep), *i.e.* emotions are at the lowest. At another extreme is the expression of extreme emotional arousal. In between, are the varying degrees of levels of emotional arousal.

Vocal expression

Most often, we judge emotions by listening to the sound of a person's voice. For example, usually laughing sound is associated with the emotion of happiness. Crying is supposed to be indicative of fear, sorrow, anger or a number of other emotions.

Bursting loudness indicates emergency state of emotional experience. Similar many more cues indicate different emotions. Such cues include loudness, pitch, tremor or break in voice, screaming sounds etc. All such changes may be a cue to an emotion, such as anger, fear, enjoyment, sorrow etc.

Like facial expression, vocal expression is also an important indicator of emotional experience. However, this expression also sometimes proves poor in the reliability of judgement about emotions. Therefore, while evaluating vocal expressions, one should be very cautious in eliminating the possibilities of misjudgement.

Postural changes or body gestures

Body postures and gestures are also important indicators of emotions. While one is in fear, he shows anger and makes aggressive gestures (clinches his fists and moves to attack). In sorrow, he turns his head downward and while in joy, holds the head high and chest out. Postural clues are usually the universal clues for identifying associated emotions. It is so because, in almost every culture, postural gestures are taken as non-verbal body language that indicates some kinds of associated emotions. However, like facial and vocal expressions, postural clues also often fail to maintain consistency in indicating emotions.

15.7 JUDGING A SITUATION

In view of the inconsistency in interpreting emotions on the basis of either facial or vocal or postural expressions, many researchers are of the opinion that emotions can be best judged by viewing the situation in totality. The whole situation adds many cues than what can be obtained by either of three expressions—facial, vocal or postural. These expressions lack uniformity and therefore, any one expression cannot reliably indicate the involved emotions accurately. All these expressions together provide relatively more accurate signals to judge the involved emotions.

To be more accurate, psychologists also give emphasis on taking stock of the situation along with the patterns of different expressions—facial, vocal and postural. To illustrate, suppose a person's facial expression seems to indicate frightened state (facial expression), he is crying for help (vocal expression) and he is found fleeing (postural expression). At the same time, it is also observed that somebody with weapons in his hand is speedily following the fleeing man (situation) on the basis of all these, one can reliably conclude that the fleeing man is having the emotion of fear as his life is in danger while the speedily following man with weapons in hands is in aggression. Thus, it is obvious that accurate judgement of emotion involves not only the patterns of expressions but also the situation of the environment in which particular patterns develop.

In essence, accuracy of judgement about emotion is dependent upon totality rather than patterns of expressions alone.

15.8 THEORIES OF EMOTION

One of the puzzling questions about emotion is that what and how physiological responses play a role in our conscious experience of emotions such as the feelings of pleasure, displeasure or elation etc.? Some view that bodily changes directly follow the perception of emotion arousing situation and our awareness of these changes is 'emotion'. Others view that both—the emotional experience and bodily changes are set off simultaneously by a lower brain mechanism known as hypothalamus. Still others view the level of arousal or activation plays important roles. Though, the controversy regarding whether the emotional experiences follow the bodily changes or the two occur simultaneously is still an unresolved issue, however, these divergent views have greatly extended our knowledge. Some of these views are discussed hereinbelow:

15.8.1 The Common Sense View

The common sense view holds that the sequence of process in emotion of an average person follows different steps. First, we perceive an emotion producing situation. Second, we become aware and feel emotions. Third, the emotional reactions are initiated. Thus, the sequence is:

Sensing (perceiving) of emotional situation → Awareness and feeling of emotion, i.e. conscious experience → Initiation of emotional activity (response)

This sequence may be explained with the help of an example. If we ask a person to describe what goes on when fire breaks out in a house of his next door neighbour. He would describe the following sequence—the sight of the fire is perceived as fearsome, immediately he knows and feels afraid because he perceives the situation as dangerous. Finally, he makes a response-accelerated heart beat. This is the common sense view of emotion.

In essence, the common sense view of emotion states—'we lose our future, are sorry and weeping, we meet a bear, are frightened and run, we are insulted by a rival, are angry and strike.*

But, James does not consider this simple sequence correct and therefore proposed a different view.

15.8.2 James–Lange Theory

William James and **Karl Lange** together share common view of emotion and therefore, it is known as **James-Lange** theory. These two physiologists are of the view that bodily changes directly follow the perception of an emotional situation and our awareness of the bodily changes give the experience of emotion. Therefore, the common sense view can be more rationally put as—**'we feel sorry because we cry, angry because we strike, afraid because we tremble...'** (James 1890, p. 448). James further elaborates that **'it is not the case that we cry, strike and tremble because we feel sorry, angry and fearful'**.†

In support of this view, the theorists cite the introspection reports that while doing an emotional role, the actors experience associated emotions. For example, when they display anger, bring about some behavioural expressions of anger and consequently, the experience of anger is aroused.

Lange holds the view similar to James with the difference that James assumes visceral organs and glands as the venue of emotional disturbance while **Lange** considers vaso-motor mechanisms as significant.

---

* Ruch, L. *Psychology and Life*, Scott. Foreman and Company, 1970, p. 426.

† James, W., *The Principles of Psychology*, Vol. II, New York, Holt, 1890, p. 448.

Physiological bases of James–Lange view

The entire sequence of emotional experience and behaviour according to James and Lange follow the physiological sequences as shown in **Figure 15.2**.

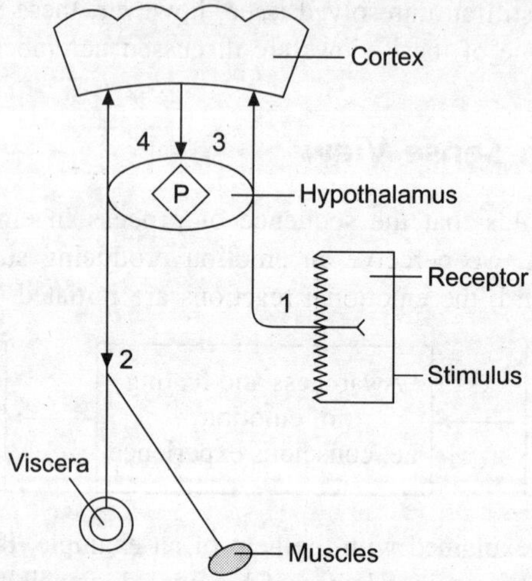

FIGURE 15.2 Physiological bases of James-Lange Theory.

Receptors get activated to the emotion provoking stimuli and an afferent nerve impulse is generated which is conveyed to the cerebral cortex through afferent fibres. This produces perceptual experience of the situation and efferent impulse is generated which is conveyed to the visceral organs and the vaso-motor organs (muscles and glands) resulting in activation of these organs causing emotional behaviour. Again afferent impulse about activation of responding organs is conveyed to the cerebral cortex and thus, the individual has the experience of the relevant emotion that correspond to the emotional behaviour. The entire sequence has been shown in Figure 15.2.

From Figure 15.2 it is evident that the conscious experience of emotion follows the sequences as follows:

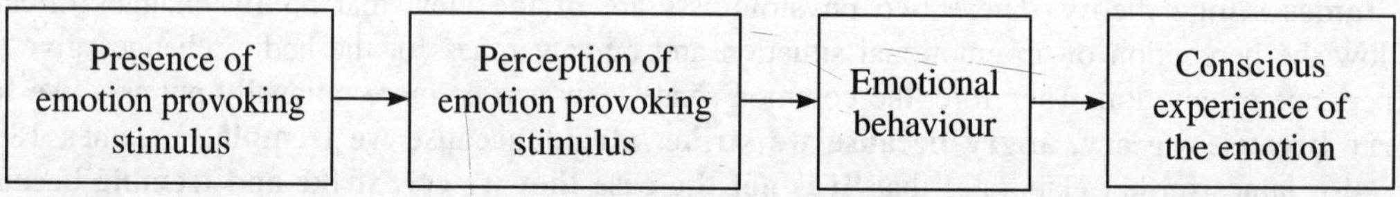

Thus, the theory assumes that the **conscious experience** of emotion is preceded by **emotional behaviour**. To quote James—**my theory is that bodily changes follow directly the perception of an exciting fact and that the feeling of the same changes as they occur is the emotion'** (James, 1890). This means to say that the **felt emotion is nothing but perception of bodily changes.**

Critical comments

James–Lange theory is significant in the sense that it lays emphasis on bodily changes as the antecedent factor of emotional experience. Prior to these, bodily changes were considered as the consequence or outcome of emotion. However, the theory suffers from certain serious pitfalls which are as follows:

(i) Wundt on the basis of his studies on conscious experience refutes the contention of James and Lange. Wundt cites certain instances in which he found that in experimental situations, if the experience of emotion is withhold temporarily, emotional behaviour too ceases. Thus, awareness of emotional behaviour cannot be assumed to be the basis for emotional experience.

(ii) Most often, we report the experience of an emotion even without displaying emotional behaviour, viz. when an officer rebukes his subordinate he experiences the emotion of anger even then he remains calm, i.e. does not display emotional behaviour, but experiences the emotion.

(iii) Major objections to the theory come from **Cannon**. He pointed out that:

   (a) Bodily changes of one emotional state do not differ significantly from another, whereas we are able to distinguish different emotional experiences very clearly.

   (b) Internal organs are relatively insensitive structures and also show inaction in comparison to conscious experience. Hence, bodily changes cannot be thought as a source of emotional experience.

   (c) When a person is artificially induced to bodily changes (by injecting adrenalin), it does not produce experience of true emotion.

   (d) James and Lange assume a kind of reflex relation between perception of an emotional situation and accompanying emotional behaviour. But as **Worcester** argues, this is not always true. For example, when we perceive the presence of a tiger in a jungle or road, we tend to run away. However, the sight of the same animal in a zoo does not evoke running behaviour, instead one tends to approach the animal. In the first instance we tend to run away because we experience fear while on the second occasion, we tend to approach because we do not experience the emotion of fear.

Thus, James-Lange theory is not totally true. However, the theory is a landmark in the study of emotion because it could pave the path in advancing our knowledge about such a complex psychological process.

15.8.3 Cannon–Bard Theory

Walter, B. Cannon (1927), a Harvard psychologist while refuting the contentions of James–Lange used a case study to substantiate his views contrary to James and Lange. A woman's neck was fractured in an accident (she fell from a horse). This caused injury to her spinalcord and the nerves connecting the brain was damaged. Owing to the injury, she was unable to feel anything down the neck. But, the woman reported experiencing normal emotions. Cannon argued, when electrical signals from body are necessary to experience emotion, then how is it possible for the woman to experience joy, grief or displeasure. This and a few more instances form the ground to refute **James–Lange** premise.

Cannon offered an alternative theory in the year 1927 which later was experimentally substantiated and extended by a researcher **Philip Bard** (1928). Thus, theory is known as **Cannon–Bard Theory**.

According to this theory, the thalamus plays central role in emotion. Emotional stimuli are received by the receptors and sensory impulses are conveyed to the centre (spinalcord and brain). Before the impulses get to the upper levels of brain, it must pass through thalamus. Similarly, impulses from upper levels of brain getting into the effectors also must pass through thalamus. Cannon holds that thalamus sends impulses simultaneously to the cerebral cortex (upper level of brain) and to the other parts of the body. Hence, experience of emotion is resultant of simultaneous arousal of the cortex and sympathetic nervous system. Thus, the experience of emotion and accompanying bodily changes occur at the sametime in which thalamus plays a very important role by relaying the impulses received from receptors to the cerebral cortex and impulses coming from cerebral cortex to the organs of response (viscera and muscles).

Follow-up investigations have made it clear that the **hypothalamus** rather than **thalamus** is the important centre for integrating to and fro the emotional experiences. Hypothalamus is a group of nerve centres situated beneath the thalamus. This subtle part has been found to elicit fear or anger in many animals. Neurologists have also observed the significance of this part in reference to emotion. On having established its prominence, hypothalamus is assumed as the **seat of emotion** by the followers of Cannon and Bard. According to Cannon–Bard view, the emotional sequence is as follows:

Perception of emotional situation → Thalamus/Hypothalamus takes over the signals and are sent simultaneously to cortex and other parts of the body → We have both, the knowledge and feeling of emotion and bodily changes simultaneously

Physiological bases of Cannon–Bard theory

From the above sequence of emotion, it is clear that the **felt emotion** and accompanying **body reactions** are independent of each other. However, the two are triggered simultaneously. In physiological terms the sequence can be diagrammatically represented as in **Figure 15.3**.

Figure 15.3 shows that on stimulation of the impulses follow path 1 and pass through

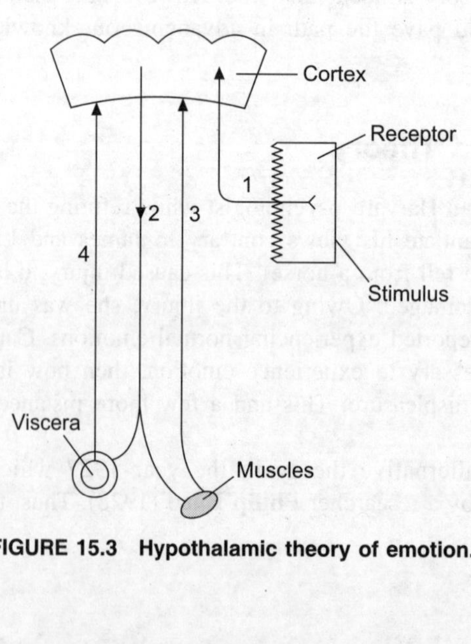

FIGURE 15.3 Hypothalamic theory of emotion.

hypothalamus (P). This causes the arousal of hypothalamic impulse (acquired and/or unacquired) which is relayed simultaneously to the cortex vide path 4 and also to the viscera and muscles—the organs of response vide path 2. Path 3 is the connecting path between the cortex and the hypothalamus and thereby the hypothalamic impulses are controlled and regulated.

The physiological bases of the theory clearly show that

(i) First we perceive the presence of emotional situation and soon the receptors are stimulated.

(ii) Perception of the emotional situation arouses hypothalamic impulses which get into the cortex and visceral/muscular organs simultaneously. Thus, the experience of the emotion and body reaction takes place simultaneously.

Critical comments

No doubt, Cannon–Bard theory meets with the shortcomings of James–Lange theory as it provides answers to the issues raised by critics. However, certain facts are contrary to the theory which are mentioned hereinbelow:

The theory lays too much emphasis on hypothalamus whereas the fact is that involvement of several other parts of nervous system have also been found equally significant. This has been substantiated in several experimental studies in which the hypothalamus was artificially stimulated by exposing the subjects to some emotional situations and their emotional reactions were compared to the control group of such subjects who were exposed to emotional situations in a natural way. Some of the noted differences were:

"Artificially aroused emotional behaviours were relatively short-lived, more stereotyped, less adaptive, more restricted and less situation oriented."

Differences like these obviously suggest that in a natural state, in addition to hypothalamus, other parts of nervous system also get involved. Therefore, the researchers such as, **Lashley**, **Lindsley**, **Amold** etc. opine that the experimental studies do not lend much support to assume hypothalamus as the seat of emotions.

The researchers further noted that the hypothalamus is also incapable in maintaining the tension arising out of emotion for longer duration.

Thus, this theory is also not able to explain the entire fact of emotion and, therefore, cannot be regarded as a preferred theory of emotion.

15.8.4 Activation Theory

D. Lindsley (1951) proposed still another theory of emotion which is popularly known as **activation theory of emotion**. It is also called **central theory** because it lays greater emphasis on central nervous system. **Lindsley** assumes that the state of emotion is nothing but heightened state of activity of the nervous system, particularly the higher brain—**cerebral cortex**. 'Hightened activity' means increased rates of discharge of neural impulses, specially in the **reticular formation** region of the brain stem.

Lindsley explains his views on the basis of **sleep arousal** dimension. On the one extreme of the dimension is the state of sleep in which the activity of the organism is very low, the cortex is relatively inactive, sympathetic system discharges are very low and muscles are relaxed. During this state, the emotion is at the lowest ebb. But when the organism is in a very intense emotional state, he is on another extreme **hightened arousal state**. In this state, the nervous system is most active. In the former state, the nervous system does not receive any sensory feedback while in the latter state, sensory feedback is continuous, rapid and frequent. Such feedbacks further increase the activity level of the nervous system.

According to Lindsley, what we call, **emotion** is in fact, high level of activation. According to him, though thalamus is important because it co-ordinates the activities of nervous system as a whole. However, it is wrong to claim that hypothalamus is the key organ of emotion. Rather, different parts of the cortex are actively involved.

This theory further says that basically motivations and emotions are hardly separable. Their separation in experience is only a matter of custom and convention. Custom and convention make us learn to label various levels of activation and accompanying feelings as **anger**, **fear**, **hunger**, **sex** etc.

Critical comments

Activation in fact, is not a complete theory because it presents the role of only a small part of the brain as to what goes on during the state of excitement or arousal. Some other parts too have been found to be actively involved during emotion, such as the **limbic system**.

On the basis of activation of nervous system alone, it is difficult to distinguish emotional state from non-emotional state as the state of activation is commonly found in other psychological processes such as motivation, perception and other cognitive processes.

Activation theory holds good in explaining behavioural aspects of emotion. But, it miserably fails to account for the experience aspect of emotion which is in no way less important in understanding emotional behaviour.

15.8.5 Cognitive Theory of Emotion

Cognitive theory is closely related to **James–Lange Theory**. This theory has been proposed by **Stanley Schachter** and **Jerome Singer** (1962). The theory assumes that the **felt emotion** is interpretation of stirred-up bodily state of arousal. This theory is also called **two-factor theory** because the theory holds that emotions have two ingredients—physical arousal and cognitive labelling. They presume that our experience of emotion grows from awareness of our present state of arousal. They also assume that bodily state of arousal for many emotions is much the same. Even when some differences in the physiological changes in different states exist, it is difficult to sense different emotions on the basis of physiological changes alone.

The autonomic changes are ambiguous and therefore, any kind of emotional feeling can be felt. But, the fact is that we actually interpret the physiological changes in relation to perceived situation, i.e. we have cognition about the physiological state as well as the experience of the particular emotion. Thus, the sequence of events according to this theory are shown in **Figure 15.4**.

Schachter and Singer in support of their theoretical formulations cite an example as below.

'Imagine a man walking alone down a dark alley. A figure with a gun suddenly appears. The perception (cognition) **'figure with a gun'** in some fashion initiates a state of physiological arousal. This state of arousal is interpreted in terms of knowledge about dark alleys and guns and the state of arousal is labelled as **'fear'**. Similarly, a student who unexpectedly learns that he has **Phi-Beta** Kappa and may experience a state of arousal which he labels 'joy'. (Schachter and Singer, 1962, p. 380).*

* Schachter, S. and Singer, J.E. (1962), "Cognitive, social and physiological determinants of emotional state". *Psychological Review*, 69, pp. 379–399.

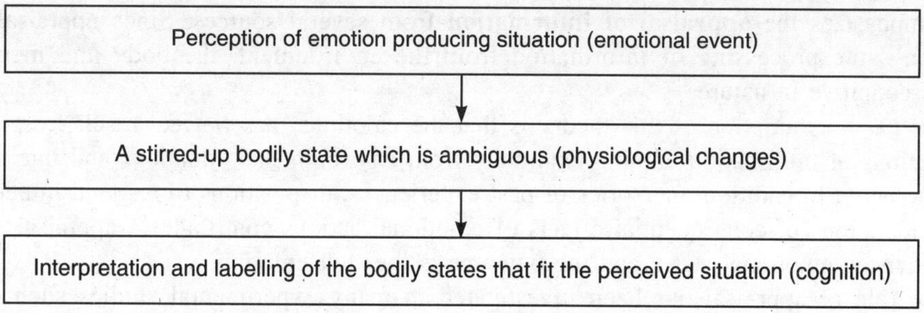

FIGURE 15.4 Cognitive theory of emotion.

Schachter and Singer tested this theory in an experiment using chemical injections. The experiment indicated the importance of cognitive factors in emotion. This experiment was conducted on college students (males) employing a clever experimental procedure. The subjects were told that they (experimenters) were investigating the effects of **superoxin** (a mythical vitamin supplement) on vision. Some were given the injections of **Placebo** (inert salt solution with little effects on physiology), some were injected epinephrine (adrenaline—a hormone) that produces arousal, physiological state such as increased blood pressure, heart-rate etc. *i.e.* a state of stirred up. Some subjects were accurately informed about the arousal effects of the drug. It was expected that they would attribute their feelings of arousal to the injection. Others were told nothing about the expected effects of the injection hence, were 'ignorant' about its effects. It was expected that these subjects would attribute their felt emotions in accordance with what they perceived about the happenings in the situation.

To an extent, the results were in the direction of the experimenter's expectation. When put in a situation of happiness, the ignorant subjects showed more happiness (euphoria) than the informed subjects. Ignorant subjects tended to feel angrier in anger arousing situation than the informed subjects. This difference was noticed in the similar state of physiological arousal.

Cantor et al. (1975) in their studies have also confirmed the findings of Schachter and Singer by inducing physiological arousal in other ways, such as physical exercise.

Both of these experiments demonstrated the importance of cognitive factors in emotion.

In essence, the theory assumes that though physiological arousal is an essential factor in emotion, but it is guided by cognitive factors. Present cognition including evaluations based on past experience provides a frame work within which one understands and labels his feelings (Schachter, 1963)

Critical comments

Cognition theory of emotion is supported by both informal and experimental evidences. It provides an explanation of different types of emotional feelings which accompany similar physiological states. However, this theory too is not complete in itself as most of the things remain unanswered. Besides, this theory also need to be supported by some more extensive research findings.

15.8.6 Cognitive Appraisal Theory of Emotion

Schachter–Singer's cognitive theory describes the cognitive thoughts involved in interpreting the perceived state of arousal. **Richard Lazarus** (1970) has proposed another cognitive theory. This theory emphasizes the **appraisal of information** from several sources. Since appraisal involves 'cognition'—the processing of information from the environment, the body and memory, this theory is cognitive in nature.

The basic assumption of this theory is that the emotions that we feel result from appraisals or evaluations of information coming externally from environmental situations and internally from within the body. In addition, memories of past experiences, dispositions to respond in certain ways and considerations of consequential effects of emotional actions contribute in appraisal process of the experienced emotional states and the outcome is the 'felt emotion'.

The role of appraisal has been investigated in many experimental studies such as that of **Specimen et al.** (1964).

This theory also assumes that **reappraisal** of emotion provoking situation is an important part of this cognitive theory. Reappraisal is also a way of coping with stressful situation. For example, suppose you are called by your boss in the office. This situation at first creates apprehension. But, suppose that when you enter his chamber, he informs you that he likes to recommend your name to be assigned with another job by granting promotion for which your consent is needed. Here, reappraisal occurs and your apprehension is likely to change in happiness. So, it is this change in emotion that occurs from minute to minute and from day to day. In stressful situations reappraisal becomes a way of coping with the stress.

Reappraisal often involves defence mechanisms such as rationalization, denial, sublimation etc. This helps in reducing the intensity of emotional experiences.

15.8.7 Theory of Relationships among Emotions

As we have seen, emotions are ill-defined states of living being and are of different natures, distinct, intermingled and go on changing constantly. This poses a problem for the psychologists to describe and study them well.

Robert Plutchik (1970, 1980) has proposed a descriptive theory of emotion that concerns with primary basic emotions. This theory also describes the way in which these emotions can be mixed together.

To show the interrelationship between emotions, **Plutchik** assumes that they differ in three ways: (i) intensity, (ii) similarity to one another and (iii) polarity or oppositeness. He has presented a **spatial model** that represents the relationships among emotions as represented in **Figure 15.5**.

Figure 15.5 shows a theoretical model portraying the dimensions of human emotion. Each vertical, wedge-shaped segment—the one composed of the subsegments–grief, sadness, and pensiveness, for example—represents a primary emotion. Intensity of the primary emotions is shown from the top down in each segment. Conflicting emotions are placed opposite each other around the figure, while similar emotions are placed near each other around the figure. The eight segments of this model (grief, sadness and pensiveness are in one segment for example) represent eight primary emotions which are derived from evolutionary processes and hence, have adaptive value.

Within each primary emotion segment, are the strongest varieties of emotions (shown at the top of the segment) while the progressively weaker varieties of emotions are shown at the bottom of the segments. For example, the grief segment is polar to—opposite from the ectasy segment. Further, the grief segment borders on primary-emotion segments with more similarity to grief than those farther away.

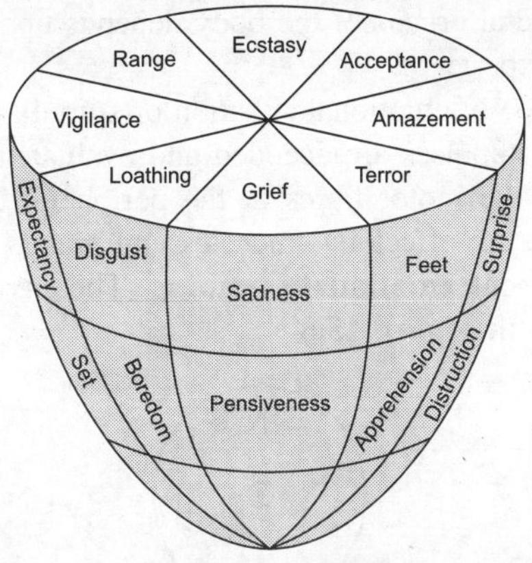

FIGURE 15.5 Dimensions of human emotions.

The emotions that are opposite to each other, conflict while the emotions which are closer to each other are complementary.

Usually, people rarely experience pure emotions. In view of this, the model provides a good description of mixed and conflicting emotions.

15.9 ROLE OF NERVOUS SYSTEM IN EMOTION

While describing the nature of emotion, it has been stated that emotion is an acute state of disturbance of the organism as a whole. That is, the emotionally aroused organism is aroused all over. There is an overall reaction in the receptors, muscles, internal physiological organs and nervous mechanisms. As a result, some kind of changes occur in the functions of various body organs including nervous system. We shall now consider the role of various neural mechanisms in emotion.

15.9.1 Role of Peripheral Nervous System (PNS)

Peripheral nervous system consists of fibres of afferent and efferent neurons and form a channel that carries information to and from central nervous system (CNS). Thus, it is concerned mainly with receptors and effectors.

The receptor–effector mechanisms

Receptors are found in almost every part of our body which on stimulation become activated and make the organism aware of the surrounding. Thus, the external receptors (eyes, ears, nose, tongue and skin) are necessarily involved in emotion. Any emotion provoking situation first activates these receptor mechanisms. Receptors of our muscles also get activated when we move and thus, make us aware of the emotional responses. Running, struggling, trembling etc. overt emotional responses activate the receptors found in muscles, joints, tendons etc. Receptors are also found in our internal organs. Receptors in the abdominal regions are called 'viscera'. Various kinds of emotionally aroused reactions, such as nausea, palpitation, feelings of contractions in the body or similar other changes in the visceral organs of the body depends upon impulses originating in these organs and their awareness or experience.

Receptors sense the presence of emotional situation or stimuli, convey the impulses originated in them to the centre where the impulses are decoded and evaluated as **emotional** and the kind of emotion is experienced through the motor fibres in the peripheral channel, appropriate emotional response impulse is conveyed to the effectors—muscles and glands and thus, the organism makes **emotional response** to the present **emotional stimulus**. The involvement of receptor–effector mechanism in emotion is shown in **Figure 15.6**.

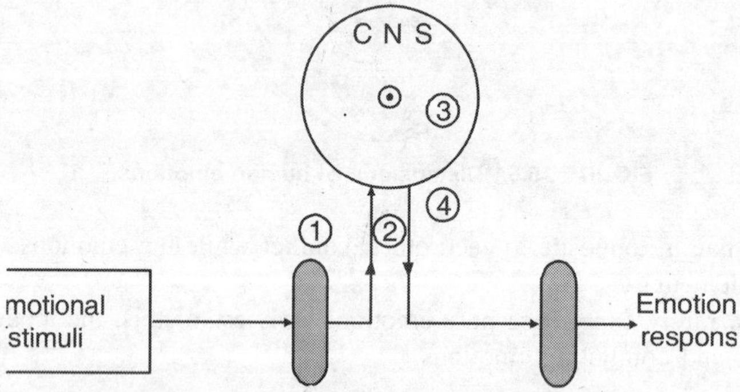

FIGURE 15.6 Receptor–effector mechanism.

Figure 15.6 shows the following steps:

(a) Receptors sense the emotional situation.
(b) Sensory impulses are conveyed through afferent fibres to the CNS.
(c) Emotion is experienced through motor fibre.
(d) Motor impulses are conveyed to effectors through motor fibres.
(e) Effectors get activated and emotional response is generated.

15.9.2 Role of Central Nervous System (CNS)

Impulses from receptors travel into the central nervous system (CNS). Some go up the spinal cord while others enter the brain via spinal cord directly. The CNS integrates the sensory information of the emotion provoking stimuli, interprets them and takes cognizance of the emotional situation, assigns a label to the emotional experience and directs the organs of response to display a particular kind of emotional response appropriate to the emotional situation. Thus, CNS plays a significant role.

Impulses from receptors to the upper levels of brain pass through lower brain known as **Thalamus**. Beneath it is situated a group of nerve centres—called **hypothalamus**. Hypothalamus serves three important functions in emotions. These are as follows:

(i) Impulses from receptors to cerebral cortex pass through it. Impulses from viscera and muscles also pass through it.
(ii) Impulses also come to the hypothalamus from cerebral cortex. For example, when we rememb́r or think of an emotion provoking situation, impulses are initiated and pass through it.
(iii) Impulses are sent to viscera and muscles. These are motor impulses.

Many psychologists consider hypothalamus as the seat of emotion because, it also exerts control over voluntary muscles in emotion. It has been observed that disease or lesion or tumour in the hypothalamic region causes emotional apathy, somnolence (sleepness) and even narcolepsy (an epileptic disease characterized by extreme sleepiness).

Limbic system

In addition to hypothalamus, a complex group of structures known as **limbic system** is also found directly involved in regulating and co-ordinating stronger emotions such as anger, fear and pleasure. The term 'limbic' comes from Latin word meaning **'border'**. The structures of this system form a 'ring' or 'border' around the brain stem as it enters the forebrain. Experimental researches have demonstrated that damage to some of the structures of this system cause great changes in the emotional behaviour of animals such as making tame animals wild or wild animals tame. Stimulation of certain parts of the limbic and hypothalamic systems has been found to produce behavioural patterns much like those occurring in naturally aroused emotions. **Heath** (1964) has also found that electrical stimulation of portions of the limbic system and hypothalamus, as well as other brain regions is rewarding to animals and pleasurable to human beings. In addition, the ascending reticular activating system (ARAS) is also found involved in emotional arousal.

Thus, it is evident that central nervous system do play a very significant role in emotion.

15.9.3 Autonomic Nervous System (ANS)

The physiological changes in emotion, such as sweating, rapid heartbeat, rise in blood pressure and so on are controlled by autonomic nervous system (ANS).

The ANS has purely motor functions. ANS is divided into two parts—sympathetic and parasympathetic. Functions of the two divisions are antagonistic to each other. For example, hyper-functioning of sympathetic nervous system accelerates the activities of autonomic functions of various body systems (*e.g.* circulation, respiration, digestion, sweating, etc). Such hyper-functioning results in rise of heart rate or pounding of heart, rapidity in breathing, throbbing temples, excessive secretation of adrenal hormones, rise in the level of blood glucose etc. Just reverse is the case with parasympathetic division of ANS. Its hyperfunctioning lowers down the activities of internal organs. Antagonistic function of ANS is useful in the sense that through it very effective control of visceral organ is possible and this plays a significant role in adjustive behaviour during emotions. While one division (sympathetic division) accelerates the visceral activities, another inhibits it and thus, results in effective coping with the emotional situation.

15.9.4 Glandular Involvements in Emotions

Sympathetic system also responds to the emotional situation by activating the adrenal gland resulting in hyper discharge of hormones—epinephrine (adrenaline) and norepinephrine (noradrenaline). Nerve impulses in the sympathetic system reaching adrenal glands, located on the top of the kidneys, cause the secretion of those hormones. Epinephrine affects many structures of the body. For example, in the liver it helps in mobilizing sugar into the blood and thus, makes more energy available to brain and muscles. It also stimulates heart to beat (cardiac surgeons use epinephrine to stimulate heart when it is weak or stops functioning). In the skeletal muscles also epinephrine helps to mobilize sugar resources so that the muscles can be used more rapidly. Thus, epinephrine adds energy to the sympathetic system to function more energetically. The major effect of norepinephrine is to constrict peripheral blood vessels and thus, raise blood pressure.

Similarly, in emotions, many other glandular functions such as thyroid, pituitary glands also get involved.

From the above description of the involvement of various body mechanisms, it is obvious that emotion is a very complex process. Perhaps this is the reason that often it becomes very difficult to differentiate between emotional and non-emotional state in terms of physiological changes alone.

15.10 PHYSIOLOGICAL MEASURES OF EMOTION

To measure the physiological changes in emotion, sensitive electronic equipments are used. One of such techniques is called **polygraph** through which the minimal changes occurring in the nervous system of the subject can be measured. It provides electrical signals which are recorded on a moving roll of paper. 'Polygraph' simultaneously provides several physiological measures. But this technique has more particularly been found useful in measuring electroderminal activities. When ANS is aroused, sweat glands in the palms of the hands begin to release moisture. We know that water is a good conductor of the electricity. Therefore, if a tiny electricity is passed across subject's palm, the slightest change in conductance becomes detectable. The electric current which is passed is too weak to be felt.

Similarly, to measure heart, blood pressure or functioning of cerebral cortex, we use ECG (electro-cardiogram), sphygmanometer and EEG (electroencephalogram), etc. To measure breathing, we use pneumograph and so on.

15.10.1 Polygraph and Lie Detector

Polygraph technique has also been found useful in detecting lie. In testing lie detection, the electrodes are placed on the chest, palms, shoulders and fingers and connected with a polygraph instrument. First, the person being tested is asked neutral questions to know and determine baseline on the polygraph. It is followed by questions relating to the crime which would indicate **guilty knowledge** which is supposed to be known only to culprits. Thus, the two graphic records—**baseline graph** and **guilty knowledge graph** are compared and the involved physio-logical changes are detected by analyzing the differences which may be an index of the guilt being committed by the culprit.

However, psychologists do not rely much on this technique because similar nature of physiological arousals are found in several kinds of emotional states such as joy, pain, anxiety etc. Moreover, people differ widely in such arousals. Therefore, any conclusion on this basis cannot be considered as definite. It becomes difficult to detect the extent to which the subject is true or lie in his statement.

15.11 EMOTION AND COMPETENCE

In social affairs, self-efficacy and efficient or competent emotional expressions are considered central to competent emotional functioning of the individuals. **Emotional competence** relates to emotionally good adjustment involving emotion eliciting social interactions. It makes us effective, confident and better adapted to the environment. The emotional competence is an ability to respond with others in the social environment emotionally with applying the knowledge about emotions to relationship with others. This knowledge includes encouraging positive emotions and discouraging the negative ones. At the same time, giving a healthier and creative direction to our emotional expressions is also a part of emotional competence. Persons rich in these abilities are able to persist in the face of difficulties arising out of long-term emotional dynamics and are able to effectively adjust in social situations.

Recently, a concept of **emotional intelligence** (EI) has been proposed. This includes persistence in the face of frustrations, delaying of gratifications, regulation of mood and exercise of adequate control over impulses. Emotional intelligence helps to adjust with life circumstances. Emotional intelligence is also indicative of **emotional maturity**. Behaviour disorder in fact reflects emotional immaturity.

15.12 EMOTION AND CULTURE

Studies have revealed that the most basic emotions are inborn and do not have to be learned. Psychologists in general hold the notion that emotions, especially facial expressions have strong biological ties. For example, children who are usually impaired from birth and have never observed the smile or seen another person's face, still smile or frown in the same way that children with normal vision do.

But, cross-cultural comparative studies have shown that learning plays an important role in emotions. This role is played in two important ways. Firstly, cultural learning influences the expression of emotions more than what actually is experienced. For example, some cultures encourage free emotional expression while others teach people through modelling and reinforcement to express little of their emotions in public.

Secondly, learning has a great deal to do with the stimuli that produce emotional reactions. It has been shown that people suffering from irrational fears (phobia) of elevators, automobiles, and the like have learned these fears through modelling and classical conditioning or avoidance conditioning. Accordingly, these emotions are also subjected to be unlearnt through modelling or conditioning procedures.

Cultural variations have also been noted in experiencing emotions. For example, in American culture, the nature of emotion is determined by subjective feelings while in other cultures, it is defined in terms of relationship between man and his environment.

Thus, the nature of emotion and the intensity with which it is expressed is culturally determined.

SUMMARY

- Emotion is a complex pattern of arousal that involves physiological activation, conscious awareness of feeling and specific cognitive label that describes the process.
- Some basic emotions are anger, fear and love. Anger is aroused when motives or desires get frustated. Anger arousing situation and mode of expression changes with age.

- Fear is usually caused by sudden and/or unexpected strange situation. Like anger, fear arousing stimuli also shift with age. Some fears are unlearned while most fears are learned through conditioning.
- Love and affections are also very common emotions which are considered significant for human life. Like anger and fear, love also undergoes changes with age.
- Emotions bring about several physiological changes—both internal and external.
- Internal physiological changes include changes in the functioning of internal visceral organs such as heart, lungs, respiratory functions, digestive system, sweating etc.
- External changes are reflected through facial expressions, vocal expressions and changed body postures and gestures.
- To explain certain puzzling questions about emotions, several theories have been proposed. These include—James–Lange theory, Cannon–Bard theory, Lindsley's activation theory, Schachter–Singer's cognitive theory and Cognitive appraisal theory.
- None of these theories is complete in themselves. Recently, Plutchik has proposed a model theory of relationship among emotions.
- Since in a state of emotion an individual is aroused as a whole, the peripheral, central and autonomic nervous systems along with glandular functioning are actively involved and play important roles in regulating and controlling emotional behaviours.
- Emotional competency is an important phenomenon of human life which refers to the ability to have control over emotional feelings and expressions.
- Emotion, though is an innate process of arousal, is largely determined by cultural factors. Hence, cultural variations are found.

Part IX

Individual Differences

CHAPTER 16

Intelligence

16.1 INTRODUCTION

Up to this point, we have presented the organism in general and man in particular. This general picture sketches the various ways of human behaviours, *i.e.*—what he does, how he does and why he does. In course of describing humans in general, we have become aware of the fact that our cognitions, affective feelings and the action tendencies widely differ from one another. This means that there exists individual differences in all our activities and psychological processes. In other words, individuals differ in their patterns of adjustment. This revolutionary idea (individual differences) was put forth by **Galton** and **Cattel** on the basis of their extensive works done during the later part of 19th century. It was a revolutionary idea indeed, because since then, a number of psychologists and scientists of other disciplines turned their focus towards measurement of various human capabilities such as aptitudes, attitudes, interests, intellectual abilities, dimensions of personality and so on. Thus, the **individual** becomes the focal point of attention and therefore, individual dispositions become the major area of research studies. Further, such an interest also led to the development of increased interest in devising various psychological tests based on psychometric principles and a new branch of psychology—**psychometric**—could emerge which is considered as one of the greatest contributions of psychology.

The revelation of individual differences suggests that in order to have complete under-standing of adjustive behaviour, the psychologists and the students of psychology so to speak, should study the individual first in isolation and then in relation to other individual in group.

The present chapter therefore deals with one of the important characteristics of individual differences—**Intelligence**. The study of intelligence in this chapter involves two basic paths. One path is called **ideopathic** and the other is known as **nomothetic**. Following the ideopathic path, psychologists have developed highly valid, reliable and sophisticated tests of intelligence to measure and study the faculty of mind of an individual. In **nomothetic** path the measured levels of intellectual abilities are related to other individuals and thus, a general principle of intelligence is formulated to describe individual's behaviour.

16.2 NATURE AND DEFINITION OF INTELLIGENCE

Intelligence is perhaps the most common word of everyday usage. In our dailylife situations, we often classify people either as intelligent or dull. We very frequently say—he is very intelligent, he is dull, where has your intelligence gone? and so on. Such usage of the term denotes that the term intelligence is a most popularly used common word of our everyday life and that this word is used to describe a wide variety of activities involving capabilities to do the activity. For example, when we classify someone as intelligent or dull, we do so on the basis of our common belief of expectations about a wide varieties of activities that an intelligent person would be supposed to perform while a dull person would not be able to do. The former would be expected to learn a difficult task and that too quickly as compared to latter. We also believe and expect that an intelligent person would be able to adjust to new and unfamiliar situation while the latter will have difficulty in adjusting. The intelligent person is further expected to solve new and complicated problems more conveniently whereas a dull person would utterly fail in solving such problems. Similarly, an intelligent person can make minute observations between old and new while a dull person cannot. An intelligent person is also supposed to have a power to think abstractly which a dull person cannot.

From the above, it is construed that intelligence can be understood in terms of various activities of a person. Though, it would be wrong to assume intelligence in terms of these activities alone, these activities are merely signs (significates) of intelligence. Intelligence in fact, is something more than these signs (significates).

Intelligence is also thought as powerful faculty of mind owing to which, human beings have been able to gain dominance over the animals and are considered as the distinct creatures of animal's kingdom. Despite this, it is also important to note that individual differs in this highly developed trait. People differ in their ability to understand complex ideas, to adapt effectively to environment, to learn from experience to engage in various forms of reasoning and to overcome obstacles. Often our judgements about the intellectual competencies of people bases on these and related characteristics and accordingly label them as being more intelligent or less intelligent.

One salient characteristic feature of intelligence is that it is not limited to any particular activity, domain or context. Rather, it is manifested in every activity such as school tasks, performance of a task, social interaction, solving some intricacies of matter or problem, decision-making, performing dailylife activities in an arranged and systematic way, observing economy of efforts and so on. Hence, it is a **general ability**.

For long, the study of intelligence was confined to the cognitive domain. In recent years, however, understanding about nature of intelligence has drastically changed. It is now believed that intelligence is not **unidimensional** rather it is **multidimensional** which has many facets. The recentmost views on the nature of intelligence also include the affective and social domains. In view of such social contexts, emphasis on different aspects of intelligence varies from one culture to another and in view of multidimensional features, intelligence is considered as **global** capacity and not any 'single entity'.

Since, intelligence is a popularly common term of our dailylife usage, and this term is used to denote abilities involved in performing a wide variety of everyday life activities. For a large number of research psychologists, more particularly those who are connected with research studies in the areas of child psychology or educational psychology, **intelligence** is assumed as a central topic of research.

16.2.1 Defining Intelligence

There are several synonyms of the term intelligence, such as the **capacity, talent, aptitude, discrimination, acumen, shrewdness, mental acuteness, comprehension, ability** etc. In Indian contexts too, words such as **buddhi, pratibha, prajna, medha, dhi, chaturya** etc. are used as substitutes for the term intelligence. These various synonyms of the words in general refer to various kinds of abilities such as ability to understand, reasoning power, mental alertness, ability to grasp relationships, ability to form good associations, ability to grasp the complexities of problems and solve them etc. Thus, it is obvious that the concept of intelligence is complex enough and multidimensional in nature that represents boundless potentialities of human beings. Hence, giving a precise definition of this concept is very difficult. However, different psychologists have chosen different aspects of intelligent behaviour and attempted to define intelligence accordingly. For the sake of convenience, these definitions can be grouped in to four different categories as mentioned hereinbelow:

(i) Definitions that define intelligence as an ability to learn.
(ii) Definitions that define intelligence as an ability to adjust.
(iii) Definitions that define intelligence as an ability to think abstractly.
(iv) Definitions that define intelligence in terms of global capacity.

Ebbinghaus, **Thorndike** etc. define intelligence as an ability to learn or **profit from past experience** or to **form good association**.

Stern, **Kagan** and **Haveman**, **Cruze** etc. have tried to define intelligence in terms of ability to adjust to new and unfamiliar situations. Some of these psychologists have explained intelligence by combining the ability to learn and adjust. For example, **Kagan** and **Haveman** have defined intelligence **as the ability to profit from past experience to learn new infor-mation and to adjust to new situations**.

A third group of psychologists (Terman, Rex and Knight, Munn) emphasise **the use of symbolic process and think abstractly** as an important aspect of individual's intelligent behaviour. For example, **Terman** holds that **an individual is intelligent in proportion to his abilities to carry on abstract thinking**. Similarly, **Munn** defines intelligence as **versatility in the use of symbolic processes. Rex** and **Knight** while defining intelligence have also put emphasis on the capacity for rational and constructive thinking directed towards attainment of some end.

Finally, the fourth group of psychologists views intelligence as **global capacity**. In this group are included **Stoddart** and **Wechsler**. Stoddard defines **intelligence as the ability to undertake activities that are characterized by (a) difficulty (b) complexity (c) abstractness (d) economy (e) adaptiveness (f) social value (g) the emergence of originals and (h) to maintain such activities under conditions that demand a concentration of energy and resistance to emotional forces.**

Thus, Stoddart in his definition has included most of the aspects of intelligent behaviour and hence, tends towards versatile (or flexible) functions performed by intelligence in making adjustments with the situations and finding solutions to the problem with concentration and resistance to emotional forces.

Wechsler does hold global view of intelligence. He defines intelligence in the following terms.

Intelligence is the aggregate or global capacity of an individual to act purposefully, to think rationally, and to deal effectively with his environment. This definition incorporates all other three groups of definitions, i.e. intelligence as an ability to perform and learn, to think and to adapt. In this sense, Wechsler's definition is appropriate one.

Similarly, **Howard Gardner** (1986) has defined intelligence as **the ability or skill to solve problems or to fashion products which are valued within one or more cultural settings.**

On analysing the above and other definitions it is indicated that intelligence consists of three general classes of skills or abilities which are as follows:

(i) Adapting to new situations and changing task demands.
(ii) Learning or profiting optimally from experience or training.
(iii) Thinking abstractly using symbols and concepts.

More recently, **Robert Sternberg** (1997), a pioneer in the field of intelligence research has defined intelligence as follows:

> **Intelligence comprises the mental abilities necessary for adaptation to, as well as shaping and selection of any environmental context.**

Sternberg's definition goes beyond the adaptive nature of intelligence. According to him, intelligence is not merely reacting to the environment (in the form of adapting) but it also involves actively selecting and shaping the environment. Thus, in course of adapting to the environment, the individual also brings changes in the contexts of the environment (shaping) according to his/her likings. For example, suppose someone goes to visit a relative's house on holidays. Initially, he behaves according to their expectations. Slowly, he begins to suggest certain specific changes in the environment (shaping) as per his own personal taste. However, he finds it difficult to bring changes in the environment due to various constraints. In that case an intelligent person tries to find another suitable environment (**selection**) such as going to another relative's house or choosing to stay in a hotel.

At this point, it must be noted that intelligence is not simply an ability that a person possesses, but also the use of these abilities in real life is far more important. In view of this, Sternberg's definition appears appropriate.

The second important thing in Sternberg's definition is that the landscape of environmental contexts changes over time, therefore the process of adequate adaptation, selection and shaping involve lifelong process of learning right from infancy to the entire span of one's life.

In view of the afore-cited definitions and their explanations and also that intelligence is an allround ability reflected in various activities, in conclusion, it can be defined as below:

> **Intelligence is a general ability of global nature which is expressed in great varieties of activities that different persons are able to perform whether a simple labourer or a distinguished scholar.**

This definition encompasses within almost all characteristic features of intellectual ability and put forth the purposive nature of intelligence. Hence, the definition seems most convincing and appropriate.

16.3 THEORIES OF INTELLIGENCE

We have seen that intelligence is versatile in nature and as such, there is no agreement regarding definition of intelligence.

Currently, research studies on intelligence have proceeded on two fronts. On the one front, psychologists continue to explain and define intelligence. On the other front, psychologists are actively busy in constructing the tests of intelligence even before reaching an agreement on what is being measured. They simply hold **Intelligence is what intelligence tests measure**. Consequently, a number of theories have been propounded and also quite a good number of intelligence tests have been constructed which are being used.

In the present section, attempts will be made to explain the structure and nature of intelligence in the context of several theoretical formulations which will be followed by description of some important tests of intelligence.

To explain what intelligence actually refers to quite a good number of distinct theories have been propounded. Some of the important such theories are being described hereinbelow:

16.3.1 Some Classical Approaches or Theories of Intelligence

Two-factor theory of Charles Spearman

Spearman (1927) proposed a 'two-factor theory' of intelligence. According to him, intelligence consists of two factors—**general (g)** and **specific (s)**. This theory maintains that all intellectual activities share a common factor that we call 'g' factor which is characterized by **mental energy**. The theory assumes that this 'g' factor is a common factor found in all different kinds of activities we do and this is the reason that we find a close relationship between different human activities. For example, a good test on memory, reasoning and other abilities parallel a similarly high score on each of these ability tests. This high positive correlation between different abilities is attributed to the presence of 'g' factor in almost similar amount in all these activities or abilities.

But, Spearman also realized that correlations between different tests of abilities are never perfect (i.e. +1.00). To explain this, Spearman has suggested the existence of another factor in addition to 'g' factor. This another factor is termed as **specific factor** or simply 's' factor which is unique to each test.

Spearman claims that different abilities such as mechanical, musical, arithmetic, spelling and similar other abilities require certain amount of 'g' and hence, this factor is found in all these activities eventhough, the intercorrelations are not very high.

's' factor is specific factor which shows special abilities. For example, an individual may have 'g' factor and at the same time, he may possess longer magnitude of capabilities in some specific activities, such as arithmetic, spatial abilities, music etc. An individual's tested intelli-gence reflects the amount of 'g' as well as the magnitude of various 's' factors which is strictly specific to single activity.

Spearman also holds that individual differences in intelligence is largely due to the differences in magnitude of 's' factor because, in a normal individual, the level or magnitude of 'g' factor is almost normal in every individual. **Figure 16.1** shows this pattern.

Later researchers, however, criticise the two-factor theory on several counts such as applicability, poor inter-correlations, unusefulness of 'g' factor and involvement of multifactors. But, Spearman's methodology and search for 's' factor through analysis to explain test results are enduring contributions. Further, his technique for factor analysis is regarded as the most valuable and outstanding contribution to psychological testing.

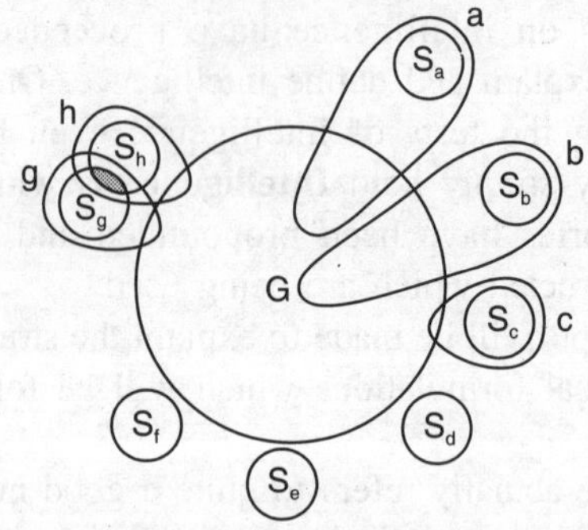

FIGURE 16.1 Relationship between 'g' and 's' factors conceptualized by Spearman.

Louis Thurston's primary ability theory

Thurston, L. (1935) advanced the theory of primary abilities (PMA) which states that intelligence consists of nine major abilities (factors), each of which is relatively independent of the others. These factors are as follows:

(i)	Spatial relations	(S)
(ii)	Perceptual speed	(P)
(iii)	Numerical ability	(N)
(iv)	Verbal comprehension	(V)
(v)	Memory	(M)
(vi)	Word fluency	(W)
(vii)	Inductive reasoning	(I)
(viii)	Deduction	(D)
(ix)	Reasoning	(R)

Thurston calls all these as the primary mental abilities (PMA).

Later on **Thurston** (1943) revised his thoughts and rejected two primary abilities—**induction** (I) and **deduction** (D). Thus, finally he stated only seven fundamental abilities SPNVMWR as the main constituents of intelligence.

Thurston also devised a battery of tests to measure these abilities which is known as 'the test of primary mental abilities' (PMA) and is still widely used.

Critical comments

However, its predictive power is no greater than other tests of general intelligence such as Wechler's scales. In fact, Thurston's conception of basic elements of intelligence are not completely independent. Different primary abilities are found significantly intercorrelated to each other and thus, lend support to Spearman's conception of 'g' factor. Moreover, the number of factors identified by factor analysis are dependent upon the nature of items choosen. Other investigators using different test items suggest many more factors. For example, **Guilford** (1911) has identified approximately 120 unique intellectual abilities and proposed as **multifactor theory** of intelligence. Further, **Garrett** (1946) sees the elemental view of 'g' factor as controversial and doubted its significance. Garrett found that 'g' factor is more prominent in primary school children which gradually decreases with growing age. Hence, the concept of 'g' factor in intelligence creates doubts.

J.P. Guilford's factor analysis theory

J.P. Guilford (1961) on the basis of more than two decades of factor analytic research, proposed a box-like model which is called **tridimensional theory** of intelligence. This theory is more popularly known as **structure of intellect model** which stands out in sharp disagreement with Spearman's 'g' factor and Thurston's concept of **primary abilities**. **Guilford** holds that in Thurston's primary mental ability model, many aspects of intelligence tend to be ignored when items are lumped together to form tests. An item in a test of verbal ability is distinguished from that which is non-verbal. The distinction is on the basis of **content** of the test item. He further opines that items of a test should not be distinguished in terms of content alone but also in terms of operations and products. Thus, Guilford classified intellectual factors in three ways—content, operation and product.

Content: Content refers to the kind of information involved. He has identified four types of contents:

(a) *Figural*: Involving concrete objects.
(b) *Symbolic*: Information represented by means of symbols such as words or signs of mathematics.
(c) *Semantic*: Involving meaning. It includes such factors as verbal comprehension and general reasoning.
(d) *Behavioural*: This resembles Thorndike's social intelligence, *i.e.* ability to deal with people.

Operation: There are five types of operations that can be performed on a particular bit of information. These are as follows:

(a) *Cognition:* Understanding or comprehending the information.
(b) *Memory:* Recalling the past event or experience.
(c) *Convergent production:* Arriving at a correct solution to the problem provided.
(d) *Divergent production:* Devising a number of possible solutions to the problem posed by information.
(e) *Evaluation:* Involves judgements as to accuracy, goodness, suitability or workability of the solutions to the problem.

Products: Guilford further states that each of the four contents may take six different forms. These forms are called product (results) of operations applied to each content. These products are as follows:

(a) *Units:* A single item of information
(b) *Class:* A group of units with common property forming a class.
(c) *Relation:* Information reflecting relationship between two things.
(d) *System:* Information involving number of parts as a complex system.
(e) *Transformation:* Transformation involves some sorts of changes.
(f) *Implication:* Involving possibilities offered by a piece of information.

Thus, if the number of factors containing in all these three dimensions (contents—4 factors, operations—5 factors and products—6 factors) are multiplied together, the total number of factors come to 120 (4×5×6).

Guilford's above model is comparable to the height, width and depth of a cube as shown in the following cubic scheme of Guilford's factors (**Figure 16.2**).

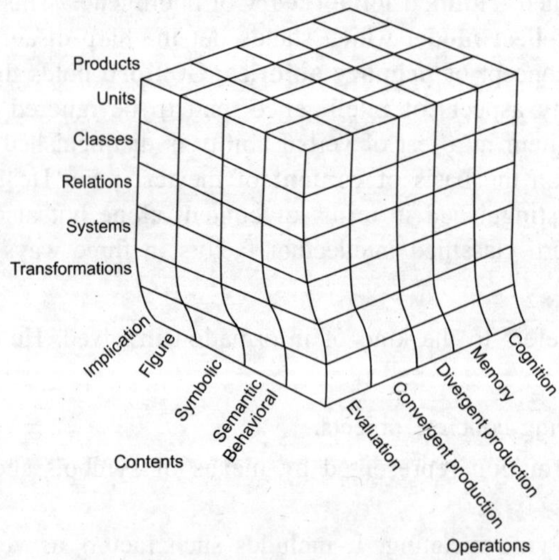

FIGURE 16.2 Guilford's ability factors.

To explain the three dimensions (contents, operations and products) of intellect, let us consider an example. Suppose that a subject is given a list of 100 **unrelated** words to study and is asked to recall the same after sometime. The 'contents' of this test is **semantic** because it involves words—a symbol, which has a meaning. The operation is **memory**—recalling the past. The product is what the subject recalls, *i.e.* list of words or units.

Similarly, suppose a subject is given anagram test. List of 5 lettered combinations (*e.g.* ANELR, PEPAL, BTAHI, ERLCA etc), and asked to rearrange the letters to form familiar words (learn, apple, habit, clear etc.). In this example, the content is **symbolic**, the operation is 'cognition' because it requires recognition of information which is in a disguised form and the product is the familiar word (*i.e.* unit).

Critical comments

Guilford's model has met with certain severe criticisms on the following grounds:

1. Guilford has included large number of factors in his model because he has broadened the concept of intelligence which from practical point of view is not suitable. Any test of intelligence with so many factors would be very complex and impracticable.
2. Some experiments comparing the results of conventional intelligence tests with results of tests designed to measure divergent thinking have shown that high creatives tend to be high in IQ but the same is not true and vice versa.
3. Factor analysis is not likely to give clear picture of the exact number and nature of intellectual abilities. In fact, the number of abilities obtained through factor analysis

depend upon specificity of test items. For example, if one wishes to measure specific activity—**memory**, he would be required to design tests of auditory memory, memory for printed words, memory for geometrical figures and so forth. On the contrary, in most of the instances, a fairly small number of well-defined abilities (such as described by Thurstone) serve the purpose of predicting one's success in job and also to specify variations in age, socio-economic status and cultural background.

4. The concept of general ability holds true as per available evidences. Therefore using so many factors in an intelligent test is not of practical significance.

Thorndike's multifactor theory

Thorndike (1926, 1927) has severely criticised Spearman's concept of 'g' factor and proposed a **multifactor theory**. He assumes that intelligence is in fact, a composite of a various abilities and hence, the assumption of 'g' factor is a nonexistent concept. Thorndike's theory is also termed as **synthetic theory of intelligence** because according to this theory, intelligence is a combination or synthesis of multiple ability factors. Clarifying his position, Thorndike has stated in his famous book on educational psychology that **the mind is a host of highly particularized and independent faculties**. Intelligence according to him is the sum total of various such smaller independent faculties and each faculty is related to some kind of cognitive functions and intelligence as we measure and describe is a synthesis of all such smaller abilities.

As regards intercorrelations between different factors of intelligence, Thorndike assumes that this correlation owes mainly to commonalities of abilities. To understand it, let us take an imaginary example. Suppose, there are two tasks—task 'A' and task 'B'. Performance of task A requires the abilities 1, 3, 4, 7, 8, 10 and 13 while task B involves abilities 2, 3, 6, 7, 9 and 10. Now since, certain abilities (e.g. 3, 7 and 10) are commonly involved in both the tasks, possibilities of high correlations between the two exists. As the number of common abilities are increased, higher intercorrelations may be obtained. Thorndike believes that in almost every intellectual task, some of the abilities are common and this causes the intercorrelations between different subtests of an intelligence test.

Thorndike has classified intellectual functioning into three major categories. These are social intelligence, concrete intelligence, and abstract intelligence.

Thorndike has also developed as test of intelligence, called CAVD test which includes four simple abilities namely,

C = Completion (sentence completion ability)
A = Arithmetic (arithmetical ability)
V = Vocabulary (vocabulary ability)
D = Direction (ability to understand direction)

If we examine closely, the test tasks selected by Spearman and Thorndike resemble with each other. Hence, difference between them is merely theoretical.

Critical comments

1. Thorndike's theory in fact is an imaginary theory because his views suffer from lack of uniformity. On the one hand he talks of various abilities while on the next occasion he also makes a reference of 'g' factor.

2. Multifactor approach is not sufficiently substantiated whereas sufficient evidences are available in favour of Spearman's 'g' factor.
3. Spearman's and Thorndike's approaches differ in theoretical formulations. How-ever from the point of view of practical implications, there exists no sharp difference.

Horn and Donaldson's approach

Horn and **Donaldson** (1980) have proposed **developmental model** of intelligence. They have attempted to classify intelligence in two types—**fluid intelligence** and **crystallized intelligence**—and argue that the direction of intelligence varies with age development of developing individuals.

By **fluid intelligence** they mean flexible thought that is independent of culturally based content. By **crystallized intelligence** they mean the degree to which an individual has mastered the knowledge and skills of the culture.

The propounders of this theory assume that the fluid intelligence declines over the period from young adulthood to old age whereas the crystallized intelligence increases with age. But the fluid-crystallized model of age change is not much clear and hence, it is merely a hypothesis which is supported only by a few cross cultural studies. However, the notion is subject to testification through longitudinal studies.

According to 'Horn' and 'Donaldson', the fluid intelligence includes creative ability to think, ability to reason abstractly, capacity to make inferences from given data, insight or understanding of relations etc. which gradually decline from young adulthood to old age. To measure such type of intelligence, the tests are constructed by selecting analogical and classificatory problems. Fluid intelligence is also more genetically determined than environmentally.

The crystallized intelligence on the other hand develops out of learning and experience and also capacity to retain them. Thus, it is more environmentally influenced than genetically. To measure crystal intelligence, tests containing vocabulary and general information are used.

A few longitudinal studies have indicated that crystal intelligence relatively remains stored in long term memory for longer duration than fluid intelligence, i.e. the crystal intellectual matters are not decayed easily. However, a sharp decline in both types of intelligence occurs above the 70 years of age.

Theory of Arthur Jensen

Arthur Jensen (1969) has advanced a theory of two levels of intelligence—level-I and level-II. Level-I denotes associative learning (e.g. learning and memory). These activities involve minimal transformation of the stimulus input prior to the outcome or response.

Level-II refers to a general class of abilities involving effective transformation or manipulation of stimuli as evidenced in higher order learning, such as reasoning and problem solving.

Hierarchical theory

We have till now presented a brief description of several factor theories, but hardly we can know as to which of these various theories can provide the best account of intelligence. However, both types of theories—'g' factor theory and various multifactorial theories seem to be true in certain respects. We can identify some abilities which are independent of one another. At the same time, we also find some correlations among the factors, suggesting that they share some commonness—

'g' factor. In view of this, **Vernon** (1950) has suggested to combine the two types of theories together and presented **hierarchical theory** of intelligence.

In hierarchical theory, intelligence is portrayed as **pyramid**. At the top of the pyramid is 'g' (general intelligence) which is reflected in all kinds of intellectual activity. Underneath it (g at the top) are several moderate specific abilities like Thurston's primary abilities. At the bottom of the pyramid are larger number of highly specific abilities as conceived by Spearman—the 's' factor.

This hierarchical theory borrows from several factor theories to form a **multilayered view** of intelligence—a view that appears the most reasonable of all other views.

16.3.2 Contemporary Approaches to Intelligence

The classical approaches of intelligence emphasized the cognitive abilities and defined intelligence in terms of single index of cognitive ability. This view has undergone major changes. As we have defined earlier, intelligence is a global ability, not unitary. Hence, there are many **intelligences** rather than single intelligence. These several intelligences are displayed by individuals while solving everyday life situation problems. Accordingly, many new approaches to intelligence have been put forward. Some of the important such approaches are as follows:

Theory of multiple intelligence

This theory has been proposed by **Howard Gardner** (1983). It is based on three following basic principles:

(a) Intelligence is not a single or unitary entity rather there exists multiple intelligences—each distinct from others.

(b) These intelligences are not interrelated rather independent of each other. Thus, if a person is good in one type of intelligence, it does not mean that he will be equally good or bad in other types of intelligences.

(c) Different types of intelligences interact. This means that different types of intelligence work together in providing solution to the problem.

Gardner has so far identified 8 different types of intelligences which may be found in different proportions in different persons. The prominence of one type of intelligence over the others is usually determined by the particular situation or context. These 8 types of intelligences are as follows:

(i) **Linguistic intelligence:** This is related to reading, writing, listening, talking, understanding etc. Poets or literates exhibit this type of intelligence better than others.

(ii) **Logical-mathematical intelligence:** This type of intelligence is more concerned with abstract reasoning and manipulation of symbols involved in numerical problems. It is exhibited in scientific works.

(iii) **Spatial intelligence:** This kind of intelligence is used in navigating in space, forming, transforming mental images. Sailors, engineers, surgeons, pilots, car drivers, sculptors and painters are found more highly developed in spatial intelligence.

(iv) **Musical intelligence:** Persons with musical intelligence show sensitivity to pitch and tone required for singing, playing an instrument, composing and appreciating music etc.

(v) **Bodily-kinesthetic intelligence:** It involves skills and dexterity for fine co-ordinated motor movements such as those required for dancing, athletics, surgery, craft making and the like.

(vi) **Interpersonal intelligence:** It requires understanding motives, feelings and behaviours of other people. Sales people, politicians, teachers, clinicians and religious leaders have high degree of interpersonal intelligence.

(vii) **Intrapersonal intelligence:** It is related to understanding one's self and developing a sense of identity. Persons with strong will power and self-esteem possess higher level of intrapersonal intelligence.

(viii) **Naturalistic intelligence:** It is related to recognizing the flora and fauna and making a distinction in the natural world. It is more possessed by hunters, farmers, tourists, students of biological sciences and the like.

In essence, Gardner's theory describes different types of intelligences used in different context. Though, genetically, every individual has the potentiality to exhibit these different types of intelligences as per the demands of the practical situations or contexts. However, the environmental opportunities play a significant role in deciding the prominence of a particular kind of intelligence in different individuals. Thus, environmental interaction is significant and in this sense intelligence functions in the form of semi-autonomous mechanism. Each kind of intelli-gence is in encapsulēd module in the brain which functions according to their independent regulatory and functional procedures. This is one reason that in the case of injury to brain, certain specific kinds of intelligence is damaged while other kinds may remain intact. For example, when Wernicke's area is damaged, linguistic intelligence get damaged while other kinds of intelligences remain intact.

Evaluation: Gardner's approach in fact deals with the practical use of intelligence in different kinds of activities. Therefore the approach is more pragmatic or purposive than simply description of structured elements. It is concerned with intellectual faculty.

However, psychologists have commented on certain kinds of intelligence, more particularly the interpersonal, intrapersonal and naturalistic intelligence. Despite this, the theory makes it obvious that intelligence should not be dealt with only in quantitative terms but also it should be understood in a wider sense—what and how does intelligence function?

In the light of this theory, the scientists of the day have began to realize that intelligence has two aspects—cognitive and specific functional aspects concerned with practical use of intellectual abilities.

16.3.3 Some Process-oriented Approaches to Intelligence

Till now, we have viewed intelligence in terms of its componential parts and the way these parts fit together. An alternative approach taken by several influential theorists focusses on the intellectual processes, *i.e.*, the pattern of thinking that people use while reasoning and solving problems. These theorists in fact use the word cognition or cognitive process instead of intelli-gence. These theorists are more interested in how a problem is solved and figure out the answers rather than the number of right answers one gets. Further, the process-oriented theorists focus on the development of intellectual processes, i.e. the changes that occur as the individual mature.

Some of the well-known process-oriented theories are described briefly herein below:

Piaget's theory

Jean Piaget (1970) views intelligence as adaptive process involving interplay of biological maturity and interaction with the environment. He views intellectual development evolved through different stages of cognitive development and processes such as understanding the laws of nature, principles of grammar and mathematical rules. The cognitive processes and developmental stages are described in greater detail in Chapter 13 (Thinking).

Bruner's theory

Jerome Bruner (1973) is also a process-oriented theorist who sees intellectual development as a function of growing internal representations. According to Bruner, small kids possess highly action-oriented form of intelligence. They 'know' an object only to the extent that they can act on it. When the babies grow to younger age, begin to know things by perceiving them and therefore, influenced by vividness of perceptual characteristics of an object or event. Older children and adolescents know things internally and symbolically. This means that they become able to devise internal symbols or representations of objects and events and to hold these mental images in mind. Bruner was also interested in exploring the influences of the environment on these growing abilities, more particularly the rewards and punishments received for using specific intellectual skills in a specific way.

Information processing theory

R.J. Stenberg (1985) proposed a new process-oriented theory of intelligence which is known as **Triarchic theory of intelligence**. The theory attempts to understand the cognitive processes involved in solving problems.

Triarchic theory consists of three subtheories of intelligence such as,

(a) Componential
(b) Experiential and
(c) Contextual

Componential subtheory: It refers to three kinds of internal mental mechanisms or components that cause intelligent behaviour. These components serve three different functions:

(i) **Meta components:** Meta components are the executive processes which are involved in planning strategies, monitoring progress and allocating external and internal resources to solve problems.
(ii) **Performance components:** This refers to the processes used to perform a task or solve a problem. The existing intelligence tests in fact, are concerned mainly to measure this componential aspect of intelligence.
(iii) **Knowledge acquisition components:** These are the processes used in learning.

Experiential subtheory: This sub-theory focuses on the relationship between person's inner mental world and outer external world. This aspect of intelligence is concerned with the effects of intelligence on one's experience as well as the effects of person's interaction with the environment on intelligence. This aspect of intelligence has additive value in **creativity** involving novelty and originality to the overall aspect of intelligence. A creative individual may not perform well on a test of intelligence but such individuals are able to combine and recombine his various experiences in a unique way.

Experiential sub-theory also assumes that experiential aspect of intelligence is an ability that **automatises** or **make routine** tasks that are done repeatedly. For example, reading is an automatised task which is carried out largely without conscious thought. Playing music is also an example of automatised activity.

Contextual sub-theory: Contextual sub-theory deals with the ways, people shape their environment effectively and make most of the available resources. Contextual intelligence is like **street smarts** or **situationally smart**. It refers to the effective management of the self as well as everyday life business. In other words, contextual intelligence refers to **practical intelligence** which is reflected in activities such as implementing, using, applying and seeking relevance.

Triarchic theory is represented diagrammatically in **Figure 16.3**.

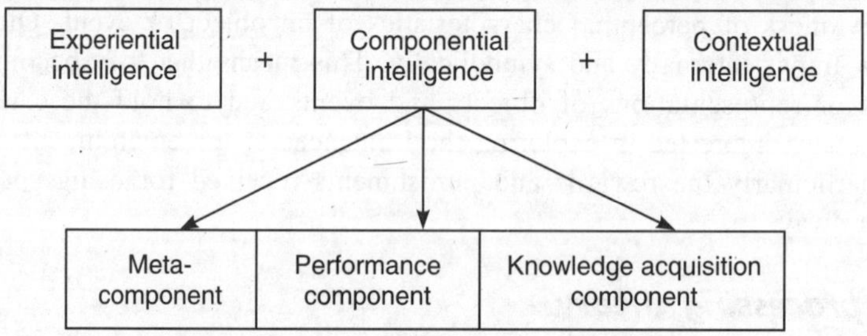

FIGURE 16.3 Triarchic theory of Stenberg.

An updated theory of intelligence propounded by Indian psychologists: PASS model

Extending the information processing approach of intelligence, **J.P. Das**, **Nagleri** and **Kirby** (1994) have proposed a new theory known as **'PASS'** model. PASS refers to four kinds of mental processes which are processed in course of intellectual functioning. These are Planning (P), Attention arousal (A), Simultaneous (S) and Successive (S) cognitive processing.

This theory is based on **Luria's** analysis of brain structures (1966, 1970, 1973, 1974, 1980). Luria has described cognitive processes within the framework of three functional units of cerebral cortex. The first function unit is cortical arousal and attention, the second is information coding using simultaneous and successive processings and the third unit provides planning, self-monitoring and structuring of cognitive activities. Luria's work on the functional aspects of brain structures served as the basis of PASS model and was used as a blue print for defining the important components of intellectual competence.

It is assumed that the cognitive processes that occur within the three functional units are responsible and involved in all cognitive activities. According to Luria, the three functional units are located in three different areas of the brain. The first unit—arousal attention—is located in the brain stem, the second functional unit responsible for receiving, analysing and storing of information through the use of simultaneous and successive processing is located in the occipital-parietal area of the brain while the third unit is located in the prefrontal areas of the frontal lobes of the brain. Frontal lobes synthesise the information and thus, through the process of planning, rogramming, regulation and verification of behaviour are provided and are responsible for problem olving behaviours and capacity for self-monitoring.

Thus, PASS model theory is based on three basic components which are briefly outlined ereinbelow:

Arousal and attention: Arousal is the basis for initiating an activity. Arousal forces us focus our attention in particular direction. As we know, attention is selective recognition of a articular stimulus (information) and inhibiting the responses to stimuli which are irrelevant. This lective function depends on sufficient arousal state. Intelligence involves sufficiently arousal and lective attention and then moves on to the second component—simultaneous and successive ocessings. For example, suppose you are travelling in a train. After a shortwhile you hear a ying sound coming from a part of the compartment. This crying sound arouses you and your tention is selectively directed towards the direction of the sound. Though, there are several other nds of sounds in the train, but your attention is drawn selectively towards the crying sound ly. This means that the stimulus that sufficiently arouses, attention is selectively drawn to that imulus only.

Simultaneous and successive processing: The second functional unit immediately comes activated for further processing of the attended information. It involves simultaneous d successive processings. Simultaneous processing is survey ability. This involves relating the fferent elements of information with each other. Successive processing involves integration of muli into a specific serial order in which each component is related to the next, i.e. **successive nthesis**. For example, when your attention is drawn to the crying sound coming from a part of train compartment, you try together several informations on the basis of which you gather that crying passenger has become victim of pick-pocketing. This information provides a number informations which are related together simultaneously and then arranged in successive rial order forming a chain of information and these are evaluated. Such S-S (successive and nultaneous) processings may be related to any of the modalities—visual, auditory, olfactory, statory or tactical. Similarly, such processings may be found in any higher order cognitive ocesses—verbal or non-verbal, direct perceptions, retention of information etc.

Planning: This process provides for programming, regulation and verification of behaviour. is also concerned with regulation of voluntary activity, impulse control and various linguistic lls such as spontaneous conversation. This functional unit also provides for the most complex ects of human behaviour including personality and consciousness (Das, J.P. 1980). Moreover, nning is an activity directed by local goal (as in performing an action) and also by overreacting tivation of the individual. In order to create plans and execute them, we are guided by processed ormation as well as attending to the relevant features of a problem or a situation. Thus, planning ends on the three other components of PASS theory.

Based on PASS theory, Das and Nagleri have also devised a cognitive assessment system AS) test that consists of verbal and non-verbal items. The test is administered on the testee either ough visual or auditory channels. This test is applicable on children ranging in age from 5 to 11 rs to measure their cognitive states.

There are many other information processing theories of intelligence or cognitive functions. group of psychologists called 'neo-Piagetians' have rewritten Piaget's theory of cognitive elopment in information processing terms—the terms that resemble the terms used to describe nputers. For example, **Jaun Pascual Leone** (1983) has expanded Piaget's notion of **'scheme'** distinguished between **action schemes** and **executive schemes**. **Action schemes** are similar to specific repeatable intellectual sequences. **Executive schemes** are similar to plans and strategie Such schemes are also referred to as **intellectual software** as distinct from **intellectual hardwa** —resources such as attention and memory.

The neo Piagetians opine that people's software grows more sophisticated as they mature wi their schemes expanding in complexity and their amount of available mental energy increasin Neo Piagetians claim that such changes promote the growth of intelligence.

Other information processing approaches focus on the rules involved in intelligent behavio (e.g. Siegler, 1983), or the skills required for various tasks (e.g. Fischer, 1980).

Despite the differences between different information processing theories of intelligenc one thing is common in all these approaches. Information processing theories in general bre intelligence into component processes and explore how the processes change over the course development.

16.4 ASSESSING INTELLIGENCE

Historically, the work of a **French** man **J. Esquirol**, in 1838 on mental disorders is consider to be the beginning of modern mental testing. However, **Sir Francis Galton**, an Englishman considered to be the father of mental tests. In 1884, Galton attempted to measure intelligen by administering a battery of tests which measured such characteristics as head size, strength hand grip, breathing capacity, reaction time, visual acquity and memory for visual forms. Gal believed that simple sensory, perceptual and motor responses were the key aspects of intelligen **J.H. Cattell** is credited with introducing the term mental test. The works of Galton and Catt together paved the way for further studies on intelligence.

From what has been discussed earlier, it is evident that there exists a great disagreem with regard to nature and definition of intelligence. Despite this, quite a good number of tests intelligence and aptitudes have been developed which can predict general pattern of performan identify the talents and discover the capabilities to solve problems and also the ability to adjust w the complex environment. The first systematic attempt to develop a test of intelligence was m by **Alfered Binet**, a Frenchman at the request of the French Ministry of Education in 1904. He v asked to serve on a commission to discover the educationally backward children to segregate th and arranging special classes for them. This task obviously meant development of an object test of intelligence for measuring and categorizing school children in terms of the level of me development. Since then, a sort of **movement** in the field of mental testing and intelligence construction began and by now quite a good number of objective, reliable, valid and standard t of intelligence have developed.

All the tests of intelligence are not alike. Some tests are such that can be administered individual basis while some can be applied in group situations. Some of these tests are verbal w some are non-verbal and performance. Hence, the tests of intelligence are divided into catego as appended in **Table 16.1**.

The above-mentioned tests are only a few cited as example. The number of tests under e category are much more. Out of the above named few tests, some of the important ones which most commonly used are being described below.

Before we begin with the description of some of the important tests of intelligence, it se important to know certain concepts that are indicative of intellectual abilities. These concepts **mental age** (MA) and **intelligence quotient** (IQ).

TABLE 16.1 Classification of intelligence tests

Individual tests		**Group test**	
Verbal tests	*Non-verbal or performance tests*	*Verbal tests*	*Non-verbal or performance tests*
(i) Binet Simon intelligence scale (ii) Stanford Binet scale (iii) Modified Stanford Binet scale	(i) Pinter Peterson performance scale (ii) Alexander's intelligence test battery (a) Passalong test (b) Block design test (c) Cube construction test (iii) Porteus maze test (iv) Form board test (v) Wechsler-Belleve test	(i) Army alfa test (ii) NGCT and AGCT (iii) Mohsin's test of general intelligence (iv) Dr. Singh's general test battery (v) Jalota's test of intelligence (vi) M.C. Joshi's test of general intelligence	Army beta test

Mental age (MA): As we have seen, the first attempt to measure intelligence was made by Binet. He used the concept of **mental age** (MA) which refers to an individual's level of mental development related to the environment in which the individual lives. Binet argued that a mentally retarded child would perform like a normal child of a younger age.

He compared mental age (MA) with **chronological age** (CA) or biological age or the age from birth. A bright child has an MA above his CA while a dull child has an MA below his CA.

Intelligence quotient (IQ): In the year 1911, **William Stern** suggested that in order to better understand the intellectual abilities in quantitative form, it is desirable to convert the level of mental development (MA) into a 'ratio' or quotient by converting the MA and CA quantities into proportional ratio values. In view of this suggestion, the concept of **IQ** could be devised in the year 1912.

Intelligence quotient or IQ refers to a child's mental age divided by chronological age $\left(\frac{MA}{CA}\right)$ and multiplied by 100—a constant ratio assumed to be normal or average level of intellectualdevelopment. Thus:

$$IQ = \frac{IQ}{CA} \times 100$$

If the mental age is the same as the chronological age, then the individual's IQ will be 100 (normal or average). If mental age is above CA then IQ is more than 100, i.e above average and if the mental age is below the chronological age, then IQ will be less than 100, i.e. inferior as compared to normal children of that age in the population. For example.

$$MA = 6, CA = 6 \quad IQ = \frac{MA}{CA} \times 100, \frac{72 \text{ months}}{72 \text{ months}} \times 100 = 1 \times 100 = 100$$

(Average in intelligence)

$$MA = 8, CA = 6 \quad IQ = \frac{MA}{CA} \times 100, \frac{96 \text{ months}}{72 \text{ months}} \times 100 = 1.33 \times 100 = 133.33$$

(Superior in intelligence)

$$MA = 6, CA = 8 \quad IQ = \frac{MA}{CA} \times 100, \frac{72 \text{ months}}{96 \text{ months}} \times 100 = 0.75 \times 100 = 75$$

(Inferior in intelligence)

16.4.1 Individual Verbal Tests

Individual verbal tests are those which contain verbal problems and constructed through the use of language. Hence, called **verbal**. Secondly, these tests are so designed that these can be applied only on one individual at a time, i.e. these cannot be administered in group situation. Hence, called 'individual tests'. Some of these tests are described below:

Stanford–Binet scale

Stanford–Binet scale is one such test which is the first test of intelligence designed to measure aptitude involved in primary education.

With the association of Simon, Alfred Binet published his first test called Binet-Simon test in the year 1905. The test contained various problems relating to verbal, perceptual and manipulative abilities. The scale consisted of 30 subtests which were arranged in order of increasing difficulties.

The test was found most useful and therefore, caught the attention of American psychologists. In 1916, **Terman** brought out a revised version which came to be known as **Stanford-Binet test**. Since Terman was working in Stanford University where he revised the scale, it is named after Stanford. This ultimately became a model for many tests of intelligence which were developed subsequently.

Termans' revision of the original Binet's scale was based on Binet's idea of mental level and suggestions of **William Stern** (German psychologists) developed the concept of **mental age** (MA) in relation to **chronological age** (CA). Thus Terman employed wholly a new concept and presented the idea of **intelligence quotient** (IQ).

This test is so popular that it has undergone further revisions in the years 1936 and 1961. The fourth and latest revision of the test has been published in 1986. In the earlier revisions only a general composite score was computed to reflect one's IQ. In the last revision, in addition to a composite score, the individual's responses in four content areas namely verbal, reasoning, quantitative reasoning, abstract/visual reasoning and short-term memory are also obtained.

In order to determine mental age (MA), the scale consists of a series of subtests arranged according to age level (chronological age). When a child is tested, the tester first finds the highest level of subtest on which the child passes all the items. The age specified for that subtest is called **'basal age'**. Then the child is given to subtest meant for next older age and continue to give older and older age level tests untill the child fails to give the correct answer for any of the items in a particular age level subtest. This ultimate age is called **ceiling age**. When the results are tallied the obtained score of the child tests his **mental age** (MA). For example, if a 6-year-old child passes all the items for age 5, half those for age 6 and none of those for age 7. Here the basal age is 5 years (60 months), ceiling age is 7 years while the mental age (MA) would be 5 years, + 1/2 years, i.e. 66 months. Suppose the child's chronological age is 72 months (6 years). Hence, on the basis of the obtained scores, the child's mental development is 6 months less than his actual biological age. His IQ will be determined using the formula:

$$\frac{\text{MA}}{\text{CA}}\times 100 = \frac{66 \text{ months}}{72 \text{ months}}\times 100 = 91.67 \text{ or } 92$$

Note here that IQ value shows the relative position of the subject's intelligence in the population of average individuals of the same age. **Thus, IQ is merely a device used to indicate relationship of an individual in intelligence to general population (Cruze).**

Students should also note that an IQ test is an **interval scale** and not **ratios** (often loosely used). In IQ there is no fixed starting point as is there in measures of distance or weight. So, it is inaccurate to treat IQ as ratio scores. For example, an IQ of 160 on an intelligence test does not possess twice the amount of intelligence from one who has a score of 80.

Since IQ is an interval scale of measurement we need norms to interpret the IQ scores of an individual, i.e. the normal level of intellectual performance of the group of the same category of individuals in the population is required.

Stanford–Binet scale has a norm table for mental age and thus the mental age is determined.

Evaluation of the Stanford–Binet scale

Binet's scale has been subjected to several revisions (1911, 1937, 1961, 1972, 1986), each time either with a new set of items or scoring system. Owing to these changes, it is intriguing indeed to make an objective evaluation if one looks at the background view of earlier pioneers of intelligence testing. For example, Terman holds that one who performs poorly on his test were unlikely to improve as their problems are inherited–'dullness seems to be racial or at least inherent in the family stocks from which they come'.* On the other hand, Binet felt optimistic about these French children who performed poorly on the test and emphatically asserted that their scores were not fixed. So, he suggested segregated courses could help, correct their weaknesses.

Terman's attitude is not shared by many psychologists today. However, judging from objective points of views, Terman's Stanford–Binet Test has high reliability. Most of the coefficients are more than .90. Norms have been improved and the test also meet the validity and standardization criteria.

16.4.2 Wechsler Adult Intelligence Scale (WAIS)†

In 1930, David Wechsler provided another test of intelligence. This test differs from Binet's test on two counts—(a) It provides more data. Wechsler created items measuring performance in verbal as well as non-verbal tasks and (b) he designed his first scale for adults and later on in the year 1956, he developed a separate test for children called Wechsler intelligence scale for children (WISC)—revised version WISC-R and also for pre-school children called WPPSI.

Like Stanford–Binet Test, WAIS is also an individual test, *i.e.* taken by one person at a time under trained tester. Also like Stanford, it contains wide varieties of subtests. The subtests are categorized into two groups—verbal and performance. There are 6 verbal and 5 performance or non-verbal subtests.

But, Wechsler's test also differs from Stanford test. Unlike Stanford–Binet scale, the sub-tests are not selected according to age. Wechsler has developed separate tests as detailed below:

(i) Wechsler Adult Intelligence Scale (WAIS) for use on adults with age range from 17 years to old age people.
(ii) Wechsler Intelligence Scale for Children (WISC) for use on children ranging from 6 years to 16 years of age.
(iii) Wechsler pre-school and primary scale of intelligence (WPPSI) for use on children ranging from 4 to 6 years of age.

* Terman (1916), pp. 91–92.
† The latest revised version of the scale is called WAIS-R.

The detailed nature of subtests in WAIS is shown in **Table 16.2**.

TABLE 16.2 Nature of subtests in WAIS

Verbal subtests	*Performance subtests*
(i) Information	(i) Picture arrangement
(ii) General comprehension	(ii) Picture completion
(iii) Memory span	(iii) Block design
(iv) Arithmetic reasoning	(iv) Object assembling
(v) Similarities	(v) Digit symbol
(vi) Vocabularies	

The subtests can be scored separately to enable the examiner to compare the examinee's abilities in various categories. Moreover, the verbal and performance categories can be separately scored to obtain independent IQs on each.

Hence, the test is useful in measuring the intelligence of those who due to lack of opportunities, are poor in verbal abilities such as foreigners or poorly educated. The test is also useful in locating the mental troubles in the case of brain injuries or mentally ill persons.

IQ is determined by standard score (z scroes). In order to obtain z score, the mean and standard deviations are obtained and then equivalent standard score (z score) is obtained. In this case standard scores are called deviation IQs.

Wechsler has standardized his test on a fairly large number of sample (1700) selected proportionately from different geographical and racial subgroups of 7 age categories ranging from 16 to 64 (16–22, 23--29, 30–36, 37–43, 44–50, 51–57, 58–64). The normal distribution of scores served as the norms for assigning standard scores or deviations to derive deviation IQs.

Obviously, Wechsler's scale is not age-based and unlike Stanford–Binet scale, it is a point scale because each correct answer of the test item carries point and IQ is derived on the basis of the total number of credit points earned by the examinee.

Wechsler set the mean of the score equal to an IQ of 100 with 1 SD in score point as equal to 15 IQ points in the normal distribution. Thus, if the examinees score has SD of 1 point below the average or mean score of others in this group, his IQ is set at 85 (IQ-Mean). Similarly if he is 1 SD above mean his IQ is set at 116.

The distribution of IQ on the test is tied directly to the normal distribution curve. The percentage of individuals having IQs below average, above or between any IQ values can be readily predicted from the normal curve. The classification of intellectual categories on the basis of IQ values is shown in **Table 16.3**.

TABLE 16.3 Distribution of IQ categories

IQ	*Classificatory category*	*Percentage*
Above 130	Very superior	2.2
120–129	Superior	6.7
110–119	Bright normal	16.1
90–109	Average	50.0
80–89	Dull normal	16.1
70–79	Borderline	6.7
Below 70	Mentally retarded	2.2

Further breakdown of the distribution of above average IQs is shown below:

WAIS IQ	110	113	119	125	128	135
% Higher	25	20	10	5	3	1

From the above, it is evident that above 1% people have IQ above 135, 10% above 119 and so on.

Evaluating Wechsler's scale

1. **Reliability:** Reliability coefficients for full scale is reported higher than .90. This means that overall scores are likely to vary very little even when the same inidvidual is tested on two different occasions. But, the reliability scores on subtests are relatively weaker. Therefore, those who are interested in identifying strengths or weaknesses of specific abilities must be cautious enough and keep eyes on the reported reliabilities of the subtests. For example, it is quite possible that a 16-year-old boy may not perform well in object assembly test on one occasion but he may perform quite good on the next occasion. The reliability coefficient for this subtest is comparatively low (.52) as per the manual for WAIS-R.
2. **Validity:** The manual discusses nothing about validity. However, other studies have checked correlations between test and academic grades and job performances. Typically, people in white collar jobs averaged higher in verbal scores than performance scores. Whereas skilled blue collar workers attained higher scores on performance than verbal subtests (Hetarazzo, 1972, p. 254). Wechsler scores are well-correlated with Stanford–Binet scale.

16.4.3 Group Intelligence Tests

In course of mental testing movement, psychologists soon began to realize that in most situations group tests of intelligence are either desirable or absolutely essential. For instance, in armed services, quite a large number of people need to be tested each year. In schools and colleges also, the entering students need to be tested in mass. To meet such needs, group tests have been developed.

World War I furnished the impetus for first large scale efforts to develop group tests and psychologists devised two such tests **Army Alfa Test (AAT)** and **Army Beta Test (ABT)**. The AAT was designed for measuring the literates who were conversant with English language while the ABT was designed for measuring the intelligence of illiterates or those who were not well conversant with English language.

Around the World War II, Army psychologists taking full advantage of the advances being made in the field of mental testing, made a drastic revision of the above two tests and renamed as **Army General Classification Test (AGCT)**. It consists of 4 subtests (i) verbal ability, (ii) spatial comprehension, (iii) arithmetic computation and (iv) arithmetic reasoning. The scoring is similar to **Stanford–Binet Test (SBT)**. Average score is kept 100 with SD 20.

Psychologists working in naval wing also developed a similar classification test in terms of intelligence for the new recruits. This test is known as **Naval General Classification Test (NGCT)**. However, NGCT has average score of 50.

Later on defence service psychologists replaced AGCT and NGCT with new test which is known as **Armed Forces Qualification Test (AFQT)**.

Some group tests for civilians have also been developed by **Arthurotis** in 1922 designed primarily to select people for jobs in business and industry. One of the best known such tests in the 'OTIS' self administrating test of mental ability (OTIS-SA). This is a sort of 4-page pencil paper test that can be administered simply with a stop-watch. It can be taken and scored within a time limit of 20–30 minutes. The scores have been correlated on Stanford–Binet Test (SBT) and as such, if one so desires, can convert them to equivalent IQs. The test emphasizes verbal and reasoning factors.

A number of other tests have also been designed such as Scholastic Aptitude Test (SAT), Dr. Mohsin's General Intelligence Test of Brightness (GIT), Dr. Singh's VNART (Verbal, Numerical, Arithmetic, Reasoning Test), Dr. M.C. Joshi's test of general intelligence, S. Jalota's test of intelligence etc.

Evaluating group tests of intelligence

Though, group tests of intelligence serve good many purposes of mental testing, the abilities of large number of people can be tested at a time and hence, economical in time, such tests suffer from certain flaws. These are as follows:

(i) In a group situation, instructions given to examinees may not be well understood by some of them in the group. Such examinees are difficult to be located and therefore, are subjected to make errors. Thus flaw occurs. Scores obtained by such examinees suffer from confident reliability.

(ii) Group tests of intelligence measure general intelligence ('g' factor). Therefore, a high score on such tests does not necessarily predict one's potentiality to succeed in all kinds of jobs requiring some special abilities ('s' factors). Each job requires some special abilities.

(iii) Some of the group test scores are not compatible with individual test. Hence, one's IQ on two kinds of tests are not comparable.

Performance/non-verbal tests

Some tests have been so designed which can be applied on illiterates, very young children and aged persons, i.e. on those who are poor in using language intelligence. Some of the popular tests in this category are mentioned hereinbelow:

(i) Form board test (FBT): It consists of a tray with compartments of different sizes and 10 blocks corresponding to the size formed in the tray. The examinees are required to place each block in the appropriate compartment of the tray. Three trials are taken and each trial with a minimum time consumption are scored.

This test is useful for young children, mentally retarded children and also those who are mentally ill.

(ii) Picture complete test (PCT): In such tests, incomplete pictures are presented before the examinee who are required to complete them by filling in the missing parts by selecting out of several alternative picture figures. **Raven's Progressive Matrices (RPM)** is one such test. In RPM, one incomplete pattern is given. Testees have to find one out of six available alternative figures which will complete the pattern. Scoring is done on the basis of time taken and errors made.

(iii) **Alexander's performance battery:** This battery consists of 3 tests—**Pass along test of Alexander**, **Block design test of Koh** and **Cube Construction Test of Gaw**. Each test is further divided into subtests. Pass along test has 9 subtests, block design has 10 sub-tests and cube construction has 3 subtests. Each subtest can be separately used, however, IQ is determined on the basis of the scores obtained on the whole battery.

Some other tests such as Porteus maze tests, Wechsler's tests, Pinter Perterson performance scale etc. are also in use. But, to describe them all within the limitations of this book is not possible. Readers are advised to consult separate books on **Mental Testing**.

Wechsler's test has already been described earlier in Section 16.4.

16.5 CULTURE FAIR TESTS

During the recent past few decades the test developers began to realize that the tests constructed so far have cultural impacts which were unlikely to be profitable in measuring intelligence of all individuals of all times and places. This realization turned their interests towards devising intelligence tests in a new way which can be administered on all individuals of all societies and all the time with faireness. Fairness here refers to **equality of opportunity or chance for all test takers**, i.e. that cannot deprive or penalize subjects coming from culturally different backgrounds.

Among such tests are the tests constructed by (i) Cattell (1949) called culture free test, (ii) Davis-Eells Games (1953) called culture fair test and (iii) the Kaufman Assessment Battery for children–K–ABC (1983).

Raymond B. Cattell and his wife constructed the test early in 1930s which was published by the Institute of Personality and Ability Testing (IPAT). Cattell agreed with Spearman's 'g' factor which he termed as **fluid general ability** (means an overall capacity that could flow like water into many different situations). He holds that the existing intelligence tests such as Stanford–Binet Test, measure **crystallized intelligence**, *i.e.* the skills that root to a particular time and place (like crystals on the sides of a glass). Stanford–Binet Test is one such test that measures subject's ability in English but not the general ability that lie behind learning all other languages.

The earlier form of Cattell's Test (IPAT test) was called **culture free test**. But, Cattell soon realized that the test in fact, is not free from social fabrics. So, on subsequent modifications and revisions, he termed it as **culture fair test**, *i.e.* the test can be fairly administered on subjects of all cultures and societies.

The test has three levels—one test is meant for children from 4 to 8 years and mentally retarded. Second level applies to children of 8 to 14 years and average adults. The third level aims at high school students and superior adults.

16.5.1 Evaluating Cattell's IPAT Test

Though, Cattell himself considers his test as a major success because it yields similar scores when used in different societies/countries. However, judging from objective standards, one should be cautious enough in drawing conclusions because of variations in the range of reliability and validity coefficients depending on the criteria used. The test-retest reliability is reported 0.80 and above. But when measured by other means, the obtained reliabilities are lower. Validity coefficients also vary depending on the criteria used. When compared to other tests, the validity coefficients vary from 0.34 to 0.85. When school grade is used as criteria, the validity coefficient again varies from

0.23 to 0.46. Cattell has himself realized that his test may not predict school grades. Predictions on the basis of IPAT are likely to vary from occasion to occasion.

16.6 SOME INTELLIGENCE TESTS CONSTRUCTED IN INDIA

Indian psychologists interested in the field of mental testing came to realize that the tests designed and developed in foreign countries cannot be fairly administered on Indian samples because of the difference in socio-cultural milieu. Though, during the recent past, attempts have been made to construct culture fair tests, however, these tests also do not prohibit the cultural ingrains in absolute sense. Culture fair tests only ensure equal opportunity or chance to complete for desirable positions in the society and fairness consists in giving everyone a chance to compete, however unprepared they may be. On the other hand, some believe that equal opportunity means guaranteeing equal proportions of many different groups in desirable positions and fairness consists of somehow constructing the tests that will consist of problems that are equally common and equally motivating to all segments of socio-cultural groups and that they must express these problems in symbols that are culturally common.

Hence, there exists a difference in the views about the nature of equal opportunities which a culture fair test is supposed to ensure.

Considering the above, development of intelligence tests in India has for long been one of the popular academic pursuits. First such efforts was made by **Herbert Rice** in 1922 who standardized Binet's performance scale in Lahore which was named as **Hindustan Binet Performance Point Scale (HBPPS)**. Later in the year 1929, **J. Mcnery** constructed a verbal test in Hindi, English and Urdu languages. **V.V. Kamat** an Indian psychologist also designed a test in Kannad and Marathi languages.

Sohan Lal has also devised an intelligence test for school children in the year 1942. **S.S. Jalota** and **S.K.D. Pandey** jointly developed a group test of intelligence in Hindi which is most popular test in India. In addition, **C.M. Bhatia** in the year 1953, **Dr. S.M. Mohsin** in the year 1954, **Dr. R.N. Singh** in the year 1968, **Long** and **Mehta** in the year 1966, also devised intelligence tests. Out of these, Dr. Mohsin's test which is used for diagnosing the index of brightness (IB) of school children applicable for children of class VI to X is very popular test even today. This test provides two types of IBs—age-based IB and class-based IB. The test also provides percentile norms separately for age and class which shows the relative position of the testee in the population of his age and class groups. The test consists of 6 subtests with verbal items in increasing order of difficulty.

Dr. R.N. Singh's test is known as VNART, i.e. verbal, numerical, abstract reasoning test.

In addition M.C. Joshi has also developed a test of general intelligence.

Subsequently, a number of intelligence tests were either developed originally or were adaptations of tests developed in the West.

Some tests developed in India are given in **Table 16.4**.

TABLE 16.4 Some tests of intelligence developed in India

Verbal	*Performance*
1. Group test of intelligence—PRAYAG MEHTA	1. Adaptation of Wechsler adult performance intelligence scale—R. RAMALINGASWAMY
2. Group test of mental ability—G.S. JALOTA	2. Draw a man test—PRAMILA PATHAK
3. Indian adaptation of Binet–Simon scale —S.K. KULSHRESHTHA	3. Performance test of intelligence—C.M. BHATIA
4. Test for general mental ability—M.C. JOSHI	
5. Bihar test of intelligence—S.M. MOHSIN	

16.7 IQ CONSTANCY

Often question arises as to whether IQ of an individual remains stable? The entire concept of IQ presupposes that an individual maintains his relative position in his group as he grows older. Quite a good number of studies have been done to determine whether or not this is the case. The conclusion in general is that if other conditions (health, type of education, home environment, stress etc.) are equal, IQ does remain stable. However, very young children are exceptions because in them the potentialities are more variable. To support this, **Table 16.5** presents correlations between IQ obtained from some individuals at different ages (Jenson, 1973).

TABLE 16.5 Retest age in years

Test age in years	7	10	14	18
2	0.46	0.37	0.28	0.31
7		0.77	0.75	0.71
10			0.86	0.73
14				0.74

In Table 16.5, correlations between IQs obtained for some individuals at different ages have been shown. The correlations between an IQ at the age of 7 is shown 0.77 at the age 10 and 0.71 at the age 18. The size of correlation appears to decrease as years between testing increases.

A review of several studies shows that though IQs remain stable, in most cases, large shifts after about the age 7 is found. This happens particularly due to some marked changes in the environment and learning opportunities. Such shifts are in both directions positive as well as negative (better or worse). **Boyley** (1970) in a longitudinal study of large number of individuals from birth to 36 years of age found shifts in IQs of more than 15 points, though, the associated variables for such shifts are not easy to specify. In general, emotional and motivational factors appear to play major role (Sontag and others, 1958).

In conclusion, it can be said that IQ is not very stable in the pre-school years (Sontag and others, 1958). However, in most cases, IQs finally stablize fairly well by the time, basic language skills are acquired, i.e. by second or third grade (age 7 to 8). But, at this age also, some sizable shifts depending upon the influence of certain factors cannot be outrightly ruled out.

16.7.1 Factors Affecting Changes in IQ

Changes in IQ may occur which can be attributed to following major factors.

(i) **Time interval between two testings:** It has been observed that if the time interval between two testings is pretty long, changes in IQ level is more readily noticed than when the time interval is relatively less (Sontag, Baker and Nelson, 1958).

(ii) **Age:** Age is also an important factor that influences constancy of IQ during pre-school age (approx. 2 to 3½ years of age) changes or variations in IQ is very rapid. Perhaps, lack of knowledge of language is a contributing factor for such changes in IQ. As the child's age grows, he begins to acquire language skills more efficiently and thus learns larger amount of vocabularies that express his mental potentialities and thus, the level of IQ also increases. In this context, **Kangas** and **Broadway** (1971), **Kendler** (1974) etc. researchers have reported that the coefficient of correlation in IQs of 4 years to 15 years of age varies between .54 and .90. This shows that as one grows older, the range of correlations relatively decreases but becomes stable to the average level.

(iii) **Physiological disturbance:** Some specific physiological states such as hyposecretion of thyroxin, brain tumour, brain trauma due to injury, prolonged illness etc. cause variations in IQ. Wheeler has gathered evidences that hypo TSH cause changes in IQ levels.

(iv) **Unusual environmental conditions:** These include the environmental opportunities such as lack of learning opportunities, constant change of environmental situations such as changes in residence, changes in availability of resources, economic status, traumatic experiences due to natural calamities etc. affect one's mental abilities and thus, changes in IQ is possible.

From the above, it is obvious that intelligence in fact is a matter of interaction of heredity and environment both. Hence, any change in environmental factors, or biological disturbances may cause one's intellectual potentialities to change.

In the Section 16.9, we shall examine the influence of heredity and environment in some greater detail.

16.8 USES OF INTELLIGENCE TESTS

Intelligence tests are very useful tools for evaluating one's level of mental development, knowing the weaknesses, making predictions, prognosticating possible improvements in deficiencies, guiding pupils to profit more from effective schooling and also in providing adequate parental support to the offsprings in learning to adjust with life situation. Intelligence tests today are very much in use in different fields such as educational institutions, industries, mental clinics, child guidance centres, recruitment of personnel for different service sectors—government/private/public undertakings, business houses etc. Following are some of the specific areas where intelligence testing is most often used:

16.8.1 Use of Intelligence Testing in Educational Institutions

Use of intelligence tests in educational institutions, particularly in schools is of great significance. As we have seen earlier, the stormy movement of test construction itself began with problems faced by authorities in France in the primary schools. The intelligence tests enable the teachers and other authorities to identify the educationally backwards and solve their problems. On the basis of periodic test scores, teachers are able not only to classify pupils into different intellectual categories, but also help them by devising special instructional programmes suited to their mental development and also enhancing the process of development to the adequate normal level.

16.8.2 Use of Intelligence Tests for Clinicians

Intelligence tests are also useful for mental clinics and clinicians outside the mental hospitals. Clinicians are able to score the intellectual levels and interpret them for diagnostic purposes, prognosis and deciding the therapeutic or rehabilitative programmes.

16.8.3 Use of Intelligence Tests for Parents

This is one of the primary utilities of intelligence tests. Almost every parent seems keenly interested n getting their offsprings tested and knowing his/her IQ. They often say I'd like to find my son's/ laughter's IQ. The family thinks he is precocious'. Such curiosities are often useful in determining he parental guidance for proper development and effective schooling of children.

16.8.4 Use of Intelligence Tests for Child Guidance Centres

ntelligence tests are also useful for those who are engaged in child guidance centres. Intelligence cores provide them with information about the unique talents of each child to the requirements f the educational courses, jobs and thus, is advantageous for both the individual and the society.

Similarly, intelligence tests are of great use in many other fields such as training centres, ecruitment or selection of personnel for different service sectors, business organizations etc. where nan's ability to work is to be assessed.

16.9 GENETIC AND ENVIRONMENTAL DETERMINANTS OF INTELLIGENCE—CONTROVERSY

16.9.1 Genetic (Heredity) and Environmental Influences on Intelligence

Whether intelligence is determined by heredity or by environment?—is a controversial issue much ke 'nature and nurture' controversy. There seems no end to the debate. The most appropriate nswer to this question would be that the two factors interact. Undoubtedly, genetic factors seem) play some basic role in determining intelligence. But how does heredity plays a role is difficult) establish on two counts: (i) It is presumed that perhaps many different genes play a role. hus, the mystery of genetics is difficult to be understood by studying merely a few genes. i) Secondly, it is difficult to conduct controlled breeding study with humans as we study about the lants or animals. Hence, psychologists and even the genetic scientists are left with no alternative ut to rely on the analysis of intelligence as it shows up in a natural way over the course of evelopment.

In view of the above facts, the researchers compare the IQs of people who differ in their egrees of genetic relatedness. For example, comparing the IQs of monozygotics Mz (*e.g.* identical vins) with the IQs of dizygotic Dz (fraternal twins). Fraternal twins on the average are identical 1 50% of their genes whereas identical twins are identical in 100% of their genes. Therefore, if ntelligence is influenced by genes, it is supposed that identical twins (Mz—mono-zygotic) would e more similar in IQ as compared to fraternal twins (Dz—dizygotics). **Scarr** (1981) has found ubstantial differences in this direction in 20 of his studies in which Mz twins were compared to z twins. These studies were conducted across various cultures such as Britain, Finland, France, ermany, Sweden and United States. Findings of all these studies in general lend support to the otion that IQ is considerably influenced by heredity.

Some other kinds of studies also provide similar conclusion. Some researchers attempted to lentify identical twins who were separated from the pair in childhood and were reared in different nvironments. The objective of such studies was to study the extent of similarity in IQs of the twin pairs. This type of studies done in three different countries showed that the correlation i IQs of separated twins ranged from 0.67 to 0.78 on a scale that ranged from 0.00 to 1.00. Suc high correlations again suggest the significance of genetic similarity that leads to similarity i intelligence.

Scar (1981) also attempted to study IQ similarities between parents and adopted childre These studies also suggested higher degree of similarity in intelligence of adopted children wit those of their biological parents rather than those of adoptive parents. However, in some of thes adoption studies, the IQs of adopted children were found tending towards adoptive parents instea of their biological parents. In such cases it was noticed that the presence of higher level of IQ of adoptive parents raised the IQ level of disadvantaged children and hence, lend support to th nurture (environmental) side of the debate. The environmental factors that seem to be significant i raising the IQ level include the factors such as nutrition, family background, qualities of schooling harmonious interrelationship and encouragement by the rearing parents.

Some researchers such as **Farber** (1981), **Eysenck** and **Kamin** (1981) and some of th earliest genetic evidences indicate some methodological errors owing to which the researche were able to establish close relationship between intelligence and genetic factors. However, w cannot outrightly ignore the influence of environmental factors because these factors also play substantial role. In the studies involving identical twins the sibling pairs who are not twins an unrelated pairs, it has generally been found that such pairs if reared together tend closer in the IQs than those who are reared separately. Further, it has also been found that those who are reare in extremely poor rearing conditions are associated with low IQ whereas those who are reared i enriched environmental conditions with better educational opportunities are associated with high IQs (Ramey and Campbell, 1979; Skeels, 1966).

In view of the above, it is evident that nature-nurture controversy is not likely to be resolve Therefore, most of the researchers now believe that 'genes' or genetic factors endow us with **reaction range**, i.e. the range of possible intellectual level that one may attain, depends partly o nature (genetic factors) and partly on the environment in which we are born and reared or nurture **The genetic endowments set the limits that we can attain while the environment determin what we actually realize or attain.** The environment in fact, provides the opportunities that c boost IQ or the level that can be achieved.

Thus, it is evident that intelligence is a product of a complex interaction of both the genet factors and environmental conditions. Probably, the maximum limit is drawn by the genetic facto within which the actual development depends upon the support from environmental conditions.

In this context, **Jacobson et al.** (1971) have also come to the conclusion that systemat learning and beneficial interpersonal experiences produce significant gains in intelligence' Hence, environment provides supplementary diet to the enrichment of intelligence.

16.10 SOME IMPORTANT ENVIRONMENTAL DETERMINANTS OF INTELLIGENCE

Among the environmental factors, some of the pertinent life situations have very extensive been studied and significant relationship has been established. Among these, a few environment correlates of intelligence are as follows:

---

* Jacobson, L.L., Benger S.E., Bergman, R.L., William J. and Greeson, L.E., *Child Development*, 197 pp. 1399–1415.

16.10.1 Gender Differences

Early studies of IQ differences between boys and girls did not find any significant difference due to difference in gender. However, some more recent studies using modern measuring devices have revealed some interesting differences. For example, **Mayer** and **Bending** (1961) in their studies found no apparent gender difference at 8th grade level but when the same subjects were retested at 11th grade, girls were found superior to boys in verbal comprehension, reasoning, number and word fluency. Girls also proved less consistent than the boys in performance and their ability test scores showed a lower correlation with school achievement.

Sweeny (1953) in a study of college students found men's superiority in solving ingenious and logical problems.

Anastasi (1958) and Taylor (1963) have also found that in some kinds of problems, men perform better than women while in some other kinds, women outperform men. In general, the researchers could note that adult males perform better in mathematical and spatial tasks, viz. men do better in understanding how parts of a machine fit together—a cognitive task requiring spatial ability or how to sail boat in a zigzag course against the wind. On the other hand, women are found to be more fluent in speaking, rote memory, have bigger vocabularies and are more sensitive to grammar.

But, none of these studies went unchallenged. If the contradictory findings are put together, it would be reasonable to conclude that boys in general excel in some primary abilities while the girls in others. Hence, if a general test is applied, this kind of difference is more likely to be cancelled out and thus, no gender difference in overall intelligence would be found.

16.10.2 Health

Generally it is believed that a child who is superior in intelligence is found inferior in health and vice versa. But, scientific studies have nullified this common belief. In fact, superior heredity is an important factor in both physical and mental superiority (**Terman**, 1925).

Many studies relating to hormone deficiencies or oversecretions, diseased tonsils or prolonged illness etc. have shown that level of intellectual functioning hardly changes during post-recovery periods. However, it is also true that good general health makes it easier to work up to one's full mental capacity (Rogers, 1922; Lowe, 1923). Thus association between health and intelligence is only to the extent that good nutrition and sound health permits full utilization of one's mental capabilities and not that it is an essential condition that brings about changes in IQ levels.

Thyroid hormonal deficiency (TSH) in infancy, however, has been reported to result in **cretinism** and is also found to interfere seriously with initial development of intelligence. Such deficiencies occurring even after 2 years of age, may also lower down the level of intelligence. But with proper and timely treatment such conditions may be corrected. As for other endocrine glands relationship between their secretions and intelligence has not yet been established. It is perhaps because studies on this aspect has very recently begun and substantial findings are still awaited. Evidences relating to pituitary disorders are also lacking.

The works of Howard and Worrell (1952) have, however, revealed some adverse effects of premature birth on the level of intelligence. But, this too can be attributed more to emotional adjustment being affected due to premature birth and over protection being provided by the parents. While rearing prematured born babies, they are considered most delicate.

16.10.3 Family Structure and Size

Quite a good number of research studies have revealed that families differ widely in their structural patterns. This include the size of the family, sex composition and sex distribution of the family, ordinal positions of the siblings, absence of parental figures nurturing by governances or other relatives are some of the important family variables that affect proper development of intellectual potentialities. It has generally been found that middle born individuals are in constant conflict with the elder and younger siblings. Such conflicts make them more competitive and that indirectly accelerates intellectual potential (Gille, 1954; Heyer, 1950). These researchers have also found negative correlations between intelligence and number of siblings more particularly in low socio-economic group. The possible reason may be that larger the number of siblings in the family, poorer are the available facilities needed for enriching intellectual abilities. Children in larger families are generally deprived of many facilities such as less money per child, deprived of proper nutrition, poor educational opportunities etc.

In different societies and families of the same society, the conventional patterns of rearing children of two sexes differ and the parental attitude towards two sexes also differ sharply. Such differences cause either positive or negative impacts on the development of potentialities. Thus, intelligence is affected by the attitude with which siblings of two sexes are reared and nurtured (Mishra, 1974).

However, the patterns of variations also depend upon various other factors such as socio-economic status, differences in racial status, parent's own intellectual and achievement orientations, cultural backgrounds etc.

16.10.4 Effects of Training

Gray and **Klaus** (1965) and **Gray** (1966) in one study found that progressive retardation in mental development may be enriched by special training. He selected two groups of children of ages 4 and 5 who were designated as T_1 and T_2 respectively. A 10-week summer session was designed to foster achievement, motivation and also to increase perceptual and language skills. The researchers also selected control groups T_3 and T_4 which had only periodic tests. For both the experimental groups (T_1 and T_2) sharp gains during special training could be noted in the case of experimental group (T_1 and T_2) while no such gain could be evidenced in the case of control group (T_3 and T_4).

16.10.5 Cultural Factors

It is increasingly realized that intellectual processes and skills are determined by socio-cultural contexts. Since successful adaptation to one's own socio-cultural milieu is considered a sign of intelligence, it is reasonable to assume that different behaviours may represent intelligence in different cultures. We, generally, observe differential patterns in different cultures with regard to certain behaviours which are considered as worthwhile or valuable. For example, in certain cultures, farming skills are considered more valuable than skills needed to become a lawyer. Accordingly, a good farmer is viewed as more intelligent than a lawyer. Thus, culture is considered as cultural genre (product). Different cultures also differ in their notions about what constitutes intelligence.

Among some of the experiments on innate cultural differences in intelligence are those of **Philips** (1912), **Kayuo** (1913), **Furguson** (1916) and others. Their findings have demonstrated that Whites are superior to Negros in their IQs.

However, most of the researchers hold the opinion that cultural differences in intelligence is not a matter of inheritance rather a matter of environmental handicaps in different societies and cultures.

Thus, we find that intelligence depends upon various factors which include both the genetic and environmental aspects of human life.

16.11 INDIVIDUAL DIFFERENCES IN INTELLIGENCE

Like many other psychological traits, intelligence is also found to be distributed in the population in such a way that most people on the basis of level of IQs fall in the middle of a normal distribution curve and only a few very high or very low scorers fall at the either extremes of bell-shaped curve—normal distribution curve (see **Figure 16.4**)

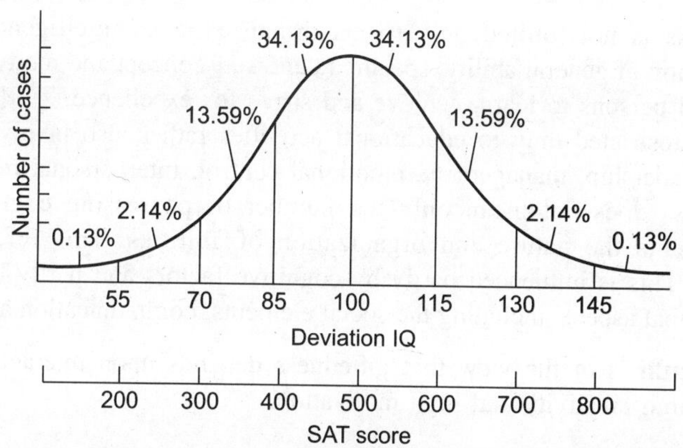

FIGURE 16.4 Normal distribution curve for IQs and SAT (scholastic aptitude test) scores.

Norms for large groups of measurements often approximate the normal curve. The numbers bove the curve give the percentage of people in each of the indicated segments, viz. 13.59% f population obtain IQ scores between 115 and 130 on the right—higher side—while similar ercentage of people obtain IQ between 85 and 70 on the left side—lower than average. Average eople score IQ of 100 ± 15 who are in the middle of the curve comprising 34.13 + 34.13% = 8.26% of the population.

From the Figure 16.4, it is evident that most people in the population are average in ntelligence (68.26%) and as high or low scorer deviates from the normal, they are categorized s superior or inferior in intelligence. However, as the distance in a level from average IQ level n either direction increases, the percentage of people in the population goes on decreasing. This hows that the superiormost intelligents or the inferiormost intelligents percentage of people are ery few (above 115 IQ and below 85 IQ).

On the basis of the normal distribution of IQ the total population can be classified as uperiormost or genius, average and mentally retarded or deficient (challenged). Till now we have discussed the various characteristic features of intelligence that concern the average intelligence Let us now consider briefly about the characteristics of other two deviants—the **geniuses** or **gifte** and **mentally retarded** or **deficients** (challenged) intelligences.

16.11.1 Giftedness (Genius)

The term **gifted** is an adjective term which refers to a person endowed with 'one gift' or man gifts; exceptionally talented or intelligent. In terms of IQ level, there is no agreed definitio of giftedness. Some consider an IQ of 120 and up to be sufficient evidence of exceptionalit others regard IQ 140 and above. The recent researchers however do not bother about a deadlir of IQ level rather take into account some salient characteristic features of exceptionally talente persons. Accordingly, they define giftedness **as superior ability in any worthwhile line human endeavour including moral, physical, emotional, social, intellectual or aesthetic li of humanity**. From this definition, it is evident that:

(i) Gifted persons exhibit high levels of performance as compared to average persons of h group.
(ii) Giftedness is not limited only to performance on an intelligence test, rather it is combination of general ability, specific talent, self-concept and motivation that predispos the gifted persons to learn, achieve and strive for excellence.
(iii) It is not restricted only to educational activities rather also involve other areas such sports, leadership, management, emotional control, interpersonal relationships etc.
(iv) Giftedness does not mean only the number of possessing cognitive abilities, rath it represents the nature and organization of abilities. This refers to the processi abilities. This is influenced partly by cognitive factors and partly by the personality a innovational aspects including the social elements, communication and ethical dimensio

Joseph Renzulli is of the view that giftedness depends upon interaction of three factors high intelligence, high creativity and high motivation.

Characteristics of gifted individuals

Gifted children show early signs of being exceptional. During infancy, such children show la attention span, good recognition memory, preference for novelty, overreactivity to sensatic and early onset of language. Following are some of the salient characteristics of gif children.

(a) A higher order in thinking process, problem solving and decision-making.
(b) Transferring skills to new problems and solving problems insightfully.
(c) Independent thinking and nonconformism.
(d) High on self-efficacy and internal locus of control.
(e) High incidence of social and emotional problems.
(f) Intrinsically motivated to achieve mastery, derive pleasure from work and possess h esteem about their intellectual capacities.
(g) Preference for being solitary and introverted.
(h) Possibility of showing giftedness in one area and poor learning in another.

Identifying gifted children

The tests of intelligence and achievement are most frequently employed to identify gifted children. Several social programmes for gifted children use rigid cutoff points such as IQs 130, 135, 150 or 160 or achievement at about 95 percentile or above. During recent times, certain various other types of data are used to identity giftedness. These include:

(a) Performance on good individual intelligence tests
(b) Expert's judgement
(c) Educational records, *viz.* achievement scores, teacher's gradings etc.
(d) Performance on group intelligence test
(e) Appraisal of social and emotional maturity and adjustment
(f) Parent's interview
(g) Individual's ambitions and drive
(h) Peer and self-nominations

Giftedness in fact is a multidimensional term. Though, differences is gifted and talented may be noticed at all levels, it is more pronounced at the secondary school level. Some gifted youngsters are just slightly above average while others are very unusual to the extent being extremely rare. Some are gifted in just one area while others show it in many areas.

Gifted children also differ in motivation and interest.

16.11.2 Intellectually Retarded or Deficient

Intellectual deficiency is referred to as mental subnormality. Such people are generally identified by two distinct characteristic features.

(i) They attain IQs below 70 on an appropriate intelligence test and
(ii) They are far poor in adaptive skills to cope with ordinary daily tasks.

During early childhood, individuals' adaptation is judged by attainment of developmental skills such as walking and talking, during school by academic and coping skills such as telling time and using money and during adulthood, by vocational performances and social responsibilities.

In accordance with the two criteria as stated above, the mentally deficients may be defined as follows:

The mentally deficients are those who in terms of performance on intelligence test are two or more standard deviations (SDs) below the mean (average) accompanied by limitations in adaptive functioning such as to cope with and common tasks of dailylife which are expected of one's age and situations.

In terms of this definition, a person having IQ less then 70 coupled with inability to manage everyday life activities like a normal person of his age are classified as mentally deficients or retarded (challenged).

As for the different levels of mental deficiencies, the main features are shown in **Table 16.6**.

TABLE 15.6 Characteristics of different levels of mental retardation

Areas of functioning	*Levels of mental retardation*		
	Mild	*Moderate*	*Severe*
IQ Range	50–70	35–49	20–34
Self help skills	Feeds and dresses self and cares for own toilet needs	Has difficulties and requires training but can learn adequate self help skills	No to partial skills but some can care for personal needs on limited basis
Speech and communication	Receptive and expressive, language is adequate, understands communication	Receptive and expressive, language is adequate, has speech problems	Receptive language is limited to good, expressive, language is limited to poor
Academics	Optimal learning environment—3rd to 6th grade	Very few academic skills—first or second grade is maximal	No academic skills.
Social skills	Has friends, can learn to adjust quickly	Capable of making friends but has difficultly in many social situations	Not capable of having real friends, no social interaction
Vocational adjustment	Can hold a job, competitive to semicompetitive primarily unskilled work	Sheltered work environment, needs constant supervision	Generally no employment, needs constant care
Adult living	Usually marries, has children, needs help during stress	Usually does not marry or have children, dependent on others	No marriage or children, always dependent on others

A point of caution in categorizing mentally deficients

While categorizing an individual's mental deficiencies, we need to take two important precautions:

(i) A person may score low on intelligence performance test because of some physiological ill states such as vision problems, hearing defects, or bad health, emotional upsets etc. Therefore, we should first examine if a person is of normal physical and mental health and then if he obtains a poor IQ it may be indicative of hindered mental growth and development.

(ii) While categorizing mental deficiencies, individual's linguistic and cultural background must be taken into consideration.

16.12 CAUSES OF MENTAL RETARDATION

Many organic conditions have been found associated with mental retardation. For example, **Down Syndrome** has been found to be associated with mild to severe retardation. Persons suffering from this syndrome display distinctive physical characteristics such as slanted eyes, stubby limbs, thin hair etc.

Down syndrome is genetically caused by possession of an extra **chromosome**.

Another cause of retardation is **Phenylke tonuria**—a kind of metabolic disorder that is caused by an inherited enzyme deficiency. If such deficiencies are not caught and treated during infancy, it may cause retardation.

Still another organic condition that can cause retardation is **hydrocephaly**, *i.e.* excessive accumulation of **cerebrospinal fluid** in skull resulting in the destruction of brain tissues.

In addition, scientists have studied various other organic or genetic factors associated with mental retardation of various natures and types.

Quite a good number of environmental factors also cause mental retardation. These include—low socio-economic status, greater marital instability, deprivation from parents during infancy, certain traumatic or shocking experiences, prolonged illness, inadequate nutrition and medical care, lower quality of schooling, too much parental expectations, recurrent failures in attaining aspired goals etc. are some of the important environmental and psychogenic factors of retardation.

16.12.1 Education and Treatment for Mentally Retarded

In general, parents come to know that their child is mentally retarded, become anxious and start worrying to adopt any measure in the hope of curing the retardation. Most often, certain dramatic stories appear in newspapers about incidents of certain cases who have been cured by certain means by tantriks, doctors or similar other professional practitioners. Such stories often catch the victim parents to be lured to make a rush in the hope of getting their child cured to a normal level of intellectual capacities. However, once, severe kind of retardation is diagnosed, cure is not possible except that by special training programme, sometimes may produce modest change in IQ level and adaptability. Such trainings may also increase some social skills.

Mentally retarded children in fact need rehabilitative programme and improvement in the environment. A friendly style of interpersonal behaviour with smile is a major asset for the mentally retarded children. In rehabilitative centres an affectionate warming environment is provided along with helping the child through affectionate fulfilment of their requirements, giving special training to do something they can. Such efforts go a long way in enhancing their abilities as well as adapting to the environment by performing dailylife activities. However, they need constant care and help in a healthier psycho-social environment and meeting their basic needs.

In sum, though education and training are not likely to cure mental retardation, but a substantial difference in personal, social and occupational adjustment may be brought about.

16.13 SPECIAL ABILITIES: APTITUDES

16.13.1 Nature

An aptitude is a combination of such characteristics that is indicative of one's capacity or ability to acquire some specific knowledge or skill. Each one of us possesses various qualities in different proportions to learn and perform. For example, acquisition of ability to learn some specific language, learning music, doing something mechanical work etc. These potentialities can be harnessed by appropriate training. In other words, suppose a person has no ability to discriminate between pitch, tone or rhythm and other aspects of sensitivity. Such persons cannot become a musician even after a great deal of training and practice. On the other hand, those who possess such abilities, they can become a good musician after training and practice.

There are very fine distinctions between intelligence, aptitude and achievement. Intelligence refers to the ability of a person to do certain thing at a given time. Aptitude refers to the potential ability to perform a task which generally consists of a combination of abilities. Achievement refers to realisation of the goal involving performance at any given point of time in a specific subject or course. Thus, **aptitudes are specilised abilities required in specific occupation and activities.**

16.13.2 Measurement of Aptitude

Aptitude tests are applied to test and predict the potential of doing something. Many aptitude tests such as clerical aptitude, mechanical aptitude, musical aptitude, scholastic aptitude, engineering aptitude, medical aptitudes etc. have been developed to predict success in specific professional areas. Each of these tests usually consists of a number of subtests. Several multiple aptitude batteries have also been developed. For example, some of the prominent and popular batteries are mentioned below:

(i) The Differential Aptitude Test (DAT)
(ii) The General Aptitude Test Battery (GATB)
(iii) Armed Services Vocational Aptitude Battery (ASVAB) etc.

The salient characteristics of one of these batteries most often used in educational settings are described hereinbelow:

The DAT (Differential Aptitude Test) was initially developed for educational and vocational guidance of students for grades 8 through 12. Later on, this battery has also been found useful for vocational counselling of young adults who are out of school and in the selection of employees. This battery consists of 8 subtests:

- Verbal reasoning (VR)
- Numerical ability (NA)
- Abstract reasoning (AR)
- Clerical speed and accuracy (CSA)
- Mechanical reasoning (MR)
- Space relations (SR)
- Spelling (S)
- Language use (LU)

J.M. Ojhas has developed an Indian adaptation of DAT. In addition, many other aptitude tests have been developed in India for measuring scientific, teaching, clerical, engineering, scholastic, medical, literary and other aptitudes.

16.14 INTELLIGENCE IN INDIAN CONTEXT

Indian thinkers have also shown their deep concern for human potentials and explored its nature in the context of self, society, the universe and also beyond all these. If we examine the Indian thinkers' views minutely, it would be clear that Indian scholars hold a **holistic** view of intelligence and encompass both the aspects of mental faculty—cognitive and non-cognitive domains—in integrative fashion. In Indian language, the term **Buddhi** is used for the English term intelligence which is broader in meaning than what intelligence means. The term *buddhi* includes the following senses:

(i) Mental vigour or power of forming and retaining conceptions and general notions.
(ii) Reason, intellect, mind, discernment and judgement.
(iii) Perception, comprehension, apprehension and understanding.
(iv) Knowledge of one's own self-conscience, will and desire.
(v) Presence of mind, ready wit and skill.

Thus, the term *buddhi* is pervasive that encompasses the cognitive, affective and motivational aspects of life. According to J.P. Das, *buddhi* refers to a mental state of alertness that wakes up the individuals to notice and recognizes the aspects of environment, enables him to understand, comprehend, evaluate, judge and decide the course and direction of action to be executed in the given situation. It also includes determination and mental efforts, discrimination and other intellectual processes of knowledge.

According to Indian thinkers, intelligent persons possess the following four kinds of competencies:

(i) **Cognitive competence:** For example, contextual sensitivity, comprehensiveness, discriminability, problem solving, effective communication and understanding the things in totality.

(ii) **Social competence:** For example, following the social norms, service to elders, obedience, helping the needy showing concern about the environment, effectiveness in interpersonal communication.

(iii) **Entrepreneurial competence:** For example, hard work, industriousness, commitment, vigilance, goal-directed behaviours, self-independence etc.

(iv) **Emotional competence:** It refers to emotional intelligence such as adequate control over emotions, honesty, politeness, realistic in approach, self-appraisal and good conduct, avoiding negative feelings and enhancing positive affects.

Thus, unlike the IQ notion of intelligence, the Indian view is not restricted only to the cognitive aspects of intellect but it also includes the socio-emotional domains and hence, Indian concept of intelligence is pragmatic, i.e. **sthir buddhi** or **pragya** (stable intellect).

'*Buddhi*' in Indian context has well been defined in Shreemad Bhagwat Gita in the following terms:

The moment an individual is able to get rid of all his desires (aspirations), impulses and begins to remain contended in the 'self' (*atman* or soul) the person is said to have attained the stage of **Sthir buddhi** or **Pragya**.* This notion obviously refers to the emotional control and enrichment of one's soul (self) as the essential aspects of *buddhi*.

Thus, the Indian concept of intelligence is pragmatic and pervasive in nature.

---

* प्रजहाति यदा कामान् सर्वान् पार्थ मनोगतान्।
आत्मन्येवात्मना तुष्टः स्थित प्रज्ञास्तदोच्यते॥
Shreemad Bhagwat Gita, Chapter 2:55.

SUMMARY

- Intelligence is a general ability of performing an activity. It is a global capacity which is demonstrated in a wide varieties of activities—learning, problem solving adaptations, abstract thinking, grasping, comprehending, making comparisons etc.
- There are several synonyms to the word intelligence, viz. ability, talent, capacity, competency, *chaturya, medha, buddhi* and many more.
- Though, intelligence has variously been defined, the most agreeable terms of definition is that it is a global capacity in which an individual attempts to shape and select the environment that fits well for his adaptation.
- There are various theories of intelligence that describe how intelligence is structured and functions.
- Some of the classical theories of intelligence are Spearman's two-factor theory, Thurston's primary ability theory, Guilford's factor theory, Thorndike's multifactorial theory, Horn and Donaldson's view, Jensen's theory etc.
- The contemporary theories of intelligence include Gardiner's multiple intelligence theory, process oriented theories of Piaget, Bruner, Sternberg's triarchic theory and PASS model theory of Das et al.
- To measure intelligence, various kinds of tests have been developed which are either verbal or non-verbal.
- The verbal and non-verbal tests are further classified into individual and group tests.
- Some of the popular tests of intelligence are Stanford-Binet test, Wechsler's tests, Form board test, picture assembly test, Alexander's performance test battery etc.
- The intelligence test scores are converted into intelligence quotient (IQ) by applying the formula $-\frac{MA}{CA}\times 100$. Mental age is obtained on the basis of norms developed from the test performance scores gathered from a large sample.
- Some psychologists have attempted to develop culture fair tests which can be fairly administered to measure the intellectual abilities of individuals across the cultures.
- Indian psychologists have also made active efforts to develop tests in Indian contexts. They have also attempted to adapt some of the foreign tests on Indian samples.
- Usually IQ rapidly changes during infancy through childhood and by later childhood it becomes stable. However, due to certain intervening factors changes by ± 15 points in IQ is possible.
- Intelligence is influenced jointly by heredity and environment both. In fact, develop-ment of intelligence is a matter of interplay of both the genetic endowments and environmental opportunities.
- In addition, intelligence is also determined by several other environmental factors such as gender difference, health, family, early learning and training and cultural factors.
- Individuals differ in the level of IQ. In population IQ level is normally distributed and classified as gifted, average (normal) and mentally retarded.
- Aptitude refers to special abilities that can be enhanced through training.
- Indian concept of intelligence is holistic and pragmatic.

CHAPTER 17

Personality

17.1 INTRODUCTION

Psychology as a scientific study of adjustive behaviour concerns itself with almost all the aspects of behaviour from simple avoidance reactions in an unicellular amoeba to the highest levels of human mental and intellectual activities. In describing various aspects of behaviour, psychologists have noted that individual differs widely from each other in feelings, emotions, cognitions and ways of responding to the various aspects and situations of the socio-cultural and physical environment in which he lives, grows and interacts. Such differences are also found in their effectiveness to respond to the situations. Everyone's social effectiveness is unique and leaves unique impressions of him on others. This uniqueness refers to one's 'personality' which marks his identity distinct from others. Psychologists try to understand the individual as distinct person—we call **Personality**.

While focusing on personality, psychologists step into a very interesting area of psychology that deals with the totality of a person's existence. It helps to understand the **uniqueness** and **commonality** found within and between the individuals.

Psychologists who specialize in the area of personality, try to measure personality, describe individual differences and assess the extent of such differences. On the basis of their study of personality, they also try to predict behaviour.

Efforts are on to understand personality and it has been the concern of thinkers for a long time. This has led to the development of several theoretical approaches and also the factors that determine the uniqueness in the person as a whole.

The present chapter focuses its attention on this important aspect of individual and discusses the various concerns—description, theoretical formulations, types, measurement of personality and the factors that determine the development of personality. This would go a long way in understanding what a piece of work is man! how noble in reason! and how infinite is faculty?*

---

* Shakespeare, *Hemlet*, Act II, Scene II.

17.2 MEANING OF PERSONALITY

In everyday talks, we very frequently discuss 'personality'. Statements like, 'he has a lot of personality', someone has no personality, 'he or she has no personality' etc. are some of the examples of our dailylife conversations in which the term personality is used. What do we mean by saying so? The phrase—'a lot of personality' refers to the attractiveness of the person in reference—particularly on initial contact with the person. 'A poor personality' refers to such attributes which are usually descarded because such attributes are either inappropriate or undesirable and hence, inattractive. The term 'no personality' means that the person does not possess any such qualities that may catch the attention of others. Thus, the above phrases refer to one's effectiveness in social situations. But, such meanings are based on superficial or surface level observations and evaluation of the person. Hence, are of little scientific values.

Another way of viewing personality is to identify some striking characteristics or attributes of a person. Thus, we refer somebody as having **aggressive personality** or **shy personality**. Such identifications of personality categories are based on certain striking features of the person that distinguishes him from others. But, such meanings too are based on superficial or surface level oservations and interpretations.

The term 'personality' is derived from Latin word—'PERSONA', menaings 'mask'—especially worn by the actors in theatres. This was subsequently adopted by **Romans**. For Romans, the word 'persona' refers to **as one appears and not as one actually is.**

But psychologists neither concern with the common usage of the term nor with its heritage. For them, the term personality refers to such characteristics of the individual(s) that distinguishes each individual with the other. Though, there seems no agreement among the psychologists with regard to any precised definition of personality, however, attempts have been made to define personality in the reference to their beliefs about the nature of the **person** as a whole (in totality). Let us try to understand the term with a workable definition offered by **'Witting** and **Williams–III' (1984)**. To quote him—**"Personality is a set of characteristics—unique for each individual—that determine a person's identity and behavioural pattens"**.* To put it in simpler terms, we may say that 'personality refers to characteristic patterns of behaviour and ways of thinking that determines a person's unique adjustment to his environment'. The word 'characteristic' here implies some sort of consistency in behaviour owing to which a person tends to act and think in a certain way irrespective of the situation. For example, one may recollect a person who seldom gets angry regardless of various provocations while on the other there may be a person who may be found to be excessively aggressive even at slightest irritation. Obviously, the behavioural pattern in the above two situations are distinct from each other which are marked by some kind of consistency. The consistency, however, is relative and specific to a particular environmental context only. If the environmental contexts change, changes in behaviour pattern may also occur. This is the reason that personality is called a **'dynamic organization'** of tendencies.

Personality is in fact, an organized pattern of tendencies specific to a person. It includes many properties such as the intellectual abilities, motives acquired in the process of growing up, emotional reactivity, attitudes, beliefs, moral values, philosophy of one's life etc. All these together form an organized pattern of the individual's 'self' and thus, become related to the person as a whole. These are referred to as the 'psycho-physical systems' or simply the **tendencies**. These are called psycho-physical because, these are 'psychological in nature but have

* Amino F. Wittings and Gunney Williams–III, *'Psychology': An Introduction*, McGraw Hills, Inc., 1984, p. 422.

'physiological base' in the individual's neural, glandular or general body states. These systems in fact, constitute the potentials for activity and, therefore, referred to tendencies.

Following the above description about the nature of personality, **'Allport'** (1937) offered a definition which is considered most appropriate even today. To quote him—**'Personality is the dynamic organization within the individual of those psycho-physical systems that determine his unique adjustment to the environment'.**

About a decade later, **White** (1948) simplifying Allport's formulations substituted the word 'psycho-physical systems' and used the term **'tendencies'** in its place. According to him—**'Personality is the organization of individual's personal patterns of tendencies'.**

Thus, it is clear that the concept of 'Personality' refers to the sum total of ways in which an individual reacts and interacts with others in the environment.

17.3 APPROACHES TO THE STUDY OF PERSONALITY

The nature of personality is very complex. Psychologists while pursuing the study of personality, share with us to answer a few questions of our common curiosities such as when some people encounter similar situation, why do they react differently? Why some people like to take risks and enjoy dangerous or adventurous situations while others prefer to spend time in reading novels, watching television or playing card games? Are these differences stable throughout one's life? They try to explore the characteristics of different personalities and also the origin or sources of such differences in personalities. Thus, the study of personality is an effort to understand, explain and predict the similarities and differences consistencies and inconsistencies, stabilities and instabilities or changes in behaviour. This has led to the development of different approaches to view personality in the totality of a person's behaviour. These approaches differ on the emphasis laid on 'what', 'why' and 'how' of behaviour and present different models of human being. Each of these models throws lights on some aspects of personality and not all the aspects. A few of such approaches are being described briefly hereunder:

17.3.1 Types and Traits: Development of Taxonomy (Trait and Type Classification)

We notice wider range of diversities in human behaviour and use labels that help in classifying personality characteristics. For example, if someone describes his intimate friend by stating that he or she is a good-natured, dependable, loyal, sociable and calm—he is using certain trait names about his friend. Psychologists do use several traits and types to describe personality. They attempt to categorize human personality by observing the behavioural patterns systematically. While doing so, they refer to certain basic types in which people are classified. These types are categories which are exclusive and do not overlap. These are discontinuous or discrete dimensions. Thus, personalities are grouped together in terms of observed similarities and put in different classificatory types.

In contrast to type approach, the trait approach, refers to certain specific dimensions along which people differ in consistent and stable ways.

A. Type approach to personality

Based on certain similarities, some expected behavioural characteristics have been subjected to typological classifications. Such efforts have been made since very ancient times. For example, the founding father of ancient Indian medical science—**Charak Sanhita** classifies people in terms of three basic elements—called **Doshas**. These are **vaat**, **pitta** and **kaph**. **vaata** is a product of **akash** (ether) and **vayu** (the air). **Pitta** emerges out of the interaction of **vayu** (the air) and the **agni** (fire) while **kapha** is produced by the joint action of **jal** (water) and **prithvi** (earth). Thus, the five biophysical components of body—the akash (ether), vayu (air), agni (fire), jal (water) and prithvi (earth, soil) together get charged with some intrinsic forces in terms of properties. The **vaata** is dry, cold, light, subtle, clear and rough. The **pitta** is slightly unctuous (oily or greasy), hot, acute, fluid, acid, mobile and poignant (stinging to taste). The **kapha** is heavy, cold, soft, unctuous (greasy or oily), sweet, stable and viscid (sticky). Each of these refers to a temperament which is called **prakriti** (nature) of the person. Thus, personality on the basis of the properties of these three **doshas** is classified into three temperamental categories, namely **vattaj**, **pittaj** and **kaphaj**.

(i) Hippocrate's classification

The Greek ancient physician **Hippocrate** also proposed typological classification of personality based on fluid or humour (liquid chemicals). Histology includes the **sanguine**, **phlegmatic** and **melancholic**. 'Sanguine' temperament is dominated by blood, the phlegmatics are dominated by phlegm while the melancholics possess black bile. Sanguines are hopeful, phlegmatics are temperamentally apathetic while the melancholics are characterized by gloomness. Hippocrate also believed that those with yellow bile are 'choleric', *i.e.* are irritable and excitable.

(ii) Somato type classification

Psychologists too have shown their interest in typological classification of personality, based on psychological attributes coupled with physique or body constitutions. Among such typological classifications, the classifications proposed by Sheldon, Krestschmer and Jung are much popular.

(i) Sheldon's classification

Sheldon (1940), a well-known constitutional psychologist studied psychological aspects of human behaviour as they are related to 'morphology' (science of body, form, structure, anatomy and physiology) of body. Accordingly, he divided human body into three types and related each type to behaviour and personality as given in **Table 17.1**.

TABLE 17.1 Sheldon's classification of body types and personality*

Body types	*Behaviour*	*Personality*
1. Endomorphy (tends to be fat)	Viscerotonia (tends to be relaxed)	Endo/Viscerotone (Fond of food, inclined to eat too much, apprehensive, insecure, amiable, sleeps well, conforms to social conventions)
2. Mesomorph (tends to be muscular)	Somatotonia (tends to be assertive)	Meso/Somatotone (Adventurous, likes strenuous exercises and cold showers, dresses informally, withstands pain easily and willingly)
3. Ectomorph (tends to be thin)	Cerebrotonia (tends to be restrained)	Ecto/Cerebrotone (A social, unamiable, lacks desire for exercise, nonadventurous, does not withstand pain easily)

* This Somato type classification of personality is based on works of Sheldon, Stevens and Tucker (1940) and Childs (1950).

(ii) Kretschmer's classification

Kretschmer (1925), a German psychiatrist, has proposed a trichotomized typology of personality based on body construction. These types are: (a) pyknic type (short and flatten), athletic (strong and aggressive) and asthenic (thin and lonely).

Kretschmer's interest grows out of working with mentally disturbed persons which were directed towards studying the personality of certain body types and associated temperaments. He has broadly classified the physical built in two main types:

(a) **Cycloid** and (b) **Schizoid**. The cycloids are temperamentally good natured, social, humorous, impulsive and moody. The schizoids, on the other hand, are unsocial, cool, reserved and close-mouthed.

He has further presented a trichotomized classification of temperament as are given below:

Pyknic Such people are short and flattened in physical built with bulged abdomen. Temperamentally such people are happy, gay and mixing.

Asthenic Lean and thin in body built. Such people are eccentric, like aloofness, remain cool and calm, dreamer, sentimental and inactive.

Athletic Well-organized and tightened muscles, widened shoulders and up chest. Physical built is good and attractive. Temperamentally these people are social, active, practical, courageous and tolerant.

(iii) Jung's classification

C.G. Jung is considered as a 'grand old man' among the personality theorists because of his suggestion that personality moves in two opposite directions—either in the direction of extraversion or in the direction of introversion (see **Table 17.2**). This concept has been adopted more widely in modern psychology than any other of his principles. The extraverted personality moves towards objective, they are practical, cares for others, ignore self interests and are sociable.

TABLE 17.2 Jung's personality types and features

	Extraversion	*Introversion*
1.	Ignores personal desires and cares for external needs or objects or persons.	Prime importance of personal needs and does not care for external needs or objects or persons.
2.	Successful adjustment with people in his immediate environment because of his interest in others.	Egocentric, not well adjusted with people in his immediate environment.
3.	Does not care for self-conscience and may tend to work for others without lust for personal gains or any kind of hesitation.	Very much careful of self-conscience and social demands have little effect upon him.
4.	These people can take pains for the welfare of others.	Not ready to take personal pains for others.
5.	Active participation in social work. Hence, they possess the ability to lead people or do social work.	Aloof from social work. Inability to lead people and take no interest in social work or affairs.
6.	Always ready to adhere to the advice given by others.	Rigid on his own ideas. Not ready to accept suggestions given by others.
7.	More likely to become hysterical.	More susceptible to obsessive-compulsive.
8.	Less sentimental. Remain balanced to criticism.	Most sentimental. Intolerant to criticism.

The introverts, on the other hand, move fast in opposite direction. His world is quiet, free fron people, and centres on subjective experiences which are quite personal (not social). Although modern psychological researchers in the area of personality has discovered a third position—**ambiversion**. However, even today, most psychologists adhere to the extraversion and intro-versio dimensions of personality.

Some of the distinguishing features of these two types of personalities are presented i Table 17.2.

Though, the extroverts and introverts differ much in their qualities of behaviour, th differences are relative and not absolute. The mode of behavioural differences depends much o the situation rather than inherent quality. In most cases, they are **ambivalent** rather than eithe purely extrovert or introvert.

(iv) Spranger's classification

Spranger (1928) has also attempted to classify personality in terms of six values as below:

- (i) **Theoretical type** Such people are knowledge oriented and work for quest of truth.
- (ii) **Economic type** Profit oriented and practical in dealings and work for accumu lation of wealth and property.
- (iii) **Aesthetic type** Such personalities are aesthetic and cares for orderly and regulate lifestyles, ways of living and loves beauty.
- (iv) **Social type** They are social and possess love, affections for others. They ar more co-operative, sympathetic and think for welfare of others.
- (v) **Political type** Such persons are power hungry. They work for authority and tr to be dominant, and assertive.
- (vi) **Religious type** Strong beliefs in spiritualism, God-fearing and pray for the we being of the universe as a whole. They are religious minded.

Spranger's classification is based on the philosophy of life which one holds. Philosophy c life determines the development of value system which shapes one's behavioural tendencies an thought processes.

Further, **Allport-Vernon-Lindzey** (1951) constructed a test of values and found that differe values lump together.

Thus, it is clear that classification of personality into types is not an easy task. Most of th classifications are based on theoretical views with which one is inclined. Personality in fact, nee to be seen in its totality and not on any single characteristic or trait or on the basis of any theor

Critical comments on typology of personality

Though, typologies are simple and appealing. However since human behaviour is complex an variable, therefore, it is very difficult to assign people to a particular type. People generally de such simple categorizations.

Typological classifications are largely based on stereotypes. Hence, lack scientific basis. I fact, personality is a unique possession of an individual. Hence, there may be as many typ of personalities as many are the people. Therefore, it is not possible to provide a concised list personality types. Moreover, personality is a dynamic organization. Hence, different types eith lump together or overlap or even moves from one type to another. Thus, typological classificati is much confounding.

B. Trait aproach to personality

Psychologists when analyse the personality of an individual, they mainly concern with identifying the behavioural attributes which are the basic components or the building blocks of personality. Trait approach psychologists believe that though human beings display a wide range of variations in their personalities yet, it is possible to see them as a combination of a smaller number of personality traits. Trait approach is akin to our dailylife experiences. For example, we attribute somebody as dependable, mixing, self-confident, co-operative and friendly. These attributions lead us to predict about an individual. This kind of thinking has prompted the trait approach psychologists to identify the primary characteristics of persons and make predictions. This is the major goal of trait theories. **'A trait refers to a relatively enduring way in which one individual differs from the other'**. Thus, traits are those attributes that function as a generalized action tendencies. Traits suggest the ranges of possible behaviours that are activated within a range according to the demands of situation. Trait approach to personality is useful in understanding personality because traits are (a) relatively stable over time, (b) consistent over situations and (c) variations in the strength and combination of traits lead to individual differences in personality.

The use of traits to describe and analyse personality has been very popular and a number of trait theories have been propounded. Let us examine a few of such approaches which are most popular:

Allport's view

Gordon Allport is considered as the champion of trait approach to personality. He proposed that 'traits' are the inherent attributes of mankind and is the ultimate reality of mankind's personality. Traits are more generalized than habits. Traits are also dynamic and determine behaviour that cause the person to approach different situations with similar goals or plans. The traits integrate the dissimilar stimuli and responses. Allport believes that the words that we use to describe a person serves as windows on the human personality. Allport and Odbert (1936) found approximately 18,000 adjectives in Webster's abridged dictionary which describe how people act, think, perceive, feel and behave. It also contains about 4000 such nouns that denote trait names such as humility, sociability, honesty and thus, describe certain general categories in which different persons can be placed in terms of common traits found in them.

According to Allport, personality is made of two types of traits—personal and general. The personal traits are those which are specific to the person because others do not posess such traits. Even the operation of personal traits are also specific or unique. This makes personality of each individual unique.

Besides, individuals also possess some such traits which may be found in other individuals also. Such traits are of generalized nature and cause similarities in personalities.

Allport also holds that the generalized dispositions or traits can be distinguished at three levels and are accordingly, categorized as (a) the 'cardinal traits', (b) the 'central traits' and (c) the secondary traits.

(a) **Cardinal traits:** The cardinal traits are highly generalized dispositions and have widespread impacts on behaviour. For example, if a person's whole life seems to be organised around honesty, it becomes a cardinal trait of his/her personality and as such, he maintains his honesty even in adverse situations. **Mahatma Gandhi's non-violence, Mother Teresa's humanitarianism, Hitler's hatred** etc. are some of the examples of cardinal traits.

(b) **Central traits:** Central traits are relatively less pervasive in effect but still quite generalized in dispositions. For example, dominance, sociability, submissiveness etc. are a few examples of generalized nature of central traits.

(c) **Secondary traits:** These traits appear in specific situations and hence are specific and narrow in effect. Such traits play a very minor role in determining personality because such traits are situationally tinged. *viz.* he likes choclets or prefers foreign car etc.

Allport opines that an individual's pattern of traits determine the behaviour. The traits are like intervening variables and thus they mediate between stimulus situation and response of the individual. If traits vary, the response to the situation also varies. For this reason, people's behaviours in similar situations on two different occasions vary. Individual differences in responding to a particualr situation is also caused by the difference in the strength of traits that are dominant differently in different individuals. Allport also believes that traits operate in unique way in each person and hence, makes his personality unique. This view is reflected in the very definition of personality offered by 'Allport'—**'a dynamic organization' of those psycho-physical systems within the individual that determine his behaviour and thought'**.

Cattell: Factorial analysis of personality

Ramond B. Cattell (1950) believed that there is a common structure found in all personalities which should be empirically determined. Cattell applied factor analysis to shortlist the huge array of descriptive adjectives found in English dictionaries to select a limited number of basic or primary traits that describes the personality of an individual.

On the basis of factor analysis, he selected 35 trait clusters which he termed as **surface traits**. He also concluded that personality consists of 16 primary or **source traits** which are the building blocks of personality. The surface traits according to him are caused by the interaction of source or primary traits. Thus, source traits are the obvious aspects of personality and are stable.

Cattell further described the source traits in terms of opposing tendencies and developed a test of personality consisting of 16 source traits (factors) which is popularly known as **16 personality factor test** (16PF test).

On the basis of factor analysis Cattell further reduced 35 clusters of traits to basic 12 pairs of bipolar dimensions. These 12 pairs of traits are presented in **Table 17.3**.*

Eysenck: The dimension of personality

H.J. Eysenck (1967) proposed that personality can be reduced merely to two dimensions. These two dimensions are biologically and genetically based that subsume numerous specific traits as shown in **Figure 17.1**.

Following are the two dimensions of personality:

(i) **Neuroticism vs emotional stability:** It refers to the degree or extent an individual has control over feelings. At the one extreme of dimension are highly neurotics characterized by hightened degree of anxiety, such people are moody, restless and lose control very quickly. On the another extreme are those who are calm, even-tempered, reliable and remain under control. Emotionally such people are stable.

* Cattell, R.B. (1950), *Personality*, New York: McGraw-Hill.

TABLE 17.3 Cattell's personality traits

Traits	*Opposites*
1. CYCLOTHYMIA (Emotionally expressive, frank, placid)	SCHIZOPHRENIA (Repressed, close-mouthed, anxious)
2. GENERAL MENTAL CAPACITY (Intelligent, smart, assertive)	MENTAL DEFECT (Unintelligent, dull, submissive)
3. EMOTIONALLY STABLE (Free of neurotic symptoms, realistic about life)	NEUROTICALLY EMOTIONAL (Variety of neurotic symptoms, evasive, immature)
4. DOMINANCE (Self-assertive, confident, assertive)	SUBMISSIVENESS (Submissive, unsure, complaisant)
5. SURGENCY (Cheerful, joyous, humorous, witty)	DESURGENCY (Depressed, pessimistic, dull, phlegmatic)
6. POSITIVE CHARACTER (Preserving, attentive to people)	DEPENDENT CHARACTER (Fickle, neglectful of social chores)
7. ADVENTUROUS CYCLOTHYMIA (Likes meeting people, strong interest in opposite sex)	WITHDRAWN SCHIZOPHRENIA (Shy, little interest in opposite sex)
8. SENSITIVE INFANTILE EMOTIONALITY (Dependent, immature, gregarious, attention seeking)	MATURE, TOUGHPOISE (Independent minded, self-sufficient)
9. SOCIALIZED CULTURE MIND (Polished, poised, composed, introspective, sensitive)	BOORISHNESS (Awkward, socially clumsy, crude)
10. TRUSTFUL CYCLOTHYMIA (Trustful, understanding)	PARANOIA (Suspicious, jealous)
11. BOHEMIAN UNCONCERNEDNESS (Unconventional, eccentric, fitful, hysterical upset)	CONVENTIONAL PRACTICALITY (Conventional, unemotional)
12. SOPHISTICATION (Logical mind, cool, aloof)	SIMPLICITY (Sentimental mind, attentive to people).

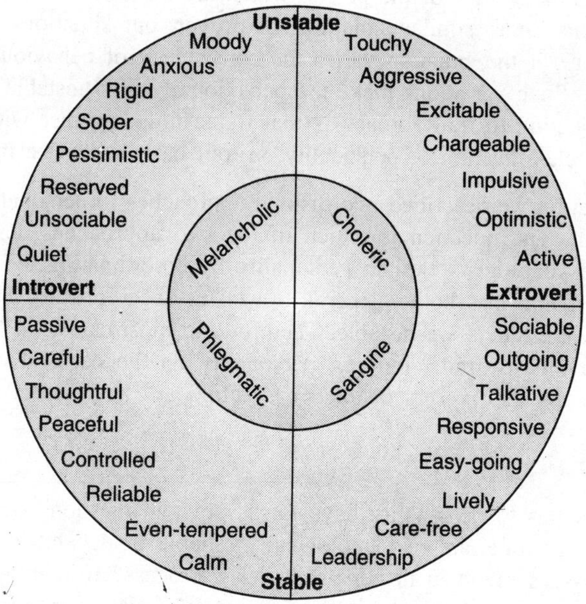

FIGURE 17.1 Eysenck's structure of personality.

(ii) **Extroversion vs introversion:** It refers to the degree to which an individual is socially outgoing or socially withdrawn. At one extreme are those who are active, gregarious, impulsive and thrill seeking while at another extreme are those who are passive, quiet, cautious and reserved.

Subsequently, Eysenck included one more dimension in his approach, namely, **'psychotism'** which he presumes an interactive product of the other two dimensions (neuroticism vs emotional stability and extroversion vs introversion dimensions). An individual scoring high on psychotism dimension tends to be hostile, egocentric and antisocial. In the eyes of others, such people are peculiar.

Eysenck is both—a trait theorist as well as a type theorist. He agrues that though people possess numerous traits, but these numerous traits get clustered into two main types of personality, i.e. extrovert and introvert. The extroverts are outgoing, active, sociable, impulsive and tough-minded persons. The introverts, on the other hand, are just opposite to extroverts. They are withdrawn, cautious, reflective, passive and tender-minded. The extroverts are also found more alert and have more sensation seeking tendencies than introverts. They learn better when aroused. They have higher level of brain chemical—dopamine—and are more suggestible. The introverts prefer loneliness and quiet environment to learn, dislike interruptions and are cautious. Such students are supposed to perform better in school tasks and learn faster even under low arousal. Threshold for pain is low in them.

Critical comments to trait approach

The trait approach is very popular approach to personality. However, it has raised many questions such as:

(i) Personality traits do not describe personality as a whole rather indicate only some dominant characteristics of the person which are relatively constant or similar on different occasions under similar situations. However, our situations are dynamic in nature and, therefore, if the situation varies the consistency of behavioural characteristics may also change. Such variations make the behavioural traits unstable or inconsistent.

(ii) Another objection to trait aproach is that traits lump together with other traits. In view of this, any classification of personality on trait basis would be misleading.

In the above section we described two distinct approaches to personality—the type approach and the trait approach. The question is which of the two approaches describe personality in a better way. Modern psychologists explain personality by co-ordinating the two approaches. They hold that personality in fact has both—general as well as specific traits. Hence, certain traits are enduring and stable while others are instable. Therefore, in most cases, the uniqueness of common behaviours reflect personality traits. Further, personality on the basis of commonness of certain tendencies or dispositions also present distinctive typological categories of personality.

Consistency of traits

Trait and type approaches to personality have raised several questions such as whether the tests that are used to measure traits are methodologically reliable or dependable, varied or are in tune with philosopohical issues involved in personality as a process? In addition, one of the pertinent methodological questions concerns about consistency of traits. Types and traits are generally thought of as source of stability in our behaviour that lead us to behave consistently across different situations and time. But, many of the studies done over the past some decades suggest otherwise. It has been found that people who are honest or calm in one situation and occasion do not remain honest or calm in another situation or occasion. Such findings suggest that type and trait approach may be misleading.

Walter Mischel (1976) has drawn the attention of the psychologists to the fact that consistency of behavioural trait varies across situations. This line of thinking has helped to promote **situationism**. This view states that behaviour is more a product of the particular situation than a product of enduring **person** as characterized by traits or types. Thus, no person is equally honest or domineering all the time and situations. We, generally, go to predict behaviour on the basis of trait but hardly can we predict what a person will do in a particular situation. At best, we may only indicate on average tendency of behaviour in a certain way across the situations. Therefore, trait theory does not describe personality features in totality because, the characteristic features of the situation is not given any consideration that plays a role in determining our behaviour. Thus, people are dependent or independent, active or passive, aggressive or calm not only because of inherent internal trait characteristics but also because of external rewards or threats inherent in the situation encountered by people. Studies done on cross-situational consistency of traits have been found to be low. The significance of situation playing a role can be seen by observing the behaviour of persons in the market, courtroom, places of worship etc.

In the light of the powerful role of situational factors on behaviour that interacts with the internal trait characteristics, Mischel (1976) view personality **as consisting of 'the distinctive patterns of behaviour' (inducing thoughts and emotions) that characterize each individual's adaptation in the situation of his/her life.***

Thus, it is obvious that human behaviour is largely determined by the situational features itself rather than the internal trait characteristics of the person.

Many psychologists however think that explaining behaviour either solely on the basis of trait or only on the basis of situation would be wrong. Instead, they prefer to adopt **interactional approach** to personality. This approach assumes that behaviour is determined by the inseparable complex interplay of situation and person factors (traits) both. Functionally, behaviour is a multidirectional interaction that occurs between an individual and the situation and hence, the individual functions as an active interactional agent in the interactional process of the situation and personal characteristics (traits).

Thus, while studying personality, the psychological meaning and its significance also need to be given due importance.

17.4 DYNAMIC PROCESS-ORIENTED VIEW OF PERSONALITY

In course of describing the trait type approach to personality, one of the philosophical questions has been raised which states that personality is not merely either the sum total of traits or the particular type in which different personalities can be fitted. Many argue that personality is much more than that. Personality is an active, dynamic interplay of motives, thoughts and feelings. It is not only a set of traits or types but is also a set of processes by which people cope with life. In view of this approach to personality, many dynamic process-oriented views of personality have been advanced. Therefore, we now turn to some of the important such theories of personality.

* Mischel, W. (1976) *Introduction in Personality*, 2nd ed., New York: Holt, Rinehart and Winston, p. 71.

17.4.1 Intra-psychic Theory

In the year 1900, Sigmund Freud published the **'Interpretation of Dreams' and introduced the system of psycho-analysis** as a theory of personality, as a therapeutic device and as a method of diagnosis. The psychoanalytic theory of personality is known as **Intra-psychic theory** that deals with the dynamic processes of the individual's psychic world which determines our behaviour. Hence, the theory is also known as **psycho-dynamic theory** of personality.

The basic difference between 'Type and Trait' approach that we have just discussed and the 'dynamic theories' to which we now take a turn is that the former approach involves a search for separable components of personality and the ways those components fit together to form a personality structure. The latter approach (dynamic approach), however, involves a search for the processes by which the needs, motives and impulses—often hidden from view—interact to produce the individual's behaviour.

The intra-psychic theory has three major parts, namely,

(i) The theory describes structure of personality comprising of three dynamic forces—id, ego and superego.
(ii) It is a theory of dynamic forces (id, ego and superego) that operates in arbitrarily divided segments of mind (psychic world)—the conscious, subconscious and unconsicous.
(iii) It is a theory of psycho-sexual development which describes the role of predominant needs and motives at different stages of child's growth and development.

(i) Structure of personality

Freud assumes that personality of an individual is a three-tier structured body of dynamic forces—'the id', 'the ego' and 'the superego'. The former (id) and latter (superego) forces are mutually antagonistic to each other while the 'ego' functions as adjusters between the two and thus, is a **balance force**.

The **id** can be understood as a composite of pleasure seeking instinct, illogical and infantile and is completely out of touch with reality.

The **superego** can be defined in terms of infantile combination of conscience and 'ego ideal' (i.e. the kind of person one wishes to become). It is socio-culturally conditioned. It functions like a judge, a jury and a policeman to exercise control over 'id' impulses.

The **ego** is a restraining or controlling force of the 'id' and operates in accordance with reality principles through logic and reason. Ego as a force of balance, delays satisfaction of a motive or channels the motive into socially acceptable outlets or pushes (represses) it. Thus, it works out the ways of behaving and thinking that are learnt for effective dealings with realities.

The 'id' is the storehouse of biologically based libidinal (sexual) energies. If it is left to itself, it would tend to satisfy the fundamental motives without any regard to reality, morals, values and norms of any kind. The superego being socially conditioned, permits satisfaction of only such motives which matches the reality and inhibits those which are dissonant to socio-cultural norms and principles of realities. Thus, superego conflicts with unrealistic demands of the 'id'. Under such conflicting states, the ego mediates and works out to resolve the conflicts without any damage to the 'self'. The conflicts arising between 'id' and 'superego' often result in anxiety and tension is created. The person under such conditions resort to 'ego defences' (defensive mechanims of ego) to reduce tension.

Thus, the functional and developmental process of personality travels through a series of conflicts and resolutions which ultimately results in uniqueness of personality. **Maddi** (1976, p. 21) terms it as a **conflict model** of personality.

(ii) The dynamics of personality or the locus of interplay of dynamic forces (id, ego, superego)

Freud while describing his ideas about personality, arbitrarily divided mind (psyche) into three territorial segments—**'the conscious'**, **'the subconscious'** and the **'unconscious'**. These are the major concepts of personality dynamics. According to Freud these segments of the 'psyche' (mind) are primarily responsible for originating all our actions, reactions and modifications. Freud holds that the infant's mind at birth is totally unconscious and the two other segments, namely the conscious and sub or preconscious gradually develop to serve the baby in course of his contacts with the realities of outer world.

The conscious segment consists of everything we are aware of at the moment. The pre(sub) conscious consists of past experiences of which we are not aware at the moment but can be easily recollected and brought to the conscious state. The unconscious consists of all memories, desires, impulses and urges which have either been pushed (repressed) into it or have never been allowed to reach consciousness. Such memories remain deep-seated and heavily guarded by conscious forces. Therefore, these cannot be easily tapped. According to Freud, unconscious is the largest segment and is the main foundation over which the whole structure of personality is built.

The urges or impulses are repressed into unconscious because of the conflicting situations arising between conscious part of ego and superego and the unconscious id. The motives of id seek conscious expression. But most of such motives cause anxiety because these are in conflict with ego and superego. Whenever such situations arise, ego pushes them into unconscious (i.e. repress them) and thus, relieves from anxiety. These repressed urges, however, remain active and are expressed in disguised form without causing much anxiety. These repressed urges are called **'unconscious motives'** which are the underlying dynamic forces in Freudian psychoanalytic theory.

(iii) Development of personality

Freud conceived personality as developing from infancy to adulthood through several overlapping stages. Broadly these stages are: (i) the pregenital stage, (ii) the latency stage and (iii) the genital stage. Pregenital stage is further divided into three substages—the oral, the anal and the phallic stage. The genital stage is also divisible into preadolescent and adolescent stages.

According to Freud, of all these different stages of development, the pregenital stage is of paramount significance because the experiences of unusual frustrations, insecurity or anxiety of any sort, if get fixated at any of the pregenital stages, become the characteristic features of later personality and manifest itself into syndromes or patterns of personality disorders during the later periods (adulthood) of development.

(a) **The pregenital stage:** This stage consists of three distinct phases—**oral stage**, **anal stage** and the **phallic stage**. The oral stage again has two subphases—sucking and biting phases. Both of these two subphases together are called the 'oral stage' which occupies much of the first year. The infant obtains pleasure by sucking, swallowing, chewing and similar other oral activities. If the infant is either prevented from or delayed in sucking or is made anxious about sucking, may acquire an oral fixation which takes the form of oral syndromes later in life such as excessive oral behaviour including greediness, dependency and passivity. Another phase is biting through teeth. The onset of this phase begins with 'weaning'—preventing the infant from sucking. Fixation of this tendency usually develops in aggressive syndromes.

As the infant grows to the age of approximately one year or more, he enters into another important phase of pre-genital stage—**anal phase**. This phase continues till aproximately 4th year of age with a transition from early **anal expulsion** to later **anal retentive phases**. During this phase (covering both the subphases), toilet training by parents and teachings to avoid 'naughty behaviours' connected with excretion poses a situation of encounter with authority. During this phase, for the first time 'id' tendencies are brought to control by 'ego' which begins to develop. Freud believes that if training is too strict (sphincter control) or encounter is stressful, it may arouse anxiety which may develop into 'anal syndrome' during adulthood and manifested in obsses-sive—compulsiveness, overconformity, exaggerated control, homosexual interests etc.

Having mastered the toilet training, child's interest turns into their genitals (phallus or sex organs). This is termed as **'phallic phase'** of pregenital stage. During this phase children develop **'romantic feelings'** of typical nature towards parental figures of opposite sexes. Such feelings are termed as **oedipus** and **electra** complexes. This phase is very crucial phase of personality development. Castration anxieties, threats of parental Jealousy and others if get fixated, develops into 'Phallus syndrome later in life such as—fear from intercourse, indecision, shyness, aggressive tendencies towards authority, phobic reactions etc. During this phase, superego also develops and child learns moral values, social norms, desirable modes of responses etc.

(b) **Latency stage:** As the child reaches the school age, he enters into a new stage called **latency stage** and the child remains under this stage till **'puberty'**, i.e. onset of pre-adolescence phase of genital stage. From psycho-sexual developmental point of view, this is the stage of 'LULL' of sexual impulses. The infantile sexual urges are repressed temporarily till it begins to reappear during **teenages**. The schooling of the children begins which provides an opportunity for exposure with outer world, learning of social norms and values, social interactions. Such primary education significantly influences the formation of personality and building of character. Hence, though the sexual urges are repressed, this stage plays significant role in the proper development of personality, including enhancing of abilities, skills and enrichment of knowledge, skills to solve problems, selecting and shaping of environment for adequate adaptability with the environment and so on. The immatured superego is matured and the child comes into direct contacts with outer realities. However, this stage is also delicate in the sense that erroneous learning processes and improper handlings of the child curiosities about the world around him may adversely affect normal development of traits and potentialities.

(c) **Genital stage:** As the child grows to the age of **puberty** he enters in **genital stage** and normal hetro-sexual interests begin to appear. His or her interest is more focussed on others rather than on the self. Thus, when the child becomes adult, plays normal adult roles in the society. However, if the frustrations owing to crude realities of life, sphincter control of consciousness etc. get fixated and normal defences are weakened, maladaptive behaviours are likely to overshadow the normal growth of personality. This stage is also crucial in facing the crisis of search for identity which needs to be handled carefully.

Thus, the way in which a child is reared by the parents and others during different stages of psycho-sexual development, smoothness in the transition of one stage to another, fixations of tendencies during different stages of development, the nature of conflicts and the manner in which they are resolved etc. all play important roles in shaping of personality. These monitor development of specific tendencies of unique character. In this context, Freud has laid emphasis on several syndromes that develop in course of psychosexual development that becomes important features of one's personality.

Two of such concepts occupy special attention with reference to personality. These are **fixation** and **regression**.

Fixation: Fixation refers to a situation when a sexual impulse is arrested at an early stage of development. It has been found that fixation occurs when conflict at any stage of psycho-sexual development is very high. Also deprivation and overindulgence at a given stage or inconsistent alterations between indulgence and depreivation may lead to fixation.

Regression: Regression refers to going back to an earlier stage of development. It is a kind of reverting to earlier stage of psychosexual development. It occurs when resolution of problems at any stage of psychosexual development is less than adequate. This causes stress that results in regression. When regression occurs, people display behaviour which is typical of that less mature stage of development.

When id impulses are strong enough, unpleasent feelings of nervousness, tension and worry take place. Ego may use defensive mechanisms such as projection, sublimation, repression, reaction-formation, identification etc. and manage the aroused tension. But often such defences fail to manage the aroused state of tension, people are subjected to the state of anxiety.

Anxiety: According to Freud, there are three types of anxiety—neurotic anxiety, objective (real) anxiety and moral anxiety. **Neurotic anxiety** is caused by severe conflict between id impulses and ego defences. **Real** or **objective anxiety** occurs when real external threat is perceived. **Moral anxiety** occurs due to conflict between id impulses and superego forces that restrains id impulses and also impose punishments such as **guilt feelings**.

Dreams: Freud in his theory of personality also considers dreams as important indicators of unconscious forces and hence, lay emphasis on interpretation of dreams. To him, **dreams are royal road to unconscious**. Therefore, by interpreting the latent contents of dreams, we may have an access to the unconscious forces that determine the underlying unconscious processes of dynamic forces and determine the kind of personality one possesses.

Thus, the intrapsychic theory of personality explains personality in terms of processes by which the dynamic forces within the psyche (mind) functions to process different instinctual tendencies and urges during the course of development from infancy to adulthood.

Critical comments

It is believed that Freud himself had a very dominant personality. He attracted many psychological thinkers and scientists and also repelled many of them. Some of the distinguished disciples of Freud who became prominent opponents of Freud include Jung and Adler. The major grounds on which Freud has been subjected to severe criticisms are as follows:

(i) Freud used various concepts in his theory which are vaguely defined.
(ii) Freud's most of the notions and concepts suffer from logical distinctions.

(iii) Freud has advanced his theory on the basis of case studies of mentally disordered people. As such, it is biased and not testable.
(iv) The techniques used by Freud have low reliability and validity. Hence, the theory is questionable.
(v) Freud's theory is based on biological instinctual tendencies. Thus, he has ignored the significance of socio-cultural contexts that play an important role in shaping and developing personality.

Despite the above shortcomings, Freud's theory had an enormous impact in understanding the **psyche** of the individual. Modern psychologists consider Freud's theory as deterministic, dynamic, developmental and structural. Hence, Freud's theory has wider implications in making empirical approach to infer behaviour of an individual.

The theory is also valuable in the sense that it reveals deeper aspects of personality which in many situations prove true.

17.4.2 Post-Freudian Developments

After Freud, many psychologists opposed the psychoanalytic theory as for them, the theory is too narrow to understand adult's personality. Freud has laid unnecessary emphasis on childhood psychosexual development, biological innate instincts and outrightly ignored the socio-cultural contexts that play a role in determining future oriented goals, hopes and plans. Consequently, psychodynamic theory has made a lead to grow in many directions, diverse emphases have appeared. These theories are characterized by less prominent roles to libidinal urges and aggressive tendencies of id. These theories have expanded the concept of ego and the trend is indicative of emergence of an **'ego psychology'** as a new frontiers of the psychology of personality. Many such theories also lay emphasis on human qualities of creativity, competence and problem solving abilities. Besides, a group of psychologists known as **'NeoFreudians'** have given attention to social determinants and conscious reality. Hence, we find that most post- Freudian theorists have made attempts to present a definite shift in focus.

With a view to develop familarity of the students regarding post-Freudian developments, a few popular such theories are being briefly discussed.

Carl Jung: Understanding the collective unconscious

Carl Gustav Jung (pronounced **Yoong**) was one of the most dependable and reliable disciples of Freud. In the year 1907, Freud wrote to Jung—**I could hope for no one better than yourself .... to continue and complete my work**.* However, Jung differed from the main track of psychoanalysis and developed his own theory known as **Analytical Psychology**.

Jung used the **word association test** as an experimental technique to study the inner psychic processes and diagnosing the complexes. Jung believed that by using this technique, he would be able to explore the unconscious much like **Freud** who explored unconscious by using **free association technique or hypnosis**. But, Jung's own finding led him away from Freud's ideas in several respects. Freud laid emphasis on sexual impulses and motives as the main driving forces of human behaviour—the prime source of libidinal energy. On the other hand, Jung laid emphasis on **'urge to live'**—a continuous life urge which is the only driving force of behaviour. This life urge

* McGuire, 1974, p. 27, cited in *Introduction to Psychology*, Morgan, C.T. et al., 1993, Tata McGraw-Hill, New Delhi, p. 582.

refers to the striving to live as well as a strive to ensure the survival of one's species. Moreover, Jung also laid emphasis on some personality structures which Freud had either ignored or not considered important.

One such structure was the concept of **collective unconscious**. Jung claimed that collective unconscious is a part of 'unconscious' that contains the premordial images—**archetypes**. These images go beyond personal experiences and hence, not individually acquired. These archetypes are hereditary. Some examples of archetypes are God, the earth mother, devil, rebirth, the young potent hero etc. These are found in myths, dreams and art of all mankind.

In addition to collective unconscious, Jung also holds the concept of **personal unconscious** which develops out of person's conscious experience that has been repressed.

Jung also proposed that human 'psyche' includes both—the **conscious** and **shadow** aspect of **conscious ego**. Thus, all major components of personality eventually work in organized manner to form a fully realized, purposeful self. This process of harmonizing the conscious and unconscious components follows a unique way in each person that leads to **uniqueness** in behavioural patterns of each individual. Jung terms this process of uniqueness as '**individuation**' owing to which, each individual has a distinct personality features.

Jung also believes that the unconscious of every female includes a masculine assertive element which he terms as **animus** and similarly the unconscious of every male includes a faminine passive element which he terms as **anima**. Therefore, in order to be constructively masculine or faminine, individuals of each sex tend to recognize and integrate these opposite sex elements again in unique ways. This is striving for unity or wholeness of the self.

Jung also describes four different ways in which we come into contact or experience the world around us. These are—**sensing**, **intuition**, **feeling** and **thinking**.

Sensing This provides knowledge about the immediate world.

Intuition This gives 'insight' on the basis of our observation of the world around us but we do not become aware of the external source of such 'insight'.

Feeling It is an expression of our affective aspects, viz. glad to meet you, I do share with your grief etc.

Thinking This is indicative of our higher order cognitive aspect of psyche(mind) that provides recognition of the objects of the world.

Jung has also classified personality into two broader categories—**extroversion** and **introversion**—for which he is popularly known as type approach theorist. He has distinguished these two types of personalities in terms of distinctive behavioural characteristics (differences between these two have been described earlier in this chapter under Section 17.3).

Jung devoted much of his time in studying such expressions of **oneness** of the self in various raditions and held that to achieve this wholeness or oneness, the individual needs to be aware of the wisdom available in one's personal as well as collective unconscious and also needs to learn to live in harmony with it. Jung had also visited India in 1930s.

Jung while describing psychic energy in the theory, took the help of **thermodynamics** from physics and has stated the three basic principles—

(i) The principle of opposites,
(ii) The principle of equivalence and
(iii) The principle of entropy.

Individuals in course of making adjustment with the environmental demands, apply these principles variously such as transfer of psychic energy from one situation to another, redistribution or allocation of psychic energy and achieving the stability.

Jung has also described four stages of personality development. These stages are childhood, young adulthood, middle age and old age. In all these stages of personality development, gradually we acquire different traits in which our experiences with the environment have significant role to play.

Critical comments

Jung's concepts of collective unconscious and archetype are considered significant contributions because these concepts enable us to understand some such specific behaviours of individuals that cannot be understood on the basis of Freud's personal unconscious. For example, to understand the creative behaviours, personal unconscious fails to throw any light. Thus, these concepts of Jung provide a new direction to know and explain the personality features of an individual.

Jung in his theory has laid emphasis on past, present and future. Thus, we can better understand the importance of situational factors and role played by the events occurring during the past, present and also the impacts of future time sequences.

Jung has also provided a projective technique to study personality which is called Word Association Test (WAT). This test is convenient to administer and dependable. Hence, a great contribution.

However, Jung's analytical approach is criticized on the ground of inconsistency and lack of systematization in detailing the dynamic processes involved in personality. The different concepts used by him are also not consistent and based on paradoxical facts.

Some psychologists also hold that Jung's ideas are mystical and complex and hence, not amenable to experimental testing.

According to **Edward Glover** (1950), Jung has proposed the concept of **archetype** which is not understandable. It is more a subjective feeling which cannot be meaningfully understood by others.

Despite the above few critical comments, Jung in his system has included many important concepts and aspects of personality and goes beyond the narrow descriptions offered by Freud. Hence, his system is considered a significant contribution in the area of psychodynamic approach to personality.

Alfred Adler's individual psychology

Alfred Adler was also a colleague of Freud and Jung but he made a departure from them and formulated a theory in different direction from those of Freud and Jung (Adler 1929, 1931).

In the background of Adler's theory, Adler cited an example of three children as narrated below:

... three children ... were taken to the zoo for the first time. As they stood before a lion's cage, one of them shrank behind his mother's skin and said, **I want to go home**. The second child stood where he was, very pale and trembling, and said, **I'm not a bit frightened**. The third glared at the lion fiercely and asked his mother, **shall I spite at it**? The three children really felt inferior, but each expressed his feelings in his own way, consonant with his own **style of life**.*

The above-cited story of three children is illustrative of the basic differences between Adler's views and those of Freud and Jung's views on the dynamics of **psychic processes**.

* Adler, A. (1931), *What life should mean to you*, New York, Putnam, p. 50.

Adler believes that people always struggle to overcome their feelings of inferiority and holds that this struggle is the most basic 'urge' of life. This urge is very potent driving force within the individual that makes him strive continuously to attain 'superiority' and mastery in the external world. However, when one fails to overcome his weaknesses and achieves some mastery or simply overemphasizes some particular inferiority, it results in **inferiority complex.**

Adler also stresses on the concepts of **'compensation'** and **'overcompensation'**. These refer to the pursuit of activities that are designed to make up or overcome the inferiority (e.g. spitting at the lion in the above story).

Ansbacher and **Ansbacher** (1956)* holds that these concepts of compensation and over-compensation have in fact a personal significance for Adler himself who was himself suffering from inferiority complex. It is reported that Adler as a child was chronically ill, weak and was intensely afraid of death. He compensated this inferiority by choosing a career of the physician so as to overcome the fear of death.

Another important concept of Adler's theory as reflected in the zoo story is the concept of **style of life**. This refers to the approach with which people want to live. Each individual creates personal style or approach to living. Hence, style of life of an individual is **highly individualized** style. This style of life grows out of one's unique sense of personal inferiorities and strategies to overcome them.

Adler further makes mention of **creative self**. Adler believes that the **individualized life style** is a creative product of the individual. Each individual has the freedom and is responsible to determine individual goal and develop the strategies to achieve the goal and cope with the situation. This concept perhaps led Adler to label his theory as **Individual Psychology**.

Further, Adler paid close attention to **birth order** that influences the development of personality. According to Adler, the 'first born begins his life as the exclusive focus of his parents. But, as soon as the next sibling is born, the first born is abruptly **dethroned**. This makes the child to feel cheated and, therefore, is likely to behave as unruly misfit. If we view the first born from positive angle of approch, the first born may develop a style of life in which they are likely to behave in a parent-like way towards the next born sibling. Similarly, Adler has described various other possibilities of developing lifestyles of second born, last born children and only born children. Though many of Adler's ideas could not be substantiated, however, his ideas could stimulate some researchers like **Dunn** and **Kendrick** (1932), **Sutton** and **Rosenberg** (1970). On the basis of their research findings, it could be discerned that the first borns have intense relationship with their parents and they tend to be more achievement oriented and self-controlled than the later borns. Adult first borns are more likely to be listed as 'who's who' while later borns tend to be less conforming, more sociable and popular. Hence, Adler's general idea about the relationship between ordinal position and personality appears tenable.

Critical comments

No doubt, Adler has made a great contribution to the psychology of personality by making a reference to some of the concepts such as inferiority feeling and compensatory behaviours, life-styles, ordinal positions etc. Hence, he admirably attempted to make a hint towards the interactional processes between the individual's psyche and the outer world in shaping and developing unique personality of individuals. Moreover, Adler also incorporated the creative

---

* Ansbacher, H.L. and Ansbacher, R.R., *The Individual Psychology of Alfred Adler*, New York, Harper & Row, 1956, p. 199.

aspects of individuals in his theory. Many psychologists viewing from the point of view of comprehensiveness and consider Adler's theory as adequate.

However, from the point of view of verifiability, the theory is not satisfactory because the basic concepts are not verifiable or testable on objective criteria.

The theory is also of limited research value as most of the Adlerian concepts except the ordinal position and feelings of inferiority do not fall within the purview of objective studies.

In addition, psychologists do not seem to come to a point of agreement on the issue of feeling of inferiority and superiority complexes—which lack general applicability in all the cases.

Thus, though Adler's departure from Freudian thought is significant in the sense that it could provide a new direction to the dynamic processing theory of personality, the theory has also certain limitations of significant nature.

NeoFreudian's view

The NeoFreudians are a group of dynamic theorists of personality who within the framework of Freud's psychoanalytic views brought certain significant modifications for which Freud was severely criticized. The major grounds of criticism were Freud's overemphasis on sex drive, undue pessimism about human nature, exaggerating the role of unconscious, for failing to consider motives towards personal growth and fulfilment, for neglect of socio-cultural forces in shaping behaviour and for lack of scientific evidences to support many of its assumptions. The NeoFreudians ventured to incorporate many of such deficiencies of psychoanalytic system and also provided a new direction to consider personality in a pervasive perspective of our socio-cultural contexts. Some of the significant contributors of this school of thought include **Fromm**, **Horney** and **Sullivan**. Let us briefly describe them one by one.

Erich Fromm: The human concerns

Fromm, being a social analyst, viewed human beings as basically 'social being' and, therefore, concerned with social influences, particularly his relationship to others. Thus, Fromm was concerned with human equalities such as growth and realizing potentials which are outcomes of a 'desire for freedom' and 'striving for justice and truth'.

Contrary to 'Freud's' biological orientations, 'Fromm' had a social orientation. He considers character too as a dominant trait of personality which develops from interpersonal experiences in the society. Character traits also has the potentials or force to shape the social processes and culture. Fromm also believed that the ideals of truth, justice, freedom etc. are the genuine strivings and not merely rationalizations.

In the year 1941, Fromm published a famous book **Escape from Freedom**. In this book, he assumes man as a social being and also made mention of **basic human dilemma**. According to him as a man gains freedom, he also feels alone and insecure. To solve this state of dilemma, Fromm has suggested the need to form a society where there is equality for every person so that each individual may get meaningfully and affectionately related to others.

Elaborting the concept of 'dilemma' Fromm has pointed out that people choose several methods to escape from feelings of helplessness that arises from striving for freedom. One such method would be the affiliation or being related to others. By relating to others, the person becomes tied to the relationship or affective love and thus, can reunite himself. Another way to get rid of dilemma is freeing oneself from the idea of becoming independent of others, *i.e.* he should set aside the idea of individualism. However, such a situation may hinder self-expression and thus, frustrating to one's self-ideals.

Basic Needs: Fromm holds that in course of interpersonal interactions, some basic needs develop. He has distinguished five such needs which are as follows:

(a) **Need for relatedness:** It refers to desire to create relationship to others through productive love. It involves mutual respect and understanding.

(b) **Need for rootedness:** It refers to the need to belong to the active world so that the person may consider himself as a meaningful organism.

(c) **Need for identity:** It refers to individual's desire to be unique so that he may be distinguished from all others.

(d) **Need for transcendence:** This is a desire to grow—involving inclination to be creative and think in a novel way.

(e) **Need for orientation:** It refers to a specific frame of reference that may develop orientation towards self and towards others.

Types of personality

Fromm considers personality as the sum of inherited as well as acquired characteristics. At the same time he has distinguished temperament from character. For him temperament is a mode of reaction which is inherited and constitutional. Therefore, it is unmodifiable. Character, on the other hand, develops through life experiences and is influenced by the socio-cultural perspectives. Thus, character is determined by physical constitution while temperament by socio-cultural influences. However, character is relatively permanent and two kinds of processes play important role in the formation of character. These are **assimilation** and **socialisation**. These two processes are called **orientation** in Fromm's terminology and are the **core of character** (Wolman, 1979).

Fromm assumes that when an individual attempts to assimilate his own character with social forces with a view to relate himself with the society, various types of personality emerges. He has distinguished five different types of personalities, each with a different character. These are as follows:

(i) **The receptive type (or character):** Such persons are 'receivers' and not 'givers'. They expect all kinds of help from others such as love, material possessions. They become too anxious when supply from others is withhold or inhibited.

(ii) **The hoarding type (or character):** Such people are selfish, a conceited fellow and orderly. They perceive outer world as threat and feel secured by hoarding (saving and keeping something).

(iii) **Exploitative type (or character):** Such persons are acquisitive by character and apply force to possess something and do not care to deprive others. They are also aggressive towards others.

(iv) **Marketing type (or character):** Such persons always think of profit and loss. Man is a commodity. They are mercenaries, *i.e.* can sell their labour, talent to earn more and more.

(v) **Productive type (or character):** Such persons are production oriented and are desirable personalities for the society. Such people are guided by genuine love, care, responsibility and creativity. They are found engaged in productive activities and are also devoted to the well-being of the society.

In essence, Fromm has presented an optimistic view of man and has laid emphasis on social and cultural factors that an individual encounters in lifetime.

Critical comments

Though, Fromm has made a significant departure from psychoanalytic view of personality, he has been criticized on the ground that his views are extremely idealistic and hence, unrealistic. Fromm has also failed to substantiate his views empirically. In view of these comments about Fromm, he is considered more as an **ethical philosopher** than a **psychologist**.

Karen Horney: Social foundations of personality

Karen Horney was a woman psychologist. Though she neither was a disciple of Freud nor she was a co-worker, however, the impact of Freudian traditions can be seen in her thoughts and views about personality. She attempted to explain the fundamentals of psychoanalysis by giving emphasis upon social and cultural forces. In the year 1923, she challanged Freudian concept of **penis envy**. Despite this, she worked within the boundaries of basic frame of references of Freudian thoughts by correcting what appeared fallacious to her.

Horney believed that the gender difference is largely due to social factors and not due to any inherent innate differences causing inferiority among the females. She advocated the idea that each sex has certain attributes which are admired by others and, therefore, neither should be viewed either superior or inferior.

With regard to psychological disorders, Horney opines that such disorders are not caused by 'fixation' of psychic energy at different stages of psychosexual development, rather it is caused by disturbed **interpersonal relationships** during childhood. When parental behaviour towards the child is indifferent, disparaging and erratic, the child feels insecured and is subjected to anxiety. Such anxieties are termed by Horney as **basic anxiety**. Thus, basic anxiety in childhood is caused by social situations in which the child feels afraid, such as, threats or domination by parents, tension and conflict between parents, requring the child to do too much, mistrust, criticism, coldness etc. When the anxiety is aroused, the child attempts to resolve it by trial and error (as one does while solving a problem). In this way, the child learns some ways to deal with anxiety and thus, forms a pattern of **neurotic needs**. A neurotic need is therefore a learnt need. According to Horney there can be any number of neurotic needs depending upon the modes a child has learned to cope with the anxiety or reduce it. Thus, if a child has learned to cope with anxiety by running to his mother for affection or approval, he may develop a neurotic need for approval or affection. Similarly, if he has learned to manage his anxiety producing situation by obtaining prestige and admiration, he may have neurotic needs for those things.

Horney further believes that in any culture, certain needs can be expected to arise because the source of anxiety tends to form repetitive pattern from one culture to another, from one family to another and from one child to another. Thus, Horney could identify ten such needs such as affection, dependency, power, prestige, achievement, self-sufficiency, acceptance, approval etc. She further emphasized that under the influence of neurotic needs, a person tends to move in either of the three directions—moving towards people, moving against poeple and moving away from people. Horney has termed these trends of movements as **neurotic trends**. Obviously, according to Horney, neurosis is not caused by inner conflicts of id, ego and superego but is the result of conflict between a person and his environment. Thus, Horney has made a major shift to consider neurosis as caused by external world rather than the individual's inner world.

Horney has also described about conflicts. According to her, the major conflict is between two incompatible needs viz. dependency and self-sufficiency are mutually incompatible needs and when these needs occur simultaneously, conflict would arise. Each one of us possesses neurotic needs in some degree. But when one fails to resolve the conflict, some need may dominate one's life and thus, he may become neurotic.

Critical comments

Horney has given emphasis on social and cultural factors and thus, tried to supplement the major shortcomings of Freud's system. Horney's approach incorporates both the biological and instinctual forces as well as socio-cultural factors in determining our personality. In this sense, her approach is **holistic** rather than **instinctual** alone (Kelman, 1971).

However, some psychologists have been critical to Horney's position.

(i) Some psychologists consider that Horney could not gain the significance as Freud could. Hence, her theoretical formulation within the framework of psychoanalytic thought could not get recognition and hence, not much significant (Lundin, 1985).

(ii) Horney's approach is partial or incomplete. It remained centred around the basic needs and the neurotic needs only. But, personality is a complex structure and functionally pervasive enough. Hence, on the basis of these two key concepts alone, personality cannot be understood fully.

In spite of the above critical remarks, Horney could make a significant shift in the dynamic process approach to personality and hence, her contributions cannot be undervalued.

Harry Stack Sullivan's approach: Interpersonal model

Harry Stack Sullivan (1953) developed entirely a different model of personality which is known as **interpersonal model** of personality. He dropped most of the concepts of Freud such as id, ego, superego, libidinal urges etc. At the same time he also took many of the Freudian concepts such as needs, tension, anxiety, unconscious motivation, defence mechanism, dream interpretation etc. Like Freud, Sullivan also stressed the significance of distinct stages of personality development.

Sullivan's theory can be represented under three major heads as mentioned hereinbelow:

Dynamics of personality: Sullivan views human beings basically as energy system that seeks to reduce tension aroused by needs. Such tensions are aroused either by needs or by anxiety. Need-aroused tensions call for integrative behaviours while anxiety-induced tensions arouse disintegrative behaviours. When needs are satisfied, tension is reduced otherwise it may lead to **apathy**. Anxiety is usually transmitted to an infant by the mother who herself may be anxious which she expresses by words or voices of mouth or behavioural actions. Such expresssions are gradually picked up by children and they become anxious.

Sullivan has also described three distinct levels or modes of cognition. These are (a) **prototaxic**, (b) **parataxic** and **syntaxic levels** of cognition. Prototaxic experiences are primitive experiences of infants which are undifferentiated, presymbolic, momentary, incapable of being conceptualized and hence, noncommunicable.

The parataxic experiences are prelogical, subjective and communicated in distorted form to others. Relatively such experiences are more differentiated than protaxic experiences of the infants. Such experiences begin to occur very early during the infancy but continue to be important mode of experience throughout the life.

Syntaxic experiences refer to meaningful interpersonal communication involving language including words and gestures.

All the above three modes of cognition occur throughout the life. However, syntaxic experiences begin to be reflected at the age of about 6 and continue to dominate in interpersonal communication throughout the life.

Enduring aspects of personality: Sullivan talks about the stability of personality. According to him, some aspects of personality such as dynamism, personification and self-system are the stable or enduring aspects of personality.

The concept of dynamism is akin to traits of personality. **Dynamism** in Sullivan's terminology refers to relatively consistent patterns of action that characterize the person through-out his life. He has divided dynamism in two types—(a) dynamism related to particular zone of the body and (b) dynamism related to tension. The former is concerned with satisfying our basic primary needs such as hunger, thirst etc. The latter class of dynamism consists of disjunctive, isolating and conjuctive dynamisms. **Disjunctive dynamism** includes distructive patterns of behaviour that is related to **malevolence**—a kind of attitude that people around us are not good rather malacious. Hence, a bad place to live in this world. The **isolating dynamism** refers to the **lust**—a biological phenomenon produced directly or indirectly by tension related to genitals. It may lead to homo or heterosexual behaviour patterns.

The **conjunctive dynamism** refers to beneficient or advantageous patterns of behaviour as is found in intimacy or self-esteem.

Personification: Personification is also an enduring aspect of personality. It refers to the self-image or the images of others. It develops or builds up out of our experiences with anxiety or need satisfaction. Satisfying interpersonal relationships produce positive image while the dissatisfying interpersonal relationships or anxiety produce negative image of the self or of others. Sullivan holds that during infancy—five elementary kinds of personification build up. These are: **good mother, bad mother, good me, bad me** and **not me.** All these personifications are determined by satisfying or dissatisfying states of interpersonal relationships including the state of anxiety. Intense state of anxiety is associated with **'not me'** type of personification which is representative of dissociation of self-accompanied by dangerous emotions or **uncanny** as termed by Sullivan.

Self-system: Self-system is the most complex and important system of dynamism. It attempts to protect the person from anxiety by maintaining interpersonal security. In this sense, self-system is **antianxiety system.** This system begins to develop around 1½ years to 2 years of age. Though, self-system attempts to protect the person from anxiety by reducing anxiety, it sometimes also interferes with ability to live constructively. It happens when the child has more experience with anxiety, his self-system becomes more inflated and separated from the rest of personality. As such, the individual is prevented from taking a realistic view and objective judgement of the situation. This interferes in constructive living.

Developmental stages

Sullivan has suggested that personality is a developmental aspect which passes through seven stages beginning from infancy to adulthood. The seven stages are: (a) infancy, (b) childhood, (c) juvenile era, (d) preadolescence, (e) early adolescence, (f) late adolescence and (g) adulthood According to Sullivan, all these stages of development are marked by certain significant changes in personality. However, changes in personality basically occur during critical periods of transition from one stage to another. Such changes are determined by the interpersonal perceptions and reactions. In other words, the interpersonal relationship is the **basic thread** that determines our personality in all different stages of personality development.

What follows from the above, Sullivan has attempted to present a very comprehensive theory of personality and is therefore widely accepted theory in which interpersonal relationship is the core of Sullivan's theory.

Critical comments

Sullivan's system is criticized for having incorporated a number of hypothetical constructs such as self-system, personification, different kinds of dynamism etc. But, this kind of criticism does not seem valid because Sullivan has used objective terms to explain these concepts. Sullivan's data were found closely related to the observations of people's interactions with others.

Erik Erikson: In search of identity

Erikson has attempted to broaden the psycho-analytic approach to personality with a focus **on** social adaptaton.

Erikson has emphasized **ego** rather than **id** and **superego**. He holds that 'ego' possesses the capacity to unify the experiences of man and his action in a meaningful and adaptive manner. Ego also possesses creative qualities and is able to provide creative solutions to the problem that we encounter. As he believes, ego is determined by both—the inner psychic forces as well as by socio-cultural influences. Erikson talks of **ego qualities** that emerge in different stages of development. Such ego qualities reflect the influence of the socio-cultural factors.

Erikson's theory has 8 stages of development. Five of these stages are what Freud has pointed out—the oral, anal, phallic, latent and genital stages. However, Erikson has added three more stages—early childhood, middle adulthood and old age. Each stage places a specific demand and poses **specific crisis** that need to be adequately resolved to foster normal development of personality. He believed—**the more successfully crises are resolved, the more healthier is the development**. These stages are given in **Table 17.4**.

TABLE 17.4 Erikson's psychological stages with corresponding crises

Sl.No.	*Age/period*	*Basic conflict (crises)*	*Optimal outcome*
1.	0 to 1½ years (Infancy)	Basic trust vs Basic mistrust	Trust is the faith that things will be alright. It develops from good care provided by reliable others (parents). A favourable ratio of trust to mistrust results in hope.
2.	1½ to 3 years (Toddler)	Autonomy vs Shame and doubt	Without a sense of self-control (autonomy) children feel shame and doubt. A favourable ratio of autonomy to shame and doubt results in self-direction with self-esteem.
3.	3 to 6 years (Preschooler)	Initiative vs Guilt	Initiative adds to autonomy—the quality of doing things just to be doing them. A series of guilt is often experienced over things contemplated or actually done. A favourable ratio of initiative to guilt results in a sense of purpose.

Continued

TABLE 17.4 Erikson's psychological stages with corresponding crises (*Continued*)

Sl.No.	*Age/period*	*Basic conflict (crises)*	*Optimal outcome*
4.	6 years to puberty (School child)	Industry vs Inferiority	Grade school children learn to win approval by making things and doing things approved of in the culture in literate societies. They learn to read. In preliterate societies they learn the skills necessary for survival. Failure to produce or do valued things leads to a sense of inferiority. A favourable ratio of industry to inferioty leads to a sense of competence and pleasure in work.
5.	Adolescence	Identity vs Role confusion	Identity refers to 'who am I?' 'what am I going to do with my life?' Questions of adolescence. Difficulty in answering those questions leads to role confusion. A favourable ratio of identity to role confusion leads to a sense of consistency.
6.	Early adulthood	Intimacy vs Isolation	Here the task is to establish lasting and loving relationships with other people. Love is the outcome of favourable ratio of intimacy to isolation.
7.	Middle adulthood	Generativity vs Stagnation	Generativity includes productivity and creativity, but here it refers primarily to preparing the next generation for life in the culture. Care is the outcome of a favourable generativity to stagnation.
8.	Late adulthood (or older person)	Ego integrity vs Despair	Ego integrity has many facets. In part, it refers to one's acceptance of one's life as what it had be. Despair, on the other hand, includes the feelings that life is too short to do much and that integrity cannot be achieved. A favourable ratio of ego identity to despair brings wisdom and the ability to face death calmly.

Table 17.4 shows that if we look at the possible outcomes, it would be evident that solving the crises associated with different stages is not always possible in positive manner. In fact, any crisis at a particular stage is bi-polar in nature with positive as well as negative outcomes. However, if a healthier solution of the crisis (conflict) is achieved, it favours relatively positive outcomes.

In addition, the cultural variations also pose difficulty in accepting any of these theories as having general applicability across the cultures.

Moreover, most of the concepts of dynamic theories are difficult to be experimentally and objectively tested.

Thus, dynamic theories alone cannot be taken as complete in themselves to describe and explain personality fully and objectively.

A general comment on dynamic process theories

No doubt, the dynamic theories that has till now been described have had a far reaching influence in understanding and knowing the psychic processes of human beings which determine the kind of personality one develops and also the way one responds to the various situations one encounters. Some of the concepts such as defence mechanism have stimulated research and gained wider acceptance. The ideas relating to the significance of childhood experiences in personality, unconscious motives and conflicts are some of the important outgrowths of dynamic theories.

Despite the above-mentioned facts, each of the dynamic theories has included some concepts which are difficult either to prove or disprove. It is practically very difficult to test oedipus and electra complexes, castration fear and similar other concepts. Most of the dynamic theories talk of disguised motives, hidden goals and indirect ways of coping. To substantiate these, the ordinary 'rules of evidences' are difficult to apply.

17.5 BEHAVIOURIST APPROACHES TO PERSONALITY

Behaviourist psychologists have attempted to explain personality based on learning principles, more particularly conditioning learning, instrumental or operant conditioning and cognitive learning.

Personality theories built on learning and behavioural principles share some important assumptions. Two of such assumptions are important and mentioned below:

(a) The first such shared assumption is that behaviours that make up personality are conditioned or learned. This means that the behavioural components of personality have their origin at some point in the learning history of the individual—often as early as childhood.
(b) Second shared assumption is that the current environmental situations help to maintain these learned behaviours.

Thus, the behaviourists try to understand personality by studying the behaviour that has originated during the learning history as well as current environmental conditions.

Learning and behavioural theorists also believe in testing their theories in objective terms. Hence, such theorists focus on observable events and behaviours that may be made clear to others how to test them. However, in cases where they are required to deal with 'unseen' processes such as 'anxiety' that occurs 'inside the person', the behaviourists violate the 'strict behaviourisim' and try to translate these processes into language designed to make them as observable as possible.

Some of the important such theories are as follows:

17.5.1 Dollard and Miller: Early Social Learning Theory

John Dollard and **Neal Miller** in early 1930s jointly ventured to test the basic idea that individual and social behaviour can be explained on the basis of learning principles. They even tried to Freud's psychoanalytic concepts into language of learning theory and attempted to test these concepts in experimental situation on rats.

For example, Freud believed that neurotic, disturbed behaviour involves conflict betwen id demands and ego/superego restraints. Dollard and Miller considered such conflicts similar to the conflicts between approach and avoidance behavioural tendencies and argued that in approaching and avoiding a certain course of action situation, we encounter a conflict. For example, when we want to get the teeth with cavity extracted by a dentist (approaching tendency), but fear the pain (avoiding tendency), conflict occurs. In such cases at first, the tendency to approach is often stronger (getting the teeth extracted) than the avoidance tendency. But, as we get closer to the 'moment of truth', the avoiding tendency is more likely to win out and we may retreat or flee from the planned action (we may cancel the idea of consulting the dentist).

Dollard and **Miller** applied this idea to a variety of human problems. As an example the researchers cite the analysis of a case of women (Mrs A) who was treated by a psychotherapist in New York.

> **The woman had a serious obsessive problem. She felt tormented particularly when she left her home alone. The idea that her heart would stop unless she counted its beats. She also feared 'something may happen to her' when she shopped and that no one would know where she was. She was so worried with these feelings and obsessed ideas that her friends began to avoid her and even her husband also threatened to leave her.**

On careful examination by the therapist, it could be revealed that these **neurotic symptoms** had developed out of her conflicting feelings about sex. On the one hand, she had a strong tendency to avoid sex because of the repeated suggestions, in stronger terms by her foster mother that sex was an evil and unclean act. Moreover, the lady had married a man of high status and higher education than her. So, she was also afraid to enjoy sex openly with him as it may make her seem **low class**. So she was extremely restrained, almost prudish in her relations with the husband. On the other hand, she had also a strong sex drive—a strong **approach tendency**. Before marriage, a dozen men had tried to seduce her and most of them had succeeded (Dollard and Miller, 1950, p. 18).* After marriage, her sexual appetites often led her what may be called **flirt with danger** (e.g. she would sometimes hitch rides with truck drivers).

Dollard and Miller interpreted her difficulties this way—she felt a strong conflict between her sexual urges (approach) and her fear of being openly sexual (avoidance). Whenever she got close to a real sexual experience, her fear of sex overdominated her desire for it resulting in shying and getting away from sexual intercourse. This situation gradually got more and more dangerous, and she became very anxious. Eventually, she found another way of avoiding sex. She developed intense fear that kept her mind totally occupied with obsessive ideas that something would happen to her and that heart might stop and she began counting every heartbeat. This prevented sexual thoughts and associated feelings. Though, this approach was upsetting in several ways, it was also rewarding in one important way—as soon as she started counting her beats, she felt better. Dollard and Miller assumes—by doing so, she was repressing the conflict. They defined Freud's concept of repression in terms of learning. According to them, repression is a learned response of **not thinking about** something that is anxiety producing. In the case of this woman, this response was rewarding as it reduces anxiety.

In essence, Dollard and Miller had attempted to redefine Freud's concepts in terms of learning principles.

17.5.2 Pavlov's Conditioning Principle

Pavlov conducted experimental studies on conditioning learning which is based on certain

* Dollard, J. and N.E. Miller, *Personality and Psychotherapy: An Analysis in Terms of Learning, Thinking and Culture*, New York, McGraw-Hill, 1950, p. 18.

observable manipulations of stimuli and responses. Pavlov has emphasized learning as a product of the pairing of responses with stimuli. As we know, a neutral stimulus and a potential stimulus (UCS), if paired together, change the situation in such a way that the previously neutral stimulus or event (now CS) alone acquires the potentiality to evoke the similar response that was earlier produced by the potent stimulus (UCS). This approach has been extended to explain and treat many abnormal behaviours such as phobic reactions, obsessions, anxiety etc. The behaviourists of classical conditioning tradition believe that most of the behavioural characteristics are learned in the manner we learn to associate our responses to a particular kind of stimulus and thus, personality features are learned attributes.

17.5.3 Skinner's Radical Behaviourism

Skinner's approach is instrumental which is concerned with the processes by which reinforcement (reward) and punishment influence the probability of behaviour. Skinner has outrightly ruled out the unobservable inner forces (e.g. needs, motives) and also the type trait aproach. Skinner in fact holds that in reality, there is no need for a concept of **personality** or any such **excess baggage** as traits and types. What we call personality is in fact a collection of **reinforced responses**. We are the kind of person because we behave in certain ways and this is because we have experience of reinforcement contingencies. Thus, analysis of stimulus conditions that control our behaviour is crucial to explain behaviour. In this sense, many psychologists consider Skinner's view as **personalityless view of personality**. Many seem to be offended by Skinner's stand while many others see Skinner's work as refreshing because this view is clear, precise and parsimonious, i.e. to rely on the smallest possible number of theoretical concepts and assumptions.

17.5.4 Bandura and Walters: Later Social Learning Theory

Bandura and **Walters** have focused on the highly efficient form of learning which is known as **observational learning** or **imitation**. They argue that observational learning does not require any direct reinforcement as has been viewed by classical and operant theorists (although they acknowledged the importance of reinforcement or at least **anticipated reinforcement** in the persistence of learned behaviour). Observational learning usually takes place in social situation involving a **model** as an imitator. Hence, often it is also referred to as **model learning** or **social learning** or **imitative learning**. The imitator observes the behaviour of the model and experience its consequences vicariously. This process is termed as **vicarious informant**. Bandura holds the view that nearly all learning (that can occur with instrumental procedure) can take place **vicariously** through modelling, i.e. by substituting oneself in the place of the model by imitating model's behaviour.

Accordingly, Bandura explains that fearful behaviours that a child learns is largely due to the fearful models and opportunities to learn or imitate such models.

Observational learning has also been used to explain and treat certain troubling problems such as phobia in addition to a variety of normal and abnormal personality patterns.

A general comment about learning and behavioural approaches to personality

Probably most psychologists would agree that many of the behaviour patterns that we call

personality are acquired or learned tendencies through conditioning or other procedures such as influenced by reward-punishment or observation of models. However, controversy does exist relating to the question whether the learning theories are sufficient to provide our enquiries about personality?

No doubt, learning theories make us to know and understand behaviour in a specific situation, but it ignores to lament upon consistencies that people show from one situation to another (Bowers, 1973). Moreover, by emphasising merely the outward observation of reinforcement would in fact diminish the perosn in personality whereas we all understand that the 'person' (innerside or psyche) has a significant role in shaping the personality of the person in such a way that each personality has certain distinguishing features that fit well with the inner self alone and not in other's self. That is why personality is dynamic organization of various psychophysical systems.

However, learning theorists counter such arguments in several ways. They assume that conditioning learning is not so simple as we understand. We learn many complex forms of behaviour through conditioning. Hence, even the intricate and subtle aspects of human pesonality can be understood in terms of conditioning procedures.

In addition, Bandura and Walters' theory of observational learning does refer to inner-cognitive processes involved in imitation and delayed performances. In fact, except Skinner, almost all learning theorists acknowledge the impact of some such powerful variables within the learner who is an active agent of the environment, learning does play a role in moulding, developing, shaping and organizing personality in some unique way.

17.6 THE HUMANISTIC THEORIES OF PERSONALITY

The humanistic approches to personality take a positive and optimistic view of human nature. It focuses on the individual's 'self' which is considered as largely responsible for what happens to the individual. Thus, humanistic view of personality recognizes the role of personal responsibility and growth and lay emphasis on the present rather than on the past. Out of several such theories, following two of them are very much popular.

17.6.1 Rogers' Self Theory

Carl Rogers' theory (1959, 1961) has grown out of his client-centred approach to psychotherapy and behaviour change. Rogers has emphasized the whole of experience which he terms as **phenomenal field** which is the subjective frame of reference of the individual. It may or may not correspond to external world.

Rogers has laid main emphasis on 'the self'. He assumes that out of the phenomenal field a **self** or 'self concept' gradually develops. This he could discern from what his clients expressed in their spontaneous thoughts (in course of client centred therapeutic session). He came to the conclusion—**it seemed clear ... that the self was an important element in the experience of the client, and that in some odd sense, his goal was to become his 'real self'** (Rogers, 1959, p. 201).* This suggests that in addition to **'present self'** there is an another kind of self known as

* Rogers, C.R. (1959), 'A theory of therapy, personality and interpersonal relationships as developed in the client-centred framework' in S. Koch (Ed.) *Psychology: A Study of Science* (Vol. 3), McGraw-Hill, New York.

ideal self—the self the person would like to be. However, when the two—present and ideal self—are incongruent, i.e. do not match to the other, person experiences trouble. Thus, the perceived self when does not match the ideal self, the individual becomes disturbed and anxiety is aroused.

Thus, gap between perceived self and ideal self is the main cause of anxiety or maladjustive behaviour. Rogers assumes that one's mental health is related to the degree to which there is cogruence or match betwen one's self and life experiences. If our self-concept is consistent with real life experiences, ourselves will be congruent and we will be well adjusted individuals. Just opposite would happen when there would be no consistency (see **Figure 17.2**).

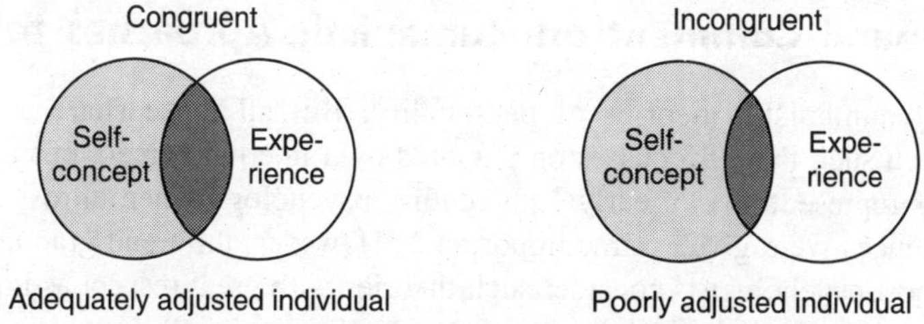

FIGURE 17.2 Pattern of adjustment and self-concept.

The situation of maladjustment (i.e. when the two are inconsistent) needs creation of an atmosphere of **unconditional positive regard** so that the person may feel accepted irrespective of what they say or do. 'Client centred therapy' attempts to create this kind of situation and Rogers claims to have achieved success in treating various disorders by applying this technique.

17.6.2 Maslow's Theory of Self-actualization

Another phenomenological theorist who emphasized development of self was **Abraham Maslow**. **Maslow** holds an optimistic and positive view of human being. Every individual has the potential to grow as he has an essential nature that 'presses' to emerge as the 'press' within the seedling to grow into a giant tree. Therefore, since each one of us is in possession of the potentials for love, joy, enriching the self-esteem and doing creative works and grow to the fullest strength, *i.e.* achieving self-actualization. In this sense, human beings are free to shape their lives and self-actualize. According to Maslow, personality is person's perceptual orientation and the hierarchies of needs to focus attention and energy. On the hierarchy of needs, a preoccupation with meeting lower order needs may lead to deficiency in orientation. Such persons remain restricted to meet only the material things that they do not have. Hence, they are likely to behave in a distorted way.

Maslow has used the term **'meta needs'** that refers to higher order needs (*e.g.* justice, goodness, order, beauty, unity etc.). The frustration of meta needs may rsult in alteration, apathy and cynicism (surliness), hate for human nature etc.

Maslow studied a good number of people who were self-actualized. Such people are found open to experiences and were in consonance with their inner world. Spontaneousness, autonomousness, independence, devotion towards goals, fresh appreciation of people and events, resistance to conformity, and sincere dedication for some genuine cause of the humanity in general are some of the characterizing features of self-actualized persons. Such people view the world more accurately because they perceive the objects of the world in relation to themselves and not as means to fulfil deficiency.

Maslow also holds that satisfaction of needs are also influenced by cultural factors. In Western societies, people are trained to focus on material satisfaction of needs and, therefore, the lower order needs are considered more important than the higher order needs like self-actualization.

In general, self-actualized persons are rare. However, people do experience the moments of self-actualization. It is termed as **peak experiences**. Such experiences are noticed in feelings of richness and highest happiness. (Details of hierarchy of need model of Maslow has been described in Chapter 14 on Motivation under Section 14.15.)

17.6.3 A General Comment on Humanistic Aproaches to Personality

There are several humanistic theories of personality. But all these share a common view of personality, i.e. each such theory focusses on person's own internal perceptions and intro-spections. Thus, the theory is representative of early 19th century psychology when introspection and analysis of personal experiences were given prime importance. However, the trend gradually turned towards objectivity. Still most psychologists consider such theories with great respect as it provides insightful reports for studying the psychological processes involved in innerself.

However, the two theories described above suffer from certain faults and need to be extensively researched to substantiate the facts.

17.7 KURT LEWIN'S FIELD THEORY OF PERSONALITY

In the light of advances being made in the areas of natural sciences, more particularly in physics, field theory of human behaviour has been proposed. The physicists use the concept of **field** to explain gravitational field, electromagnetic field etc. Some psychologists borrowed the concept of field from these sciences and tried to understand human behaviour in terms of the **topology** (space) that surrounds us.

Kurt Lewin's system has two aspects—topological and vectoral. Topology refers to the physical and psychological environment that surrounds us. Vectoral aspect describes the resolution of stress or strains within the individual.

Lewin has differentiated between psychological and physical environment and introduced the concept of **life space (LS)** to explain the nature of relation between person (P) and his environment (E). According to Lewin, life space (LS) is the whole psychological reality that determines the behaviour of an individual (B). Life space includes everything that is present in the environment and exerts its influence on individual's behaviour. This environment contains everything that lies outside the person (P), i.e. it includes the physical, psychological and social aspects. Lewin calls the person and his environment as space which in equation form is represented as follows:

$B = f\ (LS)$ and $LS = (P + E)$, i.e. behaviour (B) is a function (f) of life space (LS) and life space includes the person (P) and his environment. (E) Lewin's concept is depicted in **Figure 17.3**.

In Figure 17.3, life space consists of person (P) and psychological environment (E). The person is included within the life space but at the same time differentiated from the environment. Lewin also assumes that the person also is differentiated from within. The person is divisible in two major regions—**the perceptual motor region** and **the inner personal region.** The former lies in the periphery of circle enclosing the P whereas the latter region occupies the central part of the circle. Thus, the inner-personal region is completely surrounded by perceptual-motor region and, therefore, it has no direct contact with the outside environment. The perceptual motor region controls perceptual and motoric functions whereas the inner-personal region controls the motivational functions. Thus, the person is **heterogeneous** and not **homogeneous**.

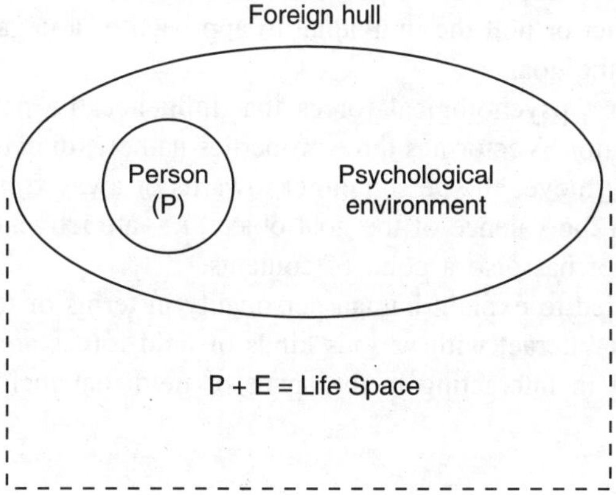

FIGURE 17.3 Life space.

Psychological environment, another aspect of life space, as shown in Figure 17.3, covers the area within the eclipse but outside the circle enclosing the person (P). Lewin has divided the psychological environment in different regions or boundaries. Some regions are permeable while others are impermeable. The permeable boundaries enable us to influence others and vice versa.

The external environment (physical E) are outside the life space and is called **foreign hull**. The boundary between foreign hull and psychological environment is permeable and, therefore, two-way communication between these two kinds of environment may occur, *i.e.* the two environmental events are likely to bring changes in each other's events.

Thus, in a nutshell, life space of a person includes himself and other persons or objects of the world as perceived by the person. It also includes ideas.

Lewin also states that life space can be divided into regions separated by boundaries. Each region contains psychological facts which are either observable or inferential such as social events, intellectual events, perceptual events etc. The boundaries of life space are of two dimensions:

(i) Nearness-remoteness dimension and (ii) Firmness-weakness dimension.

To understand these dimensions of life space boundaries let us consider an example.

A young boy wants to be an IAS officer. To achieve this goal, he must first obtain bachelor degree from a recognized university, then he will have to complete preliminary screening test (PT), then compete the main examination and finally the viva voce test of UPSC. In this example, the aspiring boy is the person (P) and goal is to become an IAS officer. In between the two, there are four regions—obtaining the bachelor degree, competing the preliminary test, main test and finally the viva voce test. Here competing the viva voce test is the near region while obtaining the bachelor degree is a remote region. Competing the main examination may be a difficult task and hence, a firm boundary while competing the PT may be relatively easier and therefore a weak boundary region. The number of boundaries in a life space depends upon the number of facts that exists at a particular time.

Lewin elaborating his concept of life space further talks of the processes by which different regions interact with each other through the process of communication and locomotion and follow certain principles such as principles of relatedness and concreteness, contemporariety.

Lewin also used the concepts of energy, tension need valence and vector. The valences may be either positive that attract or pull the individual to approach or a negative valence which pushes the person back or avoid the goal.

Vector refers to those psychological forces that influence the person to the extent that he moves in a particular direction. Vector has three properties namely, direction, strength and a point of content. Direction property moves the person either towards or away from the goal object. Strength property is correlated with the valence of the goal object, *i.e.* attractiveness or repulsiveness nature of the goal object. A vector has also a point of contents.

Hence, Lewin has tried to explain human personality in terms of totality of the space or field in which people behave or interact with various kinds of field forces and personality is determined by the processes involved in interacting in the space of field that includes the person as well as his environment.

Critical comments

Though Lewin has attempted to explain personality with a wider perspective that takes into account the totality of the situation in which the person interacts and influence each other. However, several psychologists raise several questions and passed severe criticisms to his system.

Critics of Lewin have said that his system is full of imaginary, unverifiable and untestable constructs. **Broyler** (1936, 1937) holds that Lewin's constructs are nothing more than pictorial analogies and illustrative metaphors and therefore, provide no meaningful explanation.

Lewin is also charged with misusing the mathematical concept of vector in psychology and even the topological concepts borrowed from geometry has been misapplied (London, 1944).

Critics also state that Lewin has utterly failed in specifying a clear cut relationship between life space and external environment.

Lewin has also ignored many other aspects related to personality such as past history of the individual (Garret, 1939; Leeper, 1943).

Despite the above critical remarks, Lewin's system has great heuristic value because it has generated a large number of researchers and experimenters in many areas of psychology. Lewin's system is multidimensional in scope and hence, a significant contribution.

17.8 NEW ADVANCES: FIVE-FACTOR MODEL OF PERSONALITY

In recent times, long continuous controversy with regard to the number of basic personality traits has taken a new turn and personality is being considered as consisting of a limited number of components. Consequent upon the extensive work done by **Paul Costa** and **Robert MacCrae** (1980), a new picture of five-factor model of personality has emerged. These are very often called **big five**. These big five factors are as follows:

1. **Openness to experience:** Those who are high on this factor are imaginative,

courteous, open to new ideas and interested in cultural pursuits. In contrast, the low scorers are rigid.

2. **Extraversion:** It is characterized by high indulgence in social activities, assertiveness, outgoing nature, talkativeness and fun loving. Its opposite is shy.
3. **Agreeableness:** This factor represents such traits that characterize people as helpful, co-operative, friendly, caring and nurturing. It is the opposite of hostile and being self-centred.
4. **Neuroticism:** Those who score high on this factor are emotionally unstable, anxious, worried, fearful, distressed, irritable, hypertensive. Its opposite is well-adjusted.
5. **Conscientionist:** Those who display high degree of this factor are achievement oriented, dependable, responsible, prudent, hardworking and self-controlled. Its opposite is impulsive.

This model has been considered as an important theoretical development. It is also useful in understanding the personality profile of people of different cultures. It has also been found consistent with the analysis of personality traits found in different languages and supported by the studies of personality through different methods. It is now considered to be the most promising empirical approach to the study of personality.

Costa and MacCrae also devised an inventory known as the NEO Personality inventory (NEO PI-R). It provides scores on the five-factors of personality. This inventory has been developed on the basis of extensive research that uses lexical data, describing personality in various languages to different parts of the world.

17.9 DETERMINANTS OF PERSONALITY

If we examine the course of personality development, we come across a number of forces at work which moulds and shapes our personalities in various ways. Some of these are more important during early stages of development (formation stage of personality) while some play a role later in life. In view of difficulty faced by the psychologists to cover up the **whole person** in a single theory of personality—a very intricate and complex organization of various psycho-physical systems, most of the psychologists have turned their focus of research on specific issues in personality and freeing themselves from evolving approaches to explain personality. Two of such issues involving determining factors of personality are important. These are **Genes and Personality** (nature-nurture controversy) and the **person-situation controversy**. These two issues will be discussed in this section which covers the major determining factors of personality.

17.9.1 The Nature-Nurture Controversy

Most scientists hold the view that we are what we are, partly because of our inherited biological characteristics—our nature. Others believe that it is the environment, i.e. the nurture side is much more important in making a person what he is. Researches done on both kinds of beliefs provide ample evidences in support of both the views and hence, the issue is still unresolved.

The nature-nurture debate in fact concerns with the relative impact of heredity and environment. The reality is that no one believes that either of the two alone completely determine the course of personality development and dispositions. Psychologists today seem to agree that personality is developed and shaped by the interaction of heredity (genetic factors) and environment both. Let us examine how the two groups of factors—heredity and evironment—influence personality.

Inherited predisposition

Many psychologists believe heredity as an important determinant of personality. They hold that the difference in personalities is due to the difference in inherited genes. Such claims of genetic psychologists are based on studies done on identical and fraternal (monozygotic—Mz and dizygotic—Dz) twins who have much similarities in their genetic make-up and also display similarities in psychological dispositions, such as response style, intellectual abilities, interests, emotional expressions, stress tolerance etc. For example, **Buss et al.** (1973) conducted a study on such mothers who had identical (Mz) and fraternal (Dz) twin children. The mothers were given a questionnaire on their children to fill up. The questionnaire contained items on four dimensions—emotionality (*e.g.* child has a quick temper), activity (*e.g.* child is always on the go), sociability (*e.g.* child tends to be shy) and impulsivity (*e.g.* child goes from toy to toy quickly). It was found that on all the items individual correlations for Mz were much higher than for Dz twins. Since Mz twins have 100% identical genes while Dz twins average only 50% identical genes. Hence, higher correlations in the case of identical twins seem to show that the greater similarity of genes make for similar temperaments. Subsequent researches done by others (such as **Plomin** and **Rowe**, 1977) also continue to show difference in identical and fraternal (Mz and Dz differences) twins and thus lend support to the notion of genetic influences.

However, some researchers hold the view that these studies have involved ratings by mothers who know whether their children are Mz or Dz and thus, their subjective **perceived ideas** seem to influence their ratings with respect to the extent of similarities and differences in temperament of their children. Hence, unless the influence of such variables are controlled, our conclusions based on such studies would remain only as tentative and not confirmed.

Traits, types and chromosomes

Besides child's temperament, we can also find some evidences of genetic influences on development of traits and typology. **Cary et al.** (1978) using California psychological inventory (CPI) have tried to study 18 traits of Mz and Dz twins. The study revealed average correlations obtained across several studies of Mz and Dz pairs. On every scale, Mz correlations average much higher than Dz correlations. However, in such studies again, the correlations by themselves do not show, conclusively, that personality traits have a genetic basis. Usually it is found that Mz twins are reared in similar environment than the Dz twins because of the fact that parents of Mz twins tend to treat their Mz twins alike (*e.g.,* dress them alike, provide educational opportunities alike, and so forth) whereas the Dz twins are treated differently. However, **Ludins** and **Nichols** (1976) have shown that though similarity in upbringing was not a major cause of high correlations among Mz twins, however, the similarity in upbringing strengthens the case for genetic influence. The pattern of correlations in Mz and Dz twins are presented in **Table 17.5**.

Even if we presume that the patterns shown in Table 17.5 are reflective of real genetic influences, the question is as to how does this influence operate? Do we inherit the trait **dominance** or **sociability**? Obviously, not. The pertinent question is what do we inherit that influence these traits? There is no acceptable answer to this. **H.J. Eysenck** (whose theory we have discussed earlier) has opined that the traits of extraversion and introversion dimensions are linked

TABLE 17.5 Mean Mz and Dz twin pair correlations for CPI scale*

CPI scale	Correlations (Mean)	
	Mz	Dz
Dominance	.59	.31
Capacity for status	.61	.46
Sociability	.54	.21
Social presence	.54	.28
Self-acceptance	.51	.23
Well-being	.46	.31
Responsibility	.49	.33
Socialisation	.47	.25
Self-control	.52	.30
Tolerance	.52	.32
Good impression	.48	.23
Communality	.30	.12
Achievement (conformance)	.40	.25
Achievement (independence)	.53	.37
Intellectual efficiency	.54	.38
Psychological mindedness	.43	.21
Flexibility	.50	.30
Femininity	.42	.25

to the inherited characteristics of **reticular formation**—the part of the brain that influences the individual's level of arousal. Eysenck believes that introverts usually inherit the tendency of arousal more than the extroverts and also that they have a basic need to inhibit (dumpdown) their arousal. Consequently, introverts tend to avoid extreme excitement, seek out calm, quiet conditions and remain aloof from activation caused by social interaction. On the other hand, extroverts genetically tend to be underaroused and, therefore, are attracted to excitement and social interaction. Tests of extraversion-introversion also provide fairly strong evidence of heritability. Moreover, four of the traits mentioned in CPI scales (Table 17.5) such as dominance, sociability, social presence and self-acceptance, show a very pronounced Mz-Dz difference. These traits are considered as the major components of introversion-extraversion dimension.

However, many other studies, for example, **Farber** (1981), **Bouchard** (1984) involving Mz-Dz pairs have also reflected the role of environmental factors in no way less significant than genetic endowments.

In fact, personality is not directly inherited. Genetic endowments only predispose the development of certain traits in a certain way. The development of inherited dispositions and the degree to which it develops, depend on environmental factors. Some of the differences in the inherited dispositions among the infants may be observed at an early stage, such as—one may be extremely active while another lazy, one may cry and violent and agitate most of the times while another remain so calm that often make parents anxious to consult doctors to examine if there is anything wrong with the baby. Such innate characteristics are called temperamental characteristics or traits.

* Carey, G. Gold Smith, H.H. Telkegen, A. and Gottesman, I.I. (1978), Genetics and Personality Inventories, The Limits of replication with twin data, *Behaviour Genetics*, 8, pp. 299–313.

However, most of the traits appear later under the influence of increasing environmental contacts such as schooling, membership to larger groups, meeting with various persons, adopting certain traits through experience and practice by imitating the models etc.

Personality in fact, can be taken as the **square area** of the person. To put in mathematical terms, we know that area of any space of field can be found by multiplying the length with its width (length × width = area). Similarly, **personality of an individual is an area or space (P) which is a product** of **heredity × environment**. Hence, both the genetic and environmental opportunities—play significant role.

In fact, the genetic endowments provide us with a **reaction range**—a range of possible level of different characteristics that are possible for us to ultimately reach, but achieving the possible level depends on the quality of our experience of the environment. **Curt Stern** has tried to explain the equal significance of heredity and environment in the development of personality with the help of an analogy of **rubber band**.

Stern compares genetic endowments of a particular trait to the amount of **stretch** that is possible in a rubber band. Some rubber bands have great inbuilt stretchability potential while others have relatively little. However, the amount of stretch in a rubber band will depend upon both—the basic **inbuilt stretchability** potential as well as the **amount of pressure** with which it is pulled. Similarly, the amount of any particular trait will depend upon both—the genetically endowed potential of stretchability—**reaction range** as well as the degree to which the person's environment **pulls for** the development of that trait. Hence, personality is influenced by both—the genetic and environmental factors.

17.9.2 The Person-Situation Controversy

Person-situation controversy is another major disputed issue which has extensively been researched. It concerns with the central question—the extent to which our behaviour is caused by the characteristics within ourselves and the extent to which the situation we find ourselves? This question can be examined by focusing on a key principle—**when we think or describe people's behaviour, we often tend to reduce complex reality to a few simple generalities. Walter Mischel** (1969) calls the process by which we simplify complexity as **reducing value**. To understand it **Mischel** cites an illustration as mentioned below:

> *When we observe a woman who seems hostile and fiercely independent some of the time but passive, dependent and feminine on other occasion, our reducing value usually makes us to choose between the two syndromes. We decide that one pattern is in the service of the other or that both are in the service of a third motive. She must be a castrating lady with a facade of passivity or perhaps she is a warm, passive dependent woman with a surface defense of aggressiveness.*
>
> —(Mischel*, 1969, p. 1015)

From the above illustration it is obvious that **traits** (hostile, fierce, independent, passive) and type (castrating lady) are used as simplifying devices. The trait and type approach to personality considers trait and type as useful means of identifying personality as the traits are indicative of consistent ways of behaving. But others argue that trait and type approach may generate only an illusion of consistency because people's behaviours are very complex, diverse

* W. Mischel, 'Continuity and Change in Personality', Amer. Psychologist, 1969, 24, pp. 1012–1018.

and situationally determined. As Mischel argues, **It is possible in the above example that all these traits may be found in the same person and in a particular time of reference, which of these traits occur—depends on the situation—with whom she is with, when, how and much-much more.**

This position is called **situationalism** because it emphasizes the situation, *i.e.* environmental determinants of people's behaviour.

As we notice in most of the controversies, the person-situation controversy also involves only a small number of theorists at the two extremes and many occupy the middle position. At the 'person' extreme are a few theorists of dynamic group who believe that people possess certain basic drives, motives, conflicts or tendencies that produce consistency in behaviour across various situations. At the situational extreme are the theories like Skinner who believes that the notions like traits of character and freewill is of little use and therefore should be dropped and favour the environmental situations that determine our behaviour.

However, many psychologists occupy compromising position and are positioned in the middle of the two extreme views. They argue that much of the relevant researches have been inconclusive. Most of the studies done so far show that **person characteristics** and **situation characteristics**—both influence behaviour and neither of the two alone is so important as is the interaction of the person and the situation (Bowers, 1973). This obviously means that the influence of **person factors** and **situation factors** depends on which person and which situation we observe or study. **Bem** and **Allen** (1974) have also illustrated that to predict behaviour, we can use the person trait or characteristics only some of the people some of the time.

Thus, personality is a joint function of both the personal characteristics as well as the situation available in the environment.

17.9.3 Factors of Personality

What follows from the two major controversies that we just discussed, personality or behavioural tendencies are determined by multiple factors relating to the 'person'—his genetic endowments, physical characteristics, nervous and glandular systems as well as the 'environmental' situations such as home environment, neighbourhood, school, group interrelations as well as cultural factors. In the present section, we shall be presenting a brief account of some of the important such factors.

Personal (physical) characteristics

(i) **Physique:** Constitution of physique is an important factor in personality. Physique constitutes complexion, size, physical built, general health and deformities in physique. A balanced combination of these features accounts for attractiveness (positive valence) and inattractiveness (negative valence). Usually, a slim and fair-complexioned person with other attractive features (*e.g.* facial appearance, hair style, smart dress, fairly tall etc.) are eye-catching personalities. On the other hand, those who are ugly in appearance, dark-skinned, short in height and spherical in shape are considered unattractive and are categorized as having poor personality.

Adler is of the view that physique in itself does not determine personality rather poor or good, attractive or unattractive physical features depend upon how people react. Generally people with physical deformities or ugliness are subjected to humiliation by others. Such negative attributions arouse a sense of inferiority in reaction to which one's mode of response reflects his poor personality.

(ii) **Nervous and glandular system:** Among the biological determinants, the role of genetic factors has already been discussed earlier while discussing the controversy. Therefore, in the present section, we shall be discussing about the role of nervous system, more particularly the autonomous nervous system (ANS) and hypo or hyper-hormonal secretions of the endocrine glands. These biological structures have been found closely associated with personality make-ups. The relationship between ANS and emotional expressions, drive states have been well established in several scientific studies. It has been found that individuals with strong sympathetic reactions are relatively more dependent, suggestible, dreamy and idealistic than those who are more strong in parasympathetic reactions. Such individuals are rather cool, evasive, opportunistic and independent.

Similarly, some studies done on abnormal glandular conditions provide evidences to the fact that hormones secreted by these glands (*e.g.* thyroid, adrenal, gonads, pituitary, pancreas, pineal etc.) have an impact on personality. Many of the psychologists believe that personality is a function of the extent to which glandular systems function in normal ways. For example, persons suffering from hypothyroidism (below normal level of secretion of thyroxin) are found dull, inert, and low in intelligence and also develop forgetfulness. Some psychiatrists opine that hypothyroidism is an important aeteological factor associated with schizoid personality. Conversely, hyperthyroidism (above normal secretion of thyroxin) results in quarrelsome behaviours, are over-impulsive and excited. Similarly, oversecretion of sex gland results in aggression and increased emotional reactions.

In addition to above, many more biological conditions such as changes in blood chemistry due to prolonged hunger, drug addiction, reduction of vitamins, effects of physical stressors (*e.g.* excessive exposure to bright illumination, sound, constant cough and cold, fatigue, physical harassment, pressure of overwork, ill health etc.) have also been found to have significant bearings on one's personality.

17.9.4 Social Factors of Personality

As we have seen earlier (person-situation controversy), personality of an individual is jointly determined by the **person's** personal characteristics as well as environmental situations. The environmental situations are largely man made, *i.e.* these situations are created by the people comprising the society. Thus, our social environment is a potent aspect of personality. This includes a wide variety of situations in which interpersonal interactions occur as per the demand of the social situation. It includes various aspects of the society such as the home environment, neighbourhood, school, group relations etc.

Home environment (The family)

Family is the major socializing agent of the individual. In early years, personality is moulded most rapidly in which family plays most vital and primary role in two ways—(a) it socializes the child through specific training procedures while rearing and (b) it also creates an atmosphere and provides opportunities for the child to develop and grow in a desirable direction. Some of the important characteristics that a child develops in the family by way of socialization are learning of socially valued skills—the manners, etiquettes, social poise (equilibrium), social ethics such as right-wrong, good-bad, socially acceptable-unacceptable, moral or immoral etc. (Jenis et al 1969). Though inter and intracultural variations in family environment and child rearing practices, family norms and standards are found, however, scientists in general agree that **family set-up** is one of the strongest potential aspects of our social environment that attempts to shape personality into a templet of family traditions and also rears children in the way that the child grows in to a kind of person as the family decides. The significant role of family in shaping personality is found in all cultures.

The family environment includes various kinds of situations such as **family warmth**, **learning opportunities in the family, parental attitude, interparental relations** and **relation-ships of the parents with the child, socio-economic status of the family, family traditions** etc. For example, **Jenis et al.** (1969) hold that parental training is substantially evidenced in **'sex typing'** in which male and female children develop appropriate responses and interact suitably to their gender identity. **Goldfarb** (1947) in a study of orphange children found fondling behaviour—a major factor in developing emotional responsiveness in children. **Hilgard** (1953) and **Baldwin** found that parents usually unconsciously relate their own childhood problems through their children. For example, a mother is likely to react to her son with her own childhood reactions that she used to display with her elder brother. Similarly, a father may also display his childhood experiences over to his offsprings. Parental attitudes create a particular type of atmosphere within the home which exerts influence in shaping of unique personality of the individual which is referred to as **impact of home experience.**

Within the family set-up, **imitation** is also a significant influencer of personality. Imitation is a process of social learning. **Bandura** and **Walters** (1969), on the basis of their findings, have concluded that a child learns much by imitation of the models (usually the parental figures) that include both kinds of learning—learning of general attitude as well as specific responses of the model. Children copy many of the personality characteristics of their parents such as mannerism, typical ways of coping with problems, acquiring parental habits, beliefs, attitudes, living styles, orderliness etc. Thus, despite many differences, children borrow at least some of the personality traits from their parental figure through the process of imitative learning, *i.e.* the offsprings usually carry some part of traits of their parents (model).

Over and above, many other aspects of family such as size of the family, ordinal position of the child, sex distribution, sibling rivalry, sex compositional pattern of the siblings etc. are also important familial correlates of personality (Mishra, 1974).

From the above, it is evident that family serving as a major agent of socialization process during early childhood period, play a vital role in shaping and developing of unique personality dispositions. **Family in fact lays the foundation stone upon which the personality of a person is built up later in life'.**

Neighbourhood

Next to home is the neighbour which influences personality in important ways. As the child grows to approximately 4 years of age, he comes in contact with other children of his neighbourhood. This provides an opportunity for the child to mix and interact with them. Such interactions are significant because, it brings forth the opportunities for the child to acquire some general traits as well as some specific modes of responses to adapt. This enables socially adaptive traits to develop and also to learn the acceptable modes of interpersonal interactions. Most of the aggressive or co-operative modes of responses are learned by children in course of their experiences while interacting with children and their parents in the neighbourhood.

Neighbours are of two types—**variable** and **invariable.** 'Variable neighbours' are those which change their place very off and on. Such neighbours always keep on moving or shifting. 'Invariable neighbours' are stable and do not shift from one place to other very frequently. Contacts or interactions with variable neighbours usually do not encourage development of co-operative living much, whereas stable neighbourhood permits the development of co-operation and sympathy.

School

School is also an important agent which plays an important role in moulding of personality. Schooling is an opportunity not only to acquire knowledge and skill but also to learn desirable adjustive responses with various situations of the larger world around the individual and alsc unlearn the undesirables or maladaptive modes of responses. In addition, schools also provide opportunities to achieve the genetically endowed reaction ranges to develop its fullest magnitude develop various kinds of values (e.g. moral, social, personal values), setting up the levels o aspirations and learning to take moderate levels of 'risks' to achieve the aspired goal.

Further, school provides an atmosphere where pupils are required to interact with large number of people of various levels—peers, seniors, teachers, heads of the institutions, and also ofter with the school management. Thus, it provides an environment to learn interpersonal interactions a different levels differently. Such interactional opportunities provide differing templates and childre learn to fit themselves well in all such differing templates, *i.e.* learn with whom, when and how tc react, learn good or desirable habits and unlearn the undesirable ones.

Hence, schools do play an important role in personality development.

Group interaction

As an individual grows, his contacts widens. He acquires membership of various secondary an outgroups such as clubs, different kinds of committees and institutions, political parties, etc. wher he gets an opportunity to interact with several adult members including the members of his ow professional groups. In many such situations, people interact with others vertically in hierarchia orders as well as horizontally. Different members are assigned certain definite goals and require to form a disciplined organization and discharge certain designated responsibilities. All suc opportunities provide different kinds of situations and require to bring about dynamic change in one's response tendencies to cope with the demands of the situations. In the process, a perso acquires a good number of personality characteristics and modifies his psycho-physical tendencie that best suits adjustive demands of the situation.

17.9.5 Cultural Factors

Personality is also determined by the **culture** which represents the environment in totality. Eve culture varies in its values, norms, standards, customs, traditions, institutions and art. Every cultu has unique templates in which a culture grows and personality also grows in accordance with th cultural templates which is unique to the culture in question.

Culture determines experiences of a person, the frustrations and adjustments he is required deal with. Each culture with its distinctive values, morale and ways of living, lays down its ow rules for child rearing and relationship within the family. In a sense, it dictates the characteristics a person should acquire and thus, influences personality traits—typical of the member of a particular culture.

Differences in personality due to differences in socializing norms of different cultures are best demonstrated in the studies of primitive societies. **Balinese**, for example, are characterized as introverted and emotionally blunted. They lack warm personal attachments. Each individual lives within himself. The **Naraho Indians**, on the other hand, are passive and intolerable to physical discomfort. The **Eskimos** are toilsome individuals. The **Arpesh** of **New Guinea** seem to lack egotism and competitiveness. Such differences are attributed largely to the way one is structured in his culture in course of rearing up processes.

Thus, we find that personality is determined by a number of factors—biological or physical constitution, inherited dispositions, and various socio-cultural factors. Each factor has its influence in its own way and the multiplicative product of all these factors is what we call—**Personality**.

17.10 ASSESSMENT/MEASUREMENT OF PERSONALITY

There are many situations in which we need to assess personality of a person. For example, the personnel psychologists in business organizations want to select people whose personality features are such which are desirable of a good salesmen, executives managers, marketeers etc. A psychologist in defence sectors assesses personality for important positions in the organization with a view to ascertain the characteristics or traits which are requisite attributes for the position in the organization.

Assessment of personality is also an important field for psychologists engaged in research work. Researchers test personality with a view to answer certain pertinent questions concerning personality and individual differences.

There are three general approaches to personality assessment which are mentioned hereinbelow:

17.10.1 Holistic Approach

It is an overall approach of personality assessment in which emphasis is laid upon evaluating the **person** as a whole. While evaluating the person we seek to answer the question—what sort of person one is? German military psychologists were the first to use this approach. Later on, British psychologists adopted this approach for selecting under cover agents and other strategic personnel during the last World War under the banner of **Office of the Strategic Services—OSS**.

17.10.2 Trait Approach

Trait approach in fact is a piecemeal approach which lays emphasis on the measurement of traits of personality. Psychologists who emphasize 'traits' believe personality as a **constellation of traits**. Accordingly, Cattell, Allport, Lewin, Eysenck etc. have developed tools to measure various traits of personality and describe personality in terms of the degree or level to which these traits are possessed by individuals.

17.10.3 Projective Approach

Psychologists have developed certain projective techniques for evaluating personality. Such tests also aim at assessing personality as a whole person, but the technique is indirect one. Projective techniques are powerful instruments of unearthing the **innermost** aspects of the individual's psyche or **self**. Projective measures expose certain situations before the individual. The exposed situation may be structured or unstructured upon which the individual projects his attitudes, thoughts, perceptions, experiences, feelings, emotions, tendencies, needs, impulses etc. which reflect **the kind of person one is**.

One thing must be made clear here. Increasing number of psychologists are continuously engaged in personality assessment and developing various tests to measure abilities, aptitudes, interests, traits, achievement, orientations etc. **Cronbach** (1970), however, points out a salient distinction between ability, aptitude, achievement tests and personality tests. Intelligence, aptitude and achievement tests are the tests of maximum performance, since they record the best that a person tries to do on them. Personality tests, on the other hand, are tests of **typical performance**. There are no right or wrong answer to any question or statement comprising the test. People are generally asked what they do or what is **typical** of him. Hence, personality tests are different from what aptitude or achievement tests are.

17.10.4 Some Important Measures or Tests of Personality

There are various kinds of personality measures. These may be divided into three major heads:

Behaviour study methods

According to the behaviourists, personality is made up of unique generalized habit patterns. Habit patterns are expressed in behavioural form. Hence, personality is a S-R affair (stimulus-response affair) and, therefore, in order to evaluate one's personality, observation and evaluation of expressive behaviours of individuals will be of great significance in assessing personality of an individual. Behaviourists also use **graphology** as one of the important indicators of personality.

Assessing personality features by analysing the handwriting of a person is called graphology. Though, many psychologists regard it no more valuable than palmistry or reading the tea leaves, this technique has rigorously been applied during the recent years by using appropriate scientific controls. The general conclusion has been that graphology may prove valuable in predicting personality traits.

Galbraith and **Wilson** (1964) have put forward their analysis of handwriting which shows certain typical traits of personality which can be expressed in illustrative strokes of handwriting. As a sample, following is one such analysis:

Analysis of Handwriting*

Trait and explanation	*Illustrative strokes*
Attentiveness to detail Dot close to and directly above stem of letter	
Domineeringness Lines like cross on "t" and dot on "i" slant downward and are pointed at ends	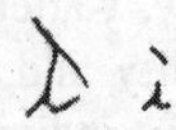

* Cited in Ruch, F.L., *Psychology and Life*, 7th ed., 1970, p. 117.

Trait and explanation	*Illustrative strokes*
Persistence Strokes made in form of loop or knot	
Self-consciousness Succession of curved or pointed strokes increasing in height	
Stubbornness Straight, rigid, braced strokes, forming point, rather than curves	

Other forms of expressive behaviour

There are some other forms of expressive behaviours too which if analyzed carefully may indicate certain important traits of personality. These include voice, gesture, posture, facial expressions, emotional outbursts etc. These and many other forms are termed as body languages of personality. Though, there has been very little research studies on the relationship between body language of personality, a few of those studies have proved that voice prints and postures definitely play a role in many **snap judgements** of personality.

Mallory and **Miller** (1958) in one study correlated the scores obtained on certain personality variables measured by self-inventory and voice prints. They found that those who score higher on dominance tended to have louder, more resonant and lower-pitched voices than those who are higher on submissiveness.

Faterson (1931) has found that poor posture people are more often found to have inferiority feeling. Though, it is difficult to judge whether poor posture has been caused by inferiority feeling or the inferiority feeling cause poor posture. However, one makes a snap judgement on the basis of body postural look. But, most of such judgements are stereotyped in nature. For example, the idea of a leader usually includes an upright, almost military bearing whereas a scholar teacher is thought as being stoop-shouldered.

Test situations: Psychologists have made attempts to place an individual under artificially structured situations and observe the response patterns to assess his personality. For example, group discussion (GD) is one such situation for personality evaluation. Today, in most of the organizations, group discussion test is very widely used for selecting candidates for executive and managerial rank. Such situations provide an opportunity to reflect one's abilities to lead, dominate/ submit, convince and other social interactional patterns.

Clinical methods

Clinical methods for assessing personality have been evolved by those psychologists who were primarily interested in measuring personality dysfunctions for clinically classifying the individuals into adaptive and maladaptive forms of personality. Some of the popular techniques of clinical evaluations are **interview, case study method,** and **projective techniques**.

(i) The Interview

Interview is a major technique of personality evaluation. This is almost a central technique of personality study by clinicians and many theories of personality have been propounded on the basis of the data gathered through interview.

In general, interviews are of two major types—**formal** or **structured** and **informal** or **unstructured**. Both of these types of interviews are used by clinical psychologists and both yield useful information about personality. These two forms of interview are also used by employers for selecting new workers (employees).

Interview is thought as an important tool in rating all personality related variables. It provides frame of reference in which all other observations are evaluated. **Cronbach** (1960) is of the view that the interviewer has at his disposal, all sorts of biographical and other data concerning the interview which directs the process of interview in terms of the kind of information, the interviewer is interested. A form of interviewe called the **stress interview**. This form of interviewee is more particularly used in detection of lies. In such cases, the interview is so designed as to discover the candidate's capacity to tolerate severe emotional and intellectual strain as on lie detection machine. The ostensible aim of lie detector is to detect flaws and make the culprit to admit that he lied. The situation is so created as to build up the tension throughout the interview session so that at the end, rapid questions in quick succession may be hurled at the candidate. The subject is not allowed any time to relax in any way. If he stands crossing his legs he is asked to uncross them. If he lowers his head to avoid light, he is asked to look up. After about 10 minutes of stress, the subject is told—'we have abundant of evidence that you have been telling lie'. This way, the culprit being intolerant to the stress and strain, admits that he had not been telling the truth.

Though, interview is an important device for evaluating personality, under certain situations, it has proved as an unpredictable device. There are a number of reasons. These are as follows:

1. **The halo effect:** This is a tendency on the part of the raters (interviewers) to be unduly influenced by a single favourable or unfavourable trait, which colours the judgement by the rater in respect of other traits to be similarly rated or evaluated. It often becomes difficult for the interviewer to isolate the behaviour he is observing from his knowledge about the individual as a whole. This produces an error in rating the individual in the direction of the raters' (interviewers') general impression of the individual being rated on the basis of interview.
2. **Stereotypes:** Stereotype refers to preconceived notions as to how people of a given race, community, class or group ought to appear or behave. Such preconceived notions or beliefs produce errors in rating the personality of an individual. Such stereotyped notions often bias the interviewer resulting in making the interviewer either too severe (hard interviewer) or too lenient in making his judgements about the person being interviewed. These errors are known as **severity error** and **leniency error** respectively.
3. **Difficulty in quantifying:** The nature of information gathered through interview is generally descriptive and qualitative. Thus, the data is not amenable to quantitative analysis and, therefore, the judgements by interviewers depend more on his subjective interpretation. Such interpretations are not objective and likely to vary from interviewer to interviewer.
4. **Faulty memory:** Sometimes the interviewer fails to recall accurately the responses given by the respondent on some previous occasion or some preceding similar item of the interview schedule. This happens because of faulty memory. Sometimes it so happens due to conscious desire of the respondent to distort or to omit the response or sometimes even without any conscious desire to do so. This produces error. However, this is not a serious limitation of the technique. Many of the limitations of interview concern the interviewer. Therefore, if the interviewer is competent and experienced, this technique would prove much useful method of personality assessment.

(ii) Case history method

In assessing personality, clinicians often desire to reconstruct the individual's past which provides some important clue about the structuring and shaping of personality during the developmental history of the particular case under reference. The clinician obtains **case history** of the individual case. The historical records are derived from two main sources—(a) biographical records and (b) auto-biography of the cases. In addition, interviews with the individual himself, his parents and other close associates (e.g. near and dear relatives, teachers, peers etc.) also provide significant information about the past life of the case. The ultimate aim of the case history is to trace the root of the trouble in personality dysfunctions (*i.e.* the stage at which it began) and also to find out the basic source of the trouble.

For clinical purposes, the technique is very useful as it involves deeper study of the case. The investigator is able to gather much information about the case under study. However, from practical point of view the method is time-taking as well as tiresome. Moreover, it requires an experienced and expert investigator.

(iii) Projective techniques

Interview or case study method of personality assessment is direct method which has certain limitations. Realizing these limitations, some psychologists have developed indirect methods of personality assessment which are called projective tests. In our day-to-day observation, we often notice shapes of cloud in the sky appearing as human face or figure of an animal. But, all individuals do not take the same meaning of the shape. To some it appears like a heavily branched trees, to some as trunk of an animal and so on. Obviously, the same shape **means** differently to different persons. The perception of the object in an unstructured situation varies from person to person. Psychologists rely upon the similar phenomenon when they use **projective technique**. The person whose personality is to be assessed is given some sets of unstructured or structured unfamiliar pictures and encouraged to interpret the given stimuli freely—**What he sees (perceives).** Thus, the subject **projects** onto them his subjective meaning of the stimuli (object). Such projections reflect individual's inner states of the **'psyche'**—consisting of the personal drives, motives or needs, emotions, perceptions, beliefs, and the positive and negative affective feelings of the person on analysing such projections, the underlying personality patterns are revealed.

Usually, three types of projective tests are commonly used. These are as follows:

(a) ***Thematic apperception test (TAT):*** **Murray** (1935) devised a projective test of personality which is known as Thematic apperception test (TAT). This test consists of 3 series of 10 picture cards (total 30 cards) each representing different situations. On the back of each picture card code numbers are mentioned which describe which card is for male or female or for both and which is for adult and children. Thus, a total of 20 cards is selected as per age and sex of the subject and testing is done in sessions with 10 cards in each session. The subject is exposed each card in order for 2 minutes and is asked to make up a short imaginary story about each picture, describing the situation, what led to the situation and what the characters felt and what would be the outcome (see **Figure 17.4**).

By evaluating the contents and the formal characteristics of each story, the test administrator tries to discover the characteristic personality pattern of the subject. Murray holds that the subject while making up the stories, establishes identification with the characters in the picture and thus, projects his personal feelings drives, needs, emotions, impulses, ideas, conflicts and thoughts. Such projections reveal the innerside covered stories of the individual.

FIGURE 17.4 A model of TAT picture.

Murray perhaps got the inspiration from **Freud's** statement—**you tell me about others, I will tell what you are**. This statement obviously describes the mechanism of **projection** which we often apply as **ego defence** against mental conflicts.

Thematic apperception test (TAT) has been subjected to tests of reliability and validity. But due to inconsistency of results, the test cannot be regarded reliable and valid. However, from clinical point of view, the test has proved its worth in detecting personality distortions, particularly, the functional distortions (Smith, 1954; Park, 1957; Singer, 1954). On the basis of their studies, they have found, Thematic apperception test findings as very useful source in differentiating the personalities of mentally ill and normal individuals, in diagnosing psycho-pathologies and also in evaluating the benefits of therapeutic techniques applied on to the mentally disordered personalities. **Brown** (1951), **Snider** (1954), **Horrall** (1957) have found TAT as an useful device in predicting the personality and educational abilities of students in schools.

As for the inconsistency due to cultural differences in TAT stories, **Mussen** (1953) opines that it is but natural. According to him, people of different cultures differ in their personal experiences associated with an event as per their own cultural frame. Hence, the inconsistency occurs.

On the whole, TAT is of great value in predicting and evaluating one's personality. For this reason, this test is most widely used even today.

(b) ***Rorschach test (RT):*** Rorschach (1942) devised another projective test. It consists of 10 cards which are series of inkblots. Five of the cards are black and white while the remaining five cards are coloured (see **Figure 17.5**). The cards vary in form, shade and complexity. The pictures are unstructured and ambiguous as we observe unstructured shades in the sky or uneven ground surface in the hill areas.

Rorschach test is relatively more objective as it proposed standardized method of scoring. Each card is presented before the subject to observe and asked—**What he sees** or **What does this remind him of?** After responding for all the 10 cards, the subject goes through them again and indicates the parts of the **inkblot** which has suggested his responses. The subject observes the cards and gives his responses describing the object which he sees, the 'location' 'determinants', 'content', 'popularity' and the 'originality'. These descriptions are the modes of scoring that provides the information about the personality structure of the individual. Such informations are not provided by clinical interviews. For example, the way a subject reacts to the colour in the blot picture may be indicative of his emotional responses to the environment.

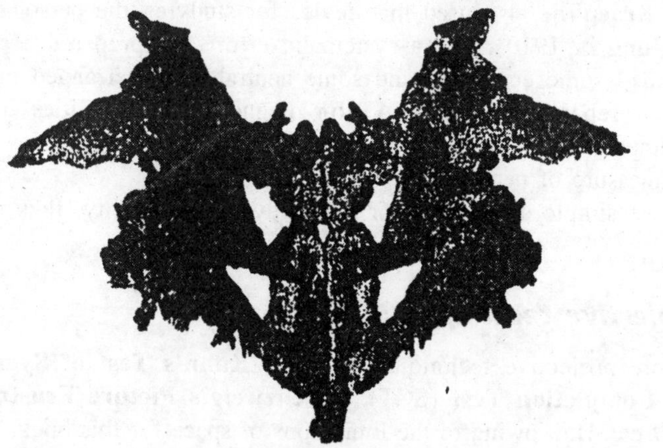

FIGURE 17.5 A model picture card of Rorschach's inkblot test.

The responses of Rorschach test (RT) are scored in two ways. Some of the scorings are objective. For example, the number of times subject responds to the part of the blot may be compared with the number of times he responds to the blot as a whole. Counting may also be done for the number of responses to the colour and movement.

Secondly, the clinicians also interpret the data subjectively. For example, while taking down the responses, the spontaneous remarks, signs of emotional upsets, symbolic meanings and postural signs of the subject are also interpreted to judge personality features involving response traits.

Though, some psychologists have attempted to use this test to predict job success, but the value of this test in such fields is not well-substantiated. **Kurtz** (1948) failed in predicting vocational subject on the basis of RT. Similar is the case with other industrial, organizational and military settings.

But, the clinicians in general agree that the test is good in understanding the personality of mentally disordered persons. However, the test lacks convincing validity.

(c) ***Word association test (WAT):*** The Word association test (WAT) is a simple and popular projective technique for evaluating personality. The test consists of selected list of some words which are presented before the subject verbally in sequential order as **stimulus word (SW)**. The subject is instructed to spell out the first (immediate) reaction response that occurs into his mind as soon as he listens the stimulus word. The spelled-out verbal reaction response of the subject is called the **response word (RW)**. The evaluator notes down RW for each SW. He also records **response time (RT)**, *i.e.* the time that intervenes between onset of SW and initation of RW. Usually this test is carried out in face-to-face situation in a peaceful atmosphere. Hence, the evaluator is also in a position to observe the accompanied reactionary expressions of the subjects reflected by changes in face, gesture, posture, loudness of responding sounds and similar other kinds of body languages. Such observations provide significant cues to correlate with the responses to judge certain personality dispositions. Hence, in this technique, data relating to RW, RT and behavioural expressions are analyzed to assess personality.

Word association test (WAT) was first devised by **Galton** in 1879. Later on, early experimental psychologists like **Wundt** and **Cattell** used this technique in the study of thinking. Clinical psychologists also became interested in introducing this technique for exploring the emotions, conflicts and guilts. **Kraepline** also used this device for studying the personality of mentally ill persons. However, **Jung** in 1910 made a systematic effort and prepared a compre-hensive list of 100 standard words—some emotional and some neutral words arranged randomly. **Kent** and **Rosanoff** (1910) also prepared standard WAT for diagnosing personalities. They also used this device to make a comparative study of neurotic and normal personalities. However, **Jung's** WAT is the most popular measure of personality.

This test is most simple and useful for the study of personality. It is more important for clinical purposes.

Some other projective techniques

There are many more projective techniques such as, **Kahn's Test of Symbol Arrangement** (KTSA), **Sentence Completion Test** (SCT), **Rosenzweig's Picture Frustration Test** (PFT), **Bender-Gestalt Test** etc. But, owing to the limitations of space for this book, it is not possible to describe all these tests in detail. Readers are suggested to consult books on **Psychological Testing** for the details of these tests.

Some Indian projective tests

Quite a good number of Indian psychologists have also come forward and developed projective tests.

Psychologists of Mysore, Madras, Allahabad, Aligarh etc. have made significant contributions in this area. **Dhapola, T.S.** (1971) used TAT with considerable success in identifying the trait of **aggressiveness**. **Sinha, A.K.P.** and **M.B. Sharma** (1971) also used TAT and RT tests on Indian sample and could explore certain traits of maladjustive personalities. **Dosajh, N.L.** also used projective techniques in guidance and counselling. **Pareek Udai** has also adapted TAT test developed by McClelland as a measure of *n* Ach. Pareek, Udai and Rosenzweig have also adapted PFT test on Indian samples. Similarly, **Pramila Pathak** has developed a Draw-a-Man-Test (DMT) to measure the intellectual aspects of personality dispositions.

Efforts are still going on by several researchers in India to develop latest projective tests. For example, **Puhan, Rath** and **Dash** (1991) proposed a projective inventory approach to measure personality that is a combination of classical projective and self report inventory—**indigenous tests** of personality. Similarly, many more psychologists are engaged in developing tests of personality in Indian contexts.

Psychometric methods

Modern psychologists are now no more dependent upon clinical methods to assess personality. They object to these methods on two important points of defect with which clinical methods, more particularly the projective techniques suffer. These are as follows:

(i) Clinical approach to assess personality is based on data obtained from mentally dis-ordered persons.
(ii) The projective techniques and other clinical methods are more qualitative than quantitative.

Though, nowadays, quantitative analysis has been initiated in interpreting the qualitative information gathered through projective measures, its reliability is very low and hence not much dependable. It is so because projective techniques is fundamentally based upon descriptive type of responses. Hence, variations in interpretations by two independent evaluators cannot be totally ruled out.

In view of the above difficulties, modern personality psychologists are actively engaged in developing quantitative, reliable, valid and standardized tools of personality assessment. Consequently, a number of psychometric tools of personality assessment have been developed. These tools are developed by following psychometric principles and scientific criteria such as reliability, validity, standardization, systematization and precision. Among these, some are paper-pencil tests while the others are rating scales. Some of the major such tools are being described below:

(i) ***Paper-pencil tests:*** For any psychological testing purposes, paper-pencil tests are most convenient tools of measurement. Such tests are economical so far time and money is concerned. According to **James et al.** (1969) abundant number of paper-pencil tests have been evolved over the past six decades and even today, large number of researchers are constantly working on devising paper-pencil tests to evaluate and assess different traits of personality. Some of the important such tests are as follows:

(a) ***Questionnaire:*** Questionnaires are used to obtain factual information relating to characteristic features of personality, behavioural characteristics, temperaments, ways of handling different situations and problems. It consists of a series of questions relating to the various aspects of personality. The respondents are required to respond to the questionnaire in certain defined categories as the contents of the questionnaire apply to the respondent. The defined categories of responses may be yes/no/doubtful categories. Thus, the respondents project their own conception of **self**, its efficacy, esteem and other dispositional characteristics, thought processes, mode of responses to the stimulus situations and the ways he attempts to solve different problems of the environment. The responses obtained in answer form are not evaluated in terms of correct or incorrect rather in terms of the degree to which particular characteristic in question form applies to him or does not apply in his case. The answers are assigned standardized scores to make it convenient for quantitative analysis. To illustrate, an example of a questionnaire is given hereinbelow:

Put a × mark in one of the boxes (Yes or No or ?) Which best applies in your case:

1. Do you feel shy in talking with members of an opposite sex? Yes | No | ?
2. Do you like to entertain members of opposite sex? Yes | No | ?
3. If given the choice, do you prefer to choose opposite sex as your marketing partner? Yes | No | ?
4. Do you feel discomfort while you are alone in the group of opposite sex members? Yes | No | ?

Questionnaires are of two types—close-ended and open-ended. In the former, the mode and category of answer is definite and limited as in the above example. In the latter type there is no definite category of answers. The respondent is free to answer in as many words/sentences as he desires. To illustrate:

1. What are the causes of students unrest?
2. What steps do you suggest to bring discipline in the campus?

In the above illustration, both the questions call for open (free) answers from the respondent.

Both the types of questionnaires (close-ended and open-ended) have their relative merits and demerits over each other. Close-ended questionnaire is advantageous in the sense that it takes little time to complete, easy to fill in, items are relatively more objective and easily scored. Open-ended questionnaires require more time, tedious in scoring, difficult to interpret and tabulate the responses. However, if the evaluator desires to gather more information and unearth the hidden potentialities, needs etc. of the respondent, open-ended questionnaire is more preferable.

Inventories: To assess personality, investigators have invented a number of inventories in which the respondent describes himself by responding to certain statements designed to know his attitudes, feelings, behavioural tendencies and underlying basic traits. Hence, it is a **self-report technique** and resembles with questionnaire with a difference that the items are not in question form and the responses are obtained in descriptive categories along a continuum scale. It also resembles standardized kind of interview in which prepared questions or statements are used in face-to-face situation. An inventory contains certain statements about the person and answers are usually given in a form that can be easily scored—often by a machine like computer, calculator etc. An inventory is generally designed to measure a single trait dimension such as extraversion—introversion dimension. So inventories have also been developed to measure several personality traits simultaneously and determine their relative magnitude or strength that indicates the dominance of various traits. Such inventories provide profile scores of the person.

Cattell (1950) has developed an inventory, called **16 personality factor (16 PF)** test. This inventory has been constructed by applying factor analysis technique and presents personality profile of the individual. The test consists of declarative statements and respondents respond to a specific situation by choosing from among given alternatives.

Currently this test is available in 5 separate forms and in one form of the test, there are 105 items. It is used for high school students to adults. In addition to 16 basic scales, there are 4 second order indices of personality. This test is frequently used in career guidance, vocational exploration and clinical testing. The 16 basic factors that it covers are as under:

Factors	*Description of dimensions*
A	Reserved vs Outgoing
B	Less intelligent vs More intelligent
C	Affected by feelings vs Emotionally stable
E	Humble vs Assertive
F	Sober vs Happy-go-lucky
G	Expedient vs Conscientious
H	Shy vs Venturesome
I	Toughminded vs Tenderminded
L	Trusting vs Suspicious
M	Practical vs Imaginative
N	Frightened vs Shrewd
O	Placid vs Apprehensive
Q 1	Constructive vs Experimenting
Q 2	Group dependent vs Self-sufficient
Q 3	Undisciplined self-conflict vs Controlled
Q 4	Relaxed vs Tensed

There are 10 to 13 items for each factor in the test:

The Minnesota Multiphasic Personality Inventory (MMPI): Hathway and **MeKinley** (1943) developed this test. This test has been found very suitable and effective in detecting psycho-pathology. It has been used in many diverse types of populations. The revised test known as MMPI 2 was published in 1989. It has 567 items in the form of affirmative statements to which the test-taker gives the responses—true or false. The MMPI 2 provides scores for 10 subscales—**Hypochondriasis, Depression, Hysteria, Psychopathic Device, Masculanity-Femininity, Paranoia, Psychesthenia, Schizophrenia, Mania** and **Social intervention.**

In India, **Mallic** and **Joshi** have attempted to develop a test similar to MMPI2 which is known as **Jodhpur Multiphasic Personality Inventory** (JMPI).

(b) **Eysenck personality questionnaire (EPQ):** This test was developed by H.J. Eysenck to assess two basic dimensions of personality-Introverted-Extraverted and emotionally stable-emotionally unstable. These dimensions subsume 32 personality traits. In subsequent works, he also identified a third dimension named psychotism. It refers to psychopathology and represents a lack of feelings for others, a tough manner of interacting with people and a tendency to defy the social conventions. A person scoring high on this dimension tends to be hostile, ego-centric and antisocial. This test is also known as **Moudsley Personality Inventory (MPI)**. Similarly, there are many more inventories such as—

(i) Edward's Personal Preference Schedule (EPPS) developed by Edward (1954)
(ii) Allport-Vernon Lindzey study of values (1951)
(iii) Bell's Adjustment Inventory (BAI) (1984).
(iv) Guilford Zimmorman Temperament Survey (GZTS) etc.

(c) **Rating scales:** One of the usual methods of knowing one's personality is to observe an individual over a period of time and record the impressions on a rating scale, a valuable device in assessing social stimulus value.

Rating scales are of two kinds—Relative rating scale and Absolute rating scale.

(i) **Relative rating scale:** Relative rating scales are used when several subjects are evaluated and assigned to a relative position in the group. **The order of merit** is an example of relative rating method. Supervisors, teachers, interviewers etc. rank the subjects in order (1st, 2nd, 3rd, 4th ... etc.) by picking out the best and then the next best and so on until all subjects are ranked in vertical hierarchical order on the trait being measured.

(ii) **Absolute rating scale:** In absolute rating scales the judge assigns a score to each individual or each trait and compare each one to some standard—independent of the group being measured. For example, an individual may be rated for **neatness** on a 5 or 7 point scale and compared to a standard to determine the degree to which the adjective applies in his case.

Absolute rating scales are of three types which are mentioned below:

- **Descriptive adjective:** This kind of rating scales simply contain certain number of adjectives or phrases that function as trait of the person or property of personality, dispositions on the right side and on the left of each adjective, blank boxes are made for putting checkmark by the rater. For example, **Figure 17.6** is a specimen illustration of this form:

Check columns			Adjectives
1	2	3	
☐	☐	☐	Industrious
☐	☐	☐	Skilful
☐	☐	☐	Dedicated
☐	☐	☐	Indifferent
☐	☐	☐	Shy

FIGURE 17.6 Descriptive adjective rating scale.

Here, the rater puts a × mark in a particular check box against each adjective according to his belief the adjective applies to the ratee. If any of the adjectives is thought not applicable, are left blank. The number above the check boxes indicates the degree in terms of favourableness, unfavourableness and neutral. However, an individual may be described in a number of ways such as yes, no, ?, most, least or inbetween etc.

- **Graphic scale:** This is also a most popular form of rating scale. In this form, the names of quality are printed on the page and a line is drawn underneath the quality name. Underneath the line, some phrases or sentences describing the rate in terms of that quality is written which varies in degree from very complementary to very uncomplementary fashion with average in the middle. The following is an example of graphic scale:

Quality of classwork: consider how well the pupil performs in class works.

Best　　With some minor errors　　Average　　Not well　　Very poor

Sometimes an alternative form by omitting the underneath line is used in which the rater simply checks the appropriate phrase as mentioned hereinbelow:

Quality	*Blank line*	*Descriptive phrase*
Learning ability	–	Extra
	–	Above average
	–	Average
	–	Tries to learn
	–	Commits errors in understanding or comprehending
	–	Poor
	–	Very poor

One of the salient features of graphic rating scale is that it provides reasonably fine discriminations and is easily convertible into total score. This enables comparisons among a number of people.

- **Forced choice scale:** This is the recentmost form of rating scale. This form has been evolved to control the chances of *leniency error* in the earlier two forms of rating.

In this form, against each adjective quality are given in groups of 4 (sometimes even more) statements about the individual. Generally, half of the statements in each group is favourable and remaining half is unfavourable. The rater is directed to pick the statement he thinks, best applies by checking in the *most like* column and also pick the statement that *least describes* the individual by checking in the *least like* column. Here is an illustrative example of this form of scale.

Below are some attributes of fraternity. Check one statement that is **most like** and one that is **least like** about an individual. For most like put ✓ in the column and for the least like put a × mark in the column.

Most like	*Least like*	*Attributes*
		A. Well-rounded
		B. Seems to think he is self-sufficient in all things for endevours to do
		C. Enjoys just being with the brothers
		D. Is not a strong influence in chapter meeting

Since, each phrase of the forced choice scale is pre-evaluated and equal number of phrases are equally popular in describing favourable or unfavourable dimensions with one that really discriminates, the chances of leniency error in checking are counter-balanced fifty-fifty.

General evaluation of rating scale: Though, rating scales are by no means far superior to other measures of personality because chance errors such as halo effect, errors of leniency or severity are controlled, however, it all depend upon the experience and proficiency of the evaluator. The greatest advantage of this method is that it is economical as far as time, money, and energy are concerned and convenient for testing in group situation.

17.11 SOME INDIAN PERSONALITY INVENTORIES

In India too, appreciable efforts have been made either to adapt the inventories on Indian samples for translating them in Indian languages and socio-cultural contexts or constructing new inventories. **Prof. S.K. Bose** of Calcutta University in the year 1964 developed a test of personality. **Dr. H.S. Asthana** of Lucknow University has also developed a modified form of Adjustment Inventory in the year 1959. **M.S.L. Saxena** in the year 1969 also constructed Adjustment Inventory to measure personality in Hindi which is known as **Vayaktitava Parakh Prashnawali**. **Dr. Mohsin** in association with **Dr. Samsad Hussain** of Patna University standardized **Bell's Adjustment Inventory** in Hindi which measures adjustment in four major areas—Home, Health, Social adjustment and Emotional adjustment. **Dr. A.K.P. Sinha** and his associates constructed an Adjustment Inventory. In addition, Jalota (1965) also standardized MPI in Hindi. **Dr. Beer Singh** had also developed **MMPI** scale in Hindi.

Dr. R.R. Tripathi had developed a Personal Performance Schedule (PPS) by taking 15 factors of personality. This is multitrait scale which includes—achievement, respect, order, exhibitionism, inhibition, succourer, dominance, abasement, encouragement, nurturence, change, hetrosexuality, difference, endurance and aggressiveness.

B.K. Muthya has also developed a Multivariate Personality Inventory—**MPI**. It measures the traits—dominance, dogmatism, self-confidence, empathy, need for achievement, introversion, neuroticism, ego ideal and pessimism. It contains a total of 50 items and is meant for adults only.

Dr. J.B.P. Sinha has also developed a Dependence Proneness Scale—**DPS**—consisting of the four basic components of personality—affection-affiliation, lack of internal control, avoiding responsibility and conformity.

Similarly, many other psychologists have developed quite a good number of personality tests and the efforts are still going on.

17.12 RELATIONSHIP OF PERSONALITY TYPES AND CARDIAC DISEASES (CHD)

In the recent times, heartstroke or attack is on the increase and almost more than 30% of the population is suffering from some kind of cardiac disorders—either organic or functional ailments. People in general seem inclined to think heart diseases as purely medical problem despite the fact that we recognize their linkage with lifestyle factors such as smoking, obesity, and inactivity. During recent years, however, a connection with personality types has emerged. Two of the specific behaviour pattern types are now known to be strongly related to increased or decreased likelihood of coronary-artery diseases. These two types are Type 'A' and Type 'B'.

Type 'A': Such persons are hard-driving and competitive. They are always in constant pressure—the pressure related largely to their own making. They strive for recognition and advancement. They undertake multiple activities with a deadline for completion. Most of the time, they may function as well-alerted man, competently and efficiently. But, when they are put under stressful conditions, they cannot control, they are likely to become hostile, impatient, anxious and disorganized. They may even fume even at a slow elevator.

Type 'B': These people are quiet and just opposite of Type 'A'. They are easy-going, non-competitive, placid, unflappable. They wither stress easily. They are comparable to the **Tortoise** in the famous story of **Tortoise and the Hare.** Type 'B' may be little dull, but are likely to live longer than Type 'A'. Thus, type 'B' may be defined as absence of Type 'A' traits.

Maier Friedman and **Ray Rosenman'** (1974) in an interesting research noticed that many of their cardiac heart disease (CHD) patients had similar personality traits, i.e. they were found to be high powered, ambitious, competitive, who seemed unable to slow down and relax. Such patients were termed as Type 'A' which refers to **action-emotion complex**.

The researchers followed both types personalities for over eight years and found that Type 'A' people were twice more likely to develop CHD than Type 'B'. It was found that Type 'A' people were equal to smokers in developing high blood pressure, higher levels of cholesterol and thus were prone to coronary heart diseases (CHD). More recent studies have shown that the critical emotional aspects related to risk of CHD was hostility and anger, irritation and resentfulness to everyday life frustrations. These emotional factors also make Type 'A' antagonistic rude, surly and uncooperative in everyday interactions.

Type C: Recent studies have also identified still another type of personality—Type 'C'—which is **cancer-prone personality**. Such people are co-operative, unassertive and patient. Such types of persons suppress negative emotions (*e.g.* anger, hostility). They comply with those in authority. It is believed that blocking of emotions release certain **neuropeptides** in the brain. This causes disturbance in homeostatic mechanism and weaken the body's capacity to defend itself from cancer cells. Some researchers tried to correlate Type 'C' personality with severity of cancer. It has been found that Type 'C' personality is more cancer-prone and more particularly lung cancer.

In this context, it is important to note that personality characteristics can influence the person's health in two ways—directly by altering the immune system and/or indirectly affecting the health related behaviours. However, the results are still inconclusive.

Friedman has also identified a **self-healing personality**. It can be defined in terms of **enthusiasm**. Such people are emotionally alert, responsive and energetic, although, they may be calm and conscientious. They are spontaneous and creative and good problem-solvers. They are also good in relationship with others and have a playful sense of humour. They develop sense of humour which is more philosophical than hostile.

Thus, it is evident that personality not only reflects one's mental health rather is also reflective of physical health.

SUMMARY

- Personality refers to the characteristics of a person that are enduring and organized psycho-physical systems that makes him unique.
- There has been quite a good number of approaches to personality such as, type and trait approach, dynamic-processing approach, neoFreudians approach, behaviouristic views and humanistic views.
- Each approach of viewing personality is based on theoretical beliefs about some aspects of personality and therefore, no single approach or theory explains personality in its totality.
- Recently, a five-factor model of personality has been advanced that consider personality as a combination of five factors—openness to experience, extraversion, agreeableness, neuroticism and conscientiousness (Paul Costa and Robert MacCrae).
- Different psychologists have also tried to classify personality into types. Though, it is an impractical proposition to present a comprehensive list of different personalities into categories or type because each person's personality is unique in itself and hence, there would be as many types of personalities as the number of people on earth.
- However, some physiologists have tried to classify personality in terms of physique and temperament while many psychologists have classified personality in terms of inherent traits that reflect consistent ways of behaving or responding.
- Krestchmer and Sheldon have classified personality on the basis of physical constitution and temperament.
- Jung has classified all personalities into extraversion-introversion categories depicting their outgoing or egocentric psychic dimensions.
- Personality does not emerge at once. Rather it follows a sequential history of development in which various hereditary, biogenic and environmental factors play significant role in shaping and developing it.

- To assess personality, different methods are employed. These include behaviour studies, clinical methods (*e.g.* interview, case history, projective methods) and psychometric methods (*e.g.* inventories, questionnaires, rating scales etc.)
- Indian psychologists have made appreciable efforts to either develop or adapt foreign tools on Indian samples.
- Recent studies have revealed that personality is also related to coronary heart diseases and cancer-proneness. Scientists have identified three such types of personalities—Type A, Type B and Type C.

Glossary

Adaptation: (i) Structural or functional changes that enhance one's survival value. (ii) In the context of psychological disorders—a term that refers to meeting the performance requirements or role demands of one's situation.

Advertisement: A way to attract the target group by providing information in a popular way towards the product goods or services.

Affect: Mood or emotion.

Alienation: Luck or loss of relationship with others.

Amnesia: Generally, any loss of memory. Often applied to situations in which a person forgets his own identity or familiarity with others including objects due to psychological or physical illness, injury, drug abuse or any other abuses.

Anorexia Nervosa: A psychological disorder characterised by loss of appetite and loss of weight and women cessation of menstruation, 'self starvation'.

Archetypes: Jung's term for contents of collective unconscious, image or symbols representing ancestral experience of human race.

Artificial intelligence: A branch of science that studies the capacity of computers to demonstrate performance. If that were produced by human beings would have demonstrated intelligence.

Attribution: The process through which we seek to identify causes behind other's behaviour.

Autism: A pervasive infantile developmental disorders viz. deficiency in language, defective reality testing, and withdrawal from society.

Behaviour therapy: Psychotherapeutic techniques based on learning principles to modify abnormal (disordered) behaviours.

Biofeed back: Use of equipments to provide immediate feedback about autonomic and somatic functional changes to the individual in whom they occur.

Bystander effect: With the increase in number of bystander, a decrease in offering help occurs and thus a good time passes before any help comes.

Cordinal trait: According to Allport—a single dominating trait of personality in an individual.

Causal attribution: The way, people attribute causes to behaviour.

Central traits: Allport's term for the traits that are less significant and pervasive than the cardinal traits of personality.

Client-centred therapy: Roger's technique of therapy which focuses on the client's present problems and feelings, emphasis on non-evaluative and accepting the client's views honestly.

Cognition: Mental process relating to thinking, decision-making, language etc. which develops through experience and knowledge seeking behaviour.

Cognitive triad: Three forms of negative thinking involving—subjective or personal views of individual's self-experience, individual's view of himself and personal view of the future of the self. According to Beck A., this leads to depression.

Cohesiveness: Those forces which are responsible for the group members to remain in the group.

Collective unconscious: Jung's views about unconscious. He opines that collective unconscious is inherited portion of unconscious which is shared by all human beings and contains ancestral thoughts, feelings, impulses that he terms as archetypes and is a significant determinant of behaviour.

Compliance: This is a form of social influence in which one or more persons not holding authority, accepts requests of one or more others.

Compulsions: A repetitive behaviour for which an individual feels compelled despite knowing that such behaviours are meaningless.

Conformity: A form of social influence in which an individual changes his attitude and behaviour to adhere to the existing norms.

Consistency: Responding to a stimulus or situation in the same way on different occassions.

Contact hypothesis: A suggestion that increased contacts with groups can be effective in reducing prejudice between them.

Correlation: Statistical procedure to determine the extent of correlations or associations between the properties or characteristics of two variables.

Correlation coefficient: A numerical value that indicate the extent and direction of correlation that exists between two or more variables.

Counseling: A supportive or helping technique to provide a client to be relieved of maladjustive problems and enable him to achieve the goal of adequate adjustment.

Crowding: A kind of mental (psychological) experience to feel cramped in a too limited space.

Culture fair test: A test of psychological processes/attributes which is relatively free from cultural biases so that the test acquires the validity of being administered on individuals irrespective of cultural or ethnic belongingness.

Defence mechanism: A mechanism of ego uncounsciously tries to restrain the unacceptable id impulses with a view to cope with and maintain harmony viz. repression, projection, sublimation etc.

Delusion: Irrational beliefs of an individual which is held by an individual despite over-whelming contrary evidences.

Depersonalisation: A kind of dissociative disorder in which there is loss of sense of self.

Depression: Mood related disorder characterized by extreme sense of unhappiness, lack of energy and several other symptoms.

Descriptive statistics: Statistical procedures used to summarise vast amount of data that can be easily understood (e.g. mean, median, graphic representations etc.)

Diathesis-stress model: A view that interaction of factors such as biological predisposition combined with life stress may cause specific disorder.

Diffusion of responsibility: A tendency of decreased initiative to extend help in emergencies in the presence of other bystanders. Greater the number of bystander, lesser is the likelihood of each individual to act or take initiative.

Dispersion: The extent of spread of scores in a distribution or deviations from mean (central point) such as standard deviation.

Displacement: Redirecting an impulse toward a less threatening or safer target, a key concept in psychoanalytic theory, a defence mechanism.

Dissociation: Split of consciousness owing to which certain thoughts, feelings and behavioural operation become independent from others.

Dyad: A social group of two individuals such as husband and wife.

Dysthymia: A chronic state of depression that lasts for several years. A moderately severe mood disorder characterised by extended period.

Ecology: A field of biology that deals with the relationship of the organism with the environment.

Electroconvulsive Therapy (ECT): A technique of shock therapy through electric current of mild nature produced by electrodes attached to a patient's head. It is effective in the treatment of severe cases of depressive disorders.

Emotional Intelligence: A cluster of abilities relating to emotional aspects of life such as recognising and controlling or managing one's own emotions and emotional impulses in handling interpersonal relationships effectively.

Empathy: Experiencing other's emotional conditions and feelings as one's own.

Enuresis (Bed wetting): Involuntary discharge of urine after the age of continence i.e. self-restraint (usually after the age of 5).

Equity theory: Person usually compares his achievements (job inputs and outcomes) with others and attempts to remove the inequality, if any.

Exorcism: Religiously inspired classical procedure of treatment with an objective to drive out evil spirits or forces and allow good spirits to get entry in the possessed person.

Extravert: One of the personality dimension that is characterised by outwards sociable characteristics as opposed to introvert's egocentrism.

Forced compliance: A situation in which an individual feels compelled to say or do things which is not consistent with his true attitudes, feelings, or desires.

Formalisation: The extent or degree to which jobs within an organisation are standardized.

Free association: A psychoanalytic technique to verbally express thoughts, feelings, emotions, images that occur to mind irrespective of their importance or relevance i.e. freely associating with repressed ideas and impulses of the unconscious.

General Adaptation Syndrome (GAS): Selye's model of reaction to stress involving three phases—alarm, resistence and exhaustion (i) Alarm—Non-specific mobilisation that promotes sympathetic autonomic nervous system's. (ii) Resistence—Organism's effort to cope with the stressor. (iii) Exhaustion—It occurs when resistence efforts fail to overcome threat and depletes coping resources.

Gestalt therapy: Humanistic approach to therapy in which a therapist focuses on helping the mentally ill persons to acknowledge hidden aspects of their thoughts and feelings.

Global warming: Increase in atmospheric temperature of the earth and oceans brought partly by various human activities that cause environmental pollution.

Great person theory of leadership: A theory of leadership which suggests that certain specific leadership qualities inherent in great men distinguish them from others in a very significant way.

Greenhouse effect: Basis of global warming. Some gases e.g. carbondioxide, methane, CFC (chloro-fluro-carbon) etc. trap the sun's heat turning the earth into a vast 'greenhouse'.

Group therapy: A therapeutic device in which a group of persons with similar problems meet together to discuss their problems with the therapist who helps them to resolve their problems through group activities such as psychodrama.

Hallucinations: A form of perception having compulsive sense of reality in absence of reality. It is an abnormal phenomenon.

Hassles: Annoying minor events of everyday life which has a cumulative effect on one's well being.

Homeostasis: State of physiological equilibriance.

Human Resource Development (HRD): A process of best utilisation of human capabilities to make them highly productive and beneficial to the organisation.

Hypocondriasis: A psychological disorder in which a person is dominantly preoccupied with fear of presumed disease despite reassurance by the doctor about non-existence of any physical disease.

Id: Impulsive force of unconscious guided by pleasure principles and oriented towards instinctual drives without caring for the realities. It is a reservoir of all instinctual wishes and impulses and accepts no reality restraints.

Impulse: An act performed without delay. In psychoanalytic terms, these acts are determined and guided by id.

Ingroup: A social group which an individual perceives as belonging to and identify as one's own. This refers to the feeling of ownness which is most characteristic feature of ingroup while others are felt outgroup—a feeling of non-belongingness with other groups.

Insight therapy: A form of group therapeutic technique that focuses on development of client's self-understanding (insight).

Intellectualisation: Solving emotional conflicts in a detached, intellectual and controlled manner. Analysis of a problem is done in purely intellectual terms and feelings or emotions are ignored.

Intelligence quotient: An index of level of intelligence computed by dividing mental age (MA) divided by chronological or biological age and multiplied by a constant 100. Thus IQ = MA/CA × 100.

Introvert: One of the dimensions of personality in which individual's interests are directed inward rather than outward (extrovert).

Job analysis: An analysis of activities and tasks involved in performing a job—knowledge, skills and abilities needed to perform them.

Latency period: A stage of psychosexual development in which libidinal interests and urges get repressed or are sublimated. This stage ranges from about 5 to 6 years of age to 10th–11th years.

Libido: A term introduced by Freud for instinctive drives or energies that motivate behaviour: the sexual energy underlying biological urges.

Life space: According to Lewin, life space (LS) is the totality of all possible events that influence an individual. It is a function of PE i.e. person and his environment.

Maladaptive behaviour: Inability of an individual to develop successful coping patterns of behaviour to deal with the environment.

Mean: A measure of central tendencies of group of sources which is an arithmetic or average value of the scores.

Median: That value or point in a distribution of scores which divides the total set of scores into two equal halves.

Meditation: A technique of turning one's concentration inward and achieving an altered state of consciousness.

Mental age (MA): Level of mental development expressed in terms of age determined by the score that he obtains while performing on a standard intelligence test for which mental age norm is available.

Mental retardation: A term that refers to mental deficiency characterized by lower level of intelligence and inability to perform normal daily routine. Now, a new term—mentally challenged is used to refer to such cases.

Minority effect: Influence exhibited by a minority on the majority of a group.

Mode: The most frequent score in a distribution. A crude measure of central tendency.

Modeling: Learning by imitating through observing others who is supposed as model.

Hood: A mild, usually transitory, emotion.

Narcissistic personality: A kind of personality disorder characterised by grandiosity, an exaggerated sense of self-importance and preoccupied with being admired.

Neurosis: A milder form of mental disorder characterised by irrational fear, hightened anxiety, poor insight and partial impairment of personality and mental conflicts.

Normal distribution curve: A graphic representation of frequency distribution showing normal distribution in which majority cluster around central point with respect to the attribute or property measured and rest spread out to two other extremes.

Normative influence: Influence of group norms because, people fear to violate those norms and behave in adherence to the norms.

Obedience: A form of social influence in which people tend to behave in conformity with commands of people in authority.

Obsession: Recurrent and persistent thoughts, impulses, ideas or images. Often these are irrational and sometimes accompanied by a compulsive act.

Organisation: A consciously co-ordinated social unit of two or more than two individuals with a common goal for achievement.

Panic: A sudden overpowering fear—'agony of terror'.

Paranoid: A psychotic group of disorder characterized by symptoms of delusions, pervasive and auspiciousness, distrust and stubborn behaviour.

Personal space: The small area around an individual considered as his own and any invasion in that area is experienced as threatening or unpleasantness.

Phallic stage: A stage of infantile sexuality (at the age of approx. 5) when erotic zone shifts to genital area and both—the boys and girls experience oedipus and electra complexes respectively.

Phlegmatic: A temperament conceptualised by hipocrates characterised by excess of phlegon resulting in calmness and listlessness.

Phobia: Irrational fear of some specific object or situation which present no actual danger.

Practical intelligence: Ability to solve daily life problems intelligently.

Prejudice: A tentative presupposed idea about a group (usually negative) which is not based on objective evaluation or facts.

Projection: A kind of ego defences in which person projects his personal feelings, attitudes, motives on others.

Proximity: Gestaltists principle of organisation according to which nearness of objects favour grouping due to which we perceive a thing as organised whole while distances in between give perception of figures apart from each other.

Random sampling: A sampling technique in which each element of the population stand equal chance of being selected or included in the sample.

Range: A measure of spreadness of scores which tells the difference between highest and lowest scores.

Rational Emotive Therapy (RET): A therapeutic device developed by Albert Alice.

Rationalisation: A defence mechanism in which individual rationalises his frustrations with a socially approved logic.

Reference group: A social group in reference to which an individual compares himself.

Regression: A defence mechanism in which a person returns back to an earlier stage of behaviour patterns. The term is also used in statistics to make predictions with the help of correlations.

Repression: A defence mechanism in which ego unconsciously touches the undesirable impulses and anxieties to unconscious state of mind to defend against frustrations.

Resistence: In psychoanalysis, the patient attempts to block the course of treatment.

Sample: A representative part smaller in size of the population selected for inferential studies.

Sanguine temperament: One of the temperamental typologies classically classified typology of Hippocrates. Characterised by warmth, ardour and hopefulness or optimism.

Schizophrenia: A type of psychotic disorders characterised by severe split of personality, hallucinatory experiences and delusions.

Self-actualisation: As Maslow describes—it is the highest order of need hierarchy. Self-actualised persons tend to utilise his potentialities fully to develop his talents and capacities. It is a motive to realise oneself as a complete person.

Self-efficiency: This term has been used by Bandura indicating one's beliefs about his/her own effectiveness and expectation that he or she can successfully conduct the required action.

Self-esteem: It refers to individual's personal judgement of one's own worth. One's towards oneself along a positive-negative dimension.

Self-monitoring: Systematic self-observation and recording of progress in a behaviour change training.

Self-serving bias: A tendency to attribute positive outcomes to internal factors or subjective factors and negative outcomes to external factors.

Shaping: Reinforcing and training the series of successive steps which lead to learning of a desired response.

Shared environmental responses: The effects of family environment which are common to all family members.

Social cognition: The process of remembering, interpreting, noticing and using social information.

Social facilitation: Tendency of people to improve performance in the presence of others.

Social identity: A person's definition of himself, self-concept in social context viz. who I am and to which group I belong to in what capacity, how I am recognised in my group etc.

Somatoform disorders: Experience of physical illness without any physiological causes of illness.

Standard deviation: Deviation or dispersion of scores which tells the extent of distance at which a particular score deviates from the mean.

Statistics: A branch of mathematics which deals with organising, treating and infering the numerical data obtained in course of observation or measurement.

Sublimation: A defence mechanism in which frustrations are manifested through socially acceptable, approved and praiseworthy actions.

Syndrome: A group of symptoms occur together in a psychological disorder and represent typical picture of the disorder.

Traits: A relatively consistent and persistent pattern of behaviour manifested in a wide range of circumstances.

Transference: In psychoanalysis, transfer of positive or negative feelings towards the therapist.

Transformational leaders: Leaders who exert greater effects on their followers and establish special types of relationship with them.

Typology: Ways of classifying individuals in discrete categories viz.—Type A personality.

Unconscious: Larger segment of mind about which an individual is unaware but has dominant influence on behaviour.

Verbal tests: Tests which contain verbal items.

Work motivation: Motivation to perform and complete a task or work.

Author Index

Abels, 256
Ach, 375
Adams, 293, 305
Adamson, 382
Adler, Alfred, 36, 440, 546, 567
Aldrich, 222
Allen, 567
Allport, Gordon, 352, 531, 534, 535
Ammons, 256
Amold, 479
Anastasi, 519
Anderson, 389
Angel, 32
Annis, 208
Ansbacher, 547
Aristotle, 28, 298, 367
Arthurotis, 512
Asthana, H.S., 583
Atkinson, 209, 325, 329, 439
Augustine, St., 29

Bacon, Francis, 28
Baddeley, 328
Bain, Alexander, 29, 33
Baker, 515
Baldwin, 569
Bandura, Albert, 118, 300, 302, 557, 569
Bard, Philip, 477
Barlow, 208
Bartlett, Fredrick, 342, 343, 352, 354
Batesan, 441
Bazren, 270
Beach, 433
Bechterve, 260
Bell, Sir Charles, 30
Bem, 567
Benedict, Ruth, 111, 121
Benet, 413
Bergen, Tin, 427
Berkeley, George, 29, 374
Berkesy, Von, 173
Berkun, 436
Berlyne, 456
Bernard, Claude, 29, 432
Bhatia, C.M., 514
Bhatt, 353
Bilodeau, 257
Binet, Alfered, 506
Birch, 382
Boardman, 222
Boring, E.G., 192, 372
Bose, S.K., 583
Bouchard, 565
Bousfield, 255
Bower, 204, 357, 558, 567
Bowler, 291
Boxton, 354
Boyley, 515
Braun, 355
Bray, 174, 257
Brier, 226
Broadbent, 235, 236
Broadway, 516
Broca, Paul, 29, 92
Bronfenbrenner, 124
Broota, 213
Brown, 192, 193, 274, 576
Broyler, 562
Bruke, 355
Bruner, James, 29, 32, 190, 209, 210, 211, 231 400, 469, 579
Bruner, Jerome, 503
Buckout, 146

Bugelaki, 276
Burke, 472
Buss, 442, 564
Butter, 436
Buxton, 305

Cain, 348
Campbell, 213, 384, 433, 445, 518
Cannon, 427, 430
Cantor, 481
Carey, G., 565
Carlson, 430
Carr, Harvey, 32
Carrol, Lewis, 373
Carroll, 355
Carry, 355, 564
Castle, van de, 226
Cattell, J.H., 123, 491, 506, 513, 578
Cattell, Ramond B., 513, 536
Cherry, 234
Chess, 114
Childs, 532
Christie, 441
Clark, 397
Clenn, 190
Coffer, 384
Cohen, 222
Collins, Allan, 339
Colrins, Mary, 163
Commins, 256
Condry, 444
Conkins, 72
Cooper, 472
Corbit, 455
Costa, Paul, 562
Courts, 255
Craik, 330, 361
Cronbach, 572, 574
Crowley, 356
Cruze, 250, 493, 508
Curry, 124

Dallenbach, 356
Dalton, John, 163
Darwin, Charles, 29, 32, 74, 472
Das, J.P., 504, 505, 527
Dash, 578
Davis, 175, 255, 430, 472, 513
Deese, 289
Descarte, Rene, 28, 367
Deutish, 234
Devolois, 167, 168
Dewey, John, 32, 384
Dhapola, T.S., 578
Dick, 194
Dollard, John, 35, 293, 301, 450, 555, 556
Donaldson, Horn, 500
Dosajh, N.L., 578
Doweling, 355
Drever, James, 163, 475, 476
Dunker, 288
Dunn, 547

Earnest, 143
Ebbinghaus, Herman, 306, 341, 342, 347, 348, 354, 493
Edridge-Green, 167
Edward, 581
Elizabeth, Loftus, 345, 347
Ellson, 472
Elwell, 257
Engen, 473
English, 372
Epstein, 432
Erickson, Erik, 37, 257, 389, 553
Esquirol, J., 506
Eysenck, H.J., 518, 536, 564, 581

Fagin, 256
Fajans, 458
Fantz, 190
Farber, 518, 565
Faterson, 573
Feather, 439
Fechner, G.T., 30
Fechner, Gustav, 144
Fernald Jr., 413
Fernald, Carmichael, 413
Fieldman, 397
Fields, 267
Filer, 222
Fischer, 506
Fitts, 304
Flourens, Pierre, 29
Foreman, 257
Foster, 356

Fox, 276
Franz, 101
French, 100
Friedman, Maier, 382, 584, 585
Friske, 456
Frober, 222
Fromm, Eric, 36, 548
Frost, 208
Funkenstein, David, 467
Furguson, 521

Gagne, Robert, 400, 410, 411
Galbraith, 572
Gall, Franz, 30
Galton, Sir Francis, 30, 32, 375, 491, 506, 578
Games, Eells, 513
Ganguli, 213
Gardner, Howard, 494, 501, 519
Garrett, 496, 562
Garry, 347
Gates, 256
Gazzaniga, 94
Geis, 441
Geldard, 178
Gellermann, 400
Geschwind, 93
Gestalt, 286
Gewirtz, J.L., 117
Giblin, Hulihan, 431
Gibson, 208, 216, 352, 380
Gille, 520
Glickman, 397
Glover, Edward, 546
Godfrey, 213
Goldfarb, 569
Goldstone, 222
Goltz, 101
Gottesman, I.I., 211, 565
Gray, 373, 520
Green, 146, 382, 411
Greenberg, 382
Greene, 444, 445
Grindley, 257
Grossman, 97
Guilford, J.P., 414, 496, 497
Gumeson, 411
Gummerman, 373
Gunney, 422, 530
Guthrie, E.R., 298, 299, 300

Haber, 373
Haier, 385
Hall, Marshall, 29
Harlow, 100, 317, 433, 436, 437
Hartley, David, 29, 33
Harton, 222
Hartzberg, 459
Hathway, 581
Haveman, 493
Heath, 485
Heatherington, 430
Hebb, D.O., 189, 208, 463
Heinz, 236
Hellyer, 327
Helmholtz, 31, 165, 225
Helson, 147, 148
Hensel, C.G.M., 226
Herbert, Rice, 514
Hering, Ewald, 166, 174
Herkovits, 213
Herman, 213
Hertz, Heinrich Rudolf, 169
Hess, Eckhard, 472
Hetarazzo, 511
Heyer, 520
Heyman, 389
Hildum, 274
Hilgard, 271, 291, 569
Hill, James, 33, 285, 436
Hiller, 450
Hillix, 297
Hilton, 388
Holt. P.R., 113
Honzik, 295
Horney, Karen, 36, 548, 550
Horrall, 576
Horton, 299, 300
Hovland, 266
Howes, 214
Hueller, 178
Hull, C.L., 193, 288, 289, 290, 291, 292, 293, 294, 295, 297, 298, 299, 300, 317, 354, 409
Hulse, 289
Hume, David, 29
Hurvich, 206
Husband, 213
Hussain, Samsad, 583
Hutten, Locher, 374
Huxley, 375

Irwin, 351, 356
Izard, 466

Jacobs, 167, 168
Jacobson, 377, 397, 518
Jalota, S.S., 514, 583
James, William, 32, 475
Jamson, 206
Janis, I.L., 113, 569
Jenkins, 446
Jenson, Arthur, 500, 515
Johnson, 409
Johnston, 236
Joshi, 581
Judid, 317
Jung, Carl Gustav, 36, 533, 544, 578

Kagan, 436, 493
Kahneman, 235
Kamat, V.V., 514
Kamin, 264, 518
Kangas, 516
Kant, 50, 158
Kaplon, 411
Katona, 316
Kayuo, 521
Keegan, J., 113
Kelman, 551
Kendler, 382, 516
Kendrick, 547
Kent, Earnest W., 158, 578
Kimble, 167, 168, 263
Kinesy, 123
King, 248, 276, 277, 401, 404, 463
Kingsley, 355
Kirby, 504
Klaus, 520
Knafer, 285
Knight, 493
Kock, 292
Koffka, Kurt, 34, 192, 197, 202, 286, 293
Kohler, Wolfgang, 34, 192, 286, 293
Kolata, 431
Kraepline, 578
Krech, 124
Kretschmer, 533
Krueger, 355
Kulpe, 375

Lahman, 222
Lal, Sohan. 514
Landon, 208
Lange, Karl, 475
Langfield, 372
Lashley, 101, 479
Lazarus, Richard, 257, 481
Leavitt, 353, 354
Leeper, 200, 208, 294, 444, 562
Lehman, 433
Lele, 353,
Leone, 505
Levonchain, 209
Lewin, Kurt, 34, 294, 457, 560, 577
Lindsay, 234
Lindsley, D., 479
Lindzey, 534
Locke, John, 29, 31
Lockhart, 320, 361
Logan, 289
Long, 409, 514
Lorenz, 427
Lowe, 519
Luchins, 381
Ludel, 176
Ludins, 564
Lundin, 551
Luria, 373, 504
Lykken, 471
Lyon, 354

MacClean, 89
MacCrae, Robert, 562
Machiavelli, Niccolo,, 441
MacWorth, 237
Madden, 382
Maddi, 456, 541
Madigan, 357
Mahi, G.F., 113
Malinowski, 212
Mallic, 581
Mallory, 573
Manning, 347
Marbe, 375
Marlowe–Crowne, 442
Marquis, 271
Martin, 354
Maslow, Abraham, 38, 453, 559
Mayer, 173, 305, 519

McClearn, 437
McClelland, 124, 353, 354, 439, 448, 459, 578
McConneld, 226
McDougall, 427
McGeoh, 248, 351, 354, 356
McGinnies, 213, 214
McGuire, 544
McKinney, 351
Mcnery, J., 514
Mechanic, 305
MeClelland, 209
Mehta, 514
MeKinley, 581
Melton, 254, 351, 452
Mervis, 405
Mill, John Stuart, 29, 31, 33
Miller, Meal, 222, 231, 293, 301, 330, 355, 358, 556, 573
Milner, 92, 100
Misanine, 433
Mischel, Walter, 539, 566, 567
Mishra, 124, 257, 520, 569
Mohsin, 514, 583
Monakow, 101
Morgan, 248, 401, 404, 446, 463, 544
Morie, 401
Moskowitz, 445
Moss, 446
Mote, 255
Muller, Johannes, 29, 30, 300, 349, 354
Munn, Norman L., 234, 329, 413, 469, 493
Murata, 256
Murdock, 327
Murphy, 209
Murray, H.A., 438, 447, 575, 576
Mussen, 576
Muthya, B.K., 584

agleri, 504, 505
ash, 148
elson, 515
ewton, Sir Isaac, 152
ichol, Mac, 167, 168
ichols, 564

dbert, 535
jhas, J.M., 526
son, 277

Orden, 410
Ormer, 356
Orth, 375
Osgood, 195, 209, 279, 292, 397, 401

Paivio, 339
Palermo, 257, 389
Pandey, S.K.D., 514
Pareek, Udai, 578
Park, 576
Parkinje, 157
Pascual, Jaun, 188, 505
Patel, 353
Pathak, Pramila, 578
Patrick, 384
Paugh, Trinkle, 295
Pavlov, I.V., 29, 255, 258, 293, 298, 556
Peiron, 188
Perin, 289
Peterson, 327
Philips, 521
Piaget, Jean, 376, 378, 398, 503
Pilzecker, 349, 354
Plato, 28
Plomin, 564
Plout, 441
Plutchik, Robert, 466, 482
Porter, 267
Postman, 190, 209, 211, 231, 305, 312
Pragya, 527
Pringer, S., 222
Pronko, 213
Puhan, 578

Quiglec, 430
Quillian, Ross, 339

Rabinowtz, 382
Ramey, 518
Ranson, 430
Rappaport, 353
Rath, 578
Ratliff, 203
Reed, 255
Renzulli, Joseph, 522
Rex, 493
Reynolds, 389

Rhine, 226
Richardson, 163
Richman, 382
Richter, 255, 427
Riesen, 208
Rivers, 163
Roberts, 316
Robinson, 361
Rodrigues, 190
Rogers, Carl, 38, 519, 558
Romanes, 436
Rorschach, 447, 576
Rosanoff, 578
Rosch, Eleanor, 402
Rosenberg, 547
Rosenland, 256
Rosenman, Ray, 584
Rosenzweig, 448
Rosh, 405
Ross, H., 117
Rovee-Collier, 357
Rowe, 564
Rozin, 431
Rubin, 201
Ruch, F.L., 248, 475, 572
Rutherford, Ernest, 174

Saltzman, 472
Sanford, 209, 401
Sarson, 256
Saxena, M.S.L., 583
Scar, 518
Scarr, 517
Schachter, Stanley, 380, 440, 480, 481
Schafer, 209
Schmidt, 177
Schneider, 235
Schoenford, 300
Scholsberg, 311
Schooler, 210
Schultz, 157
Schumsky, 257
Sears, 147, 256
Segall, 213
Senden, M., 189, 208
Senders, 305
Seward, 303
Shakespeare, 3
Shallace, 330
Sharma, M.B., 578
Sheffield, 355, 445
Sheldon, 532
Sheriff, 212
Sherrington, Charles, 96
Shiffrin, 325, 329
Shirley, 250
Shurrager, 358
Siegler, 506
Sigmund, Freud, 35, 294, 353, 458, 469, 540, 544, 576
Singer, Jerome, 480, 481, 576
Singh, Beer, 583
Singh, R.N., 514
Sinha, A.K.P., 578, 583
Sinha, J.B.P., 584
Skeels, 518
Skinner, B.F., 271, 293, 300, 301, 557
Skolnick, 431
Slobin, 379
Slucki, 267
Smith, Gold, 173, 397, 565, 576
Smoke, 409
Snider, 576
Snoddy, 353, 354
Sobel, 177
Sokolov, 397
Soloman, 207, 214, 455
Sontag, 515
Spearman, 482, 495
Spence, 293, 312
Spencer, Herbert, 29, 32, 33, 289
Spielberger, 312
Spoon, Green, 257, 274
Spranger, 534
Spurzheim, 30
Stenberg, R.J., 503
Stern, Curt, 493, 566
Stern, William, 507, 508
Sternberg, Robert, 494
Stevens, 144, 532
Stock, 222
Stoddart, 493
Stone, 250
Stroud, 255
Sullivan, Harry Stack, 36, 37, 548, 551
Sutton, 547
Sweat, 146
Sweeny, 519

Taylor, 519
Telkegen, A., 565
Terman, 493, 508, 509, 519
Terry, 264
Thomas, St., 29, 114
Thompson, 207, 473
Thomson, Robert, 374
Thorndike, Edward L., 29, 255, 271, 282, 293, 298, 300, 312, 436, 493, 499
Thoroson, 397
Thouless, 189
Thurston, L., 496
Titchner, 50
Titchner, Edward, 31, 191, 372, 374
Tolman, E.C., 293, 303
Triesman, 234, 236
Tripathi, R.R., 583
Tsai, 446
Tucker, 532
Tulving, 332, 357
Turnbull, 204

Ueda, 208
Underwood, 351, 355

Vernon, 501, 534
Veroff, 440
Vierordt, 223
Vinacke, 384, 401
Voeks, 299
von Helmholtz, Herman, 30, 173
Vonkries, 154, 157
Voth, 192, 193
Vyogotsky, Lev, 378

Wagner, 264
Wake, 468
Walf, 432
Wallach, 205
Wallas, 384
Walter, B. Cannon, 118, 477
Walters, Richard, 300, 557, 569
Wang, 255, 446
Wangensteen, 430
Warner, 446
Warrington, 330
Watson, J.B., 5, 33, 260, 269, 395, 469
Watt, 375, 382
Waught, 329
Weaver, 382
Weber, W.H., 30, 143
Wechsler, David, 493, 509
Weiner, Anderson, 457
Welch, 409
Weld, 372
Welsh, 411
Werner, 203
Wernicke, Carl, 92
Wertheimer, Max, 34, 97, 189, 192, 218, 377, 397
Wever, 173, 174
Wheeler, 516
White, 531
Whorf, Benjamin Lee, 378
Willey, 348, 396
Williams III, 286, 530
Williams, 289
Wilson, 572
Wittings, Amino F., 286, 422, 530
Wolf, 275, 352
Wolman, 549
Woodbury, 194
Woodrow, 223, 311
Woodworth, 311, 349, 356
Worcester, 477
Worrell, 519
Wright, 458
Wundt, Wilhelm, 5, 31, 41, 191, 374, 375, 578
Wüzberg, 375
Wyatt, 222

Yerks, 433
Young, Thomas, 165, 255, 431

Zener, 293

Subject Index

16 personality factor (16 PF), 536, 580
19th century psychology, 41
20th century psychology, 41
21st century psychology, 43

Absolute limen (AL), 138
Absolute sensitivity, 142
Accommodation, 153, 217, 376
Acculturation, 113, 119
Achievement imageries (AI), 439
Achromatic sensation, 154
Acoustic codes, 327
Acquired colourblindness, 164
ACTH (Adreno-corticotrophic hormone), 106
Action-emotion complex, 584
Action potential method, 97
Action schemes, 505
Activation theory, 479
Active learning, 311
Active process, 181
Activity cage method, 445
Adaptation level theory, 147
Adaptation, 376
Adrenal cortex, 106
Adrenal gland, 106
Adrenal medulla, 106
Aerial perspective or clearness, 215
Affective processes, 185
Afferent code and experience, 137
After-image, 373
    effect, 162
Age of the perceiver, 221
Agencies of socialization, 112
Aggression, 441
Agnosia, 101
Aided observation, 48, 51
Aldosterone, 106
Alexander's performance battery, 513
Alexia, 101
Alfred Adler's individual psychology, 546
Algorithms, 386
Allport's view, 535
Allport-Vernon Lindzey study of values, 581
Ambiversion, 534
Amnesia, 359
Anal expulsion, 542
Anal phase, 542
Anal retentive phases, 542
Anal stage, 541
Analytical psychology, 544
Anatomical method, 96
Anatomy of human ear, 171
Anatomy of PNS, 83
Ancient Greeks' views, 27
Androgens, 107
Anger, 467
Anima, 545
Animus, 545
Annoyance, 467
Anterograde amnesia, 360
Anticipating, 408
Anti-consolidation, 350
Anxiety, 543
    state, 312
Apathy, 551
Aphasias, 101
Apparent motion, 326
Apperception, 32
Appetitive stimuli, 263
Applied branches, 16
Appraisal of information, 482
Approach–approach conflict, 450
Approach–avoidance conflict, 450

Approaches to the study of personality, 531
Approval motive, 442
Aqueous humour, 154
Archetypes, 545
Arcuate fasciculus, 94
Arousal and directedness of behaviour (instrumental behaviour), 424
Artificial concepts, 404
Ascending reticular activating system, 88, 485
Assessing intelligence, 506
Assessment psychology, 24
Assessment/measurement of personality, 571
Assimilates, 376
Assimilation, 120, 376
Association, 309
  area, 100
Associationism, 33
Associative learning, 258
Associative reflex, 260
Asterognosis, 101
Asymptote, 261
Atkinson–Shiffrin model of memory, 325
Attainment of concepts, 407
Attainment of the goal, 424
Attending and organizing, 324
Attention as a clearness in consciousness, 230
Attention as a postural adjustment, 230
Attention as a set towards action, 230
Attention deficit hyperactivity disorder (ADHD), 241
Attention–rejection, 473
Attribution theory, 459
Auditory sensation, 168
Auditory sense organ, 170
Authoritarian—autocratic style, 114
Authoritative, 114
Autistic thinking, 369
Autobiographical memories, 346
Autographic memory, 332
Automatic processing, 232
Autonomic nervous system (ANS), 102, 485
Aversive conditioning, 278
Aversive UCR, 263
Avoidance–avoidance conflict, 451
Axon, 76

Backward conditioning, 262, 263
Backward search, 387
Ballard Williams phenomenon, 353
Bandura and Walters: Later social learning theory, 557
Barriers to creative thinking, 415
Bartlett's view, 352
Bases of transfer, 316
Basic anxiety, 550
Basic approaches or theories of motivation, 453
Basic emotions, 466
Basic human dilemma, 548
Beginning of experimental psychology, 30
Behaviour study methods, 572
Behaviourism, 33
Behaviourist approaches to personality, 555
Behaviouristic approach, 193
Bell's adjustment inventory (BAI), 581
Bender-Gestalt test, 578
Best definition, 6
Binocular cues, 217
Biological memory, 322
Bipedalism, 71
Birth order, 547
Block design test, 513
Blue-yellow blindness, 163
Bottleneck theory, 235
Bottom-up processing, 190
Brain stem, 87
Brightness, 159
  constancy, 205
  contrast effect, 164
Broca's area, 92, 101
Bruner's theory, 503
Buddhi, 526

Cancer-prone personality, 584
Cannon-Bard theory, 477
Cardiac muscles, 131
Cardinal traits, 535
Carl Jung: Understanding the collective unconscious, 544
Case history method, 575
Case study method, 58
Categories, 338
Cathexis, 294
Causes of forgetting, 354
Causes of mental retardation, 524
Central executive, 328
Central laws or principles, 199
Central nervous system (CNS), 84
  role of, 484

Central or fissure of Rolando, 90
Central theory, 393
Central traits, 536
Cerebellum, 87, 88
Cerebrospinal fluid, 525
Cerebrum, 90
Change, 239
Changes in breathing, 470
Changes in glandular responses, 471
Changes in skin temperature, 471
Characteristic features of endocrine glands, 104
Characteristics of
  concepts, 403
  creative thinkers, 411
  gifted individuals, 522
  learning curve, 254
  natural concepts, 405
  perception, 182
  scientific method, 45
Chemical method, 97
Chemoreceptors, 135
Childhood amnesia, 346
Choroid, 154
Chromatic sensation, 154
Chromosomes, 72, 564
Chronological age, 312, 507, 508
Chunking, 329, 361
Cilliary muscles, 153, 154
Classical conditioning, 258
Classical methods, 96
Clinical methods, 573
Closed-end questionnaire, 60
Coded, 324
Cognitive appraisal theory of emotion, 481
Cognitive, 293
  competence, 527
  dissonance, 442
  map, 340, 376
  style, 211
  theory of emotion, 376, 480
Collective unconscious, 545
Colour constancy, 205
Colour mixture, 161
Colour vision, 158
Colourblindness, 158, 162
Common sense view, 475
Communication skills, 251
Comparison between Gestaltist and behaviouristic approaches to perception, 195
Comparison between Hull and Tolman's theories of learning, 297
Compensation, 547
Competence, 486
  motive, 439
Competition, 118
Computer science, 25
Computerized tomography (C.T. scanning), 98
Concept, 338, 400, 402
  types of, 404
  of working memory, 328
Conclusive remarks on the relationship of psychology with other sciences, 22
Conclusive remarks regarding different methods of psychology, 64
Concrete operational stage, 399
Conditioned inhibition, 291
Conditioned response, 248, 258
Conduction, 136
Cones, 154
Conflict, 450
  model of personality, 541
Conjunctive concepts, 404
Conjunctive dynamism, 552
Conscious attitude, 375
Conscious ego, 545
Consistency of traits, 538
Constant error, 142
Construction in memory, 342
Contact comfort motive, 437
Contemporary approaches to intelligence, 501
Context, 199, 207
Contiguity, 295, 298
Continuity, 198
Continuous reinforcement, 276
Contour, 203
Contrast effect, 164
Control processes, 329
Controlled conditions of study, 46
Controlled observation, 51
Convergence, 217
Convergent thinking, 414
Cooperation, 118
Corpus callosum, 92
Cortisol, 106
Counter conditioning, 269
Cowen, 389
Cranial nerves, 83
Creative self, 547

Creative thinking, 410
  nature of, 414
Cretinism, 519
Critical comments, 543, 546, 547, 553, 562
  on typology of personality, 534
  to trait approach, 538
Cross-sectional method, 62
Crystallized intelligence, 500, 513
Cube construction, 513
Cue dependent approach, 357
Cultural barriers, 416
Cultural factors, 520, 570
Cultural influences, 213
Culture, 487
  fair test, 513
  free test, 513
Curiosity, 436
Current status of motivational psychology, 459
Current trends, 175
  in understanding colours, 168
Cushing syndrome, 106

Day care homes, 115
Decay or disuse theory, 347
Deci, 444
Deciding, 325
Declarative memory, 332
Deductive thinking, 370
Defining intelligence, 493
Defining thinking, 368
Degree of learning, 355
Delayed conditioning, 262, 263
Delayed recall, 335
Delayed reinforcement, 277
Demographic information, 47
Dendrites, 76
Dependent variables, 54
Description of major methods of psychology, 48
Designing an experiment, 55
Detecting blind spot, 155
Detection problems, 138
Determinants (factors) of classical conditioning, 261
Determinants of personality, 563
Deuteranopes, 163
Development of personality, 541
Developmental model of intelligence, 500
Developmental stages, 552
Difference between
  artificial and natural concepts, 406
  emotion and feeling, 465
  perception and attention, 187
  perception and sensation, 186
Different origins of language and thought, 378
Differential sensitivity, 142
Differential threshold or limen (DL) or just noticeable difference (j.n.d.), 139
Dimension of personality, 536
Directing role, 452
Direction of attention or determinants of attention or conditions (factors) of attention, 238
Discrimination, 266
Disjunctive concepts, 404
Disjunctive dynamism, 552
Distraction of attention, 233
Divergent thinking, 415
Diversity of field, 4
Divided attention, 232
Divided brain, 95
Division of
  attention, 232
  labour in ANS, 103
  nervous system, 82
  PNS, 82
Dollard and Miller: Early social learning theory, 555
Double or multiple approach avoidance conflict, 451
Down syndrome, 524
Dreams, 543
Drive, 425
  competition method, 446
  discrimination, 294
  physiological, 434
  reduction theory, 290, 428
  theory, 428
Drugs, 222
Dual coding hypothesis, 339
Dualism, 29
Duct glands, 132
Ductless glands, 132
Duplicity theory of vision, 154, 157
Dynamic process-oriented view of personality, 539
Dynamics of personality, 551
Dynamism, 552

Echoic or auditory sensory memory (ASM), 326
Economics, 21
Edison's discovery, 383
Edridge-Green theory, 167
Education for mentally retarded, 525
Edward's personal preference schedule (EPPS) developed, 581

Effect of learning, 208
Effectance motivation, 444
Effectors, 129, 131
Effects of training, 520
Ego qualities, 553
Einstelling in German or 'direction', 380
Elaborative rehearsal, 329, 331
Electra, 542
Electro-chemical energy, 324
Electroencephalogram (EEG), 98
Emotion, 463, 487
Emotional block, 416
Emotional competence, 527
Emotional intelligence, 487
Empathy, 119
Emphasizing role, 453
Encephalization, 71
Encoded semantically, 329
Encoding, 324
Enculturation, 112
Endocrine system, 104
Enduring aspects of personality, 552
Energising role, 452
Energizing role of motivation, 254
Engaging in deep level processing, 361
Entrepreneurial competence, 527
Environmental determinants of intelligence, 517
Environmental ethics, 34
Environmental influences on evolutionary trend, 71
Environmental obstruction or blockage, 449
Episodic memory, 332
Equilibration, 376
Equipotential theory, 101
Equity theory, 459
Equivalence beliefs, 294
Erich Fromm: The human concerns, 548
Erik Erikson: In search of identity, 553
Escape conditioning, 278
Evaluating Cattell's IPAT test, 513
Evaluating group tests of intelligence, 512
Evaluating Wechsler's scale, 511
Evaluation, 414
    of Stanford–Binet scale, 509
Evaluative thinking, 371
Evolutionary perspectives, 70
Excretion, 434
Executive schemes, 505, 506
Expectancy theory, 293
Expectations or perceptual, 212
Experience of the perceiver, 221
Experimental evidence, 189
Experimental method, 53
Experimental neurosis, 269
Exploitative type, 549
Exploration learning, 251
Exploration need, 444
Exploratory motive, 436
External changes in emotion, 473
External factors, 235, 239
Exteroceptors, 130
Extinction, 265, 275
Extraneous relevant variables, 54
Extrinsic framework of motivation, 444
Extroversion, 545
Eyewitness memory, 345
Eysenck personality questionnaire (EPQ), 581

Facial expression, 473
Factorial analysis of personality, 536
Factors affecting changes in IQ, 515
Factors affecting perception of time, 221
Factors affecting problem solving, 387
Factors in human learning, 311
Factors influencing sustained attention, 238
Factors relating to
    learning, 355
    retention or encoding errors, 355
Factors of
    concept formation, 408
    organization, 207
    perception, 206
    personality, 567
    selective attention, 235
Fallacies about psychology or psychologists, 7
False or illusory memory syndrome, 346
Familiar size, 216
Family structure and size, 520
Fear, 468
Feeling, 464, 545
Field cognition mode, 294
Field expectancies, 294
Field experiments and quasi experiments, 56
Figure and ground perception, 201
Filter theory, 236
Filter-attenuation theory, 236
First letter technique, 361
Fixation, 543
Fixed ratio of schedule, 277
Flash bulb memories, 346

Fluctuation of attention, 232
Fluid general ability, 513
Fluid intelligence, 500
Forced choice procedure of recognition, 336
Forebrain, 88
Form board test (FBT), 512
Form, 159
Formal operational stage, 400
Founding ideas of ancient times, 27
Frame of teference, 208
Free association, 35
  technique or hypnosis, 544
Free recall, 307
Frequency theory, 174
Frontal lobe, 91
Frustration aggression hypothesis, 450
Frustration of motives, 449
Functionalism, 32
Functions of motivation or role of motivation on performance, 452
Functions of nerve cells (meurous), 76
Fundamental theories of motivation, 427

Galvanic skin response (GSR), 471
Gender differences, 519
General(g), 495
General comment about learning and behavioural approaches to personality, 557
General comment on dynamic process theories, 555
General comment on humanistic aproaches to personality, 560
Generalization and discrimination, 277
Generalization gradients, 268
Genes and behaviour, 72
Genetic determinants of intelligence—controversy, 517
Genetic epistemology, 398
Genital stage, 542
Germany, 50
Gestaltism, 34
Gestaltist's approach, 192
Giftedness (genius), 522
Glands, 132
Glandular involvements in emotions, 485
Glandular system, 568
Global amnesia, 359
Goals or objectives of psychology, 11
Good figure or symmetry, 198
Gradients of texture, 216
Graphology, 572
Group, 116
  intelligence tests, 511
  interaction, 570
Guilford zimmorman temperament survey (GZTS), 581
Guilt feelings, 543
Gustav Fechner's law, 144
Guthrie's contiguity theory, 298

Habit interference, 314
Habit strengh (SHR), 290
Habitual attention, 233
Habitual blocks, 416
Hallucinations, 225
Harry Stack Sullivan's approach: interpersonal model, 551
Health, 519
Heart rate and blood pressure, 470
Helson's adaptation level theory, 147
Hering's theory, 166
Herman ebbinghaus' study, 341
Heuristics, 387
Hierarchical theory, 500
Higher order conditioning, 268
Hindustan binet performance point scale (HBPPS), 514
Hippocrate's classification, 532
Hoarding type, 549
Holistic approach, 571
Holistic view of intelligence, 526
Home environment, 568
Homeostasis, 426
Horizontal, 309
Horn and Donaldson's approach, 500
Hostile aggression, 441
Hull's reinforcement theory, 288
Hull-Spencer theory, 289
Human concern approach, 37
Human eye, 153
Human memory is an active system, 344
Humanistic psychology, 37
Humanistic theories of personality, 558
Hunger, 430
Hydrocephaly, 525
Hypnogogic image, 373
Hypnopomptic image, 373
Hypothalamus, 89, 484
Hypothetico-deductive, 288

Iconic memory or visual sensory memory (VSM), 326
Ideal self, 559
Identification, 118
Identifying, 408
gifted children, 523
Ideopathic, 491
Illumination, 413
Illusions, 223
Imaginative image, 373
Imitation, 301
Imitative learning, 300
Immediate memory chamber, 327
Immediate recall, 335
Implicit memory, 345
Implicit trial and error, 383
Important concepts of psychophysics, 141
Important environmental determinants of intelligence, 518
Important measures or tests of personality, 572
Improving creativity, 417
Improving memory, 360
Inability of the individual to attain the goal, 450
Incentives, 425
Incidental learning, 305
Inclusiveness, 198
Increment theory of learning, 292
Incubation, 413
Independent variables, 54
Indian projective tests, 578
Indifferent—uninvolved style, 114
Individual differences in intelligence, 521
Individual psychology, 36, 547
Individual verbal tests, 508
Individuation, 545
Inducing false memories, 347
Inductive thinking, 371
Indulgent—permissive style, 114
Inferiority complex, 547
Influences of motives on behaviour, 426
Information and expectation theory, 264
Information processing, 330
model of memory, 323
theory, 330
view, 323
Inherited predisposition, 564
Inhibitory potential (I), 291
Initial lag, 351
Inner ear, 171
Input, 323
Insight in thinking, 383
Insight learning, 300
Insight theory, 286
Instinct, 425
theory, 427
Instrumental aggression, 441
Insulin, 107
Integration, 120
Intellectual hardware, 506
Intellectual software, 506
Intellectually retarded or deficient, 523
Intelligence in indian context, 526
Intelligence quotient (IQ), 506, 507, 508
Intelligence tests constructed in india, 514
Intelligence, nature and definition of, 492
Intentional learning, 305
Interactional approach, 539
Interactionism, 29, 32
Interference theory, 349
Interfering effects, 356
Intermittent or partial reinforcement, 277
Internal changes in emotion, 470
Internal factors, 235
Internal or organismic or subjective determinants, 240
Internationalization, 118
Interoceptors, 130
Interpersonal relationships, 550
Interposition or superposition or covering, 215
Interval scale, 509
Interval schedule, 277
Interview, 573
method, 57
Intra-psychic theory, 540
Intrinsic framework of motivation, 444
Intrinsic motivation, 444
Introspection (self-observation), 49
Introspection, 48
Introversion, 545
Intuition, 545
Inventories, 580
Involuntary attention, 233
IQ constancy, 515
Isolating dynamism, 552

J.P. Guilford's factor analysis theory, 497
James–Lange theory, 475
Jodhpur multiphasic personality inventory (JMPI), 581

Judging a situation, 474
Jung's classification, 533

Kahn's test of symbol arrangement (KTSA), 578
Karen Horney: Social foundations of personality, 550
Karma, 116
Keyword method, 360
Kinds of images, 372
Kinds of learning, 250
Kinds of motives, 429
Kinds of neurons, 77
Kinds of transfer in learning, 314
Kinesthesis, 135
Kinesthetic sensation, 177
Knowledge of result, 256
Kretschmer's classification, 533
Kurt Lewin's field theory of personality, 560

Ladd-Franklin theory, 167
Language as determinant of thought, 377
Language development, 71
Latency stage, 542
Latent learning, 303
Lateral or fissure of sylvius, 90
Law governing propagation of action potential (nerve impulse), 79
Law of
  effect, 255, 284, 453
  exercise, 284
  finality, 307
  learning, 284
  primacy, 307
  proximity, 197
  readiness, 284
  similarity, 197
Learn how to learn, 251
Learning and maturation, 250
Learning and performance, 249
Learning curve, 253
Learning materials, nature of 313
Learning methods, 355, 446
Learning set, 317
Learning to learn, 314
Learning, nature and definition of, 247
Left hemispheres, 90, 92
Leipzig, 5
Length of time intervals, 223
Leniency error, 574
Level of aspiration, 443
Levels of processing model, 330
Life space (LS), 560
Light and shadow, 216
Limbic system, 89, 485
Linear perspective, 215
Linguistic relativity hypothesis, 378
Live versus symbolic modelling, 301
Localization theory of functions, 99
Location constancy, 206
London 1944, 562
Longitudinal method, 62
Long-term memory (LTM), 328
Louis Thurston's primary ability theory, 496
Love and affection, 469

Machiavellianism, 441
Magnetic resonance imaging (MRI), 98
Maintaining stimuli, 299
Maintenance rehearsal, 329, 331
Maintenance trials, 327
Manipulative motive, 437
Marginalization, 120
Marketing type, 549
Maslow's theory of self-actualization, 559
Mass action theory, 101
Massed and distributed learning, 310
Materials used to study verbal learning, 306
Maternal drive, 433
Mathematico-deductive theory or model of learning, 288
McClelland's imagery achievement, 448
Meaning of
  method, 44
  personality, 530
Meaningfulness of the learning materials, 354
Means-end analysis, 387
Measurement of
  aptitude, 526
  human socio-psychogenic (acquired) motives, 447
  motives, 444
  retention, 334
Mechanoreceptors, 135
Media, 115
Medulla oblongata, 87

Melancholic, 532
Memory, 322
  image, 373
  span, 358
  traces, 324
Mental age (MA), 506, 507, 508
Mental inertia, 351
Mental organization (schemas), 376
Mental set, 199
Mental set (einstelling), 375
Mentalist, 32
Meta needs, 559
Method of average error or adjustment, 140
Method of constant stimuli or method of frequency, 141
Method of extirpation or ablation, 97
Method of loci, 360
Method of stimulation, 97
Methods employed for studying time perception, 223
Methods employed in studying brain functions, 96
Methods for measuring verbal learning, 307
Methods of learning, 311
Methods of limit or minimal changes or successive exploration, 140
Methods of verbal learning, 309
Mid-brain, 88
Middle ear, 171
Milestones in the history of psychology, 41
Military psychology, 24
Minimising the interference, 361
Minnesota multiphasic personality inventory (MMPI), 581
Mnemonics using images, 360
Mnemonics using organization, 361
Modelling, 117
Modern perspectives in psychology—current views, 39
Modern psychology, 39
Modern psychophysics, 146
Modern techniques, 98
Monitoring of neural activities, 78
Monocular cues, 215
Mood, 464
Moral anxiety, 543
Motivated forgetting, 352
Motivating state within the individual, 423
Motivation, 201, 222, 312, 421
Motivational blocks, 416
Motivational cycle, 423
Motives, 426
  for activity, 436
  and emotions, 465
  and interests, 240
Motor functions, 100
Motor learning, 251
Motor patterns, 295
Motor skills, 251
Moudsley personality inventory (MPI), 581
Movement, 216, 240
Muller-lyer illusion, 142
Multifactor theory, 496
Multimode theory, 236
Multiple status, 122
Muscles, 131
Mutation, 73
Myxoedema, 106

Natural concepts, 405
Naturalistic observation, 51
Nature, 463
Nature-nurture controversy, 73, 563
Need for, 209, 425
  achievement (n Ach), 439
  affiliation (n Affil.), 440
  identity, 549
  orientation, 549
  power (n Pow.), 440
  relatedness, 549
  rootedness, 549
  transcendence, 549
Need hierarchy theory, 453
Need-drive-incentive theory, 428
Negative after-image, 162
Negative transfer, 314
Neighbourhood, 569
Neo personality inventory (NEO PI-R), 563
Neo-Freudians, 36, 544, 548
  thoughts, 36
Neo-Piagetians, 505
Nerve impulse, 69, 324
Nervous system, 75, 568
Neurons as building blocks, 76
Neuro-psychology, 23
Neurotic anxiety, 543
Neurotic needs, 550
Neurotic trends, 550
Neuroticism vs emotional stability, 536
Neurotransmitting substance, 80

Neutral stimulus, 258
New advances: five-factor model of personality, 562
New frontiers of psychology, 23
No transfer effect, 314
Nomothetic, 491
Non-availability of right cues, 357
Non-participant vs. Participant observation, 51
Non-specific (general) or generic transfer, 314

Objective anxiety, 543
Objective observation, 48
Objectivity, 45
Obstruction method, 446
Occipital lobe, 91
Oedipus, 542
Oestrogen, 107
Olfactory, 135
Open-end questionnaire, 60
Operant (instrumental) conditioning, 271
Opponent–process theory, 455
Optic nerves, 156
Optical resolution, 154
Optimal level theory, 456
Oral stage, 541
Organic amnesia, 359
Organic sensitivity, 178
Organization in memory, 338
Organizational processing in perception, 190
Orienting reflexes, 251
Origence, 411
Osburn's technique, 417
Outer or external ear, 171
Output, 325
Overcompensation, 547

Paired associate method, 309
Pancreas, 107
Paper-pencil tests, 579
Parallel processing, 231
Parallelism, 32
Para-sympathetic system, 103
Parataxic, 551
Parathyroid gland, 106
Parents or the family, 113
Parietal lobe, 91
Parkinje phenomenon or effect, 157
Pass along, 513
Passive learnings, 311
Past experience, 200
Pathways or nerve tracts, 85
Pathways to brain, 156
Pavlov's conditioning principle, 556
Peak experiences, 560
Peer groups, 114
Penis envy, 550
Perceiver's (personal) factors, 208
Perceiving, 324
  direction of sound, 221
  distance of sound, 221
Perception, nature and definition of, 180
Perception involves complex receptor and neural processes, 183
Perception is a complex mental process, 182
Perception is an active mental process, 183
Perception is immediate in nature, 182
Perception is organization of stimuli, 183
Perception is selective in nature, 183
Perception of motion, 218
Perception of time, 221
Perceptual blocks, 416
Perceptual constancy (stability), 204
Perceptual defence, 213
Perceptual experience has the attribute of constancy, 183
Perceptual experiences are also flexible, 184
Perceptual learning, 251
Perceptual organization (grouping), 196
Perceptual vigilance, 214
Performance/non-verbal tests, 512
Peripheral laws or principles of organization, 197
Peripheral nervous system (PNS), 82
Peripheral-central theory, 394
Perseveration, 350
Persona, 530
Personal factors, 212
Personal unconscious, 545
Personality less view of personality, 557
Personification, 552
Person-situation controversy, 566
Phallic phase, 542
Phallic stage, 541
Phallus syndrome, 542
Phases of skill acquisition, 304
Phenomenal field, 558
Phenomenon, points of views towards perceptual, 191
Phenylke tonuria, 524
Philosophical roots, 28
Phlegmatic, 532
Phonological loop, 328

Photoreceptors, 135, 154
Physical information, 47
Physiological bases of Cannon–Bard theory, 478
Physiological bases of James–Lange view, 476
Physiological correlates of emotion, 470
Physiological data, nature of, 47
Physiological measures of emotion, 486
Physiological motives, 430
Physique, 567
Piaget's cognitive theory, 398
Piaget's theory, 503
Picture complete test (PCT), 512
Picture frustration test (PFT), 448
Pineal gland, 105
Pinter perterson performance scale, 513
Pitch is which, 173
Pitting one drive against another, 446
Pituitary gland, 105
Place or goal learning experiment, 295
Place or resonance theory, 173
Place theory, 173
Pleasantness–unpleasantness, 473
Point of clearest vision, 154
Point of subjective equality (PSE), 142
Polygraph and lie detector, 486
Pons, 88
Porteus maze, 513
Positive after-image, 162
Positive psychology, 24
Positive transfer, 314
Positron emission tomography (PET scanning), 98
Post-Freudian developments, 544
Postural changes or body gestures, 474
PQRST technique, 361
Practical intelligence, 504
Pre-19th century psychology, 41
Pregenital stage, 541
Pre-operational stage, 399
Preparatory phase, 412
Preparedness or readiness to learn, 312
Prepotency, 239
Present self, 558
Presentative and representative, 181
Previous learning, 312
Primary and secondary reinforcement, 276
Principle of conservation, 399
Principle of entropy, 545
Principle of equivalence, 545
Principle of opposites, 545
Principle of posterity, 299
Pro-active inhibition (PI), 350
Problem solving behaviour as an information processing model, 390
Problem solving, 251, 384
Procedural memory, 334
Process of retrieval in memory, 337
Processes involved in perception, 184
Process-oriented approaches to intelligence, 502
Productive type, 549
Progesterone, 107
Projective approach, 572
Projective techniques, 575
Projective tests, 447
Prompting and anticipation method, 308
Properties or attributes of sensation, 134
Proprioceptive, 175
Proprioceptors, 130
Pro-social behaviours, 119
Protanopes, 163
Prototaxic, 551
Prototype, 402, 405
Pseudo-conditioning, 269
Psychoanalysis, 35
Psychoanalytic approach, 458
Psychological amnesia, 353
Psychological data, 48
Psychological double aspectism, 29
Psychological feedback, 257
Psychology, 3
    analytical, 36
    and anthropology, 20
    and life, 18
    natural science, 10
    and physiology, 21
    a science, 9
    and sociology, 20
    today, 22
    tomorrow, 40
Psychometric, 491
    methods, 578
Psychophysical relations and methods of study, 137
Psychophysical relationships, 158
Psychosociogenic motives, 437
Pupliometrics, 472
Purposive behaviourism, 293
Purposive learning, 305
Push and pull model, 444

Quasi-experiment, 57

Questionnaire, 579
    method, 60
    types of, 60

Radical behaviourism, 301
Rating scales, 581
Raven's progressive matrices (RPM), 512
Reaction potential (SER), 290
Reactions to frustrations, 451
Reactive inhibition (IR), 291
Real, 543
Realistic thinking, 370
Rearing practices, 119
Rebirth, 116
Recall or reproduction method, 334
Receptive type, 549
Receptor, 129, 178
    process, 184
Receptor–effector mechanisms, 483
Recognition, 335
Reconditioning, 266
Reconstration in memory, 342
Reconstruction method, 336
Red-green blindness, 163
Reduction division, 73
Redundancy of sensory cues, 206
Reflex action, 85
Reflex arch, 85
Refractory period, 79
Regression, 543
Reinforcement, 268, 290, 443
    theory, 291
Reintegration, 322
Relational concepts, 404
Relationship between behaviour and socio-cultural environment, 120
Relationship of personality types and cardiac diseases (CHD), 584
Relationship of psychology to other natural sciences, 22
Relationship of psychology with other disciplines, 19
Relearning or saving method, 336
Reliability, 46
Religion, 116
Reminiscence, 353
Renaissance of science, 28
Repetition, 239
Repetition priming task (RPT), 337
Resistance to extinction, 277
Respondent conditioning, 259
Response learning, 251, 252
Response-competition or interference theory, 351
Retention, 334
    interval, 335
Reticular activating system, 88
Reticular formation, 479, 565
Retina, 154
Retinal disparity, 217
Retrieval of similar material, 356
Retrieval related forgetting, 356
Retrieving, 324
Retroactive and proactive inhibitions, 349
Retrograde amnesia, 359
Reverse logical operations, 399
Revision, 414
Reward and punishment, 117
Reward conditioning, 278
Reward expectancy experiment, 295
Right hemisphere, 94
Right, 90
Rigidity of organization, 382
Rods, 154
Rogers' self theory, 558
Role conflict, 122
Role of
    images in thinking, 372
    language, 377
    motivation in learning, 254
    nervous system in emotion, 483
    past experience in perception, 188
    peripheral nervous system (PNS), 483
    set and direction, 380
Rorschach test (RT or BT), 447, 576
Rosenzweig's picture frustration test (PFT), 578

Salient features of classical conditioning procedure, 260
Saturation, 160
Schedule of reinforcement, 276
Schema, 339
School, 115, 570
Schools of psychology, 31
Sclerotic or sclera, 153
Script, 340
Secondary traits, 536
Selective, 181
    attention, 234, 329
    breeding, 98
Self-actualisation, 38

Self-healing personality, 585
Self-motivation, 444
Self-observation, 48
Self-report technique, 448, 580
Self-system, 552
Semantic codes, 328
Semantic level of processing, 331
Semantic means, meaning with connotations, 333
Semantic memory, 333
Sensation, 31
    nature and definition, 133
Sense, 175
    of balance, 178
Sensing, 545
Sensitivity, 141
Sensors, 135
Sensory aphasia, 101
Sensory channel: processing, 135
Sensory functions, 99
Sensory input, 323
Sensory processes, 132
Sensory stimuli, 135
Sensory-motor coordination skills, 251
Sensory-motor learning, 252
Sensory-motor stage, 398
Sentence completion test (SCT), 578
Separation, 120
Sequential method, 63
Serial processing, 235
Serial recall, 307
Serial reproduction method, 352
Set or expectancy, 240
Severity error, 574
Sex hormone, 106
Shape constancy, 205
Shaping of behaviour, 275
Sheldon's classification, 532
Shift of attention, 232
Short-term memory (STM), 327
Sign learning, 300
Sign-Gestalt, 293
Significance of classical conditioning, 270
Significance of instrumental (operant) conditioning, 278
Sign-significate, 293
Similarity of principle, 316
Similarity of technique, 316
Simple concepts, 404
Simultaneous conditioning, 262, 263
Simultaneous contrast, 164
Single photon emission computerized tomography (SPECT), 98
Single reproduction, 352
Situational tests, 448
Situationalism, 567
Situationism, 539
Size, 239
    constancy, 204
    of rational images, 218
Skill learning, 304
Skin sensation, 177
Skinner's radical behaviourism, 557
Sleep arousal dimension, 479
Sleep–tension, 473
Smell, 176
Smooth muscles, 131
Social
    behaviour, 123
    class, 123
    competence, 527
    desirability test, 442
    factors of personality, 568
    factors, 212
    learning, 302
    norms, 212
    suggestion, 212, 241
Socialization and culture, 110
Socio-biology, 74
Somato type classification, 532
Source traits, 536
Space perception of sound, 220
Span of attention, 231
Spatial model, 482
Special abilities: aptitudes, 525
Specialization of cerebral hemisphere, 92
Specific crisis, 553
Specific food need, 431
Specific transfer, 315
Spectrum, 157
Spinal cord, 84
Spontaneous recovery, 265
Spranger's classification, 534
S-R bond, 282, 293
Stable level of responding, 261
Stage model, 325, 329
Stages of creative thinking, 411
Standardization, 46
Stanford–Binet scale, 508
Status and role, 122
Steps in problem solving, 384

Stereoscopic vision, 218
Stevens' power law, 144
Stimulus characteristics, 223
Stimulus for hearing, 168
Stimulus for kinesthesis, 178
Stimulus for vision, 152
Stimulus generalization, 266
Stimulus learning, 252
Stimulus scaling, 139
Stimulus substitution theory, 264
Stimulus-response (S-R) theory, 282
Storing and holding, 324
Strategies of problem solving or thinking, 386
Stress interview, 574
Striped muscles, 131
Structuralism, 31
Structuralist's view, 191
Structure of intellect model, 497
Structure of nerve cells (Neurons), 76
Structure of neurons, 76
Structure of personality, 540
Structured interview, 57
Style of life, 546, 547
Sub-fields or branches of psychology, 13
Subject matter and scope, 8
Subjective or personal factors, 311
Successive approximation, 275
Successive contrast effect, 164
Successive reproduction method, 352
Super conducting quantum interference device (SCQID), 98
Surface traits, 536
Survey method, 63
Sustained attention, 236
Symbolic meaning, 210
Symbolic process, 185
Sympathetic system, 103
Sympathy, 119
Synaptic facilitation, 80
Synaptic functions, 80, 81
Syntaxic levels, 551
Synthetic theory of intelligence, 499
Systematization, 45

Tactile, 138
  properties, 135
Taste, 176
Temporal lobe, 91
Terminal lag, 351
Test situations, 573
Testosterone, 107
Tetranopes, 163
Thalamus, 89, 484
Thematic apperception test (TAT), 439, 447, 575
Theology, 28
Theoretical branches, 14
Theories of
  brain functions, 99
  colour vision, 165
  emotion, 474
  hearing (audition), 172
  intelligence, 494
  perception, 191
  retro/proactive inhibitions, 350
  selective attention, 236
  thinking, 393
Theory of
  Arthur Jensen, 500
  multiple intelligence, 501
  Piaget's cognitive, 398
  relationships among emotions, 482
  signal detection, 146
Thermodynamics, 545
Thermo-receptors, 135
Thinking, 376, 402, 545
  nature of, 367
Thirst, 431
Thorndike's connectionism, 282
Thorndike's multifactor theory, 499
Thought as determinant of language, 378
Threads of life, 72
Threshold or limen, 142
Thyroid gland, 106
Tip of the tongue phenomenon, 338
Tolman's cognitive theory, 293
Tools of thinking, 371
Top-down processing, 190
Topology, 560
Total colourblindness, 163
Trace conditioning, 262, 299
Trace dependent approach, 357
Trace or sign conditioning, 263
Trait, 564
  approach, 571
  to personality, 535
Transaction, 324
Transduction, 69, 136
Transfer of learning, 313
Transient amnesia, 359

Transmission of nerve impulse, 80
Transposition, 207
Treatment, 242
  for mentally retarded, 525
Trial and error in thinking, 383
Trial and error theory, 282
Triarchic theory of intelligence, 503
Trichromatic cones, 165
Trichromatic theory of colour sensation, 163
Tridimensional theory, 32, 497
Two-factor theory, 351, 459, 480
  of Charles Spearman, 495
Type approach to personality, 531
Type 'A', 584
Type 'B', 584
Type C, 584
Type E, 54
Type S, 54
Types and traits: development of taxonomy (trait and type classification), 531
Types of
  long-term memory, 332
  personality, 549
  receptors or sensory, 130

Unaided observation, 48
Unconditioned response, 258
Unconditioned stimulus, 258
Unconscious, 36
  motives, 541
Unifying process, 185
Unlearned/general motives, 435
Unstructured interview, 58
Updated theory of intelligence propounded by Indian psychologists: PASS model, 504
Urge to live, 544
Use of multiple methods and strategies, 362
Uses of intelligence tests, 516

Valence–vector theory, 457
Valency, 294
Validity, 46
Value, 210
Variable, 53
  error, 143
  types of, 54
Verbal learning, 251, 306
Verbal skills, 251
Vicarious learning, 301
Vigilance, 236
Visceral brain, 89
Visio-spatial sketch pad, 328
Visual acquity, 158
Visual adaptation, 158
Visual codes, 328
Visual sensation, 151
Visual space perception, 214
Visual threshold, 157
Vocal expression, 473
Volley theory, 174
Voluntary attention, 233

Waking vs sleeping, 356
Ward-Hovland phenomenon, 353
Warming up, 314
Weber's law, 143
Weber's ratio, 143
Wechsler adult intelligence scale (WAIS), 509
Wechsler's tests, 513
Wernicke's lobe, 92
Wernicke's-Geschwind model, 93
Wever-Bray effect, 174
Whole and part method, 310
Word association test (WAT), 577, 544
Word completion test (WCT), 337
Working memory, 327
Work-motivation, 459
Wüzberg school, 375

Yerk's-Dodson law, 237
Young-Helmholtz theory, 165

Zigarnik effect, 457